Decolonizing the Lens of Power

ross
ultures

Readings in the Post / Colonial

Literatures in English

100

Series Editors

Gordon Collier
(Giessen)

†Hena Maes–Jelinek
(Liège)

Geoffrey Davis
(Aachen)

Decolonizing the Lens of Power

Indigenous Films in North America

Kerstin Knopf

Amsterdam - New York, NY 2008

I would like to dedicate this book
to Indigenous film- and videomakers
in Canada and the United States
without whose creative work, continuous endeavours,
generous cooperation and support
this book could not have been written.
I wish to return the gift.

Meegwetch!

Cover design: Gordon Collier & Pier Post

Front cover: Hnony moccasin

The paper on which this book is printed meets the requirements of
"ISO 9706:1994, Information and documentation - Paper for
documents - Requirements for permanence".

ISBN: 978-90-420-2543-1
©Editions Rodopi B.V., Amsterdam – New York, NY 2008
Printed in The Netherlands

Table of Contents

Acknowledgements

F IRST AND FOREMOST, I wish to thank the various Indigenous film- and videomakers from Canada and the USA for creating and sharing their work, for generously supplying me with copies of their work and information material, and finally for sharing their thoughts and opinions in interview discussions. Thank you Marjorie Beaucage, Maria Campbell, Martha Carlson, Gil Cardinal, Doug Cuthand, Chris Eyre, Zacharias Kunuk, Lloyd Martell, Victor Masayesva, Shelley Niro, Alanis Obomsawin, Neil Pasqua, Debra Piapot, Evelyn Poitras, Rodger Ross, and Loretta Todd. I would also like to acknowledge the enlightening interview discussion with Métis scholar Linda Sutherland. Likewise, I wish to thank Maria Campbell, Gil Cardinal, Norman Cohn, Doug Cuthand, Chris Eyre, Zacharias Kunuk, Lloyd Martell, Victor Masayesva, and Shelley Niro for kindly granting print permission for the film stills.

My heartfelt thanks go to professor, mentor, and colleague Hartmut Lutz, University of Greifswald, for his guidance, critical commentary, long-standing support, and patience. Furthermore, I wish to thank Hans–Peter Rodenberg, University of Hamburg, for his critical counsel and back-up as well as Dirk Vanderbeke, University of Jena, for his critical advice during the early stage of the writing process.

Also, I would like to thank my fellow members of the Doktoranden-kolloquium "Group of Seven," Jörg Behrendt, Renate Eigenbrod, Heike Gerds, Christiane Kollenberg, Antje Thiersch, and Stefanie von Berg, for our intense academic discussions and exchange of ideas. Similarly, I wish to acknowledge the intellectual support of Colt Henning Schäfer and Jörg Heinke as members of my "secret graduate student colloquium." A big big thank-you also goes to Lara Christianson, who proofread the manuscript and blotted out idiomatic weaknesses. In the same vein, I wish to express my deepfelt gratefulness to Gordon Collier, technical editor of the Cross/

Cultures series, for his unconditional commitment, suggestions, and work on the final draft. I am especially grateful to my family and friends for morally supporting this project, for giving me energy and strength, and for putting up with my increasing neglectfulness.

Finally, I wish to acknowledge the financial support of the state government of Mecklenburg–Western Pomerania for a thirty-two month graduate scholarship and the German Academic Exchange Service D A A D for granting a supplementary scholarship to spend six months in Regina at the First Nations University for research purposes. Likewise, I am indebted to the Government of Canada for a six-month research scholarship for my M A thesis on documentaries by and about Aboriginal women, some ideas and insights of which also went into the writing of this book. Last but not least, I would like to thank the Gesellschaft für Kanada-Studien for financially supporting the publication of this book.

Thank you all!

Introduction

THE COLONIZATION of the North American continent went hand in hand with the development of a colonial discourse as a transmitter of colonial ideology. The contemporary North American media are dominated by this discourse, which legitimizes colonialistic policies, upholds cultural and political hegemonies, transmits the colonial view on the colonized 'others', and silences Indigenous voices and those of other marginalized groups. When concerned with Indigenous issues, stereotypes, prejudice, ethnocentrism, and tendencies to appropriate abound in colonial media discourse. Ethnographic filmmaking, Hollywood, and North American television have constructed and sustained the 'imaginary and ideological Indian', an array of dehumanizing, humiliating, and romanticizing stereotypes of the people indigenous to colonized North America. They have been defined by this Western media discourse – the colonial gaze – that has shaped perceptions of Indigenous cultures in mainstream society, furthering the notion that Indigenous cultures are inferior to the 'advanced' and 'civilized' eurocentric cultures. This idea gave way to the rejection, disrespect, racism, patronage, injustice, marginalization, and economic, political, and cultural oppression that characterize societal contact between mainstream and Indigenous societies. The effects of these contact phenomena are visible in the contemporary state of Indigenous North America. Likewise, the self-perception of the colonial subjects is channelled through this colonial gaze; Indigenous people have often appropriated the image of the imaginary and ideological Indian, which has resulted in confusion, self-denial, cultural alienation, and identity-crises.[1]

---

[1] See Heather Norris Nicholson, "Introduction" to *Screening Culture: Constructing Image and Identity*, ed. Norris Nicholson (Lanham MD: Lexington, 2003): 1.

Indigenous people are continually struggling for recognition, participation, and control over their own affairs, as the many successful land claim settlements and self-government agreements show. In the media also, they are striving for participation and productive control over the images of them that are fed into the mediascape. Their voices are emerging in all kinds of media outlets, be it television, radio, news media or film. An array of Indigenous radio stations – for example, NCI FM in Winnipeg, the Aboriginal Voices Radio network with its first station in Toronto, KNBA in Anchorage, and KINI in St Francis on the Rosebud reservation, as well as APTN, the first Indigenous television channel in the world with a country-wide broadcast license – bear witness to this self-empowering development. The 1970s, a period of intense Indigenous political activism (e.g., the takeovers of Wounded Knee and Alcatraz Island), also gave rise to Indigenous documentary films[2] which dealt with cultural and social issues and political conflicts.[3] The large-scale development of Indigenous dramatized filmmaking started in the late 1990s, with Chris Eyre's *Smoke Signals* (1998) as the first Indigenous feature film to receive national and international acclaim in the USA and the 1999 television series *Big Bear* (1998) by Gil Cardinal in Canada.

This book examines Indigenous filmmaking in North America, analyzing a variety of representative films by Indigenous Canadian and US-American filmmakers. It explores how members of colonized groups use the medium of film as a vehicle of cultural and political expression, thereby entering the dominant colonial film discourse and creating an answering discourse. The theoretical framework developed takes an interdisciplinary approach combining postcolonialism, Indigenous studies, and film studies. As Indigenous people gradually take control over the image-making pro-

---

[2] Elizabeth Weatherford, "Currents: Film and Video in Native America," in *Native Americans on Film and Video*, vol. 2, ed. Elizabeth Weatherford & Emelia Seubert (New York: Museum of the American Indian, 1988): 7.

[3] Alanis Obomsawin is undoubtedly the pioneer of Indigenous documentary film in Canada. She started in the early 1970s with the National Film Board of Canada. Her early films on cultural, social, and political issues are *Christmas at Moose Factory* (1971), *No Address* (1988) and *Incident at Restigouche* (1984). She was later to direct the seminal *Kanehsatake: 270 Years of Resistance* (1993), which depicted the Oka crisis from an Indigenous perspective and provided historical background that was generally absent from Canadian media coverage. In the USA, George Burdeau, Phil Lucas, Robert Hagopian, and Victor Masayesva are the pioneers of Indigenous documentary film, Burdeau with his six-part series *The Real People* (1976), Lucas and Hagopian with their five-part series *Images of Indians* (1980), and Masayesva with *Hopiit* (1982) and *Itam Hakim, Hopiit* (1984).

cess in the domain of film- and videomaking, they cease to be studied and described as objects and become subjects who create self-controlled images of Indigenous cultures. The book asks whether or not there is a definite Indigenous film practice and whether filmmakers tend to dissociate their work from dominant classical filmmaking, adapt to it, or create new film forms and styles by merging with and consciously violating classical film conventions. In this context, postcolonial filmic strategies, styles, and techniques are examined as well. In Bakhtin's sense, this approach presupposes that Indigenous filmmakers are constantly in some state of dialogue with Western ethnographic filmmaking and with classical narrative filmmaking and its epitome, Hollywood narrative cinema.

Since neither an academic framework for the analysis of Indigenous films nor suggestions for possible approaches are available, I was obliged to merge several different methodologies in order to create an appropriate approach to Indigenous filmmaking. The first are obviously techniques of film analysis. Because Indigenous filmmakers employ Western film technology, the tools for Western film analysis must be employed as well. Even if used for the creation of an Indigenous filmic discourse, the tools for creating this discourse remain the same (cameras, film material, video tape, editing boards/computers, sound recording machines, digital techniques, etc). The system of rules and techniques to be applied or subverted while making a film also remains the same (the 180° system, continuity, lighting, sound, frame composition, camera angles and movement, etc). Lastly, the channels of distribution are largely similar, albeit on a different scale. As there is no framework yet for the analysis of Indigenous films, there is also no specifically Indigenous film terminology with which to refer to the tools, techniques, rules, and distribution channels involved. Thus, there is currently no way to discuss film techniques and styles save Western film terminology and Western practices. I am not endorsing a set of Western film theories or modes of criticism or theory; I am making use of Western tools for purposes of analysis.[4] If I were to avoid such tools, this book would consist merely of content description.

---

[4] Of course, Western film criticism and theory find their way into film analysis indirectly because aspects of these form a 'pre-understanding' of what is known or what the author knows about film. Texts about film cannot hang suspended in a void, but must build on such pre-understandings. However, rather than paying allegiance to what David Bordwell & Noël Carroll have termed 'Grand Theory', an amalgam of doctrines derived from Lacanian psychoanalysis, structuralist semiotics, poststructuralist literary theory, and Althusserian Marxism – see Bordwell & Carroll, "Introduction" to *Post-Theory: Reconstructing Film Studies*, ed.

These Western analytical tools are joined to Indigenous Studies and Postcolonial Studies. An Indigenous Studies background is necessary to situate Indigenous filmmaking in general and the films in particular in their historical and socio-political contexts. The postcolonial approach ensures that analysis does not slip into a discourse of cultural hegemony. Rather, the postcolonial approach aims at dismantling such hegemonies and exploring the mechanisms of colonial discourse as well as strategies employed to respond to cultural hegemonies. This confluence of approaches is conditioned by the hybrid nature of Indigenous films, the subjects of analysis. Bernd Schulte holds that media, communication, and cultural studies themselves have a hybrid character, which results from the fact that hybridity as a definition of intercultural processes meets hybrid academic-analytical discourses on the cultural-theoretical and methodological level. These discourses qualify as interdisciplinary approaches to postcolonial texts, and are able to discuss phenomena of blending within the realms of culture and media, but only with due consideration of hegemonies within established cultural models and academic disciplines/theories.[5]

In this light, I have taken a selective approach to Western tools when looking at camera work, techniques, and style, utilizing them within the framework of postcolonial criticism. As well as this, I conducted interviews with Indigenous filmmakers in order to explore their views on Indigenous

---

Bordwell & Carroll (Madison: U of Wisconsin P, 1996): xiii – my analyses are indebted to neoformalist film analysis as outlined by Kristin Thompson in "A Neoformalist Approach to Film Analysis: One Approach, Many Methods," in Kristin Thompson, *Breaking the Glass Armor: Neoformalist Film Analysis* (Princeton NJ: Princeton UP, 1988): 3–46. Cf. Bordwell, who argues that instead of applying various doctrines of Grand Theory to the understanding of film, "middle-level research" and what Carroll calls "piecemeal theory" are better alternatives, as they can incorporate empirical *and* theoretical research as well as interdisciplinary theorizing about particular film phenomena without being committed to "determining philosophical assumptions about subjectivity or culture" or to "univocal metaphysical or epistemological or political presumptions." In this sense, Bordwell calls for sharply focussed, in-depth inquiry that will advance our knowledge of cinema ("Contemporary Film Studies and the Vicissitudes of Grand Theory," in *Post-Theory*, 29–30). Neoformalism is indebted to the New Historicism and requires constant modification: i.e. adaptation of its methods and inquiries to the specifics of a given film. It connects the analyses of form and content, while embedding these analyses in the historical, socio-political, and cultural contexts of the works examined. In neoformalism, viewers are not passive objects but active subjects, taking part in the construction of meaning (Kristin Thompson, "A Neoformalist Approach to Film Analysis," 6–26).

[5] Bernd Schulte, "Kulturelle Hybridität: Kulturanthropologische Anmerkungen zu einem 'Normalzustand'," in *Hybridkultur: Medien, Netze, Künste*, ed. Irmela Schneider & Christian W. Thomsen (Cologne: Wienand, 1997): 245–47.

filmmaking – also in contrast to Western filmmaking. As there is hardly any basic research on Indigenous filmmaking in North America, these interviews, together with a very small number of essays by Indigenous filmmakers,[6] help to create a self-referential body of theoretical 'secondary sources' on Indigenous filmmaking in general and the filmic works to be analyzed in particular. Including such self-referential sources was considered imperative in order to prevent hegemonic tendencies from fouling up the modes of representation adopted. These interviews find their way into analysis as comments, explanations, and personal views on various issues, chiefly the relation between oral tradition and film. Lastly, in line with the approaches applied, I had to consider my own position as a Western scholar studying Indigenous filmmaking. It was imperative that I avoid homogenizing, objectifying, and patronizing tendencies and try not to put myself in the position of the Western scholar claiming exclusive authority in explaining Indigenous filmmaking. I was, and continue to be, aware that I can only view Indigenous cinematic discourse from outside and not from within, as Beverly Singer does in her study of Native American film and video,[7]

Chapter 1 of this book sets up a parallel between Michel Foucault's notion of the 'gaze of power' and the collective viewpoint of colonial groups – hence with the colonial discourse that controls, defines, and objectifies oppressed groups. Colonial filmic discourse can thus be understood as a 'lens of power', whose two major operational instruments are Western ethnographic documentaries and Hollywood narrative films. The 'lens': i.e. film technology itself, is a neutral medium. However, its use by members of the colonialist group creates a romanticizing, objectifying, othering, and stereotyping film discourse that turns it into a colonialist instrument. Hima-

---

[6] See Marjorie Beaucage, "Aboriginal Voices: Entitlement Through Storytelling," in *Mirror Machine: Video and Identity*, ed. Janine Marchessault (Toronto: YYZ, 1995): 214–26, and "Self Government in Art to Create Anew... / Être autonome... être autochtone... se recréer," in *Video re/View*, ed. Peggy Gale & Lisa Steele (Toronto: Art Metropole & Vtape, 1996): 72–83; Victor Masayesva, Jr. "The Emerging Native American Aesthetics in Film and Video," *Film and Video Monthly Independent* (December 1994): 20–21, 27; Loretta Todd, "Three Moments After Savage Graces," *Harbour* 9 (1993): 57–62; and Christine Welsh, "Voices of the Grandmothers: Reclaiming a Métis Heritage," *Canadian Literature* 131 (Winter 1991): 15–24.

[7] Beverly Singer, *Wiping the War Paint Off the Lens: Native American Film and Video* (Minneapolis: U of Minnesota P, 2001).

ni Bannerji's concept of 'returning the gaze'[8] can be applied to the works of Indigenous filmmakers, and in that sense the filmmakers are returning the colonial gaze by creating anticolonial, autonomous media. They are thus decolonizing mainstream media discourse and the lens of power.

Chapter 2 examines the applicability of postcolonial criticism to the analysis of Indigenous filmmaking. Postcolonial theory, as applied to the analysis of film, serves to reveal underlying colonialist relations, to pinpoint latent self/other dichotomies and derived binaries, to disclose the practices of romanticizing, othering, essentializing, and appropriation inhering in colonialist discourse, and to indicate their reflection in these films. Unlike mainstream analysis, this theory evades the grip of cultural hegemonies, instead accommodating hybrid forms of self-definition and cultural expression. This chapter also warns against the danger of an essentializing position that presupposes a clearly defined 'Indigenous film aesthetic'. Werner Sollors' concept of the constructed nature of ethnicity serves as inoculation against the pitfalls of demanding 'authentic Indigenous filmmaking' (the 'authenticity trap'). In this light, Indigenous filmmaking is described as a set of hybrid practices that undermine the fetishizing tendencies of hegemonic discourse and combine Western cinematic practice and concepts of film with Indigenous narrative and performative traditions. In a survey of the history of Indigenous filmmaking in North America, the chapter develops a model which identifies four phases of development – from colonial discourse about Indigenous people, through the creation of Indigenous works under colonial dependency, to the creation of independent, autonomous works. Also traced are the salient characteristics of Third-World cinema (as outlined by Shohat and Stam) that also apply to Fourth-World films. Likewise examined is the problem of the language to use in a given film – either colonial influence can be excluded by using a traditional language, or a larger audience can be reached by using English (thereby exposing the work to colonial influence). Or ways can be sought to get round the problem, such as employing local vernaculars of English or providing subtitles for the Indigenous language. In this context, the chapter takes issue with the thesis that language variance, code-switching and so forth implant 'culture' in a text, and concludes that language variance is not a metonymic expression of culture but a metaphor of cultural difference.

---

[8] Himani Bannerji, "Returning the Gaze: An Introduction," in *Returning the Gaze: Essays on Racism, Feminism and Politics*, ed. Himani Bannerji (Toronto: Sister Vision, 1993): xxii.

Chapter 3 extensively reviews the relation between Indigenous oral tradition and film and the translatability of oral narration into electronic narration, using as examples Maria Campbell's *The Road Allowance People* (1988) and Victor Masayesva's *Itam Hakim, Hopiit* (1984). Attention is devoted to the issues that filmmakers have to cope with when recording and/or thematizing oral tradition. They need to be aware of the fact that filming removes the oral information from its original context, that the medium of film is not able to replace or to continue oral tradition, and that control over the receiver of the cultural information relayed is lost, so that it is hardly possible in this medium to observe cultural taboos and restrictions. Although similarities between the two media suggest themselves and although information in both is transmitted by visual and sonic means, the medium of film cannot replace direct human contact and fixes the information on the storage medium, whereas information within oral tradition is subject to change. Again, the issue of which language to use is of the utmost importance in this translating process.

Campell's *The Road Allowance People*, based on her collection of Métis stories *Stories of the Road Allowance People*, features traditional modes of narration, with community members assembled to listen to the tales of a travelling Métis storyteller. The film has a main sequence (the storytelling event), from which six other sequences (filmic illustrations of the stories told) depart and to which they return, yielding an underlying circular structure. Campbell solves the language problem by having her actors speak English but with a culture-specific dialect, which she also uses in her printed collection of Métis stories. The Métis vernacular interspersed with Mitchif words is the linguistic continuum within which contemporary Métis oral tradition operates. By employing this vernacular, Campbell constructs a linguistic medium which does not alienate oral knowledge from its cultural context and avoids purely colonial linguistic expression.

Unlike Campbell, who dramatizes oral tradition, Masayesva, in *Itam Hakim, Hopiit*, records the telling of a Hopi elder to create a documentary-like film about several different complexes of Hopi oral culture, including the creation myth. He illustrates the telling with archival photographs and contemplative, mesmerizing images of Hopi landscape and everyday and ritual Hopi life. Accordingly, the film is characterized by a very slow pace, achieved by long takes and long transitions. As well as this, Masayesva applies visual and sound-breaks, fragmentary filming, posterization, and slow- and fast-motion effects in order to counter the tradition of ethnogra-

phic filmmaking and to avert its romanticizing, objectifying, and scrutinizing gaze, which needs to satisfy the desire to view and explain the
culture studied. Through the slow pace and by having the narrator speak
and chant in Hopi (with subtitles), Masayesva transmits the Hopi cultural
context and is able, to a certain extent, to capture the storytelling situation
and remain largely true to the original meaning of the oral knowledge.

   The analysis of three short films – *Talker* (1996), *Tenacity* (1994), and
Overweight With Crooked Teeth (1997) – in chapter 4 exemplifies how Indigenous filmmakers thematize colonialist practices, power relations, and
clichéd reflection of Indigenous cultures in colonialistic media discourse in
North America. Lloyd Martell in *Talker*, by applying a Cree myth to the
colonialist practice of appropriation, tells a metaphoric story about the
silencing of Indigenous voices. Chris Eyre's *Tenacity* is a metaphoric representation of the encounter between colonizer and colonized through the
story of a hit-and-run accident in which a boy gets killed by a truck. With
mise-en-scène elements and cinematographic techniques, the film positions
the two opposing 'fronts' in the encounter. Shelley Niro's carnivalesque
film with the programmatic title *Overweight with Crooked Teeth* ironizes
the most prevalent Indian stereotypes that exist in literature, film, and public discourse, denouncing their exploitation in the field between eco-cult
and essentializing museum culture. The technical mimesis of the colonial
gaze serves to pinpoint the objectifying, romanticizing, and stereotyping
tendencies of Western discourse.

   Chapter 5 is dedicated to the analysis of four longer dramatic films[9] –
Honey Moccasin (1998), *Smoke Signals*, *Big Bear*, and *Atanarjuat: The
Fast Runner* (2001) – which contextualize Indigenous reality in colonialist
North America. Like *Overweight with Crooked Teeth*, Niro's *Honey
Moccasin* is a postmodern and carnivalesque piece of work. She uses conventional filmmaking techniques in subversive violation of their rules. The
film applies the grotesque not only to expose Indian stereotypes and to
parody the genre of the detective film as representative of dominant film
discourse, but also to sidestep clear narrative structures to create a digres-

---

[9] The term 'feature film', defined by Frank E. Beaver as "a full-length motion picture made
and distributed for release in movie theaters" – *Dictionary of Film Terms* (New York:
Twayne, 1994): 146 – does not apply to all four films but only to *Smoke Signals* and *Atanarjuat: The Fast Runner* and is therefore not employed here. *Honey Moccasin* is an independently made 49-minute dramatic film that is accessible through film societies, institutions,
and a distribution agency (V-tape). *Big Bear* is a three-hour mini-series made for CBC, Canadian Television.

sive, non-sustaining narrative. The 'aesthetic of hunger' here is a characteristic feature resulting from a tight budget and turned into a conspicuous stylistic trait, especially in the parody of a local Indigenous TV station. Here, and in the parody of detective movies, the multi-layered character of Indigenous humor comes to the fore, unmasking auto- and heterostereotyping practices.[10] Nevertheless, the film deals respectfully with Indigenous social ethics, as seen in the 'punishment' of the culprit with subsequent reintegration, in the presentation of the achievements of members of the community, and in the postmodern appearance of contemporary Indigenous artists. Through contextualization of Indigenous television, the screening of a film, song performances, and a one-woman show, Niro creates a modification of oral storytelling in electronic form.

The first major Indigenous motion picture in the USA, *Smoke Signals*, directed by Chris Eyre and based on Sherman Alexie's *The Lone Ranger and Tonto Fistfight in Heaven*, is a universal story (a father–son conflict) set in a contemporary Indigenous context and realized via the road-movie genre. The filmmakers, in employing the form of the conventional Hollywood narrative film, succeed with *Smoke Signals* in bringing Indigenous filmmaking to Hollywood, which was and remains the factory for Indian stereotypes in movies *per se* and has always provided the visual and sonic element in colonialist discourse. However, classical Western filmmaking is complemented with individual stylistic means and culturally motivated elements such as modernized versions of storytelling. Indigenous cultural traits are included but not explicated ethnologically – contemporary problems are shown but not discussed through a sociological lens. This film emancipates Indigenous discourse from moralizing indictment and perpetual Indian victimization, avoids the romanticization and idealization of Indigenous cultures, and presents Indigenous reality as the result of colonization without thematizing the latter anew. The contemporary setting wards off the kind of historical contextualization which Indigenous cultures have almost exclusively been subjected to in mainstream film discourse. The film is not exoticized by rituals, sweat lodges, feather costumes, dances or the like, and the filmmakers avoid contemporary Indian clichés. Intermedial references respond to neoromantic mainstream Indian movies such as *Dances with Wolves* and *Last of the Mohicans* and use satirical quotations

---

[10] The prefixes 'auto-' and 'hetero-' are employed here in relation to the dichotomy of 'self' and 'other': i.e. stereotyping the self and the other.

and comments to denounce their subtle perpetuation of Indian clichés, their fragmentation of Indigenous cultures, and their transportation of a false notion of fairness and political correctness toward Indigenous cultures.

The mini-series *Big Bear*, directed by Gil Cardinal and produced by Doug Cuthand, is the first major Indigenous film in Canada to be produced for television. It follows a classical narrative filmmaking style but applies, more than does *Smoke Signals*, an Indigenous approach that consists of filming on Indigenous reserve land and thus financially supporting the Pasqua community (which received rental revenues), hiring a large number of Cree actors and extras, employing many reserve residents on the set, and, finally, observing cultural taboos and refraining from showing a Thirst Dance. This Cree approach, coupled with a slow cinematic rhythm and efforts to underlining visually the vastness and beauty of the land, root this film firmly in Cree culture. The mini-series is based on the 1973 novel *The Temptations of Big Bear* by Rudy Wiebe and, in the fashion of historical realism, traces the era of treaty-making on the prairies and Cree chief Big Bear's protracted resistance to signing a treaty. Through the figure of Big Bear, one of the most charismatic figures in the history of the Canadian prairies, the filmmakers give an historical account of this era from an inside perspective (which, of course, cannot be a complete and universal account), describe the Cree way of life concealed behind historical 'facts', and provide insight into the drastic and devastating changes for the Cree caused by the colonization of the Canadian West. With this film, they present an historical narrative that counters Canadian historical portrayals of the figure of Big Bear, which previously depicted him as a bellicose and/or powerless chief. The film turns the tables on the traditional Hollywood language model which defined the Indigenous people as the inferior other through the 'improper' English assigned to them. Instead, it has the Cree speak proper English and the Canadian colonizers an unintelligible gibberish.

The Inuit feature film *Atanarjuat: The Fast Runner*, directed by Zacharias Kunuk, is the first Inuit dramatic film made in Inuktitut to receive both nationwide and international attention. It is an Inuit legend translated for the cinema and shot in the Arctic on digital video. Like *Big Bear*, it employs a distinctly Indigenous approach – what the filmmakers have called an "Inuit-style of community-based media production." This film was shot on Indigenous land, here Nunavut, the all-Inuit cast consists entirely of Igloolik residents, and the production also employed an almost exclusively Inuit crew, mixing expert filmmakers with film novices and involving a few southern professionals. The production money for the film benefited the local economy of Igloolik and involved local artists and elders, who re-made traditional clothing, tools, weapons, sleds, and dwellings after traditional models. Apart from its length (almost three hours), the film complies with conventional filmmaking guidelines, but adapts these to Arctic conditions and to the fact that an oral legend is being rendered. As with *Big Bear*'s portrayal of the prairies, the filmmakers succeed in conveying the harsh beauty of the Arctic landscape and the various Arctic colors and shades of snow and ice.

With respect to terminology, to speak about the original inhabitants of North America and their descendants I use the term 'Indigenous', because I believe that the other current terms are not appropriate. 'First Nations People' in Canada refers to people with 'Indian status', excluding 'non-status Indians', who are the Inuit, Métis, and some nations who did not sign a numbered treaty with the Canadian government. The terms 'Aboriginal people' and 'Native Americans/Canadians' cover all of the original inhabitants of North America. However, as these terms also have the derogatory connotation of 'primitive', I refrain from them as well. Furthermore, the term 'Aboriginal people' makes perfect sense in the Canadian context (where it is used more often than in the USA), but in a global context it could lead to confusion with the 'Aborigine', the original inhabitants of Australia. Finally, the term 'Indian' (as it is widely employed by Indigenous people themselves) is highly inappropriate, as it originates in the early colonialist context, has helped foster stereotypical notions, and also has a derogatory connotation.[11] Whenever I am referring to contemporary Indigenous people, I use the term 'Indigenous'; whenever I am referring to constructed, stereotyped and objectified images of Indigenous people, I use the term 'Indian'. With the term 'non-Indigenous', I am speaking of members of dominant mainstream North America and Europe; Asian North American, African North American, and Caribbean people are not included in this term. The terms 'filmic' and 'cinematic' are employed interchangeably to denote matters having to do with the medium of film. I am primarily dis-

---

[11] Robert F. Berkhofer, in *The White Man's Indian* (New York: Vintage, 1978), traces the constructed concept of 'the Indian' back to terminology and images employed by the colonizing powers of Spain, England, and France. He examines various academic schools which deal with Indigenous culture(s) and its (their) ranking in the cultural hierarchy and illuminates their contribution to the concept of 'the Indian'. Such schools were, for example, defenders of the theories of deficiency, environmentalism, progressivism, evolutionism, and polygenism/monogenism.

cussing filmmaking, films, and filmic discourse. Where not otherwise specified, videomaking, videos, and video discourse are subsumed under this term. With the development of digital video, one cannot easily distinguish between the two forms in terms of quality. For financial and practical reasons, many filmmakers use video technology or mix footage shot on film and footage shot on video. There is no real reason for differentiating between the two technologies, because the issue of which material and equipment is used is often not conditioned by the filmmakers' choice of styles and techniques but by the budget and conditions of location. When I am speaking of texts, I am differentiating between filmic and printed texts, as required. Otherwise, 'text' refers to both filmic and printed texts. The term 'aesthetic' is defined by the Encarta *World English Dictionary*, among others, as "the study of the rules and principles of art."[12] In this book it is employed in a related sense, to cover the principles involved in the making of filmic works: i.e. the entirety of film conventions, cultural elements, rules, techniques, and stylistic elements that influence the way in which a certain film is created.

The term 'colonization' denotes the establishment of colonies through the occupation of alien territory. The term 'colonialism' denotes a policy of a country to rule over other countries as colonies and develop trade for its own benefit. The two concepts are mutually conditional, whereas colonization is the prerequisite for colonialism. In academic discussions about contemporary colonial relations, both terms are usually employed interchangeably; however, to be correct one would have to use the term 'colonialism'. Similarly, 'colonial' and 'colonialist' pertain to actions and states relating to 'colonization' and 'colonialism', and the term 'colonialist' would be more correct for describing practices, relations, discourse and the like. According to accepted usage, I use the simpler 'colonial'. But often, in order to place emphasis on states, conditions, epistemes, practices and the like as results of colonialism, I employ the term 'colonialist'. Postcolonial writers and filmmakers in this book are original inhabitants of former European colonies and their descendants,[13] including the original inhabitants of settler nations and their descendants (i.e. Australia, Canada, New Zealand, and the USA) – not, however, Caucasian members of the colonizing powers and their descendants. Indigenous films in this book are films made by Indige-

---

[12] Encarta, *World English Dictionary* (London: Bloomsbury, 1999): 26.
[13] See also section below, "Postcolonial Theory and its Criticism."

nous people (i.e. necessarily the director or producer and, ideally, also the scriptwriter) – but not films made by non-Indigenous people based on Indigenous scripts or with Indigenous content.[14]

This book does not claim to be a comprehensive account of the whole body of Indigenous film work. Such an attempt would prove to be an impossible endeavour, as the films – encouragingly, it should be said – are as numerous as they are diverse, and the making of Indigenous films is increasing rapidly. The analysis of the films concentrates on both content and form, less as separate aspects than as reciprocally conditioning elements. For the analysis of form, I provide sequence protocols and/or detailed shot tables where necessary and useful. These are included in the Appendix.

∅ ২

---

[14] There is a current debate among filmmakers and scholars about what makes an Indigenous film; some include films with Indigenous content or those based on Indigenous screenplays.

1 The Foucauldian Lens of Power Decolonized

O NE OF THE CENTRAL THEMES of Michel Foucault's oeuvre
is the observing and objectifying gaze. In *The Birth of the Clinic*,
he describes the complicity between visual domination and the
rise of modern medicine and elaborates on the disciplinary power of *le
regard* – the gaze. He says that clinical thought, its methods and its scientific norms are defined by the "great myth of a pure Gaze that would be
pure Language: a speaking eye."[1] This speaking eye draws in all the existing information within the realm of the clinic. The more and the better it
sees, the more it becomes speech that states and teaches. "This speaking
eye would be the servant of things and the master of truth."[2] Foucault thus
equates the gaze with language and thought: a "hearing gaze and a speaking
gaze [...] all that is *visible* is *expressible*, and that is *wholly visible* because
it is *wholly expressible*."[3] He explains further:

> The gaze saw sovereignty in a world of language whose clear speech it
> gathered up effortlessly in order to restore it in a secondary, identical
> speech: given by the visible, this speech, without changing anything, made
> it possible to see. In its sovereign exercise, the gaze took up once again the
> structures of visibility that it had itself deposited in its field of perception.[4]

Thus, Martin Jay observes, "what is in fact 'seen' is not a given, objective
reality open to an innocent eye. Rather, it is an epistemic field, constructed

---

[1] Michel Foucault, *The Birth of the Clinic: An Archaeology of Medical Perception* (*Naissance de la clinique: Une archéologie du regard médical*, 1963; New York: Pantheon, 1973): 114.

[2] Foucault, *The Birth of the Clinic*, 115.

[3] *The Birth of the Clinic*, 115; emphases in original.

[4] *The Birth of the Clinic*, 117.

as much linguistically as visually, which is more or less close to the 'truth' than what is replaced."[5]

In his lecture "Orders of Discourse," Foucault shows that the "will to truth" is an instrument of institutionalized and symbolic violence, operating through convictions and 'truths' that are seemingly grounded in arguments and evidence. In this way, he is able to delineate discourse and scientific/academic qualification as phenomena of power.[6] The union of truth and power defines discourse as the agency of power and the "will to truth" as a disguised "will to power."[7] Thus, the gaze becomes speech, which becomes discourse, which becomes power. Discourse in itself is not power, but

> in every society the production of discourse is at once controlled, selected, organised, and redistributed according to a certain number of procedures, whose role is to avert its powers and its dangers, to cope with chance events, to evade its ponderous, awesome materiality.[8]

Foucault holds that this exercise of power via discourse operates through exclusion, and he identifies "three great systems of exclusion governing discourse – prohibited words, the division of madness and the will to truth."[9] The first system operates on the principle of prohibition, mainly in the realms of speech, politics, and sexuality, the second on the principle of division and rejection, and the third through the constructed division between true and false. This last division and its implicit "will to truth"

---

[5] Martin Jay, "In the Empire of the Gaze: Foucault and the Denigration of Vision in Twentieth-Century French Thought," in *Michel Foucault: Critical Assessments*, ed. Barry Smart (New York & London: Routledge, 1994), vol. 1: 206.

[6] Foucault does not provide a consistent definition of power. Rather, he analyzes various aspects of this phenomenon which can be summarized as follows: power is directed at the body of the individual, power is a network of practices, power is characterized as relation between individuals, power is decentralized, power can produce experiences and scholarly object areas, power produces disciplinary individuals, and power is inseparable from knowledge; Hans Herbert Kögler, *Michel Foucault* (Sammlung Metzler 281: Realien zur Philosophie; Stuttgart & Weimar: J.B. Metzler, 1994): 89–98. Foucault has been widely criticized for his concept of power. The most common points of critique are targeted at his ontological overrating of power, the subsequent impossibility of resistance, and his equating of power and truth (Kögler, *Michel Foucault*, 107–19). Cf., further, Axel Honneth, *Kritik der Macht: Reflexionsstufen einer kritischen Gesellschaftstheorie* (Frankfurt am Main: Suhrkamp, 1994): 168–95.

[7] Kögler, *Michel Foucault*, 81, 84.

[8] Michel Foucault, "Orders of Discourse," tr. Rupert Swyer ("L'ordre du discours") *Social Science Information* 10.2 (1971): 8.

[9] Foucault, "Orders of Discourse," 11.

governs our "will to knowledge" and the creation of discourse. Discourse is channelled, controlled, and limited by the principle of commentary, a masked, endless repetition of what has been and has not been said before, via the author as unifying principle of a particular group of writings and statements and as guaranteeing principle of their coherence, and via the principle of disciplines constituting a system of control that defines discourse's limits and the rules according to which it is employed. These principles control what is said, how it is said, and who can say it; hence they constrain the speaking subject. This system of exclusion relies heavily on institutional support: teaching, print, the publishing system, libraries, and laboratories.[10] Thus, discourse is marked by control, limitation, and exclusion. In this sense, Foucault understands scientific and academic disciplines as controlling instruments of discourse production that limit the horizon of possibilities of experience through implicit rules.[11] Shared by Foucault's three principles of exclusion is the creation of binaries and oppositions, which he has described most elaborately with the example of the polarization of reason and insanity in *Madness and Civilization.*

Such binaries and principles of exclusion can be related to North American colonial discourse. This discourse was created in the institutions of knowledge and education (presses, publishers, universities, schools etc) and has been furthered in media institutions (presses, publishers, television broadcasters, film companies etc), both in colonial England and in the later settler nations.[12] The basic constructed opposition in North American colonial discourse, on which discursive exclusion, marginalization, and objectifications rest, is that of self/other and center/margin, from which other binaries derive. This discourse defines the colonial group through difference from and in opposition to the colonized group in terms of 'race', cultural traditions, philosophy, morality, beliefs, social systems, and other factors. In the Foucauldian sense, the dominant group controls, selects, organizes, and channels this discourse. Shohat and Stam explain the tendencies within and operations of eurocentric discourse, which is colonial discourse in the case of North America, in terms of five aspects:

---

[10] Foucault, "Orders of Discourse," 8–11.

[11] Kögler, *Michel Foucault*, 82–83.

[12] On the formation of colonial discourse, see Ella Shohat & Robert Stam, *Unthinking Eurocentrism: Multiculturalism and the Media* (1994; London & New York: Routledge, 1997): 55–99.

1. it projects a linear historical trajectory leading from classical Greece to the metropolitan capitals of Europe and the USA, and it renders history as a sequence of empires from Pax Romana to Pax Americana;

2. it attributes to the West an inherent progress toward democracy;

3. it elides non-European democratic traditions, while obscuring manipulations within Western democracies and masking their part in manipulating/subverting non-Western democracies;

4. it minimizes the West's oppressive practices by viewing them as contingent, accidental, exceptional;

5. it appropriates the cultural and material production of non-Europeans while negating both their achievements and its own appropriation, in that way consolidating its own sense of self.[13]

This explanation directs Foucault's philosophico-political approach toward postcolonial experience and is paramount for the understanding of colonial media discourse and the Indigenous response to it.

The gaze/vision is the primary aspect of cognition in the medical sciences, as Foucault observes in *The Birth of the Clinic*, which leads him to suggest that the primacy of the visual is retained in the development of the human sciences.[14] Martin Jay argues: "The sciences of man, intended to help in the macro-logical control of populations as well as the micro-logical normalization of individuals, drew on the mixture of the gaze and discourse."[15] Sol Worth and John Adair make it clear that not only vision but also moving images constitute an undemanding mode of perception: "the notion of taking meaning or sense from a flow of images might be deeply ingrained in human consciousness and might make filmmaking a uniquely easy and responsive methodology to learn."[16] The messages of this flow of images are as easily understood and internalized. This concept of ocular-centrism in the realm of cognition associated with the concepts of colonialism and ethnocentrism in historical and contemporary discourse allows a parallel to be set up between Foucault's 'gaze of power' and the dominant group's viewpoint, hence with colonial discourse that observes and objecti-

---

[13] Shohat & Stam, *Unthinking Eurocentrism*, 2–3.

[14] Martin Jay, "In the Empire of the Gaze," 211.

[15] Jay, "In the Empire of the Gaze," 215.

[16] Sol Worth & John Adair, *Through Navajo Eyes: An Exploration in Film Communication and Anthropology* (1972; Albuquerque: U of New Mexico P, 1997): 258.

fies oppressed groups. Regarding the visual modalities of colonial discourse represented by photography, movies, videos, and TV broadcasts,
one can indeed speak of a lens of power, the camera representing Foucault's 'speaking eye'. Works of film, photography, and TV broadcasting
from this dominant media discourse can thus be understood metaphorically
as the lens of power with a colonialist gaze. Marianette Jaimes–Guerrero
cautions that the power of media within a controlling discourse needs to be
recognized. She holds that its systematic and systemic effectivity has made
members of both the dominant and the subaltern groups its product as well
as its victims.[17]

The two major operational instruments of visual colonial discourse in
North America are ethnographic documentaries[18] and Hollywood narrative
films, the latter being the dominant mode of dramatic filmmaking. Because
documentary form is most often falsely understood as a reflection of 'reality', truth is applied to its images, and thus the 'truthfulness' of documentary narrative is often not questioned. James Clifford holds that ethnographic texts are systems of truth through which power and history work,
and warns that ethnographic texts are inherently only partly true.[19] Homi
Bhabha observes that the 'entertaining' Hollywood discourse of the 1950s
operated with the agencies of voyeurism and fetishism, an idea that is applicable to Hollywood narrative cinema in general.[20] He applies Foucault's

---

[17] Marianette Jaimes–Guerrero, "Savage Erotica Exotica: Media Imagery of Native Women in North America," in *Native North America: Critical and Cultural Perspectives*, ed.
Renée Hulan (Toronto: ECW, 1999): 190.

[18] On ethnographic filmmaking and its criticism, see Timothy Asch, "Ethnographic Film
Production," *Film Comment* 7.1 (1971): 40–42, and "The ethics of ethnographic film-
making," in *Film as Ethnography*, ed. Peter Ian Crawford & David Turton (Manchester &
New York: Manchester UP, 1992): 196–204; Eva Hohenberger, *Die Wirklichkeit des Films:
Dokumentarfilm, Ethnografischer Film* (Hildesheim, Zurich & New York: Georg Olms,
1988); Karl–Heinz Kohl, "Abwehr und Verlangen: Der Eurozentrismus in der Ethnologie,"
Berliner Hefte 12 (1979): 28–42; Kathleen Kuehnast, "Visual Imperialism and the Export of
Prejudice: An Exploration of Ethnographic Film," in *Film as Ethnography*, ed. Peter Ian
Crawford & David Turton (Manchester & New York: Manchester UP, 1992): 183–95; David
MacDougall, "Ethnographic Film: Failure and Promise," *Annual Review of Anthropology* 7
(1978): 405–25; Bob Scholte, "Toward a Reflexive and Critical Anthropology," in *Reinvent-
ing Anthropology*, ed. Dell Hymes (New York: Pantheon, 1972): 430–57; and Ellen Strain,
"Exotic Bodies, Distant Landscapes: Touristic Viewing and Popularized Anthropology in the
Nineteenth Century," *Wide Angle* 18.2 (April 1996): 70–100.

[19] James Clifford, "Introduction: Partial Truths," in *Writing Culture: The Poetics and Politics of Ethnography*, ed. James Clifford & George E. Marcus (Berkeley: U of California P,
1986): 7.

[20] Homi K. Bhabha, *The Location of Culture* (London & New York: Routledge, 1994): 68.

concept of 'surveillance'[21] of those in control to colonial power, linking it with the "regime of the *scopic drive*": i.e. "the drive that represents the pleasure in 'seeing', which has the look as its object of desire."[22] The Foucauldian 'gaze of power' becomes the Bhabhian 'voyeuristic look' that fetishizes that which is seen by "active consent." It associates the image presented with an image contained in colonial discourse/ knowledge which is assumed to be its equivalent and thus "establishes in the scopic space the illusion of the object relation. [...] The ambivalence of this form of 'consent' in objectification – real as mythical – is the *ambivalence* on which the stereotype turns and illustrates that crucial bind of pleasure and power."[23] The fetish is a stereotype that simultaneously constructs an identity grounded on the dichotomy of mastery/anxiety and pleasure/defence because it is a form of contradictory belief, both recognizing and disavowing difference.[24] Bhabha thus defines the stereotype as the major strategy of colonialist discourse and as an ambivalent mode of knowledge and power.[25]

Foucault makes it clear that the humanities and social sciences degrade their subjects of analysis to mere objects and reveal 'truths' about them which are independent of their own self-image. This discursive 'truth' is not the individual's 'truth' of him/herself but an 'individual truth' about her/him.[26] In this sense, the analyzing and scrutinizing gaze objectifies. Thus, with the rise of human sciences, wo/man becomes both the object of scientific and academic discourse and the subject that sees and knows.[27] In colonialist visual discourse, however, the positions of knowing subject and object of knowledge were clearly defined: the first was filled by members of the dominant group and the latter assigned to members of the oppressed group. According to Foucault, vision can help to constitute an episteme

---

[21] Foucault, in *Discipline and Punish*, introduces the concept of 'surveillance' within a society and describes it with the help of Jeremy Bentham's Panopticon prison model; Foucault, *Discipline and Punish: The Birth of the Prison* (*Surveiller et punir: La naissance de la prison*, 1975; New York: Vintage, 1979).

[22] Bhabha, *The Location of Culture*, 76; emphasis in original.

[23] *The Location of Culture*, 76; emphasis in original. For Bhabha's concept of 'ambivalence', see *The Location of Culture*, 66, and Bill Ashcroft, Gareth Griffiths & Helen Tiffin, *Key Concepts in Post-Colonial Studies* (London & New York: Routledge, 1998): 12–14.

[24] *The Location of Culture*, 75.

[25] *The Location of Culture*, 66.

[26] Kögler, *Michel Foucault*, 122.

[27] Michel Foucault, *The Order of Things: An Archaeology of the Human Sciences* (*Les Mots et les choses: Une archéologie des sciences humaines*, 1966; London & New York: Routledge, 2007): 340.

without the implied presence of an observer, "of an absent sovereign or his humanist surrogate, whose gaze totalized the discursive field."[28] This episteme abstracts the gaze to an invisible and unspecifiable presence of control. In ethnographic filmmaking and Western feature films, the director, camera operator, director of photography, and crew are the direct observers, and the viewers of these films are abstracted into a seeming absence, thus becoming indirect observers. Both groups 'gaze' at the object of knowledge and constitute the unspecifiable presence of control and the gaze of surveillance and power. The camera lens, operating on behalf of this gaze, is the Foucauldian lens of power.

Himani Bannerji applies Foucault's concept of 'the gaze of power' to "racist–sexist–imperialist constructions of otherness and difference" in prevalent societies.[29] According to her, such constructions are the gaze of the dominant group, which contains unfiltered objectifying and stereotyping images of marginalized groups. She identifies the theoretical writings of marginalized scholars who analyze the social and cultural agency of ruling (coded as gender, race, and class) as "returning the gaze."[30] This concept, applied to the works of Indigenous filmmakers, permits one to view the process of filming as metaphorically returning the objectifying and surveilling gaze, because the filmmakers avail themselves of colonialist means of production (film technology) and employ them to create self-controlled images that look critically at colonialist images. They decolonize the Foucauldian lens of power by quoting, discussing, and subverting such colonialist images of Indigeneity and by projecting through this lens self-determined images free of stereotypization and objectification (be it the filmic treatment of history, political incidents, cultural events, tradition, or contemporary Indigenous experience). In this sense, the decolonized lens of power is a second, self-controlled gaze, an anticolonialist gaze. Through their production of media, Indigenous filmmakers cease to belong to the objectified group as objects of knowledge and presentation and become subjects that know and present. They create a discourse that responds to colonialist media discourse. Thus, it is appropriate to analyze their works within the framework of postcolonial theory that attempts to expose binary oppositions and the mechanisms of colonialist discourse. According to Ed-

---

[28] Martin Jay, "In the Empire of the Gaze," 213.

[29] Himani Bannerji, "Returning the Gaze: An Introduction," in *Returning the Gaze: Essays on Racism, Feminism and Politics*, ed. Himani Bannerji (Toronto: Sister Vision, 1993): xxii.

[30] Bannerji, "Returning the Gaze," xxii–xxiii.

ward Said, such counter-discursive attempts can disclose the misrepresentations of discursive power, contextualize the violence done to psychically
and politically repressed 'inferior' individuals in the name of advanced culture, and commence the difficult project of formulating a discourse of
liberation.[31] This media discourse of liberation decolonizes the Foucauldian
lens of power.

In creating this discourse of liberation, Indigenous filmmakers are always in some state of reaction to and dialogue with ethnographic filmmaking and to classical/conventional narrative filmmaking and its epitome,
Hollywood cinema. Hollywood narrative cinema has come to dominate
cinematic discourses and has substantially reinforced cultural hegemonies
around the globe.[32] There are deviations from this filmmaking convention,
mainly in other national cinemas, such as the French, the Brazilian, and the
(Asian) Indian, but also within Hollywood cinema. Nevertheless, these deviations are often based on reactions to Hollywood film, hence Hollywood
cinema is a latent constant factor in global cinema. Indigenous filmmakers
see themselves as responding to this colonial cinematic discourse, which
developed a tradition of stereotyped, objectified, romanticized, and homogenized representation of Indigenous people and which has created noto-
rious clichés of them in the Western media.[33] The most prevalent ideologi-

---

[31] Edward W. Said, "Foucault and the Imagination of Power," in *Foucault: A Critical Reader*, ed. David Couzens Hoy (Oxford & New York: Basil Blackwell, 1986): 153.

[32] I work with Susan Hayward's definition of the concept of classical narrative cinema, which she equates with Hollywood cinema. Her definition covers several aspects: cinematic style serves to explain, not to obscure; the narrative is presented as reality; this filmic 'reality' is ideologically charged; cause and effect move the narrative along; the narrative achieves closure at the end; the narrative is psychologically, hence individually, motivated; representa-tion of the successful completion of the oedipal trajectory is central; spatial and temporal con-tinuity are paramount; cinematic techniques, such as shots, lighting, color, editing, sound, and mise-en-scène, must not draw attention to themselves but manufacture realism [an illusionist reality]; narrative and characters are goal-oriented; continuity is essential; the natural effect achieved through three-point lighting supports the naturalness of filmic realism; and sound serves to reinforce meaning, such as danger and romance; Hayward, *Key Concepts in Cinema Studies* (London & New York: Routledge, 1996): 45–49). Cf. also David Bordwell, "Clas-sical Hollywood Cinema: Narrational Principles and Procedures," in *Narrative, Apparatus, Ideology: A Film Theory Reader*, ed. Philip Rosen (New York: Columbia UP, 1986): 17–34.

[33] On the representation of Indigenous people in Western media, including narrative and ethnographic films, see Gretchen Bataille & Charles L.P. Silet, "The Entertaining Ana-chronism: Indians in American Film," in *The Kaleidoscopic Lens: How Hollywood Views Ethnic Groups*, ed. Randall M. Miller (n.p.: Jerome S. Ozer, 1980): 36–53; Ward Churchill, "Smoke Signals: A History of Native Americans in Cinema," *LiP Magazine* (1998): http://www.lipmagazine.org/articles/revichurchill_35_p.htm; Ward Churchill, "Fantasies of the

cal element of dominant media discourse that Indigenous filmmakers react to is the stereotypical visualization of 'Indians'. Early Hollywood usually represented Indigenous people in two groups that reflected a stereotypical dichotomy: one docile and submissive, ready to cooperate with the army and/or settlers, and the other fierce, ready to attack, take hostages, and kill (and, of course, take scalps). Very often, Indians were an indefinite mass attacking settlers, coaches, camps, and the like. Most often, their linguistic abilities were restricted to a monosyllabic and/ or "pseudo-poetic" babble, as Friar and Friar call it.[34] If Indian characters were singled out, they were stoic and taciturn and sometimes mystic kidnappers. Even today, mainstream films sometimes make use of Indigenous cultures/figures as composing exotic and enthralling backgrounds and elements for plots with non-Indigenous protagonists – for example, *Dances with Wolves* (1990), *The Last of the Mohicans* (1992), and *Natural Born Killers* (1994).

The genesis of the stereotypical Indian begins with the colonization of the Americas. Robert Berkhofer explores the way in which present-day Indian clichés are grounded in early colonial discourse: i.e. in the writings of Spanish and English colonizers and explorers such as Christopher Colum-

---

Master Race. The Cinematic Colonization of American Indians," in Churchill, *Fantasies of the Master Race: Literature, Cinema and the Colonization of American Indians* (San Francisco: City Lights, 1998): 167–224; Daniel Francis, *The Imaginary Indian: The Image of the Indian in Canadian Culture* (Vancouver, British Columbia: Arsenal Pulp, 1992); Philip French, "The Indian in the Western Movie," *Art in America* 60 (July–August 1972): 32–39; Ralph Friar & Natasha Friar, *The Only Good Indian: The Hollywood Gospel* (New York: Drama Book Specialists, 1972); Jacquelyn Kilpatrick, *Celluloid Indians: Native Americans and Film* (Lincoln: U of Nebraska P, 1999); Hartmut Lutz, *"Indianer" und "Native Americans": Zur sozial- und literarhistorischen Vermittlung eines Stereotyps* (Hildesheim, Zurich & New York: Georg Olms, 1985); Hartmut Lutz, "'Indians' and Native Americans in the Movies: A History of Stereotypes, Distortions, and Displacements," *Visual Anthropology* 3 (1990): 31–48; Rosalind C. Morris, *New Worlds from Fragments: Film, Ethnography, and the Representation of Northwest Coast Culture* (Boulder CO: Westview, 1994); John E. O'Connor, *The Hollywood Indian: Stereotypes of Native Americans in Films* (Trenton NJ: New Jersey State Museum, 1980); Louis Owens, *Mixedblood Messages: Literature, Film, Family, Place* (Norman: U of Oklahoma P, 1998): 99–131; Hans–Peter Rodenberg, *Der imaginierte Indianer: Zur Dynamik von Kulturkonflikt und Vergesellschaftung des Fremden* (Frankfurt am Main: Suhrkamp, 1994); Peter C. Rollins & John E. O'Connor, ed. *Hollywood's Indian: The Portrayal of the Native American in Film* (Lexington: UP of Kentucky, 2003); Beverly Singer, *Wiping the War Paint off the Lens: Native American Film and Video* (Minneapolis: U of Minnesota P, 2001); Fatimah Tobing Rony, *The Third Eye: Race, Cinema, and Ethnographic Spectacle* (Durham NC & London: Duke UP, 1996); and *Native Americans on Film and Video*, ed. Elizabeth Weatherford (New York: Museum of the American Indian, 1981).

[34] Ralph Friar & Natasha Friar, *The Only Good Indian: The Hollywood Gospel*, 178.

bus, Amerigo Vespucci, Richard Hakluyt, Thomas Hariot, John Smith, and the minister Alexander Whitaker.[35] Berkhofer points out that these accounts of the inhabitants of the New World tended to be contradictory and inconsistent. They featured them either as insolent, cruel, treacherous, loose/libidinous, and living in anarchy-like communities without laws and governance, or as handsome, friendly, hospitable, brave, dignified, loving, and modest people. Indigenous cultures were measured against non-Indigenous cultures, and 'characteristic' Indian features were derived from aspects of European cultures that Indigenous cultures were lacking, and, vice versa, from aspects of Indigenous people that Europeans were lacking and abhorred. These opposing images served to sustain the observers' image of their own societies and whatever image of the Indian was needed for the observers' judgement.[36] Hartmut Lutz also points out that eurocentric clichés about the Indigenous people of North America oscillate between the two extremes of the 'bloodthirsty red devil' and the 'noble savage'.[37] This polarity results from the fact that stereotypes are constructed in such a way that they can apply to practically any individual in a given group.[38] Early Puritan chronicles reflect this polarity of perception of Indigenous people: there is the "physically hard-working, honest, and proud Indian" alongside the "superstitious devil-worshipper."[39] Current Indian clichés have arisen chiefly from Puritan thought, early Puritan writings, and the descriptions of early explorers, who measured Indigenous culture against European morality and values. Indigenous culture was judged against the twin criteria of Christianity and civilization.[40] Gesa Mackenthun holds that early colonizers in the Caribbean similarly constructed a dichotomous myth of the 'peaceful Arawaks' and the 'ferocious Caribs' (also 'Cannibals') as two different ethnic groups. She writes that "the Caribs – protectors of the desired gold – proved a legitimate impulse for colonial aggression (now 'defense') as well as a justification for the failure of obtaining the desired object (due to the danger of being eaten)."[41] The dichotomy legitimized colonial intervention

---

[35] Robert F. Berkhofer, *The White Man's Indian* (New York: Vintage, 1978): 3–22.

[36] Berkhofer, *The White Man's Indian*, 19–20, 27–28.

[37] Hartmut Lutz, *"Indianer" und "Native Americans"*, 3.

[38] Lutz, *"Indianer" und "Native Americans"*, 9.

[39] *"Indianer" und "Native Americans"*, 131.

[40] Berkhofer, *The White Man's Indian*, 10.

[41] Gesa Mackenthun, *Metaphors of Dispossession: American Beginnings and the Translation of Empire, 1492–1637* (Norman & London: U of Oklahoma P, 1997): 62.

in favor of the Arawaks, who had to be "defended" against the Caribs in "knightly fashion." In this sense, the myth of the "man eaters" and "gold keepers" supported official colonial policy, to the extent that Queen Isabel decreed that "Cannibals" could rightfully be enslaved, because the "'good' Indians were dying so fast."[42] This decree then began to be understood as a right to enslave any "potentially cannibalistic" inhabitant of the 'discovered' islands.

It becomes clear that such dichotomies of the good and the evil Indian have always existed in eurocentric discourse. They were constructed myths legitimizing colonial policies and defining European civilization, including its religion and moral values, as a role model for the beginnings of a developed New World society against the background of the 'other primitive' societies. Although present clichés still move between two extremes, their quality has shifted to either the notion of the 'dumb, drunken, lecherous, and lazy Indian' or the 'nature-loving spiritual traditionalist' and 'exotic lover'. The polarities of stereotypical notions still work in such a way that they can accommodate almost all members of present Indigenous cultures in the space between the two extremes. Berkhofer considers the image of the 'drunken, poor, and degraded Indian' to be a third major "White image" of the Indian.[43] Since the notions of the 'bloodthirsty red devil' and the 'noble savage' do not as readily apply to contemporary imagery of Indigenous cultures,[44] they need to be regarded as the basic stage of image-making from which the present pejorative and romanticized stereotypes evolved.[45] Similarly, the 'Indian princess', 'squaw drudge', and 'tawny temptress' became the 'suffering helpless victim' or the 'loose squaw', all clichés still prevalent in Western thought and discourse.[46] Jacquelyn Kilpatrick identifes three categories of stereotypes of Indigenous people in West-

---

[42] Mackenthun, *Metaphors of Dispossession*, 62.

[43] Berkhofer, *The White Man's Indian*, 30.

[44] Exceptions are the polarized presentation of the Sioux and Pawnee in *Dances With Wolves* (1990) and of the Mohicans and Hurons in *The Last of the Mohicans* (1992).

[45] On the creation and operation of stereotypes, see also Homi K. Bhabha, "The Other Question: Difference, Discrimination and the Discourse of Colonialism," in *Out There: Marginalization and Contemporary Cultures*, ed. Russel Ferguson et al. (New York: New Museum of Contemporary Art & Cambridge MA: MIT Press, 1990): 85; Bhabha, *The Location of Culture*, 79; Jacquelyn Kilpatrick, *Celluloid Indians: Native Americans and Film* (Lincoln: U of Nebraska P, 1999): 1–15; and Ella Shohat & Robert Stam, *Unthinking Eurocentrism: Multiculturalism and the Media* (1994; London & New York: Routledge, 1997): 178–219.

[46] See Janice Acoose, *Iskwewak: Kah' Ki Yaw Ni Wahkomakanak: Neither Indian Princesses nor Easy Squaws* (Toronto: Women's Press, 1995): 55.

ern film: mental, sexual, and spiritual. She explains that Indian enemies or
sidekicks were presented as innately less intelligent than their Euro-American counterparts and that "this lack of mental prowess may have something
to do with the image of the Native American as intensely sexual – more
creature than human, more bestial than celestial."[47] The "spiritual Indian"
then became emancipated from his role as "primitive heathen," shifting
toward the "nature-based noble savage" and, latterly, to the "natural ecolo-
gist."[48] In her report on Aboriginal-language broadcasting in Canada, Jennifer David states:

> Stereotypes of the alcoholic on welfare, the wise elder, the squaw, the prin-
> cess, the noble savage, and the warrior are just a few of the images that the
> media perpetuates through advertising, typecasting, and exclusion of con-
> temporary portrayals of Aboriginal people [...] there are very few programs
> where Aboriginal people are not cast in stereotypical roles.[49]

These imaginary and ideological Indians have been "as real, perhaps more
real, than the Native American of actual existence and contact," says Berkhofer.[50] And Amanda Cobb notes:

> American popular culture has been so saturated for so long with represen-
> tations of Hollywood Indians that those representations have become a
> litmus test by which non-Native people judge whether or not an actual
> Native person is 'really Indian'.[51]

As Foucault suggests, vision dominates cognition and the acquisition of
knowledge; consequently, the implications of clichéd visual images influence and spread into all other discourses. In this respect, subaltern films almost necessarily become reflexive, engaging in dialogue with the established body of belief and method and directly or indirectly discussing
established cinema[52] and the imaginary Indian developed in this discourse.
Through this dialogue, each new film extends and alters filmic discourse in

---

[47] Jacquelyn Kilpatrick, "Introduction" to Kilpatrick, *Celluloid Indians*, xvii.

[48] Kilpatrick, "Introduction" to Kilpatrick, *Celluloid Indians*, xvii–xviii.

[49] Jennifer David, *Aboriginal Language Broadcasting in Canada: An overview and recommendations to the Task Force on Aboriginal Languages and Cultures* (Debwe Communications Inc., 26 November 2004): 9 at http://www.aptn.ca

[50] Berkhofer, *The White Man's Indian*, 71.

[51] Amanda J. Cobb, "This Is What It Means to Say *Smoke Signals*: Native American Cultural
Sovereignty," in *Hollywood's Indian: The Portrayal of the Native American in Film*, ed. Peter C.
Rollins & John E. O'Connor (1998; Lexington: UP of Kentucky, rev. ed. 2003): 217.

[52] Shohat & Stam, *Unthinking Eurocentrism*, 279.

general and Indigenous filmic discourse in particular. Bhabha argues that this dialogue must transcend the mere recognition and displacement of stereotypical images and engage with their effectivity in the construction of fetishized colonialist identification, "with the repertoire of positions of power and resistance, domination and dependence that constructs colonial identification subject (both colonizer and colonized)."[53] On the basis of an understanding of the colonial "processes of subjectification" that are made possible and plausible through stereotypical discourse,[54] subaltern film discourse must redirect the colonial discourse's effectivity of constructing colonial images, identities, and subject positions and thus dismantle and deconstruct hetero- and autostereotyped images and identities.

Gerald Vizenor, in outlining his concept of trickster discourse, draws on Mikhail Bakhtin's and Tzvetan Todorov's theories of dialogism. According to Bakhtin, the context of an utterance is an integral part of it; an utterance consists of a verbal and an implied part:[55]

> The living utterance, having taken meaning and shape at a particular historical moment in a socially specific environment, cannot fail to brush up against thousands of living dialogic threads, woven by socio-ideological consciousness around the given object of an utterance; it cannot fail to become an active participant in social dialogue. After all, the utterance arises out of this dialogue as a continuation of it and as a rejoinder to it.[56]

In his discussion of Bakhtin's ideas, Todorov explains:

> The most important feature of the utterance, or at least the most neglected, is its *dialogism*, that is, its intertextual dimension. [...] Intentionally or not, all discourse is in dialogue with prior discourses on the same subject, as well as with discourses yet to come, whose reactions it foresees and anticipates.[57]

---

[53] Homi Bhabha, *The Location of Culture* (London & New York: Routledge, 1994): 67.

[54] Bhabha, *The Location of Culture*, 67.

[55] Tzvetan Todorov, *Mikhail Bakhtin: The Dialogical Principle*, tr. Wlad Godzich (1981; Minneapolis MN: U of Minnesota P, 1985): 41.

[56] Mikhail Bakhtin, "Discourse in the Novel," in Bakhtin, *The Dialogic Imagination*, tr. Caryl Emerson & Michael Holquist (*Voprosy literatury i estetki*; Austin: U of Texas P, 1990): 276–77.

[57] Tzvetan Todorov, *Mikhail Bakhtin: The Dialogical Principle*, x; emphasis in original; quoted in part by Gerald Vizenor in "Trickster Discourse: Comic Holotropes and Language Games," in *Narrative Chance: Postmoden Discourse on Native American Indian Literatures*, ed. Vizenor (Norman & London, U of Oklahoma P, 1993): 191.

And later: "There is no utterance without relation to other utterances, and that is essential."[58] In the same sense, Valentin N. Voloshinov, drawing on Bakhtin, holds:

> No utterance in general can be attributed to the speaker exclusively; it is the *product of the interaction of the interlocutors*, and, broadly speaking, the product of the whole complex *social situation* in which it has occurred.[59]

Applying this theory to anticolonialist and colonialist discourses, it becomes apparent that on the subject of the imaginary and ideological Indian, which was created in early colonial discourse and developed and maintained through endless citation and repetition of such utterances, Indigenous discourses constantly engage with colonial discourse. Utterances of the imaginary and ideological Indian are never applicable to a single source within colonialist discourse but exist only in the context of this colonialist discourse, in the sum of their production, channelling, distribution, and reception. These utterances depend on interaction between several sources within colonialist discourse and on dialogue with the recipients, who are both colonizing and colonized subjects.

This idea of dialogue between discourses and interaction between interlocutors leads Vizenor to develop the idea of the trickster as a sign "in a postmodern language game" "that becomes a comic holotrope, a consonance of sentences in various voices, ironies, variations in cultural myths and social metaphors."[60] The dialogue between discourses and interlocutors on the same subject can have ironic, playful moments that reveal distinctions and differences of views and beliefs. To Vizenor, these interlocutors in trickster narratives are the author, narrator, characters, and audience.[61] In filmic trickster narratives, these are scriptwriter, director, producer, characters, and audience (defining the filmic pendant of the narrator is tricky). Trickster discourse relies on "two consciousnesses that do not fuse"; its "essential and constitutive element is the relation of a consciousness to

---

[58] Tzvetan Todorov, *Mikhail Bakhtin: The Dialogical Principle*, 60; quoted in part by Gerald Vizenor in "Trickster Discourse: Comic Holotropes and Language Games," 191.

[59] Valentin N. Voloshinov, *Freudianism: A Marxist Critique*, tr. I.R. Titunik (*Frejdizm*, 1927; New York: Academic Press, 1975): 118; quoted. in Tzvetan Todorov, *Mikhail Bakhtin: The Dialogical Principle*, 30, quoted in part by Gerald Vizenor in "Trickster Discourse: Comic Holotropes and Language Games," 191; emphases in Todorov.

[60] Vizenor in "Trickster Discourse: Comic Holotropes and Language Games," 190, 192.

[61] "Trickster Discourse: Comic Holotropes and Language Games," 191.

another consciousness, precisely because it is *other*."[62] It is the dialogic friction between the Western and Indigenous consciousness that reveals ironies and disparities, seemingly playful and humorous but with a more serious message in their wake. Trickster discourse pokes fun at all inter-locutors; its subversive potential lies in its ability to demonstrate disparities in a playful and comic manner. In the dialogism between Western and In-digenous discourses, these ironies and disparities are centered on the imagi-nary and ideological Indian, historical and contemporary.

Trickster discourse

> provides a means to contest tragic narratives on Indian history, social science monologues on Indianness, and a belief in the ultimate extinction of the tribes. It is thus a comic mode of discourse that emphasizes survival, adaptability, and humor.[63]

Vizenor says that "the opposite of a comic discourse is a monologue, an utterance in isolation, which comes closer to the tragic mode in literature and not a comic tribal world view."[64] He holds further that "the trickster bears no evil or malice in narrative voices. Malice and evil would silence the comic *holotropes*."[65] In consequence, he sees hegemonic monologues, the grand narratives of Western discourse, as tragic and as oppositional to discursive dialogue that is invested with laughter, postmodern playfulness, and comic relief and that thus becomes trickster discourse. The trickster is

> freedom in a comic sign [...] imagined in narrative voices, a communal rein to the unconscious, which is comic liberation.[66]

And:

---

[62] Mikhail Bakhtin, "Avtor i geroj v esteticheskoj dejatel' nosti" ["Author and character in aesthetic activity"], in Bakhtin, *Estetika slovesnogo tvorchestva* [The aesthetics of verbal creation] (Moscow: Iskusstvo, 1979): 77–78, quoted in Tzvetan Todorov, *Mikhail Bakhtin: The Dialogical Principle*, 99–100; quoted by Gerald Vizenor in "Trickster Discourse," *American Indian Quarterly* 14.3 (Summer 1990): 282; emphases in Todorov.

[63] Paul Pasquaretta, "Introduction" to Pasquaretta, *Gambling and Survival in Native North America* (Tucson: U of Arizona P, 2003): xiv.

[64] Gerald Vizenor, "Trickster Discourse: Comic Holotropes and Language Games," 191.

[65] Gerald Vizenor, "A Postmodern Introduction," in *Narrative Chance: Postmoden Discourse on Native American Indian Literatures*, ed. Gerald Vizenor (Norman & London: U of Oklahoma P, 1993): 13; emphasis in original.

[66] Vizenor, "A Postmodern Introduction," 13.

Laughter over that comic touch [...] would not steal the breath of destitute children; rather, children would be healed with humor, and manifest manners would be undermined at the same time.[67]

Trickster discourse thus liberates and heals both speaker and listener,[68] both colonizing and colonized subject. Indigenous film discourse, in this logic, employs trickster strategies in its dialogue with Western film discourse on the imaginary and ideological Indian. It often plays with viewers' expectation of the celluloid Indian and is thus able to playfully challenge preconceptions about Indigeneity. In this way, trickster discourse helps to decolonize the lens of power.

ᚹ ᚹ

---

[67] Gerald Vizenor, *Manifest Manners: Narratives on Postindian Survivance* (1994; Lincoln & London: U of Nebraska P, 1999): 83.

[68] Paul Pasquaretta, "Introduction" to Pasquaretta, *Gambling and Survival in Native North America*, xiv.

2 | A Postcolonial Approach to Indigenous Filmmaking in North America

In the face of Eurocentric historicizing, Third World and minoritarian film-makers have rewritten their own histories, taken control over their own images, spoken in their own voices. It is not that their films substitute a pristine "truth" for European "lies," but that they propose counter-truths and counter-narratives informed by an anticolonialist perspective.[1]

WITH THIS STATEMENT Shohat and Stam summarize one important aspect of the global process of decolonization, which is the creation of anticolonialist media. Postcolonial criticism deals chiefly with literature, but it is justified to open up the employment of postcolonial theory to the field of film and video as well. The study of films/videos will move in a similar direction because postcolonial filmmakers are subject to the same cultural hegemonies and (post) colonial conditions as writers: i.e. the socioeconomic, historico-political, and cultural contexts of production – in short, postcolonial experiences that condition the production process – are the same. The decolonization of the media chiefly involves raising Indigenous voices and creating self-controlled media in the process of asserting Indigenous identity, cultural values, and historical and contemporary experiences. As well as this, it involves contesting the grand Western narratives of Indigenous history, ethnography, and sociology. In this way, Indigenous filmmakers strive to work against assimilation through Western media discourse and against the appropriation of Indigenous discourse. Within these works of anticolonialist media, filmmakers attempt to break down stereotypes and preconceived notions of Indigenous cultures established by Western media discourse.

---

[1] Ella Shohat & Robert Stam, *Unthinking Eurocentrism: Multiculturalism and the Media* (1994; London & New York: Routledge, 1997): 249.

Needless to say, the creation of anticolonialist media requires Indigenous filmmakers to have control over film production, and, if possible, over distribution and broadcast as well.

Basic Concepts of Postcolonial Theory

In applying postcolonial theory to forms of Indigenous cultural expression, it is necessary to comprehend fully the underlying colonialist relations that are to be dismantled. These are older, direct colonial relations and contemporary, indirect colonialist manifestations, which are often termed neocolonialism. Here, dependency theory can be helpful.[2] Against the imperialist-loyal modernization theory, which attributes the underdevelopment of former colonies to their "lack of certain qualities [...] such as drive, entrepreneurial spirit, creativity and problem-solving ability," this theory sees the global structure of domination as the reason for underdevelopment and states that these countries are prevented from industrial development by the forces of global capitalism.[3]

Postcolonial theory, which ideally should be grounded on the dependency model, attempts to reveal (neo)colonial forms of economic and political domination that characterize(d) the relations between centers and colonies. But it additionally addresses cultural and mental colonization, of

---

[2] C. Richard Bath & Dilmus D. James, for example, apply dependency theory to examine the reasons for economic underdevelopment in Latin America, with a special focus on Chile; Bath & James, "Dependency Analysis of Latin America: Some Criticism, Some Suggestions," *Latin American Research Review* 11.3 (1976): 6, 19–26. On dependency theory, see also Sangeeta Ray & Henry Schwarz, "Postcolonial Discourse: The Raw and the Cooked," *ARIEL: A Review of International English Literature* 26.1 (January 1995): 147.

[3] Bill Ashcroft, Gareth Griffiths & Helen Tiffin, *Key Concepts in Post-Colonial Studies* (London & New York: Routledge, 1998): 67–68. The dependency model is echoed in Anne McClintock's definition of colonization: "*colonization* involves direct territorial appropriation of another geopolitical entity, combined with forthright exploitation of its resources and labor, and systematic interference in the capacity of the appropriated culture (itself not necessarily a homogeneous entity) to organize its dispensations of power"; McClintock, "The Angel of Progress: Pitfalls of the Term 'Post-Colonialism'" (1992), in *Colonial Discourse and Post-Colonial Theory*, ed. Patrick Williams & Laura Chrisman (1993; New York: Columbia UP, 1994): 295; emphasis in original. Cf. also Aimé Césaire's definition of colonialism and Stuart Hall's definition of colonization: Césaire, "From *Discourse on Colonialism*" (1972), in *Colonial Discourse and Post-Colonial Theory*, ed. Williams & Chrisman, 178; Hall, "When Was 'the Post-Colonial'? Thinking at the Limit," in *The Post-Colonial Question: Common Skies, Divided Horizons*, ed. Iain Chambers & Lidia Curti (London & New York: Routledge, 1996): 249.

which the main aspects are the replacement of Indigenous languages and the destruction of Indigenous collective and individual identities in colonized countries. Colonialist language and text production, as agencies of colonial power, have the potential to misrepresent, subjugate, and denigrate, and it lies in the nature of discourses of power that these texts produced by the group in control mirror their hegemonic views of subaltern groups. As one major instrument, colonization of the mind works mainly through the simultaneous production and distribution (i.e. education) of colonialist texts, where the colonial subjects 'learn' and internalize cultural hegemonies.[4] These hegemonies are already inscribed in early European colonial texts in the second half of the sixteenth century, which were largely travel reports, accounts of conquest, and descriptions of the New Land (mainly India). Their English translations and the compilations of English and non-English travel reports by the Protestant minister Richard Hakluyt (*Divers Voyages Touching the Discoverie of America* of 1582 and *The Principall Navigations, Voiages and Discoveries of the English Nation* of 1589) anchored the colonialist mission in Anglo-European historical and geographical consciousness.[5] This textual mapping of the *terra incognita* formed the beginnings of English and North American colonial discourse.[6]

Coincident with the rise of English imperialism was the rise of the English novel and of 'English' as a scholarly discipline,[7] both being prerequisites of mental colonization. In line with this argument, Bhabha denotes English literature (and subsequent institutions) as "a signifier of authority,"[8] thus confirming the concept of English education and books as major tools in the process of colonization. Frantz Fanon examines the relation between colonizer and colonized on the psychological level. In concert with Octave Mannoni, whom he both acknowledges and fiercely criticizes, Fanon ar-

---

[4] Cf. Ngũgĩ wa Thiong'o, "The Language of African Literature" (excerpt from *Decolonising the Mind*, 1986), in *Colonial Discourse and Post-Colonial Theory*, ed. Williams & Chrisman, 442–43, and Peter Hulme, *Colonial Encounters: Europe and the Native Caribbean, 1492–1797* (London: Methuen, 1986): 2.

[5] Gesa Mackenthun, *Metaphors of Dispossession: American Beginnings and the Translation of Empire, 1492–1637* (Norman & London: U of Oklahoma P, 1997): 22–23.

[6] Cf. Elizabeth Gross, "Criticism, Feminism and the Institution: An Interview with Gayatri Chakravorty Spivak," *Thesis Eleven* 10–11 (1984–85): 175.

[7] Bill Ashcroft, Gareth Griffiths & Helen Tiffin, *The Empire Writes Back: Theory and Practice in Post-Colonial Literatures* (London & New York: Routledge, 1989): 3.

[8] Homi K. Bhabha, "Signs Taken for Wonders: Questions of Ambivalence and Authority under a Tree outside Delhi, May 1817," *Critical Inquiry* 12.1 (Autumn 1985): 149–50.

gues that in contact with the colonizer the colonized takes on a "dependent behavior," and as soon as "he forgets his place, if he takes it into his head to be the equal of the European, then the said European is indignant and casts out the upstart – who, in such circumstance [...] pays for his own rejection of dependence with an inferiority complex."[9] He concludes, quite sardonically, "that the white man acts in obedience to an authority complex, a leadership complex, while the Malagasy obeys a dependency complex. Everyone is satisfied."[10] This inferiority complex drives the colonized individuals into a neurotic situation and caters to their colonized minds. Beside the "authority complex" as pendant to the colonized's "inferiority complex," Mannoni diagnoses the "Prospero complex" in the colonizers' mind, a neurotic tendency that suggests that they themselves or things dearest to them are sure to suffer loss or violence at the hands of the colonized.[11]

One precursor of postcolonial theory is Edward Said's critique of 'orientalism', an occidental practice of constructing a homogeneous image of the Orient through historical, cultural, political, ethnic, aesthetic, academic, and sociological discourses, overshadowing and excluding other discourses in the Occident as well as in the Orient. This established set of ideas assuming the superiority of European cultures over non-European cultures is the basis for European cultural hegemony; in Said's words: "the hegemony of European ideas about the Orient, themselves reiterating European superiority over Oriental backwardness."[12] Thus, cultural hegemony and orientalism are mutually conditional. People in the Orient appropriate and internalize this Western construct about their cultures through any of the discourses named and consequently develop colonized minds. As dependency theory explains for centers and colonies, there are two poles, the Occident and the Orient, and their relation is characterized by power, domination, and the complex hegemony that the first exerts over the latter. The orientalist ideology penetrates the socio-economic and political sector of both Western and 'Eastern' societies.[13]

---

[9] Frantz Fanon, *Black Skin, White Masks*, tr. Charles L. Markman (*Peau noire, masques blancs*, 1967; tr. New York: Grove, 1967): 93.

[10] Fanon, *Black Skin, White Masks*, 99.

[11] Cited in *Black Skin, White Masks*, 107–108.

[12] Edward W. Said, *Orientalism* (London: Routledge, 1978): 7.

[13] In Said's study, orientalism also covers Western representations of North African societies.

The similarities between orientalism and colonialism are obvious. Both invoke the urge of European hegemony for self-legitimization, the difference being that colonialism is conditioned by the occupation/subjugation of alien territory and its inhabitants whereas orientalism, according to Said, represents an occupation/subjugation of ideologies and minds, also grounded, however, in British (French etc) imperial rule. Both also live off the construction of an other, the oriental/colonial other, subjects of orientalist/colonialist discourse. The colonialist dichotomy of 'self and other' finds an echo in Said's contention of the "Orientalist's presence and the Orient's effective absence." Ashcroft et al. state the consequences of this:

> [Orientalism's] practice remains pertinent to the operation of imperial power in whatever form it adopts; to know, to name, to fix the other in discourse is to maintain a far-reaching political control.[14]

Orientalism is one major aspect of world colonialism and the two have to be observed in relation to each other. If one looks at the following discussion by Said of orientalism, one can validly replace the term 'Orientalism' with the term 'colonialist ideology':

> [Orientalism] is, above all, a discourse that is by no means in direct, corresponding relationship with political power in the raw, but rather it is produced and exists in an uneven exchange with various kinds of power, shaped to a degree by the exchange with power political (as with a colonial or imperial establishment), power intellectual (as with reigning sciences like comparative linguistics or anatomy, or any of the modern policy sciences), power cultural (as with orthodoxies and canons of taste, texts, values), power moral (as with ideas about what "we" do and what "they" cannot do or understand as "we" do). Indeed, my real argument is that Orientalism is – and does not simply represent – a considerable dimension of modern political-intellectual culture, and as such has less to do with the Orient than it does with "our" world.[15]

Said distinguishes between latent and manifest orientalism which Bhabha identifies as content – the unconscious repository of fantasy, imaginative writings, and essential ideas, and as form – the historically and discursively determined, diachronic aspect.[16]

---

[14] Bill Ashcroft, Gareth Griffiths & Helen Tiffin, *Key Concepts in Post-Colonial Studies* (London & New York: Routledge, 1998): 169.

[15] Edward Said, *Orientalism*, 12.

[16] Homi K. Bhabha, *The Location of Culture* (London & New York: Routledge, 1994): 71–72.

Postcolonial Theory and its Criticism

Postcolonial theory has been harshly criticized for homogenizing differing chronologies and localities, for downplaying contemporary neocolonial and global domination, for mistakenly insinuating the end of colonialist re-gimes, and for blurring the realms of subaltern and mainstream within the settler cultures by undifferentiated inclusion of the latter in the field of post-colonial study. One major point of criticism concerns the term 'postcolonialism' as suggesting a stage after colonialism which, however, is not achieved by any of the nations concerned except the non-Indigenous groups in settler cultures.[17] Colonialist forms of domination still exist in the

---

[17] Cf. Vijay Mishra & Bob Hodge, "What is Post(-)Colonialism?" (1991), in *Colonial Discourse and Post-Colonial Theory*, ed. Williams & Chrisman, 284; Ella Shohat & Robert Stam, *Unthinking Eurocentrism: Multiculturalism and the Media* (1994; London & New York: Routledge, 1997): 39–41; Anne McClintock, "The Angel of Progress," 292–94; Stuart Hall, "When Was 'the Post-Colonial'? Thinking at the Limit," 242–54; and Kwame Anthony Appiah, "Is the Post- in Postmodernism the Post- in Postcolonial?" *Critical Inquiry* 17.2 (Winter 1991): 348. Shohat and Stam point out that the term blurs perspectives (*Unthinking Eurocentrism*, 39), whereas 'colonial discourse' refers to the discourse created by colonizers, 'postcolonial discourse' may refer to a discourse created by (ex)colonizers (e.g., mainstream Canadians/Americans) and (ex)colonized (e.g., Indigenous people in North America) in the colony or by (ex)colonizers (e.g., British) and (ex)colonized (e.g., Indigenous people in the diaspora) in the mother country. Furthermore, there are non-Western immigrants (e.g., Indians, Pakistanis, Chinese) living in diaspora in North America, which are included in the term 'postcolonial'. McClintock notes that the term insinuates a linear development in which one stage replaces the next, from 'pre-colonial', through 'colonial', to 'postcolonial', involving a commitment to linear time and to the idea of development as well as playing down continuities of colonial power; McClintock, "The Angel of Progress," 292, 294. Sangeeta Ray and Henry Schwarz, on the other hand, suggest not to view the term 'postcolonialism' merely in association with the qualitative states of 'colonialism' and 'after colonialism', but "also as the philosphico-cultural departure from the larger homogenizing logic of European modernity itself"; Ray & Schwarz, "Postcolonial Discourse: The Raw and the Cooked," *ARIEL: A Review of International English Literature* 26.1 (January 1995): 150. Peter Hulme reasons that the 'post' in postcolonial has a temporal and also critical dimension which enables the examination of colonial conditions. According to him, postcolonial "refers to a *process* of disengagement from the whole colonial syndrome, which takes many forms and probably is inescapable for all those worlds have been marked by that set of phenomena: 'postcolonial' is (or should be) a descriptive, not an evaluative, term"; Hulme, "Including America," *ARIEL: A Review of International English Literature* 26.1 (January 1995): 120; emphasis in original. Hulme's plea for the inclusion of America in postcolonial studies brought forward in this article is ambiguous and does not take the colonial experience of its Indigenous population into account. The Indigenous population of North, Central, and South America clearly is to be included in postcolonial studies. The inclusion of non-Indigenous North America must be dismissed on the grounds that, first, they were not a colony in the sense of being occupied by another nation but, like Australia, Canada, and New Zealand, they

guise of the power relations operating within the global context and in former colonies. It is a dangerous fallacy to believe that independent or, rather, non-European governments in former colonies (except the settler cultures) have full control over the country and also exert their political power for the benefit of their citizens. Political decolonization does not necessarily include economic decolonization, and many countries have undergone only partial decolonization.[18] In a nutshell: economic imperialism as a form of neocolonialism has largely replaced colonialism;[19] and an understanding of these global power relations on the basis of the dependency theory enables us to see the current continual exploitation of the Third and Fourth World.

As the British and other European empires were breaking apart, the US empire, on a quite different scale, was on the rise. US imperialism with its various forms of economic, military, political, and cultural influence and interference is comparable to a colonialist regime – "imperialism-without-colonies."[20] Additionally, many of today's postcolonial governments are infiltrated by nepotism and corruption because officials have gone through colonialist schools and have bought into colonialist ideologies. Shohat and Stam define this new sort of colonialism thus:

---

were in the process of settling new territories and colonizing the people indigenous to theses territories. Second, non-Indigenous US-America and Canada do not, in any repect, share with subaltern nations/groups the condition of being oppressed/dominated/marginalized /defined as inferior by another nation/group; only, before they achieved independence from the British Empire their situation was similar to a certain degree. The situation of non-Indigenous Central and South America is different and the issue of their inclusion remains open to debate. I suggest taking the term 'postcolonialism' in the way Hulme perceives it and in the way Stuart Hall understands 'post-marxism' and 'poststructuralism': the prefix 'post' for him does not mean closure or abandonment of an era or area; instead, it is a reference point, with critical thought grounded on a set of established problems; Lawrence Grossberg, "On Postmodernism and Articulation: An Interview with Stuart Hall," *Journal of Commonwealth Inquiry* 10 (1986): 59. Consequently, in postcolonial studies, the aspects of producer, control, and character of discourse constantly change and need to be assessed for each specific context.

[18] Anne McClintock, "The Angel of Progress," 295.

[19] Cf. Julia Emberley, *Thresholds of Difference: Feminist Critique, Native Women's Writings, Postcolonial Theory* (Toronto: U of Toronto P, 1993): 5–7.

[20] McClintock, "The Angel of Progress," 295–96.

a conjuncture in which direct political and military control has given way to abstract, semi-indirect, largely economic forms of control whose linchpin is a close alliance between foreign capital and an Indigenous elite.[21]

This points to the relevance of the dependency model. In former settler countries like Australia, Canada, New Zealand, and the USA, the relation between Indigenous local and national leadership as elites and their sub-altern are sometimes characterized by the same issues, although here the neocolonial situation is more apparent, by virtue of the fact that the colo-nized nations do not have economic or political power nationally. They do not belong to the so-called 'Third World'[22] as Latin American and African countries but to the 'Fourth World'.[23] Colonialist infiltration of Indigenous

---

[21] Ella Shohat & Robert Stam, *Unthinking Eurocentrism*, 17. Cf. also Fanon, who holds that tribal dictatorships, Third-World governments marked by corruption, nepotism, and pre-varication, sabotage national economies and upset their structures. They "hasten to send the people back to their caves" and are the "true traitors in Africa"; *The Wretched of the Earth*, tr. Constance Farrington, intro. Jean–Paul Sartre (*Les damnés de la terre*, 1961; New York: Grove, 1963): 144–47.

[22] 'Third World' denotes, in Western discourse, colonized, neocolonized, and decolonized nations, characterizing them as 'backward', 'underdeveloped', and 'primitive'. The term was coined by Alfred Sauvy in the 1950s, referring to commoners as the revolutionary 'third estate' of France (Ella Shohat & Robert Stam, *Unthinking Eurocentrism*, 25), and was con-solidated at a 1955 conference of representatives of former African and Asian colonies in Bandung, Indonesia, and accepted as underscoring these countries' sovereignty as well as setting them off from the First and Second Worlds. It is appropriate to apply 'Third World' to former colonies, for it aptly transmits political hierarchy and "refers to the colonized, neo-colonized, decolonized nations, and 'minorities whose structural disadvantages have been shaped by the colonial process and by the unequal division of international labor'" (Shohat & Stam, *Unthinking Eurocentrism*, 25). Still, as with other key terms, 'Third World' is criticized for evoking cultural hierarchies, homogenizing different cultural, political, historical, and gender experiences, and masking similarities with the Fourth World and Indigenous people in both the First and Third Worlds. Nevertheless, if there is differentiated use of the terms 'Third World' and 'Fourth World', I suggest that the last-mentioned concern can be ignored.

[23] The term 'Fourth World' was first used by George Manuel and Michael Posluns in *The Fourth World: An Indian Reality* (Don Mills, Ontario: Collier–Macmillan Canada, 1974), and denotes discrete cultures that are subject to imperial domination within the nations that colo-nized their traditional territories. It thus chiefly covers Indigenous cultures of Australia, Canada, New Zealand, and the USA but could also be used for Indigenous cultures in Latin America. Cf. also Shohat & Stam, *Unthinking Eurocentrism*, 32. Anne McClintock defines this situation as internal colonialism, "where the dominant part of the country treats a group or region as it might a foreign colony; McClintock, "The Angel of Progress," 295. See also Julia Emberley, *Thresholds of Difference*, 17–19. The term was consolidated through use by such scholars as Gordon Brotherston, *Book of the Fourth World: Reading Native Americans Through Their Literature* (Cambridge: Cambridge UP, 1992), Ward Churchill & Winona LaDuke, "Native North America: The Political Economy of Radioactive Colonialism," in *The*

leadership is conditioned by the fact that the colonizers largely abolished traditional forms of leadership in North America and imposed new leadership systems which were reminiscent of the elective European ones. Recent problems of nepotism and corruption within tribal and band leaderships seem to reveal that these forms of governance are not meeting the needs of Indigenous nations and are inadequate replacements for traditional forms of governance.

There are critical voices who see the danger of postcolonial theory in the fact that although it was born out of the need for a theory that would incorporate the diversity of literary and cultural traditions in (ex-)colonies, it is on the brink of being appropriated by eurocentric literary theory simply as an antithesis to mainstream theories.[24] In the same vein, it is problematic that postcolonialism is often seen in relation to postmodernism and, more concretely, that it is often regarded as evolving out of the latter. According to Linda Hutcheon, the object of analysis for postmodernism is the subject that is defined by humanism, while for postcolonialism the object of analysis is the colonized subject: i.e. defined by the processes of imperialism/ colonialism.[25] The appropriation of postcolonial discourse by postmodern discourse ensures academic hegemonies; conversely, it enables the inclusion of settler discourses into postcolonial discourse. The hierarchy established between the two discourses endangers the critical historiopolitical and socio-economic agenda of postcolonialism.[26] In this sense, postcolonialism and postmodernism need to be differentiated.

State of Native America: Genocide, Colonization, and Resistance, ed. M. Annette Jaimes (Boston M A : South End, 1992): 241–66, Emmanuel Nelson, "Fourth World Fictions: A Comparative Commentary on James Welch's *Winter in the Blood* and Mudrooroo Narogin's *Wild Cat Falling*," in *Critical Perspectives on Native American Fiction*, ed. Richard F. Fleck (Washington D C : Three Continents, 1993): 57–63, and Arnold Krupat, "Postcoloniality and Native American Literature," *Yale Journal of Criticism* 7.1 (1994): 163–80); the latter calls this condition 'domestic imperialism'.

[24] Thomas King, "Godzilla vs. Post-Colonial," *World Literature Written in English* 30.2 (1990): 11–12; and Anne McClintock, "The Angel of Progress," 292–93. Arguments defending postcolonial theory in this regard are presented by Sangeeta Ray & Henry Schwarz, "Postcolonial Discourse: The Raw and the Cooked," 150, and Peter Hulme, "Including America," 120.

[25] Vijay Mishra & Bob Hodge, "What is Post(-)Colonialism?" 281.

[26] Cf. Mishra & Bob Hodge, "What is Post(-)Colonialism?" 282–84, and Patrick Williams & Laura Chrisman, "Colonial Discourse and Post-Colonial Theory: An Introduction," in *Colonial Discourse and Post-Colonial Theory*, ed. Williams & Chrisman, 13.

Nevertheless, it would be academic colonialism to classify texts according to conventional categories – as modern, postmodern, postcolonial, or
traditional (meaning both literary traditional and Indigenous traditional),
and to arrange them hierarchically. Rather, a mix between two or more of
these categories and approaches is applicable to subaltern texts.[27] In the
field of film and video, such categorization becomes even more unreason-
able, not least because the concepts of traditional, modern, postmodern, and
postcolonial cannot be readily applied to this medium. Traditional, conventional narrative films informed by Hollywood practice, which may contain
some postmodern elements such as intermediality, are perceived as being
the norm, while films informed by unconventional and digressive styles
tend to be regarded as experimental. Films and videos by Indigenous filmmakers might draw on traditional forms of cultural expression, but might
also employ a conventional style and include postmodern elements, while
at the same time being postcolonial films and videos. It can be useful to
analyze postcolonial literary and filmic texts with some of the tools of postmodernist criticism in order to discover innovative features – of structure,
intermediality, and narrative patterns, for example. If postmodernism is
harnessed to the analysis of Indigenous texts, this needs to be done in relation to postcolonialism, thus ensuring that traditional hegemonic structures
engulfed in postmodernism have no agency in the analysis but are its
object.

In addition, the homogenizing tendencies within postcolonial theory are
fallacious. There are substantial cultural, socio-economic, and historico-
political differences in the various postcolonial contexts, as well as gender,
religious, and age differences. Very often in the context of settler cultures,
subaltern/ Indigenous and mainstream/non-Indigenous experiences are not
distinguished.[28] In order to unify varied colonialist experiences in different

---

[27] There are certainly postcolonial texts with traditional, postmodern, and postcolonial elements – for example, Thomas King's *Green Grass, Running Water*. Srinivas Aravamudan
finds that Salman Rushdie's *Satanic Verses* can be postmodern and postcolonial (cited in
Mishra & Hodge, "What is Post(-)Colonialism?" 283). Stephen Slemon argues that a postmodern and postcolonial analysis of a text brings forth different results. As suggested by
Mishra and Hodge, both modes of analysis can support each other by drawing attention to
features/meanings that the other analysis did not expose as well as by including some of the
findings of one approach as basic elements from which the other approach can depart ("What
is Post(-)Colonialism?" 283).

[28] Cf. Arnold Krupat, "Postcoloniality and Native American Literature," *Yale Journal of
Criticism* 7.1 (1994), and Shohat & Stam, *Unthinking Eurocentrism*, 38–40. Cf. also fn. 17 in
this chapter.

parts of the world into one theoretical framework, the theory has fallen into the trap of concentrating on one generic experience and applying an approach that is dictated by that generic experience. The initial goal of decentralizing theoretical inquiries has been lost sight of. Thus, in employing this theory, one has to place the works to be analyzed in their cultural, geographical, historical, and socio-political contexts in order to avoid homogenization. In this regard, it is imperative to define which cultural group is included in the postcolonial approach. Another aspect of criticism is the often undistinguished and abstract usage of phrases like 'postcolonial condition', 'postcolonial space', 'counter-discourse', and 'postcolonial other'. These terms run the risk of becoming empty buzzwords, generalizing where differentiation is essential for analysis. Above all, the concept of 'counter-discourse' may distract too much from existing colonialist situations and concentrate too much on texts.[29]

Nevertheless, cultural and mental colonization operates preeminently through the oral, written, and visual texts that make up colonial discourse. Colonial discourse, in Bhabha's words, is

> an apparatus that turns on the recognition and disavowal of racial/cultural/historical differences. Its predominant strategic function is the creation of a space for a "subject peoples" through the production of knowledges in terms of which surveillance is exercised. [...] It seeks authorization for its strategies by the production of knowledges of colonizer and colonized which are stereotypical but antithetically evaluated. The objective of colonial discourse is to construe the colonized as a population of degenerate types on the basis of racial origin, in order to justify conquest and to establish systems of administration and instruction.[30]

It is obvious that postcolonial theory addresses textual works that create counter-discourses that respond to colonial discourses, which have produced, and continue to produce, collective identities alienated from Indigenous roots and turned into colonized mentalities. Colonialist ideas and principles, via discourse practices, enter subaltern minds and influence their mind-set, ideas about their own cultures, and understanding of power-relations: "They had the power to make us see and experience ourselves as

---

[29] See Anne McClintock, "The Angel of Progress," 293, and Mishra & Hodge, "What is Post(-)Colonialism?" 278.

[30] Homi Bhabha, *The Location of Culture*, 70.

'Other'."[31] Any textual counter-discourse battles this mental adaptation to colonialist thought-structures and works toward the decolonization of those minds. This mental decolonization of the mind involves not only acknowledgment and dismissal of this stereotypical other but also an "understanding of the processes of subjectification made possible (and plausible) through stereotypical discourse."[32] As an alternative to 'counter-discourse', Said offers the term "discourse of liberation."[33] I apply the term 'answering/responding discourse', because subaltern discourses respond actively to colonialist discourse by mimicking and parodying it, quoting from and referring to it, and/or subversively playing with it, hence correcting it. Parts of this corresponding discourse are also more politicized texts, often informed by political events. Barbara Harlow calls such writing "resistance literature": i.e. "a political and politicized activity";[34] in this way, literary texts become constitutive elements in the political struggle.[35] Consequently, self-controlled literary and filmic discourses, whether subversive and playful or realist and politicized or both, are intertwined with agendas of political decolonization. In this sense, postcolonial theory and criticism attempt to dismantle colonialist relations, expose cultural hegemonies, and explore strategies of textual subversion and correction. Furthermore, such theory looks at how these texts decentralize history and overcome manichaean dichotomies by introducing notions of 'syncretism' and 'hybridity'.

If one is aware of the critical aspects discussed here, then postcolonial criticism proves to be a very good tool for analyzing Third- and Fourth-World printed and filmic works as well as the underlying economic, social, and political relations in the context of which these texts are created and to which they react. If examined not simply as counter-discourses and writing/filming against hegemonic power, postcolonial texts in North America prove to be hybrid discourses with many more influences than colonialism. Their creation is conditioned by the various possible ethnic backgrounds and cultural specifics (including colonial ones), diasporic and neocolonial

---

[31] Stuart Hall, "Cultural Identity and Cinematic Representation," *Framework: A Film Journal* 36 (1989): 71.

[32] Bhabha, *The Location of Culture*, 67.

[33] Edward W. Said, "Foucault and the Imagination of Power," in *Foucault: A Critical Reader*, ed. David Couzens Hoy (Oxford & New York: Basil Blackwell, 1986): 153.

[34] Barbara Harlow, in her study *Resistance Literature* (1986), cited in Julia Emberley, *Thresholds of Difference: Feminist Critique, Native Women's Writings, Postcolonial Theory* (Toronto: U of Toronto P, 1993): 21.

[35] Emberley, *Thresholds of Difference*, 21.

experiences, degrees of acculturation, class and gender differences, matters of education, age, and urban or rural (reservation) setting. This extended form of study concedes to textual practices greater freedom for creation and offers more aspects and facets for interpretation. The artificial creation of such binaries as discourse/counter-discourse and colonialism/postcolonialism and their maintenance in related discourses upholds inherent cultural hegemonies that dominate literature and film studies. One has to view postcolonial discourse not only as anticolonialist but also as including colonialism, evolving out of colonialism, and in dialogue with colonialism. One can thereby pay due attention to the continuities of colonialism and circumvent the presentation of colonialism and postcolonialism in terms of linear development and leaps in quality. Postcolonialism further enables a decentering of theory, with scholars from different cultural backgrounds (including colonial and colonized groups) and different academic affiliations (different schools of theory) catering to contemporary debate, and with their contributions being used as starting-points for further dialogue in the field.

In view of the homogenizing tendencies of postcolonial theory discussed here, it becomes necessary to define who is included in the application of the theory. The concepts of Third and Fourth World are useful categories here: i.e. people belonging to any kind of colonized culture (excluding Caucasian settler cultures) are postcolonial in the sense of the theory. In the case of North America, this definition includes Indigenous people and non-Caucasian immigrants, whereas Indigenous must be defined by their own standards and neither by the US-American blood-quantum rule nor the Canadian status system.[36] This open definition, of course, runs the risk of letting impostors and wannabes pass as Indigenous, but it certainly enables the concept of hybridity to gain a foothold in analysis and moves away from essentializing reductionism. Furthermore, the content of Indigenous textual and filmic expression must not be limited to Indigenous issues. Such practice creates an 'authenticity trap',[37] ready to neglect Indigenous expression without explicit Indigenous content and thus furthering essentialist tendencies and cultural dichotomies and hegemonies. A thriller about

---

[36] Here I work with a concept of individual and collective self-definition and rely upon Indigenous individuals and communities to interrogate the concept of identity. There is an ongoing discussion about how Indigeneity should be defined; such a definition usually involves individual affiliation with a nation/band, recognition by the nation/band of this affiliation, and the ability to trace ancestral lines.

[37] This term was introduced to me by Hartmut Lutz in a personal conversation.

the KGB in Russia, a film drama about a high-school teacher in Jamaica, or a crime novel set in India,[38] in my judgement, have to qualify as Indigenous texts so long as they are written, directed, or produced by an Indigenous person.[39] In the field of documentary filmmaking, Indigenous filmmakers also create works that have no Indigenous content, mostly when such films are commissioned work.[40] To my knowledge, there are no feature films yet by Indigenous filmmakers that do not deal with Indigenous experience, presumably owing to the fact that at this early stage of development in an Indigenous dramatic film tradition filmmakers still feel the need to react to Hollywood film discourse, Western ethnographic and anthropological discourses, and other Western discourses that have constructed the imaginary Indian. Whatever the choice of content, Indigenous writers and filmmakers occupy, according to Gareth Griffiths, the difficult and ambivalent position of having to integrate both, recuperating the traditional and contesting the profile of Indigenous identity in dominant political and cultural space.[41]

Postcolonial Conditions in North America

The colonization of North America involved land appropriation supported by military power, the introduction of a capitalist economy, and the imposition of eurocentric religions, cultural practices, and values and morals. All

---

[38] These are only random examples and do not represent cornerstones of an area in which Indigenous practice has to move.

[39] The following example illustrates how Indigenous and non-Indigenous practice in classifying Indigenous content as a major category proves to be essentializing and discourages the creation of Indigenous films/videos beyond the realm of Indigenous experience. The short film *Talker* by the Saskatchewan filmmaker Lloyd Martell has a metaphoric plot centered on a character who is defined neither as Indigenous nor as non-Indigenous. This character is played by a non-Indigenous actor. Nevertheless, according to Martell, the film deals with the silencing of Indigenous voices. Martell was disqualified from the category of Best Aboriginal Film at the 1996 Yorkton Short Film and Video Festival and from the category of Best Native Film at the 1996 Santa Fe Film Festival on the grounds that his film does not have Indigenous content. Instead, two non-Indigenous filmmakers with productions on Indigenous issues/experience won these awards (personal conversation with Lloyd Martell). These incidents indicate a great deal about essentializing practices in the film and video industry and about film institutions facilitating and sanctioning the kinds of cultural appropriation that non-Indigenous filmmakers engage in.

[40] For example, Rodger Ross in Regina and Doug Cuthand in Saskatoon, Saskatchewan.

[41] Gareth Griffiths, "The Myth of Authenticity: Representation, Discourse and Social Practice," in *De-Scribing Empire: Post-Colonialism and Textuality*, ed. Chris Tiffin & Alan Lawson (London & New York: Routledge, 1994): 74.

of these factors contributed to the 'generous' project of bringing 'civilization' and 'enlightenment' to Indigenous populations. Indigenous barter economies based on the production of use-value were replaced by the Western market economy based on the production of exchange-value, which fostered the transition to a state of economic dependency among Indigenous inhabitants. In the case of Indigenous North America, the 'civilization project' was implemented largely and most devastatingly via the boarding /residential schools system, where Indigenous children were taken from their traditional homes and brought to these schools to be educated. One could rather speak of indoctrination with European religion, culture, morality, and values. Often the children were exploited as cheap labor force. Most schools strove toward becoming self-supporting and profitable, and children did, for example, seamstress, farm, construction, and road building work.[42] They generally could not go home for long periods of time and were forbidden to speak their traditional languages and practice their traditional religions.[43] Thus, they were most effectively alienated from their families, cultures, and religions and were transformed into assimilated subjects. These cultural hybrids reflect the colonized minds, discussed above, which facilitated the legitimization of colonialist politics.

In a postcolonial sense, Canada and the USA, like Australia and New Zealand, enjoy unique status. On the one hand, they have, as former British colonies, experienced a marginalized position and the need for self-assertion against the British Empire (the USA through the War of Independence and Canada, New Zealand, and Australia via the Dominion status granted by the British Crown). On the other hand, they based this struggle for self-

---

[42] See Frank Schumacher, "Colonization through Education: A Comparative Exploration of Ideologies, Practices, and Cultural Memories of 'Aboriginal Schools' in the United States and Canada," *Zeitschrift für Kanada-Studien* 26.2/49 (2006): 104.

[43] On boarding/residential schools, see, for fictional life-story texts: Basil Johnston, *Indian School Days* (Toronto: Key Porter Books, 1988), and *Behind Closed Doors: Stories from the Kamloops Indian Residential School*, ed. Jack Agness (Kamloops, British Columbia: Secwepemc Cultural Education Society, 2000); and, for non-fiction: J.R. Miller, "Reserves, Residential Schools, and the Threat of Assimilation," in Miller, *Skyscrapers Hide the Heavens: A History of Indian–White Relations in Canada* (1989; Toronto: U of Toronto P, 2000): 125–47; Olive Patricia Dickason, *Canada's First Nations: A History of Founding Peoples from Earliest Times* (Don Mills, Ontario: Oxford UP Canada, 3rd ed. 2002): 315–19; Jorge Noriega, "American Indian Education in the United States: Indoctrination for Subordination to Colonialism," in *The State of Native America: Genocide, Colonization, and Resistance*, ed. M. Annette Jaimes (Boston MA: South End, 1992): 371–402, and Schumacher, "Colonization through Education," 97–117.

assertion on colonialist politics towards the Indigenous populations of the territories they occupied. This internal colonialism has turned the Indigenous inhabitants into a marginalized and oppressed group within the country whose territories were once solely theirs, and thus, they became the last link in the chain of colonialism. The former francophone settlers in eastern Canada have yet another colonial history: they share with anglophone Canadians the experience of colonizing Indigenous territory and dominating the Aboriginal population and they share with the Indigenous population the historical experience of being politically and economically dominated by mainstream English Canada.

Having gained independence from the British center, Canada and the USA developed new national identities and national literatures grounded, among other things, on difference from Great Britain. However, the English language and British literature were the 'gold standard' for all varieties of English[44] and literatures of those countries which had split off from the Empire. Ashcroft et al. describe the relation between the British Empire and these settler cultures as one of a "stream–tributary" or a "parent–child" relation, in which the "children" suffered from an inferiority complex, being as they were neither as old and experienced nor as important and substantial as the "parent."[45] Most importantly, these "offspring" cultures experienced rootlessness, displacement, and a mismatch between language and geography, resulting in the adaptation of the imported language to the alien landscape.[46] This ever-present "inauthenticity" of the "new word"[47] led to an ongoing struggle for a national literary identity. The inherent dilemma was that it had to be defined through its difference from the literature of the imperial center; at the same time, it had to be oriented towards the literature of Empire because it was criticized and judged by British literary standards.

The rise of the English novel and English imperialism is coeval with the 'golden age' of English children's literature.[48] Jo–Ann Wallace argues that

---

[44] Ashcroft, Griffiths and Tiffin (*The Empire Writes Back*) use a decapitalized 'english' for the language of the settler cultures and a capitalized 'English' for British Standard English. In order to avoid confusion, this differentiation is not upheld in the present study.

[45] Ashcroft, Griffiths & Tiffin, *The Empire Writes Back*, 16.

[46] *The Empire Writes Back*, 140.

[47] *The Empire Writes Back*, 140.

[48] Jo–Ann Wallace, "De-Scribing *The Water-Babies*: 'The Child' in Post-Colonial Theory," in *De-Scribing Empire: Post-Colonialism and Textuality*, ed. Chris Tiffin & Alan Lawson (London & New York: Routledge, 1994): 172.

European ideas equated the concept of the 'primitive' as associated with children with the concept of the 'primitive' as associated with Aboriginal inhabitants of the colonies. "The child as a kind of noble savage" (and 'the noble savage as child') thus entered children's literature, which in turn was utilized to educate children in the colonies and in the mother country. The trope of the 'Indigenous cultures as children' was thus established and maintained in transatlantic Western discourse.

> The child, like the savage or the primitive, is pre-literate (the word "infant," from the Latin *infans*, meaning literally "without speech"). [...] It is as "primitive," then, that "the child" represents to the West our racial as well as our individual past: the child is that "ancient piece of history" [...] whose presence has left room, if not for theories, then for the parent–child logic of imperialist expansion.[49]

To substantiate her argument, Wallace quotes Bhabha, who holds that colonial discourse directs the colonizer to "be the father and the oppressor," and notes further that "an idea of 'the child' is a *necessary precondition* of imperialism – that is, that the West had to invent for itself 'the child' before it could think a specifically colonialist imperialism."[50] Subsequently, the trope of 'primal people as children' in colonial discourses legitimized colonialist politics and promoted mental colonization.

This parent–child concept is reflected in the politics of the young American and Canadian nations. They almost simultaneously transferred their experiences as 'wards' and/or 'children' of Great Britain to the dealings with or, rather, handling of the inhabitants of the occupied territories.[51] The

---

[49] Wallace, "De-Scribing *The Water-Babies*," 175; emphasis in original.

[50] "De-Scribing *The Water-Babies*," 176; emphasis in original.

[51] Exemplarily in the *Cherokee vs. Georgia* case of 1831, Indigenous people were declared a "domestic dependent nation," comparable to the status of a "ward to the federal government"; Vine Deloria, Jr. & Clifford M. Lytle, *American Indians, American Justice* (Austin: U of Texas P, 1983): 4–5. What seemed to be a clever judicial move at the time (ensuring Indigenous rights under federal law which would protect them against individual states) expressed the colonizers' notion of Indigenous people being inferior, childlike, and at their mercy. On the guardianship role of the US government, see also Deloria & Lytle, *American Indians, American Justice*, 35–45, and Alice B. Kehoe, *North American Indians: A Comprehensive Account* (Englewood Cliffs NJ: Prentice Hall, 1992): 196. The Canadian government dealt with Indigenous matters on the basis of the Indian Act of 1876, a compilation of all previous policies and legislation on Indigenous people and their land. This law placed Indigenous people under the guardianship of the Canadian government, which represented the authority of the British Crown. Previously, Indigenous people had been granted sovereignty by the Crown through the Royal Proclamation Act of 1763. Canada's bond with the British

Canadian and US governments secured control and title over the colonized territories with the exception of the small portions of land, which were reserved for the remnants of the Indigenous population through eleven treaties in Canada (1871–1921) and approximately 370 treaties in the USA (1778–1871) as well as the Dawes Act (1887) and its amendment (1891). However, even on these reserves and reservations,[52] Indigenous people did not have control over their affairs. Indian agents and later the Bureau of Indian Affairs (USA) and the Department of Indian Affairs and Northern Development (Canada) were put in charge of the governments' 'wards'. These patriarchal policies resulted, for example, in the weakening and destruction of the Indigenous farming economy, previously encouraged by assimilation policies.[53] Ward Churchill and Winona LaDuke, further, assign decreasing Indigenous self-sufficiency to the "systematic transfer of economic power to the neocolonial structure lodged in the US/tribal council relationship."[54] Another aspect of economic domination and exploitation is the continued uranium and coal-strip mining on or close to Indigenous territories and the resulting environmental damage (e.g., in the US Southwest and northern Saskatchewan in Canada).[55] Although in both countries the governments attempted with different policies (the US policies of Indian

---

Empire through the Commonwealth resembles the 'parent–child' relation, which then was imposed upon the Indigenous population in a similar way as in the USA.

[52] The pieces of land set aside for the Indigenous population in order to clear the rest of the land for the incoming settlers are called 'reserves' in Canada and 'reservations' in the USA.

[53] In Canada, Indigenous farmers were not allowed to participate directly in the market, and their products could only be sold through an Indian agent. In the USA, stock reduction programs in the 1930s were implemented to counteract the effects of 'overgrazing' reservation land by tribally or individually owned cattle, with the result that since 1935 "more than one-half of all Indian livestock resources have been eliminated"; Ward Churchill & Winona LaDuke, "Native North America: The Political Economy of Radioactive Colonialism," 244. Such a policy proved to be most devastating for nations such as the Navajo, who derive their income largely from sheep-raising.

[54] Churchill & LaDuke, "Native North America: The Political Economy of Radioactive Colonialism," 244–45.

[55] In 1980 there were forty-two uranium mines and seven uranium mills on the Navajo reservation and in adjacent areas, with seven new uranium projects under construction. Here, tribal councils were tricked with promises of jobs and profit-sharing into agreeing. The devastating effects of this radioactive colonialism were dramatically high occurrences of lung cancer, leukemia, birth defects, and chemical and radioactive contamination of surface water. On radioactive colonialism, see also Churchill & LaDuke, "Native North America: The Political Economy of Radioactive Colonialism," 241–66, and Ward Churchill, *Fantasies of the Master Race: Literature, Cinema and the Colonization of American Indians* (San Francisco: City Lights, 1998): 85.

Reorganization 1928–45 and self-determination 1961 to the present,[56] and Canadian policies of self-determination and Indian self-government[57]) to enhance the autonomy and decision-making power of Indigenous people, they have never changed the assimilationist and patronizing protocol. Furthermore, the unclear specification of respective rights in the treaties has caused constant tensions between Indigenous individuals/groups and the states/provinces or non-Indigenous individuals, often resulting in court cases. These have usually concerned land rights, water rights, and hunting and fishing rights. In short, Indigenous nations are/were inhibited from freely developing economically and politically as autonomous nations.

Key Concepts of Postcolonial Theory

In concert with illuminating the cultural, historical, and political specifics of North American postcolonial nations, it is also necessary to explain how key concepts of postcolonial theory are applied. The most exploited term, 'the colonial other', has acquired various connotations in its career as a fashionable academic concept. Ashcroft et al. argue that the colonized subject has been defined as 'other' through discourses such as primitivism and cannibalism, constituting literally the existent binary separation between colonizer and colonized and subsequently reinforcing the primacy of colonial cultures[58] in the psychological dichotomy of self and other. They distinguish between the 'other' and the 'Other', the former referring to "the colonized others who are marginalized by imperial discourse, identified by their difference from the center and [...] become the focus of anticipated mastery by the imperial 'ego'." The 'Other' stands for "the imperial centre, imperial discourse, or the empire itself."[59] In this definition, the colonial 'other' exists only through the gaze of the imperial 'Other', and its dependent identity is constructed through imperial discourse. This forming of colonial subjects is referred to as 'othering', an orientalist/colonialist practice by which the existence of the 'Other' is sanctioned. Thus, as Gayatri

---

[56] Vine Deloria, Jr. & Clifford M. Lytle, *American Indians, American Justice*, 12–24.

[57] James S. Frideres, *Native Peoples in Canada: Contemporary Conflicts* (Scarborough, Ontario: Prentice Hall Canada, 1993): 407–63.

[58] Bill Ashcroft, Gareth Griffiths & Helen Tiffin, *Key Concepts in Post-Colonial Studies*, 169.

[59] *Key Concepts in Post-Colonial Studies*, 170.

Spivak explains, 'other' and 'Other' are produced at the same time and are dialectically interdependent.[60]

Robert Berkhofer traces the othering of people indigenous to the North American continent to the historical eurocentric convention in settler cultures of measuring Indigenous cultural, social, religious, and political practices against the constructed eurocentric concepts of civilization, religion, and morality. They applied counter-images of themselves to describe Indigenous people and vice versa,[61] which resulted in manichaean dichotomies of primitive, savage, heathen, Satan, bad/evil, and emotion on one side and developed, civilized, Christian, God, good, and reason on the other.[62] The concept of oppositional thinking that Fanon calls "manicheism delirium"[63] reflects the Western construct of self/other and is applicable to Western discourse about all colonized cultures including Indigenous people in North and South America, Africa, Australia, and New Zealand. This self/other dichotomy served settler cultures to stand out from something 'other' and inferior and to define themselves through this difference as superior beings. The same dichotomy of "thesis and antithesis"[64] was the basis of settler cultures' national identity.

The manichaean dichotomy of self/other becomes culturally lethal at the moment in which colonial subjects construct their identity within the borders of this binary and hierarchized opposition: i.e. their culture, history,

---

[60] *Key Concepts in Post-Colonial Studies*, 171.

[61] Robert F. Berkhofer, *The White Man's Indian* (New York: Vintage, 1978): xv, 27.

[62] Fanon develops the theory of manichaean thinking that characterizes Western thought and upholds Western hegemony. Manichaeism is an ancient dualistic religious belief that separates matter and spirit as well as good and evil; Encarta, *World English Dictionary* (London: Bloomsbury, 1999): 1147. Working from this dualistic belief, Fanon concludes that Western thought divides ideas, cultures, societies, moral values into binary oppositions with a positive and negative pole, the main opposition being White and Black. "Good–Evil, Beauty–Ugliness, White–Black [...]. Blackness, darkness, shadow, shades, night, the labyrinths of the earth, abysmal depths, blacken someone's reputation; and, on the other side, the bright look of innocence, the white dove of peace, magical, heavenly light" (*Black Skin, White Masks*, 183, 189). Shohat and Stam also apply the eurocentric trope of lightness/darkness, as derived from the Enlightenment ideal of rational clarity, to manichaean thinking that understands European cultures as being "deep and profound" and non-European cultures as "shallow and 'superficial'": "Earlier religious Manicheisms of good and evil became transmuted into the philosophical binarism of rationality/light versus irrationality/darkness. Sight and vision are attributed to Europe, while the 'other' is seen as living in 'obscurity,' blind to moral knowledge" (*Unthinking Eurocentrism*, 140).

[63] *Black Skin, White Masks*, 183.

[64] Ashcroft, Griffiths & Tiffin, *The Empire Writes Back*, 3.

religion, value systems are filtered through colonial discourse and are shaped according to cultural hegemonies. They see themselves from the perspective, through the 'lens', of the colonizer. As seen earlier, the colonial subjects learn and internalize cultural and political hegemonies through colonial discourse and assume a victim role, appropriate cultural clichés and hierarchies, and understand themselves as inferior pendants to the imperial subjects – the colonized mind is thus born and passed on to following generations. The imperial self exoticizes its other, which becomes the basis of colonial identity, and further manipulates the construction of colonial subjectivity. These invented colonial identities and colonized mentalities are not only manifest in the discourse of the oppressor but, more perilously, appropriated into the discourse of the oppressed.[65] Anthony Kwame Appiah warns against self-exoticization and the celebration of oneself as other as well as against the commodification of culture as the manufacturing of otherness.[66] Sara Suleri deplores being treated as an "otherness machine,"[67] which leads Appiah to conclude that postcolonial intellectuals are

> always at the risk of becoming otherness machines, with the manufacture of alterity as our principal role. Our only distinction in the world of texts to which we are latecomers is that we can mediate it to our fellows.[68]

If the role of postcolonial scholars and writers in postcolonial discourse is seen as constructing alterity[69] to Western discourses, postcolonial criticism indeed nurtures neocolonial hegemonic tendencies on the academic plane.

In the analysis of postcolonial film, as well, the definition of the eurocentric West (occidental discourse) as 'self' and the non-West (oriental discourse) as 'other' consolidates hegemonic ideology. Mitsuhiro Yoshimoto reasons that this self/other opposition does "not only fix the non-West as the object to be appropriated, but also transform[s] serious political issues

---

[65] On self-hatred and self-imposed alienation as effective aspects of the colonized mind, see, for example, Howard Adams, *Prison of Grass: Canada from a Native Point of View* (Saskatoon, Saskatchewan: Fifth House, 1989): 141–49.

[66] Appiah, "Is the Post- in Postmodernism the Post- in Postcolonial?" 356.

[67] Quoted in Appiah, "Is the Post- in Postmodernism the Post- in Postcolonial?" 356.

[68] "Is the Post- in Postmodernism the Post- in Postcolonial?" 356. See also Gayatri Chakravorty Spivak, "Can the Subaltern Speak?" (1988), in *Colonial Discourse and Post-Colonial Theory*, ed. Patrick Williams & Laura Chrisman (New York: Columbia U P, 1994): 76.

[69] Often, the terms 'otherness' and 'alterity' are used alternatively in postcolonial discourse. Ashcroft et al. explain that the term 'otherness' has its roots in the philosophical context, whereas 'alterity' shifts focus to the material and discursive context (Ashcroft, Griffiths & Tiffin, *Key Concepts in Post-Colonial Studies*, 11–12.).

into bad philosophical questions," and that it furthermore is a "disguise for a legitimation of Western subjectivity."[70] To avoid such academic colonialism, the terms 'other' and 'otherness/alterity' must be inscribed with an additional significance that implies a struggle against the construction of an exoticized other as a commodity of Western academia (and also of a Western art market). Bhabha suggests surmounting the fallacies of cultural diversity, exoticism, and essentialism by acknowledging an open cultural 'third space', an international culture that stresses not difference but hybridity:

> for me the importance of hybridity is not to be able to trace two original moments from which the third emerges, rather hybridity to me is the 'third space' which enables other positions to emerge. This third space displaces the histories that constitute it, and sets up new structures of authority, new political initiatives, which are inadequately understood through received wisdom.[71]

Decolonized subject positions beyond the colonial positions of "power and resistance, domination and dependence"[72] can exist in this third space. Thus, the third space replaces Western epistemology with an anticolonialist epistemology that is, however, still entangled in Western discourse, its methods, and schemes of validation. In a hybrid space, cultures mingle as well as engage in a "mutual contamination of imaginary purity both in the colonial and the postcolonial scenario."[73] Bhabha assigns cultural meaning to this space between cultures and views the productivity of internal differences that are denoted by the dichotomous constructions inside/outside, dominant/dissident, mainstream/subculture, and global/local as dynamics of hybridization, replacing colonialist, racist or nationalist conceptions of excluding the other.[74] Consequently, we have to understand Bhabha's hybrid and third space as operating simultaneously on both the physical/empirical and the epistemic level.

---

[70] Mitsuhiro Yoshimoto, "The Difficulty of Being Radical: The Discipline of Film Studies and the Postcolonial World Order," *boundary 2* 18.3 (Fall 1991): 251.

[71] Homi Bhabha, "The Third Space: Interview with Homi Bhabha," in *Identity: Community, Culture, Difference*, ed. Jonathan Rutherford (London: Lawrence & Wishart, 1990): 211. Cf. also Bhabha, *The Location of Culture*, 37–39.

[72] Bhabha, "The Third Space," 67.

[73] Monika Fludernik, "Introduction" to *Hybridity and Postcolonialism: Twentieth-Century Indian Literature*, ed. Fludernik (Tübingen: Stauffenburg, 1998): 13.

[74] Fludernik, "Introduction" to *Hybridity and Postcolonialism*, 13.

Ashcroft et al. caution not to employ the concept of 'hybridity' simply as a signifier of cultural mixture or shared postcolonial condition, as this might obscure existing cultural hegemonies and power-relations as well as dehistoricizing and de-locating cultures "from their temporal, spatial, geographical and linguistic contexts."[75] Monika Fludernik reminds us that the term 'hybridity' had a racist connotation (as racial 'impurity') within colonial discourse in the nineteenth century.[76] In the same vein, the term 'syncretism', which has also been used to designate the processes and results of cultural mixing, was open to pejorative use (mainly for 'impure' religious tendencies) and underwent shifts in connotation. In the realm of postcolonial analysis, both terms have come to be rehabilitated and the critical use of these concepts with regard to their origins has proved indispensable.[77]

Nevertheless, considering the unbalanced power-relations between center and margin that are still prevalent in today's settler cultures, acknowledged models of syncretism and hybridity can easily mutate into a veiled threat of appropriation and cultural exploitation. Indigenous people in North America have to engage in an ongoing fight against the appropriation

---

[75] Ashcroft, Griffiths & Tiffin, *Key Concepts in Post-Colonial Studies*, 119.

[76] Monika Fludernik, "Introduction" to *Hybridity and Postcolonialism*, 10.

[77] Christopher Balme traces the connotative development of the term 'syncretism', much as Fludernik looks at the career of the term 'hybridity'; Balme, "Inventive Syncretism: The Concept of the Syncretic in Intercultural Discourse," in *Fusion of Cultures?*, ed. Peter Stummer & Christopher Balme (Cross/Cultures 26, ASNEL Papers 2; Amsterdam & Atlanta GA: Rodopi, 1996): 9–18; Monika Fludernik, "The Constitution of Hybridity: Postcolonial Interventions," in *Hybridity and Postcolonialism: Twentieth-Century Indian Literature*, ed. Monika Fludernik (Tübingen: Stauffenburg, 1998): 19–53. See also Ellis Cashmore, ed. *Dictionary of Race and Ethnic Relations* (1984; London & New York: Routledge, 4th ed. 1996): 164–66. Frank Schulze–Engler warned in a lecture that the terms 'hybridity', 'syncretism', and 'creolization' are not be used interchangeably, since they originated in different discourses – 'creolization' in linguistic discourse denoting the mixture of languages, 'hybridity' in biological discourse, denoting crossbred animals and deriving from this the mixed offspring of different races, and 'syncretism' in religious discourse denoting the mixture of different religious beliefs. (This lecture was held at the Autumn Summer School of the Association for the Study of the New Literatures in English in Berlin, 2002.) Alternatively, Christopher Balme offers the concept of 'inventive syncretism', which "assumes a view of cultural change that is fundamentally dynamic, that presupposes openness and a creative utilization of disparate, heterogeneous cultural products" ("Inventive Syncretism," 9). In postcolonial discourse, the concept of 'hybridity' is revalorized as a concept of cultural diversity in which "racist 'impurity' has been reinscribed as subversive multiplicity and as progressive (but not unidirectional) agency" (Fludernik, "The Constitution of Hybridity," 21). In the present study, the term 'hybridity' is employed in Bhabha's sense, overcoming political and ideological dichotomies and conveying the notion of a space between cultures within which cultural differences, commonalties, and confluences can operate.

of spiritual and cultural elements into mainstream literature and film.[78] In the merging of two literary/filmic discourses, the more powerful one always dominates or swallows the disadvantaged one, so that self-assertion against appropriation is an ever-present issue. But, as Emberley says, the demanded incorporation of Indigenous cultural productions into industrial media itself is a hybrid process. She holds that this process is not merely an unprecedented overlay of 'traditions' but an ongoing effort to overcome the epistemic violence[79] of colonial discourse which, on the one hand, has ignored and, on the other, has appropriated Indigenous cultural traditions, relegating them "to a wasteland of stereotypical by-products."[80]

The concept of hybridity is important in the application of postcolonial theory to literature and media-making in North America, because many creators of such works are of mixed ethnic background and cannot meet essentialist demands for authenticity. Likewise, because of Western colonialism and domination, there cannot be any 'pure' Indigenous cultural expression, as Indigenous cultures have developed under the influence of Western culture and philosophy. Demands for the recovering of precolonial and uncontaminated traditions tend to preclude hybrid practices and generally deny cultural continuity and development.[81] They negate processes of transformation that arose from the imposition of Western civilization and its religion, morality, and value-system upon Aboriginal cultures. Within a hybrid context, the space between cultures offers room to probe cultural differences, commonalties, and/or amalgamation. As well as this, various

---

[78] Examples of the literary appropriation of Indigenous spiritual culture are the works of Hyemeyohsts Storm (*Seven Arrows*), Ruth Beebe Hill (*Hanta Yo*), Gary Snyder, Lynn Andrews, and Carlos Castañeda; see Hartmut Lutz, "Confronting Cultural Imperialism: First Nations People are Combating Continued Cultural Theft," in *Multiculturalism in North America and Europe: Social Practices – Literary Visions*, ed. Hans Braun & Wolfgang Klooss (Trier: WVT, 1995): 139. More recent examples of cultural and/or spiritual appropriation are Tony Hillerman's Chee/Leaphorn mystery novels and W.P. Kinsella's Ermineskin/Fencepost novels. Of the numerous films that engage in cultural and/or spiritual appropriation, one can name Elliot Silverstein's *A Man Called Horse* (USA, 1970), Kevin Costner's *Dances With Wolves* (USA, 1990), Errol Morris's *The Dark Wind* (USA, 1991), Oliver Stone's *Natural Born Killers* (USA, 1994), Bruce McDonald's *Dance Me Outside* (Canada, 1994), and Jan Egleson's *Coyote Waits* (USA, 2003).

[79] The term 'epistemic violence' was coined by Spivak in her essay "Can the Subaltern Speak?" (1988), in *Colonial Discourse and Post-Colonial Theory*, ed. Williams & Chrisman, 66–111.

[80] Julia Emberley, *Thresholds of Difference*, 19.

[81] Cf. James Clifford, *The Predicament of Culture: Twentieth-Century Ethnography, Literature, Art* (Cambridge MA: Harvard UP, 1988): 14.

practices and techniques of cultural expression have room to be negotiated in a hybrid space. On the epistemic level, the hybrid space allows critical evaluation of Western discursive practices and the creation of an anticolonialist discourse that draws on both Western and subaltern experience, values, and philosophy. The very idea of a hybrid space indicates that there is no 'pure' and 'authentic' culture and cultural expression and that authenticity is a construct that gives way to a hegemonic view of Indigeneity. Emma LaRoque,[82] like Suleri, underscores the immense pressure that is put on Indigenous writers, scholars, and artists to create texts or art that is different from or 'other' than mainstream culture. But she makes it clear that Indigenous cultures are as dynamic as others, so that the claim of 'authenticity' cannot hold. She also points to the fact that, after five hundred years of colonialism and imposition of Western ideology, culture, and economy, it is ridiculous to request 'authentic Indigenous imagery'. Here, the term 'authenticity trap' assumes heightened significance with respect not only to expectations of Indigenous content as such but also to mistaken demands for 'authentic' quality in texts and, even worse, proof of an 'authentic' ethnic background on the part of the producer of a text.[83]

The question of authenticity is intertwined with the question of ethnicity. Ellis Cashmore defines an ethnic group as "possessing some degree of coherence and solidarity composed of people who are [...] aware of having common origins and interests," and as "a self-conscious collection of people united, or closely related, by shared experiences."[84] Werner Sollors shows that ethnicity is a constructed and invented phenomenon, which he relates to the "recognition of the general cultural constructedness of the modern world" and "to widely shared, though intensely debated, collective fictions that are continually reinvented."[85] He does not reject the existence of physical and cultural differences conditioned by 'race' and 'ethnicity',

---

[82] LaRoque presented these views at the joint conference of the Canadian Association for American Studies and the Western Literature Association in Banff, October 1998.

[83] Cf. also Leslie Marmon Silko, "Videomakers and Basketmakers," *Aperture* 119 (Summer 1990): 73.

[84] *Dictionary of Race and Ethnic Relations*, ed. Cashmore, 119.

[85] Sollors, "Introduction: The Invention of Ethnicity," in *The Invention of Ethnicity*, ed. Sollors (New York & Oxford: Oxford U P, 1989): x–xi. See also Sollors, *Beyond Ethnicity: Consent and Descent in American Culture* (New York & Oxford: Oxford U P, 1986): 20–36, and Sarita Malik, "Beyond 'The Cinema of Duty'? The Pleasures of Hybridity: Black British Film of the 1980s and 1990s," in *Dissolving Views: Key Writings on British Cinema*, ed. Andrew Higson (London & New York: Cassell, 1996): 204.

but says that these differences are constructed because one group *defines* its difference vis-à-vis other groups on the basis of racial and/or ethnic characteristics. These differences allow the crystallization of hierarchies, thus enabling this one group to claim hegemonic status over others. Consequently, because of the *definition* of differences in terms of racial and/or ethnic characteristics, 'race' and 'ethnicity' are produced and constructed. Sollors further makes it clear that the term 'ethnicity' has replaced the discredited term 'race'[86] and that ethnicity has ever since served to define otherness.[87] The belief in ethnicity goes hand in hand with the notion that ethnic groups are natural, real, eternal, stable, and static entities that have always been in existence and that are focussed on their own threatened preservation and survival.[88] Ethnicity is stressed to resist assimilation to the melting pot.[89] In this sense, Sollors questions a perceived cultural homogeneity, an 'ethnicity' that "emphasizes 'authenticity' and cultural heritage [...] at the expense of more widely shared historical conditions and cultural features, of dynamic interaction and syncretism."[90] Furthermore, an unbalanced stress on ethnicity neglects aspects of class, gender, sexual orientation, religion, age, and education in the analysis of oppressive differences. Distinguishing between 'consent' and 'descent', Sollors holds that race is not the same as ethnicity, but one aspect of ethnicity.[91] Drawing on the work of Milton M. Gordon, he argues that physical differences are often associated with race and cultural differences with ethnicity and, most importantly, that these differences rely on perception.[92]

---

[86] Werner Sollors, *Beyond Ethnicity: Consent and Descent in American Culture* (New York & Oxford: Oxford UP, 1986): 38.

[87] Sollors, *Beyond Ethnicity*, 25.

[88] Werner Sollors, "Introduction: The Invention of Ethnicity," xiii–xiv.

[89] Sollors, "Introduction: The Invention of Ethnicity," xiv.

[90] "Introduction: The Invention of Ethnicity," xiv. Christopher Balme understands cultural homogeneity, an "authentic ethnicity," as a Western conceptual construct (Balme, "Inventive Syncretism, 17).

[91] Werner Sollors, *Beyond Ethnicity*, 6, 36–39.

[92] Werner Sollors, "Foreword: Theories of Ethnicity," in *Theories of Ethnicity: A Classical Reader*, ed. Sollors (Houndmills & London: Macmillan, 1996): xxx. Ward Churchill criticizes Sollors harshly for reducing 'race' to a mere aspect of ethnicity, for homogenizing differences of descent, and for suggesting that one bypass the concept of 'ethnicity' by calling for kinship and cultural codes as keys for definition; Churchill, *Fantasies of the Master Race*, 137–47. Sollors argues that ethnicity exists in the minds of people because of practices that distinguish between groups culturally, politically, and economically. These practices generate conflict. Race and ethnicity are constructed because one group defines itself and its hegemony through differences from other groups that rest on concepts such as race and ethnicity. Churchill's

Cashmore also understands an ethnic group as a cultural phenomenon with positivist tendencies of identification and inclusion, but race as attributes of one group with negative tendencies of dissociation and exclusion.[93] In this sense, groups of people are defined and differentiated through cultural codes and descent. Cultural and racial differences come to the fore through unbalanced power-relations and the exercise of political, economic, and social domination by one group over another that is born of ethnocentric notions.[94] Only because one group defines another group as other (and inferior) on the grounds of visible and otherwise perceivable differences, these differences – ethnic, racial, cultural – gain meaning and are constructed. In this sense, Cashmore holds that an ethnic group is always a reaction to material conditions.[95] There are conflicts centered on race and cultural differences, which Sollors also concedes.[96] According to Fredrik Barth, the ethnic *boundary* defines the group and not the cultural content that it encloses.[97] However, current tendencies within cultural criticism run counter to this argument, holding that boundaries between distinctive groups are blurred and that in-between, hybrid spaces exist between them. Drawing on Charles Olson's postmodern 'open field' poetics, Helmbrecht Breinig and Klaus Lösch introduce a model of 'cultural core elements' which serve "as a gravitational force recognized by the members of the group as well as by outsiders and sufficiently specific in their combination of components to mark difference from other cultures."[98] Following this thought to the end, it appears that the gravitational forces as defining cultural elements become weaker the further they are from the core, and the core elements themselves are not static. This model allows cultural identity to be seen as "relational,

---

approach, by contrast, does not consider invention and construction as cultural phenomena, concentrating instead on the reality and visibility of racial and ethnic differences. The disagreement between Sollors and Churchill is rooted in this difference in *modus operandi*; their approaches are not strictly comparable.

[93] *Dictionary of Race and Ethnic Relations*, ed. Cashmore, 120.

[94] On ethnocentrism, see, for example, *Dictionary of Race and Ethnic Relations*, ed. Cashmore, 289.

[95] *Dictionary of Race and Ethnic Relations*, ed. Cashmore, 123.

[96] Werner Sollors, "Introduction: The Invention of Ethnicity," xv.

[97] Cited by Werner Sollors, *Beyond Ethnicity*, 27.

[98] Helmbrecht Breinig & Klaus Lösch, "Introduction: Difference and Transdifference," in *Multiculturalism in Contemporary Societies: Perspectives on Difference and Transdifference*, ed. Helmbrecht Breinig, Jürgen Gebhardt & Klaus Lösch (Erlangen: Universitäts-Bund Erlangen–Nürnberg, 2002): 20.

produced by interaction and negotiation."[99] Cultural groups in the homeland and in the diaspora, especially their younger generations, continually
reinterpret ethnic identity and negotiate new ethnic groups and identities in
processes of assimilation, hybridization, modernization, and the reincor-
poration and maintenance of traditional traits. Indigenous people in North
America are one group in terms of a shared colonial history and the shared
experience of political, economic, and social marginalization and oppression. But they consist of numerous different groups in terms of cultural
traditions and histories. Moreover, contact and mixing between various Indigenous cultural groups, between Indigenous and other cultural groups,
including Caucasians, results in constant hybridization and negotiation of
identity. Thus, Indigenous identities are defined and created in constant
dialogue with historical and traditional identities and in constant interaction
with other 'ethnic' groups (including Caucasians) and colonialist experience. It is in this sense of a constant reinterpretation of cultural identification that the terms 'ethnic' and 'ethnicity' are employed in this book.

   Spivak links the demand for authentic quality in texts to neocolonial
strategies that offer a deal to non-Western intelligentsia: inclusion in Western discourse in exchange for delivery of 'authentic' cultural practices:

> Neo-colonialism is fabricating its allies by proposing a share of the centre in
> a seemingly new way (not a rupture but displacement): disciplinary support
> for the conviction of authentic marginality by the (aspiring) elite.[100]

Indigenous discourse as "fetishized cultural commodity" and "mythodolo-
gized authentic," in Griffiths' words, enables subtler control of dominant
discourse. According to him, the "specific employment of this [alter/
native] meta-text under the sign of the authentic" furthers the exclusion of
the many and complex Indigenous voices, past and present.[101] In the case of

---

[99] Breinig & Lösch, "Introduction: Difference and Transdifference," 20.

[100] Gayatri Chakravorty Spivak, "Poststructuralism, Marginality, Postcoloniality, and
Value," in *Literary Theory Today*, ed. Peter Collier & Helga Geyer-Ryan (1990; Cambridge:
Polity, 1992): 222; quoted in Sangeeta Ray & Henry Schwarz, "Postcolonial Discourse: The
Raw and the Cooked," *ARIEL: A Review of International English Literature* 26.1 (January
1995): 163. Cf. Jean Franco, who compares the works of Third-World elite writers to cultural
recycling that removes cultural practice from its context; Franco, "Beyond Ethnocentrism: Gen-
der, Power and the Third-World Intelligentsia" (1988), in *Colonial Discourse and Post-Colonial
Theory*, ed. Patrick Williams & Laura Chrisman (New York: Columbia UP, 1994): 361.

[101] Gareth Griffiths, "The Myth of Authenticity: Representation, Discourse and Social
Practice," 76. Cf. the case of Lloyd Martell's film *Talker*, as discussed in chapters 2 and 4 of
the present study.

North America, a fetishized Indigenous discourse would be a mere pan-Indian text (printed and cinematic) that excludes diverse, digressive, and nonconformist practices. These arguments essentially question any claim to authenticity, welcoming instead the notion of hybrid cultures and discourses.

Hall offers the concept of 'articulation' as an alternative to 'hybridity'. According to James Clifford, it avoids an organic connotation and is more tactical and political.[102] The approach asks how ideological elements cohere with others within a discourse, and whether or not they become connected to certain political subjects – always and at specific conjunctures.[103] It is a form of connection which, under certain conditions, can unite different elements. Most important, argues Stuart Hall, such a linkage is not necessary, determined, absolute, and essential:

> So the so-called 'unity' of a discourse is really the articulation of different, distinct elements which can be re-articulated in different ways because they have no necessary 'belongingness'.[104]

The approach asks how ideological elements cohere with others within a discourse, and whether or not they become connected with certain political subjects – always and at specific conjunctures.[105] For Indigenous filmmaking in North America, this articulation-approach discloses the conjuncture of a certain cultural practice, a certain colonialist experience, a certain social, economic, and political condition, and a certain mode in which Western media technology is employed to form a new discourse; in each film, Indigenous filmic discourse is negotiated anew. Clifford points out that the issue of authenticity is irrelevant to the articulation-approach,[106] since various elements constitute a new discourse. This latter discourse is subject to constant change, for some elements will disconnect and other, new ones will connect according to specific circumstances. In regard to "articulated sites of indigenization," Clifford acknowledges that the sense of being connected to the land is more than simply discursive: "There is a

---

[102] James Clifford, in Robert Borofsky, "Valuing the Pacific: An Interview with James Clifford," in *Remembrance of Pacific Pasts: An Invitation to Remake History*, ed. Borofsky (Honolulu: U of Hawai'i P, 2000): 97.

[103] Stuart Hall, "On Postmodernism and Articulation: An Interview with Stuart Hall," ed. Lawrence Grossberg, *Journal of Commonwealth Inquiry* 10 (1986): 53.

[104] Stuart Hall, in Lawrence Grossberg, "On Postmodernism and Articulation," 53.

[105] Stuart Hall, in Grossberg, "On Postmodernism and Articulation," 53.

[106] James Clifford, in Borofsky, "Valuing the Pacific," 97.

nondiscursive reality of attachment and belonging as well," which adds a sense of continuity to this new shifting discourse.[107]

By contrast, Spivak, in an interview, has suggested employing a "strategic essentialism" in order to combat cultural hegemonies and oppressive systems. "You pick up the universal that will give you the power to fight against the other side and what you are throwing away by doing that is your theoretical purity."[108] She argues that it is of paramount importance to take a stand rhetorically against the discourses of essentialism; but "strategically we cannot."[109] Ashcroft et al. say that, for Spivak, a strategically employed essentialism might at certain points promote the renewal on the part of colonized cultures of the dignity and value of precolonial traditions, on their way to becoming self-confident nations.[110] Strategically essentialist views have always been employed in Indigenous land claims in North America, and Griffiths describes such strategic use of authentic Aborigine voices in a dispute over mining in Western Australia. He warns, though, that such subaltern writing/speech under the sign of 'authenticity' is still contained in the discourse of the oppressor and defines it as an "act of 'liberal' discursive violence."[111] In this light, suggestions for strategic essentialism have to be taken with great caution, because they disguise colonialist control of subaltern discourses and because they can easily encourage fundamentalist and nationalist ideas which, among other problems, promote an entrenchment of fronts and undermine the concept of hybrid spaces. A strategic essentialist approach by Indigenous filmmakers also harbors the danger that they might repeat clichés and romantic notions about their own cultures, as they are presented in dominant media discourse. Griffiths is concerned that, through such practices, the "possibilities for winning the larger discursive battle may be lost even as local 'tactical' victories may be won."[112] In the same vein, nativism, the politically charged drive to go back to precolonial traditions, will have homogenizing and essentializing effects, since colonialism has often created culturally mixed groups (Chicana/os, intertribal mixtures, Caucasian–Indigenous and

---

[107] Clifford, in Borofsky, "Valuing the Pacific," 98.

[108] Gayatri Chakravorty Spivak, in Gross, "Criticism, Feminism and the Institution: An Interview with Gayatri Chakravorty Spivak," 184.

[109] Spivak, in Gross, "Criticism, Feminism and the Institution," 184.

[110] Ashcroft, Griffiths & Tiffin, *Key Concepts in Post-Colonial Studies*, 79–80.

[111] Gareth Griffiths, "The Myth of Authenticity," 70–71.

[112] Griffiths, "The Myth of Authenticity," 76.

African–Indigenous mixtures) that are in danger of being left outside of a nativist scheme. Similarly, nativism has dichotomous effects, as it consciously reaffirms differences between Indigenous and other experiences. Essentialist and nativist tendencies also run the risk of limiting the decolonizing vector of cultural and, especially, political development.[113]

Like 'hybridity', 'articulation', and 'cultural core elements', the concept of 'transdifference', as introduced by Breinig and Lösch, circumvents nativist, essentialist, and simplistic binary views by advocating a non-linear understanding of cultures and subcultures that builds on differences. Differences must not be ignored as divisive modes but understood as oscillating modes of constructing meaning. While transdifference resists binary models,

> the term refers to whatever runs 'through' the line of demarcation drawn by binary difference. [...] Thus, the concept of transdifference interrogates the validity of binary constructions of difference without completely deconstructing them.[114]

These differences, crucial for identity-formation, are of intersystemic (between cultural systems) and intrasystemic character (within a cultural system).[115] Similar to the process of disconnecting and connecting new elements that form a 'new discourse' of articulation, the ongoing reproduction of cultural systems is a palimpsestic process: "in the cycles of reproduction the excluded has to be re-inscribed and overwritten again and again in order to neutralize its destabilizing threat," thus reproducing moments of transdifference.[116] This concept differs from that of hybridity, in the sense that the latter devalues cultural differences as confining binaries that are to be deconstructed, whereas transdifference evaluates differences as necessary elements for the construction of cultural meaning. While Breinig and Lösch explain hybridity as having validity in the specific historico-political contexts of postcolonial experience, they assign transdifference to "all situa-

---

[113] Cf. Frantz Fanon, who, in his analysis of national culture, warns that any going back to precolonial culture by 'native intellectuals' in order to create national works of art is reminiscent of exoticism, confines pieces of art/literature to the past, and might generate stereotypical reproduction; "On National Culture" (excerpt from *The Wretched of the Earth*, 1961/1967), in *Colonial Discourse and Post-Colonial Theory*, ed. Williams & Chrisman, 41–44.

[114] Helmbrecht Breinig & Klaus Lösch, "Introduction: Difference and Transdifference," 23.

[115] Breinig & Lösch, "Introduction: Difference and Transdifference," 24.

[116] "Introduction: Difference and Transdifference," 25.

tions of intercultural contact and interaction."[117] In the same vein, hybridity seems to denote cultural negotiation/ mingling in a narrower sense of cultures with the common denominators of ethnicity and/or nationality (owing to political valency of these terms), whereas transdifference understands cultures and subcultures in a wider sense of these terms, including, along with ethnicity, such denominators as age, religion, political affiliations, class, gender, and sexual orientation.[118] This understanding allows for multitudinous group identities that interfere, overlap, mingle, connect, and disconnect in a constant process of contestation and redefinition.

In order to clarify this interfructuating tangle of cultural concepts, one must understand that the discussed cultural concepts are not diametrically opposed to each other. They all acknowledge the existence of cultural differences and binaries that serve essentialist and hegemonic purposes, and they all acknowledge the existence of spaces, modes, and moments of identity-construction that lie beyond these binaries. The concepts differ in their theoretical understanding of how cultural identities are constructed and defined and subsequently in their applicability to certain phenomena. Regardless of how cultural meaning is constructed theoretically, certain dimensions remain crucial – acknowledging the existence of innumerable varieties of cultural expression; giving the subaltern a voice; and asserting constantly negotiated cultural identities within colonial discourses.

Spivak draws attention to the fact that colonized subjects who gain a position that enables them to "speak out" are still entangled in the self-serving hegemonic system of colonial discourse which utilizes cultural binaries and differences to construct them as colonized subaltern subjects. Creating a decolonized discourse is not simply a matter of "speaking out," but must be a conscious attempt, first, to understand the processes by which colonization of the mind through colonial discourse has functioned (what Spivak refers to as "epistemic violence") and, secondly, to undermine their operational mechanisms from within the postcolonial domain. Essentialist ideas are liable to impair this conscious process. Spivak reasons as follows:

> in subaltern studies, because of the violence of imperialist epistemic, social and disciplinary inscription, a project understood in essentialist terms must traffic in a radical textual practice of differences. The object of the group's investigation, in the case not even of the people as such but of the floating

---

[117] "Introduction: Difference and Transdifference," 30.
[118] "Introduction: Difference and Transdifference," 30.

buffer zone of the regional elite–subaltern is a *deviation* from an *ideal* – the people or subaltern – which is itself defined as a difference from the elite.[119]

She thus draws attention to the fact that in the moment in which a subaltern individual or group gains a voice in (post)colonial discourse, it ceases to be subaltern and forms the "elite–subaltern" and "buffer group" in the space between subaltern and colonialist. She illustrates this shift in group status by drawing on Ranajit Guha's scheme of four different groups in Indian society: 1. dominant foreign groups (elite); 2. dominant Indigenous groups on the all-India level (elite); 3. dominant Indigenous groups at the regional and local levels (buffer group); 4. "people" and "subaltern classes."[120] According to Spivak, the object of subaltern studies is not the fourth group, the "real subaltern," who are defined by difference from the other three groups, but the third group, who are an aberration of the "ideal" and mediator between the subaltern and the elite groups. In line with the definition of Guha and Spivak, writers, filmmakers, journalists, and politicians of a given colonized group, who by emancipation have gained a voice with which to speak out, belong to the third or even the second group. Spivak says that these act "in the interests of the latter [the dominant all-India groups] and not in conformity to interests corresponding truly to their own social being."[121] But then, what is left as the object of postcolonial studies? The "real subaltern" in Spivak's sense do not have a voice and an opportunity to gain discursive attention. And those who do, do not belong to the fourth group any longer, since at the very moment at which they obtain a voice by publishing a text or releasing a video/film, they slip from the fourth group into the third or even second. In Spivak's words, "The postcolonial intellectuals learn that their privilege is their loss."[122]

In this sense, postcolonial studies include the third and fourth group, and to a certain extent the second group, as they share some forms of oppression with the other two. One must be aware that postcolonial filmic and textual practices stem from individuals who have ceased to belong to a

---

[119] Gayatri Chakravorty Spivak, "Can the Subaltern Speak?" 80; emphasis in original.

[120] Spivak, "Can the Subaltern Speak?" 79. This scheme is also applicable to social and colonial strata in North America, where the first group is the dominant mainstream, the second the dominant Indigenous groups and leaders on the national level, the third the dominant Indigenous groups and leaders on the local and regional levels, and the fourth the subaltern Indigenous groups.

[121] Spivak, "Can the Subaltern Speak?" 80.

[122] "Can the Subaltern Speak?" 82.

'real' subaltern group and who have gained the privilege of voice. That they act 'in the interests of the dominant group' cannot be confirmed, as the analysis of the films in this book will show. There is no clear distinction between these groups, since filmmakers and writers of marginalized groups might be privileged politically, culturally, and economically, but they might also experience the same effects of colonialist oppression in the very same areas as others who have no voice. Consequently, the zone of transgression between these groups must be considered, along with the geopolitical and socio-economic contexts of the texts analyzed.

Postcolonialism and Film Analysis

As seen earlier, filmmakers from the Third[123] and Fourth World experience the same postcolonial conditions and are subject to the same cultural hegemonies as writers and artists. Indigenous media are often devalued, since there is no coherent set of experiences as in Western culture.[124] Filmic practice is subordinated to Western conventions of analysis and reception as well. Thus, Bordwell and Thompson classify the Japanese filmmaker Yasujiro Ozu as a modernist, neglecting the fact that his deviation from classical Hollywood cinema and his tendency to violate spatial continuity and yet to masterfully employ graphic matches and matches on action might be due to a link between his films and traditional Japanese art rather than to his modernist tendencies (which, however, should not be denied here).[125]

Western scholars apply a Western concept of analysis to postcolonial/subaltern practices, since appropriate analytical tools are lacking. E. Ann Kaplan notes that Western scholars "are forced to read works produced by the Other

---

[123] There exists a controversial term, 'Third Cinema', used by the Argentine documentarists Fernando Solanas and Octavio Getino for filmmaking that opposes dominant-industrial ('First') and independent-auteurist ('Second') cinema; Julianne Burton, "Marginal Cinemas and Mainstream Critical Theory," *Screen* 26. 3–4 (1985): 6; I shall refrain from using it here. Burton uses the terms 'marginal cinema' and 'oppositional cinema' ("Marginal Cinemas," 6–7), whereas I employ either 'postcolonial filmmaking' or 'Third- and Fourth-World filmmaking', distinguishing between colonized but now politicall independent countries and internally colonized nations existing within the sphere of a dominant country. Further, the term 'filmmaking' does not limit genre and the material and techniques employed (as suggested by 'cinema') but covers documentary, short, experimental, and feature works produced in both film and video technology.

[124] Loretta Todd, dir./writ., *Through the Lens: Changing Voices*, prod. Gretchen Jordan Basto & Fumik Kiyooka (Canadian Broadcasting Corporation – CBC, Canada 1998; 60 min.).

[125] Mitsuhiro Yoshimoto, "The Difficulty of Being Radical: The Discipline of Film Studies and the Postcolonial World Order," *boundary 2* 18.3 (Fall 1991): 244.

through the constraints of [their] own frameworks/theories/ideologies."[126] Julianne Burton explains that in the Third World a framework for the critical analysis of filmic practice did not materialize because there is no division between film production and critical reception/theoretical analysis, as in the Western sphere. Essays on filmmaking are usually written by filmmakers themselves "whose theoretical propositions derive from the concrete practice of attempting to make specific films under specific historical conditions."[127] The situation in the Fourth World is similar. Thus, the application of Western film analysis harbors the danger that Western scholars adapt Third- and Fourth-World filmic practice to their own understanding of film, re-imposing cultural hegemonies and distorting meanings. In the sense of the dependency model, Burton describes the relation between postcolonial/marginal cinematic practices and mainstream cinematic theory thus:

> another instance of the asymmetrical nature of cultural exchange between the developed and underdeveloped spheres, since the metropolitan sector imports and consumes the "raw materials" produced in the Third World (films, in this case) more easily than peripheral sectors can import and consume the manufactured products of the developed sector (in this case, theoretical and critical writings).[128]

One could argue that, according to Roland Barthes,[129] every film, novel, poem, and piece of art develops a momentum and order of its own, independent of the author and driven by the analysis and reception undertaken by various critics, readers, and viewers. However, this anti-authorial approach does not meet the needs of Third- and Fourth-World discourses, because it is apt to occlude particular cultural and political contexts and decolonizing strategies born out of these contexts.[130] Nevertheless, as dis-

---

[126] E. Ann Kaplan, "Problematizing Cross-Cultural Analysis: The Case of Women in the Recent Chinese Cinema," *Wide Angle* 11.2 (1989): 42, quoted in Mitsuhiro Yoshimoto, "The Difficulty of Being Radical," 245.

[127] Julianne Burton, "Marginal Cinemas and Mainstream Critical Theory," 4.

[128] Burton, "Marginal Cinemas and Mainstream Critical Theory," 4.

[129] Roland Barthes, "The Death of the Author," in Barthes, *Image – Music – Text*, ed. Steven Heath (New York: Hill & Wang, 1977): 142–48.

[130] The ideas of Barthes, Foucault, and Derrida on the removal of the authorial subject are discussed comprehensively in Seán Burke, *The Death and Return of the Author: Criticism and Subjectivity in Barthes, Foucault and Derrida* (1992; Edinburgh: Edinburgh UP, 1999). In the context of the Third and Fourth Worlds, Jean–Paul Sartre's application of the notion of free subjectivity in his model of the engaged author and the politically committed writer is quite helpful (Burke, *The Death and Return of the Author*, 11).

cussed earlier, for postcolonial film analysis it is necessary to combine a critical application of 'classical' tools for film analysis with postcolonial theory. Classical film analysis here serves to study technical (camera work, salient methods, lighting), structural (narrative features, motifs, form), and stylistic features. Postcolonial theory needs to be employed for the assessment of these features and, of course, for the analysis of content. As Bernd Schulte suggests, such an interdisciplinary approach is capable of discussing products of cultural and cinematic mixture.[131]

A focal point of this combined approach must, however, be the classical Hollywood cinema, since Western fictional cinema has been dominated historically by this film practice.[132] It has been the shaping norm for many national cinemas and still influences filmic production and reception on a global scale. Since Hollywood cinema clearly upholds Western supremacy, the export of Hollywood films throughout the world ensures the dissemination of eurocentric ideologies and the cultural export of US imperialism. Shohat and Stam employ the phrases "Hollywoodcentrism" and "imperializing film culture of the US"[133] to denote North American colonialist film practices, which need to be undermined by oppositional practices in the creation of postcolonial films. Judith Mayne argues:

> The classical Hollywood cinema has become the norm against which all other alternative practices are measured. Films which do not engage the classical Hollywood cinema are by and large relegated to irrelevance. Frequently, the very notion of "alternative" is posed in the narrow terms of an either–or: either one is within classical discourse and therefore complicit, or one is critical of and/or resistant to it and therefore outside of it.[134]

Burton, too, insists on the inseparability between dominant and marginal filmic practice in an ongoing, partly disguised, dialogue:

---

[131] Bernd Schulte, "Kulturelle Hybridität: Kulturanthropologische Anmerkungen zu einem 'Normalzustand'," in *Hybridkultur: Medien, Netze, Künste*, ed. Irmela Schneider & Christian W. Thomsen (Cologne: Wienand, 1997): 245–47.

[132] David Bordwell & Kristin Thompson, *Film Art: An Introduction* (1979; New York: McGraw–Hill, 1997): 108.

[133] Ella Shohat & Robert Stam, *Unthinking Eurocentrism*, 29, 282. These authors warn against understanding Hollywood as the *primum mobile* of film history, as this view reduces other national cinemas to mere mimicry of Hollywood (29–30). Nevertheless, its global influence cannot be denied; moreover, Bollywood's film practice mixes "Hollywood continuity codes and production values with the anti-illusionist values of Hindu mythology" (29–30).

[134] Mayne, *Kino and the Woman Question* (Columbus: Ohio State UP, 1989): 3; quoted in Yoshimoto, "The Difficulty of Being Radical," 254.

Mainstream cultural manifestations appropriate marginal creativity without acknowledging (and often actively concealing) the source. Oppositional cultural practice defines itself as a denial of and an alternative to dominant practice, a stance which requires constant monitoring of its adversary. Dominant or mainstream cultures thus establish the terms of oppositional or marginal cultures to a significant degree.[135]

On the one hand, postcolonial filmmaking is driven by the need to deviate and differentiate itself from mainstream filmmaking; on the other, the binary reception of filmic practice needs to be dissolved and the concept of hybrid filmic practice introduced. Hybrid film practice in regard to Indigenous filmmaking needs to be understood in the Bhabhian sense of creating a third space, where Western film technology, conventions, and genres mingle with Indigenous usage and negotiation of these, infused with content that derives from various Indigenous constructions of cultural meaning as well as structures, styles, and techniques that are informed by traditional and modern Indigenous cultural practice and expression. A great deal of today's non-Western and also some Western films (I am thinking here of avantgarde and *auteur* cinema – for example, films by Atom Egoyan, David Cronenberg, Quentin Tarantino, Jim Jarmusch, David Lynch, and the Coen brothers) are for the most part amalgamations of classical film techniques and individual techniques and/or deviations from classical film conventions. These are sometimes highly stylized films which nevertheless adhere to basic rules of classical film. But one has to differentiate between the deviation of avantgarde and Indigenous filmmaking, since the former belongs to the colonial and the latter to the subaltern sphere.[136] Furthermore, with the rise of Third- and Fourth-World film, Indigenous traditional art and narrative concepts as well as other cultural elements find their way into films, so that hybrid film practices emerge on various planes.

Many former colonies (e.g., India, Brazil, Cuba) have developed their own national cinemas informed by traditional art, religious and cultural values, and socio-historical specifics. Although these features also shape Indigenous films, an Indigenous national cinema[137] in North America has not been able to develop, chiefly because Indigenous nations are not politically independent and autonomous nations, and, further, because the

---

[135] Julianne Burton, "Marginal Cinemas and Mainstream Critical Theory," 11.

[136] Burton, "Marginal Cinemas and Mainstream Critical Theory," 6.

[137] Here the term 'cinema' includes documentary and dramatic work produced with film and video technology.

"imperialist center of film production" is situated on the same continent. Indigenous filmmakers, more than any other postcolonial filmmakers, are compelled to create work in relation to Hollywood practice. Since Hollywood was and remains the industry which, from works of print culture, has most shaped Western clichés about the colonized nations of North America through misrepresentation, distortion, romanticizing, exoticizing, and muting in filmic domestications of the 'savage', and since this classical narrative cinema dominates the North American film industry, it is this industry against which Indigenous filmmakers measure their practice. As some see themselves trapped in the oppositional binaries of center/margin and self/other, they can only regard their filmic practice as either conformist or nonconformist. Others find ways to create a space between the two, in which their works move to interrogate film conventions and explore filmic digressions. Still, most Indigenous filmmakers in North America feel constrained to relate to Hollywood in some way, and there are varying degrees of deviation from mainstream cinema.

The Development of Fourth-World Film

Like postcolonial literature in Indigenous North America, the development of postcolonial films has also gone through various stages. The first stage is formed by colonial filmic discourse about the colonial subjects. The beginning of moving pictures at the end of the nineteenth century was also the beginning of ethnographic filmmaking and modern anthropology. In 1895 the Lumière brothers sent cameramen to Indochina and North Africa to bring "back images of the world." These early cinematographers (for example, Felix Mesguich and Raoul Grimoin–Sanson), in search of exotic locations with action, often staged scenes with 'local' actors[138] – a practice that was to be continually repeated, most notoriously by Edward S. Curtis and Robert J. Flaherty. One of the first pieces of visual anthropology was created by Alfred Haddon, leader of the 1898 Cambridge expedition to the Torres Straits, off the coast of Queensland, Australia. He took a kinematograph with him and shot four minutes of Aborigine dances and fire-making. This generation of anthropologists regarded the camera as their 'micro-

---

[138] Martine Astier Loutfi, "Imperial Frame: Film Industry and Colonial Representation," in *Cinema, Colonialism, Postcolonialism: Perspectives from the French and Francophone Worlds*, ed. Dina Sherzer (Austin: U of Texas P, 1996): 20–21.

scope' or 'telescope', which would capture and preserve their work as well as lend it 'objective' character. In the 1920s, anthropology became less iconographic and anthropologists began to see that the medium of film was manipulative and would not assist them in developing anthropology as an 'objective' science such as physics or biology.[139] Very often in such films, dances were staged, dancers were wearing cardboard masks, people acted out their daily chores and hunting in pre-contact clothes and were not permitted to use tools that they had acquired through Western contact. However, the making of ethnographic films (mostly in documentary form) continued and developed further, so that it became one major aspect in the process of mental colonization and the creation of a discursive exotic other.[140]

Indigenous people of North America were filmed for the first time by Thomas Edison's company in the short films *Sioux Ghost Dance* of 1894 and *Esquimaux Village* of 1903.[141] At the beginning of the twentieth century, the former U.S. Department of the Interior, which was later to become the Bureau of Indian Affairs, commissioned anthropologists to collect film footage about Indigenous people. Early American ethnographic films were composed out of this footage. They include *Life and Customs of the Winnebago Indians* (1912), *See America First* (1912), and *Indian Dances and Past Times* (1912).[142] Edward S. Curtis produced his epic saga about the Kwakiutl, *In the Land of the Head Hunters*, in 1914. Various other ethnographic films followed – for example, *History of the American Indian* (1915) by Rodman Wanamaker, documenting rites and ceremonies, *Indian Life* (1918), *Nurse Among the Tepees* (1920), and a few color documentaries shot in the 1920s, such as *The Land of the Great Spirit*, *Life in the Blackfoot Country*, and *Heritage of the Red Man*. In 1922 Robert Flaherty released his largely staged film *Nanook of the North*, which attempted to describe Inuit life by following Nanook and his family on their hunting

---

[139] Paul Henley, "Fly in the Soup," *London Review of Books* (21 June 2001): 35.

[140] In order to pinpoint the subject/object relation in ethnographic films, the French ethnographic filmmaker Jean Rouch reversed the ethnographic scheme in one of his films. In *Chronicle of a Summer* (1960), he has an African man examine the habits and body characteristics of the 'Parisian Tribe'; Henley, "Fly in the Soup," 36.

[141] Amy Lynn Corbin, "Native American Narrative and Experimental Film: Aesthetics of Activism and Resistance" (BA Hons. thesis, College of William & Mary, 1997): 7; Ian Morgan, "American Indians in Film: Changing Portrayals," at http://www.lucidscreening.com /2006/11/american_indians_in_film.php

[142] Richard M. Barsam, *Nonfiction Film: A Critical History* (Bloomington & Indianapolis: Indiana U P, 1992): 45.

trips and everyday activities. In the 1960s, the anthropologist Asen Balikci produced a documentary series on the Netsilik Inuit, focussing on life and survival in the Arctic. The Netsilik Eskimo Project consists of twelve films, each dealing with a special aspect of Inuit life. All of these early ethnographic films belong to a stage of development in which individuals from the colonial group were making films about individuals from the colonized group. These films clearly resemble a colonialist subject/object relation (filmmaker/filmed) with its underlying self/other dichotomy. Later, numerous other ethnographic films were produced. Today there is a large market in the governmental and educational sector for documentaries about Indigenous cultures and issues. Indigenous filmmakers only have a small share of this market and these neo-ethnographic films[143] compete, often victoriously, for space against autonomous documentaries by Indigenous filmmakers.

Already at the beginning of the twentieth century, there were two Indigenous filmmakers, James Young Deer (Winnebago) and Edwin Carewe (Chickasaw). Both of them made a series of commercially successful films, including *Cheyenne Brave* (1910), *The Yaqui Girl* (1911), *Lieutenant Scott's Narrow Escape* (n.d.), and *Red Deer's Devotion* (n.d.) by Young Deer, and *The Trail of the Shadow* (1917) and *Ramona* (1928) by Carewe.[144] These men are probably the first Indigenous filmmakers in North America, but their accomplishments largely went unacknowledged. Their careers as directors were short-lived and they did not seem to influence the media (mis)representation of Indigenous cultures of their time. Indeed, Young Deer's work was informed by contemporary Hollywood practice and depicted Indian attacks with simplistic plots, celebrating male heroism and unrequited love.[145] These two early Indigenous filmmakers were unable to initiate the production of Indigenous films on a broader scale; Indigenous filmmaking was suspended for half a century. Over this same time-span,

---

[143] The term 'neo-ethnographic films' is employed because, although there is a raised awareness of Indigenous cultural, political, and economic issues, the colonialist subject/object relation has not changed with the production by non-Indigenous filmmakers of videos/programs with Indigenous content. Cf. also Loretta Todd, who holds that contemporary mainstream documentaries with Indigenous content still have an ethnographic tone and seem to scrutinize Indigenous cultures (Todd, unpublished interview, 1998).

[144] Ward Churchill, "Smoke Signals: A History of Native Americans in Cinema," *LiP Magazine* (1998): 1 at http://www.lipmagazine.org/articles/revichurchill_35_p.htm; Beverly Singer, *Wiping the War Paint Off the Lens: Native American Film and Video* (Minneapolis: U of Minnesota P, 2001): 15–16. The sources do not specify whether these are documentary or feature productions, however, titles and context suggest that they are feature films.

[145] Beverly Singer, *Wiping the War Paint Off the Lens*, 16.

until the late 1970s, Hollywood studios released approximately 2,000 feature films with 'Indian' content, and between 1950 and 1970 some 2,500 were made as television segments.[146] These numbers convey the dimensions of mainstream Indian imagery as it developed into a lopsided stereotypical discourse. As indicated earlier, these stereotypes include the whole range of clichéd notions of 'the Indian', between the 'poles' of the 'noble savage' and 'bloodthirsty devil' as well as between the 'poles' of the contemporary 'drunk and lazy Indian' and the 'handsome exotic womanizer', greatly exceeding the sexual qualities of Euro-American/Canadian lovers. In the same vein, westerns, by relaying the cowboy(settler)/Indian dichotomy, were 'mapping the *terra incognita*' in media discourse.

The 1966 project "Navajos Film Themselves" in Pine Springs on the Navajo reservation marked the beginning of the second stage of Indigenous media development.[147] The anthropologist John Adair and the communication-science professor Sol Worth trained six Navajos how to use film cameras and how to cut and splice, and asked them to make a film about Navajo life. The Navajos had till then been hardly exposed to film (except for the art student Al Clah), and Worth and Adair did not teach them about the concept of film. They studied how the Navajos used film as a form of cultural expression, how they structured their view of the world through film, and the ways in which their films differed from those made by non-Indigenous people, including film novices. The Navajos made a series of silent films on subjects that they thought important and appropriate for capture on film. Like 'as-told-to' autobiographies, this project can be seen as marking a stage in which individuals from the colonized group were making films in collaboration with members of the colonizing group, whereby the latter remained in control. Although it is clearly a patronizing project and independence from imperial control could not be gained, it must be understood as a step in the process toward decolonized media-making.

Itam Hakim, Hopiit by the Hopi filmmaker Victor Masayevsa can be regarded as one of the first fully self-determined documentaries. Masayevsa made his commemorative film on the occasion of the tricentennial of the Pueblo Revolt in 1680. It was released in 1984 by IS Productions (Masayesva's film company) in collaboration with ZDF (Zweites Deutsches Fernsehen, the German public broadcaster that commissioned and funded

---

[146] Ward Churchill, "Smoke Signals: A History of Native Americans in Cinema."

[147] Cf. Sol Worth & John Adair, *Through Navajo Eyes: An Exploration in Film Communication and Anthropology* (1972; Albuquerque: U of New Mexico P, 1997).

the film). According to Masayesva, ZDF gave him a free hand.[148] Like-wise, the films of Shelley Niro (*Honey Moccasin, Overweight With Crooked Teeth*), Chris Eyre (*Tenacity*), Lloyd Martell (*Talker*), and Zacha-rias Kunuk (*Atanarjuat: The Fast Runner*)[149] reflect the creation of indep-endent Indigenous media, thus marking a third stage, one that comes closest to decolonized media-making.

In a fourth stage of Fourth-World filmmaking, collaboration between mainstream and subaltern filmmaking is adopted as the mode of produc-tion; of prime importance here is the fact that the dynamics of decision-making power in the process of creation are in balanced relation. In 1971, Alanis Obomsawin (Abenaki) directed her first documentary film at the National Film Board of Canada (NFB) and has since then been making documentaries about Indigenous social and political issues in a spirit of ad-mirable perseverance. She is a pioneer of Indigenous filmmaking and re-vered in the Indigenous filmmaking community. Her films have won thirty-nine national and international awards and honorable mentions and she has received twenty-six personal achievement awards, including five honorary doctorates.[150] Many other Indigenous filmmakers have followed suit in making documentaries within major companies, in Canada mainly with the NFB.[151] The films *Smoke Signals* (dir. Chris Eyre) and *Big Bear* (dir. Gil Cardinal), the first major motion pictures made by Indigenous filmmakers in the USA and Canada, were likewise made in collaboration with main-stream film companies and/or distributors. The screenplay of *Smoke Sig-nals* and the text it was adapted from were written by an Indigenous author (Sherman Alexie), whereas *Big Bear*'s was co-scripted by an Indigenous and a non-Indigenous author (Gil Cardinal and Rudy Wiebe respectively), on the basis of a then still controversial novel by Wiebe. On the one hand, these films cannot be regarded as fully autonomous; on the other, nor do they belong to the second stage, since here the collaboration is self-chosen and is largely restricted to providing technical and financial support. With

---

[148] This information was provided in a personal conversation with Victor Masayesva, Jr.

[149] In some of these examples, there are still non-Indigenous individuals involved in the production process. Nevertheless, control over production remained with the Indigenous film-makers, and the films are not made in cooperation with non-Indigenous production com-panies, so that they do not belong the fourth group.

[150] CitizenShift, Alanis Obomsawin: "Awards and Honours" at http://citizen.nfb.ca/extraits /media/Alanis_awards.pdf

[151] Some filmmakers, such as Marjorie Beaucage and Victor Masayesva, purposely avoid mainstream film companies and create documentaries independently.

such collaborations, co-producers, camera persons, editors, sound editors/ managers and other crew members are often part of the respective mainstream company, but what counts is the fact that producer and/or co-producer, director, and scriptwriter belong to the colonized group. Collaboration with major film and distribution companies has become necessary, and is indeed sought, because Indigenous companies do not (yet) have the financial means to produce films on an nth-million-dollar budget; also, some filmmakers do not regard it as important to exclude mainstream involvement in the making of their films. To them, such collaboration is fruitful in the creation of Indigenous media products.[152]

Indigenous filmmaking began as a "cinema of duty" discourse, which Cameron Bailey defines as "social issue in content, documentary-realist in style, firmly responsible in intention," positioning its subjects "in direct relation to social crisis" and attempting "to articulate 'problems' and 'solutions to problems' within a framework of center and margin, white and non-white communities. The goal is often to tell buried or forgotten stories, to write unwritten histories, to 'correct' the misrepresentations of the mainstream."[153] To a large degree employing the documentary mode, Indigenous filmmakers deal with social and political issues and present historical and cultural narratives from within the subaltern discourse. The documentary mode has been favored because this genre requires much lower budgets and because the major funding sources have traditionally supported documentaries.[154] Steven Leuthold outlines three other reasons for the prevalence of documentaries:

> the place of documentaries in education, the natural adoption of electronic media documentaries by members of traditionally oral cultures, and the desire to document disappearing cultural practices.[155]

---

[152] Cf. the interviews with Gil Cardinal (1998), Doug Cuthand (1998), Lloyd Martell (1996 and 1998), and Rodger Ross (1996 and 1998), all unpublished.

[153] Cameron Bailey, "A Cinema of Duty: The Films of Jennifer Hodge de Silva," *Cine-Action* 23 (Winter 1990–91): 4, quoted in Sarita Malik, "Beyond 'The Cinema of Duty'? The Pleasures of Hybridity: Black British Film of the 1980s and 1990s," in *Dissolving Views: Key Writings on British Cinema*, ed. Andrew Higson (London & New York: Cassell, 1996): 204.

[154] Steven Leuthold, *"Telling Our Own Story": The Aesthetic Expression of Collective Identity in Native American Documentary* (Ann Arbor MI: UMI, 1992): 145, 153, repr. as Leuthold, *Indigenous Aesthetics: Native Art, Media and Identity* (Austin: U of Texas P, 1998).

[155] Leuthold, *Indigenous Aesthetics*, 153.

As educational broadcasters have also shown an interest in airing Indigenous documentaries, and as tribal/band councils and the Canadian government commission Indigenous filmmakers to produce videos about important events and about conditions on reserves, as well as to make videos with
community profiles, the production of documentary work is nurtured by
this emerging market as well.[156] In this regard, Elizabeth Weatherford has
observed:

> Documentary has long been the genre of choice for Native directors con-
> cerned that Native American history and contemporary viewpoints lack
> authentic representation in American society.[157]

Tied in with the constraints of the 'cinema of duty' is what Kobena Mercer
calls the "burden of representation," an urgent need to comment on *all*
social and political problems and correct *all* misrepresentations in one
film.[158] This burden, which many pioneer Indigenous filmmakers will be
familiar with, harbors the danger of succumbing to essentializing and
moralizing tendencies. Filmmakers have not always succeeded in warding
off such tendencies.

In the last few years, there has been a movement away from social and
political realism in documentary form to a dramatized mode in which filmmakers stay close to conventional filmmaking but also experiment with
style, techniques, narrative forms, metaphoric plots, and a humorous subversive play with the dominant media discourse. I call this discourse the
'cinema of pleasure' in contrast to the 'cinema of duty'. At present, both
cinematic approaches coexist; where they mix, this is not the exception –
rather, it is becoming the shaping norm. The movement toward the dramatic mode was enabled by filmmakers' growing interest in the subversive
potential of cinematic fiction as well as by their entrepreneurial spirit in
starting up small independent film companies and their ability to commit
mainstream companies to cooperative projects.

The release of Indigenous feature films has increased in the past few
years. *Naturally Native* (1997) by Valerie Red Horse and Jennifer Wynne
Farmer was financed with Indigenous monies – casino profits invested by

---

[156] See Rodger Ross (1996, unpublished interview).
[157] Elizabeth Weatherford, "The Public Eye, Native Media-Making: A Growing Potential,"
Native Americas: Akwe:kon's Journal of Indigenous Issues (Spring 1996): 56.
[158] As cited in Sarita Malik, "Beyond 'The Cinema of Duty'?" 206.

the Mashantucket Pequots.[159] The film *Tushka* (1996) by Ian Skorodin is labelled as the first all-Indigenous feature production. Shirley Cheechoo's *Bear Walker* (1999, re-released as *Backroads*, 2000), Sean Morris' *Kusah Hakwaan* (2001), and Zacharias Kunuk's *Atanarjuat: The Fast Runner* (2001) and *The Journals of Knud Rasmussen* (2006) are the first Indigenous features to be shot partly or wholly in an Indigenous language – English and Cree, English and Tlingit, and Inuktitut respectively, with English subtitles.[160] Sherman Alexie has adapted his collection of poetry *The Business of Fancydancing* (2002) for the screen, and also directed the production. Last but not least, Chris Eyre has followed up *Smoke Signals* with *Skins* (2002), *Skinwalkers* (2002), *Edge of America* (2003), *A Thief of Time* (2004), and *A Thousand Roads* (2005). The latest Indigenous feature productions are Shirley Cheechoo's *Johnny Tootall* (2005), Gil Cardinal's television mini-series *Indian Summer: The Oka Crisis* (2006), Sterlin Harjo's *Four Sheets to the Wind* (2007), and Shane Belcourt's *Tkaronto* (2007).

These recent developments indicate that Indigenous filmmaking is on the threshold of claiming a firm share of the media industry and becoming a full-scale and internationally acclaimed film tradition. These feature films show that Indigenous filmmaking is not only a matter of adapting Western filmmaking techniques to Indigenous themes and creating mixed film codes but that the film sources can be of mixed origin as well. *Smoke Signals*, *The Business of Fancydancing*, and *Skins* are based on texts by Indigenous authors, but *Big Bear*, *Skinwalkers*, *A Thief of Time*, and *The Journals of Knud Rasmussen* are based on texts by non-Indigenous authors, Rudy Wiebe, Tony Hillermann, and Knud Rasmussen. The first two are big names in the appropriation debate, and the choice of their texts indicates that emphasis is being put not so much on *which* texts are adapted for the screen but on *how* they are adapted. In this sense, the filmic translation of texts belonging to colonialist discourse might be understood as a double act

---

[159] Beverly Singer, *Wiping the War Paint Off the Lens*, 92. The Mashantucket Pequots in Washington receive nearly half a billion U S dollars in annual revenues from their casino and have begun to support and invest in Indigenous filmmaking; Ward Churchill, "Smoke Signals: A History of Native Americans in Cinema."

[160] Cf. the schedule of the Annual Taos Talking Picture Film Festival – Native Cinema Showcase (2002) at http://www.ttpix.org/native_copy.html, and *V O X of Dartmouth* (5 November 2001): 8. Kunuk's *Atanarjuat: The Fast Runner* was produced entirely by Igloolik Isuma Productions and *The Journals of Knud Rasmussen* was co-produced with Denmark's Barok Film.

of decolonizing. It is conceivable that in the near future all-Indigenous productions funded by Indigenous finance capital will be a common affair, and
Indigenous filmmaking will have its grand entry into the mainstream industry as fully decolonized and self-controlled media.

Teshome Gabriel lists three phases in the development of Third-World
film: 1. "unqualified assimilation"; 2. the "remembrance phase"; and 3. the
"combative phase."[161] The first phase is characterized by identification with
Hollywood, its objective being to entertain and make profits. The themes
are largely adventure, romance, and comedy. Narrative and technical style
are fully subordinated to Hollywood conventions to create an illusionistic
reality. In the second phase, the film industry experiences an indigenization: i.e. ex-colonized groups gain control over production, cast, exhibition,
and distribution. They thematize contemporary problems, culture, traditions, and history, often by drawing on folklore and mythology. The (re)
turn to traditional values and themes, however, runs the risk of romanticizing the past and conveying essentialist and nativist attitudes. The style in
this phase still exhibits conventional traits but adapts to meet thematic and
culture-specific concerns. Finally, in the third phase the film industry is a
government/nation-owned institution, managed, operated, and run for and
by the people – a cinema for mass participation. Technical and artistic perfection are not primary, and thematically the films concentrate on the lives
and struggles of Third-World peoples. Here, film is consciously employed
as an ideological tool and the filmmaker, fully conversant with the concerns
of a mass audience, is its spokesperson. Thus, a political agenda dominates
rather than one of entertainment and aesthetic production. Gabriel stresses
the fact that these phases are subject to certain dynamic constraints and that
there is a buffer zone between them.

This scheme is useful in order to delineate the continuing process of the
development and decolonization of Third-World films but, for obvious
reasons, it cannot be applied wholesale to Fourth-World films. Fourth-
World nations have not gained political independence and are still under
colonialist rule. They are not recognized nation-states, so they are unable to
develop a national cinema and a state-owned film industry. Thus, phase 3
in Gabriel's model is irrelevant for the Fourth World. Nor are the other two
phases clearly traceable in Indigenous filmmaking in North America. Assi-

---

[161] Teshome H. Gabriel, "Towards a Critical Theory of Third World Films" (1989), in
Colonial Discourse and Post-Colonial Theory, ed. Patrick Williams & Laura Chrisman
(1993; New York: Columbia UP, 1994): 341–45.

milation to the dominant industry of phase 1 only concerns the techniques of filmmaking and (with some exceptions) not the content. One can state unreservedly that Indigenous films largely deal with cultural traditions, history, and contemporary experience, often including elements from the oral tradition and folklore, much as Gabriel suggests for phase 2. With regard to style, both adherence to and conscious avoidance of Western film conventions are widespread in contemporary postcolonial filmmaking in North America, as well as a combination of both. Thus, Indigenous film does not develop homogeneously in the direction of a national cinema but is characterized by heterogeneous strategies with respect to technique, conventions, and film genres.

For Indigenous filmmakers, decolonization starts when they take their image-making and self-representation into their own hands, creating decolonized cultural, historical, and political discourses, and become progressively emancipated from the Hollywood-dominated industry. This decolonizing process works in a twofold manner: first, as a political struggle, through the creation of self-fashioned images and an anticolonialist rewriting and filming of history; and, secondly, as an aesthetic struggle, through defiance of and/or negotiation with established conventions of feature and ethnographic film.[162] Julianne Burton's differentiation between a capitalist and a non-profit mode of production[163] is also helpful here. Whereas Gabriel's phase 3 is based on a non-profit mode of production which is non-competitive and permits shifting perspectives and mass participation, the first two phases seem to be grounded on a capitalist mode of production. In phase 1 particularly, competition and market orientation dominate film production, while today's Third-World filmmaking, as classified in phases 2 and 3, is marked by a transition from a non-profit to a capitalist mode of production.[164] Indigenous filmmaking, too, has to be likewise understood as a capitalist mode of production, since the domain in which it operates is inescapably capitalist.

The 'parent–child' relation between mainstream governments and their colonial subjects in North America is also demonstrated by the fact that there

---

[162] In the field of postcolonial media, a clear distinction between documentary and fictional films/videos cannot always be made, since many filmmakers create mixed forms outside Western genres and avail themselves of the form of the docudrama, which, as the term suggests, often mixes fact and fiction by re-enacting historical/contemporary events.

[163] Julianne Burton, "Marginal Cinemas and Mainstream Critical Theory," 11.

[164] "Marginal Cinemas and Mainstream Critical Theory," 11.

still seems to be a paternalistic notion that Indigenous people cannot speak
for themselves, and that they do not have the potential for making qualitatively good films. This paternalism, coupled with prejudices and institutional
and structural racism, fosters a situation in which all kinds of obstacles bar
the subalterns' way to autonomous films. Production companies, broadcasters, and funding agencies often do not trust Indigenous filmmakers, reason-
ing that they are not properly trained, that they are not reliable or organized
enough, or that they do not have the knack for making good films.[165] As a
result, projects with Indigenous content are often placed in the hands of non-
Indigenous filmmakers. Documentaries, television series, and feature films
with Indigenous content are made *for* them instead of *by* them. For example,
the Canadian federal government endeavors to support Indigenous film practice by assigning monies to big film companies and broadcasting corporations, such as SaskFilm, Telefilm, the Canadian Broadcasting Corporation
(CBC), Canadian Television (CTV), and the NFB, for the promotion, production, and broadcasting of Indigenous film and video productions. But
most often the monies are not given directly to Indigenous filmmakers but
are distributed through these non-Indigenous companies, so that the above-
mentioned paternalism takes hold.[166] The NFB has the greatest share in
Canadian documentary production. On the one hand, it has been supportive
of Indigenous documentary, through its "Challenge for Change"[167] and
"Studio One" programs, which have trained and guided Indigenous media
producers in the creation of documentaries. In 1996, the decentralized
"Indigenous Filmmaking Program" emerged from "Studio One" and
finances Indigenous documentary projects four times a year. In March
2005, the NFB launched the "First Stories" program, where aspiring Indigenous filmmakers are trained and selected documentarists make films
with an NFB producer.[168] On the other hand, the NFB upholds hegemonic

---

[165] Kerstin Knopf, "Aboriginal Women and Film in Canada," 7–8. See also Beverly
Singer, *Wiping the War Paint Off the Lens*, 9 and unpublished interviews with Marjorie Beaucage (1998), Lloyd Martell (1996 and 1998), Debra Piapot (1996), Evelyn Poitras (1998), and
Rodger Ross (1996 and 1998).
[166] Kerstin Knopf, "Aboriginal Women and Film in Canada," 10. See also interview with
Rodger Ross (1996 unpublished).
[167] Elizabeth Weatherford, "Currents: Film and Video in Native America," *Native Americans on Film and Video*, vol. 2, ed. Elizabeth Weatherford & Emelia Seubert (New York:
Museum of the American Indian, 1988): 7.
[168] "DPR 2005–2006 – National Film Board of Canada: Section II – Analysis of Program
Activities by Strategic Outcome," at http://www.tbs-sct.gc.ca/dpr-rmr/0506/NFB-ONF/nfb-
onf02_e.asp

structures, since it seldom supports experimental or feature projects but only conventional documentaries and is usually responsible for providing the producer for a project.[169] Katherine Monk observes of the NFB that it

> ghettoizes the Aboriginal experience within a government institution [...] and limits not only the exposure of the art to a wider audience, but [...] the content of the work to fact-based, documentary exposés of real-life scenarios.[170]

Likewise, in the USA the Native American Public Telecommunications, Inc. (NAPT) supports the production, promotion, and distribution of Native (educational) media and provides training opportunities for American Indians and Alaska Natives.[171] It allocates funds for Indigenous projects to both Indigenous and non-Indigenous media makers. There have been concerns on the part of Indigenous media producers that NAPT also funds projects by non-Indigenous media producers as long as Indigenous media producers play key roles in the production process. As such a policy promotes tokenism, Indigenous media producers believe that such funding for Indigenous projects should be allocated to them alone, after which they could decide for themselves whether to engage non-Indigenous participation in a given project.[172] It is only in the past few years that there seems to have been some recognition of Indigenous filmmaking potential and a gradual shift toward entrusting Indigenous image-making to Indigenous hands.

But Indigenous and non-Indigenous voices are still far from being balanced in the mainstream media, as Jennifer David observes in a report on Aboriginal language broadcasting in Canada:

> The issue of appropriation is also a common issue for Aboriginal people in the media. Well-intentioned non-Aboriginal people are often asked to comment upon or categorize Aboriginal people or situations, leaving Aboriginal people without a voice and creating a void in the media where Aboriginal people are being seen and discussed, but not consulted or asked to contribute in a significant way. Finally, Aboriginal artists – performers, writers, producers, directors – are often excluded from mainstream television altogether, and have had to find access to media through Aboriginal-specific venues such as

---

[169] Kerstin Knopf, "Aboriginal Women and Film in Canada," 15. See also Rodger Ross (1998 unpublished interview).

[170] Katherine Monk, "First Takes: Our Home and Native Land," in Monk, *Weird Sex and Snowshoes and Other Canadian Film Phenomena* (Vancouver CA: Raincoast, 2001): 49.

[171] "Native American Public Telecommunications," at http://www.nativetelecom.org /mission.html

[172] Beverly Singer, *Wiping the War Paint Off the Lens*, 40.

APTN. Much-touted programs such as *North of 60* and *The Rez*, while employing Aboriginal people and telling Aboriginal stories, were still a product of a mainstream network, subject to higher management decisions and editorial control based on audience preferences and network policies. These decisions are made without consultation with Aboriginal people; mainstream television thus provides no consistent window on Aboriginal reality.[173]

With respect to film conventions, classical documentary and Hollywood narrative cinema constitute the shaping norm in both the USA and Canada. In economic terms, Hollywood and the North American mainstream also control the cinema market and the television sector. The Indigenous-run broadcaster Aboriginal Peoples Television Network (APTN) (formerly TVNC) in Canada has only a minimal share of the public television sector. Nevertheless, this minimal share of air space and access to viewers is controlled by Indigenous people employing basic Western television conventions while at the same time catering to culture-specific concerns. Tele-Vision Northern Canada (TVNC) emerged in 1992 after determined lobbying on the part of various Indigenous organizations and with the support of government funds. As a consortium, it integrated the Inuit Broadcasting Corporation (IBC), five other local Indigenous broadcasters, the Northwest Territories and Yukon governments, the National Aboriginal Communications Society, and the CBC Northern Service.[174] It ran education, children's, communal and political discussion programs, documentaries, and short features tailored to Northern communities. TVNC aired in various Northern Indigenous languages besides English and French.[175] In 1999, TVNC became the Aboriginal Peoples Television Network (APTN), with a country-wide broadcast license. It is financially backed by the Canadian government's Northern Native Broadcast Access Program and the Northern

---

[173] Jennifer David, *Aboriginal Language Broadcasting in Canada: An overview and recommendations to the Task Force on Aboriginal Languages and Cultures* (Debwe Communications, 26 November 2004): 10, online at http://www.aptn.ca

[174] "History of the Inuit Broadcasting Corporation" at http://www.inuitbroadcasting.ca /history_e.htm

[175] Kerstin Knopf, "Geschichte filmen: Die Perspektive kanadischer indigener Filmemacher(innen)," *Zeitschrift für Kanada-Studien* 19.1/35 (1999): 181. On the development of television broadcasting in the Canadian North, see John Greyson and Lisa Steele, "The Inukshuk Project / Inuit TV: The Satellite Solution," in *Video re/View: The (Best) Source for Critical Writings on Canadian Artists' Video*, ed. Peggy Gale & Lisa Steele (Toronto: Art Metropole & Vtape, 1996): 57–63, and Lorna Roth, "Television Broadcasting North of 60," in *Images of Canadianness: Visions on Canada's Politics, Culture, Economics*, ed. Leen d'Haenens (Ottawa: U of Ottawa P, 1998): 148–66.

Distribution Program, but is financed mainly through advertising and sub-
scriber fees.[176] As the first national Indigenous television network in the
world, its programs consist of Indigenous documentaries, news shows, live
coverage of special events, feature films, children's series and cartoons,
youth shows, cooking shows, educational programs, and programs on culture, traditions, dance, and music. These programs are broadcast in English,
French, Inuktitut, Cree, Micmac, Ojibway, Mohawk, Dene, and other Aboriginal languages. The shares of program languages are sixty percent English, fifteen percent French, and twenty-five percent Aboriginal languages
with six hundred dialects.[177] Aside from being broadcast by this Indigenous
station, Indigenous media works are generally shown at Indigenous film
festivals such as the Dreamspeakers Film Festival in Edmonton, the ima-
gineNATIVE Film and Media Arts Festival in Toronto, the Winnipeg
Aboriginal Film and Video Festival, the American Indian Film Festival in
San Francisco, the Annual Taos Talking Picture Film Festival, the Native
American Film and Video Festival at the NMAI in New York, and Two
Rivers Native American Film and Video Festival in Minneapolis. Beside
presenting filmic works, these festivals are forums for discussion, network-
ing, and exchanging ideas among filmmakers.

The Aboriginal Film and Video Arts Alliance (AFVAA) and the Aboriginal Media Industry Professionals Association (AMIPA) in Canada, the
Native American Producers Alliance (NAPA), and the Native American
Public Broadcasting Consortium (NAPBC; now NAPT) in the USA are
organizations which create a network for and of Indigenous filmmakers,
support their projects, and work against the exclusion, silencing, and appropriation of Indigenous voices in the film and video industry. NAPBC was
founded in 1977 with funding from the Corporation for Public Broadcasting

---

[176] Whiteduck Resources and Consilium, *Northern Native Broadcast Access Program
(NNBAP) & Northern Distribution Program (NDP) Evaluation: Final Report*, 29 at http:
//www.aptn.ca.

[177] APTN webpage at http://www.aptn.ca; Personal conversation with Kent Brown,
Human Resources Director with APTN in September 2004. For an account of the devel-
opment of Indigenous film and televisionmaking in Canada, see Lorna Roth, "The Aboriginal
Peoples Television Network (APTN) – Going National," in Lorna Roth, *Something New in
the Air: The Story of First Peoples Television Broadcasting in Canada* (Montreal & Kingston,
Ontario: McGill–Queen's UP, 2005): 201–18 and Kerstin Knopf, "Aboriginal Women and
Film in Canada," 6–28. For an overview of the development of Indigenous film- and tele-
vision-making in the USA, including the founding of several institutions and the creation of
specific programs by various TV broadcasters, see Beverly Singer, *Wiping the War Paint Off
the Lens*, 33–44.

(CPB), the Public Broadcasting Service (PBS), and thirty other public television stations. In 1995, it was renamed Native American Public Telecommunications, Inc. (NAPT). It operates the largest library for Indigenous
video programs in the USA, provides structural support and access to
national funding sources for emergent Indigenous filmmakers, and provides
small-scale funding.[178] Film centers such as the American Indian Film Institute (AIFI), which hosts the annual American Indian Film Festival, the
Center for Media, Culture, and History at New York University, and the
Native Voices Public Television Workshop in the USA similarly support
the work of Indigenous filmmakers, partly through funding.[179] Indigenous
filmmakers also have access to funds for media production through, for example, the Canada Council, the Canadian Television Fund, APTN, and the
NFB in Canada and the CPB in the USA. However, as of 1998 less than
two percent of media funding in Canada was devoted to the work of Indigenous filmmakers.[180]

Many filmmakers start within dominant documentary companies in
order to get a foothold in the industry. Later, they either stay and become
largely autonomous filmmakers within such companies (one example being
Alanis Obomsawin, the highly respected staff director of the NFB) or they
move on in order to engage in projects under their own control, as Loretta
Todd and Gil Cardinal have done. Some filmmakers avoid mainstream
companies altogether and start their own small independent companies.
Examples include Victor Masayesva (IS Productions), Shelley Niro (Turtle
Night Productions), and Zacharias Kunuk (Igloolik Isuma Productions).
Such small Indigenous film companies can also engage in collaborations
with mainstream film companies, as was the case with Gil Cardinal's
Kanata Productions and Doug Cuthand's Blue Hill Productions for *Big
Bear*. Projects realized in co-production with non-Indigenous filmmakers
and film and distribution companies such as the *Alaska Native Heritage
Series* (1972), *The Native American Series* (1974), various NFB documentaries, the mini-series *Big Bear* (1998), and the feature films *Smoke Signals*
(1998) and *The Journals of Knud Rasmussen* (2006) have the potential to
overcome cultural hegemonies entrenched in the film industry because both

---

[178] Steven Leuthold, *Indigenous Aesthetics*, 148, 151; Beverly Singer, *Wiping the War
Paint Off the Lens*, 39. See also discussion of NAPT's funding policy earlier in this chapter.
[179] See Beverly Singer, *Wiping the War Paint Off the Lens*, 42–43.
[180] Loretta Todd, dir./writ., *Through the Lens: Changing Voices*, prod. Gretchen Jordan Basto
& Fumik Kiyooka (Canadian Broadcasting Corporation – CBC, Canada 1998; 60 min.).

sides have desired to collaborate and usually have an equal voice in the decision-making process.

Strategies of Postcolonial Filmmaking

Ella Shohat and Robert Stam have delineated several strategies for the making of decolonized films, of which a few will be presented here.[181] These strategies avoid oversimplified categorization and overlap with each other. There is, to begin with, the 'aesthetic of hunger', created by Brazilian filmmakers who turned the absence of technical and financial resources as well as the lack of marketing possibilities into a tool and hallmark of their films. This feature is not restricted to Brazil but applies also to films in other Third- and Fourth-World territories. The 'aesthetic of hunger' often appears in sparse or low-key lighting,[182] with basic camera equipment, long takes, a basic audio track avoiding lavish musical scoring, and the frequent use of a hand-held camera because a tubular track and/or dolly is not available. Often, shots can only be taken once because of the high costs of film material, or the films are shot entirely on video.[183] For these reasons, the films often radiate an air of unprofessionalism. Needless to say, most of these films do not hire star actors but non-professionals, which may result in somewhat contrived dialogue and acting.

Another strategy is the integration of traditional orality: first, as narrative formula in which characters or the plot present (traditional) oral accounts, myths, and legends or elements thereof; and, secondly, as a structuring formula in which a non-linear digressive narrative shapes the form, and the film comes to resemble an oral account. In the latter case, the film form is characterized by circular structure, repetitions, pauses, and/or a slow rhythm, all echoes or imitations of oral rhetoric.

---

[181] Shohat & Stam, *Unthinking Eurocentrism*, 256–60, 279–85, 297–302, 302–306.

[182] By contrast, commercial cinema usually employs three-point (high-key) lighting.

[183] With the development of digital video, video technology made a significant qualitative leap and can now be compared to film in terms of quality. For example, the Inuit filmmaker Zacharias Kunuk and the cinematographer Norman Cohn shot *Atanarjuat: The Fast Runner* and *The Journals of Knud Rasmussen* entirely on digital video (not least due to Arctic conditions), with no loss of artistic quality. Similarly, the Filipino filmmaker Auraeos Solito (Kanakan Balintagos) shot his feature debut *The Blossoming of Maximo Oliveros* (2005) and his second feature *Tuli* (2006) entirely on digital video. Much less expensive than film technology, digital video allows subaltern and up-and-coming filmmakers to create feature-length films that achieve artistic quality similar to that of feature films shot on film.

On another level, reflexivity and self-reflexivity subliminally control the filming as every postcolonial filmmaker communicates with an established body of filmic and printed colonialist and postcolonial texts in the form of quotations, allegories, parodying mimicry, and/or references. In this respect, every postcolonial film becomes a piece of filmic reflection and critique as well as an instance of possible decolonizing strategies. Often, in the Brechtian manner of the *Verfremdungseffekt*,[184] filmmakers accentuate the medium of film and its techniques, creating a rupture in the illusion of reality[185] within a film, and thus focussing on the filmmaking process itself.

---

[184] Brecht understands the 'Aristotelian' or 'dramatic' narrative form as one that creates a powerful illusion of reality, operating chiefly through empathy and/or identification with protagonists and events, which then obscure any broader or more critical perspective on social or other conflicts that generate the narrative; Murray Smith, "The Logic and Legacy of Brechtianism," in *Post-Theory: Reconstructing Film Studies*, ed. David Bordwell & Noël Carroll (Madison: U of Wisconsin P, 1996): 130–31. This 'illusion of reality' (see next footnote) freezes conflicts rooted in reality, which feed narratives, into fictitious space and hinders a critical approach outside of this fictitious space. According to Brecht, this illusion is achieved by a linear chain of cause and effect organized around a central character and is realized through mimetic detail in setting and costumes and an almost realistic performance style that replaced the formulaic gestures of nineteenth-century theatre (Smith, "The Logic and Legacy of Brechtianism," 131). In order to frustrate empathy and character identification, Brecht introduced the 'alienation effect' or 'estrangement effect' into the epic theatre in the 1930s, employing it chiefly in political theatre. The goal of this *Verfremdungseffekt* is to facilitate a more 'estranged' and 'distantiated' response and to destroy illusionistic reality ("The Logic and Legacy of Brechtianism," 130) by using various stylistic means: disruption of the temporal and spatial flow of the action; the interplay of dialogue, music, and singing; not an identifying but a demonstrating way of acting; renunciation of interior design and all means of creating atmosphere (lighting); visible stage technique etc. The de-illusionist theatre places emphasis on showing processes and facts, and focusses on the medium in order to expose historical and political contradictions, dialectical laws of reality, and the standpoint of social realism; Günther Schweickle & Irmgard Schweickle, *Metzler Literatur Lexikon* (Stuttgart: J.B. Metzler, 1990): 486. The stylistic means employed are meant to make audience and actors keep a critical distance from the play and check their identification with the characters and action; J.A. Cuddon, *A Dictionary of Literary Terms and Literary Theory* (1976, Oxford: Basil Blackwell, 3rd ed. 1991): 21. See also James Monaco, *How to Read a Film: The Art, Technology, Language, History, and Theory of Film and Media* (1977; Oxford: Oxford UP, 1981): 35–36. In the works of Indigenous filmmakers, this effect is not a political element (save in the broadest sense) but primarily a stylistic element. This alienation effect is not always a conscious choice, but can arise out of strategic differentiation from conventional filmmaking.

[185] The notion that narrative cinema and theatre produce an illusion of reality or, for the spectator, "the illusion of being present at a fleeting, accidental, 'real' event" (Brecht, quoted in Smith, "The Logic and Legacy of Brechtianism," 132) is contested by some film critics, such as Smith himself ("The Logic and Legacy of Brechtianism," passim). Smith argues that emotion and reason cannot be regarded as dichotomous or antinomous, since viewers do not mistake the events presented for an immediate reality that concerns themselves, otherwise they would inter-

This alienation effect is achieved by such tactics as non-linear narratives, collage-like structures (combination of newsreel, documentary footage,

---

vene or even flee the location where the dramatic event is presented. Different emotions are to be distinguished by distinct cognitive acts of evaluation on the part of the viewer, and "emotion is integrated with perception, attention, and cognition, not implacably opposed to any of them" ("The Logic and Legacy of Brechtianism," 132–33). Drawing on Russian Formalism, Smith holds that aesthetic representation does not involve a rejection of reference to the social, cognitive, or affective dimensions of existence and that the engagement of emotion in the realm of aesthetic representation [and perception] is defamiliarized (133–34). In the same vein, Gregory Currie rejects the idea of film's presenting an illusionistic reality, on the grounds that viewers of a film do not act as if they believed the filmic events were affecting their reality (which would mean they felt endangered by murderers, explosions, catastrophes and the like). Over and above this, viewers of a film do not necessarily identify with the position of an invisible narrator (i.e. the camera), because, according to Currie, shots are only rarely taken from a psychological point of view (Currie, "Film, Reality, and Illusion," in *Post-Theory: Reconstructing Film Studies*, ed. Bordwell & Carroll, 331–32). Currie distinguishes between cognitive and perceptual illusions, cognitive illusion being false belief and mistaking something for what it is not – e.g., fata morgana, Ponzo illusion, Müller–Lyer illusion (see James Monaco, *How to Read a Film*, 127, 162) – and perceptual illusion as a process "when experience represents the world as being a certain way, when in fact the world is not that way and the subject knows it" ("Film, Reality, and Illusion," 334). To my mind, the theses of cognitive and perceptual illusionism do not invalidate the idea that film creates the illusion that the events presented are or could be real. Currie's concept of 'perceptual realism' is helpful here. It does not "claim that cinema presents objects and events isomorphic to those that exist in an observer-independent world, but [claims] that, in crucial aspects, the experience of film watching is similar to the ordinary perceptual experience of the world": in short, "*our* experience of film watching is similar to *our* perceptual experience of the world" ("Film, Reality, and Illusion," 329; emphasis in original). Both Currie and Smith argue that viewers naturally do not feel endangered by being presented with frightening, horrific, and catastrophic events, but there is nothing said about political and historical events or events that concern human relations. I would argue that narrative film does not present events as if they were the immediate reality of the spectator (since viewers can distinguish between fictitious presentation and their own reality), but film can present events as realistic and as if they *could* happen in reality or happen *in a different time and space* from that in which viewers are situated. The degree to which viewers identify with characters or filmic events depends, of course, on the subject of the film (it seems more likely with the subject of human relations and less likely with historical, political, or science-fiction subjects that are not part of the everyday experiences of the average film-goer). It depends, furthermore, on viewers' capacity for empathy and emotion and the extent to which they are psychologically willing and able to replace their own identity and reality temporarily with those of filmic characters and events; lastly, it depends on the quality of mimesis and seamless presentation of the film itself. I also understand the concept of filmic illusionistic reality in terms of the fetish character of narrative filmic presentation, which seeks to obfuscate "the labor underlying cinema and provides us only with ideology, that is, 'the imaginary relation of men to their real conditions of existence'" (Stephen Heath, quoted in Murray Smith, "The Logic and Legacy of Brechtianism," 136–37). Seamless presentation in narrative film obscures the technology that produces this illusionistic reality, which can be dissolved by the alienation/ estrangement effect. It is in the sense of the last part of the discussion that the concept of film as presenting an illusion of reality is employed throughout this book.

and/or photographs with fictitious footage), extreme and mobile framing, unconventional camera angles, inconsistent camera-work and characters looking into the camera, an uneven editing pace, the connection of diegetic and non-diegetic sounds, unfaithful sound, incorporation of traditional orality and magical occurrences, ostentatious acting, the film continuing after its closing credits, and the burlesquing of mainstream filmic texts. This self-reflexivity in films creates a metanarrative or, rather, a metafilm which describes ways of resistance to accepted film practices.

Last but not least, there are acts of carnivalesque subversion in films. These may appear as literal thematizations of carnival and masquerade.[186] But more commonly, postcolonial filmmakers develop a carnivalesque film style, by grossly violating established filmmaking conventions. They may purposely employ jump cuts, a digressive narrative or digressive narrative threads without closure, a re-shooting of the same scene, a jamming camera, and/or have the film running out in the middle of a shot. At this point, carnivalesque subversion ties in with self-reflexive cinema, both being strategies of performing resistance to classical film conventions. Carnivalesque film style, further, betrays its roots in Caribbean and Latin-American carnival, where the enslaved and oppressed, disguised in costumes, ridiculed and parodied their masters and oppressors. Before it was engulfed by commercialism, carnival served as a platform for protest against inequities and oppression in colonialist societies. Although commercialism has entered the scene of carnival, its inherent subversiveness can be charged with new meanings and harnessed to the creation of other forms of cultural expression. Shohat and Stam explain carnivalesque film as follows:

> carnival embraces an anticlassical esthetic that rejects formal harmony and unity in favor of the asymmetrical, the heterogenous, the oxymoronic, the miscegenated. [...] In the carnival esthetic, everything is pregnant with its opposite, within an alternative logic of permanent contradiction and non-exclusive opposites that transgresses the monologic true-or-false thinking typical of a certain kind of positivist rationalism.[187]

In short: carnivalesque film advocates an aesthetic of digression and flaws, or what Western film conventions understand as flaws.

---

[186] On carnival, see, for example, Helen Gilbert & Joanne Tompkins, *Post-Colonial Drama: Theory, Practice, Politics* (London & New York: Routledge, 1996): 78–87.

[187] Ella Shohat & Robert Stam, *Unthinking Eurocentrism*, 302.

In the CBC program *Through the Lens: Changing Voices* by Loretta Todd (1998), filmmakers belonging to different marginalized groups in Canada talk about their individual decolonizing strategies. These include, among others: applying diversity through characters, settings, cultural traits, forms, and styles (Yasmin Jiwani), creating films that are different from mainstream films in terms of techniques and narrative structures and creating new film forms (Paul Wong says that he bastardizes documentary and other pure film forms). In the same vein, Marjorie Beaucage says that she needs to invent a documentary film form that is not fast and where the sound is very important, because Indigenous cultures are oral cultures. Karin Lee introduces mythical characters and David Odhiambo explains that he needs to come back to the body and work against the stereotype of black male sexuality.

Postcolonial filmmakers for the most part face four major dilemmas. First, in order to raise their voices and explore decolonizing strategies, Indigenous writers and filmmakers must to a certain degree assimilate to colonialist modes of literary and filmic practice. They have to make use of colonialist means of production such as film technology, including cameras, film material / video tape / digital film or disks, editing boards / computers, television sets and projection screens, as well as colonialist marketing systems: namely, publishing houses, literary magazines, distribution and broadcasting companies, the internet etc. Thus, they remain entangled in a state of dependency on hegemonic colonialist institutions and in a capitalist mode of production. Very often, filmmakers approximate Western conventions of filmmaking which facilitates recognition by the mainstream. Only those whose works are acceptable by mainstream standards are being acknowledged and promoted. However, approximation to Western forms of expression is often sought by the filmmakers and should not be viewed as a blemish on this Indigenous film discourse.[188] After all, Indigenous people in North America live in Western capitalist societies and experience and live with these values, 'norms', and ways of representation.

Secondly, through the imposed self / other dichotomy, Indigenous writers and filmmakers enjoy a certain freedom concerning Indigenous settings and stories. However, 'freedom' is misleading, an authenticity trap, because

---

[188] For example, Thomas King has been widely criticized by Indigenous voices for assimilating his writing style to contemporary Western (postmodernist) style. Alexie and Eyre (*Smoke Signals*) and Cardinal and Cuthand (*Big Bear*), too, have been criticized for using mainstream film conventions that hamper the creation of non-Western, Indigenous media.

Indigenous content is regarded as the core characteristic of Indigenous textual and filmic works. Indigenous content makes these works *different* and *other* and contributes to a 'new cultural diversity' appropriated into mainstream literature and film discourse. As demonstrated earlier, this view is essentializing and confining, and serves only to nurture hegemonic structures. Aside from the content, Indigenous writers and filmmakers have to go by eurocentric conventions: i.e. for mainstream broadcast/screening, a film has to be made according to mainstream standards of style, structure, narrative, and length. The films will be judged in accordance with a eurocentric critical framework, and they must usually be either in English/French or provide subtitles. Thus, in order to realize their projects, Indigenous filmmakers have to move knowingly into a state of dependency on the colonial center. Even if there were/are Indigenous publishers, literary magazines, broadcasters, production and distribution companies and an Indigenous framework for criticism, Indigenous practice would still be dependent on the mainstream market and Western notions of marketability.[189] As long as cultural and economic hegemonies rule, Indigenous writers and filmmakers will not be able to free themselves fully from imperial control.

Thirdly, there is what Faye Ginsberg calls the Faustian dilemma regarding cultural groups which have been largely unexposed to Western influences. Here, people from secluded communities avail themselves of Western film technologies for self-assertion and self-expression; at the same time, they are introducing into their communities technologies which might promote disintegrative alienation from traditional knowledge and values.[190] Scholars like James Weiner and James Faris argue that Western (film and) video technology are tools of cultural indoctrination and that through their use non-Western cultures adopt Western ontology intrinsic to these Western media. By contrast, Ginsberg and Terence Turner hold that the use of Western technologies does not necessarily mean assimilation to

---

[189] For example, as A P T N orients its program structure toward mainstream television in terms of temporal guidelines (starting on the hour or half-hour, inserting the same amount of advertising blocks with a similar rhythm), the films and programs aired here have to comply with mainstream conventions. Similarly, because this channel derives a major share of its revenues from advertisement, the environment for such ads, the programs, cannot be uninteresting and offensive in terms of content to both Indigenous and non-Indigenous viewers; nor, in terms of form and style, can they deviate greatly from accepted television program standards.

[190] Faye Ginsberg, "Indigenous Media: Faustian Contract or Global Village?" *Cultural Anthropology* 6.1 (1991): 96.

Western conventions and philosophies, that (self-)representation is equally an Indigenous and a Western practice, and that video is a tool for cultural preservation and communication as well as for the rejuvenation of deracinated cultural traditions. Indigenous video makers, so Ginsberg, produce their own work and can use this Western medium in order to critique the culturally destructive effects of Western mass media.[191] What cannot be ignored in this debate and what inheres in Ginsberg and Turner's arguments is the phenomenon of continuous cultural change and development from within cultures and because of external (Western colonialist) influences, including the adoption of Western technologies according to Indigenous philosophies.

And finally, there is the issue of which language is to be employed, a matter that will be discussed in the next chapter.

Postcolonial Language Use

The Sapir–Whorf Hypothesis holds that there is a close connection between language and culture and that "'the structure of a human being's language influences the manner in which he understands reality and behaves with respect to it'."[192] Fanon links the use of the colonial language to assimilation:

> To speak means to be in a position to use a certain syntax, to grasp the morphology of this or that language, but it means above all to assume a culture, to support the weight of a civilization.[193]

---

[191] John Palatella, "Pictures of Us: Are Native Videomakers Putting Anthropologists Out of Business?" *Lingua Franca* (July–August 1998): 50–55.

[192] Robert H. Robins, "The Current Relevance of the Sapir–Whorf Hypothesis," in *Universalism versus Relativism in Language and Thought: Proceedings of a Colloquium on the Sapir–Whorf Hypothesis*, ed. Rik Pinxten (The Hague: Mouton, 1976): 99–100. Other filmmakers, writers, and scholars also see language/communication and culture as being inseparable – for example, Marjorie Beaucage (1998, unpublished interview), Umberto Eco, *A Theory of Semiotics* (Bloomington & London: Indiana U P, 1976): 22, Yoshihiko Ikegami, "From the Sapir–Whorf Hypothesis to Cultural Semiotics: Some Considerations on the 'Language–Culture Problem'," in *Scientific and Humanistic Dimensions of Language*, ed. Kurt Jankowsky (Amsterdam & Philadelphia P A: John Benjamins, 1985): 219, and Berkeley Peabody, *The Winged Word: A Study in the Technique of Ancient Greek Oral Composition as Seen Principally through Hesiod's "Works and Days"* (Albany: State U of New York P, 1975): 168. See also my discussion of the Sapir–Whorf hypothesis in chapter 3.

[193] Frantz Fanon, *Black Skin, White Masks*, 17–18.

According to Fanon, colonialism restricts Indigenous languages, thus de-stroying cultures and creating cultural alienation. He says that speaking the colonial language implies an acceptance of colonialist consciousness and colonialist values, which creates a gap between the colonized's body and mind, and the colonized subject becomes assimilated to the colonizers' cul-ture and alienated from his/her mother culture. To put it in a nutshell: ac-cepting the colonial language creates alienated identities.[194] Ngũgĩ wa Thiong'o also insists that language is a carrier of culture. He defines the colonial language as a tool for mental subjugation and alienation:

> [using the colonizer's language] is like separating the mind from the body so that they are occupying two unrelated linguistic spheres in the same person. On a larger social scale it is like producing a society of bodiless heads and headless bodies.[195]

The mismatch between language and place that the settler cultures faced upon entering the new continent is of a different quality for Indigenous people. Many nations still live on their traditional homelands[196] but through debatable legislative acts have been forced onto small portions of land that are a mere fraction of the territories they had occupied before European contact. Also on the tide of assimilation policy, Indigenous children were put into residential/boarding schools to be 'educated' in a European way, to learn a 'proper' language – English – and to profess a 'civilized' religion – Christianity. As discussed earlier, in these schools the children were not allowed to speak their own language and were punished for doing so. To save their children from punishment and teasing, Indigenous parents often avoided speaking and teaching their native language to their children. As a result, Indigenous languages were for a long time on the brink of being wiped out. What becomes clear, then, is that Indigenous people were not, and still are not, struggling with a mismatch between an imported language and an alien landscape, as the settler cultures did, but with a mismatch be-tween a semantically inadequate imposed colonial language and a fairly restricted native land-base. While colonialist writers in North America write in their mother tongue on a different continent, Indigenous writers are compelled to write in the colonial, formerly alien, tongue on their restricted

---

[194] *Black Skin, White Masks*, 18–25.
[195] Ngũgĩ wa Thiong'o, "The Language of African Literature," 451.
[196] Except those who were forced to move to the Oklahoma territory after the Indian Re-moval Act of 1830.

traditional territory. According to Ngũgĩ, they face another mismatch, one that cuts deeper into identity and self-recognition and is a partial mismatch between a foreign colonial language and Indigenous cultural traditions resulting in cultural alienation. As the settler cultures struggled for a literary identity in a new country (in a position of power), Indigenous cultures struggled, and continue to struggle, with a colonial language for a literary identity in their own colonized country (in the position of the marginalized). The same applies to filmmakers.

The language–culture thesis is plausible in the case of secluded, traditional communities where the Indigenous language is the first language and the colonizing one is only marginal, if spoken at all; or in the case of first-generation colonized peoples. However, applied undifferentiatedly to the study of works of Indigenous filmmakers in North America, whose communities are penetrated by Western influences and are often based in urban areas, this thesis is essentializing. Many of the filmmakers grow up speaking only English,[197] and many are not able to understand or speak their traditional language; nor do they want to. As all cultures are in flux, today's Indigenous cultures are amalgamations of Indigenous and Western habits, religions, traditions, techniques, media, and languages. Before contact, Indigenous people in North America had numerous different languages and dialects of roughly twelve language stocks, and colonial English became the intertribal lingua franca. In regard to Africa, Chinua Achebe draws similar conclusions:

> There are not many countries in Africa today where you could abolish the language of the erstwhile colonial powers and still retain the facility for mutual communication. Therefore those African writers who have chosen to write in English or French are not unpatriotic smart alecks with an eye on the main chance – outside their own countries. They are by-products of the same process that made the new nation-states of Africa.[198]

In this sense, it is essentializing to proscribe the usage of English and to restrict the production of cultural expression – in print and film / video – to the traditional Indigenous languages. The development of Indigenous forms of expression incorporating English[199] must find approval in the postcolo-

---

[197] As this book deals with Indigenous films in the English-speaking part of North America, references to colonial languages are only made to English and not to French.
[198] Chinua Achebe, "The African Writer and the English Language" (1975): 57, in *Colonial Discourse and Post-Colonial Theory*, ed. Williams & Chrisman, 430.
[199] According to Ashcroft, Griffiths and Tiffin, *The Empire Writes Back*, this 'English'

nial context, even though it is a colonial language. Such linguistic usage must not be devalued as culturally alienated. It is in this spirit that Salman Rushdie advises postcolonial writers not to use English the way the English did but that "it needs remaking for our own purposes. [...] To conquer English may be to complete the process of making ourselves free."[200] Kobena Mercer attributes subversive power to the creolization of master and subaltern language-codes, as such creoles "decenter, destabilise and carnivalise the linguistic domination of 'English'."[201] Gerald Vizenor also sees the colonial language as a carrier for textual resistance:

> The English language has been the linear tongue of colonial discoveries, racial cruelties, invented names [...] at the same time, this mother tongue of paracolonialism has been a language of invincible imagination and liberation for many people of the postindian world. [... It] has carried some of the best stories of endurance, the shadows of tribal survivance, and now that same language of dominance bears the creative literature of distinguished postindian authors in the cities.[202]

As Rushdie and Mercer suggest, many subaltern writers use different strategies such as code-switching, glossing, inserting untranslated words, interlanguage or syntactic fusion[203] in order to resolve the mismatch between colonial language and native place. Ashcroft et al. assign to such language variants a potential to create difference, separation, and absence from the norm of the colonizing language as well as the potential to construct a contrastive counter-discourse. Such difference from the colonial language in monoglossic texts is achieved through changes in lexis, orthography, grammar, and syntax.[204] This difference or "overlap of language" occurs when texture, sound, rhythm, and words from the mother tongue are introduced

---

would not be capitalized and become 'english'.

[200] Salman Rushdie, "Imaginary Homelands" (1982), in Rushdie, *Imaginary Homelands: Essays and Criticism, 1981–1991* (New York: Granta, 1992): 17.

[201] Kobena Mercer, "Diaspora Culture and the Dialogic Imagination: The Aesthetics of Black Independent Film in Britain," in *Blackframes: Critical Perspectives on Black Independent Cinema,* ed. Mbye B. Cham & Claire Andrade-Watkins (Cambridge MA: MIT Press, 1988): 57, quoted in Stuart Hall, "Cultural Identity and Cinematic Representation," *Framework: A Film Journal* 36 (1989): 80.

[202] Gerald Vizenor, *Manifest Manners: Postindian Warriors of Survivance* (Hanover & London: UP of New England, 1994): 105–106.

[203] Ashcroft, Griffiths & Tiffin, *The Empire Writes Back,* 59–77.

[204] *The Empire Writes Back,* 57.

into the colonial tongue.[205] At the same time as cultures mingle linguistically, this introduction of cultural expression into a colonial language creates a gap and confirms the distance between cultures:

> The articulation of two quite opposed possibilities of speaking and therefore of political and cultural identification outlines a cultural space between them which is left unfilled, and which indeed locates the core of the cross-cultural text."[206]

But there remains the risk of devaluing vernacular forms as colloquial, idiomatic, or simply wrong English in the face of 'correct' Standard English. Such devaluation not only creates difference but also sustains the colonialist hierarchy between languages or different forms of English. Derek Bickerton suggests seeing language "as a dynamic process evolving through space and time":

> It follows that to speak of "dialects" or even perhaps "languages" may be misleading; these terms merely seek to freeze at an arbitrary moment, and to coalesce into an arbitrary whole, phenomena which in nature are ongoing and heterogenous.[207]

Although dismissed as non-Standard English, heterogeneous vernacular forms become central in the postcolonial context and demand a language theory which treats them not as marginal variants of a central language but as forms equal to the latter. Bickerton calls such theory a metatheory "that takes linguistic variation as the center rather than the periphery of language study."[208] This kind of theory also creates the framework for abrogating Standard English as the language norm for Third- and Fourth-World cultures, where English is the official language. Looking at W.D. Ashcroft's statements about African writers and their fusion of colonial and mother tongue, one must conclude that the acknowledged thesis – that the semantics and syntax of the colonized language metonymically inscribed in the colonial language thus embody the culture's world-view or introduce the colonized culture into the printed or filmic text – cannot be substantiated for Indigenous films in North America. This is because Standard English

---

[205] W.D. Ashcroft, "Is That The Congo? Language as Metonomy in the Post-Colonial Text," *World Literature Written in English* 29.2 (1990): 4.

[206] Ashcroft, "Is That The Congo?" 4.

[207] Derek Bickerton, "The Nature of a Creole Continuum," *Language* 49.3 (1973): 643.

[208] Bickerton, "The Nature of a Creole Continuum," 642. See also Bill Ashcroft, Gareth Griffiths & Helen Tiffin, *The Empire Writes Back* (London & New York: Routledge, 1989): 47.

with its syntax, semantics or pronunciation modified through another language reveals nothing about the specific culture that informed this linguistic
medium and because the relationship between the untranslated non-English
word and the culture of its origin is missing. This privilege is reserved for
the complete and not fragmented use of the Indigenous language. Thus, the
gap or difference created by language variance is a metaphor of cultural
difference and not of culture. Language variance, code-switching, glossing
and similar strategies abrogate colonialist culture by disrupting the linguistic dominance of English in a text, but they do not inscribe culture in the
same text.
    Indigenous filmmakers have the choice of either employing their tradi-
tional language or the language of the colonizers. Each choice has its advantages and drawbacks. On the one hand, films made in English can reach
a far larger audience than films made in the respective Indigenous language.
If a film records or dramatizes in English, it submits the subject-matter, to a
certain extent, to the colonialist context and adapts it to mainstream needs. It
cannot transmit original contextual meanings of the translated words and the
respective cultural background that their originals contain. But this concern is
only valid so long as the traditional language is still well used. As already
indicated, there is the possibility of using vernacularized forms of the colonizers' language which have developed in the communities concerned. Such
usage secures a wider audience and prevents the film product from surren-
dering wholly to colonialist influence. Schulte holds that authors not writing
in their mother tongue consciously accept the loss of cultural meaning that
creolized and vernacular forms cannot make up for.[209]
    On the other hand, using an Indigenous language means a higher degree
of self-determination and decolonization in the process of filming and its
cinematic result.[210] Still, if a film is made in an Indigenous language, a

---

[209] Bernd Schulte, "Kulturelle Hybridität: Kulturanthropologische Anmerkungen zu einem
'Normalzustand'," in *Hybridkultur: Medien, Netze, Künste*, ed. Irmela Schneider & Christian
W. Thomsen (Cologne: Wienand, 1997): 250.
[210] Examples of feature films made in Indigenous languages are *Yawar Mallku [Blood of
the Condor]* (Bolivia, 1969), in Quechua, Aymara, and Spanish, and *Ukamau* (Bolivia, 1966),
in Quechua and Spanish, both made by Jorge Sanjines in collaboration with Indigenous
people (Shohat & Stam, *Unthinking Eurocentrism*, 33). In *The Battle of Algiers* (1966) by
Gillo Pontecorvo, the Algerian characters speak Arabic, with subtitles (*Unthinking Eurocentrism*, 252), so that they stand out against the incomprehensible babble that was assigned
to them in European feature films set in Arabic-speaking countries. Thus, they no longer exist
merely as an exotic background for a European narrative. In North America, *Bear Walker* by
Shirley Cheechoo (Canada/USA, 1999), *Kusah Hakwaan* by Sean Morris (USA, 2001), set

large part of the prospective audience (including Indigenous people from the same or another cultural group) may not be able to access the content. There is the possibility of adding translating subtitles or voice-overs, but this method is problematic. Storytellers and characters speaking in the Indigenous language create a certain aura, a certain space, time, and energy, which would be disturbed and even spoiled through voice-overs and subtitles.[211] The subtitles distract the viewers' attention from the image; a voice-over drowns out the voice of the character or storyteller and even falsifies it by creating a different aura and energy. In addition, voice-overs carry ethnographic film practice in their wake, in which Indigenous people were objectified and were usually not given a voice; instead, narrative voice-overs explained *for* them, describing their cultures from *outside*. The next problem is that the making of a fictional film in the Indigenous language requires that the actors, the filmmakers, and a substantial part of the crew be fluent or at least knowledgeable in the language. But it is not a given fact in Indigenous North America that there are enough people who are both suitable for such jobs and speak their traditional language.[212] If Indigenous actors simply study the part in the Indigenous language of the character they portray, the result might not always be very convincing, at least to speakers of the respective language. Thus, filmmakers will have to weigh the pros and cons regarding language-use with the intended audience in mind.

✄ ꙙ

---

in a modern Tlingit community, and *Atanarjuat: The Fast Runner* by Zacharias Kunuk (Canada, 2001) are the first features to employ an Indigenous language (Cree, Tlingit, Inuktitut with English subtitles).

[211] Marjorie Beaucage (1998, unpublished interview).

[212] According to the Canadian census of 2001, twenty-four percent of the Indigenous population (individuals who identified themselves as North American Indian, Métis, or Inuit) is able to conduct a conversation in a traditional language; this number fell from twenty-nine percent in 1996. But this decline in language knowledge is not characteristic for all Indigenous languages in Canada: "eight of the fourteen languages with at least 2,000 speakers in 2001 had increased since 1996, while six languages showed declines" (2001 Census: analysis series – "Aboriginal Peoples of Canada: A Demographic Profile," at http://www12.statcan.ca /english/census01/products/analytic/companion/abor/pdf/96F0030XIE2001007.pdf).

According to the US census of 2000, 14.4 percent of all American Indian and Alaska Natives five years and older speak a traditional language at home (calculation done by author on numbers given in "Characteristics of American Indians and Alaska Natives by Tribe and Language: 2000," at http://www.census.gov/prod/cen2000/phc-5-pt1.pdf).

3 Oral Tradition as Reflected in Film

Connections Between Oral Tradition and Film

THROUGH COLONIZATION and the ensuing influence of the dominant Western culture, Indigenous oral tradition has been seriously enfeebled and replaced to a certain degree by writing and print. The European colonizer, in its attempt to 'civilize' and 'educate' the people who were indigenous to the North American continent, severely interfered with and even destroyed the traditional function of the family and of Indigenous society as a whole. Because the children were put in residential/boarding schools, the Indigenous cultures were cut off from their future generations – almost a death sentence. Apart from alienating the young people from their cultures, languages, and families, it also alienated them from the way in which a family functions. They lost their parenting skills, and they could not be taught how to pass on knowledge in traditional ways.[1] Thus, the function of oral tradition as a transmitter of culture, values, and beliefs was seriously undermined, along with its moral and didactic function. The introduction of writing and print through European contact also weakened the role of storytellers and the oral storage and transmission of cultural knowledge. Walter J. Ong explains:

> By storing knowledge outside the mind, writing, and, even more, print downgrade the figures of the wise old man and the wise old woman, repeaters of the past, in favor of younger discoverers of something new.[2]

---

[1] Marjorie Beaucage (1998, unpublished interview).

[2] For further discussion of residential/boarding schools, see the section on "Postcolonial Conditions in North America," ch. 2 above.

Nevertheless, the tradition of oral storytelling continues. More and more people are becoming aware of the wealth of oral culture and efforts are being made by Indigenous communities to revive this tradition. However, Western colonization has radically altered the circumstances and needs of Indigenous communities: many Indigenous people are not able to speak or understand their traditional languages; many live in urban areas where their modes of life have adapted to a Western pace and rhythm and where access to elders and storytellers is diminished; and especially the younger genera- tions have been absorbed into a Western way of life. The latter contrasts strongly with the traditional one – they attend Western public (and private) schools, or Indigenous schools which to a large extent have Western-dominated curricula and learning environments. The young people are greatly influenced by dominant North American media and engage in Western leisure activities. All this severely impairs the continuity of Indige- nous oral traditions and has to be kept in mind when exploring modes of Indigenous cultural survival in a modern context.

My original working hypothesis was that there is a link between oral tradition and film/video, since the latter medium works with means similar to those of the oral tradition. In both communicative traditions, information is transported through visual and sonic effects. The television/VCR/DVD player/computer and screen/projector are interconnective transmitters of information by visual and audio means. This indirect producer/audience contact would be similar to the direct contact between storyteller and audi- ence in the oral tradition. I assumed thus that film and video would be a much more appropriate medium for preserving oral tradition than the medi- um of print. Ong would seem to support this hypothesis:

> This new orality [electronic media] has striking resemblance to the old in its participatory mystique, its fostering of a communal sense, its concentration on the present moment, and even its use of formulas.[3]

Marshall McLuhan suggests:

> Because of its action in extending our central nervous system, electric tech- nology seems to favor the inclusive and participational spoken word over the specialist written word.[4]

---

[3] Ong, *Orality and Literacy*, 136.
[4] Marshall McLuhan, *Understanding Media: The Extensions of Man* (New York & Scar- borough, Ontario: Mentor, 1964): 85.

McLuhan also states that electronic societies tend to be more like oral societies than literate ones.[5] Thus, I presumed that film and video technologies could be used to continue the tradition of oral transmission of knowledge in a modified way, adapted to the changing needs of Indigenous communities under Western influence. Indigenous people welcomed the era of electronic media at least as much as their non-Indigenous contemporaries did,[6] and growing access to electronic media facilitates and furthers the creation of technologized means of communication alongside traditional ones.

However, while doing research and talking to filmmakers, I realized that my approach was one-sided and centered in my own European way of thinking. If there is a relation between oral tradition and film and video, it is much more complex and multi-layered. It is important to look at oral tradition in its historical and cultural context and to consider its function as a philosophy, and to be aware of the restrictions imposed by cultural taboos and other constraints. One needs to note which stories are being told, what they are about, why and how they are being told, and who is entitled to tell stories. Thus, the first object of analysis should be the nature of oral tradition in its relation to Indigenous and Western culture.

Oral Tradition

The tradition of orally communicating cultural and historical knowledge is not just the expression of a culture and a literature in the Western sense but a complex of a culture's traditions, histories, language, religion, philosophy, and mythology. Berkeley Peabody explains oral traditions as song traditions:

> [these] seem to be sung independently of ideas as we understand them, and independently of individual consciousness as we know it. Such song traditions seem to endure through time without memorization, as we practice it, and without the aid of writing or other material recording devices. The continuing process of such oral composition we call an *oral tradition*.[7]

---

[5] Eric Michaels, "Constraints on Knowledge in an Economy of Oral Information," *Current Anthropology* 26.4 (1985): 505.

[6] There are, of course, reservations about, and even resistance to, electronic means of communication in both cultures.

[7] Berkeley Peabody, *The Winged Word: A Study in the Technique of Ancient Greek Oral Composition as Seen Principally through Hesiod's "Works and Days"* (Albany: State U of New York P, 1975): 1; emphasis in original. Peabody chiefly examines Hesiod's *Works and Days* and Homer's *Iliad* and *Odyssey*, exploring oral tradition as consisting only of sung tradition and supporting his arguments with reference to the oral composition of bards in primal

However, in most primal cultures, it is not only sung and/or poetic texts that belong to the oral tradition, as Peabody assumes, but also spoken prose texts. In the Indigenous cultures of North America, the oral tradition is tightly interwoven with the everyday life of the people in the form of songs, chants, ceremonies, dances, speeches, stories, and legends. It includes all literary genres in the Western sense, from lyric and ritual poetry in songs, chants, and ceremonies, through prose legends, tales, and speeches, to the dramatizing or performing of a story by one or several persons:

> the oral tradition encompasses all kinds of formats and genres, ranging from large public dramatizations to private and personal tales, and encompassing a ceremonial as well as a popular mode.[8]

Andrew Wiget distinguishes between oral narratives (creation myths, trickster and other tales), oratory (speeches and ceremonial oratory), and oral poetry (lyric and ritual poetry) as genres of the Indigenous oral tradition.[9] Oral narratives can stem from the creation mythology of the particular culture; they can be legends about cultural heroes (e.g., Hero Twins) and spiritual beings (e.g., Lakota Woman, Spider Woman, Changing Woman); they can be animal stories, stories about the little beings that exist in the same environment as humans;[10] and they can be community and family stories about important events and funny incidents. Some stories are sacred and can only be told at certain times of the year, most often in winter. Many stories are told in a very humorous way and are sometimes performed, and thus possess great entertainment potential.

In an oral culture, the spoken word has much more power, magic, and complexity than it has in a literate culture:

> The fact that oral peoples commonly and in all likelihood universally consider words to have magical potency is clearly tied in, at least unconsciously, with their sense of the word as necessarily spoken, sound, and hence power-driven.[11]

---

societies around the world. Still, I believe that one can also apply his findings to the spoken tradition of the (contemporary) oral continuum, and I shall accordingly be employing some of his conclusions.

[8] Hartmut Lutz, "Native Literatures in Canada Today: An Introduction," *Zeitschrift der Gesellschaft für Kanada-Studien* 10.1/17 (1990): 30.

[9] Andrew Wiget, *Native American Literature* (Boston MA: Twayne, 1985): 1–43.

[10] Debra Piapot has explained that, in her Cree culture, there is a body of stories about the Little People (unpublished interview, 1996).

[11] Walter J. Ong, *Orality and Literacy*, 32.

Although the spoken word has lost much of this power and magic in our
literate industrial culture, it is still the basis for the written mode, since
thoughts are bound to the spoken word in the first place:

> in all the wonderful worlds that writing opens, the spoken word still resides
> and lives. Written texts all have to be related somehow, directly or in-
> directly, to the world of sound, the natural habitat of language, to yield their
> meanings. [...] Oral expression can exist and has mostly existed without any
> writing at all, writing never without orality.[12]

In Indigenous cultures, the spoken word embodies collective philosophy,
passing on cultural knowledge, histories, and traditions. Some Indigenous
cultures even attribute magical and mystic power to the spoken word;[13]
"language is not only a reflection of outer-lingual reality, but it has a power
to create and change reality itself."[14]

In order to retain and to retrieve cultural knowledge, thinking and communicating contains mnemonic patterns as a basic structure to which
knowledge is attached.

> Your thought must come into being in heavily rhythmic, balanced patterns,
> in repetitions or antitheses, in alliterations and assonances, in epithetic and
> other formulaic expression, in standard thematic settings [...] in proverbs
> which are constantly heard by everyone so that they come to mind readily
> and which themselves are patterned for retention and ready recall.[15]

Ong suggests on the basis of other scholars' findings (Parry, Lord) that the
Homeric poems *Iliad* and *Odyssey*, as creations of an oral culture, could
only be composed and recited because of such mnemonic patterns, especially standardized formulae, themes, and phrases.[16] He draws on Peabody
when he says that: "the true 'thought' or content of ancient Greek oral epic
dwells in the remembered traditional formulaic and stanzaic patterns rather
than in the conscious intentions of the singer to organize or 'plot' narrative
in a certain remembered way."[17] It is appropriate to assume that other oral

---

[12] Ong, *Orality and Literacy*, 8.

[13] Anna Lee Walters, *Talking Indian: Reflections on Survival and Writing* (Ithaca N Y :
Firebrand, 1992): 11–12.

[14] Hartmut Lutz, "The Circle as Philosophical and Structural Concept in Native American
Fiction Today," in *Native American Literatures*, ed. Laura Cotelli (Pisa: Servicio Editoriale
Universitario, 1989): 89.

[15] Ong, *Orality and Literacy*, 34.

[16] *Orality and Literacy*, 22–23.

[17] *Orality and Literacy*, 145.

cultures, even if they do not employ stanzaic patterns, depend on formulae, themes, and phrases in order to retain oral information.

Catherine Littlejohn enumerates some of the mnemonic patterns found in Indigenous cultures:

> things connected with certain places, or buildings, geographical or geo-
> logical formations, objects handed down from generation to generation such
> as pieces of clothing, medicine bundles, songs, parfleche designs, etc.[18]

According to the filmmaker Loretta Todd, these patterns can be the character of space, light, and sound at the moment in which the storytelling
takes place.[19] Constant repetition of lines and phrases, a preconditioned set
of expressions, recurrent characters (e.g., Coyote, Iktome, Raven, Old Man,
Spider Woman, Buffalo Woman), alliterations, redundancy, and structured
loudness, pitch, and timbre in the storyteller's voice are mnemonic patterns
as well. Redundant elements and continuous repetition are likely to appear
tiresome and annoying to a Western mind and are very often omitted when
written down and printed.[20] "Since redundancy characterizes oral thought
and speech, it is in a profound sense more natural to thought and speech
than is sparse linearity," writes Ong,[21] also suggesting that instead of being

---

[18] Catherine Isabel Littlejohn, "The Indian Oral Tradition: A Model forTeachers" (MA thesis, University of Saskatchewan, College of Education, 1975): 31.

[19] Unpublished interview, 1998.

[20] An excellent example of how oral texts can be translated into print is Harry Robinson's *Write It On Your Heart*. The editor, Wendy Wickwire, writes in the introduction that she "searched for a representational style to capture the nuance of the oral tradition – the emphasis on certain phrases, intentional repetition, and dramatic rhythms and pauses"; Robinson, *Write It On Your Heart: The Epic World of an Okanagan Storyteller*, ed. Wickwire (Vancouver, British Columbia: Talonbooks / Theytus, 1989): 16). Wickwire adheres closely to the oral text as it was told, setting the stories in lines reflecting Robinson's speech rhythm, and she does not edit out repetitive phrases. She puts in paragraphs, line breaks, indentations of different lengths, and retains the dialogue character of certain passages. She also retains the numerous repetitions of single words, such as 'and', 'they', 'he', and 'that', which she generally posi-tions at the beginning of a line. At first glance, the text looks like poetry. On the translation of oral tradition into print and from traditional languages into English, see Dennis Tedlock, "On the Translation of Style in Oral Narrative," in *Smoothing the Ground: Essays on Native American Oral Literature*, ed. Brian Swann (Berkeley: U of California P, 1983): 57–77; Jeffrey F. Huntsman, "Traditional Native American Literature: The Translation Dilemma," in *Smoothing the Ground*, ed. Swann, 87–97; *On the Translation of Native American Lite-ratures*, ed. Brian Swann (Washington DC & London: Smithsonian Institution Press, 1992); and *Coming to Light: Contemporary Translations of the Native Literature of North America*, ed. Brian Swann (New York: Vintage, 1994).

[21] Walter J. Ong, *Orality and Literacy*, 40.

linearly structured, oral texts (be it tales, speech, ritual or lyric poetry) revolve around narrated events and have a circular structure. Berkeley Peabody, too, observes that oral memory and a linear narrative structure are not
compatible.[22] According to him, the redundant and repetitive character of
oral texts is grounded in a particular context:

> the environmental conditioning and prompting of utterances in an oral tradi-
> tion consists of the very messages that the singer is going to retransmit. The
> songs a singer hears, from which he learns his specialized language, already
> exist formulated in the very code that he will use when he himself sings.[23]

It appears that an oral presentation by a storyteller is but the public remembering of the things s/he knows. Memory does not work in strictly linear
and chronological patterns. Thus, oral texts do not have a stringently organized narrative in temporal sequence.[24] The narrative may make roundabouts
and short cuts; it may trail off from the central story line and may contain
various loose ends. Since categories in a Western sense are alien to people
in oral cultures, they "use stories of human action to store, organize, and
communicate much of what they know."[25] Ong holds further that oral narratives are essential in an oral culture, since they can embody a large amount
of cultural knowledge in "relatively substantial, lengthy forms that are
reasonably durable."[26]

Knowledge of an oral culture must be spoken and repeated again and
again lest it get lost. Thus, oral tradition depends on continuous repetition.

> Written words are a residue. Oral tradition has no such residue or deposit.
> When an often-told oral story is not actually being told, all that exists of it is
> the potential in certain human beings to tell it. [...] Sustained thought in an
> oral culture is tied to communication.[27]

The stories and historical accounts that are being told over and over again
change under pressure of historical and contemporary events. Past and present are absorbed into the stories, and new events are continually being incorporated. Oral historical knowledge is thus constantly updated by the

---

[22] Berkeley Peabody, quoted in Ong, *Orality and Literacy*, 145.
[23] Peabody, *The Winged Word*, 172.
[24] Walter J. Ong, *Orality and Literacy*, 147.
[25] Ong, *Orality and Literacy*, 140.
[26] *Orality and Literacy*, 141.
[27] *Orality and Literacy*, 11, 34.

storytellers. The content of stories and the way of telling them might also vary according to the specific situations:

> Stories change, and the teller, the audience, the occasion, the time all combine to create a new version. There is not just one way to tell a story. Each person creates their own story as they listen.[28]

Similarly, Peabody holds that,

> despite stylized behavioral patterns, every singing of a song is a unique performance. [...] The conditions of each singing are different; the experimental state of a bard [...] does not remain static through time; therefore, the accidents of thematic development and expansion do not remain constant. Such variations in input cause each singing of a song to vary. A singer is behaviorally conditioned, but he is not a closed field.[29]

Wickwire warns against an essentialist academic approach to oral stories which would seek the "purest essence" of North American oral tradition and would regard the incorporation of post-contact historical events as tarnishing a previously untouched cultural expression. The result of such an approach might be that "modern contaminants" are edited out and the vibrant oral culture that lives not least because of constant change and adaptation is frozen and turned into a cultural artefact in print.[30] Such purist assumptions are another aspect of the 'authenticity trap' and hinder cultural development. Peabody offers an explanation of how changes in the content of oral composition are manifested linguistically:

> The divergent rates of change that distinguish informational cores from the semaphoric features of language enable traditional thought to adapt semantically to perceptual conventions current in a particular society at different times. The need for recurrent composition (due to the absence of fixed texts) and the feedback of a singer's phenomenalized perception into his own singing enable traditional thought to remain continuingly meaningful for its society with an elegance denied to written records. Semantic adaptation and

---

[28] Marjorie Beaucage, "Aboriginal Voices: Entitlement Through Storytelling," in *Mirror Machine: Video and Identity*, ed. Janine Marchessault (Toronto: Y Y Z, 1995): 218. See also Lee Maracle, *Sojourner's Truth and Other Stories* (Vancouver, British Columbia: Press Gang, 1990): 133; Julie Cruikshank, "Oral Tradition and Oral History: Reviewing Some Issues," *Canadian Historical Review* 75.3 (1994): 411; and Walter J. Ong, *Orality and Literacy*, 42.

[29] Berkeley Peabody, *The Winged Word*, 176.

[30] Harry Robinson, *Write It On Your Heart*, 23.

transformation do not necessarily require change in the fundamental substance of traditional thought, only its reinterpretation or reformulation.[31]

The oral culture is carried and passed on by storytellers and elders who can be either women or men, chosen by their community and given the responsibility of retaining, sharing, and teaching cultural knowledge and history. The community looks up to them for spiritual guidance.[32]

Storytelling works according to an Indigenous copyright system which is based on trust, as Alexander Wolfe explains in the introduction to his *Earth Elder Stories*.[33] Storytellers tell their own stories, or a story must be given or traded to them. The storyteller begins by naming the original creator of the story and recounting how s/he got to tell the story, thus giving credit to the originator.[34] Usually the storyteller's account is accompanied by gestures and facial play, and often a storyteller will get up and act out parts of the story or different characters, for the human performance adds entertaining elements to it and can be essential to its understanding. Ong notes that "oral memory differs significantly from textual memory in that oral memory has a high somatic component" and that "bodily activity beyond mere vocalization is not adventitious or contrived in oral communication, but is natural and even inevitable."[35] In the course of the account, interaction between singers/storytellers and the audience is developed in the form of sight contact, gestures, and mimicry, as well as rhetorical questions on the part of the storyteller and approving interjections and murmurs, supplemental information, and interruptions on the part of the audience. "Narrative originality lodges not in making up new stories but in managing a particular interaction with this audience at this time," says Ong.[36] Thus, in each new storytelling situation not only the story itself but the nature of the interaction between storyteller and audience alters as well. Performances of stories are judged much more by the "extent and complexity of their thematic development than by the uniqueness of their particular themes."[37] This

---

[31] Berkeley Peabody, *The Winged Word*, 178.

[32] Lloyd Martell (unpublished interview, 1996).

[33] Alexander Wolfe, *Earth Elder Stories: The Pinayzitt Path* (Saskatoon, Saskatchewan: Fifth House, 1988).

[34] Marjorie Beaucage, "Aboriginal Voices: Entitlement Through Storytelling," 218–19.

[35] Walter J. Ong, *Orality and Literacy*, 6–66. Debra Piapot likewise explains that body performance is an essential element of oral storytelling (unpublished interview, 1996).

[36] Ong, *Orality and Literacy*, 41–42.

[37] Peabody, *The Winged Word*, 180.

argument supports the idea that stories are most often known to their listeners and that the act of the telling and not the content of the story is the important element from which entertainment is derived.[38] Another major feature of oral tradition is its fostering of communal contact; it unites people in groups.[39] Oral culture allows irrelevant memories to be discarded – a mechanism to protect the culture's essence. Subsequently, things remembered form the core of this culture, and equilibrium is maintained by jettisoning thoughts/knowledge that have become unnecessary.[40]

For a long time, Indigenous oral tradition was not considered a substantial body of cultural expression comparable to national literatures, because it was neither written down nor published and did not meet the norms for literature in the Western sense. Texts from the oral tradition were not taken seriously by literary scholars, were regarded as 'quaint' and 'exotic', and were considered merely as appropriate for children and as material for ethnological research.[41] This disregard for and neglect of Indigenous oral tradition by scholars persisted until the 1960s, when George Clutesi published *Son of Raven, Son of Deer: Fables of the Tse-Shaht People*, a collection of tales from the Nootka oral tradition in British Columbia. Other Indigenous authors, such as Edward Ahenakew, Joseph Bruchac, Maria Campbell, Alfonso Ortiz, and Alexander Wolfe, followed with publications of legends and tales from their own cultures or compilations of stories from several Indigenous cultures. Not surprisingly, only when the appearance of oral tradition was assimilated to Western standards in the form of print did it start to be taken seriously by literary scholarship. But in this transition it lost its fundamental feature of being oral; and one would have to find another term for the printed versions of formerly oral texts than 'oral literature', which is an oxymoron. However, for want of a better term, 'oral literature' is still being used widely.

---

[38] On the interaction between storyteller and audience as well as on story performance, see also Andrew Wiget, "Telling the Tale: A Performance Analysis of a Hopi Coyote Story," in *Recovering the Word: Essays on Native American Literature*, ed. Brian Swann & Arnold Krupat (Berkeley, Los Angeles & London: U of California P, 1987): 320–25.

[39] Walter J. Ong, *Orality and Literacy*, 69.

[40] Cf. Catherine Littlejohn, "The Indian Oral Tradition: A Model forTeachers," 29; Marjorie Beaucage, "Aboriginal Voices: Entitlement Through Storytelling," 218; and Walter J. Ong, *Orality and Literacy*, 46.

[41] Hartmut Lutz, "First Nations Literature in Canada and the Voice of Survival," *London Journal of Canadian Studies* 11 (Special Issue on Aboriginal Peoples, 1995): 62.

Peabody holds that because the Homeric texts *Iliad* and *Odyssey* were found (through the application of a set of tests developed by Albert B. Lord) to stem from an oral tradition, oral tradition can be considered as the basis of the Western literary and cultural heritage.[42] This conclusion, which applies to the European oral tradition the position of a body of *Ur*-texts, undermines Western academic positions that in general marginalize oral texts as being minor when compared to printed Western ones. But this argument can only weaken such an academic position that prioritizes print over orality, not one that prioritizes Western cultural expression over non-Western cultural expression. Addressing Homeric scholarship, Albert Lord suggests thoroughly examining all elements of traditional poetry to explore their depths and hidden recesses. But his appeal also applies to criticism and assessment of the oral tradition of non-Western cultures:

> We must be willing to use the new tools for investigation of multiforms of themes and patterns, and we must be willing to learn from the experience of other oral traditional poetries. Otherwise "oral" is only an empty label and "traditional" is devoid of sense. Together they form merely a façade behind which scholarship can continue to apply the poetics of written literature.[43]

The Indigenous oral tradition is a means of cultural self-identification and social definition. Beyond being the essence of cultural knowledge, it serves didactic and healing purposes and transmits moral values and patterns of behavior. Stories, legends, and myths are believed to be partly true, and the line between truth and myth is blurred. Benjamin Lee Whorf explains thoroughly the blurred correlation between the realms of objectivity and subjectivity in Indigenous thought:

> As the objective realm displaying its characteristic attribute of extension stretches away from the observer toward that unfathomable remoteness which is both far away in space and long past in time, there comes a point where extension in detail ceases to be knowable and is lost in the vast distance, and where the subjective, creeping behind the scenes as it were, merges into the objective, so that at this inconceivable distance from the observer – from all observers – there is an all-encircling end and beginning of things where it might be said that existence, itself, swallows up the objective

---

[42] Berkeley Peabody, *The Winged Word*, 5.
[43] Albert Bates Lord, "Homer as Oral Poet," *Harvard Studies in Classical Philology* 72 (1968): 46, quoted in Peabody, *The Winged Word*, 8–9.

and the subjective. The borderland of this realm is as much subjective as objective.[44]

He makes it clear that the Hopi distinguish between certain qualities of truth and that this distinction is inherent in the Hopi language:

> It is the abysm of antiquity, the time and place told about in the myths, which is known only subjectively or mentally – the Hopi realize and even express in their grammar that the things told in myths and stories do not have the same kind of reality or validity as things of the present day, the things of practical concern.[45]

Oral tradition permeates the borderland between objective and subjective truth. This Indigenous concept of truth, however opposed to a Western one, must not be understood as negotiable and adaptable to circumstances and to the storyteller's judgement. Edward Ahenakew describes the role of story-tellers in Plains Cree culture and their adherence to reality in the transmission of historical knowledge according to his concept of truth:

> An Old Man dared not to lie, for ridicule that was keen and general would have been his lot, and his standing as a teller of authentic events would have suffered. He dared not lie, for there were always other Old Men on the re-serve or in the encampment who would contradict him readily, and who would delight in doing that. Of necessity then, his veracity had to be un-impeachable, and this, together with well-developed powers of observation, made him an authentic repository for the annals of his people, a worthy medium through whom the folklore of previous generations could be trans-mitted.[46]

Similarly, Wickwire explains that in Okanagan storytelling stories were not made up and that they describe personal experience or accounts of personal experience, no matter how long ago.[47]

The above discussion indicates that oral tradition presents truth insofar as storytellers do not lie and have never invented the stories of their people. However, this truthfulness is situated somewhere in the borderland between

---

[44] Benjamin Lee Whorf, *Language, Thought, and Reality*, ed. John B. Carroll (London: Chapman & Hall, New York: John Wiley & Sons, & Cambridge MA: Technology Press of MIT, 1956): 63.

[45] Whorf, *Language, Thought, and Reality*, 63–64.

[46] Edward Ahenakew, *Voices of the Plains Cree*, ed. Ruth M. Buck (1973; Regina, Sas-katchewan: Canadian Plains Research Center, U of Regina, 1995): 10.

[47] Harry Robinson, *Write It On Your Heart*, 16.

the 'real' and the 'legendary', so that truth in the Indigenous context is something different from truth in the Western context. It becomes problematic when the different cultures have to find common ground in their understanding of truth. It is inherent in the nature of colonial history that the culture in power, usually the colonialist Western culture, determines the guidelines for this assessment. Julie Cruikshank suggests that oral tradition as subjective truth must not be evaluated against a Western definition of truth:

> Broadly speaking, oral tradition (like history or anthropology) can be viewed as a coherent, open-ended system for constructing and transmitting knowledge. Ideas about what constitutes legitimate evidence may differ in oral tradition and scholarly investigation, and the explanations are certainly framed differently. They cannot be compared easily, nor can their accuracy or truth value necessarily be evaluated in positivistic terms. From this perspective, scholarly papers can be understood as another form of narrative structured by the language of academic discourse.[48]

Her argument is supported by Renato Rosaldo:

> oral sources are cultural documents that organise perceptions about the past, and not containers of brute facts. All facts are culturally mediated. Stories people tell about themselves should thus be conceived less as documents to be restored than as texts to be read. One must study historical consciousness because it is the medium through which oral testimonies present the shape of the past.[49]

According to Rosaldo, oral accounts rely on the context in which they are relayed; the information extracted is void of cultural meaning. Consequently, the oral account, when removed from its telling context, loses its original meaning and, in particular, its original claim of truth.

Cruikshank further relates the Western handling of Indigenous truth and of orally transmitted knowledge to the Delgamuukw court case, in which the Gitksan and Wet'suwet'en nations of British Columbia tried to apply oral accounts about the boundaries of, and trails through, their traditional territories as evidence in land-claim negotiations (their argument was dismissed, in the most racist of terms). She concludes: "The inescapable lesson seems to be that removing oral tradition from a context where it has self-evident power, and performing it in a context where it is opened to

---

[48] Julie Cruikshank, "Oral Tradition and Oral History: Reviewing Some Issues," 408.
[49] Renato Rosaldo, "Doing Oral History," *Social Analysis* 4 (1980): 97.

evaluation by the state poses enormous problems for serious understanding of its historical value."[50]

Filming Oral Tradition
What does Cruikshank's argument mean for the filming of oral story-telling? The medium of film runs the risk of removing oral tradition from its context of self-evident power and truth, in recorded as well as drama-tized versions. This is, among others, a question of the control of spectator-ship. Whereas the cultural knowledge in such a film shown to an Indige-nous audience, even from another community or nation, still remains within its context of axiomatic truth, the same film shown to a Western audience is dislodged from this context and opens up room for critique and discussion of its inherent subjective truth. Cruikshank argues:

> oral tradition cannot be treated simply as evidence to be sifted for "facts"; they are told from the perspectives of people whose views inevitably differ depending on context, social position, and level of involvement. Too often, the notion of community history presumes homogeneity of opinion and interest that does not exist now and cannot be assumed to have existed in other times and places.[51]

In exploring the nature of a relation between oral tradition and film, it is necessary to look at several aspects that distinguish the two media. Oral tradition is least accessible to the colonizer,[52] because when this cultural knowledge is transmitted in Indigenous languages they thereby serve as a secret code. Oral tradition is not congenial to Western modes of knowledge transformation (recording, print) but is a medium of the moment. As soon

---

[50] Julie Cruikshank, "Oral Tradition and Oral History: Reviewing Some Issues," 413. On oral tradition, see also Basil Johnston, *The Manitous: The Spiritual World of the Ojibway* (Toronto: Key Porter Books, 1995): xv–xxiii; Hartmut Lutz, "The Circle as Philosophical and Structural Concept in Native American Fiction Today," 88–90; Hartmut Lutz, "Native Literatures in Canada Today: An Introduction," 30–33; Hartmut Lutz, "Canadian Native Literature and the Sixties: A Historical and Bibliographical Survey," *Canadian Literature* 152–53 (Spring, Summer 1997): 175–79; Harry Robinson, *Write It On Your Heart*, 17–28; Kenneth M. Roemer, "Native American Oral Narratives: Context and Continuity," in *Smoothing the Ground*, ed. Swann, 39–54; and Andrew Wiget, "Native American Oral Literatures: A Critical Orientation," in *Dictionary of Native American Literature*, ed. Wiget (New York & London: Garland, 1994): 3–18. For the most substantial discussion, see Andrew Wiget, *Native American Literature*, 1–43.

[51] Julie Cruikshank, "Oral Tradition and Oral History: Reviewing Some Issues," 414.

[52] Jörg Becker explained this in a lecture about publication in the Third World (University of Osnabrück, 1979).

as words are spoken, they are gone, and, with them, the information they contain, which cannot be retrieved later (except in the same mode with a new telling). Only when oral information is transformed into the Western media of print and video/film can it be retrieved again and again without the authority of the sender. Walter J. Ong argues that present-day high-tech culture generates a new orality, the existence of which is based on telephone, radio, television, and other electronic devices which exist and function only through the development of writing and print.[53] Such a "secondary orality," as he calls it, stands in contrast to the orality of pre-contact cultures that did not develop writing and print, which he refers to as "primary orality." Through this terminology he implies a hierarchy between oral tradition and film and video with regard to the sonic mode of communication.[54] As much as the medium of film and video seems to be akin to oral culture, it is even more dependent on the medium of print, so that it is closer to the latter. John Cipolla explains:

> Insofar as type of content is concerned, both television and graphics [graphic literacy] have similar space and time binding properties. [...] Graphic literacy, as an aspect of individual socialization, tends toward producing a different logic as regards these concepts [space and time binding functions in primary literacies]. The literacy of television, in this respect, would seem to carry the logic of graphic literacy.[55]

And Ong maintains that secondary orality "is essentially a more deliberate and self-conscious orality, based permanently on the use of writing and print, which are essential for the manufacture and operation of the equipment and for its use as well."[56] Finally, one must not forget that print and film technologies are a product of the industrial development of Europe. The commonality between print and film also resides in the fact that both

---

[53] Walter J. Ong, *Orality and Literacy*, 11. Ong's argument is supported by Marshall McLuhan, who also maintains that film is fully dependent on print culture: "Even the film industry regards all of its greatest achievements as derived from novels. [...] Film, both in its reel form and in its scenario or script form, is completely involved with book culture"; McLuhan, *Understanding Media: The Extensions of Man* (New York & Scarborough, Ontario: Mentor, 1964): 250).

[54] Cf. also Eric Michaels, "Constraints on Knowledge in an Economy of Oral Information," *Current Anthropology* 26.4 (1985): 505.

[55] John Cipolla, "Mass Media as Language: The Sapir–Whorf Hypothesis and Electronic Media," in *Universalism versus Relativism in Language and Thought: Proceedings of a Colloquium on the Sapir–Whorf Hypothesis*, ed. Rik Pinxten (The Hague: Mouton, 1976): 308.

[56] Walter J. Ong, *Orality and Literacy*, 136.

are colonialist means of expression, in contrast to the oral tradition as expression rooted in the colonized cultures.

The translation of oral tradition into print and film removes it from the
specific context in which it was conveyed. Renato Rosaldo argues that
"oral traditions can't be stored with the idea that their meanings can be determined retrospectively; their meanings emerge from how they are used in
practice."[57] This poses a problem for the adaptation of oral tradition to film,
since films are most often viewed in another context, usually another time
and space, than when and where they were made. Film and video can mirror the image of a storyteller surrounded by people; it can capture gestures,
motions, and facial play. It can visualize the enactment of stories or
legends. A film can reflect the narration of the storyteller, along with repetitions, redundancies, and pauses; it can transmit the sound of the voice, its
loudness, timbre, and pitch, as well as subtle and drastic changes in vocal
tonality and their effects upon the audience. As well, it can transmit background noises. (These, admittedly, are also the primary stock-in-trade of
that long-established Western media genre, the radio play.) Film can, to a
certain extent, show interaction between the storyteller and audience, but
the film itself cannot interact with the audience. Film is not able to capture
the atmosphere of a storytelling situation, the influence of surroundings,
and the effect that the interplay between storyteller and atmosphere has on
the audience. Although it transmits image and sound, it cannot directly convey smell, temperature, or felt motion (despite the occasional, and often
comical, experiments on the part of Hollywood and Imax to realize these –
extraneous – pseudo-subjective 'sensurround' dimensions). Held captive on
a tape or digital storage medium, the storyteller is in another place at another time from that experienced by the audience. Surroundings and atmosphere that might influence his/her telling cannot be experienced by the
spectator. Thus, the separation of the oral information from the context in
which it is relayed endangers the rendering of the specific meaning of the
account. Also, in regard to the concerns touched on above, film and video
fail the oral tradition. Once stories, historical accounts, and performances
are recorded on film or video, they are locked into the medium and cannot
change over time as they would in a traditional context. Since every word
has a specific meaning in a specific cultural and situational context, these

---

[57] Renato Rosaldo, "Doing Oral History," *Social Analysis* 4 (September 1980): 91, paraphrased by Julie Cruikshank, "Oral Tradition and Oral History: Reviewing Some Issues,"
Canadian Historical Review 75.3 (1994): 409.

specific meanings are also lost in the electronic/mechanical rendering of the same word.

Walter Benjamin put a powerful, minutely reasoned, and now universally familiar case for a major shift in the culture of modernity: that every piece of art loses its particular aura when reproduced mechanically.[58] He suggested that the act of reproducing art not only objectifies works of art and changes their effect and quality but that this act itself becomes an art process.[59] Applying the unique value of a piece of art to its foundation in ritual,[60] in which it receives its original and initial practical value, he does not regard this alienation from original value as a drawback but acknowledges that the 'emancipation' of the art work from ritual allows multiple opportunities for its exhibition and that it can thus democratically foster access to it among the broader public. The reproduction of the original is removed from tradition; and it can move toward its recipients, changing and adapting to them.[61] Benjamin's argument, when applied (as he himself does) to the translation of oral tradition into filmic media, suggests that if oral storytelling is filmed, it definitely suffers a loss of its specific aura and the discrete character of time and space in which the event occurred. Through the process of filming, the storytelling becomes an object, its effect and quality are changed, and it is alienated from its original source. Still, the adaptation of oral tradition to the medium of film and video at the same time fosters easier dissemination of it. More people, be it members of the same or other Indigenous groups or members of non-Indigenous groups, will have access to it. Despite the loss of original cultural and situational context, oral cultural knowledge can be preserved and stored for future generations; translated into film, it can be used to teach about a particular culture as well as to bridge gaps of communication between different cultures.

---

[58] Walter Benjamin, *Das Kunstwerk im Zeitalter seiner beliebigen Reproduzierbarkeit* (*Zeitschrift für Sozialforschung* 5.1, 1936; Frankfurt am Main: Suhrkamp, 1963): 13; tr. by Harry Zohn as "The Work of Art in the Age of Mechanical Reproduction," in Benjamin, *Illuminations*, ed. & intro. Hannah Arendt (tr. 1968; New York: Schocken, 2007): 221.

[59] Benjamin terms this 'process reproduction" (*Das Kunstwerk im Zeitalter seiner beliebigen Reproduzierbarkeit*, 11, 20; tr. Zohn, 219–20, 225).

[60] Here, Benjamin seems to be referring to 'ritual' both in a spiritual sense and as an act of creation.

[61] Benjamin, *Das Kunstwerk im Zeitalter seiner beliebigen Reproduzierbarkeit*, 12–13, 16, 20; tr. Zohn, 220–21, 223–24, 225.

Eric Michaels suggests that the direct connection between speech and speaker during oral storytelling allows a choice of who constitutes the audience,[62] hence control over the information:

> Aboriginal orality depends upon exploiting and controlling, by segmenting each step of the communication process: sender/message/receiver. This control is realised in social and economic terms as differences of value associated with the right to speak, the right to know, and the right to hear.[63]

Accordingly, one major problem in the translation of oral tradition into film and video is posed by constraints on the filming of sacred items, dances, designs, ceremonies etc as well as limitations on which oral information can be relayed. Michaels illustrates this issue with four cases concerning filming in Australian Aborigine communities, where councils had to decide whether or not certain dances could be filmed, footage of certain items could remain in a film or had to be edited out, etc. In the same connection, he outlines the problem that the filming of elders poses for the community. In Aborigine communities, as in some other Indigenous communities around the globe, the name of a dead person must not be uttered; there is a replacement word that can be used instead if the person was named after an object or if other persons go by the same name. As soon as filmed persons die, the images of these persons have to be edited out of the film or the film has to be locked away for a certain time.[64] This constraint might result in major difficulties in handling such films. It is customary with Aborigine films now to screen a warning for Aborigines and Torres Strait Islanders that the film about to be shown might contain images of deceased persons.

If Indigenous people control every aspect of the filmmaking: i.e. if they themselves shoot the footage and if they supervise distribution and screenings, then these taboos can be respected and cultural impositions met. However, if such productions get out of the hands of Indigenous people, adherence to such restrictions is endangered and taboos may well be violated, for control is lost over who gets to see the films/videos, hence who gains access to this cultural knowledge. For example, Victor Masayesva explains in an interview that for his film *Itam Hakim, Hopiit* he had to stage the part of the storytelling where Macaya the storyteller was relaying the Hopi creation myth. He says in an interview (2001) that there were con-

---

[62] Eric Michaels, "Constraints on Knowledge in an Economy of Oral Information," 505.

[63] Michaels, "Constraints on Knowledge in an Economy of Oral Information," 507.

[64] "Constraints on Knowledge in an Economy of Oral Information," 505–507.

cerns that the Hopi children, who made up the audience, might hear this myth. In the filmic space of *Itam Hakim, Hopiit*, the oral tradition undergoes alienation because recording takes the oral account out of the context in which it was relayed. It also undergoes manipulation, since Masayesva stages or 'fakes' this part of the telling: i.e. the children were not in the room when Macaya was filmed telling this myth, but were edited in as audience later. By contrast, in the cultural space Masayesva does not alienate the oral tradition from its context by controlling the audience: i.e. observing a cultural taboo and not allowing the children to hear this myth. Nevertheless, Masayesva was in a position to control who the audience was during the filming but obviously had no say in who the audience should be during screening after the film went to the commissioner of ZDF in Germany.[65]

Michaels also mentions another aspect which has to be considered while transmitting oral knowledge through film and video:

> It is precisely the ability to restrict access to information that gives Aboriginal Australian orality its economic focus. Oral information can be exchanged only so many times before it loses its value.[66]

Thus, in the case of oral cultural knowledge, filmed material must remain under the control of the makers or subjects of the film in order to retain its value. This control is endangered by continuous rendering of filmed material outside the realm of the Indigenous community. As discussed earlier, in North American Indigenous communities, many stories are sacred and can only be told at a certain time of the year. Time and space must be right for the telling. This means that some films containing oral testimonies can only be shown to a certain audience and at a certain time as well. Only when an Indigenous community retains control over the product can such constraints be granted due consideration.

The separation of oral testimonies from their sources through recording means a gradual loss of control over who composes the audience once distribution processes set in. The degree of control might be fairly high in some cases and low in others. A community might decide to commission a filmmaker to record an elder or elders talking about the community's cultural history and the film/video remains within the community. This would mean maximum control over the product and the cultural knowledge stored. However, in most cases, such films/videos are distributed through

---

[65] ZDF (Zweites Deutsches Fernsehen) is a public national broadcaster in Germany.
[66] Eric Michaels, "Constraints on Knowledge in an Economy of Oral Information," 509.

channels that lie outside of the communities' control. They might be
screened at film festivals, might be acquired by public and university libraries, or might be shown on public educational and national TV channels
such as SCN, CBC, and APTN.[67] In these cases, the control over spectatorship is quite minimal and responsibility for what sort of oral knowledge
is recorded lies with the elders and filmmakers.

As for making Indigenous films in general, the issue of language is
crucial to the translation of oral tradition into film, and is related to the
issue of removing the oral account from its original context. If a film records oral testimonies in the traditional language without provision of subtitles or voice-overs, a large part of the prospective audience (including
individuals from the same cultural group who do not speak the language)
would not comprehend the immediate content of the testimony. But recording in the traditional language means resisting colonialist influence and
remaining true to the original meaning of the spoken words.[68] Peabody suggests that a separation between traditional thought and its linguistic vehicle
is uncharacteristic of oral tradition, because the cultural knowledge and
context, which he calls traditional wisdom, *is* the composition or its source,
not its content.[69] The words remain in their spoken contexts in order to
render their original meaning: "it is true that a text in any language is more
or less dependent on the context of its use for the satisfactory fulfillment of
its communicative function."[70] A language contains a particular world-
view, as findings by various scholars suggest. Whorf writes:

> language first of all is a classification and arrangement of the stream of
> sensory experience which results in a certain world-order, a certain segment

---

[67] SCN (Saskatchewan Communications Network), CBC (Canadian Broadcasting Corporation), APTN (Aboriginal Peoples Television Network). APTN is the first Indigenous
TV channel with a country-wide broadcast license. Showing a program with elders narrating
oral history on this channel secures commercial control but not control over access to this oral
knowledge.

[68] Lloyd Martell outlines in an interview (1996) that while recording oral storytelling one
elder insisted that he relay oral accounts in Cree so that the younger people who watch the
video receive these messages in their traditional language, even though they might not be able
to understand them right away.

[69] Berkeley Peabody, *The Winged Word*, 168.

[70] Yoshihiko Ikegami, "From the Sapir–Whorf Hypothesis to Cultural Semiotics: Some
Considerations on the 'Language–Culture Problem'," in *Scientific and Humanistic Dimensions of Language*, ed. Kurt Jankowsky (Amsterdam & Philadelphia PA: John Benjamins,
1985): 220.

of the world that is easily expressible by the type of symbolic means that language employs.[71]

Apart from disconnecting the oral testimony from its narrational context by translating it into an electronic language frozen on celluloid, tape, or DVD, the original language employed can transmit at least part of the aura, space, and time of the narrational situation. A film in the original language can even induce members of the respective community to learn their traditional language, thus bringing them closer to their culture and, at the same time, giving them access to a more integral message. Translated into another language, the specific sense of the words spoken cannot be rendered accurately, or will even be missed. Still, translations via subtitles or voice-overs tend to be useful in providing the gist of what is being said. As indicated in "Postcolonial Language Use" (chapter 2 above), subtitles tend to disturb and distract from the images, and voice-overs even alienate the storyteller's voice and the aura s/he creates. But in most cases either choice might be a good alternative to limiting the audience to speakers of the respective traditional language.

The situation is a little different with dramatizing oral tradition on film. Here again, the filmmaker has the choice of either having the characters speak in the traditional language, with or without subtitles and voice-overs, or having them speak English. Dramatizing the event in the traditional language means staying partly true to the original meaning of the spoken words and character of a storytelling situation. Since oral accounts, through the act of dramatizing, are separated from their original contexts, it depends on the filmmaker to create atmosphere, space, and time that s/he feels are appropriate for the particular storytelling session. It is up to her/his judgement which language to use. As discussed earlier, using the traditional language requires that all the actors and the filmmaker(s) speak the language. Again, the images and atmosphere would either be disturbed by voice-overs or subtitles; or if the filmmakers go without such, the film dialogue would not be understood by a considerable part of the audience, including members of both their own and other Indigenous groups. On the other hand, dramatizing an oral account in English ensures a large audience but also the colonizer's access to it (depending on distribution), since the account employs a lingua franca and is captured on tape/celluloid/digital disk to be retrieved again and again. Such material loses the cultural con-

---

[71] Benjamin Lee Whorf, *Language, Thought, and Reality*, 55.

text and content otherwise contained but retains the content of the oral testimonies themselves and can provide an idea of what storytelling is like. A filmmaker might sacrifice the originality of the spoken words in favor of disseminating the oral knowledge and presumably trying to make the concept of oral tradition comprehensible to mainstream audiences as well as to Indigenous individuals who are estranged from their traditional languages and cultures. S/he might try to create a similar atmosphere with the choices remaining to her/him: the essence of the story, interaction between storyteller and her/his audience in the film, images and sonic effects such as the voice of the speaker, background noises, music, and others.

   Speaking to Their Mother (1992) is a documentary about Indigenous protest against clear-cutting and centers on the Cree artist Rebecca Belmore's protest piece, a giant megaphone made of wood. During the Wiggins Bay blockade in 1992, the megaphone sat on top of a hill overlooking the clear-cut area and elders spoke through it to the land.[72] The maker of the film, Marjorie Beaucage, does not use voice-overs or subtitles when the elders talk in Cree. To her, the sound of the elders' voices is important and also the connection between the speakers and the land, which is inherent in the words of the Cree language. In the case of her film, she felt that subtitles and voice-overs would have alienated the film from the image it created. In Victor Masayevsa's *Itam Hakim, Hopiit* (1984), an elder, Macaya, renders the oral accounts of Hopi creation and history in Hopi, and the director provides subtitles for non-Hopi speakers. In her dramatized version on Métis stories *The Road Allowance People* (1988), Maria Campbell uses English but has the characters speak a Métis dialect of English. All three filmmakers negotiate their choices, and in different ways stay true to their Indigenous language in order to transmit as much of the context in which the words were spoken and the world-view they represent.

   In the medium of film, as in print, filmmakers search for forms in which to represent the oral tradition and are concerned with retaining features of that tradition. Narrative mnemonic patterns are crucial for conveying oral information. This prompts the question of whether or not film and video can adhere to oral narrative patterns, and, if they do, how these are presented. Oral narrative patterns can be relayed on a one-to-one basis by recording elders in documentary mode, with appropriate editing and perhaps supported by an appropriate style and structure (e.g., a circular structure, re-

---

[72] V-tape – Online Catalogue at http://www.vtape.org/catalogue.htm

spectful camera angles and camera distance, or slow editing pace). A filmmaker who dramatizes oral storytelling has to make sure that a given passage in the script resembles the patterning of oral narrative, again perhaps
supported by an appropriate style and structure. Alanis Obomsawin, in an
interview (1996), points to the fact that while recording elders telling myths
and stories, the time factor is crucial. As traditional storytelling may last
several hours, a filmmaker only has a limited time frame in which to present this storytelling. The editing process then obliges the filmmaker to
condense, during which the structure of the oral account may change and
oral narrative patterns may get lost (e.g., redundancies, repetitive phrases).
By choosing what to present and how to present it, the filmmaker can steer
the content of the message relayed as well as its narrative patterning.

With respect to African cinema, Manthia Diawara argues that the process of dramatizing oral tradition results in deep structural transformations
in the narrative points of view.[73] Depending on how the film dramatizes
oral storytelling, this argument is also applicable to the North American
context. When the film features a storyteller as a character who tells stories
(e.g., *The Road Allowance People*), the film camera, cinematographer,
scriptwriter, and director (and possibly even the set designer, producer et al.
as well) as a group become the storyteller / narrative instance and acquire
authority over the cultural information transmitted. This in turn reduces the
authority that the storyteller wields in a physical storytelling event to a
mere repetitive function, where s/he repeats what the first group's authority
has crystallized as oral information to be transmitted. The reason for this
unfortunate circumstance is to be sought in the techniques of making
dramatized films. When a storyteller does not appear as storyteller character in the film but only as narrative voice,[74] then the storyteller seems to
gain authority, in contrast to the former instance, as s/he appears as authorial narrative voice. But this authority is an illusion, as the filmmaking group
has authority over the cultural information transmitted and not the interposed narrating voice, which is still controlled by the filmmaking group. In
both cases, the filmmaking group decides whether and how the stories told
are illustrated by images and/or sequences where the stories are acted out.
In a documentary film that records a physical storytelling event (e.g., *Itam
Hakim, Hopiit*), the authority over the information transmitted and the illus-

---

[73] Cited in Ella Shohat & Robert Stam, *Unthinking Eurocentrism*, 299.
[74] Panikpak in *Atanarjuat: The Fast Runner* could partly serve as an example here, but she
has a double function as narrator and character.

tration of that information are divided between the filmmaker (or filmmaking group) and the storyteller. The filmmaker decides what s/he wants the storyteller to tell and what images s/he might use for illustration; the storyteller, nevertheless, chooses what and what not to tell and how to tell it; and the filmmaker has final authority over the information through editing.

Wiget explains that a storyteller has three different roles to play during a storytelling performance. First, the storyteller has a *social role* as an individual whose social status is clearly defined through his/her ancestry and through his/her position as matriarch, elder, or storyteller, and this role in turn helps to validate him/her as a "competent and legitimate communicator of traditions." The second is the *narrative role* that s/he assumes and maintains during the performance by responding to a request for a story and by affirming her/his authoritative position through narration and metanarration – comments about the story, for example. The third is a *narrated role*, as the storyteller performs the account and assumes the identity of characters in the story. The shift between narrative role and narrated role is signalled through either quotative keys (e.g., "then he said") or paralinguistic keys (e.g., change of voice and volume).[75] These three roles do not change during the recording of an oral performance; they are the only ones reflected through the filmmaker and film technology, which then become the locus of authority over these roles. When an oral performance is dramatized, the social role of the storyteller becomes fictitious, as actors might not normally be trusted storytellers and elders in their physical and non-fictitious lives. The narrative role still exists, but is dependent on the interpretation of the filmmaking group, chiefly the scriptwriter and the director, about how it should be presented. Finally, the narrated role might vanish from the script altogether or might be retained – again, depending on the filmmaking group. Needless to say, the last two roles also become fictitious and their textual basis might not have as its model a physical storytelling event. In the case of dramatizing oral tradition, these three roles of the storyteller are to an even greater degree subject to the authority of the filmmaking group.

As oral tradition constantly involves post-contact colonial events, it is interesting to see how these influence or change oral narrative patterns. In passages dealing with colonial history and the effects of colonialism, narra-

---

[75] Andrew Wiget, "Telling the Tale: A Performance Analysis of a Hopi Coyote Story," 319–20; emphasis in original.

tive patterns might adapt to the colonialist context (e.g., become more linear, be less redundant and repetitive), which might show in the film version as well (e.g., different sound and background noise/music, alienating post-production effects, a different editing pace, different angles and camera distances).[76]

On the reception of Indigenous oral tradition, Julie Cruikshank says:

> Indigenous people who grew up immersed in oral tradition frequently suggest that their narratives are better understood by absorbing the successive personal messages revealed to listeners in repeated tellings than by trying to analyse and publicly explain their meanings.[77]

In my view, this need can be fulfilled with the medium of film and video, since films and videos that capture oral tradition are usually made in reflective, non-analytical mode and mirror it in different ways. Films and videos can be played over and over again; and with video and DVD technology one can without much effort go back and forth to review certain passages. As we have seen, Ong holds that secondary orality, like primary orality, fosters a certain group dynamic. It unites viewers and listeners, in contrast to print, which tends to separate reading individuals from one another (except at public readings, of course). He admits, though, that this technologized orality generates groups immensely larger than those of primary cultures.[78] However, electronic media, too, certainly have the inherent quality of separating individuals, for film, video, radio, email, computer technology, and interactive media also have a tendency to be utilized in isolation.

Filmmakers Talk About the Relationship Between the Media of Oral Tradition and Film

In interviews, I asked various Indigenous filmmakers to characterize the relation between oral tradition and film. Further, I asked whether or not they believe that oral tradition can be translated into film.[79] The filmmakers responded in various ways, most reacting positively and agreeing that while

---

[76] Cf. Julie Cruikshank, who looks at how oral tradition incorporates "Indigenous concepts of colonial history"; "Oral Tradition and Oral History: Reviewing Some Issues," 417.

[77] Cruikshank, "Oral Tradition and Oral History: Reviewing Some Issues," 403.

[78] Walter J. Ong, *Orality and Literacy*, 136, referring to McLuhan's "global village."

[79] In the following I present excerpts from these interviews, which were conducted by the author between 1996 and 2001.

they are not the same media, they are similar and that translation of Indigenous oral tradition into the medium of film and video is possible.

Marjorie Beaucage (Métis)

K.K.: What do you feel is the relation between oral tradition and filmmaking? I have understood that Aboriginal filmmaking draws upon the oral tradition.

M.B.: Of course.

K.K.: The main difference between oral tradition and filmmaking is that film is a technical medium in the first place, and it cuts off the interaction between storyteller and audience.

M.B.: Well, you don't cut it off because the storyteller is still present in a way that he puts the story together; it's just a different form... . I think you have to explore different ways to do that. I don't think it's impossible. It works ... we still haven't done enough to know ... how to transform the story into this form. There are not enough people who have done it. [...] But elements of it are there in films ... it's not done to the extent of perfection. With oral storytelling, we don't have the experience as filmmakers well enough to be experts, like the expertise of a master storyteller. The only way you can do it is by doing it.

Because when I'm telling a story, you got your own story going on in your head; so you try to make a film that will help people to do that and to connect with their own stories. That's what an oral storyteller does, [s/he] makes that energy work by throwing in a little humor, throwing in a little something that keeps you alive and alert. (1998)

Martha Carlson (Yurok)

M.C.: Film and oral tradition seem to be similar mediums. Indians are natural storytellers. That's something that's part of their tradition. If they're not telling stories in the oral tradition, they'd be leaving pictographs all over the place, telling them in a visual sense. Indians have a long history of being able to depict stories either visually or orally. So, there's a connection between the two traditions. (1999)

Doug Cuthand (Cree)

D.C.: I think as Indian people we are storytellers by our nature; it's a gift we have in our culture. Storytellers are revered, they are honored. So, being a good storyteller is our part of being a good filmmaker. That's what you're doing, you're telling a story; but you are doing it on many different levels. And that's what I like about it.

K.K.: So, Aboriginal filmmaking kind of feeds off the oral tradition?

D.C.: Very much so, yes. The interview I [am doing] is oral. People telling a story, people telling you something, is oral. Then you just work that into a script. And it's just a continuation of the oral tradition. (1998)

Lloyd Martell (Cree)

L.M.: Part of my traditional training that I received from my family and my people is storytelling; they taught me about storytelling and oral stories. And one problem that I have is that we have to find a way to tell these stories to our children, to our communities, to other communities and to the non-Indian people to start something going. You have the responsibility to do it; you are going to have to find whatever you feel is the best way to do that. It's been my experience that the best way to do that is through television, radio and those kinds of things. At one time, traditionally, we gathered on an annual basis and we had the opportunity to tell our children our stories. But it's not there anymore, our kids live all over the place. We are all scattered around the country and we can't come together to tell those stories in traditional ways. We need to put it onto the airwaves, where it's available for the people to hear.

I feel very strongly that in terms of storytelling and in terms of our history, our oral history – we don't have a written history – that the best way to tell it is through the large media. I think that in terms of that media probably the best one is video, television, and visual media, because in the past we had our stories. They would be told at certain times of the year, and they would be told only at night around the fire, when we were out camping and those kinds of things. Those all added to the story, and we didn't tell a story in the middle of the day, because people wouldn't learn the message unless it's told in the night by the fire. We need the sounds of the night and the smells and to see the person and the gestures and the facial expression. If you just read the story it's hard to get the intent of the story, it needs to be acted. And through the video we can add sounds, sites, visual expression, gestures ... we can't add smells. We don't have that technology [*laughs*], but as much as we can add to it in order to tell a story, those become the best vehicles.

At one time it was really unheard-of bringing cameras into our ceremonies, and it still is to some degree, you don't bring cameras into ceremonies. [...] And we've seen a movement with the elders – they've recognized what video can do. If our people are running a camera, they see that a good message can be gotten out of there, and that our children and our grandchildren can better understand it. So they have started to call on us to put a lot of their stories onto videotape.

Like I said, I believe that video is an extension of the oral tradition. Of course, the oral tradition is still alive, and we can still practice that. Whenever we get the option we should practice our oral tradition, and tell our stories, and tell our history, and go to the gatherings. But in lieu of that, the second bout is a video. It captures as much of life as we can. And I think that in the future multimedia, CD-ROM, and interactive is going to add more to it. It's a recording, but it has another layer of flexibility. (1996)

Victor Masayesva (Hopi)

V.M.: I think superficially there are connections, and you can make the case with oral and visual experience, right? And of course it takes time, and it's not as if, let's say, a time like the solar calendar, it's predictable, it always has to happen in regard to that, and this performance creates its own time. Superficially yes, certainly there are those connections, but beyond that I don't know what you're really asking. (2001)

Shelley Niro (Mohawk)

K.K.: How do you see the relation between Aboriginal filmmaking and the oral tradition, if there is any link?

S.N.: I think that there is a big relation. The only difference is the technology, but to me that's nothing new. We are born in this century, and it's part of who we are.

K.K.: So, do you feel that film is kind of a continuum of oral tradition in a modern sense, with a modern technique?

S.N.: Yes. That's what I think. (1998)

Alanis Obomsawin (Abenaki)

K.K.: Do you think that there is a link between oral tradition and film and video?

A.O.: It depends. It's much more than a link, because images and sound are very much parts of all that's happening in our life, especially sound. Elders would tell stories and the younger ones would listen for hours. That was how the teaching was done. They would organize theater-like gatherings with imaginarry performances, dances, masks, for stories to be told. Because of the culture that all people are living in now, you have to take advantages of new technologies. If you look at the children, they are always watching television. This is why film and videomaking is so important; you have to make good films that the young people have a chance to see. It is very important to get our stories and to get our message through images to the people, especially to children. It's a very powerful place to be, to give a message. (1996)

Debra Piapot (Cree)

K.K.: Would you say that Aboriginal video and filmmaking is a form of oral tradition, or is it something different?

D.P.: I don't think they're one and the same thing. I think that filmmaking feeds off of oral storytelling. [...] I don't think that oral stories are the same as the medium of film. But what is important is that we're trying to find the best way possible to translate this oral story to the medium. I think that the translation can be done depending on what your particular interest and mind from an Aboriginal perspective is, and entirely depending on what you see individually as your own vision. (1996)

Rodger Ross (Cree)

K.K.: Oral tradition has been to a certain extent replaced by written litera-ture through colonialism. Would you say that film and video could some-how continue oral tradition because this medium also works through audio and visual effects?

R.R.: Exactly; that's one of the reasons I got into it, because I wanted to put some of those on video. The elders need to be heard; not everything I do, of course, evolves around that, but at some point we do have elders on video. We like to get them involved in what we do. In a video that we shot last year, we dealt with kids, and the video was basically about pre-schools in Aboriginal communities. Urban communities are dealing specifically with First Nations, and Aboriginal people in urban centers set up their own pre-schools and teaching kids, getting them ready for school. But as part of that project there is a big cultural content; [... schools] have their own elders. They used to come in on a daily basis and spend time with the kids and teach them about sweetgrass ceremonies and how to pray and how to smudge, those types of things. Once I got them on video, it's there forever and it'll never be lost now.

That's something I'm really proud of. My whole purpose leads back to that; it's to get that type of thing on video, so that we can keep it, so that it'll always be ours and so that nobody can take it away. Video keeps a lot of that oral tradition. I'd love to do some stuff on storytelling, but there's only certain times of the year when you could do that, and that's in winter. You got to shoot specifically around winter time to get the storytellers to be able to tell the stories. That's, to me, keeping alive the oral tradition and a better access, because the stories will always live but the storytellers won't always live. I'd like to get some storytellers that are around now so that fifty, sixty years down the road somebody is telling a story and when they die, you can take the tape and say: "That's the person that taught me that story." (1996)

Because we need to keep that history, we need to keep the oral tradition alive. I'll find a different way to it through the films, and the productions that I do. But they're not the traditional ways; it's not the way things used to be done. I'd like to be able to just sit down at an old man's house for a weekend and let him talk, let him say what he needs to say, talk about the things in the past. Our people need to address the past, it's not always pretty, it's not always the romantic thing that non-Natives see. (1998)

Loretta Todd (Métis, Cree)

I guess oral tradition is just a way of the storytellers being able to [...] make you conscious of the word by making you conscious of the space you are in. They make you conscious of the sense of smell, the air you feel on your skin, they make you conscious of this earth beneath your feet, they make you conscious of who is sitting next to you; they make you very conscious of the space you happen to be in as the story is being told. They also make you very conscious of the space that the word was told in in the first place.

I realized, in a sense, that is what I want to do with film, that I would sort of conjure up that place, and make that place so sensual, so full of senses, that the memory is stimulated. Film has the capacity to do that, again, film is a two-dimensional space that has the capacity to help create essential experience. I think in that way it replicates the oral tradition. I don't think it'll ever take the place of oral tradition, but it can replicate some of the techniques that are used in the oral tradition.

I guess that's the relationship; it's not to duplicate oral tradition but to use some of its tools and its richness to help make the film a more sensual experience. I think that's sometimes what happens; you're just keeping those little things in all of us sort of alive, helping to keep them exercised. In other ways film and oral tradition have similarities – the way they use past, present, and the future. Past, present, and future are very movable. I guess those are the ways in which there are those similarities. (1998)

The answers of the filmmakers vary to the extent that they have different ways of defining the affinities between the two media. Some state that Indigenous filmmakers are natural storytellers by creating films (Carlson, Cuthand) and that making films is an electronic continuation (Carlson, Cuthand, Niro) or extension (Martell) of the oral tradition. Beaucage and Piapot say that Indigenous film draws on oral tradition and Ross finds that film/video keeps a lot of its character. Although Indigenous orality can never be truly re-created on film, as most agree, Beaucage and Todd hold that the medium of film contains elements or techniques of oral tradition, and filmmakers have to experiment with how to translate one into the other. Masayesva limits a connection to the oral and visual experience but says that oral storytelling creates its own time. Cuthand explains that oral tradition and its rendering on film should have the same temporal structure:

Doug Cuthand (Cree)

K.K.: Do you also think that film has the same patterns as oral tradition? Would people make films according to how people would tell stories? Or are these two totally different things?

D.C.: Yes, I've had some problems sometimes doing some of my stories, because I've edited them without regard to the timing. I did a documentary on a gathering of elders up in LaRonge in Northern Saskatchewan. It's a one-hour documentary. And in the business you make your cuts very short, very short clips, the story rolls along very fast, you can't lose your audience.... Anyway, with this elders' documentary, the elders have their own pace. Time doesn't really mean that much to them, they get up very early and go to bed very late; and they do a lot of things in the course of the day. And so, in putting this thing together I found I wasn't pacing myself like I normally do. I've got to have these long cuts of people talking, I'll let the camera linger on things, nature; we took a lot of shots of birds and trees and water, just around the camp. And normally, you put up a shot in five to eight seconds on the screen, but here I put shots up to twenty seconds at a time. You just slow the pace right down; and it matched the pace of life and the pace of the story. And white people find it slow. But I find it very healing to watch; it just shows a different pace of life. (1998)

Some filmmakers find it crucial to keep oral history alive – even the painful and unromantic parts. Martell and Ross believe that they are able to do this through electronic media. Martell and Obomsawin stress the fact that the electronic media that a growing number of people have access to can help to reach Indigenous people, especially children, but find it just as important to reach non-Indigenous communities (Martell). They think it necessary to get oral testimonies on tape and celluloid to preserve cultural knowledge for the younger generations (Martell, Obomsawin). Masayesva talks about how the elder, Macaya, took part in the editing process and was well aware of the possibilities of manipulation through editing:

Victor Masayesva (Hopi)

K.K.: Did you stage the storytelling situation with the kids as audience?

V.M.: Definitely the "emergence story." The "emergence story" is a series of texts, and it actually got ritual aspects – it's not a public thing. The story was actually told with the kids not there. We established the storytelling thing by cutting pictures of him together with pictures of the kids. And when he was aware that we needed to add that, he was pretending that he was talking to those kids about that story. (2001)

Poitras and Todd question the term 'oral tradition' and doubt that the concept is well understood:[80]

Evelyn Poitras (Cree, Saulteaux)

I think that we have yet to see what is going to develop, you know, a distinctive Aboriginal way of storytelling. There is so much discussion on our side of how [...] oral storytelling can transcend into ... this development where it is just natural. [...] Just because we shoot something it is not the same as traditional oral storytelling [...]. [There is] much more we would have to learn to see how that might work. But right now, personally, I don't see any example of that. It's very hard for me to say, because I don't know if that's the goal, either. But I think that there is just that kind of assumption – that just put an Indian behind the camera and that's oral storytelling. I don't think that's true. [...] I don't even like to use the word 'oral' – I mean, it's 'storytelling'. It's a habit to say 'oral'; it's just kind of weird. [...] I think in particular about one uncle, who is very gifted. And he is always saying: "You have to write my story, you have to write my life story." [...] There is no way that I can translate his character into written words. And maybe I could try to show it in video, and even in that I don't think I could capture what he is, or who he is. [...] You just have to spend time with him and he has to trust you as well; once you have that, then his storytelling is an experience that he can offer, I think. And I can't translate that; I don't think I could interpret that. (1998)

Loretta Todd (Cree, Métis)

I think it's just something that's there and I don't think that everybody really understand oral tradition. It's a word that has sort of flown out, it becomes too easy to just use it as a more or less Native feature – the 'oral tradition' – and that's where our filmmaking goes ... people haven't really thought about what that means. What is the oral tradition? It's nothing wrong with the artists who carve or make beadwork; they open themselves to the many forces that happen to make those artworks well. I think as filmmakers we experience different forces and we have to look at what oral tradition is, not to kind of break down as many elements, but to sort of look at it in terms of the skills that are required to be good at it. (1998)

Poitras is not so positive as the others about the translation of oral tradition into film. Although she leaves its possibilities open and states that

---

[80] Of course, I must ask myself at this point if I understand the concept of oral tradition. I have to admit that, having not grown up in a culture where this tradition has been kept alive, I cannot fully grasp the nature of it. In my judgement, I can only rely upon depictions of friends and filmmakers and upon scholarly essays.

filmmakers still have to learn how this would work, she feels that she cannot capture the aura of her uncle, a storyteller, on film. Although her answers differ a little bit in tone, they do not contradict the statements made by the other filmmakers, who also say that the aura and atmosphere of oral testimonies cannot truly be rendered, and that filmmakers still have to experiment to find ways of making such a transition. Marjorie Beaucage is somewhat skeptical:

> we are trying to take what happens in the oral tradition and re-create it on film – you can't. There is something that can't be re-created on film. Like the energy of the storyteller…. How does a storyteller work in oral tradition? They create a space and a time and an energy, right. How do you re-create that space, that time? It's not linear. (1998)

It would seem, then, that my initial hypothesis has turned out to be somewhat off-beam. Although there is a link between the two media, the medium of film and video is not a natural continuum of oral tradition; it cannot convey the human touch. There are different powers, dynamics, and energies working in both media.[81] Film might show interaction between storyteller and audience, as seen earlier, but the film itself can interact with the audience in very limited ways. Film is not able to capture the atmosphere of a storytelling situation. As Lloyd Martell so rightly pointed out in an interview (1996), it transmits images and sound but not smell or temperature. Frozen on celluloid or tape, the storyteller is in another place at another time than the audience. Surroundings and atmosphere that might influence his/her telling cannot be experienced by the audience. Film and video constitute a retrievable medium, durable in contrast to an oral account, which vanishes after the sound of the voices recedes. Like sound, it exists at the same time as it disappears. The medium of film and video does not replace or continue oral tradition; it might feed off oral culture as a different form that takes up some of its characteristics.

> The comprehension of culture as it relates to Native filmmaking comes from the storytelling approach that always pays homage to the past but is not suspended there.[82]

Many Indigenous people believe that legends and traditional stories should be told by a storyteller and not in a film. Others are convinced that film and

---

[81] See Walter J. Ong, *Orality and Literacy*, 101.
[82] Beverly Singer, *Wiping the War Paint Off the Lens*, 9.

video are new means of preserving oral tradition and of passing on cultural knowledge. Filmmakers are being asked by elders to record them while telling stories from cultural history in order to keep them for future generations. It is important that they tell these stories in their traditional language, because, quite apart from the concrete information, it is their cultural contexts that are being transmitted. If a story is translated, it can lose little nuances of expression, subtle differences in meaning, or even its larger meaning. It would also disrupt the correlation between the storyteller and the philosophico-cultural world s/he lives in. Nevertheless, one must bear in mind that because Indigenous North America in general experiences a loss of traditional languages as a result of colonialist history, stories and oral history are to a large extent also communicated in English; likewise the rendering of such oral communication. Electronic media as secondary orality can become a tool to preserve and pass on primary orality.[83]

Oral tradition is expanded by literature and film but continues to exist alongside these two media. Since everything is in constant flux – people, cultures, languages, traditions – the way of relaying culture, values, and traditions changes, too. One can understand Indigenous film and video as a form of cultural expression that evolved out of combining oral culture with new technologies, with artists translating stories of the past and the present into film and video. Some of the interviewees (Carlson, Cuthand, Martell, Niro) say that any documentary or dramatized film is a kind of modified storytelling.[84] Thus, film and video might be regarded as new expressive forms of oral tradition. In that sense, filmmakers are storytellers and utilize the form of film and video to create images and to tell stories.[85] Film and video are a new medium alongside oral tradition, passing on cultural knowledge, constructing a world-view, constructing identity, and providing cultural self-identification and social definition. In the way that storytelling is a tradition preserving and passing on cultural knowledge, making films is like electronic storytelling. When used to transmit oral tradition, the

---

[83] The Indigenous broadcaster APTN acts upon this notion and carries a number of programs (e.g., *Tamapta, Haa Shagoon, Our Dene Elders*, and *Nunavimiut*) that feature elders speaking in their traditional language or in English about their personal histories, cultural traditions, colonial history, residential school experience, or simply telling stories.

[84] Evelyn Poitras challenges this notion and says that a film by an Indigenous filmmaker is not automatically a way of storytelling (unpublished interview, 1998).

[85] See Alexie, quoted in Jeffrey Ressner, "They've Gotta Have It: What Spike Lee's Film Did For African Americans, *Smoke Signals* Aims to Do For Native Americans," *TIME* (29 June 1998): 2; Marjorie Beaucage, "Aboriginal Voices: Entitlement Through Storytelling," 214.

medium of film carries stories of the past and the present, be these historical accounts, cultural or political events, social issues, or dramatized stories. Film transports individual stories of filmmakers and stories of how people interact with their surroundings.[86] As Marshall McLuhan so aptly stated in 1964, "The medium is the message." This notion allows us to understand the medium of film and video less as a continuation of oral tradition than as an extension of it. The message, in this sense, is not the oral tradition, but the "change of scale or pace or pattern"[87] that film and video hold for the communication of oral cultural knowledge.

A documentary film records an oral account in a certain space and at a certain time, it renders it at another time and mostly in another space. Even if the rendition takes place at the same location, certain qualities of the environment and atmosphere that characterize the space at a given time have changed. Through its inherent technical ability to record and render at different locations, film technology removes the recorded storytelling from its 'natural': i.e. cultural, ethnic, geographical, and social context. The mechanical and electronic intermediaries tape, film, digital disk, VCR, DVD player, computer, film projector, television, and computer screen further distance the recorded product from its original context. A dramatized film stages an oral account – it does not present a physical storytelling. The authority of the storyteller over the oral knowledge is reduced in film and video, as it is shared with the filmmaker in the documentary form and ceded to the group of filmmakers in the dramatized form. Films and videos can be played again and again but they lock the oral information in a rigid state. Film and video technology can only reflect oral tradition (content, function, and mode) as much as its own limits allow.

Like orally transmitted knowledge, the information in film is transported through visual and sonic means – the viewers of a film and the audience of a storyteller see and hear the storyteller talk and perform his/her tale, and in dramatized versions the viewers additionally see and hear the performance film itself. Like the information in the oral tradition, the filmic information is organized in mnemonic patterns, reflected in content and technique. In their content, documentary film and video usually adopt the adapted and modified mnemonic patterns contained in the storyteller's talk and might keep oral patterns such as repetition and digression.

---

[86] Cf. Marjorie Beaucage, "Aboriginal Voices: Entitlement Through Storytelling," 216.
[87] McLuhan, *Understanding Media: The Extension of Man*, 24.

memory, as it guides the oral poet, often has little to do with strict linear presentation of events in temporal sequence. The poet will get caught up with the description of the hero's shield and completely lose the narrative track.[88]

A dramatic film can render these patterns in the script for the storyteller. It might also contain loose ends and may digress from the storyline. It might not be a linear and chronological presentation of the subject but, rather, have a circular structure. Filmmakers can also create electronic mnemonic patterns: e.g., repeated visual and sonic motifs, repeated camera angles or camera movement, similar composition of several images, similar transition between shots, and salient post-production effects such as posterization and fast and slow motion. Certain elements of the film or video, e.g., atmosphere, images, incidents, can also serve as basic mnemonic patterns.

As seen earlier, Renato Rosaldo warns against the assumption that oral knowledge can be stored on tape/celluloid, for the meaning of an oral text arises out of the practice of oral tradition.[89] Considering the fact that film alienates the oral account from its natural context, one must understand a recording of an oral account as a duplicate or copy of an original. Viewers must accept losses of originality, aura, and meaning associated with the cultural context. Still, films that record elders telling stories and talking about the nation's history are largely made in order to preserve the cultural and historical teachings and the traditional language for future generations. Many filmmakers see their responsibility in that objective (Martell, Obomsawin, Ross). Although there are potential losses, the purpose of such films is to function as a repository of oral cultural and historical knowledge. Oral tradition in its didactic function relays knowledge and teaches; the medium of film can be used to teach, too, only in a different way, adapted to the needs of contemporary society. Thus, Indigenous filmmakers have, like storytellers, an enormous responsibility to reflect society and to preserve and pass on cultural knowledge.[90]

When looking at films which have translated oral tradition into film, it would prove useful to consider a set of questions that arose during the exploration of the relation between the two media. One may not be able to

---

[88] Walter J. Ong, *Orality and Literacy*, 147.
[89] In Julie Cruikshank, "Oral Tradition and Oral History: Reviewing Some Issues," 409.
[90] Cf. Lloyd Martell (unpublished interviews, 1996 and 1998); Alanis Obomsawin (unpublished interview, 1996).

answer all the questions, but simply keeping them in mind may help to find out how oral tradition is reflected in or translated into these films:

1. How does the film reflect oral tradition and an oral storytelling event?
2. Is the film faithful to the particular context in which this oral knowledge is traditionally passed on?
3. Can the film qualify as a form that organizes perception according to modes of oral tradition, or is it merely a repository of cultural knowledge meant to be retrieved later?
4. Does the film record oral accounts, or does it dramatize such accounts?
5. Does the film adhere to specific oral narrative structures/patterns, and if so, how are they translated into the film?
6. How are the three roles of storytellers realized in the film?
7. In which language are the oral accounts rendered?
8. How does the film reflect the incorporation of colonial history into the oral account?
9. What information can Indigenous and non-Indigenous people take from the film?

The Road Allowance People

The 48-minute film *The Road Allowance People* (Canada, 1988) by the Métis filmmaker, writer, and activist Maria Campbell is one example of the adaptation of the Indigenous oral tradition to the medium of film. Campbell's film stages a potential storytelling event, having characters act out the parts of the storyteller and of the audience. The following analysis will consider matters of content, narrative technique, and film style. The film is based on Campbell's *Stories of the Road Allowance People*, a collection of Métis tales. She uses the stories "Joseph's Justice" and "La Beau Sha Sho," which form the two parts of the film. The film is set in a contemporary context with a storyteller traveling to a community and community members assembling in the evening to listen to his stories.

The film combines elements of the documentary and narrative film tradition.[91] At the beginning, during the transition between the two parts, and at

---

[91] It would seem logical to apply the term 'docudrama', but as it is a fixed term denoting

the end, Campbell narrates, providing introductory and later explanatory information about Métis history and oral storytelling. Her documentary-style narration is juxtaposed with the partly diegetic (in the main sequence) and partly voice-over narration (in the interposed sequences) of the story-teller, whose narration is clearly associated with the dramatized part of the film. At the beginning, the film provides a printed text that introduces viewers to the Métis' attempt to found an independent nation, with the re-sulting hostile reaction of the Canadian government. The military conflict that arose became known as the Riel or North West rebellion, ending with the Battle of Batoche in 1885.[92] The opening credits are superimposed on a tracking shot showing a man riding slowly through a snowy forest. Next comes a shot of a truck, followed by a POV shot from inside the truck onto the road and a tracking shot sideways showing the moving truck and the driver. These introductory shots are accompanied by Campbell's voice-over narration, explaining the meaning of the previously dubbed song and the tradition of storytelling. The film still appears to be a documentary until the dialogue in the ensuing shots reveals that it has changed into a drama-tized story. Since the film returns to the documentary mode with the epi-logue, documentary narration frames the dramatized film and formally suggests that the film could be understood as an educational narrative film.

Dramatizing Community Storytelling
The narrative space[93] of the film is defined as that of a Métis community in Saskatchewan, because the introductory voice-over narration acquaints the viewers with the history of the Métis, and further because one of the first

---

feature films that deal with actual historical, mostly political, events (e.g., *The Missiles of October* [1974], *Fear on Trial* [1975], *JFK* [1991]), it is inappropriate to use it in this context. Although the film dramatizes physical storytelling and stories that exist in Métis oral tradition, the storytelling here is not an historical but a fictitious event. On 'docudrama', see Frank E. Beaver, *Dictionary of Film Terms* (New York: Twayne, 1994): 116–19, and James Monaco, *How to Read a Film: The Art, Technology, Language, History, and Theory of Film and Media* (1977; Oxford: Oxford UP, 1981): 397–98.

[92] The Métis resistance and historical events leading to it are comprehensively outlined by Howard Adams, *Prison of Grass: Canada from a Native Point of View* (Saskatoon, Sas-katchewan: Fifth House, 1989): 46–97.

[93] The concepts of narrative time and narrative space are employed in the sense of the time and locale in which the narrative is situated. There is also the on-screen space that is created anew for each sequence. However, since screen time as temporal relations and screen space as spatial relations are aspects of classical continuity, they are discussed only where they deviate from the 'norm'.

shots shows a young man driving up to a gas station, where a sign of the Saskatchewan Greyhound Bus company is posted. The narrative time is also specified. The shots introducing the storyteller and also other shots throughout the film show that it is winter. While the people are talking about the stolen bell of Batoche, one woman states that it would be great if the thief could also reclaim the stolen Métis land as easily. Somebody turns this statement into a joke by answering: "no problem, we'll just get Brian and the boys drunk." This joke indicates that it is the era of Brian Mulroney's government (1984–93). Since the film was made in 1988, the narrative time is thus defined as one winter between 1984 and 1988. As is done in conventional filmmaking, Campbell clearly defines spatial relations. The first sequence, after the introduction of the storyteller, starts with establishing shots, one featuring the house from outside in a long shot, and several others inside, in the kitchen–living room, conveying spatial relations between the characters. The initial shots also convey the atmosphere in the room by showing people talking and playing cards, tea boiling and soup cooking on the stove. Later, all interposed sequences start with a long shot which functions as an establishing shot.

The storyteller Alcid (Harry Daniels) is introduced in a twofold way, at first riding a horse and seconds later driving a pickup truck. Here, the past is juxtaposed with the present. The man on the horse is photographed in exactly the same camera position as the same man in the truck. The background also remains exactly the same. Both shots are connected by a dissolve so that the storyteller on horseback seems to be transforming into the storyteller in the truck and during the dissolve the man on horseback seems to be driving the truck (Figs. 1.1–1.4). With these two shots, Campbell illustrates the transformation from traditional storytelling to modern storytelling, which has adapted according to historical changes. The social role of Alcid as a storyteller is fictitiously established, simply because he is presented as a revered storyteller through the storyline and through continual cinematic focus on him telling stories (Figs. 1.5–1.6). His fictitious narrative role is prominently featured when he is prompted to tell stories by the audience and thus assumes responsibility for an oral performance and when he is consequently shown telling stories. He constantly reaffirms his authoritative narrative role through metanarrative comments such as: "The story of Batoche is about Louis and Gabe and Joseph. And even now the story of Batoche is about the people who went to Ontario to get the bell, […] That's another story. I'll tell you that another time," and "My old grandfather told me that story and Joseph told it to him." Wiget writes: "Response to both her [the storyteller's] metanarrative questioning and to the narration reaffirms her narrative role."[94] In this sense, Alcid's narrative role is also maintained by his metanarrative questions and the responses to it, for example: Alcid: "He was on his way home from the trap line when that English General ... What's his name again?"/ Girl: "Middleton."/ Boy: "Yes his name was General Middleton."/ Alcid: "That's right. General Middleton." Alcid's fictitious narrative and social roles as storyteller are underscored through this teller/audience interaction and collaboration. Alcid assumes a narrated role when he slips into the roles of his characters and imitates their words. The shift between these narrative and narrated roles is indicated by quotative keys rather than by change of voice and volume. Nevertheless, Alcid underlines his talk and the shift between the roles with gestures and facial play. The next example shows the continual shift between these roles:

> Well, when General Middleton got his horse settled down, he climbed off, and he said to Joseph: "Batoche has fallen and your leader has surrendered. And all those men here, they are under arrest. And you, my good man, you are under arrest too." "Well," Joseph said: "if I'm a good man, why're you arresting me?" The General doesn't like that but he is a gentleman, so he doesn't lose his temper. Then he tells Joseph: "The charge is high treason.' Joseph, he doesn't know what high treason means, but it sounded pretty dangerous."

Campbell thus also re-establishes the three roles storytellers have during a physical oral performance in her electronic rendition of a potential story-telling event.

The narrative starts with the storyteller coming into town. Word of his arrival spreads and several people from the community gather in the house of the family that the storyteller is visiting. They all sit together and talk, until one boy asks Alcid to tell a certain story, upon which two boys start quarrelling about whether or not the story is about Joseph, about Riel and Dumont, or about the stolen bell of Batoche. Through this incident, Camp-bell shows that people often know the stories beforehand and that stories are retold many times. As conveyed in the film, stories function as an ar-chive from which cultural knowledge is repeatedly retrieved. This knowl-edge is constantly updated by the different storytellers, who change the

---

[94] Andrew Wiget, "Telling the Tale: A Performance Analysis of a Hopi Coyote Story," 321.

stories and incorporate events from recent history and the present. Thus, storytellers constantly reassess history in the cultural context and intertwine past and present. The incident also reveals that people enjoy listening to the same stories over and over again for entertainment because each storyteller adds a different flavor and has a different way of telling and performing.

Oral storytelling derives its entertaining and teaching character from the interaction between storyteller and audience. This interaction is quite often illustrated in the main sequence, in which Alcid asks his audience about facts of the story (e.g., he asks about the name of the General who fought the Métis in the North West rebellion). Very often people throw in little comments or fill in information that goes with the story. For example, one boy brings the photograph of a group of Métis arrested after the rebellion, and another boy adds that General Middleton was knighted in England. Teaching without didacticism and including the audience's knowledge in the form of little added details is the tradition of Indigenous storytelling[95] as exemplified in the film. At some points, members of the audience take over and puzzle together what they know about the stolen bell of Batoche, Joseph, and the fiddler Jonas. The interaction between storyteller and audience, which is not just verbal but also visual and sonic, is also formally transmitted through inserted shots of faces in the audience. Campbell thus creates imaginary lines of action between the storyteller and the respective person. She also shows that storytelling is not a tightly organized event but that it is interspersed with people making remarks off the story-line, people telling jokes, people playing music and dancing. When an Irish fiddle player knocks on the door, he is welcomed and integrated into the group. Alcid even includes an Irish element in his story by talking about an Irish lawyer who is marginally involved in the historical events, thereby suggesting the readiness of storytellers to incorporate new elements into their accounts. This incorporation of the Irish story reflects a certain solidarity between peoples who were both historically oppressed by the English colonial power and continue to be so in a different way.

When Alcid starts to tell his story about Joseph, Riel, and Dumont during the Métis resistance in Part One, entitled "Joseph's Justice," the film switches to a scene in black and white that enacts the trial of Louis Riel. The characters from the main-sequence audience are also the audience wit-

---

[95] Elizabeth Weatherford, "To End and Begin Again: The Work of Victor Masayesva," *Art Journal* (Winter 1995): 52.

nessing the trial, all dressed in the fashion of the day (Figs. 1.7–1.8). Campbell thereby blends both sequences to stress the similarity of situations in
which an audience watches a 'performance' in an abstract sense. This
merging of audiences disrupts seamless presentation, accentuates the fact
that the events are staged, and destroys the illusion of film presenting an
outer reality. Campbell cuts back to the main sequence, where Alcid continues his story, talking about Gabriel Dumont and Michelle Dumas. The
next interposed black-and-white sequence illustrates this part of the story.
Then the film returns to the main sequence where the Irish fiddle player
enters the circle and somebody plays the Red River Jig. After Alcid is
given a red jacket and a sash, which the women made for him, the first part
of the film ends.

   Part Two, "La Beau Sha Sho" starts with a long shot of a leafless tree
under a black sky illuminated by the Northern lights and complete with
drifting fog and the howling of a wolf. Campbell's documentary-style narration talks about the importance and the power of both storytellers and
fiddle players in Métis communities. She explains that fiddle players often
traded their souls for music and bewitched people, especially young women. Campbell visualizes her talk by photographing a room in which alter-
nately a fiddle player sits on a bench playing and a young woman listens
and dances to the music. All shots are in the same camera position and
camera distance, so that they actually look as if shot at the same time and
same place, and both figures seem to be in the same room (Figs. 1.9–1.11).
They appear and disappear through dissolves, as if by magic.[96] With the

---

[96] The merging of the magical and the real often occurs in the works of Indigenous authors
and filmmakers around the globe. By having the fiddle player and the woman appear and disappear, Campbell translates this coexistence of natural and supernatural elements in Indigenous
belief/reality into the medium of film. However, I would shy away from calling the technique an
expression of 'magical realism'. The art critic Franz Roh coined the term in 1925, praising post-
expressionist painting that acknowledges the "magic of being." According to him, the new mode
of painting contains a "radiation of magic, that spirituality, that lugubrious quality throbbing in
the best works of the new mode, along with their coldness and apparent sobriety" and "constitutes a magical gaze opening onto a piece of mildly transfigured 'reality'" – Roh, "Magic Realism: Post-Expressionism" (1925), tr. Wendy B. Faris in *Magical Realism: Theory, History,
Community*, ed. Lois Parkinson Zamora & Wendy B. Faris (1995; Durham NC & London:
Duke UP, 5th ed. 2005): 20. 'Magic/al realism' came to be understood as a "movement that
sought to capture the beyond-rational, inner meaning of immediate, exterior reality" – George R.
McMurray, "Magical Realism in Spanish Fiction," *Colorado State Review* 8.2 (Spring–Summer
1981): 7, quoted in Robert Franklin Gish, "La Llorona, Magic Realism, and the Frontier," in
Gish, *Beyond Bounds: Crosscultural Essays on Anglo, American Indian, and Chicano Literature*
(Albuquerque: U of New Mexico P, 1996): 111. The concept was taken up by the Venezuelan

writer Arturo Uslar Pietri ("La Llorona, Magic Realism, and the Frontier," 111) and the Cuban writer Alejo Carpentier. The term 'magical realism' describes the coexistence of magic and reality in Indigenous cultures of the Americas and attempts to grasp the complex nature of this interplay. Magic is part of reality because people believe and thus create truths on a different level from what Western logic can accommodate. Carpentier writes that the cognition of magic first of all requires belief – Carpentier, "On the Marvelous Real in America" (1949), tr. Tanya Huntington & Lois Parkinson Zamora in *Magical Realism: Theory, History, Community*, ed. Parkinson Zamora & Faris, 86. McLuhan explains why the dichotomy of magic and reality in primal cultures appeared as mere superstition to a Western mind: "Nonliterate people register very little interest in this kind of 'efficient' cause and effect [cause and effect as sequence], but are fascinated by hidden forms that produce magical results. Inner, rather than outer, causes interest the nonliterate and nonvisual cultures. And that is why the literate West sees the rest of the world as caught in the seamless web of superstition" (*Understanding Media*, 251).

Carmen Galarce states that the concept of a heterogeneous and mythic world was born in the very moment of the European discovery of the New World. She makes it clear that the conquistadors were men searching for medieval and Renaissance wonders such as Eldorado or the Fountain of Eternal Youth which were occupying the European imagination in that age. Gesa Mackenthun outlines how, in addition, accounts of the Golden Age as found in the writings of Hesiod, Ovid, and Virgil inhabited medieval thought and subsequently hindered any objective assessment of climatic and agricultural conditions that the seafarers encountered in the New World. Confusing reality with ideological construct, early colonizers failed to engage in customary agriculture but waited for the eternal bliss "finally found on earth" to materialize, resulting in disastrous famines; the French colony founded by Ribault in 1564, for example, experienced a famine two years later. Mackenthun argues that such myths preconditioned the early colonizers' perception of the New World, which then entered into their writings as corroborations of the myths of Eldorado and the Golden Age. They presented the new continent as a terrestrial paradise and land of plenty as well as a place where the laws of nature and logic seemed suspended, and where wonders, legends, myths, and reality went hand in hand. It remains an open question whether they distorted their accounts on purpose in order to legitimate their journeys, to create glorious accounts of themselves, or to delude new potential settlers, or whether their perceptions were indeed twisted, confusing New-World reality with contemporary fiction of a life without labor. Galarce concurs in suggesting that the germ of the Latin American novel could be found in the accounts and chronicles written from the enthralled and blinded imagination of the first navigators. See Gesa Mackenthun, *Metaphors of Dispossession: American Beginnings and the Translation of Empire, 1492–1637* (Norman & London: U of Oklahoma P, 1997): 36–43; Carmen Judith Galarce, *La novela chilena de exílio, 1973–1987: El caso de Isabel Allende* (Santiago de Chile: Departamento de Estudios Humanísticos, 1993): 131.

Miguel Ángel Asturias and Alejo Carpentier started to intertwine magical phenomena with reality in their fiction, as one aspect of American Indigenous cultural expression. Since then, the term 'magical realism' has appeared in literary critiques of writers of the Americas such as Gabriel García Márquez, Isabel Allende, and Ana Castillo. "The term 'magic realism' seems to have become a catch-all in the literary world to describe a 'Latin American' style of fiction in which real action is tinged with dreamlike surrealism"; Martha Frase–Blunt, "New Regard for Hispanic Authors," *ASN* 34 (September 1994): 41. However, Latin American writers who do not avail themselves of a 'real-magical' style such as Sandra Cisneros and Francisco Goldman complain that they are categorized as 'magical realists' along with García Márquez. It seems as though the concept of 'magical realism' has become an effective marketing strategy for publishers of Latin American writers since García Márquez and Carpentier paved the way. Western reception and

magical appearances and her story about such Métis fiddle players who entered Faustian contracts and who in turn enchanted young women, Campbell introduces a mythic element into her film and animates a legend that is
part of the Métis oral tradition.

The next sequence is set outside the house, where a boy and a girl play
tag. Their laughter is juxtaposed with the howling of the wolf, which
creates an eerie atmosphere. The boy startles the girl, upon which she runs
back to the house. A mysterious man in front of the door stares at her,
scaring her even more. When, back in the house, the Irish fiddle player
plays an Irish tune, the little girl gets frightened. Campbell reveals in different close-ups that the song is uncanny to her, and that she snuggles up to
her mom, seeking 'shelter'. These three situations in which the girl is terri-
fied sustain the mystic element; and especially the last incident alludes to
the myth about Métis fiddle players bewitching young women.

The fiddle players – there are three of them, including the Irishman –
have a contest about who plays the Red River Jig best. After the contest
Alcid continues his story about how the old storyteller Jonas brought the
tune "La Beau Sha Sho" to the Métis. The story is first illustrated by a
sequence showing Jonas walking his horse through a snowy forest. A quick
cut back to the main sequence features Alcid telling the part of the story in
which Jonas dies and goes to heaven. Then Campbell interprets this talk
with a sequence showing Jonas on his death-bed, followed by a sequence
set in heaven: Jesus sits in the foreground drinking wine, while Jonas
stumbles around in the back until Jesus waves him over. Both talk and
drink wine from a golden jug and golden goblets, obviously enjoying themselves (Fig. 1.12). Here, a blasphemous tone enters the film, for Jesus drinks
to his mother Mary while talking without respect about his father. He says

---

literary criticism of 'real-magical' fiction have thus redefined the meaning of the concept
'magical realism' and have appropriated it in accordance with hegemonic critical discourses. The
term now confines the interplay of reality and the magical to texts and movies, and denies an
interweaving of the two in the thought and everyday life of Indigenous cultures. For Indigenous
people, there was no binary opposition between the spiritual and the material. The concept of
'magical realism' comes into the picture "wherever a veneer of European civilization is imper-
fectly blended with hidden layers of primitive cultures" (Gish, *Beyond Bounds*, 111). Calling
something magical that is not perceived as magic in another culture constitutes a border between
two cultures. Although the term attempts to subvert the strict demarcation between the supernatural and the material world, it actually constructs a new border between these two which in
Indigenous cultures does not exist. On 'magical realism' (and its essential differentiation from
Carpentier's original specification, 'marvellous realism'), see also Irlemar Chiampi, *El realismo
maravilloso* (Caracas: Monte Ávila, 1983).

that he is glad that Jonas came along so that he has somebody to drink with, for nobody else does – they are all scared of "his old man." The blasphemous tone is maintained by Jesus expressing regret that "they" banned all the fiddles along with the devil so that there are only harps left in heaven. This statement places the Métis, whose culture incorporates the fiddle as an essential element, on the side of the devil in the Puritan dichotomy of good and evil.[97] This stereotypical concept is ridiculed and the oppositional binaries likewise blurred through the ironic twist of having Jesus (associated with good) and Jonas (associated with evil) drinking wine together and blaspheming. Furthermore, "somebody" in heaven has made a mistake, for Jonas was not supposed to die and is just visiting heaven. Jesus says that he has a tune in his head for Jonas to take back to earth, one that he cannot play on a harp because it is meant to be a fiddle tune. So he teaches it to Jonas, drumming on his golden wine jug and singing along (Fig. 1.13). That is how Jonas brought "La Beau Sha Sho" to the Métis. This part of the film illustrates how stories of the oral tradition often explain how natural and geographical things, as well as things of social significance – here the song "La Beau Sha Sho" – came into being or to the people: for example, 'that is how the bear lost its tail' or 'that is how this boulder came here'.

The ironic treatment of the appropriated Christian elements in Métis culture, first, denounces the fact that fiddle playing was banned by the Church because it was associated with superstition and, secondly, mirrors the symbiotic relation of Christian and Indigenous religions as it exists in many Indigenous communities today. With the storyteller entering heaven and drinking wine with Jesus, the realm of Indigenous religion enters the realm of Christian religion and is put on the same level with the latter. Metaphorically, Jesus' teachings in the form of the song depend on the storyteller Jonas for dissemination among the Métis/Indigenous people on earth. Thus the colonizer's religion depends on a mechanism of the colonized's tradition to disseminate their teachings among the colonized. The filmic syncretism can be understood as Campbell's strategy to illustrate Indigenous–Christian syncretism and the ambiguous relation of the Métis to Christianity. On the one hand, the Métis came into being through contact and intermarriage between Indigenous people and European Christian (mainly French and Scottish) trappers and fur traders. The Métis are a

---

[97] For a discussion of the genesis of Indian stereotypes in Western thought and its dichotomy of the good and evil Indian, see chapter 1.

hybrid people, and Christianity is thus part of their culture. Furthermore, the missionary work and the residential school system have done their work in converting many people to Christianity. On the other hand, many Métis remain at a critical distance to Christianity because it has undermined social structures in traditional societies and has alienated generations of children from their parents and subsequently from their culture. Today, religious syncretism is widespread, not only in Métis communities, and Indigenous religious elements are incorporated into church services. As Campbell says in an interview, "You have the priests doing ceremonies, they are going to sweat lodges [...]. So the priest ends up becoming the shaman in the community."[98]

After briefly cutting to the main sequence between two heaven sequences, the film moves to the main sequence one last time. In accord with the end of Alcid's story, the film ends with a high-angle shot taking in the whole room and all the people who surround the storyteller (Fig. 1.14). Then several clips of the film are repeated with superimposed closing titles. Campbell's narration in the epilogue describes such traditional gatherings for storytelling around Christmas time.

As the trickster is inseparable from Indigenous oral tradition, Campbell implicitly includes this figure as well. When the people talk about the stolen bell of Batoche, they joke around, asserting that the thief drove a red pickup truck with Saskatchewan license plates, thus hinting that Alcid is the thief. However, the thief of the bell is untraceable – he is elusive like the trickster in Indigenous mythology. At another point, Alcid describes the old storyteller Jonas: "The old man was always dying and going to heaven. But when he came back, he always had a song. Even the old people didn't know if he was telling the truth or not." The ability to change forms, to die, and to be reincarnated is also a feature of the trickster in different Indigenous oral cultures. In both cases, a storyteller is linked to the trickster, and thus mythical powers are applied to him. This helps Campbell to further root the film in the Indigenous tradition of oral storytelling.

With her film, Campbell not only teaches about oral storytelling but also conveys different aspects of Métis culture. One is, for example, the fact that several people assemble in a house to socialize and to listen to someone telling stories – the cinematic focus being on a social gathering. They also

---

[98] Hartmut Lutz, *Contemporary Challenges: Conversations with Canadian Native Authors* (Saskatoon, Saskatchewan: Fifth House, 1991): 47.

play fiddle and piano music and dance to it. A metonym of Métis music is the Red River Jig, which is played twice in the film and to which the little girl, a woman, and Alcid are jig-dancing. Jonas and Alcid wear sashes, Alcid beaded moccasins, and Jonas a beaded vest, all of which belong to traditional Métis dress. Other cultural markers are transported via the setting. The Métis flag with the Moebius strip and a star blanket decorate the walls. Through Alcid's story about Riel, Dumont, and Dumas, Campbell reassesses Canadian history, especially Métis resistance, from a Métis perspective. She politicizes oral storytelling in order to comment on colonial Canadian historiography and presents a Métis history discourse as an answering discourse. Also, the joke about reclaiming Métis land by "getting Brian and the boys drunk" is a political statement, which must not be dismissed as just a joke to relax the atmosphere. It also has to be regarded as an indictment of the European occupation of Indigenous North America. The joke is a wonderful example of Indigenous humor, which is often self-deprecating and borders on black humor, and which helps the Indigenous people to cope with painful experiences, in this case the conquest of their land. It also alludes to the fact that Indigenous people were first made dependent on European goods and alcohol while at the same time their traditional food sources were diminished or destroyed, and then chiefs and band leaders, sometimes under the influence of alcohol, were compelled into signing treaties that guaranteed the government title to great chunks of Indigenous land.

The narrative of the film does not arise out of a story in the conventional sense but is entirely motivated by the dramatization of oral tradition on film through the relaying of the two stories. The film also deviates in a number of other aspects from conventional narrative films. The characters do not have opposing goals or conflicting personalities which could generate conflict or a certain dynamic. Nor do they have appointments or deadlines requiring them to fulfill a certain task in a certain time limit, which are crucial for building a motivated and suspenseful cause–effect chain.[99] The narrative time is unlimited toward the end, so that the narrative flows smoothly. Throughout the film, the viewers are supplied with unrestricted story information: i.e. they know as much as any character in the plot. Even more so, the viewers are provided with sequences that interpret the stories being told,

---

[99] David Bordwell & Kristin Thompson, *Film Art: An Introduction* (1979; New York: McGraw–Hill, 4th ed. 1997): 90–101, 109.

which the characters in the main sequence itself can only create in their own imagination. Thus, the film employs a style of authorial narration that results in a total lack of suspense and surprise.[100] The particular film 'story' of Alcid arriving in town and telling stories does not require any suspenseful narration. Rather, the character of the narration arises out of the nature and pace of oral storytelling. There is no need to resolve plot-lines at the end of the film; the closure of the last story marks the closure of the film. Thus, it becomes obvious once more that the motivation and dynamic of the narrative line goes back to the stories being told and oral storytelling in general. Furthermore, if one does not count Alcid as a main character but as a narrator, all the figures in the film have the same importance to the plot: i.e. their participation in the plot is equally balanced. That means that there are twenty-four characters in the film (including double roles and not counting the extras), which by far exceeds the recommended seven to eight important characters in conventional filmmaking.[101] The film does not focus on a few main characters but on a whole community, which makes it communal storytelling through the medium of film and sets it off against mainstream films.

Circular Structure and Color Symbolism as Stylistic Devices
The most apparent feature that contrasts with mainstream films is the circle as the underlying structure of the film. Campbell creates a main sequence (the scene in which the people meet in one house and listen to the storyteller), from which six other sequences illustrating the storyteller's two stories depart and to which they return. Often, the illustrating sequences are cut between shots of the same person, so that they begin and end at the same point of the main part. Thus, the film has one linear and two circular narrative lines that revolve around the first. In this structure, Campbell reflects an Indigenous understanding of cyclical time that is a structural element in the oral tradition.

    Another salient stylistic means is Campbell's color symbolism. The color red recurs as a motif in various contexts. At the beginning, the storyteller on the horse has a red jacket and a red saddle blanket, then he transforms into a modern storyteller in a red truck. He now wears a red checkered shirt and is later given a red jacket and a red sash. Jonas, the old story-

---

[100] Bordwell & Thompson, *Film Art*, 102–103.
[101] Bordwell & Thompson, *Film Art*, 395.

teller, wears a red sash, too; one community member wears a red headband and a red shirt; and, last but not least, Jesus wears a red cloth around his waist. In the sequences when Jonas walks through a snowy forest and when he visits Jesus, Jonas' red sash and then Jesus' red cloth belt contrast with the subdued colors of the settings (white snow, dark leafless trees, a dark horse, a whitish surreal setting of heaven, Jonas' dark clothes, and Jesus' blue garment). The color red relates the characters of the different sequences to each other and figuratively represents the Métis, for they call themselves the Red River people. The color motif also helps to unify most of the sequences that illustrate Alcid's story and to connect them formally with the main sequence. Also, Jonas' red sash and Jesus' red cloth belt link these two characters; here, the color motif maintains the Indigenous–Christian syncretism and the blurring of the good/evil binary that the same sequence implies with the characters' meeting.

Twice in the film, individual sequences are linked with the main one through a graphic match (match cut) and through dissolves back to the same person. The graphic match occurs when the film for the first time cuts to an illustrating sequence. The last shot of the main sequence features a girl in the audience in a medium shot, and the first shot of the Riel trial sequence shows the same girl in the court-room audience in the same camera position and camera distance, both shots connected by a dissolve (Figs. 1.15–1.17). At other points, Campbell achieves the transition between the main sequence and the others through a dissolve from a certain person or the whole group of storyteller and audience to the inserted sequence, and then back through a dissolve to the same person or the whole group. Thus, she usually ends an illustrative part where it began, in this way supporting the underlying formal structure of several interposed sequences departing from and returning to a main sequence. These dissolves and the graphic match nicely relate the events of the sub-sequences to the events of the main sequence.

A Métis Vernacular

Campbell solved the language problem by having her actors speak English but with a culture-specific dialect, which she also used in her printed collection of Métis stories. Throughout the film, Alcid talks in this Métis vernacular: "Me I never saw him without that sash," and "Joseph, he never trusted them Englishmen." Two passages from the collection of Métis

stories further illustrate this vernacular and show how Campbell also im-
plements it in the printed medium:

> "You know Jonas" dah Jesus say "Your a damned good fiddle player. Me I
> always want to play dah fiddle but I never have a chance. When dah Lucifer
> he get kicked out he take all dah fiddles wit him an all we got now is harps."
> [...] Dah General he don like dat very much an he say "Dah charge hees
> high treason." Joseph him he don know what dat word treason he mean. But
> he say it sound awful dangerous so he talk real careful jus in case hees got
> someting to do wit shooting. Dem soldiers you know dey got guns an he say
> dey look like dey wan to use dem. Joseph you know him he don trus dah
> Anglais. He never trus dem in hees whole life.[102]

The Métis vernacular is the linguistic continuum in which contemporary
Métis oral tradition operates beside Mitchif. Another choice would have
been Mitchif, a creole language of Cree, Ojibway, French, and English, but
that choice would have limited the audience. By employing the Métis
vernacular interspersed with Mitchif words, Campbell constructs a linguistic medium which does not alienate the oral knowledge from its cultural
context and avoids purely colonial linguistic expression. In an interview she
explains that she tries to "put the Mother [Earth] back in the language":

> I've been working with dialect for about 10 years, and a lot of my writing
> now is in very broken English. I find that I can express myself better that
> way. I can't write in our language because who would understand it? So
> I've been using the way that I spoke when I was at home, rather than the
> way that I speak today. And the way that I spoke when I was at home was
> what linguists call today "village English" – you know, very broken Eng-
> lish. It's very beautiful but it took me a long time to realize that. Very
> lyrical, and I can express myself much better. I can also express my com-
> munity better than I can in "good" English. It's more like oral tradition, and
> I am able to work as a storyteller with that.[103]

Final Remarks

Except for the unconventional narrative, as motivated by storytelling, Campbell follows conventional filmmaking guidelines. However, as the narrative is
usually the most important component of a mainstream film, this exception
sets *The Road Allowance People* off against conventional films. The inter-

---

[102] Maria Campbell, *Stories of the Road Allowance People* (Penticton, British Columbia:
Theytus, 1995): 64, 113.
[103] Hartmut Lutz, *Contemporary Challenges*, 48–49.

play of two different film modes, the documentary and the dramatic film, is also a striking element. Furthermore, Campbell employs a cultural-specific Métis dialect of English so that she can undermine the colonial lingua franca. Thus, with the use of the Métis language and a narrative that is based on the Indigenous traditional mode of narrative, Campbell limits colonial influence on her film.

The idea of dramatizing oral storytelling in the sense of showing the act of storytelling in film is very ambitious and, to my knowledge, there is no other film yet in North America that does this.[104] Filming oral storytelling seems to be a natural continuum of the oral tradition, as several filmmakers have pointed out in the interviews. Many filmmakers (Masayesva, for instance) make documentary-style films in which they record an elder speaking about tribal history and telling stories. Campbell goes a step further and dramatizes the act of telling and the events being recounted. With her printed collection of stories and with her film, she translates oral tradition into two different media. The book and the film show that she is trying out new ways of preserving oral cultural knowledge and of carrying on the tradition of oral storytelling in other media.

The film, nevertheless, has some weak points, which can be traced to the very limited budget of the film and to the fact that Campbell explores possibilities of how to adapt a century-old tradition to a modern technical medium. She deliberately uses non-professional actors (except for Harry Daniels as Alcid): i.e. Métis community members who re-enact things that are part of their lives. The events in the film, especially the dialogue, often appear contrived, and the characters appear at times artificial and wooden; their inexperience as actors becomes noticeable. The presentation of Métis culture often slips into cliché because some metonymic items in Métis culture, such as the Moebius strip, a star blanket, and the gift of a sash, are displayed ostentatiously and placard-style. By contrast, the fiddle-playing and jig-dancing look natural and intertwined with Métis life. One notices that the actors feel at ease re-enacting the music-playing and dancing parts as opposed to acting out dialogue. They are absorbed in the fiddling and dancing, so that the camera seems to be ignored at these moments. When criticizing the film, one needs to consider the originality of the attempt, the deliberate choice of non-professional actors, the low budget, and Camp-

---

[104] *Atanarjuat: The Fast Runner* tells an oral legend but does not dramatize an oral storytelling situation as *The Road Allowance People* does.

bell's apparent approach of creating this film from within the community. Aside from being actors, community members helped to prepare the settings – an old lady, for example, designed the flowers and the background of the heaven sequence.[105] The inclusion of the community in the film as well as the film's focus on the community create communal storytelling in the medium of film. The partly circular structure roots the film more deeply in the oral tradition, in which stories end where they begin.[106] The film thus represents Campbell's understanding of storytelling and her method of carrying on oral tradition.

Itam Hakim, Hopiit

Itam Hakim, Hopiit: In Recognition of the Hopi Tricenntenial (USA, 1984) is a 58-minute documentary by the Hopi filmmaker Victor Masayesva. The film was made in 1984 by IS Productions (Masayesva's production company) and was commissioned by the German public broadcaster ZDF. It was presented at the Chicago International Film Festival the same year and won the Gold Hugo Award.[107] In contrast to the previous film, *Itam Hakim, Hopiit* [*We someone, the Hopi*] does not dramatize a storytelling situation but records one. The Hopi elder and storyteller Ross Macaya is filmed telling parts of Hopi and his clan and personal history to a group of Hopi children.[108] The following analysis is based on the detailed shot analysis provided in the Appendix, which lists the visual and sonic content, camera techniques, and shot length.[109]

---

[105] See Campbell in Loretta Todd, dir./writ., *Through the Lens: Changing Voices*, prod. Gretchen Jordan Basto & Fumik Kiyooka (CBC; Canada 1998).

[106] For the symbolism of the circle in Indigenous cultures, see Hartmut Lutz, "The Circle as Philosophical and Structural Concept in Native American Fiction Today," 85–100.

[107] Documentary Educational Resources at http://www.der.org/films/itam-hakim-hopiit .html

[108] See also the analysis of *Itam Hakim, Hopiit* by Steven Leuthold, *Indigenous Aesthetics: Native Art, Media and Identity* (Austin: U of Texas P, 1998): 116–30. In many respects our readings of this film are similar, in others they differ (e.g., the explanation of the fast-motion sequence).

[109] Sonja Bahn–Coblans, in "Reading with a Eurocentric Eye the 'Seeing with a Native Eye': Victor Masayesva's *Itam Hakim, Hopiit*," *Studies in American Indian Literatures* 8.4 (Winter 1996): 58–60, gives a film protocol of *Itam Hakim, Hopiit* at the end of her article, which roughly shows visual content, camera techniques, and the soundtrack. However, I believe that this protocol is insufficient for a detailed analysis intended to capture Masayesva's film style. Thus, my analysis table renders a shot-for-shot analysis of the film.

As in *The Road Allowance People*, the narrative of the images is subordinated to the filmic rendering of oral tradition: i.e. the storyteller's talk. All the shots in the film either show the storyteller and/or his audience, or they convey visual information interpreting the sonic information of Macaya's voice. The latter are organic shots[110] of the Hopi surroundings, shots mirroring Hopi life, and shots illustrating Spanish colonization. The film is subdivided into six parts according to the content of Macaya's narration:

1.	shots 1–11	Macaya's childhood;
2.	shots 17–19	a song about the antics of a young prairie dog;
3.	shots 20–55	the Hopi creation myth;
4.	shots 56–105	the history and chants of the Bow Clan (Macaya's clan);
5.	shots 107–137	the Spanish Conquest and the Pueblo Revolt of 1680;
6.	shots 138–180	a Hopi harvest festival with religious songs and dancing.

The second and the last part need to be regarded as narrative parts like the others, for they narrate through images. Furthermore, songs are one form of oral tradition and their lyrics narrate as well. In spite of the grouping according to content, all the parts have to be understood as belonging together, because in the oral tradition the storyteller's explanation of where the story or myth to be told came from and his/her personal introduction are inseparable from the story or myth itself. In the same vein, one cannot clearly detach the telling of the Hopi creation myth from the telling of the history of the Hopi after conquest, because all the information mingles to shape the nation's history. Indigenous thought does not distinguish between mythic events and 'real' events as Western thought does. Physical heroes may become mythic heroes, and mythic heroes are believed to have existed. Myth and reality are always intertwined.[111]

---

[110] The term 'organic' here denotes natural images that show none or hardly any human traces: i.e. images of landscapes, plants, and animals.

[111] Cf. the discussion of magical realism, fn 96 above.

Hopi Myths and Stories in Film

The storyteller Macaya is introduced by particular visual means in the initial sequences. The first shots feature, in close-up, a pair of feet in black Converse shoes walking on dry cracked earth to a water hole. Hands draw water with a bucket. Only after these introductory shots do viewers see a man walking with the bucket against the backdrop of the Arizona landscape, the Hopi homeland. The long shot that follows takes in a straight horizontal line that divides the sky from the mesa cliff. The walking man connects these two opposite spaces (Figs 2.1–2.4). Shots follow that show the watering of plants and, later, weaving and chanting inside his home. Only then is he shown telling the story. This visual introduction corresponds to the obligatory verbal introduction of the storyteller in the oral tradition. While the visuals present him fragmentarily, sound introduces him right from the beginning, when his voice is heard talking about his childhood. His narration runs through almost the whole film and is only interrupted by his chants, by the music of dances, and by baroque Spanish military music and a baroque concerto by Vivaldi. The three different storytelling roles are present in this film. It is clear that the late Macaya is known as a respected elder and storyteller to the audience of children and to Hopi viewers of the film who are from the area where he lived. Macaya helps maintain his social role by introducing himself, his clan, and, eventually, the knowledge that he shares. His narrative role is established through his continuous narration and a metanarrative comment at the end, in which he indicates his awareness of his role as narrator.[112] As in *The Road Allowance People*, the shift between his narrative and narrated roles is signalled by quotative keys and not so much by paralinguistic keys. For example, when Macaya talks about Hopi creation, he says:

> So they sent the men again and said: "Maybe this time somebody will talk." When they arrived, it was not the same man. He looked like a Hopi. He had long hair. He wore turquoise jewellery. And they asked him: "Was it you who did not talk to us the last time?" "Yes, it was me," he answered in Hopi.[113]

---

[112] Because the subtitles are not a one-to-one translation of Macaya's accounts, it is difficult to detect other metanarrative remarks.

[113] Personal translation of the German subtitles, which read: "Sie schickten also wieder die Männer los und sagten: 'Vielleicht wird dieses Mal jemand sprechen.' Als sie dort ankamen war es nicht derselbe Mann. Er sah genauso aus wie eine Hopi. Er hatte langes Haar. Er trug Schmuck aus Türkisen. Und sie fragten ihn: 'Warst du der, der das letzte Mal nicht mit uns sprach?' 'Ja, das war ich,' antwortete er auf Hopi."

Masayesva sustains Macaya's social and narrative role by showing him intermittently as he narrates, sometimes embedded in the Hopi landscape (Figs. 2.5–2.6).

Analyzing the visual imagery of the film is the most challenging task. In order to sort out the considerable number of predominantly beautiful photographic images, these were assigned to different themes, and the occurrences of each simply counted. Of the 181 shots in the film, 121 shots feature people, body fragments, and things associated with people (e.g., tools, drums). 59 shots are organic shots that show the natural surroundings of the Hopi – these are 22 shots featuring animals and 37 shots presenting views of the mesa landscape, plants, and other landscapes. There are 33 landscape shots, 19 shots of cornfields, corn plants, or corn kernels, 4 shots of lightning, and 5 shots of the moon and moonrise. 10 shots feature water and 11 rain, rain clouds, wet earth, and plants in the rain.[114] This assignment of visual themes, of course, cannot take into consideration that there are also many shots which show a person or an animal against a landscape backdrop, thus mingling the themes of people and landscapes but counting as shots with people. For a documentary film that is not centered on nature, one-third organic shots without human beings is a quite considerable proportion.

As discussed earlier, oral communication in Indigenous cultures is tied to mnemonic patterns which function as the basic structure into which the sum of oral information is integrated. In the way that geological formations and geographical sites serve as such patterns, Masayesva provides images of the very localities Macaya is talking about as visual mnemonic patterns. These form one group of shots that is directly related to the talking. When his speech revolves around the Alosaka Mountain with clouds directly growing out of it, Masayesva provides a shot of the very same mountain with clouds on top (Fig. 2.7). Buildings may also function as mnemonic patterns, and the filmmaker integrates shots of Macaya's house, of houses in Old Oraibi,[115] and of Anasazi ruins (Figs. 2.8–2.10). At other times, the visuals do not correspond directly to the landscapes contextualized in Macaya's talk; they could be seen as substitute mnemonic patterns. For example, Macaya talks about the earth trembling and of water rising and flooding the earth, which is matched by a long shot showing a flood washing away great chunks of earth – it looks as if a mountain wall were col-

---

[114] These numbers do not amount to 59, because of overlaps and the presence of human beings in some of the shots.

[115] Victor Masayesva, Jr. (2001, unpublished interview).

lapsing beneath the flood (Fig 2.11). His talk about waves coming from afar and pushing earth ashore to create new land is matched by a shot of waves rolling on a beach. Accompanying the talk about the wanderings of the Bow Clan in alien territory are shots of alpine mountains and forests. To match the sections on the Spanish conquest, Masayesva stages a few men in Spanish military dress of the day riding on horseback through the Hopi landscape, complete with the sound of Spanish military music. In the system of visual mnemonic devices, these would be fictitious mnemonic patterns. There is a primal logic in all this:

> oral cultures must conceptualize and verbalize all their knowledge with more or less close reference to the human life world, assimilating the alien, objective world to the more immediate, familiar interaction of human beings.[116]

The conceptualization and verbalization of the objective world in Hopi culture are modified through filmic visualization in a technologized oral culture. Masayesva combines the verbal integration of the outside world and the verbalization of Hopi knowledge (in Macaya's talk) with visual integration and conceptualization in the film (the Alosaka mountain, the Anasazi ruins, Old Oraibi, the flood, the waves, Spanish horsemen).

A second group of shots forms the water- and corn-imagery group. The 21 shots of rain and water manifest the importance of this element in Hopi life. Water wets the earth and nourishes the corn, the subsistence crop of the Hopi. Thus, water is essential for Hopi survival in this arid land. What looks to be randomly arranged shots of water/rain is a visualized cyclical continuum: the earth has dried out, rain clouds bring rain, the rain moistens the earth and makes corn and other plants grow (Figs. 2.12–2.14).[117] The plants feed various animals, and the animals and corn in turn feed the people, who have to keep natural forces in balance by living in accordance with the spirit-world and by ceremonially asking for rain. Gary Witherspoon explains that in Navajo[118] mythology "the rain from the sky is analogically associated with semen, and its intrusion into the earth causes reproduction, birth, and the sprouting of new life."[119] Masayesva visualizes

---

[116] Walter J. Ong, *Orality and Literacy*, 42.

[117] These images are not cut one after the other.

[118] The comparison between Hopi and Navajo culture at this point is justified by the fact that they live in the same arid territory and, consequently, that the climatic conditions are similar. Masayesva confirmed this relatedness in a personal interview.

[119] Gary Witherspoon, "Cultural Motifs in Navajo Weaving," in *North American Indian Anthropology: Essays on Society and Culture*, ed. Raymond J. DeMallie & Alfonso Ortiz

this analogy by abstracting falling corn kernels into an image of pelting rain – rain as symbolic semen and corn that is nourished by the rain become one in the image (Fig. 2.15). According to Carl Gorman (Navajo), there is a "he-rain" (large pelting drops, penetrating the soil, which are thought to inseminate the earth) and a "she-rain" (soft, tiny drops, wetting the soil, which are thought to nurture the earth).[120] Masayesva's image suggests 'he-rain', thus confirming this Navajo concept of rain.

With his corn imagery (19 shots), Masayesva renders the horticultural cycle – planting the corn, watering the plants, growing them, harvesting the corn, knocking the kernels off the cob, grinding them, making cornbread (Figs. 2.16–2.24).[121] Corn is a key element not only in the physical quotidian of the Hopi (cornmeal is the basic ingredient for bread, and the Hopi produce various items out of dried corn leaves) but also in spiritual Hopi life. There are special dances to honor the Corn Mother, cornmeal is sprinkled on the face and body parts in certain ceremonies, and corn plays a crucial role in Hopi creation myths. The planting of the corn follows an ancient tradition: six corn seeds have to be planted very deeply (one for each direction – East, West, North, South, zenith, nadir). Then the Hopi conduct dances in order to ask the spirits for rain so that the corn can grow. There are rain songs reserved only for this occasion. Helmut Gipper holds that there is a cyclical continuum in Hopi life:

> Let us [...] consider the Hopi cycle of the ceremonial year, the Hopi road of life, the world view of the people reflected in the events during the year and during the life of the individual. Here we find evidence for the predominance of a cyclic conception of time combined with a dual conception of human life on earth and the "life of the dead" in the underworld.[122]

Jerrold Levy explains that the Hopi ceremonial year is synchronized with the horticultural cycle and that priestly societies perform weather-control functions.[123] Through the corn imagery and images of ceremonial dances,

---

(Norman & London: U of Oklahoma P, 1994): 364.

[120] Personal account of Gorman during an interview conducted by Hartmut Lutz in 1980; see Lutz et al., *Achte Deines Bruders Traum: Gespräche mit nordamerikanischen Indianern, 1978–1985* (1987; Osnabrück: Druck- und Verlagskooperative, 1997).

[121] These images are not cut one after the other.

[122] Helmut Gipper, "Is There a Linguistic Relativity Principle?" in *Universalism versus Relativism in Language and Thought: Proceedings of a Colloquium on the Sapir–Whorf Hypothesis,* ed. Rik Pinxten (The Hague: Mouton, 1976): 225.

[123] Jerrold E. Levy, "Hopi Shamans: A Reappraisal," in *North American Indian Anthropology: Essays on Society and Culture,* ed. Raymond J. DeMallie & Alfonso Ortiz (Norman &

Masayesva shows this synchronization of the horticultural and ceremonial cycle in his film. The images shown also suggest that the tending, harvesting, and grinding of the corn, as well as the making of bread, are still done in traditional ways in some Hopi villages.

Apart from the water/rain and corn imagery, there is a third group of shots that convey the natural surroundings. Recurring shots show the sky, a moonrise and the wanderings of the moon, sunsets, corn plants moving in a rain storm, puddles of water in the mesa stone, flying geese and other animals. There are six shots of a captured eagle, two close-ups of a rattlesnake, three shots of deer, one of grazing buffalo, and five of sheep, including two showing the butchering of one. Besides corn, sheep are a major subsistence source for the Hopi, the eagle and the snake are sacred animals to Indigenous people, and deer and buffalo are a supplementary food source. Shots of the second group with water and corn imagery taken out of the storytelling context and cut together generate sense, for they describe cyclical events in Hopi life and form a second narrative alongside Macaya's narration. The organic shots of the third group and some shots of the first group could also be understood as generating meaning apart from the storytelling, in the sense that they form a third narrative that depicts the Hopi environment. The three converging narratives transmit a cultural semantic translated into the semantic of film.

Three shots of ancient Anasazi ruins in the Canyon de Chelly function as signifiers of Hopi ancestors (e.g., Figs. 2.10–2.11). In the opening shot of the ruins, in the creation-myth section, Masayesva shows the places where the Anasazi lived while Macaya is speaking about the people's founding of a village and waiting for a sign to show them their home. The two other shots of ruins belong to the Bow Clan section, in which Macaya is talking about the wanderings of the clan. All three shots are long shots or extreme long shots, are either from a high or low angle, and are all executed in connection with camera movement. In the first shot, the camera zooms out, in the second the camera pans right, and in the third it tilts up. The ruins bear witness to an extinct people; however, the filmmaker brings movement into these shots through his camera work, so that the shots are not static – thus

---

London: U of Oklahoma P, 1994): 321, 324. In other primal cultures, the horticultural cycle also determines everyday life and cultural expression in the form of oral accounts, songs etc. For example, Renato Rosaldo explains that the annual horticultural cycle is an integral part of oral texts among the Ilongots of the Philippines (Rosaldo, "Doing Oral History," 92).

implying that the Anasazi are not a dead culture but that they live on in the Hopi and other Southwestern Indigenous cultures.

In the Bow Clan section, Masayesva includes fourteen shots of sepia-toned photographs taken by non-Indigenous photographers at religious dances, probably in the 1940s (shots 89–105).[124] They are combined with the sound of the howling mesa wind, which enlivens these static photographs. Although Macaya's voice is heard talking and later chanting, there are no subtitles translating what is said. Thus, viewers have to rely on their own senses to grasp the meaning of Macaya's words. Masayesva says that through the photographs he was able to go back to these dances, something he could not otherwise do, since nobody is permitted to photograph or film these dances anymore. Along with Macaya's song of the society that conducted the dances, the filmmaker tries to approximate the dances. He also addresses Hopi viewers, warning (as he has indicated in an interview, 2001) that there was an agreement that this ceremony had to stay in Old Oraibi, a message that, of course, slips by non-Hopi viewers. At the same time, he addresses Western viewers by pointing out that non-Indigenous photographers, as members of the colonizing group, had taken advantage of their position of power and had taken photographs of religious ceremonies, such as the snake dance and the corn dance, without respecting cultural constraints and taboos. The Hopi in particular were a people sought after by photographers, for they were said to have kept their culture and 'exotic' rituals through the years of Spanish and Anglo-American conquest. The Hopi are a secluded people, and were to a certain extent able to resist cultural colonization. Such photographs mirrored the Hopi as ethnographic objects, satisfying the eurocentric scopic greed for the 'exotic' other. It seemed that it was not enough to colonize a people politically and economically; their culture, too, especially the spiritual and mythical, had to be penetrated and exposed.

There has been a felt need on the part of Indigenous peoples to assuage the pain of this expropriation:

---

[124] Sonja Bahn–Coblans, "Reading with a Eurocentric Eye the 'Seeing with a Native Eye'," 51. The photographs are courtesy of John Wilson, Joe Mora Photo Collection, Southwest Museum, and H. Voth Photo Collection. The number of shots in this sequence does not correspond to the number of recontextualized photographs and with the number of photograph shots, as some shots feature the same photograph and some shots in this sequence do not feature an archival photograph.

Masayesva, like many Native filmmakers and video-makers, including
Dean Curtis Bear Claw, Fidel Moreno, Diane Reyna, and Edward Ladd,
does not so much repudiate as recontextualize archival photography, reclaiming his own histories from the museum's deep freeze of Native Americans as metonyms of a "timeless past."[125]

I would go further and argue that Masayesva subverts the objectifying ethnographic look by projecting these images through yet another lens, his
own camera. The objectifying gaze of the colonizer is manipulated by the
second projection of the image through the lens of the colonized. The subversion in the photograph sequence is achieved visually through camera
movement and sonically through Macaya's narrating and chanting and the
dubbed sound of howling mesa wind. Macaya's voice transmitting cultural
oral knowledge and the mesa wind put these photographs back into the
Hopi cultural context. Of the ten recontextualized photographs, only two
are filmed with a still camera that allows easy visual access. By contrast,
two are filmed with a zoom-in, four with a zoom-out, two with a pan, and
one with a tilt. Also, three photographs have a framing mask, in two the
image is blurred, and Masayesva presents detail sections of two photographs. The camera movement and these last techniques prevent calm observation of these photographs and thus avert the objectifying ethnographic
gaze, the Western scopic drive, and they also make viewers aware of the
second camera gaze and its manipulation.

   In the harvest-festival sequence at the end of the film (shots 162–180),[126]
Masayesva intensifies his manipulation of images – but this time of contemporary dances. If we look at the process comparatively, both sequences
(the sequence with recontextualized archival photographs of Hopi ceremonies and the harvest festival sequence) have the same theme – religious
dancing. However, the photographs are in black and white, the dance
images in color; the photographs of dancing people are frozen images, but
filmed with a mobile camera, whereas the dancing people are moving
images, also filmed with a mobile camera (over 8 pans, several tilts, and 8
zooms of 19 shots that visually feature the harvest dancers) and with added
fast motion. The threefold movement of moving people, mobile camera

---

[125] Fatimah Tobing Rony, *The Third Eye: Race, Cinema, and Ethnographic Spectacle*
(Durham NC & London: Duke UP, 1996): 213.
   [126] In the grouping of shots, I have assigned shots 138–180 to the Hopi harvest festival.
The difference results from the fact that the narration of the festival starts in shot 138 and that
the first shots in this part mainly feature the harvesting and processing of corn.

frames, and fast-motion effect, combined with accelerated montage, intensifies movement and announces that the Hopi have a living culture as opposed to many Western views, which see them as an exotic cultural enclave
frozen in the past. This intensified movement means a radical break in the
film, which had hitherto relied on contemplative images and a slow editing
pace. The filmic tools with which Masayesva renders the harvest dances
also mean a break in the conventions of ethnographic filmmaking, which
tends to employ a cinematography that facilitates easy visual access to what
is presented. Before Masayesva adds fast motion to the images of harvest
dancers, he introduces the dancers through fragmentary filming via the
framing of heads, torsoes, legs, and feet. Although this fragmentary or
metonymic filming frustrates visual access to the whole body, it nevertheless facilitates access to details. Thus, Masayesva counters ethnographic
filmmaking methods of providing establishing shots, shots of groups of
dancers, and whole bodies before venturing into detail, but he cannot completely prevent the scopic drive. Masayesva's instrumentarium makes
viewers aware of ethnographic filmic tools, or, at least, makes them realize
that there is a difference in visual presentation, a difference that cconveys
Masayesva's subversive criticism. Viewers might be puzzled at the sight of
these jiggling bodies but, seen as an answer to eurocentric photography
romanticizing the Hopi and to ethnographic filmmaking scrutinizing and
patronizing its objects, Masayesva's filmic tools largely frustrate the
romanticizing and scrutinizing gaze that needs to satisfy the scopic drive,
the desire to see everything. As well as this, they pinpoint the filmic tools
with which this gaze has been facilitated and expose and disrupt the
Foucauldian 'lens of power'.[127]

Masayesva's filmic treatment of Spanish conquest and the Pueblo Revolt
differs greatly from the rest of the film. Color posterization, different
angles, continuous camera movement, and Spanish military music cause a
violent break in the smooth flow of the film. In the last photograph shot, of
a Hopi priest performing a ceremony (105), Macaya's chanting ebbs away.
It is a straight shot with the camera zooming out of the photograph. Then
follows a long take (30 sec.) in total silence – a spider spins a web around a
grasshopper (Fig. 2.25). It is taken in close-up, from a straight angle, and
the still camera sustains the silence of the shot. Thus, the shot initiates the

---

[127] On Foucault's concept of the 'lens of power' and Bhabha's concept of the 'scopic
drive', see chapter 1.

break in the sonic and visual flow of the film achieved by the sudden entry of baroque Spanish military music and the glaring artificial colors of staged Spanish horsemen. With this violent break, Masayesva visually and sonic-ally illustrates the beginning of Spanish conquest and attempts to re-create its suddenness and ferocity as experienced by the Hopi. The shot may also be seen as a visual metaphor for the beginning of the colonization of the Hopi people – the spider (the Spanish) spinning a web around the grass-hopper (the Hopi). Nevertheless, the spider is a spiritual being in the myth-ology of many Indigenous nations, and it is usually associated with the In-digenous in a non-Indigenous context. Thus, the metaphor is rather ambi-valent and does not allow such an oversimplified interpretation. After the spider shot come seven shots featuring a re-enactment of Spanish conquis-tadors riding through the mesa landscape (Figs. 2.26–2.27). Through color posterization, the images appear surreal, in different blazing colors ranging from purple, over blue, green and yellow. The first four shots are taken from a low angle in order to visualize their military superiority. All of them are taken with a moving camera, either panning or tracking, and all of them are accompanied by the baroque military music and the rattling and gallop-ing sound of horses. Macaya does not narrate in any of these shots. After the sixth follows a posterized shot in close-up of a wolf in a trap, trying to get free. The caption of the shot reads "Pueblo Revolt 1680," and Macaya starts talking about the conquest and the revolt. This shot may also serve as a metaphor for the Spanish conquest, the wolf symbolizing the Hopi people in the trap of the European colonizers. Later, a fast-motion posterized shot shows black silhouettes against a red backdrop: two Spanish soldiers on horses whipping or killing people at their feet, with which Masayesva again metaphorically visualizes the subjugation of the Hopi (Fig. 2.28).

    Then he provides shots of Hopi runners at a community competition interspersed with shots of rain clouds, lighting, the setting sun, and corn plants (Fig. 2.29) – shots pointing to the contribution of runners to the suc-cess of the Pueblo Revolt, taking messages back and forth between the single Pueblo communities.[128] The shots that stand for the resistance of the Pueblo people are not posterized. The filmmaker clearly distinguishes be-tween the shots of the subjugating Spanish and shots of things connected with the Hopi. Everything that is close, familiar, akin to the Hopi appears in natural colors, while everything that is alien, intrusive, conquering appears

---

[128] Elizabeth Weatherford, "To End and Begin Again: The Work of Victor Masayesva," 50.

surreal, in artificial blazing colors. A very long take (1.24 min.), not posterized, illustrates the defeat of the Spanish, symbolically expressed by
several cinematic means. The horsemen are now filmed in an extreme long
shot, in which they appear as tiny figures within the grandiose mesa landscape (Fig. 2.30). They no longer gallop or trot as in the shots illustrating
the conquest, but ride in slow gait. The low camera angles in the conquest
shots are now replaced by a high angle, and the military music is replaced
by Vivaldi's *Concerto for Baroque Trumpet*, a rather melancholy tune in
comparison to the previous one.

   Like Campbell in *The Road Allowance People*, Masayesva in *Itam
Hakim, Hopiit* illustrates characteristic elements of the oral tradition. He
conveys that storytellers work with regard to an Indigenous copyright system. Macaya starts by telling his personal tale and talking about his father
and later about his own clan of storytellers. Thus, he discloses how he came
to know this cultural knowledge he now passes on. It is impossible to tell
from the film whether or not the children are familiar with the Hopi creation myth and recent history in this oral form,[129] nor are viewers acquainted
with the motivation for this storytelling event. What becomes obvious,
though, is the fact that the oral tradition works as an archive for a nation's
historical and cultural knowledge, for Macaya speaks of Hopi creation,
about Spanish conquest, and about the successful Pueblo Revolt, after
which a council of local nations ruled the territory for twelve years before
the Spanish reoccupied the territory. He talks about traditional Hopi life:
traditional corn growing, his own clan, traditional Hopi society, the Ahl
brotherhood; and he chants traditional songs – all information handed down
from generation to generation. Thus, the film mirrors the function of oral
tradition in preserving and teaching cultural and historical knowledge.
Apart from the technical disadvantages that recording oral storytelling
brings, the film lives up to the requirement that oral tradition be rendered as
faithfully as possible.

   As oral storytellers work post-conquest historical events into their accounts, so do the people incorporate such events metaphorically into their
ceremonies. Verbal and somatic expressions consistently integrate physical
history into mythic past:

---

[129] The children were not allowed to hear the emergence myth and cannot be familiar with
this part of Hopi history (Victor Masayesva, Jr., 2001, unpublished interview).

In such ways as this [the Pueblos depict the coming of the Spanish in their dances], throughout the year, the Pueblos take important events of the past that intruded upon them and freeze them into place, as it were, by anchoring the historical events onto symbolic vehicles of expression that are traditional and that, thereby, lock those events comfortably onto their own cultural landscape.[130]

Alfonso Ortiz further explains that Pueblos create images of non-Pueblans in their mass public ritual dramas. Masayesva does the same in a modified way when he interprets the Spanish invasion with cinematic means and thus gives Macaya's account of it visual and sonic substance.

Like Campbell, Masayesva makes it clear that oral storytelling is not a tightly organized event but one that allows interruptions, interaction between storyteller and audience, and that takes a tolerant attitude towards inattentive members of the audience. The children in Macaya's audience whisper and giggle, laugh and nudge each other, run around and play. When one boy accidentally drops a glass lamp-shade with which the children were playing, Macaya keeps on talking and ignores the incident. He performs the stories by interspersing his talk with chants that complement the information he relays. Only narration and chant together make up the oral storytelling experience and can transmit oral cultural and historical knowledge. Just as oral tradition is performative, the film itself becomes performance, its imagery illustrating the talk and the soundtrack of chant, talk, and background noises all performing the spoken words.

Translated Slowness as Stylistic Device

Already in the first few shots, it becomes clear that the film is different from most other documentaries. It has a slower pace and relies more on organic shots and artistic shots (shots that are reminiscent of art photography) than conventional documentaries. As noted by other critics,[131] these shots indicate that Masayesva came to film through photography: i.e. he also works as a photographer and has published two volumes of Hopi

---

[130] Alfonso Ortiz, "The Dynamics of Pueblo Cultural Survival," in *North American Indian Anthropology. Essays on Society and Culture*, ed. Raymond J. DeMallie & Alfonso Ortiz (Norman & London: U of Oklahoma P, 1994): 303.

[131] Sonja Bahn–Coblans, "Reading with a Eurocentric Eye the 'Seeing with a Native Eye'," 47–60; Kathleen M. Sands & Allison Sekaquaptewa Lewis, "Seeing with a Native Eye: A Hopi Film on Hopi," *American Indian Quarterly* 14.4 (1990): 387–96; Elizabeth Weatherford, "To End and Begin Again," 48–52.

photography.[132] He tends to use long takes and a slow editing rhythm, reinforced by the continuous usage of dissolves which ensure soft transitions between the images. The shots have an average length of 19 seconds with only 40 of 181 shots being between one and ten seconds. Ten of the latter are part of the fast-motion section at the end of the film, in which the filmmaker employs accelerated montage for the fast motion of his images. Four shots are over one minute and two over two minutes long. Kathleen Sands and Allison Sekaquaptewa Lewis have mentioned Masayesva's willingness to sustain an image, and apply it to his work as a still photographer.[133] The long takes give the narrative space a long time to develop. Combined with the slow editing rhythm, they adjust the film to a slower pace of life and a traditional Indigenous understanding of time, which are subordinated to the natural cyclical continuum of life, as also suggested by Sands and Sekaquaptewa Lewis:

> continuous action is not his style. Rather, he focuses on individual moments – faces, subdued movement, long shots of the mesa-top villages, elements of nature – each image completing an idea before it fades into another connecting or contrasting moment.
>
> Masayesva's long attention to the peach boughs may also be related to an attitude toward pace and focus on particular detail that is cultural specific, much as the dominance of coming and going is culturally distinctive in the Navajo film. Meditation is the mood of the film; the pace of life at Hopi is slow, repetitive, and contemplative.[134]

Most shots of the mesa landscape have a similar composition, with clearly defined lines. The main compositional feature is a horizontal line, either in the middle or in the lower half of the frame, which either divides one mesa from the other, the mesa from the sky, or the mesa or water from the horizon. There are twenty such shots with clear forms and straight lines, usually without people. When there are people in these shots, they appear as tiny little figures against the backdrop of the magnificent landscape. While anybody could take shots like this (mesa landscapes feature straight lines, after all), the reiteration of this motif in shot composition reveals a Hopi way of seeing surroundings and can thus be regarded as an example of Hopi pat-

---

[132] Victor Masayesva, Jr., *Hopi Photography, Hopi Images* (Tucson: Sun Tracks & U of Arizona P, 1984); Victor Masayesva, Jr., *Husk of Time: The Photography of Victor Masayesva* (Tucson: U of Arizona P, 2006).

[133] Sands & Sekaquaptewa Lewis, "Seeing with a Native Eye: A Hopi Film on Hopi," 392.

[134] "Seeing with a Native Eye," 392.

terns of perception. The shot composition with tiny figures in the imposing landscape is a filmic embodiment of the Indigenous concept of wo/man as just a minor part of the natural universe (Fig 2.31).

Masayesva tends to refrain from establishing shots (e.g., of such filmic spaces as the house interior and fields) or shots introducing the whole object that is filmed (e.g., the weaving loom, or a person). Rather, he first films single parts and later provides a shot of the whole filmic object or subject. At the beginning, the storytelling takes place in a house which is not clearly defined. There is only one shot conveying spatial relations in the house but it follows fragmentary shots of Macaya's body, fragments of the interior, and a few shots outside. At first one sees a corner with a cast-iron stove, then the weaving storyteller from behind and his hands weaving; only then follows an oblique shot of Macaya weaving. The next one is a portrait-like shot of the man (Figs 2.32–2.36). Then Macaya's audience is introduced by a shot of the children playing and later of them sitting on a bed and listening (Fig. 2.37). Macaya starts chanting while the camera is trained on his hands in close-up as he pounds the rhythm (Fig. 2.38). Only in shot 20 is he for the first time actually seen telling the stories (Fig. 2.39); here he begins telling the Hopi creation myth, and various shots start to illustrate his words.

Altogether, Masayesva employs 70 long and extreme long shots, 52 medium shots, and 91 close-ups.[135] There are thus more long shots and close-ups than medium shots, which is different from most conventional documentaries, in which medium shots (e.g., in interviews) and long shots (e.g., of landscapes and cityscapes) predominate. Masayesva's style tends to move close to the subject/object in order to abstract it by not showing the whole. He is inclined to film either body fragments or a person in a long shot or extreme long shot, who is often just a tiny little figure in the frame. In both ways, the person cannot be recognized and scrutinized as easily as in a medium shot and American shot. He very often films hands and feet in close-up and pays filmic attention to otherwise irrelevant details, such as a spider, a bough with blossoms, and a kerosene lamp. As already mentioned, in the introductory shots the viewer sees just the feet of Macaya walking upon the dry mesa earth toward a waterhole. Later, when Macaya chops wood (shot 14), Masayesva, instead of using medium camera distance,

---

[135] Their sum exceeds the total number of shots because of the frequent zooming, which may result in a long and a medium shot in one take.

films the man in close-up, tilting the camera up so that, once again, he isolates body parts. In shot 54 he films the digging of a hole with a planting stick in close-up. Again the foot of the boy is central to the image. At the beginning of the Bow Clan section (shots 57–58), the filmmaker captures the lower legs and feet of people walking. In the harvest-festival sequence (shots 169–180), he films the heads, torsoes, legs, and feet of the dancers (Figs. 2.40–2.43), and whole persons only when he adds the fast-motion effect (Fig. 2.44). Also Bahn–Coblans suggests that there are sharp contrasts of distance and closeness and macro- and micro-effects in Masyesva's filmic work.[136] Unlike ethnographic films, one favorite subject of which have often been the dances of the people being studied, Masayesva only shows body parts and later whole bodies in fast motion in the harvest-festival sequence, so that his film does not have a depicting and scrutinizing character at all with the atmosphere of the public dances getting lost. Instead, Masayesva very often focusses on the feet of the dancers, showing how the people stomp their feet exactly according to the drumbeat. A superficial interpretation would apply this stress on feet to the notion of the people's connection with the earth through their feet. This thought might well be correct, but there are also other reasons for filming feet. Masayesva holds that in the initial images he wanted to draw attention to the black Converse shoes of the elder as a strong image of old Hopi people; as well as this, he wanted to suggest that Macaya is a humorous guy and thus make the viewers sympathize with him.[137] Tobing Rony sees the film's introductory shots of Macaya's feet walking as resisting an ethnographic film aesthetic.[138]

In the same vein, the high number of long shots and close-ups is part of Masayesva's filmmaking style. This style counters conventional documentary and ethnographic filmmaking (as was seen earlier), which would provide establishing shots or shots of the whole object to be filmed, usually in an American, medium, or medium-long shot, before venturing into detail. In concert with Masayesva's fragmentary cinematography, his focus on hands and feet, and his reluctance to film whole bodies in medium shots, his preference for long shots and close-ups, all largely evades a surveilling

---

[136] Sonja Bahn–Coblans, "Reading with a Eurocentric Eye the 'Seeing with a Native Eye'," 50.

[137] Victor Masayesva, Jr. (unpublished interview, 2001).

[138] Fatimah Tobing Rony, "Victor Masayesva, Jr., and the Politics of Imagining Indians," *Film Quarterly* 48.2 (1994–1995): 25.

and objectifying gaze and curbs the Western scopic drive.[139] This style can
also be attributed to his culture, where one does not "violate the silences."
Masayesva explains, in the foreword to his edition of Hopi photography:

> I would risk generalizing. Hopis are very private, often secretive people who
> understand the value of silence and unobtrusiveness. Even if you are a Hopi
> photographing a Hopi, you will not confront the silences. The subjects would
> not expect you to, knowing that you are a Hopi. And if you are a Hopi, you
> would not be in the confrontational situation in the first place. As a Hopi, you
> cannot violate the silences, just as you would not intrude on ceremony.[140]

When Masayesva uses medium shots to film people, he does so with a certain pattern. Macaya and the Spanish soldiers are filmed four times each in
a medium shot, the children 13 times, and the harvest dancers 9 times.
Considering that Macaya was filmed 19 times and the Spanish soldiers 12
times altogether, the four medium shots each are negligible. Half of the
shots of harvest dancers (9 out of 17) are done as medium shots; however,
most of them, again, only show body fragments, so that they cannot serve
to visually describe the people completely. Of the 24 shots of children, 13
are medium shots, and these are not fragmented. The shots showing women
knocking corn kernels off the cobs, sieving and grinding the corn, and
making cornbread are also taken in medium camera distance. In contrast to
the dance sequences, Masayesva here shows how these things are done,
which is reminiscent of the films of Navajo film novices made in 1966.[141]
Of the 22 animal shots, only three (eagle, deer, buffalo) are medium shots,
and of the 37 landscape shots only two (of waves rolling upon a beach, of
the sun setting on a lake) are in medium camera distance, although landscape shots are conventionally executed in long and extreme long shots,
which is conditioned by this object of film/photography itself. It becomes
apparent that Masayesva mostly uses unconditioned medium shots to film
playing and dancing children and people doing daily chores. This fact
might be attributable to his aim of highlighting the storytelling audience
and also the processing of the corn. His focus is on the Hopi landscape,
which is captured in many long and extreme long shots combined with
abundant pans. He is interested in presenting as much of the land as pos-

---

[139] See also Fatimah Tobing Rony, *The Third Eye: Race, Cinema, and Ethnographic Spectacle* (Durham NC & London: Duke UP, 1996): 212–16.

[140] Victor Masayesva, Jr., *Hopi Photography, Hopi Images*, 10.

[141] See the discussion of the Navajo films later in this chapter.

sible and in showing the merging of individual landmarks with the mesa landscape, communicating a Hopi sense of place and his own view of Hopi land.

The camera perspectives in *Itam Hakim, Hopiit* are basically conventional. With 117 straight, 14 oblique right and 20 oblique left angles as well as 18 high angles and 15 low angles, the film stays within the range of the customary. The camera angles are thus no stylistic device here. However, the camera movements can be regarded as such. Masayesva's technique is conspicuous for continuously zooming in and out of images, as well as for frequent pans and tracking shots. He uses 51 pans, 14 tracking shots, 23 zoom ins and 42 zoom outs. These movement shots total 130, by far exceeding the 50 shots where the camera remains still while filming. This frequently employed mobile framing is quite unusual in conventional documentary filmmaking. The numerous pans and zooms are especially striking to a eurocentric eye and are part of Masayesva's filmmaking style. The technique of panning and zooming stresses the direct, immediately active character of the camera gaze and emphasizes the technical aspect of film as product, which viewers usually tend to ignore. They most often take an illusion of reality (dramatic films) and a reflection of reality (documentaries) for granted and forget the fact that film – including documentary film – is a medium open to manipulation by the maker through various techniques, such as montage, editing, sound, camera angle, and perspective. Masayesva often blurs the images, abstracting them into the unrecognizable. Sometimes clearly focussed images become blurred, sometimes blurry images become focussed, and at other times the images move from being clearly focussed to being blurry, then to being focussed again. His motive for doing this might be to dissociate the image from clear visual messages and to guide the viewers' attention to other contexts than the visual. The blurring of images, the frequent mobile camera, and fragmentary filming appear to be employed in the sense of the Brechtian alienation effect; once again, they counter ethnographic filmmaking and its scrutinizing gaze.

There are four visual breaks in the film, partly combined with sound-breaks. They are not necessarily in concordance with the different parts of the film, and they are more or less noticeable, disturbing the smooth flow of the film and signalling that something new is going on. The first visual break appears between shots 60 and 61, where the images become milky and seem to show an alien landscape. Here, Masayesva films alpine forests for the first time, and Macaya describes the wanderings of the Bow Clan into different territories. The second visual break occurs with shot 89, which introduces the photograph sequence. The break is achieved through the sepia-toned black-and-white photographs, which contrast with the previous color shot of rain clouds and the mesa. The third visual break is combined with a sonic break in shot 107. Color posterization and the sudden entry of Spanish military music 'tell' the viewers that another force is entering the filmic events. The fourth visual break is accompanied by a sonic change and occurs in shot 169. Here, the images of the harvest dancers are sped up in post-production. The music of the dance becomes distorted into the typical fast-motion noise one hears while forwarding or rewinding a cassette player without hitting the stop key. The drum beat is also accelerated and mixed with the fast-motion noise.

The first and the last shot of the film are the same – two people working in a cornfield against the backdrop of a reddish sky – but the introductory shot is a still, while the last shot is a regular motion shot (Fig. 2.45). It has the effect of being in slow motion, since the preceding shots of the dancers at the harvest festival are in fast motion. Because Masayesva uses the same shot as an introductory and final image, the film goes back to where it started. This allows one to see the film as having a circular structure, formally confirming or pointing up the cyclical processes of the content. Choosing a framing shot which shows the harvest of corn stresses the utmost importance of this crop for Hopi subsistence and the fact that Hopi life is synchronized with the corn cycle. Again, this supports the thesis that the corn- and corn-plant imagery is an important element of visual expression in Hopi culture.

Masayesva's film reveals characteristics similar to the Navajo films of the "Navajos Film Themselves" project.[142] Filming walking feet, cracked

---

[142] John Adair and Sol Worth implemented the "Navajo Film Themselves" project, where they taught Navajo film novices how to operate film cameras and how to edit. The films produced were *A Navajo Weaver* (20 min.) by Susie Benally, *A Navajo Silversmith* (20 min.) and *The Shallow Well* (20 min.) by Johnny Nelson, *Old Antelope Lake* (15 min.) by Mike Anderson, *The Spirit of the Navajo* (20 min.) by Maxine and Mary Jane Tsosie, *Intrepid Shadows* (15 min.) by Al Clah, and *Second Weaver* (originally untitled; 10 min.) by Alta Kahn, Benally's mother, who had been taught by her daughter how to make a film. There are also the practice films *The Swing* by Benally, *The Monkey Bars* by Clah, *John Adair Hangs Out the Laundry* and *The Boys on the Seesaw* by the Tsosie sisters, *The Piñon Tree* and *The Ants* by Anderson, *The Navajo Horse* and *The Summer Shower* by Nelson, which all usually run about two minutes. The project is comprehensively described and analyzed in Sol Worth & John Adair, *Through Navajo Eyes: An Exploration in Film Communication and Anthropology* (1972; Albuquerque: U of New Mexico P, 1997). The films *A Navajo Weaver, A Navajo*

earth, rain clouds, and immediate surroundings is reminiscent of these films. So is the filmic description of natural cycles (dry earth – rain – growth) as well as cycles of processes (sheep – wool – rugs; corn plants – watering and harvest – corncobs – cornflour – bread – ceremonies) within the respective culture. The general tone in *Itam Hakim, Hopiit*, created to a large extent by the slow pace and lingering images, also resembles the style of the Navajo film students. The manipulation of images is another shared feature. In the creation-myth part, the director has pointed out in an interview (2001), Macaya was play-acting, pretending to speak to the children, and the shots of the children as audience were inserted in post-production.[143] In contrast to the Navajo films, Masayesva frequently employs facial close-ups of Macaya and of the children in the audience. However, like the Navajo films, no person looks directly into the camera (except one boy and Macaya once very briefly, Fig. 2.36). Like the Navajo filmmakers, Masayesva is concerned with conveying an Indigenous holistic understanding of the world. He also focusses on narrative space through the frequent long shots and neglects temporal relations and narrative time. The viewers are never cued as to what time of the day it is, nor whether the sequences are shot or edited in chronological order. This phenomenon might be rooted in the Hopi language, which, Whorf explains, does not contain any gram-

---

Silversmith, and *Second Weaver*, in particular, painstakingly describe the whole preparatory process for making a Navajo rug and a piece of silver jewellery. For example, Benally includes shots of sheep being shorn, of her mother carding, spinning, and washing the wool, collecting plants and roots for dyeing, dyeing the wool, again washing and drying it, rolling it into balls, then preparing the loom. The actual weaving takes up only a minimal amount of screen-time and Western viewers are quite puzzled when all of a sudden the finished rug is presented without their having actually seen much weaving. The film thus makes clear how ideas can differ greatly about how a film on weaving should be made, which in turn goes back to the differences between Western and Indigenous world-views. The film illustrates well how, to the Navajos, the preparation process is inseparable from the actual weaving and that the weaving cannot be shown in isolation. To them, the whole process of creation matters; the films thus reflect the Navajo world-view, which understands life as cyclical and all things as interconnected. Some of the other films, too, depict whole cycles of creation and life – that of plants, for example. Masayesva's filmic attention to Macaya's walking feet might likewise be seen in connection with the long walking sequences in the Navajo films, and the filmmakers' focus on feet and walking as well as on cyclical processes can be understood as arising from similar world-views. Since the Hopi and Navajo are geographically and culturally related, their mode of visual expression is also related and contributes to a similar film aesthetic (Victor Masayesva, Jr., unpublished interview, 2001).

[143] Clah, for *Intrepid Shadows*, films water coming from a hose and uses that as an image of rain, and he makes a spider's web out of cotton thread and pretends that this is an actual spider's web.

matical forms or expressions that reflect a concept of time as Western cultures know it. There is no distinction between past, present, and future. Instead, Hopi verbs have nine voices and nine aspects, one of which is
spatial.[144] However, there is controversy among linguists about Whorf's
thesis.[145] Masayesva himself (interview, 2001) is not convinced of Whorf's
conclusions and says that there are only a few cases in which they can be
demonstrated. Thus the language structure cannot serve as an appropriate
explanation of the issue of narrative time and space in Masayesva's film.
One must also keep in mind that conventional documentaries do not always
consider temporal relations, either. The explanation is, rather, that traditional Hopi and Navajo, like other Indigenous cultures, have a strong sense
of place and a cyclical understanding of time that shows in the films as a
focus on filmic space and a disregard for chronological order and temporal
relations.

This consideration brings us to the matter of the audience intended.
Some critics[146] hold that *Itam Hakim, Hopiit* was initially made for a Hopi

---

[144] Benjamin Lee Whorf, *Language, Thought, and Reality*, 57, 51.

[145] For example, Helmut Gipper maintains that "an exhaustive analysis of Whorf's own
controversial papers on the conception of time and space in Hopi [...] reveals that such pro-
voking statements of his, as 'The Hopi language contains no reference to 'time,' either explicit or implicit' [...], are misleading, and even false. The Hopi language does indeed contain
a considerable number of expressions referring to space and time"; Gipper, "Is There a Linguistic Relativity Principle?" in *Universalism versus Relativism in Language and Thought:
Proceedings of a Colloquium on the Sapir–Whorf Hypothesis*, ed. Rik Pinxten (The Hague:
Mouton, 1976): 220. In regard to time and space he writes: "4. Contrary to Whorf's opinion,
expressions for spatial relations are used metaphorically in a temporal sense, in other words,
there are space–time metaphors as in Indo-European languages. [...] 7. There are grammatical
means in Hopi to express present, past, and future, though the Hopi thinking seems to be
governed by a bipartition of time ('present'+'past' and 'future') instead of the tripartition of
time ('past'–'present'–'future') we are accustomed to. [...] 10. There seems to exist – or at
least to have existed – a special word for 'time', which, however, Whorf – and my informants
– denied" (221–24). Although Gipper explicitly presents arguments against Whorf's writings,
he also admits that, according to his own research, past and present seem to be mingled and
neither of his informants could confirm his hypothesis that there is a term for 'time'. John
Cipolla maintains in this regard that the "primary literacies deal almost exclusively with the
here and now, the present. Their time and space binding functions are loose, inexact, open to
individual interpretation and manipulation"; Cipolla, "Mass Media as Language: The Sapir–
Whorf Hypothesis and Electronic Media," in *Universalism versus Relativism in Language
and Thought*, ed. Pinxten, 308.

[146] Steven Leuthold, "An Indigenous Aesthetic? Two Noted Videographers: George Bur-
deau and Victor Masayesva," *Wicazo Sa Review* 10.1 (Spring 1994): 40–51; Fatimah Tobing
Rony, "Victor Masayesva, Jr., and the Politics of Imagining Indians," 20–33; Elizabeth
Weatherford, "To End and Begin Again: The Work of Victor Masayesva," 48–52.

audience exclusively, for Macaya narrates only in Hopi. Masayesva has explained in an interview (2001) that since the film was commissioned by a German broadcaster, the 'paying' audience was German. Nevertheless, he consciously applied a Hopi approach, of which language is one aspect:

> But we still felt like if we make a program about Hopi we have to deal with Hopi approaches. I mean language is definitely a part of that. That I chose Hopi did not necessarily mean that I was only making it for Hopi. But that was the language of that experience, so it had to be in Hopi.

The film was also screened locally in Hopi communities and, since some children were not fluent in Hopi, he created a version with English subtitles in 1985/86. Viewers realize during the course of the film that the subtitles do not provide a one-to-one translation of Macaya's account but only summarize or generalize information. There is a whole narrative section (the photograph sequence) where the filmmaker does not add subtitles at all. The translation leaves out the continuous repetitions and paraphrases that characterize the rhetoric of oral tradition. Masayesva explains (interview, 2001) that he was providing summaries in the subtitles and that he could not translate the lyrics of one song because of cultural taboos.

Nonetheless, it is clear that Hopi viewers are cued to see the film quite differently from Western viewers or Indigenous viewers from other nations: i.e. a Hopi viewer as a cultural insider constructs a different meaning of the film than a non-Hopi viewer does. A Hopi viewer would grasp certain gestures and facial play, recognize the surroundings, geographical sites, certain songs and dances, ideally understand the language and subsequently the original message of Macaya's account, and s/he would apply a different significance to the visual imagery and sonic presentation than a non-Hopi viewer. Every mind is conditioned by its culture and mother tongue: i.e. cultural codes shape and influence cognitive patterns. As Max Black says, cultural codes form a "system of associated commonplaces" according to which members of a certain culture would associate the same context and apply the same or a similar meaning to a certain word.[147] Worth and Adair apply this principle to the medium of film:

> films could be classified in a crude way according to differences in the *structure* of the response of different audiences to specific film *structures.* That is, aspects of the structure or pattern in a film seemed relevant to the

---

[147] Max Black, *Models and Metaphors: Studies in Language and Philosophy* (Ithaca N Y : Cornell U P , 1981): 40.

cognitive processes employed in dealing not only with film, but with other modes or media of communication as well.[148]

A Hopi Voice and Sound

Sound is another technical means of creating the specific character of *Itam Hakim, Hopiit*. The range of sounds consists of four basic elements: Macaya's voice talking and chanting (122 shots),[149] the sound of singing and drums at the dances (49 shots), the sound of the howling mesa winds (33 shots), and the baroque Spanish military music and Vivaldi's *Concerto for Baroque Trumpet* (11 shots). Most other sounds are faithful sounds which sonically support the visual context of Masayesva's imagery. Macaya's intriguing voice narrating the history of the Hopi nation throughout the film constitutes its basic tonality, in quality as well as in quantity. It is the most dominant sonic element (in 122 shots out of 181), even though the image of Macaya himself appears only 19 times. This Hopi voice is a leitmotif lending the film its character and bearing its verbal message. His voice not only functions as a sound bridge, as faithful sound, and as a supplemental element, but has its own function as a carrier of sonic information – which indeed has primacy with regards to the objective of the film.

By having the narrator speak and chant in Hopi (with subtitles), Masayesva embeds the cultural knowledge transmitted in the technical medium of film in the Hopi linguistic and cultural context, and the words in Macaya's account retain their original meaning. By employing the Hopi language and the slow pace, he is able, to a certain extent, to capture the storytelling situation and stay largely true to the original sense of the oral knowledge. At the same time, Masayesva resists using the colonial language, which would have modifed the information's original meaning. Although he avails himself of a Western means of expression (film technology), he keeps the grade of assimilation to Western influences very low. He is director, photographer, producer, and partly distributor; further, he denies the colonial lingua franca. Weatherford suggests that "visual language and the Hopi language are his tools for eloquence."[150] Whorf has indicated how a

---

[148] Sol Worth & John Adair, *Through Navajo Eyes*, 19; emphasis in original.

[149] Because chants are also a form of the oral tradition in which cultural knowledge can be transmitted, for the analysis of sound there is no distinction made between Macaya talking and chanting.

[150] Elizabeth Weatherford, "To End and Begin Again: The Work of Victor Masayesva," 49.

phrase may receive different meanings when translated into another language and consequently into another cultural context, supporting his hypothesis with an example from Hopi grammar, in which the phrase 'begins doing' together with different verbs switches between several fundamental categories of meaning, hence several English translations. "This tends to confirm [...] that the Hopi observer conceives the events in a different manner from the one whose native language is English."[151]

Macaya's voice may strike the viewers as being monotonous, for it has a very slow rhythm that is supported by the slow editing. Both lend the film a characteristic lingering pace. The coordination of imagery and sound forms what Sergei Eisenstein has called a "synchronization of senses."[152] In this respect, the voice narrating in Hopi, combined with the lingering pace and images from Hopi daily life and surroundings, cues the viewers to accept a Hopi understanding of time and space.

The drums and the songs of the harvest dances are other characteristic sounds of Hopi culture. As discussed earlier, the religious dances are an essential ingredient in the cycle of Hopi life. Through these dances and songs, the people ask for rain and good harvests and also thank the Corn Mother for giving the corn to the people. The sound of drums and singing becomes the supplemental sonic information for the harvest-dance shots. It also works as a sound bridge and adds the concept of religious dancing to other shots – for example, the primarily organic shots of the clouds and the bird (shot 138), the full moon (shot 139), the setting sun (shot 140), the butchering of a sheep (shots 142–143), and the shots depicting the making of cornbread. According to Masayesva, the form of songs and chants also serves mnemonic purposes: "song forms are repetitive, serving memorization, stability and repetition like the mnemonic designs of computers, tape recorders and computer chips."[153] Songs are sonic mnemonic patterns that structure oral performance and the film, but as oral performance the songs themselves contain such patterns as structuring clues. Masayesva defines song thus:

---

[151] Benjamin Lee Whorf, *Language, Thought, and Reality*, 104.

[152] Cited in David Bordwell & Kristin Thompson, *Film Art*, 316, from Eisenstein, "Synchronization of Senses," ch. 2 of *The Film Sense*, tr. Jay Leyda (1947; San Diego CA: Harcourt, Brace, 1970): 73.

[153] Victor Masayesva, Jr., "The Emerging Native American Aesthetics in Film and Video," *Film and Video Monthly Independent* (December 1994): 21.

a prompting device for our memories, there is a certain consistence in song patterns, these songs are very structured. There is always some kind of reference so that you'll know what kind of song it is if you are at the beginning or at the end of it. That's what I mean by "mnemonic patterns." (interview, 2001)

In this regard, songs and ritual chants also serve to conceptualize and verbalize the objective world and are transformed into an electronic secondary orality in the film.

Another sound-motif is the ever-present howling mesa wind that shapes the Hopi cognition of space. It appears in combination with the landscape shots, transmitting the sonic essence of the mesa. But it also works as a sound bridge and creates a certain atmosphere in other sequences. For example, it enlivens the frozen images of Hopi religious dances in the photograph sequence and embeds them afresh in a Hopi cultural context. Finally, the Spanish military music as well as Vivaldi's baroque concerto, which complete the shots of the Spanish riders, are the only non-diegetic sounds in the film. They characterize the Spanish, for it is the music of seventeenth- and eighteenth-century Europe and of the era when Spanish colonialism in Central America and the southern and western parts of North America was in full force.[154] Since this use of non-diegetic music means a sonic break in a film that has previously used diegetic sound, the European music becomes the signature tune of the colonizing forces and sonically symbolizes Spanish intrusion into Hopi culture.

According to V.F. Perkins, sound brings with it a new expressive function, "a new sense of the value of silence."[155] Using this expressive force, Masayesva does not add sound to three shots. One is the very first shot, a still of two silhouettes working in a field. Here, the silence of the shot does not have a very strong effect, for it is the beginning of the film and there are no shots with sounds before this one. But the second time (shot 12), there is a brief moment when Macaya's face is filmed looking into the camera without sound. Very often, traditional Indigenous people do not like to be filmed in close-up, and if they are, they avoid direct eye-contact with the camera. As the sound generally helps to direct the viewer's attention to special visual elements, the technique of providing no sound emphasizes

---

[154] The Baroque age was c.1600–1770; Vivaldi lived between 1678 and 1741.

[155] Paraphrased by Bordwell & Thompson, *Film Art*, 318, from Perkins, *Film as Film: Understanding and Judging Movies* (1964; Harmondsworth & Baltimore MD: Penguin, 1972): 54.

the shot as a special moment in the film, because it is the only time that Macaya looks directly into the camera. Even more striking is the silence in shot 106, which might serve as a metaphor for Spanish colonization and which, together with shot 107, creates a visual and sonic break. Before this shot, the viewer heard Macaya chanting, then there is a sudden silence for 20 seconds, interrupted by a bird's whistle in the last ten seconds of the shot, then followed by the startling entry of Spanish military music. The silence becomes even more noticeable in contrast to the full-scale sounds in the previous (105) and following shot (107). It increases the effect of the visual imagery and foreshadows the transition to the Spanish-conquest part. In the last shot (181), Masayesva uses this technique of sound-break a fourth time. It cannot be clearly grouped with the previous three shots, for it does have sound (the subdued voices of the two people working in the cornfield). However, the effect of a sound-break is still there, because after the accelerated montage, fast motion, and unnerving fast-motion noise in the dance sequence, the film seems to drop suddenly into complete silence.

Genre Discussions

Sands and Sekaquaptewa Lewis group Masayesva's first film *Hopiit* (1981) with the bio-documentary genre, a term coined by Sol Worth, which he elucidates in *Through Navajo Eyes*. He defines a bio-documentary as a film that mirrors the maker's cognition of the world and subsequently her/his values. Such a film does not objectify the culture featured, but is a subjective cultural expression distinct from ethnographic patterns and also distinct from a consciousness of art:

> A Bio-Documentary is a film made by a person to show how he feels about himself and his world. It is a *subjective* way of showing what the *objective* world that a person *sees* is "really" like. In part, this kind of film bears the same relation to documentary film that a self-portrait has to a portrait [...]. In addition because of the specific way that this kind of film is made, it often captures feelings and reveals values, attitudes, and concerns that lie beyond conscious control of the maker. [...] The Bio-Documentary method suggests that at times it is fruitful to get away from an examination of man as object and try to learn more about him as subject.[156]

Itam Hakim, Hopiit could also be understood as a bio-documentary. Its focus on oral storytelling and its visual imagery transmit Masayesva's cog-

---

[156] Sol Worth & John Adair, *Through Navajo Eyes*, 25–26; emphasis added.

nition of his culture and surroundings, of Macaya, and of the value Hopi
culture accords to different things such as corn and corn plants, animals, the
moon, the mesa earth, rain clouds, and ceremonies. Whorf sees the Hopi
metaphysical expression of the subjective realm in the cultural semantics of
the word 'hope' or 'hoping'.

> The word is really a term which crystallizes the Hopi philosophy of the uni-
> verse in respect to its grand dualism of objective and subjective; it is the
> Hopi term for SUBJECTIVE. [...] As anyone acquainted with Hopi society
> knows, the Hopi see this burgeoning activity ["hoping"] in the growing of
> plants, the forming of clouds and their condensation in rain, the careful
> planning out of the communal activities of agriculture and architecture, and
> in all human hoping, wishing, striving, and taking thought; and as most
> especially concentrated in prayer, the constant hopeful praying of the Hopi
> community [...] prayer which conducts the pressure of the collective Hopi
> thought and will out of the subjective into the objective.[157]

Whorf's findings make it clear that Hopi language is deeply rooted in Hopi
culture and religion and vice versa. The visual imagery of *Itam Hakim,
Hopiit* reflects this philosophy and is Masayesva's subjective way of mirroring the objective Hopi world. Another Hopi person is sure to come up
with another subjective way of presenting the Hopi, and a non-Hopi person
with an even more distant mode of presentation. Steven Leuthold objects
that "the question of a distinct biodocumentary genre becomes more complex when applied to experienced native producers and directors."[158] He
points out the fact that the makers of bio-documentaries (usually Worth's
students) were all novice filmmakers and that Sands and Sekaquaptewa
Lewis base their assessment partly on the fact that *Hopiit* is Masayesva's
first film. However, I feel that the question of whether or not a film is the
first or nth film of a filmmaker cannot serve as a criterion for a conclusion
about a film's bio-documentary nature. Rather, the criteria for this assessment are visual patterns, camera work, style, and the overall atmosphere of
the respective film. Not every Indigenous filmmaker making a film about
his/her culture automatically creates a bio-documentary. There are many
who apply an absolutely straightforward documentary style and many who
apply this documentary style mixed with their own stylistic features. But
even a documentary done in conventional style still mirrors a subjective

---

[157] Whorf, *Language, Thought, and Reality*, 61–62; emphasis in original.
[158] Steven Leuthold, "An Indigenous Aesthetic?" 45.

way of seeing and expresses the values of its maker. Where shall one draw
the line and decide what is a subjective mode of cognition and how much
of the values, attitudes, and concerns of the filmmaker is transmitted via the
visual and sonic information? How subjective must a documentary be in
order to qualify as bio-documentary? Thus, I believe it is useful to look
closely at Worth' definition of bio-documentary and weigh the individual
elements of his definition against the the respective film analyses.

Essential for this discussion is the content and focus of the film. It is easy
to see Masayesva's identification with Hopi culture, his values, attitudes,
and concerns, in *Itam Hakim, Hopiit*. But what about the documentary
films by Alanis Obomsawin? Her film *Incident at Restigouche* (1984)
covers the political and military clash between the Canadian state and
police and Micmacs protesting against fishing regulations. Her film *Kaneh-*
satake: 270 Years of Resistance (1992) features a similar confrontation
between the Mohawks and the provincial Quebec and federal Canadian
governments, which lasted almost three months. Does Obomsawin as an
Abenaki identify culturally with the Micmacs and the Mohawks? Can she
present *their* values, concerns, and attitudes with *her* subjective way of
seeing? If one takes two of her other films, *Mother of Many Children*
(1977) and *No Address* (1988), other influencing factors become visible.
The first is a film about women in different Indigenous nations. Can Obomsawin as an Indigenous woman express values, concerns, and attitudes of
other Indigenous women with *her* subjective angle of vision? Does she, in
order to do this, adapt *her* subjective view to that of *other* Indigenous
women, if that is possible at all? *No Address* is a film about the lives and
needs of homeless Indigenous people in Montreal. Does Obomsawin as an
Indigenous person from another class identify with the situation of homeless people there? And can she thus present their values and concerns? It is
easy to see, then, that Obomsawin's films are not bio-documentaries, but
that a bio-documentary is a film about the maker's own culture and/or environment. But often Indigenous filmmakers grew up alienated from their
own culture – they may have been raised in another nation, another part of
the country, in an urban environment, or even with non-Indigenous foster
parents. Can these filmmakers still represent a culture-specific subjective
way of seeing? I believe that the decision whether a film can be classified
as bio-documentary should depend on the content, focus, and style of the
respective film – and on the political, social, and cultural factors that influence the making of the film as well. To come back to the initial question of

whether or not *Itam Hakim, Hopiit* can be considered as a bio-documentary, I would suggest that it can be regarded as such in view of the guidelines that Worth provides.

Discussion of the bio-documentary leads to the question of how Masayesva's film differs from conventional documentary films.[159] A number of critics (Bahn–Coblans, Sands and Sekaquaptewa Lewis, Tobing Rony) agree that *Itam Hakim, Hopiit* is not a documentary in the conventional sense of focussing on factual information or instruction.[160] Instead, it focusses on cyclical events in nature and in the Hopi horticultural and ceremonial year and presents ritual not as an analyzed aspect of Hopi life but as an essential element for Hopi survival on the arid land. It avoids 'talking–heads' sequences; the shots of Macaya talking do not feature him in a 'head-to-shoulder shot' where he looks in the direction of the camera lens but, rather, from oblique angles or from the side and/or with his face in half-shade. They always present him as embedded in his environment – his house, his audience, the mesa. The film does not contain explanatory voice-over narration nor any interview sequences (Macaya's narration is not an interview). Its slow editing pace, the long takes, the contemplative imagery, and the lingering soundtrack (except in the Spanish-conquest and dance sequences) lend the film a special atmosphere which seems to mirror a Hopi understanding of time and space. Paula Gunn Allen holds that "those reared in traditional American Indian societies are inclined to relate events and experiences to one another [...] and view space as spherical and time as cyclical."[161] Masayesva translates this spherical space and cyclical time into his film. The special atmosphere is created by image composition, camera work, editing pace, sound, and several other techniques. Masayesva employs his visual imagery holistically to show the space in which the

---

[159] In discussing conventional documentary, it is useful to provide an idea of what the term 'conventional documentary' means in this context. I base my comments on Leuthold: "Assumedly, traditional documentary refers to a 'talking heads' format which consists of a great deal of onscreen narration and interview sequences and a linear narrative structure" ("An Indigenous Aesthetic?" 47). Of course, Beaver's definition applies as well: "A nonfiction film. Documentaries are usually shot on location, use actual persons rather than actors, and focus thematically on historical, scientific, social, or environmental subjects." (Beaver, *Dictionary of Film Terms*, 119).

[160] Kathleen M. Sands & Allison Sekaquaptewa Lewis, "Seeing with a Native Eye," 393.

[161] Paula Gunn Allen, *The Sacred Hoop: Recovering the Feminine in American Indian Traditions* (Boston MA: Beacon Press, 1986): 58–59, quoted in Sonja Bahn–Coblans, "Reading with an Eurocentric Eye the 'Seeing with a Native Eye': Victor Masayesva's *Itam Hakim, Hopiit*," *Studies in American Indian Literatures* 8.4 (Winter 1996): 50.

Hopi, particularly Macaya and his audience, exist. He also renders the cycles of natural forces and corn that shape Hopi time. This creation of spherical space and cyclical time is precisely what Robert Silberman calls romantic:

> Masayesva's videos are romantic in outlook and basically similar in form to standard documentaries, leading one to conclude that Masayesva has incorporated the dominant culture's romantic view of Indians into his own videos.[162]

Silberman bases his claim on the fact that Masayesva avoids any sign of modern civilization in his film (there are no stores, no television sets, no machine tools, no modern institutions, seldom cars), thus deliberately presenting a traditional way of Hopi living. Silberman further criticizes Masayesva's "sweetness" and "sentimentality" in the presentation of old people, children, and landscape, defining such a "pantribal aesthetic rooted in views of nature and the idealization of the past" as a "re-assimilation of a romanticized non-Indian aesthetic."[163]

I hope to have shown with the previous analysis that the argument that Masayesva employs a conventional documentary or ethnographic film style is invalid.[164] It is much harder to deal with the argument that he re-appropriates a Western romanticized notion about an Indian nature ethic and mythic past. To start with, Silberman is right to argue that Masayesva excludes familiar elements of modern civilization from his film. This fact is reminiscent of the Navajo films of 1966. However, the filmmaker does *not* painstakingly remove every sign of modern civilization from the Hopi space: i.e. there are a kerosene lamp, tins, a metal bunk, an axe, a metal planting stick, a clothesline, a stove, a fridge, a pickup truck, a plough, several pairs of modern shoes, and contemporary clothes. He does *not*, as ethnographic filmmakers have repeatedly done, stage traditional Indigenous life but films Macaya's environment as it is. This is a film about a tradi-

---

[162] Robert Silberman, "Victor Masayesva and the Question of a Native American Aesthetic," paper presented at College Art Association Conference, Chicago, 1992, paraphrased in Steven Leuthold, "An Indigenous Aesthetic? Two Noted Videographers: George Burdeau and Victor Masayesva," *Wicazo Sa Review* 10.1 (Spring 1994): 45.

[163] Silberman, "Victor Masayesva and the Question of a Native American Aesthetic," quoted in Leuthold, "An Indigenous Aesthetic?" 46.

[164] Leuthold discusses at length the danger of applying the concept of a Western conventional documentary to non-Western modes of communication: i.e. Indigenous filmmaking ("An Indigenous Aesthetic?" 40–51).

tional man and the cultural knowledge he imparts, hence Masayesva picks out elements of Hopi life that are still done in traditional ways (also by Macaya himself) partly with modern tools. The reverence for the portrayal of the old man and the children springs from Indigenous philosophy, which places a high value on the young and the elderly.[165] Their special relationship stems from the traditional way of the elders teaching the young ones, which is also the topic of the film. Obviously, Masayesva did not intend to make a documentary about the Hopi nation as a political body with government-built houses, schools, banks, and a tribal office. Furthermore, there is probably no school, store, or any other public building in Macaya's immediate surroundings. Silberman criticizes the film's "longing for an idyllic, mythic, legendary past in the face of the increasingly impersonal, secular, industrial, and urban life that developed during the 19th and 20th centuries."[166] But he overlooks here the fact that instead of ongoing colonization and westernization of Indigenous cultures, the Hopi are still a very secluded and traditional people. They have not yet incorporated the concept of an American-style constitution[167] and government, they have excluded tourists from their ceremonial dances, they have kept traditional forms of life to a large extent, they certainly do not enjoy the economic advantages of industrialization (the coal mining on Hopi territories is just another aspect of cultural and economic exploitation and is still in the hands of private corporations and/or under federal control),[168] and they definitely have not experienced any urbanization of their communities. Thus, the human alienation in industrial and urbanized areas that Silberman is talking about can hardly apply to the Hopi. When Silberman claims that this film expresses a longing for an idyllic and romanticized past in contrast to a fast-paced, industrial, and urban life-style, one has to ask who is influenced by this fast-paced, industrial life and is seeking some ersatz religion in a mythic Indigenous past and traditional lifeways – certainly not the storyteller and the filmmaker. Leuthold discusses the irreconcilable Western and Indigenous views of certain shots of landscapes, cultural and religious activities, portraits etc. that are branded 'romantic' and 'visionary' respectively:

---

[165] Leuthold, "An Indigenous Aesthetic?" 46.
[166] "An Indigenous Aesthetic?" 46.
[167] Alfonso Ortiz, "The Dynamics of Pueblo Cultural Survival," 301.
[168] The Hopi Tribe – Office of Mining and Mineral Resources at http://www.hopi.nsn.us/mining.asp

The problem, then, is one of understanding what "romantic" might mean within the context of native ethno-aesthetics, within native views of the relationship between art and life. In a paradoxical collapsing of different aesthetic and ethical systems, natives take the very characteristics that non-natives associate with romanticism – reverent shots of the land, homage to tradition, themes of spirituality and family – as some of the essential ingredients of a native way of seeing. This is what the transference of a Western critical perspective leaves out: the possibility of a different aesthetic, and ethical, system.[169]

Masayesva explains that he did not intend to project any romantic picture of the peaceful and harmonious Hopi. In the first part, Macaya tells of a conflict-ridden period in Hopi history, and his description of the Pueblo Revolt also dispels any romantic view of the Hopi. Masayesva says:

> The description [in the first part] was about a time when Hopi attacked other Hopi people. They killed them and destroyed that village. That was my way of declaring to the Hopi audience and eventually to who ever might ask that this is going to be different. I'm not going to treat us as the people of peace and harmony, we've killed each other in the past. (interview, 2001)

Robert Nelson uses the term "geographical realism" to describe an element that often exists in texts by Indigenous authors. He suggests:

> As fictions, these texts take as an inviolable referent the physical landscape, one that exists prior to the fiction and then comes to exist (the way referents can be said to "exist") within the fiction as well. For both the writer creating the fiction and the fictional protagonist discovering or creating violable identity, the physical landscape functions in these works as a dependable constant.[170]

These writers, as well as Masayesva, take what Arnold Krupat calls a "geocentric" and "indigenist" approach. In line with Vine Deloria, Krupat explains that there are discrete principles governing the writings of a group of Indigenous authors, principles which are "said to derive from the special relationship to the land that indigenous peoples everywhere are presumed to share."[171] This indigenist world-view exists side by side with a nationalist and cosmopolitan world-view and does not present *the* Indigenous ap-

---

[169] Steven Leuthold, *Indigenous Aesthetics*, 120.

[170] Robert M. Nelson, *Place and Vision: The Function of Landscape in Native American Fiction*, vol. 1 (New York: Peter Lang, 1993): 6.

[171] Arnold Krupat, "Nationalism, Indigenism, Cosmopolitanism: Critical Perspectives on Native American Literatures," *Centennial Review* 42.3 (Fall 1998): 620.

proach. Krupat cites Arif Dirlik, who holds that the indigenist approach
does not simply draw on the spiritual relationship to the land but that this
"ecological sensibility" also "calls for a transformation of the spatial ar-
rangements of colonialism or postcolonialism. Indigenism [...] challenges
[...] the system of economic relations that provides the ultimate context for
social and political relationships: capitalist or state socialist."[172]

The label 'romanticism' is an oversimplified generalization that neglects
an inherent bond between the people and the natural world, a cyclical way
of life, dictated by natural forces, which still applies to many Hopi people,
and a holistic philosophy which many Indigenous people still respect. Because it is hard, if not impossible, for a Western mind to grasp this concept,
Western thought often applies the closest approximating concept it has for
such a phenomenon, which is the negatively weighted term 'romanticism'.
Similarly, as many Western people have lost a certain connectedness to the
land and a holistic philosophy, or believe that Western culture has lost
them, many Western people romanticize this aspect of Indigenous belief
and synchronized way of life, which is otherwise largely disapproved of by
academia. But it is erroneous to simply transfer the criticism of Western
romanticizing of Indigenous culture and philosophy to an Indigenous context, thereby constructing an ostensibly Indigenous romanticizing of Indigenous culture. No doubt the latter exists, but autoromanticization should be
treated differently from heteroromanticization; the same critical framework
of the one phenomenon should not be imposed on the view of the other.
Neither phenomenon should be homogenized; both need to be seen in relation to the specific contexts in which they occur. Non-Indigenous scholars
should take care not to try and squeeze patterns related to territorial ethos
and holistic philosophy, in whatever Indigenous expressive genre or medium, into approximating Western concepts; modern Western thought does
not have a framework with which to conceptualize these. Both groups, one
denying and the other affirming such a territorial ethos and holistic philosophy, risk overriding and misrepresenting Indigenous beliefs. Further, it is
illogical to reproach an Indigenous filmmaker who has grown up immersed

---

[172] Arif Dirlik, "The Past as Legacy and Project: Postcolonial Criticism in the Perspective
of Indigenous Historicism," *American Indian Culture and Research Journal* 20.2 (1996): 21,
quoted in Arnold Krupat, "Nationalism, Indigenism, Cosmopolitanism: Critical Perspectives
on Native American Literatures," *Centennial Review* 42.3 (Fall 1998): 621. Cf., further,
Leuthold, who brings the aspect of land control and access to physical locations into the discussion (Leuthold, "An Indigenous Aesthetic?" 50).

in his culture, who speaks his traditional language, and who, while doing his work, maintains very close ties to his community, with expropriating a romanticized Western construct of an Indigenous territorial ethos when he never lost his own in the first place.

Final Remarks

At the end of the film, Macaya comments on the necessity of filming oral accounts in order to preserve them for future generations: "I have told you a lot, and you have learned a lot. These stories have to be recorded in order for the children to remember them. The children will see them and improve them. That's how it will be. It won't stop anywhere."[173] With these re-marks, the narrative most notably crosses over into a metanarrative that de-scribes and comments on the film. Here and in remarks throughout the film, Macaya asserts his position as storyteller and authoritative instance (the narrative role). The remarks also legitimize the purpose of this film and position it firmly among the voices who call for the translation of oral tradition into film to preserve cultural knowledge, even at the risk of freez-ing this tradition inflexibly in a single moment. The last part underscores the fact that in oral tradition accounts are constantly 'under construction', incorporating improvements that might result from political, economic, social, and cultural changes. The last sentence echoes the circular structure of the film and stresses the cyclical and continuous nature of the oral tradition.

Masayesva presents his subject-matter with camera work that does not allow scrutiny and romanticization and simultaneously counters ethnogra-phic filmmaking. He makes extensive use of high and low angles, mobile frames, long shots, extreme long shots, and close-ups, and is inclined to avoid establishing shots. Accordingly, he applies a 'synchronization of senses' by combining a steady soothing sound with a slow rhythm of con-templative, often organic images, creating a tonality that runs counter to standard notions of a documentary. Although his images most often seem to spring from artistic photography, he does not apply an artistic approach purposely. Posterization, fast-motion effects, and visual and sound-breaks

---

[173] Personal translation of the following statement in the German version: "Ich habe eine Menge erzählt, und ihr habt eine Menge gelernt. Diese Geschichten sollen aufgezeichnet werden, damit die Kinder sich an sie erinnern. Diese Kinder werden sie sehen und sie noch verbessern. So wird es sein. Es wird nirgends aufhören" (Victor Masayesva, Jr., dir./prod./ writ., *Itam Hakim, Hopiit*, USA, 1984).

are stylistic features that are employed for certain purposes. However, any other filmmaker would be prepared to use these techniques. They are thus part of Masayesva's filmmaking style for this film, but cannot be seen as a certain filmmaking aesthetic. His visual imagery of carefully composed shots presents cyclical Hopi life and the natural surroundings. Again, this cyclical pattern in Masayesva's films is rooted in the Hopi conception of time and their synchronization of the horticultural and ceremonial year with the cycle of the land. Along with the mnemonic verbal patterns contained in Macaya's talk and chants, Masayesva creates mnemonic visual patterns, recurring compositional elements such as the horizontal line and the motifs of corn, corn plants, rain, water, and animals. Cinematographic mnemonic patterns are the frequent zooms, pans, and tilts, dissolves between most shots, and the considerable number of long shots and close-ups.

Masayesva says that an Indigenous film aesthetic is influenced by traditional forms of expression; or, to him, there is a clear connection between oral tradition and the technologized medium of film: "If we indigenous filmmakers were to showcase our differences, we would infuse film with the same reverence which we have for our oral and performing traditions."[174] He holds that the oral tradition – not only narrative forms but also "dance, song, ritual, ceremony and worship" – corresponds best to film. Masayesva himself sketches what he believes an Indigenous film aesthetic may be:

> Rejecting the Hollywood blueprint, we will find alternatives to a cuts-only format and explore special optics instead of prime lenses. Native language would be essential to this expression of the Native American experience. Character motivation would reflect our understanding of the world. The technical conventions of filmmaking would shift, evidenced in how we use a 360° pan to tell a story, rather than show facility in a physically complicated move; where we begin and end a sequence without drawing attention to complicated dolly track configurations, but showing why motion must follow a certain order; how we look at motion itself; how the transition between the events are not clichés – shots of moving cars to reach the next set or situation – but expressions of the rhythms of a unique order: falling rain, a newborn foal, mature grasslands, or a personal object or item infused with ancient meaning. This new film logic driving the Native American aesthetic

---

[174] Victor Masayesva, Jr., "The Emerging Native American Aesthetics in Film and Video," 20.

would permeate technique, style, dramatic continuity; narrative would begin, conclude, cut, and be extended without didacticism.[175]

Masayesva's assessment of a possible Indigenous film aesthetic is born out
of his own filmic work, particularly *Hopiit* and *Itam Hakim, Hopiit*.[176] The
slow editing pace, long takes, dissolves, and fragmentary filmmaking run
counter to a conventional 'cuts-only' format, while the use of the Hopi language with subtitles limits any linguistic colonialist infiltration of the film.
The depictions of Macaya embedded in his cultural context, together with
images telling of the unique Hopi order of existence, make for an essential
electronic chronicle of Hopi oral knowledge.

᭐ ᭥

---

[175] Masayesva, Jr., "The Emerging Native American Aesthetics in Film and Video," 21.

[176] Masayesva's other films, such as *Imagining Indians* (USA, 1992), *Pot Starr* (USA,
n.d.), and *Ritual Clowns* (USA, 1988), betray a style that does not correspond to the two
films' slow, lingering imagery. Here, he experiments with animation, visual metaphors, color
frames, speed, and several images in one frame.

4 Short Films

T HIS CHAPTER looks at the characteristics of three Indigenous short films and explores how decolonizing strategies manifest themselves in this genre. Short films have long lost their minor status as fillers and films preceding features in movie theatre programs. They have now become a frequented cinematic medium. Their presentation is largely restricted to film festivals and minor, often independent, distribution. For some Indigenous filmmakers, the short-film genre has proven to be a stepping-stone to feature films (e.g., Chris Eyre). Short films require far lower budgets than feature films and independent filmmakers can experiment with and explore film drama without being compelled to enter into cooperation with non-Indigenous filmmakers and film companies for financial reasons. In this way, colonialist influence can be limited to the means of production in the direct process of creation. The following three films were all made by independent Indigenous filmmakers and partly with their own small Indigenous production companies.

Talker

Talker (Canada, 1996) is a 13-minute short film produced by the Cree film-maker Lloyd Martell. The film won a 1995 National Screen Institute Drama Prize and the Golden Sheaf Award for Best Sound and Best Saskatchewan Production at the 1996 Yorkton Short Film and Video Festival.[1] It is a Cree myth adapted to a modern context and constructed with symbolism and metaphoric meanings. Martell explains in an interview:

---

[1] N S I Drama Prize Teams at http://www.nsi-canada.ca/dramaprize/participants.html; Talking Dog Studios at http://www.talkingdogstudios.com/awards/

> In Cree history there is a character called Weesaykeechak, the trickster. The trickster always teaches a lesson. [...] I took the trickster myth, and it was a little bit adapted, and it takes the outline of a trickster story. The traditional story that I relied upon is a story about how you have to be careful when you tell someone else's story. The whole intent was to try a trickster myth on the film community, and tell the film community that they have to be careful when they tell someone else's story, that maybe they're shutting those people out by telling their story and making up their own. I took that trickster myth and I put it into a modern-day context, and told it. (1998)

By translating this trickster myth into film, Martell connects the Indigenous oral tradition with contemporary techniques of communication. Here electronic media as a secondary orality are established as a way to preserve and pass on traditional oral culture – primary orality – as well as to transform it into a political instrument and means of cultural expression.

On a first viewing, the film seems to have nothing to do with Indigenous issues, for there is no Indigenous character in the plot. But a closer look reveals that the plot serves as a metaphor for the silencing of Indigenous voices in the mainstream filmmaking community and mainstream society in general. The film tells the story of a cab driver (played by a non-Indigenous actor) who feels isolated and needs human contact. He needs to talk to somebody but encounters only rejection. He seizes an opportunity to be hired as a talk therapist in a mental-health clinic – but again does not get to talk at all. The receptionist and the doctor who hires him do not let him talk and often answer for him. Even the mental patient to whom the cab driver is supposed to give psychological treatment through talking does the talking for him, because the cab driver has been instructed not to say anything. Significantly, the film *Talker* depicts a person hired as a 'talker' who does not get to say a single word throughout the whole film. In order to emphasize this fact, words associated with 'talking' are often repeated in the dialogue. 'Talker' occurs four times, 'talk' or 'talking' four times, 'say' four times, and 'tell', 'speak', and 'own voice' each once. These words ironically pinpoint the fact that the cab driver is not allowed to speak.

From the mise-en-scène, the viewer can deduce that the film is set in a city in winter. Since there are no shots that could provide opportunities to identify landmarks of the city where the film is set, it becomes clear that the narrative space is meant to remain opaque and serves as the stage for a metaphoric plot. Winter is chosen as narrative time to convey a sense of a harsh, cold, stoic reality as background for the plot and because winter is the time for storytelling in Indigenous cultures (interview with Martell, 1998). A magazine cover on a table in the common room has the title *The Year in Pictures 1972*. It may suggest that it is winter 1972/73 but it may as well be an old magazine. It transports the plot into a state of suspended time, as if, in this narrative space, time were standing still. As the narrative space, the exact narrative time is insignificant to the plot and serves to abstract the events of the film.

The detailed shot analysis in the Appendix serves to give a rough overview of the film's content but, even more, allows recognition of editing techniques, montage pattern, camera perspectives, distance, and movement. My detailed analysis in this chapter concentrates on the visual rather the sound.[2] Martell divides his film into four scenes by conventional fades: scene 1 – shots 2–22; scene 2 – shots 23–28; scene 3 – shots 29–47; and scene 4 – shots 48–79. The number 'four' is considered sacred and recurs in various Indigenous mythologies. For example, the medicine wheel has four sections and consists of four circles, the world consists of four basic elements (earth, water, fire, sky), there are four seasons, Indigenous cultures of the Southwest pray to four sacred mountains, and the mythologies of Southwestern cultures talk about four worlds the people had to pass in order to reach the fifth – the present – world. Thus the film's very structure, too, bears spiritual meaning and roots the film in Indigenous philosophy.

To specify montage patterns, one can assign different letters to the individual shots according to their visual content, like the analysis of rhyme schemes in poetry. This is done in the last column of the analysis table (Appendix); with each new scene the same letters are assigned anew. This breakdown of shots into repeating 'lines' reveals Martell's use of parallel montage in the first and fourth scenes. Silbermann, Schaaf, and Adam define parallel montage as follows:

> Connection of several shots, at least four, where one of the connected shots appears over and over again according to the same pattern after a certain succession of the others: i.e. the first (*anaphora*), the nth (*epiphora*), or the first and the nth (*complexio*).[3]

---

[2] A film shot consists of the interplay of image, dialogue, music, and background noises. However, I feel that an analysis of the visual level including mise-en-scène and cinematography are sufficient for my purpose.

[3] Personal translation of the following German statement: "Verbindung mehrerer Einstellungen, mindestens vier, bei der eine der verbundenen Einstellungen nach einer bestimmten Abfolge der anderen immer wieder in gleicher Weise erscheint; und zwar die erste (*Anapher*),

In the first scene, 'line' *a* (the cab driver's eyes with exactly the same camera distance, angle, and movement) appears four times after the succession of lines *b*, *c*, *d*, and *e*: it is an anaphoric montage pattern. At the same time it is an epiphoric pattern, for *d* (hooker and pimp in the back seat: camera distance remains the same; camera angle changes, but the camera moves only once), which is the nth shot, appears seven times after the succession of lines *a*, *b*, *c*, and *e*. Scene four employs a modified *complexio* pattern, for *c* and *d* alternate after the introductory *a* and *b*. Scenes two and three are cut together according to the pattern of simple associative montage or *annominatio*, which Silbermann, Schaaf, and Adam explain thus:

> It is technically the simplest of the montage patterns introduced here. Any kinds of shot with different content are linked via editing or superimposition. Only the effect of the succeeding visual content generates meaning through their connection.[4]

There are also detectable patterns at work in the use of the temporal length of shots. Shots that carry an important message are noticeably longer than the others, ranging between 19 and 52 seconds. These are shot 22, in which the pimp is spitting on the cab's windshield, shot 25, in which the cab driver reads a paper and a fly is annoying him, shot 27, in which he sees an ad and calls the mental hospital, shot 30, which shows his encounter with the mental-hospital receptionist, shots 36 and 37 in the common room, and finally shot 49, in which cab driver and patient meet. The three shots in which doctor, assistant, and cab driver descend a stairway (40–42) are of almost the same length, creating a consistent rhythm for the descent. In scene four, Martell applies accelerated montage between the alternating shots of the cab driver and the patient. Shots 50 through 67, except for three, have a length of between 4 and 20 seconds, the average length being 6.81 seconds. Thereafter, the length of the shots decreases markedly to 2 or 3 seconds in shots 68 to 78, the average being 2.52 seconds. The accelerated editing pattern imposes a faster pace on the film and works to heigh-

---

die n-te (*Epipher*) oder die erste und die n-te (*Complexio*)"; Alphons Silbermann, Michael Schaaf & Gerhard Adam, "Theoreme der Filmanalyse," in *Filmanalyse: Grundlagen – Methoden – Didaktik* (Munich: Oldenbourg, 1980): 53.

[4] Personal translation of the following German statement: "Von der Technik her gesehen ist sie die einfachste der vorgestellten Montagefiguren. Durch Schnitt oder Überblendung getrennt werden beliebige Einstellungen verschiedenen Inhalts gekoppelt. Allein die Wirkung der aufeinanderfolgenden Bildinhalte läßt diese bedeutungsmäßig in Verbindung treten" (Silbermann, Schaaf & Adam, "Theoreme der Filmanalyse," 55).

ten tension and to foreshadow the climax of the film – the joint scream of cab driver and patient at the end. In scene one, accelerated montage is used more obliquely, for the length of the shots featuring the cab driver's eyes (*a*) before he almost hits a woman on the sidewalk shrinks from 8.37 to 0.75 seconds and is 2.28 seconds after the incident. In the scenes of the cab driver's encounter with the pimp and hooker and later with the patient (both shot mainly in classical shot/reverse-shot pattern), the shots showing him (*a* and *c*) are generally shorter than those featuring the pimp and hooker (*d*) and the patient (*d*) respectively. This editing pattern reinforces the film's message that the cab driver does not speak but the others do.

There is no discernible pattern in the relation between camera distance and the temporal length of shots: i.e. one cannot say that long shots stay on the screen longer than medium shots and even longer than close-ups. However, one can say that the shots with important information (see above) are realized through considerable camera movement as well as different camera angles and positions. Thus, the mobile camera and varying camera angles and position further emphasize the content of the shots. They are almost all medium shots and medium close-ups, which is probably due to the fact that more than half of the shots in the film are medium shots (21) and medium close-ups (26), followed by close-ups (20), leaving only six long shots and seven extreme close-ups.

Throughout the film, Martell adheres to classical continuity. Only shots 37 (medium close-up) and 38 (close-up) are connected by a jump cut,[5]

---

[5] Unintentional jump cuts are considered poor editing among filmmakers, showing disregard for continuity. Hollywood narrative cinema, in particular, rules out jump cutting because it has a disconcerting effect. However, jump cuts are used by contemporary filmmakers to achieve various effects such as to startle the viewer, "to enliven the rhythm" (Bordwell & Thompson, *Film Art*, 403), or "to advance the action in a scene without regard for transitional devices (Beaver, *Dictionary of Film Terms*, 202). "Time-shattering jump cuts" are employed to express "the scrambled life-styles of modern screen characters" (Beaver, *Dictionary of Film Terms*, 201). Jean–Luc Godard, in *À bout de souffle* [*Breathless*] (1960), uses jump cuts to bring rhythm into a monologue by Michel, his main character. The jump cuts also result from Godard's *nouvelle vague* disregard for classical film conventions. Martell employs the jump cut to focus on the medium of film itself and to stress the camera gaze. He destroys the illusion that film presents a reality, which conventional filmmaking normally creates, and alienates the viewer from his/her expectations of film in the sense of the Brechtian *Verfremdungseffekt* (see previous chapter, fn 183). In this sense, he also makes the viewer uncomfortable and foreshadows the inconvenient message of the film. The jump cuts may also be used as a device to play around with mainstream film critics' notion that Indigenous filmmaking is unprofessional – a notion, of course, that is based on half-truths. On the one hand, the tradition of Indigenous filmmaking is very young and has to cope with scant regard and systemic

where the head of the doctor seems to be 'jumping' at the viewer. It repeats formally the content of shot 37, in which the doctor startles the waiting cab driver by his sudden appearance. Martell applies classical reverse-angle shooting, adhering to the 180° system (also part of the continuity approach) in shots 2 through 8, 15 through 21, and 50 through 78. This reverse-angle shooting is crucial for introducing the viewer to the spatial relations of the scene and to create an axis of action between the respective characters. In addition to reverse-angle shooting, in the fourth scene the camera distance is crucial to the effect generated. The change of distance, from medium shot to medium close-up to close-up to extreme close-up, has the camera, and subsequently the viewer, move closer and closer to the faces of the characters. It implies that the characters' facial expressions become more crucial for the message of the shots. The intruding camera gaze mimics the observant look of the doctor and serves as a metaphor for intrusion of any kind into the characters' minds.

The extreme facial close-ups imply that the camera and subsequently the viewer can look into the psyche of the respective persons. The series of extreme close-up shots 2, 8, 10, and 16 (Figs. 3.1–3.4) discloses through

---

barriers. The fact that some films may seem contrived, flat, trite, or amateurish is often due to very limited budgets and the inexperience of filmmakers. Such flaws can be easily tolerated in regard to the unique situation of postcolonial filmmakers who have to assimilate to and meet the expectations of mainstream filmmaking in order to find acceptance. At the same time, they want to gain public attention for the Indigenous experience and create a space for it in the mainstream media. On the other hand, there are many examples that prove the opposite (e.g., Alanis Obomsawin, Doug Cuthand, Loretta Todd, Chris Eyre) and show that flaws and amateurish weaknesses belong to the previous stage in the development of Indigenous filmmaking, which has now passed. Martell's jump cut could have been used to rebel against or stretch conventional filmmaking rules. Last but not least, the use of jump cuts by an experienced filmmaker like Martell can be understood as part of an "Indigenous film code." This goes back to the 1966 "Navajos Film Themselves" project, where untrained Navajos made a few films with the startlingly extensive use of jump cuts, which exemplified their way of perceiving the environment. The jump cuts in these films mirrored part of their lives and suggest a different cognitive pattern in Indigenous cultures; Sol Worth & John Adair, *Through Navajo Eyes: An Exploration in Film Communication and Anthropology* (1972; Albuquerque: U of New Mexico P, 1997): 171–75, 284. The Métis filmmaker Marjorie Beaucage says in an interview: "And jump cuts, and all those kinds of things are not important ... they don't matter, they [Innu people who, under the direction of Beaucage, made two videos to express their voice in the struggle against the Voisey's Bay Nickel Company, which attempted to begin nickel mining in the territory where Innu people live] don't even see them. [...] So what if it's the same shot? We are creating an illusion that life is seamless .... See, that's the thing, just have an illusion, video is all an illusion .... So, my life isn't perfect, my life jumps around too" (unpublished interview, 1998).

the cab driver's eyes how his state of mind changes from being calm, to nervous and alert, to being startled and horrified because he almost hit the woman, and finally to being emotionally drained after the incident. Shots 75 and 76 (Figs. 3.5–3.6) are reverse-angle shots, taken in extreme close-up, of the cab driver's and patient's eyes. Their eyes reveal fright and terror, as both release their frustration and mental despair in a joint scream. In accord with these extreme facial close-ups, Martell employs reaction shots. The technique of extreme facial close-ups is applied fairly often by filmmakers (e.g., Ingmar Bergman[6]) in trying to explore the psychological states of their characters. The close-ups further transmit a sense of the camera, and the viewer, encroaching upon the character.

In five shots (4, 14, 19, 25, 27), a rear-view mirror frames the eyes of the respective people. These shots also enhance the effect of looking into the mind of a person, for the camera concentrates on the eyes as a main vehicle for facial expression and as 'door to the mind'. In shot 25 (Fig. 3.7), the camera shows the inside of the car and the cab driver with half of his head from behind. The main point of focus, the cab driver's eyes, is concentrated on the small frame-segment of the rear-view mirror, which shows how the cab driver is tensely following the fly with his eyes and looking annoyed at the tramps beside his car. Further, these rear-view mirror shots become a visual motif and enable composition in depth. For example, shot 4 (Fig. 3.8) shows the streets through the cab's windshield and the eyes of pimp and hooker in the rear-view mirror. Another example of deep-space photography[7] is shot 35 (Fig. 3.9), a low-angle long shot that takes in the full length of the main hallway of the hospital. Here, the deep-space photography permits four different actions to take place on four planes of one axis – the hospital hallway: a male nurse wheeling a stretcher in the front, the receptionist at her desk, the cab driver walking down the hallway, and a person in a white coat moving around in the back. Similarly, deep-focus

---

[6] I am referring here mainly to *Viskningar och Rop* [*Cries and Whispers*] (Sweden, 1972) and *Persona* (Sweden, 1966).

[7] For the concept of deep-space photography, see Beaver, *Dictionary of Film Terms*, 103, and Bordwell & Thompson, *Film Art*, 195–96 and 220–21. It is not to be confused with deep-focus photography, in which all actions on the various planes are in sharp focus (see the glossary in the Appendix). Classic examples of deep-focus photography (implemented by its inventor, the cinematographer Gregg Toland) can be found in Orson Welles' *Citizen Kane* (USA, 1941), mainly the scenes in which the contract is signed, in which a dinner on a long table takes places, in which young Kane is signed over to his guardian, and in which Kane and his wife are positioned far apart in their huge church-like living room.

photography allows the filmmaker to provide visual information on several planes within a single shot, the difference being the focus. Examples of deep-focus photography in Martell's film are shot 27 (Fig. 3.10), which shows the back of the cab driver's head in the front plane, the dashboard and his eyes in the rear-view mirror on the middle plane, and the approaching tramps on the rear plane, and shot 36 (Fig. 3.11), which painstakingly reveals all the items in the common room on different planes.

Some of the film shots exhibit a striking symmetry, also called bilateral symmetry.[8] Shot 29 frames the entrance and part of the hospital building symmetrically, making it appear as an unwelcoming castle. The low-angle long shot of the hallway (35) is almost symmetrical vertically and horizontally, so that the vanishing point, the end of the hallway to where the cab driver moves, is in the middle of the frame. Martell also tends to arrange the figures in compositional balance. The heads of pimp and hooker fill out either side of the rear-view mirror in shots 4 (Fig. 3.8) and 19. Shots 5 (Fig. 3.12) and 7 frame them in such a way that the distance between them is the same as the distance between either head and frame margin. In shots 41, 42, and 45, Martell arranges the doctor, his assistant, and the cab driver with a similar symmetry. The visual symmetry in the shots is taken up in the cinematography of some parts of the film. Shots 50 through 78 are symmetrical owing to the reverse-angle shooting, camera distance, camera movement, camera direction, and camera perspective of the alternating shots. This symmetry becomes most obvious in shots 77 (Figs. 3.13–3.14) and 78 (Figs. 3.15–3.16), in which the camera first focusses extremely closely upon the eyes and then tilts down to reveal the screaming mouth of both patient and cab driver. After the reverse-angle shooting between the faces of cab driver and patient, Martell cuts to an ashtray made of clay in the shape of a face with an open mouth (Fig. 3.17). The match cut to the ashtray complements the graphic match between the screaming faces of cab driver and patient and stresses the mental terror they experience. As occasional graphic matches, bilateral symmetry, compositional balance, and reverse-angle shooting ensure graphic continuity in the film.

Martell uses many high and low camera angles to convey a sense of looking at things from oppositional and unnatural perspectives. First of all, such extreme camera angles put the viewer in a more detached observer-

---

[8] On bilateral symmetry and compositional balance, see Bordwell & Thompson, *Film Art*, 191.

like position, further stressing the medium of film and disrupting the illusion that film presents reality by utilizing an alienation effect similar to the
one Brecht created. Secondly, these camera angles leave the viewer outside
of the filmic events, contrasting with Hollywood film practice, which
usually attempts to draw the viewer into the filmic events and thus blur the
division between reality and filmic fiction. Thirdly, this technique explores
unusual points of view, suggesting ways of seeing that differ from straight-
on viewing and that are used to create a certain atmosphere. The very low
angle in shot 35 (Fig. 3.9) has the figures on the different planes appear
taller than they are. The vertical lines of the hallway, such as door frames,
walls, and pillars, are mirrored in the polished floor, so that the hallway
seems to be higher and narrower than it is. The doubling of the length of
vertical lines and the deep-space photography create a claustrophobic effect
by having it appear like a long tunnel. Fourthly, the high and low angles
exemplify secondary camera looks. In shot 36 (Fig. 3.11), the high angle
out of one ceiling corner of the common room suggests that the camera is
an observation device filming the cab driver's reactions to various items in
the room and the doctor's sudden appearance.

Shots 22, 30, 37, 43, 47, and 49 indicate that Martell tends to apply
dolly shots, tilts, and pans where cuts would also have been appropriate.
Together with high and low angles, these camera movements present characters and mise-en-scène elements in an unusual way. The cab driver is
introduced in shot 2 with only his eyes framed in the rear-view mirror; and
until shot 27 the viewers get only to see his eyes and the back of his head.
The full man is shown in shot 28 in scene two, but the shot is from an extreme high angle. Shot 29 shows him from a straight angle walking towards
the hospital entrance, but from behind. Shot 30 scrutinizes him through
close-ups of body parts. It starts with the camera focussed on the cab
driver's feet in front of the reception desk. Then the camera tilts up waist-
high until it reaches his right hand clutching the newspaper, stays there for
a while, then pans right to reveal items on the desk, moves further right to
show a pencil sharpener in the hands of the receptionist, whose head is
shown through a last tilt (Figs. 3.18–3.21). Shot 39, halfway through the
film, shows the main character's whole face and shot 43 is the first time the
whole person is shown facing the camera at a straight angle. This fragmentary or metonymic introduction of the main character and his full presentation rather late in the film, supported by camera movement and extreme
angles, counters the general Hollywood practice of introducing characters

at the beginning and with a variety of shots that can sufficiently describe them.[9] Martell's mobile framing also plays out in shot 49, which is a 360° track shot. The camera is positioned in a corner of the room, focussed on the strapped patient in the right upper frame, with the figure of the cab driver blurred in the left lower frame. Then it moves to the right around the patient and the table, never letting the patient out of focus, until it is fixed again in the same corner of the room in the same position and focus where it started, having described a whole circle.

Throughout the film, Martell employs extreme high-key lighting, which reinforces the sense of coldness introduced through the setting. Also, the light illuminates every little nook and cranny, so that nothing can evade the camera's eye. The hallway and the stairway of the hospital are bathed in bright light, and when the cab driver reaches the door behind which the patient is waiting for him, his silhouette vanishes into the darkness of the fade-out. The room in the cellar where patient and cab driver meet is less brightly lit, and thick beams of light from outside divide the room. The extreme high-key lighting in the upper floors of the hospital, especially on the stairway (Figs. 3.22–3.24), is juxtaposed with the low-key lighting in the basement (Fig. 3.25) and thus characterizes both spaces as different worlds. Martell comments on his use of light:

> I used a lot of light because I wanted to really show what was actually there; [...] there was one stairway which had to symbolize the descent of the characters, the descent of the characters from the real world, their real world that they lived in, into this ... almost like a dungeon. It was so critical that that light was put in that stairway, because that was like an avenue of hope for the character, an avenue of opportunity. I wanted that to be bright like the light of the end of the tunnel. And he [the cab driver] entered into that and followed that light. And in going up to that light he ended up in this darkness. (interview, 1998)

Martell achieves an outstanding quality of high-key lighting with lighting equipment that is unusual for a low-budget short film. His shifts between very high-key and low-key lighting are an outstanding characteristic of his film.

The main sound in the first and second scene, which is carried through the rest of the film as a minor soundtrack, is a mixture of radio broadcast, the cab's C B radio, and the whispering voices in the head of the cab driver.

---

[9] Of course, there are also exceptions to this general statement.

This mixture alone is auditory stress. In the third scene, voices of tramps, of people talking, and of children laughing are added to this mixture. Characteristic screams in the mental hospital while the cab driver is waiting in the common room further test his mental endurance. This mixture of sound and voices returns in the fourth scene and is completed with the sound of a buzzing fly. Already very disturbing and nerve-wracking for the viewer, the sound reflects the cab driver's increasingly enervated state of mind and matches the message of the visuals. The sounds in the hospital become amplified in the cab driver's head and mix with his inner voices. These voices and sounds compensate for the silence of society and become louder and louder. They bounce back and forth between the patient's and the cab driver's minds, as suggested by the oscillating sound. The cab driver would need to talk to release the voices, lest they drive him mad, but he cannot. He is ordered not to talk by the printed instructions handed to him earlier. The patient becomes disturbed because the talk therapist does not speak to him. This drives both of them over the edge, and the sounds and voices in their heads explode into a joint scream.

Some mise-en-scène elements carry a symbolic message. White miniature shoes dangling from the rear-view mirror in the cab foreshadow the cab driver's dealing with a doctor and hospital. A buzzing fly often symbolically indicates a character's poor state of nerves; the annoying fly in scene two does this, foreshadowing dealings with a mental institution. A mobile with clowns and a doll's-head sharpener, clichéd as they might seem, suggest that people (here Indigenous people) are simply puppets in a larger society where invisible forces pull the strings. The introductory shot of the second scene starts by showing snowy roofs, then slowly tilts down to show the sign of a Western Furs Ltd. store, as well as the large painted store name above the door. Here, the sign and letters are employed as a metonym of the Canadian fur-trade era, when the colonization of Indigenous people and the first serious changes in traditional pre-contact societies began.[10] It thus serves as a reference to Canada's colonial past.[11]

The mental clinic is a metaphorical construct of a dehumanized society; the doctor, his assistants, and the receptionist are its executive powers. A pimp, a hooker, and homeless people – themselves outcasts of society – are

---

[10] For the fur-trade era, see fn 33 in this chapter.

[11] Although the film occludes the narrative space, an analytical approach that includes the production of a work allows this conclusion because Martell is Canadian and the film's reception occurs mainly in Canada, save for screenings at International Film Festivals.

used to design a background for the character's alienation. It is interesting
that the hooker is a transvestite and the pimp is a woman. With this cast,
Martell plays with the viewers' expectations and defies clichéd notions of
people in the prostitution business. He also relates to recent tendencies in
the Indigenous sex trade, where it is not unusual for pimps to be women
and for hookers to choose their own pimps.[12] The filmmaker purposely
chose a mental-health clinic as a metaphor for control and surveillance in
society, because psychiatrists are most able to influence and manipulate
people's minds (interview, 1998), thus also referring to mental colonization. This metaphor is sustained in the sequence in which the receptionist
sharpens a pencil with a doll's-head sharpener. The camera is trained on the
head, which is turned around and around in the receptionist's hands, the
pencil poking into the 'ear' of the sharpener (Fig. 3.20). Similarly clichéed,
it yet visualizes symbolically the fact that most citizens are controlled by a
political and economic elite and are subject to manipulation by them. The
metaphor even suggests that this society does not want to deal with the
problems of the individual, for the receptionist fakes an automated message
manager. She could talk to the people who call but is ordered not to. By
exaggerating the message of this sequence, the filmmaker makes fun of
these automated message systems but also implies how civil and social
services and individuals become more and more alienated in contemporary
society. The rejection of the individual by society is epitomized by the
receptionist, who shrugs and says: "People, who can deal with them?" Both
the patient and the cab driver become the guinea pigs for the doctor's experiments with the human mind – when the cab driver is left alone in the
common room, his movements are recorded. He is startled by the doctor's
sudden appearance, is later (mis) guided by the brief insufficient instructions as to what he has to do as a 'talker', and is finally confused and
angered by the order not to say anything. Thus, the doctor is testing out the
point at which the cab driver will break. The patient also tries to manipulate
the cab driver by telling a sick story. The contrast between the (extreme)
high-key lighting in the clinic and the low-key lighting in its cellar stands in
for a metaphorical world and underworld and their respective 'residents' –
receptionist, doctor, assistant vs. cab driver (Indigenous people) and patient
(and pimp, hooker, tramps) as second-class citizens. With his setting, plot,

---

[12] This fact was made known to me by Jo–Ann Episkenew of Regina, Saskatchewan, in a
personal conversation.

and camera work, Martell, in a way, translates into film Foucault's ideas about doctoral authority, the objectifying gaze, surveillance, and discursive control outlined in chapter 1.

Martell sees the pimp, the hooker, the tramps, the doctor, and the receptionist as representatives of mainstream society, which silences the Indigenous community, symbolized by the cab driver. He explains:

> I told it [the trickster myth] through the life of a cab driver, who wanted to talk. And he, I guess, epitomizes the Indian people. Why did he want to tell his story? He wanted to tell his story, he wanted to talk; and no one would ever let him talk. They wouldn't let him speak, they would ask him a question and they answered for him. That symbolizes the film community, who asks something of the Indian people, who asks: "We want to tell an Indian story." But they're not going to listen to you. They listen what that story is, they then repeat it and say what they think it is. [...] What I was doing was taking the cab driver who wanted to talk, his desire to speak and tell his story and gave him an opportunity. Like a window of opportunity, like a lot of Aboriginal filmmakers think they have the opportunity to make a film, they think: "Now I get the time to tell my story." And then the producers and everybody else take control of it; and the Aboriginal person, whose story was to be told, gets shut out. That's what happened to the cab driver in the story obviously, so you can relate. [...] In the traditional myth the trickster always has almost supernatural capabilities. So I selected a profession where ... a doctor in a mental institution doing research work, experimental work almost in a sense of supernatural ... not supernatural but unrealistic capabilities as to what he can do with people. Based on the fact that he is supposed to be doing scientific research, he can toil with people's lives, emotions etc. and see how it plays out, and base his research on that. That is why the trickster character is a doctor. (interview, 1998)

The figures of the pimp, the hooker, tramps, doctor, and receptionist exemplify mistrust, indirect racism, indifference, and patronage of Indigenous people by the state and non-Indigenous individuals. The aggressive question of the pimp (whether the cab driver speaks English) and their abrupt exit from the car signal mistrust and covert racism toward people of color. The pimp's spitting on the cab's windshield is a strong expression of open personal racism. Indifference is signified by the receptionist faking the automated message manager and by her cool appearance. Again, patronage by the state is depicted by the doctor's giving terse orders without sufficient explanation and not expecting questions and answers and by instructing the cab driver not to talk. The patient, too, dominates the meeting with the cab driver and gives instructions. The hesitant visual introduction of the main character supports the message that the character is not given a chance to introduce himself but that everybody (the pimp, the hooker, receptionist, doctor, and patient) assesses him only by his appearance and does not give their hasty (prejudiced) judgement a second thought. Here, the cab driver's experience approximates a shared Indigenous experience that Martell pinpoints.

This metaphoric story implies that mainstream society does the talking for Indigenous people; it does not let them speak and instead answers for them. More concretely, it refers to the patronizing policies and tokenizing practices of funding agencies in the Canadian film industry. Often, Rodger Ross told me in a 1998 interview, Indigenous filmmakers and their projects are rejected, or if film companies place a project in the hands of an Indigenous director, they tend to secure a share of control through a non-Indigenous producer or in some other form. Government agencies very often tie their funding of films with Indigenous content to the prerequisite that an Indigenous person – producer, director, or advisor – has to be part of the project. Once the project is confirmed by the funding agency, the Indigenous person involved very often has to struggle for control during filming and to have a say in the outcome of the project. Lloyd Martell and Rodger Ross have both confirmed in interviews (1996) that a director is frequently hired as a 'token Indian'. In this sense, the film becomes a metafilm that comments on practices within the film industry. The metaphor also refers to the appropriation of Indigenous voices in the film and video industry:[13] i.e. the fact that many non-Indigenous filmmakers present an Indigenous voice or view by making films (features and documentaries) with Indigenous content. In *Talker*, Martell creates a didactic analogy to the trickster story that admonishes people not to tell someone else's story, in order to expose the politicking that goes on within the filmmaking community. The filmmaker epitomizes the silencing of Indigenous voices through the order the cab driver receives in capital letters: SAY NOTHING (Fig. 3.26).

---

[13] On the appropriation of Indigenous voices, see Hartmut Lutz, "Cultural Appropriation as a Repression of Peoples and Histories," in Lutz, *Approaches: Essays in Native North American Studies and Literatures* (Beiträge zur Kanadistik 11; Augsburg: Wissner, 2002): 75–82, and Hartmut Lutz, "Confronting Cultural Imperialism: First Nations People are Combating Continued Cultural Theft," in Lutz, *Approaches*, 83–97.

Martell includes several intermedial references to mainstream films.[14] The setting of *Talker* is reminiscent of Milos Forman's *One Flew Over the Cuckoo's Nest* (1975), from Ken Kesey's novel of the same title. There, too, a mental-health institution stands for present-day society as controlling and manipulating people's minds. An individual without mental problems enters this space and fails because of his inability to assess the system's manipulative and controlling power. Like shot 35 in *Talker*, Forman's film also contains long shots of the hallway of the mental ward. These shots make individuals appear very small in relation to the hall, thus visualizing how patients are under control and locked in, their individuality restricted. The descent of doctor, assistant, and cab driver down the stairway of the hospital, while the doctor is explaining and giving orders to the talk therapist (Figs. 3.22–3.24), alludes to Jonathan Demme's *Silence of the Lambs* (1991). In that film, the psychiatrist responsible for Hannibal Lecter leads the FBI agent down into the dungeon-like basement of the hospital where the serious cases are kept, also giving instructions on the way down. The buzzing fly in the second scene of *Talker* is a crucial element in the introductory sequences of Sergio Leone's Italo-western *C'era una Volta il West* [*Once Upon a Time in the West*] (1968). Leone also makes extensive use of facial close-ups, mostly showing only the eyes and the nose of the respective character. This intermediality expresses sympathy with Leone's films, which are not only a radical break with the American western genre but also with the genre of the Italo-western.[15] This break reaches its climax in Leone's *Il Mio Nome è Nessuno* [*My Name is Nobody*] (1973), in which Leone, besides parodying some classical elements of the American western, has the Italian western, embodied by Nobody (Terence Hill), prepare a glorious exit and death for the American western, embodied by Jack Beauregard (Henry Fonda).[16] Martell thus pays homage to a filmmaker who mimics and ridicules the classical American western, itself the main vehicle for pejorative and stereotypical filmic presentation of Indigenous people.

By presenting an Indigenous experience without Indigenous characters, Martell blurs the self/other binary prevalent in Indigenous–mainstream relations and avoids evoking cultural hierarchies and exoticization. Choosing not to use Indigenous characters to present an Indigenous story is also a

---

[14] See the discussion of intermediality in "Cinematic Dialogue With Hollywood," next chapter.

[15] Joe Hembus, *Das Westernlexikon* (Munich: Wilhelm Heine, 1997): 610.

[16] I am grateful to Dirk Vanderbeke for pointing out this fact to me.

political statement, relating to the essentialist categorizing of Indigenous art, film, and literature in both Indigenous and mainstream society.[17] Although the traditional story is set in a modern context, narrative time and space are occluded in order to abstract the plot. The filmmaker blurs the background as a portrait photographer does in order to focus on his metaphoric story. Instead, symbolic mise-en-scène elements enhance the impression of a surreal setting. Martell's approach to filming a traditional story involves various cinematic techniques. Parallel montage and accelerated montage, reverse-angle shooting using the 180° system, compositional balance, and the continuity approach – all indicate that Martell mainly adheres to classical filmmaking rules. A jump cut, extreme lighting, frequent usage of tilts, pans, and dolly shots, high and low camera angles, extreme facial close-ups, rear-view mirror shots, a 360° shot, and the fragmentary introduction of the main character are his individual touches – none, however, alien to conventional filmmaking. They cannot be considered unique features of Indigenous filmmaking, but the interplay between the classical and the individual develops a certain dynamic and constitutes a prime example of modern, technologized Indigenous storytelling.

Tenacity

Tenacity (USA, 1994) is a 9-minute short film by the Cheyenne/Arapaho filmmaker Chris Eyre. It won an award at the Native American Film and Video Festival at the NMAI in New York City in 1995. Like *Talker*, the film relates to colonialist relations in North America. This film treats by analogy the encounter between colonizer and colonized through the story of a hit-and-run accident in which an Indigenous boy gets killed by a truck driven by non-Indigenous men. The stage is a quiet stretch of road on the

---

[17] The issue of what is Indigenous art, literature, and film is a central one, involving discussions among and between both Indigenous and non-Indigenous people in North America. While some critics consider works of art with clearly Indigenous content to be Indigenous, to others it is necessary that the artist, writer, or filmmaker be Indigenous: i.e. an Indigenous person can write a novel with non-Indigenous content and that novel would be considered to be Indigenous literature. What Martell means here is that a film without Indigenous characters can relate Indigenous experience and be an Indigenous film. By having a non-Indigenous character as the main character, he poses the question to the film community of what makes an Indigenous film. At the same time, he challenges essentializing ideas that Indigneous art, film, and literature have to be about Indigenous issues. See ch. 2 above, fn 39, for examples of categorial discrimination by film juries against Martell.

Onondaga Indian reservation in upstate New York.[18] But as in *Talker*, the film's mise-en-scène does not reveal the whereabouts of the narrative space, implying that real and symbolic encounters like this one did, could, and do happen everywhere in the colonized world. If one considers the ethnic background of the filmmaker, one can conclude that this neutral space stands for North America, where internal colonialism and racism are still the major reasons for the marginalization of Indigenous people. In this way, Eyre translates into film what he feels Indigenous and non-Indigenous relations are in the Americas.

The lighting in the film is a soft yellow-grey, reminiscent of the sepia tone of old photographs. In an interview, Eyre has said that he wanted to draw a parallel with Edward S. Curtis's numerous photographs of Indigenous people and capture the same look and feel.[19] Yet this time it is an Indigenous person behind the camera telling a story. Curtis wanted to record a 'dying race', because he assumed that Indigenous people and their way of life would soon become extinct.[20] Instead of recording elements of life in dying cultures as he intended to do, he froze romanticized images of living cultures in his photographs. Western contact was usually blended out and no trace of Western influence detectable – only implicitly, as the reason for their 'vanishing'. Eyre reverses positions: he tells a story happening in a living culture and centered on a deadly encounter between individuals of the colonizing and colonized cultures. While the death of one boy stands for the colonization of the original North American inhabitants and the concomitant ethnocide and genocide, the boy who survives is the vehicle of cultural recuperation and continuation.

With mise-en-scène elements, Eyre constructs gradually building tension and foreboding, as in an epitasis leading to a dramatic climax. The opening sequence introduces the viewer to the peculiar atmosphere that is present throughout the whole film. Everything seems to be quiet – dead quiet – although birds are singing and the wind is blowing. This motif of death runs through the whole film. The first shot of a power-line post looming over a prayer-stick with feathers and cloth pieces tied to it (Fig. 4.1) – both could be seen as metonyms of the non-Indigenous and Indigenous culture – reveal the antagonism that is nurtured throughout the film; as well, they are

---

[18] Mary K. Bowannie, "Tenacious Focus," *Aboriginal Voices* 1.4 (Fall 1994): 11.

[19] Bowannie, "Tenacious Focus," 11.

[20] Christopher Cardozo, *Native Nations: First Americans as Seen by E.S. Curtis*, ed. Cardozo (Boston MA: Bulfinch, 1993): 6.

a metaphoric illustration of contemporary power relations in North America. After the opening credits, the film starts with a tracking shot in slow motion of two boys running through the woods. Slow-motion shots are often used to evoke dreamlike states, to offer a non-traditional way of viewing, to stress lyrical or key sequences, or to enhance dramatic contrast.[21] The slow motion here intensifies dramatic contrast and polarizes the boys' slow movements against the comparably fast movements of the two men in their truck when they appear later. The tracking shot then changes into a slow-motion POV shot mediating the vision of one of the boys. The sound complements the visuals: i.e. the boy's breathing, his footsteps, and the crackling of twigs are amplified to suggest that the boy is hearing these sounds. Eyre combines lighting, sound amplification, and the slow-motion effect to make the environment an abstract timeless backdrop to the action.

The boys run to their playground – several deserted car wrecks. The whole area is a site of destruction and abandonment – the roadside and adjacent woods are practically littered with car wrecks and rusty bins (Figs. 4.2–4.3). These images foreshadow and follow the hit-and-run accident, and stand as metaphors of culture-clash. Equipped with helmets, goggles, and toy guns, the boy start playing war. They play a game of death in a place that itself has an air of death about it, created by the sepia-toned pictures, the metal garbage, and the artificial silence. The boys are suddenly startled by the decaying corpse of a dog lying by the roadside (Fig. 4.4). Like the war game, the dead dog reiterates the death motif running through the rising action. The dog, which has probably been killed by a car, predicts another death on the road. On the metaphoric level, it evokes the death of Coyote, the mythical trickster in the Indigenous oral and literary tradition. As Coyote is a cultural hero that survives all disasters, which s/he has sometimes created him/herself (even Western colonization and influence), his dog-death here makes little sense within an Indigenous understanding of the figure and must thus be seen as evoking the broader death of Indigenous oral tradition, literature, and, in a wider sense still, Indigenous cultures.

While Eyre has the boys wondering how the dog died, he starts crosscutting to an advancing truck zigzagging on the road (Fig. 4.5). Instantly the viewers know that the driver must be either drunk or in a reckless mood. Although it is daylight, there are four hunting lights burning on the roof of the truck. Thus, the truck radiates an aggressiveness which further fore-

---

[21] Frank E. Beaver, *Dictionary of Film Terms*, 314–15.

shadows the deadly encounter. Another shot shows a young woman in a prom dress lying, apparently drunk and helpless, in the back of the truck. Because she is also at the mercy of the two young men, her figure draws parallels between women and Indigenous people, both dependent subjects of patriarchal society. However, in contrast to the Indigenous boys the prom queen is just being taken for a ride and ridiculed; she does not get hurt.[22] Although she is treated as inferior, she is still considered one of them. Thus, Eyre illustrates the fine lines between different social and ethnic groups drawn by mainstream society. White Anglo-Saxon Protestant (WASP) males are on the top and Indigenous women and children are on the bottom rung of the social ladder. Eyre here denounces existing social hierarchies by illustrating the power that one group exercises over the others.

Sensing approaching danger, the boys hide in the roadside bush, from where they can survey the road. When the truck pulls over and stops in front of them, the crosscut sequences are joined. Two men get out and pee, realized also through low-angle POV shots from the boys' hide-out (Figs. 4.6–4.7). These shots, too, are metaphoric of existing power relations in North America, stressed by the standing position of the men and the crouching position of the boys, and supported by the partly low camera angles. The frightened boys only dare to leave their hide-out when the truck is gone; encouraged by the growing distance, one of them starts shooting after it with his toy gun. The driver, in the rear-view mirror, sees the boy shooting in their direction, and instantly turns around. Seeing the truck coming back, the boys start running away in the opposite direction. When the truck has reached the boys, the driver gets out and slaps and pushes the boy who has shot until he falls to the ground. Then the other boy shoots at the men and the truck several times. When the truck leaves, the boys believe that they have gotten off lightly – but the truck returns and the boys have to run again. A high-angle shot from the driver's cab showing the boys cuts to a slow-motion shot of one boy running followed by his slow motion POV in which he sees the blurred image of the other running in front of him (Figs. 4.10–4.11). These juxtaposed shots further reinforce the depiction of representative power relations: the two adults supported by a truck, itself a power symbol, versus the two boys without the support of a

---

[22] Another reading might suggest that she has been sexually harassed or raped; according to this reading, the young woman would be socially inferior to the men but still be part of their cultural group and above Indigenous men in the constructed social hierarchy.

machine ensuring power and speed. Reinforcing this opposition is the sound of the machine becoming faster versus the sound of human breathing.

Determined to face the intruder this time, one boy positions himself in the middle of the road and awaits the approaching truck. Cuts inside the driver's cab reveal the nervousness and unyielding stubbornness of the driver. Uttering a determined "I'm not moving," the driver steers straight for the boy. Neither party budges an inch, both tenaciously awaiting the encounter, as in a duel. By crosscutting between both 'fronts' and presenting their POVs at the other party, Eyre drives the dramatic tension to the limit. At the very last second, the driver slams on the brakes and swerves the vehicle sharply, but too late: he has hit the other boy. The camera is trained on his helmet which has come off during the crash and which is now spinning on the road until it comes to rest, suggesting the boy's death.

As in previous sequences, Eyre uses cinematic means to transmit the manichaean power metaphoric.[23] The crash is realized through respective high- and low-angle POV shots of the driver and the standing boy and of shots into the driver's cab as well as low-angle shots of the truck and its tires (Figs. 4.8–4.9; 4.12–4.15). Another low-angle shot shows the second boy coming to the scene of the accident. He takes off his helmet and his goggles: the war is over, the boys have lost. The game that had started so playfully has become deadly serious. Another high-angle shot out of the driver's cab down to the boy who is kneeling beside his companion suggests who is superior and who celebrates a sad victory (Fig. 4.16). With the words "I'll get help" the driver gets back into the truck and leaves the paralyzed boy at the scene of death. When the truck has left, the boy realizes what has happened and runs feebly after it. This last shot is a tail-on shot out of the back of the departing truck – the flight from the offenders' viewpoint. The camera is trained on the running boy until it tilts down to show the moving road in close-up (Figs. 4.17–4.19). With this final sequence, Eyre intends to transmit the message "'that the American public doesn't take the responsibility for what they've done to Native People [...] whether it was then or now'."[24] In this sense, Eyre's film is an indictment of the colonial history of the Americas.

---

[23] See ch. 2 fn 62 above for discussion of the Fanonesque 'manichaean'.

[24] Eyre, quoted in Mary K. Bowannie, "Tenacious Focus," 11.

To play out the inferiority/superiority metaphoric, Eyre uses low- and high-angle shots, characterizing sound, speed variation, focus variation, and power symbols in association with the respective group. Cinematography and mise-en-scène position the two opposing 'fronts' of the encounter:

Indigenous	vs.	non-Indigenous
children	vs.	adults
crouching	vs.	standing
intimidated	vs.	self-assured
watching	vs.	pissing
toy guns, plastic helmets	vs.	truck/machine
sound of human breathing	vs.	sound of accelerating truck
blurred vision	vs.	sharp focus
low-angle shots	vs.	high-angle shots
slow motion	vs.	normal running speed
powerlessness	vs.	power.

In *Tenacity*, Eyre tells a metaphoric story of colonial conquest. He starts with pre-contact intertribal warfare, which, in the face of lethal colonial warfare and the sheer numbers of Indigenous people killed, seems, rather, to have been playful (the boys' war games). The dead dog, or death of Coyote, functions as a bad omen. During the initial years of contact, Indigenous people were also reluctantly and curiously watching what the new-comers were doing, stalled as these were by physical needs in their project of settlement – their inability to provide themselves with enough food (here, the men have to stop the truck in order to take a piss, watched by the boys concealed in the roadside bush). The woods, the playground of the boys, is defined as Indigenous space cut through by the road, the space of the intruder, standing here for pioneer settlements, trails, and later the railroad. The metal garbage, too, is metonymic for European settlement. Ensuing warfare because of continuous encroachment upon Indigenous lands and resources and an ideology that justified Euro-American expansionism ('Manifest Destiny'), on a par with military superiority (the truck) led to genocide and ethnocide in Indigenous North America (illustrated by the beating and crash sequences). As the film suggests, the killed, beaten, and assimilated peoples were left to themselves to deal with the consequences of these clashes while the colonizers continued their progress (the young men get into their truck and leave). This metaphoric tale is realized largely according to classical filmmaking conventions (narrative, framing, editing)

which are, nevertheless, combined with unconventional and individual implementation of images, lighting, and sound. The filmmaker negotiates oppositional positions of the characters through POVs at the other party, high
and low camera angles, and, again, sound. These technical possibilities for
creating filmic binaries visualize manichaean oppositions that characterize
the Indigenous and the mainstream in colonial discourse. Whereas Martell
avoids the self/other dichotomy, Eyre stresses the oppositional binaries of
center/margin and self/other that uphold Western hegemonies in North
America.

Overweight With Crooked Teeth

The 5-minute short film *Overweight With Crooked Teeth* (Canada, 1997)
was written and directed by the visual artist and filmmaker Shelley Niro
(Mohawk) and produced by Niro and Dan BigBee, Jr. (Comanche). It is
based on a poem by Michael Doxtater (Mohawk) of the same title.[25] The
film, like the poem, dismantles stereotypical assumptions about Indigenous
people which are prevalent in mainstream North America. It is not a film
that transmits its message through subliminal allusions or indirect references but one that blatantly attacks such clichés, parodying them with
macabre humor and a large portion of self-irony. The programmatic title,
by referring to two attributes that are incompatible with the romanticized
beauty of Indians, promises that the film will be a satirical indictment of
such stereotypes.

    The film consists of several vignettes that are framed by two correspond-
ing sequences. The vignettes illustrate the individual lines of the poem,
which is read by Lily Shangreaux in voice-over. The lines run as superimposed captions across the middle of the screen. In order to match the
lines, most vignettes feature an Indigenous character (mainly Michael Doxtater himself) posing or acting out one aspect of the Western imaginary
Indian. In some vignettes these captions ostentatiously confirm the image
and in others they question and parody it. Through the composition of
images and the spoken words, the vignettes call to mind preconceived ideas
of the imaginary Indian, look at them critically, and brutally tear them
apart. Often, the opening shots of these vignettes represent the respective
cliché by showing Doxtater as a stereotypical Indian, and subsequent shots

---

[25] The poem is provided in the Appendix, below.

show him doing exactly the opposite of what the Indian cliché suggests he
should be doing. The vignettes introduce these clichés only to counteract,
ironize, or twist them seconds later, repeating and mimicking stereotypes in
order to denounce them. In the manner of Vizenor's trickster,[26] Niro ridicules aspects of the imaginary Indian by mocking viewers' expectations of
a 'screen Indian'. This mockery is fortified by Doxtater's masquerade and
overdone acting and the caption "What were you expecting anyway?" at
the beginning. This short film employs the strategy of "deconstruction of
stereotypes through excess."[27] Niro accumulates enactments of stereotypes
and takes them out of their contexts of hegemonic discourse so that she is
able to ridicule them and to disclose their falsity and dependency on colonial discourse. They become emptied of their clichéd meaning.

The vignette images are often shown through an iris that gradually opens
the view on the image and then closes in on it. These iris shots, telescope-
like gazes, can be understood as a reference to the colonization of the Americas, for the telescope as a metonym of seafaring can denote the 'discovery' of the New World. Moreover, this telescopic gaze stresses the
camera lens between the viewer and the images presented. It evokes the
colonialist gaze at 'the other', the Foucauldian lens of power, which is
manifested in the eurocentric gaze at colonized 'exotic' people to be studied through film, video, and still camera. The iris shot is an old-fashioned
technique typical of the silent-film era, and, because it is registered by the
viewer as an expansion and contraction of frame borders, it echoes the use
in early studio photography of oval fading-out of the borders in portraits. In
this way, the iris shots also refer to the work of photographers of the nineteenth and the early twentieth century, who contributed to the visual imaginary Indian and the trope of the romantic yet vanishing Indians. Some
photographers contributed to the construction of the stereotype of the
'noble savage', such as Emma Freeman, who staged her models "in an
invented pastiche of 'Indian' costumery," "with signature props of Indian
authenticity,"[28] and in postures romanticizing and stylizing an Indian 'noble

---

[26] On trickster discourse, see chapter 2.

[27] Mark Shackleton mentioned this strategy in a lecture given at Greifswald University,
Germany, in January 2003.

[28] Susan Bernardin, "Capturing and Recapturing Culture: Trailing Grace Nicholson's
Legacy in Northwestern California," in Susan Bernardin et al., *Trading Gazes: Euro-American Photographers and Native North Americans, 1880–1940* (New Brunswick NJ & London: Rutgers UP, 2003): 170–71.

and savage' past (e.g., one hand shading the eyes or gazing thoughtfully into the distance). Others, such as Edward S. Curtis, pursued the goal of capturing and preserving 'authentic' images of Indigenous people. Being usually beautiful images, these photographs invoke an idyllic noble past and sentimental clichés about dying Indian cultures and thus cater to the trope of the 'vanishing Indian'. Mary Schäffer, infatuated with 'primitive Indian cultures' and viewing Indians as picturesque individuals, nevertheless establishes a more humanizing tone in her portrayal and often shows self-confident subjects who gaze with friendly openness into the camera.[29] Jane Gay's photographs of Nez Perces are similarly counter-narratives to Curtis', Vroman's, and Choate's colonial visual discourse. Her photography renounces the picturesque Indian in grand landscapes and reveals processes of assimilation, the deprivation of the Indian land base, and the "civilly disobedient responses of the Nez Perces."[30] Photography of Indige-

---

[29] For example, Schäffer's two photographs of Sampson Beaver's family (husband, wife, and infant) picture this nuclear Indigenous family in the woods in front of birch trees and not a dwelling. Their dress is a mixture of Western and Indigenous attire. Rather refreshingly and like others of her subjects, the three people smile and look self-assuredly into the camera, which suggests a fairly confident relationship between photographer and subject. Clearly not suppressing evidence of colonial contact and not staging a mythologized pre-contact Indian life, she nevertheless presents her subjects within the framework of colonial cultural codes and ideology: the nuclear (not extended) family as a domesticated version of the 'noble savage in the wilderness'. Schäffer, in her "longing for a 'wild free life'" and "fascination with the 'primitive'," travelled the Canadian Rockies in the early 1900s, exposed herself to the hardships and discomforts of travelling on horseback and camping out, and befriended Stoney families that bestowed on her an Indian name: Yahe-Weha, or Mountain Woman. Her photographs "attempt a counter-archive to the flattened and depersonalized images of Indians taken by Edward S. Curtis, Adam Vroman, John N. Choate, and other would-be chroniclers of the 'vanishing race' of Native North Americans." And yet, the Beaver family photographs "reference[s] Schäffer's sentimental investment in Indian families and her fascination with the stereotypical and colorful trappings of 'the Indian'"; Lisa MacFarlane, "Mary Schäffer's 'Comprehending Equal Eyes'," in Susan Bernardin et al., *Trading Gazes: Euro-American Photographers and Native North Americans, 1880–1940* (New Brunswick NJ & London: Rutgers UP, 2003): 26, 110–16, 146.

[30] Gay's photography during the Nez Perce allotment lacks spectacular backdrops and picturesque Indians posing in regalia with 'signature props' such as weapons, pottery, basketry, and the like. She treats and presents her subjects "more equivocally" in Western clothing, doing farm work or assisting in surveying, and shows the 'wilderness' transformed into a space of Western and Indigenous habitation, including grassland, farmland, surveyed land, fences, walls, settled towns, tipis, log houses, and a well. "Whether in natural surroundings or fully demonstrating their civilized accomplishments, her Nez Perce subjects look uncomfortable, off balance, or temporary"; Nicole Tonkovich, "'Lost in the General Wreckage of the Far West': The Photographs and Writings of Jane Gay," in Bernardin et al., *Trading Gazes*, 34, 50, 55. They are not a sentimentalized culture of the past but a culture in enforced transition.

nous people subtly reflects the state's relations with them. Faris, for example, argues that photographers of the Navajo at the turn of the century
created a surveillance mode through profile and *en face* photographs, commonly used for photographs of criminals. This kind of photography "implies control, supervision, command, rule, test, defeat, arrest."[31] After the
Navajo had been confined to reservations and no longer presented a threat
to the state, the photographers changed to an aestheticizing register, which
is still prevalent in today's Navajo photography. This photographic discourse (initiated by the photography of Laura Gilpin) of "washed and clean
and in-their-place Navajo" is "a persistent means of imaging that is quite
popular, and one that makes them (or parts of them) creatures of turquoise,
velvet, sky, feathers, silver, sheep, blankets, red rocks."[32] Growing social
awareness in the USA brought forth the dignified-victim discourse (Leonard McCombe), objectifying drunk, disturbed, poverty-stricken, assimilated, and dying Indians.[33] Thus, Western photography continues to be a
vehicle for transporting clichés, and the examples discussed show how
photography, echoing changing Indian policies, changed their tone from
portraying the stereotypical 'doomed noble savage' to the stereotypical dichotomy of the 'nature-loving spiritual traditionalist' and the 'drunken,
poor, degraded Indian'.

The opening sequence of *Overweight With Crooked Teeth* shows a road
with trees on either side in an extreme long shot. The camera is fixed on the
road, where Doxtater can be seen walking toward the camera. His approach
is realized with several fades to black. Niro has him soon appear close to
the camera, bowing down and moving so close to the lens that it seems as if
he is going to crawl inside it (Figs. 5.1–5.3). His face in close-up becomes
blurred – a prelude to the content of the subsequent vignettes, which visualize, blur, and distort Indian stereotypes. This sequence is thus an introductory framing device. In concert with the caption asking "What were you expecting anyway?" the blurry-image effect also forces the viewer to revisit
assumptions about Indians that are derived from knowledge of ethnographic films and Hollywood narrative films that present Indigenous cultures.
Instead of moving toward the image, the camera is fixed and the image to

---

[31] James C. Faris, "Photographing the Navajo: Scanning Abuse," *American Indian Culture
and Research Journal* 20.3 (1996): 68.

[32] Faris, "Photographing the Navajo: Scanning Abuse," 69.

[33] "Photographing the Navajo: Scanning Abuse," 76.

be shot approaches it. This reversal conveys a sense of the viewer's being approached by the film and the question it poses.

The first vignette shows Doxtater in a medium close-up, sitting sideways toward the camera. Wrapped in an 'Indian-pattern blanket', with braids and a feather on the back of his head, he is holding a stuffed bird and is talking to it, while Shangreaux asks "A noble savage?" Doxtater slowly turns to face the camera, sporting a cruel, gloating smile, and simply drops the bird (Figs. 5.4–5.5). Then an oval black and white photograph of Sitting Bull appears embedded in a colored geometric design, the likes of which have come to be pan-Indian signifiers. A brief dissolve to Doxtater in a posture reminiscent of those of photographed Indian chiefs is followed by another dissolve to a medium close-up of Doxtater, again masquerading as a cliché Indian, complete with an Indian-patterned blanket and feathers, and speaking. But it is Shangreaux's voice here, saying: "The earth and I are one." The viewer's sudden awareness of a lack of fidelity – the sound is unfaithful to its source – is usually employed for comic effect.[34] Here, it is not used simply to amuse the audience but to emphasize the critical mockery of pan-Indian signifiers, such as feathers and geometric and flowery designs, and of the romantic trope of the Indian nature-lover. The dissolve also reinforces the mockery and the subversion, as it overwrites the image of Sitting Bull's photograph in the geometric design, standing in for the imaginary Indian of Western media discourse, with Niro's mock-image of the same (Figs. 5.6–5.8). In carnivalesque fashion, Doxtater appears as the clichéd Indian and parodies his own image. He finishes a bag of chips and, with a rebellious facial expression, throws the empty bag into the woods (Figs. 5.9–5.10). This vignette takes apart the romantic cliché of the Indian as 'noble savage' who has a special spiritual relation with nature that Western people supposedly lack. On the surface, the image suggests that Indians are 'one with earth and nature' and that they can talk with animals. But the dressing-up and the acts of killing the bird and polluting the forest parody it and are like a blow in the face of the 'good old' stereotype. Of course, these acts are exaggerated, the sequences overdone. But it is mainly through exaggeration that Niro can question the stereotypes in the viewer's head.[35]

---

[34] Bordwell & Thompson, *Film Art*, 329.

[35] Many Indigenous people did, and do, have a certain territorial ethos intertwined with religious belief and everyday life. In traditional societies, the people lived in harmony with nature and considered the land they lived on as sacred. This belief has been partly retained, but it has to be differentiated from the cliché of the 'nature-protecting noble savage'. The rela-

Those viewers who are not aware of their stereotypical thinking might start watching mass-media products more critically, and those who are aware of it at least get a good laugh out of it.

The next vignette shows a child with a white fur cap, while the caption across the screen reads: "Like we're not supposed to think / Just react" (Fig. 5.11). Like the Western Furs Ltd. sign in *Talker*, the fur cap alludes to the era of the fur trade in Canadian history, when the first results of conquest and colonization, such as changes in traditional Indigenous societies and traditional gender relations, began to take effect.[36] Staging a child in this

---

tion to the land is variously reflected in early and contemporary Indigenous texts such as those by Black Elk (I would consider the as-told-to text *Black Elk Speaks* as his own writing), Ruby Slipperjack (*Honour the Sun*), and Vine Deloria (*God is Red: A Native View of Religion*). Robert M. Nelson proposes that in Indigenous fiction "place, understood as a living physical landscape invested with the same type and degree of spirit as humanity, has the power to shape the identities of the People, individually and collectively, whose lives take place there"; Nelson, *Place and Vision: The Function of Landscape in Native American Fiction*, vol. 1 (New York: Peter Lang, 1993): 133. This relationship has changed with the concept of ownership introduced by the capitalist system. Indigenous nations have to fight in land-claim settlements and court cases for land titles and are forced to enter the same basic relation to the land that Western people have: ownership as a prerequisite for inhabitation. As the Indigenous relation to the land was changed, Western thought (mainly in North America and Europe) developed a romanticized concept of an Indian nature ethic and a special spiritual relationship between Indigenous people and the land. This notion often develops an esoteric character. It serves to compensate spiritually for a link currently missing between Western people and their natural surroundings, which people have come painfully to realize lately after being confronted by the effects of the structural destruction of the earth such as global warming and the ozone hole. Westerners who seek some kind of ersatz religion that can lead them back 'to the roots' or 'back to nature' find an appropriate source in tribal religions that embody life in harmony with the land and all living creatures. The belief in a Western-constructed Indian territorial ethos can satisfy the need for reconnection with nature and compensate for a spiritual void. Many Indigenous people themselves have appropriated this sentimental idea of being one with the earth and all living things, for it is a positive and flattering stereotype and appears to be a concept disguised as tradition. The task is to differentiate between the romanticizing cliché of all Indians being nature-lovers, on the one hand, and the Indigenous traditional concept of living in harmony with nature and a sense of belonging to a certain piece of land, on the other. In her film, Niro tries to demonstrate this differentiation.

[36] On the Canadian fur-trade era, see: Margaret Conrad, Alvin Finkel & Cornelius Jaenen, *History of the Canadian Peoples*, vol. 1: *Beginnings to 1867* (Toronto: Copp Clark Pitman, 1993): 98–102 and 455–62; Arthur J. Ray, "Fur Trade History as an Aspect of Native History," in *Readings in Canadian History*, vol. 1: *Pre-Confederation*, ed. R. Douglas Francis & Donald B. Smith (Toronto: Holt, Rinehart & Winston of Canada, 1990): 49–63; Robin Fisher, "Indian Control of the Maritime Fur Trade and the Northwest Coast," in *Readings in Canadian History*, vol. 1: *Pre-Confederation*, ed. Francis & Smith, 79–92; and William J. Eccles, "The French Fur Trade in the Eighteenth Century," in *Interpreting Canada's Past*, vol. 1: *Pre-Confederation*, ed. J.M. Bumsted (Toronto: Oxford U P, 1993): 207–30. On the

sequence epitomizes the ward-like status of Indigenous people in Canadian
and US-American societies. The caption thus plays into the notion of Indigenous people being a dominated and marginalized group in mainstream
society, able merely to react to, but not control, national policies regulating
them.
    The caption of the third vignette, "Like we're peripatetic pagans / Stroll-
ing through a steaming forest after a June rain," suggests the notion of
beaded and feathered Indians walking aimlessly through a forest (Fig.
5.12). By staging three Indigenous children walking in wonder through the
woods, Niro again invokes the ward-like status of Indigenous nations but
also pokes fun at the eurocentric idea that all Indigenous nations were
nomadic and did not 'use' the land, which in turn legitimized colonialist
policies. The parodic character of this shot, in concert with the contemporary clothing of the kids, stresses the gap between the imaginary and contemporary Indigenous experience. As in the first vignette, the images counteract the caption, thereby conveying the message that Indigenous cultures

---

destruction of egalitarian pre-contact societies and the resulting impairment of the status of
Indigenous women as effects of colonization, see: Ron Bourgeault, "Women in Egalitarian
Society," *New Breed Journal* (Métis Society of Saskatchewan, January–April 1983): 3–8;
Ron Bourgeault, "Race, Class and Gender: Colonial Domination of Indian Women," in *Race,
Class, Gender: Bonds and Barriers*, ed. Jesse Vorst et al. (Society for Socialist Studies: A
Canadian Annual 5, 1989): 87–115; Linda Sutherland, "Citizen Minus: Aboriginal Women
and Indian Self-Government, Race, Nation, Class and Gender" (MA thesis, University of
Regina, 1995); Silvia van Kirk, *Many Tender Ties: Women in Fur-Trade Society, 1670 –
1870* (Winnipeg, Manitoba: Watson & Dwyer, 1980); and Silvia van Kirk, "'Women in Be-
tween': Indian Women in Fur Trade Society in Western Canada," in *Out of the Background:
Readings on Canadian Native History*, ed. Robin Fisher & Ken S. Coates (1988; Toronto:
Copp Clark, 1996): 102–17. Van Kirk, along with Jennifer Brown, was the first historian to
examine the role of Indigenous women in the Canadian fur-trade era. Van Kirk explains that
Indigenous women at that time entered into a unique position as 'women in between', exploited by both Indigenous and European males. She describes how Indigenous women were
indispensable as translators, negotiators, and intermediaries between the trading parties. Furthermore, the wives of the non-Indigenous traders taught them to survive in the wilderness,
supported and comforted them, and bore them children. At the same time, van Kirk illustrates
the gradual loss of autonomy experienced by these women as a result of their position as 'women in between'. Bourgeault goes further, examining not only gender differences but also
emerging class and 'race' differences in the process of the destruction of egalitarian Indigenous societies. With the introduction of private property (furs as exchange commodities), the
colonizing society gradually imposed their capitalist system and ideology on the colonized
societies. Thus, the egalitarian form of societies was destroyed and the traditional political and
economic autonomy of women was undermined. The Indigenous value system based on use-
value changed into a system based on exchange-value. Indigenous people were introduced
into the system as an exploited labor force.

are as contemporary and modern as mainstream cultures. Costumes with beads and feathers[37] as well as a special spiritual relationship with nature belong to a eurocentric construct of a sentimentalized Indian past.

The fourth vignette features a pickup truck from the back as it drives away. This time the caption ostentatiously reads (rather, screams): "Not supposed to FART / or SCREW / Or what we're supposed to be … / People with weaknesses" (Fig. 5.13). Again, the image refers to contemporary Indigenous people, who seem to prefer driving pickup trucks, which makes sense, considering the pathetic state of most reserve and reservation roads. The caption, on the one hand, ironizes Indian museum culture as established in Western society, in which Indigenous cultures appear to be dead and stiff like waxworks. On the other hand, it ridicules the romanticized notion of the 'noble savage', which denies its object any sexuality and bodily functions. By presenting these 'taboo' words, which are usually not associated with the idealized Indian, in red and pink, Niro emphasizes them to debunk this idea of the sanitary (and diplomatically polite and 'decent') 'noble savage.' The capitalized vulgarisms create an initial resistance in the viewer to being confronted with such physical needs. The film is again overdoing its critical irony – which, however, works precisely by screaming out this message. The caption, Debra Piapot has pointed out (interview, 1998), also exemplifies the fact that many Indigenous people themselves love to make jokes about physical needs and bodily functions.

The next two vignettes employ posterization – having the images appear in unnatural colors (here, bright orange and light blue) so that one can only make out silhouettes. The posterization effect abstracts the images and makes the figures appear surreal. At first, the camera pans through a forest and is finally trained in a medium close-up on a figure, whose facial features appear reddish orange. He is aiming at something and pulling the trigger, while the caption comments: "Victims of a lotta bad breaks / Like the repeating carbine rifle" (Fig. 5.14). Here, the text ironizes voices that reduce colonization of the North American continent to a combination of unfortunate circumstances, such as the European invaders' possessing rifles and cannons, which formed the basis of their military superiority. The color posterization also estranges the image, warning the viewer not to take

---

[37] Beads and feathers are, of course, still part of traditional costumes worn at powwows and formal events such as political negotiations. On these occasions, the beads and feathers possess no romantic overtones, assuming instead social and political significance, since they are strong contextual markers of cultural consciousness.

media images, especially images of the constructed imaginary and ideolo-
gized Indian of Western media discourse, at face value.

In the seventh vignette, the camera shows a person sitting and reading,
while the shot that follows closes up over the person's shoulder to reveal
the cover page of the text, Darwin's *The Origin of Species* (Fig. 5.15). With
the image of an Indigenous person reading Darwin together with the caption: "Charles Darwin / Same thing," Niro plays on the ambiguous connection between Indigenous people and Darwinism. On one hand, Darwin's
evolutionary theory took apart the basis of Christian religion, the Western
myth of human creation. His theory of common descent showed that all
organisms have descended from common ancestors by a continuous process of branching.[38] It thus offered itself as a vehicle with which to attack
the church as an institution for legitimizing the colonization of the Americas. Pope Alexander VI provided the European colonizer with "dominion
over the 'New World'" by acknowledging the right of "the sovereigns of
Castile and Aragon to acquire and Christianize the islands and *terra firma*
of the new regions."[39] Even before Social Darwinism, the people living in
the New World were described as being an inferior race – for example, by
Juan Ginés de Sepúlveda, a fierce defender of the Spanish right to conquest.[40] In England, the legalization of conquest was deduced from an
Elizabethan Protestant doctrine "declaring the English in covenant with
God to bring 'true' (as opposed to Spanish) Christianity to 'heathen natives'." This concept was further supported by the writings of Sir George
Peckham, who established a doctrine which entitled the English to conquer
the Indigenous people and dispossess them of their lands if they refused to
trade.[41] The Pope validated the conquest of foreign land on condition that
Christianity be spread among the conquered peoples.[42] Colonization and

---

[38] *Dictionary of Race and Ethnic Relations*, ed. Ellis Cashmore, 94.

[39] Glenn T. Morris, "International Law and Politics: Toward a Right to Self-Determination
for Indigenous Peoples," in *The State of Native America*, ed. M. Annette Jaimes (Boston MA:
South End, 1992): 59; emphasis in original.

[40] On the debate among Spanish scholars such as Juan López de Palacios Rubios, Matías
de Paz, Bartolomé de Las Casas, and Sepúlveda about the rights of the people indigenous to
the New World, whether or not they should be considered human beings, and the Rights of
Conquest doctrine, see Morris, "International Law and Politics: Toward a Right to Self-Determination for Indigenous Peoples," 58–62.

[41] Morris, "International Law and Politics," 62–63.

[42] Vine Deloria, Jr., "Trouble in High Places: Erosion of American Indian Rights to Religious Freedom in the United States," in *The State of Native America*, ed. M. Annette Jaimes
(Boston MA: South End, 1992): 271.

the forcible christianization of the Indigenous population became causally connected. Early colonizers did not see their expansionist and christianizing policies as acts in their own right but regarded them as a fulfillment of God's commands, supported by scholars and Christian institutions of the day:

> To rule is really to submit, in the first instance, as an obedient believer of God's command and, in the second instance, as a helpless pawn abiding by Nature's laws governing the races of man. The White races [...] never felt superior in an absolute sense since they yielded to the Christian Bible and to Nature's demand in commanding inferior races.[43]

But while Darwinism deconstructs the basis of the Christian belief in the creation of humankind, hence the Christian legitimization of conquest, it does the same with Indigenous creation mythology, for the theory in its scientific approach excludes any kind of mythic and oral account of creation:

> When secular science defeated Christian fundamentalism, in its victory it was able to promulgate the belief that all accounts of a creation or of spectacular catastrophic events were superstitions devised by ignorant peoples to explain the processes of the world around them. The defeat of Christianity foreclosed the possibility that any other tradition that had accounts of past Earth events could join in the enterprise to explain to an increasingly global society the origins of the planet and of our race.[44]

On the other hand, Darwin's laws of 'natural selection' were developed in such a way that they sanctioned theories of inferior and superior races. Most Darwinist thinkers equated biological evolution with cultural evolution. Physical anthropologists of the day declared 'races' other than the Caucasian (the 'chosen race') to be inherently inferior and primitive, based upon their findings after studying the size of the brain, the shape of the skull, and the nature of the suture (phrenology and craniometry).[45]

> Darwinian biology only seemed to confirm further the conventional wisdom. Ascent up the ladder of social evolution was closely linked to mental

---

[43] Sidney Willhelm, "Red Man, Black Man, and White America: The Constitutional Approach to Genocide," *Catalyst* 4 (Spring 1969): 3–4, quoted in James S. Frideres, *Native Peoples in Canada: Contemporary Conflicts* (Scarborough, Ontario: Prentice Hall Canada, 1993): 466.

[44] Vine Deloria, Jr., *Red Earth, White Lies* (Golden CO: Fulcrum, 1997). 24.

[45] Robert F. Berkhofer, *The White Man's Indian*, 57–58.

capacity, and mental capacity was presumed a function of brain or cranial size.[46]

Darwinism stimulated the idea that, in the genesis of humankind, the human species passed through different hierarchically ranked stages. The European cultures had already reached the highest stage, whereas Indigenous cultures[47] still remained in the lower primitive stage. This contrast 'naturally' explained their inferiority and thus justified European dominion. In North America, the conclusions of physical anthropologists, coupled with Social Darwinism, worked to justify aggressive colonial expansion, and thus sanctioned cultural and economic subjugation of Indigenous peoples and African Americans. In the same vein, the notion of 'Manifest Destiny' was being promoted even before Darwin's seminal text. Originally coined by Jacksonian democrats in the 1840s to justify expansionist policies to the west and southwest of the USA, it became a cover-up term sanctifying any acts of expropriation (including Indigenous territory) in North America.[48] Alice Kehoe states that the notion of the Indians' being inherently and hopelessly inferior "was an application of Social Darwinism":

> the school of thought that believed the contemporary world powers had achieved their position through natural selection of races with superior genetic endowments for the development of civilization.[49]

Darwin's conclusion that "natural selection affected males and females as a function of their roles in reproduction and/or from resource competition" led to the "principle of sexual dimorphism,"[50] developed and maintained in

---

[46] Berkhofer, *The White Man's Indian*, 59.

[47] The term 'culture' underwent a change of meaning with the work of the anthropologist Franz Boas, who introduced the concept of 'cultural pluralism', stressing the diversity of cultures. Before this, scholars had used the term 'culture' in the singular sense, seeing all human cultures as one entity (Berkhofer, *The White Man's Indian*, 63–64). Indigenous cultures were perceived as one culture by Euro-American scholars, and cultural diversity in the Americas was acknowledged only with the advent of the 'cultural pluralism' concept. Of course, the concept of 'culture' has been and still is widely debated by critics and there are many different views and theories of the meaning of 'culture' and of how 'culture' and 'group identity' are constructed. For the complexity of the issue, one might compare the cultural concepts of hybridity, articulation, transculturalism, and transdifference.

[48] Hartmut Lutz, *"Indianer" und "Native Americans": Zur sozial- und literarhistorischen Vermittlung eines Stereotyps* (Hildesheim, Zurich & New York: Georg Olms, 1985): 182.

[49] Alice B. Kehoe, *North American Indians: A Comprehensive Account*, 91.

[50] Gilbert Herdt, *Third Sex, Third Gender: Beyond Sexual Dimorphism in Culture and History*, ed. Herdt (New York: Zone, 1994): 25.

colonial discourse. The advance of this principle and stress on the repro-
ductive aspect of sexual relations invited essentialist sex and gender definitions, culminating in the ideas that 'male' and 'female' are innate structures
in all forms of life and that heterosexuality is inevitably the necessary and
highest form of evolution.[51] This dimorphic principle does not only 'other'
and exclude gay and lesbian, transsexual, and transgender identities, it also
demonizes such personalities and views them as inferior, immoral, and unnatural. Darwinian thought, in this domain, has nurtured othering, subjugat-
ing, hegemonic ideas about Indigenous (and, indeed, 'advanced') cultures
and groups that do not identify exclusively with dimorphic categories.

After the evocation of European military might and Social Darwinism
and its legitimization of racial and sexological theories, Niro's film fash-
ions links to other 'bad breaks' that Indigenous people fell victim to –
European diseases. The caption "Small Pox / Influenza" refers to yet
another aspect of the process of colonizing Indigenous North America.
These diseases serve as metonyms for the various viruses and bacteria the
colonizers brought to the New World, such as measles, cholera, typhoid,
scarlet fever, diphtheria, and mumps. Between 1520 and 1900, ninety-three
serious epidemics and pandemics resulting from European contact ravaged
Indigenous North America, radically reducing populations.[52] Historically,
non-Indigenous scholars have tended to downplay this onslaught through
disease as "a sort of 'natural disaster', induced, but never intended by
Europeans."[53] However, there were cases where diseases were deliberately
introduced. For example, blankets infected with smallpox had been given to
the Ottawas and other nations of Pontiac's confederation in 1763 in order to
defeat this military alliance. Probably in the same manner and for the same
purpose, member-nations of the Iroquois confederation were infected by
small pox in 1717 and in 1731–33, which devastated their numbers.[54] The
French-American fur-trader Francis A. Chardon argued that the US army
also distributed infected blankets among the North-Dakotan Mandans at
Fort Clark in 1837, causing a devastating epidemic among the Plains

---

[51] Herdt, *Third Sex, Third Gender*, ed. Herdt, 28.
[52] Lenore A. Stiffarm & Phil Lane, Jr., "The Demography of Native North America: A
Question of American Indian Survival," in *The State of Native America*, ed. M. Annette
Jaimes (Boston MA: South End, 1992): 31.
[53] Stiffarm & Lane, "The Demography of Native North America," 32.
[54] "The Demography of Native North America," 32.

Indians.[55] With these primitive biological weapons the enemy could be eliminated without much effort. What the USA was fighting so aggressively and militantly (and unjustifiably) in the two Iraq wars, the country had itself engaged in during the Indian wars – the use of biological weapons and weapons of mass destruction. Such expressions of outrage at malicious wrongdoing on the part of the US army are complemented by voices offering a basis for future mutual understanding and recognition. Georges Sioui does not absolve history, stating categorically that the epidemics were the main cause of the severe reduction of the Indigenous population.

> Since first coming into contact, both carriers and receivers have suffered from an inability to recognize the true instigators of the great disaster in which they have been plunged; to recognize this situation would serve, not only to indict the guilty party but also and most importantly to enable all of us to work together toward a reorientation of human thought.[56]

Doxtater is next shown in the darkness of the night looking at some phoney comet, together with the caption: "Halley's comet." Here, Niro mocks the eurocentric trope of the colonized blanketed in mental darkness before European 'civilization' brought them enlightenment, which then promoted the colonialist idea that Indigenous people are innately less intelligent. This enlightenment, basically an Indigenous turn toward eurocentric beliefs and knowledges, entailed an adaptation to the eurocentric framework of thought about and view of different cultures – mental colonization. The last lines of the poem – "Victims of a lotta bad breaks / Like the repeating carbine rifle / Charles Darwin / Same thing / Small pox / Influenza / Halley's comet" – cynically insinuate that these 'bad breaks' (military might, Social-Darwinist ideology, (un)intentional introduction of diseases, mental colonization) are something like natural disasters and developments, not intended yet working for the benefit of the European colonizers. The poem and the film critically allude to the often postulated notion that these were 'just' natural and logical consequences of the settling of the 'empty space' of North America. With Doxtater and Niro ironizing European military superiority, Social Darwinism, diseases, and European education as 'bad breaks', they emphasize the fact that not these aspects

---

[55] *Chardon's Journal at Fort Clark, 1834–1839*, ed. & intro. Annie Heloise Abel, intro. William R. Swagerty (Lincoln: U of Nebraska P, 1997).

[56] Georges E. Sioui, *For an Amerindian Autohistory*, tr. Sheila Fischman (*Pour une auto-histoire amérindienne* 1991; tr. Montreal & Kingston, Ontario: McGill–Queen's UP, 1992): 4.

were the essence of colonization, but that the trope of Manifest Destiny, the 'divine right' to conquer and dispossess, and the belief in European cultural, civil, religious, and moral superiority were the driving forces behind the colonization of the Americas, which then was supported by and produced these effects.

The final framing sequence of *Overweight With Crooked Teeth* reverses the first one by having the camera trained in close-up on Doxtater, who is again dressed in ordinary clothes, and having it then pull away from him until he appears as a small figure in a long shot (Figs. 5.16–5.19). Whereas in the initial sequence a still camera films the approaching Doxtater, now a hand-held camera producing shaky images is used. The image retreats from the viewers, releasing them to ponder the contextualized clichés and Niro's cinematic deconstruction thereof. Again the telescope-like gaze invokes the colonialist gaze of power but accentuates the fact that Niro's gaze is not objectifying as in Western film discourse. Her iris shots and the captions across the screen continually restrict visual access and thus frustrate any objectifying gaze. In contrast to colonialist visual discourse with its appropriating gaze, here it is an Indigenous person behind the camera who processes enactments of the imaginary Indian through a camera under her own control, and who creates a second, fresh, anticolonialist gaze. The decolonized gaze returns an image of Indigeneity that is stripped of objectifications and stereotypes. Since the film is made by an Indigenous filmmaker and since Indigenous humor to a great extent depends on self-irony, the telescope gaze also demonstrates a critically humorous look at themselves by Indigenous people. The caption asks once more: "What were you expecting anyway?" as if to sum up the messages of the film. It also demands, through the filmic deconstruction exercise undertaken, that viewers measure their preconceived ideas about Indigenous cultures against those dismantled in the film.

Niro's short film is quite unconventional. There is no continuing plot; instead, several vignettes with different content are strung together episodically. The film is reminiscent of a home-video clip, since the setting and acting betray a minimalistic approach that associates it with the 'aesthetic of hunger'. The unconventional elements in Niro's approach include such various stylistic means as the telescope/iris shots, blurring of images, color posterization, and a contrapuntal voice-over. On the one hand, these devices serve to make the viewer aware of the camera gaze and the fact that film is a manipulative medium. They keep a distance between viewer and

film in order to create the objectivity needed for appropriate absorption and
judgement of the filmic presentation. On the other hand, these devices are
technical vehicles of criticism, so that the stylistic means fully support the
film's content. In this short film, Niro puts on trial five hundred years of
European colonization of the Americas, with certain vignettes dealing with
aspects or results of the conquering process: the decimation and conquest of
the Indigenous population through warfare (repeating rifle) and epidemics
(small pox) as well as Indigenous economic dependency as established by
the fur trade (fur cap). Further, she attacks Indian stereotypes based on, or
leading to, eurocentric treatment and (mis)representation of Indigenous cultures in science, history, literature, and the media. Engaging Vizenor's
trickster discourse, Niro ostentatiously, even grotesquely, stages stereotypical notions in order to ridicule them instantly. At the same time, she commissions what Bhabha explains as the effectivity of colonial stereotypes
and their construction of colonial identities and subject positions – a
'dynamic of clichés': she presents clichés for their recognition by viewers
and ridicules them instants later, so that the effectivity of clichés is redirected toward their deconstruction.[57] After purging the cliché of its inscribed
meaning, the film reinscribes the scaffold (the image) with a new meaning.
Thus, some vignettes in the film 'outwit' the viewer by delivering the unexpected. The film startles the viewer and creates a gap between the generally associated image of 'the Indian' and images of how Indigenous people
see themselves. This gap has to be closed through an effort of critical re-
assessment on the part of the viewer. In this way, the film succeeds in dismantling present-day 'Indian' clichés and undermining the self/other
dichotomy cultivated by mainstream media.

☙ ☙

---

[57] On Bhabha's idea of employing and redirecting the effectivity of colonial stereotypes,
see chapter 2.

Figures

1.1

1.2

1.3

1.4

1.5

1.6

Road Allowance People (© Halfbreed Inc.)

1.7

1.8

1.9

1.10

1.11

1.12

Road Allowance People (© Halfbreed Inc.)

1.13

1.14

1.15

1.16

1.17

Itam Hakim, Hopiit (© IS Productions)

2.1

2.2

2.3

2.4

2.5

2.6

2.7

2.8

Itam Hakim, Hopiit (© IS Productions)

2.9

2.10

2.11

2.12

2.13

2.14

2.15

2.16

2.17

2.18

2.19

2.20

2.21

2.22

2.23

2.24

Itam Hakim, Hopiit (© IS Productions)

2.25

2.26

2.27

2.28

2.29

2.30

2.31

2.32

Itam Hakim, Hopiit (© IS Productions)

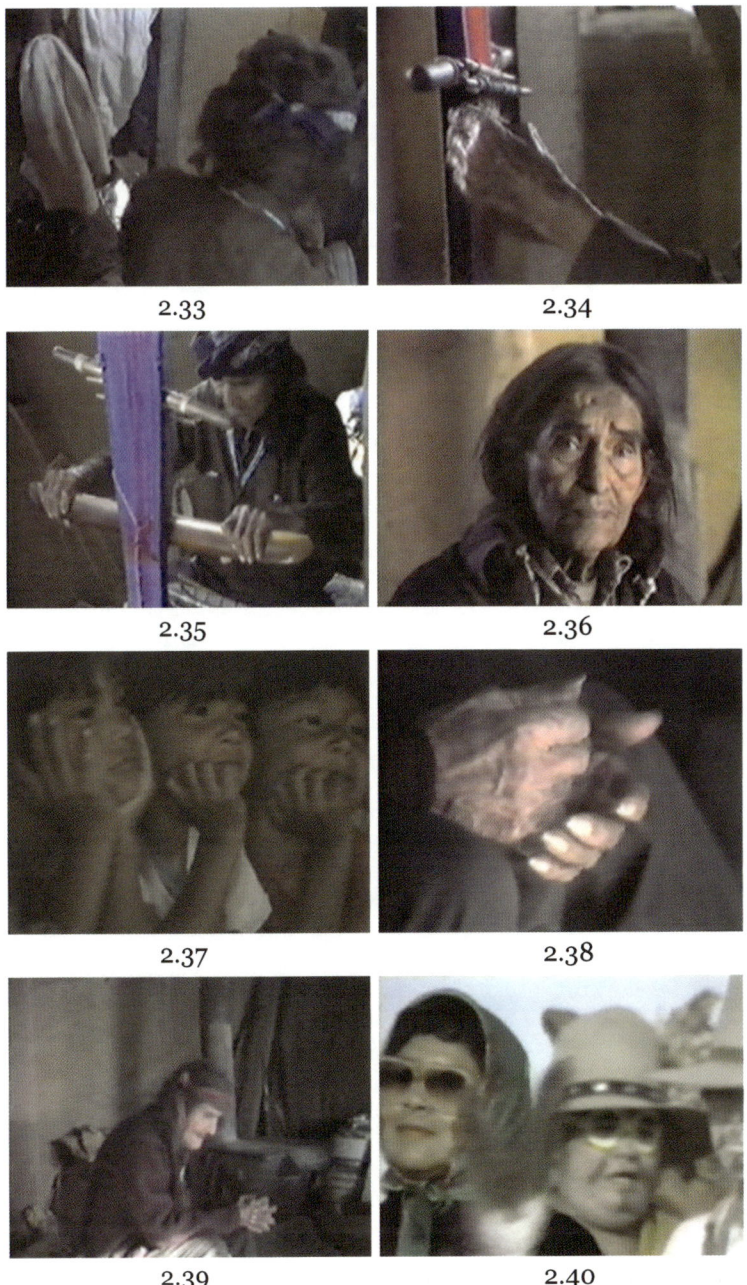

2.33

2.34

2.35

2.36

2.37

2.38

2.39

2.40

Itam Hakim, Hopiit (© IS Productions)

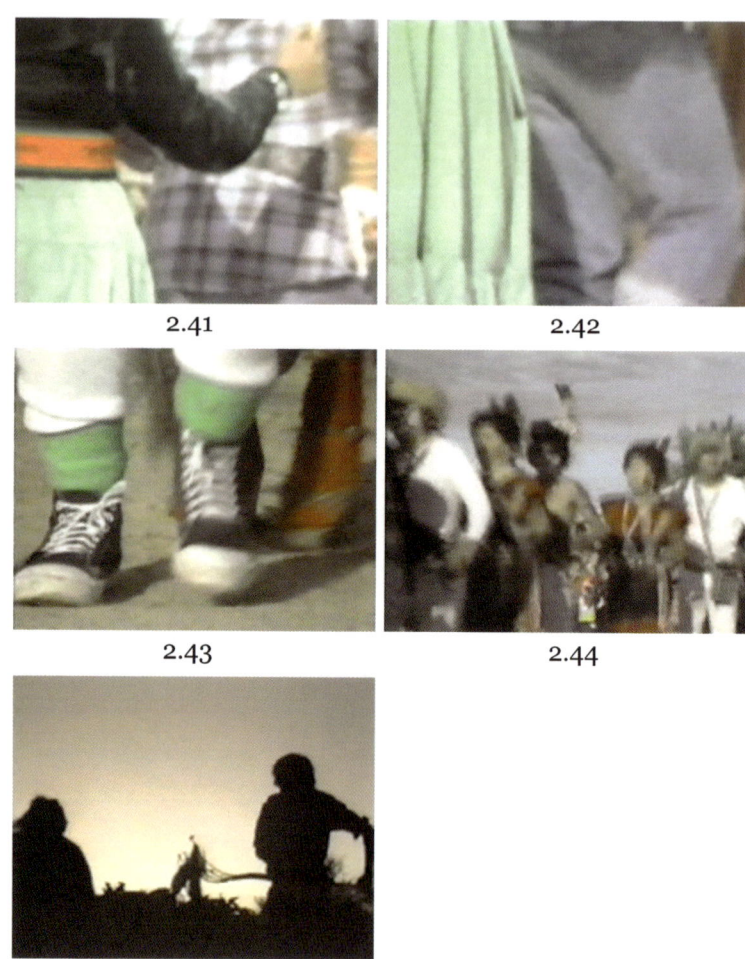

2.41

2.42

2.43

2.44

2.45

Talker (© Lloyd Martell)

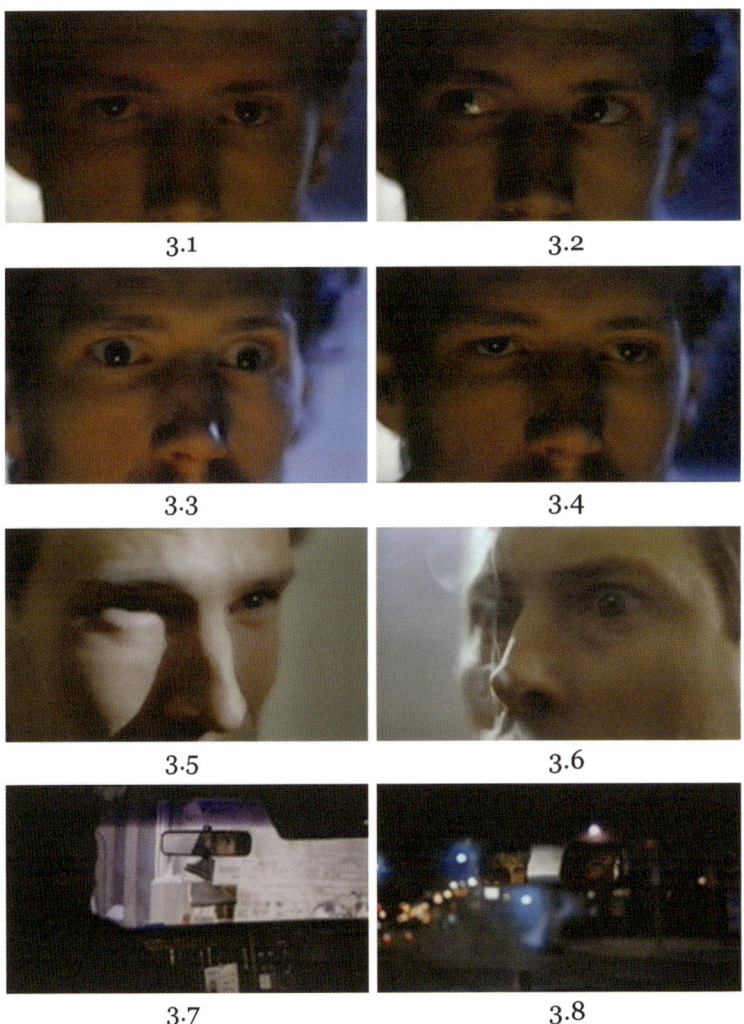

3.1

3.2

3.3

3.4

3.5

3.6

3.7

3.8

Talker (© Lloyd Martell)

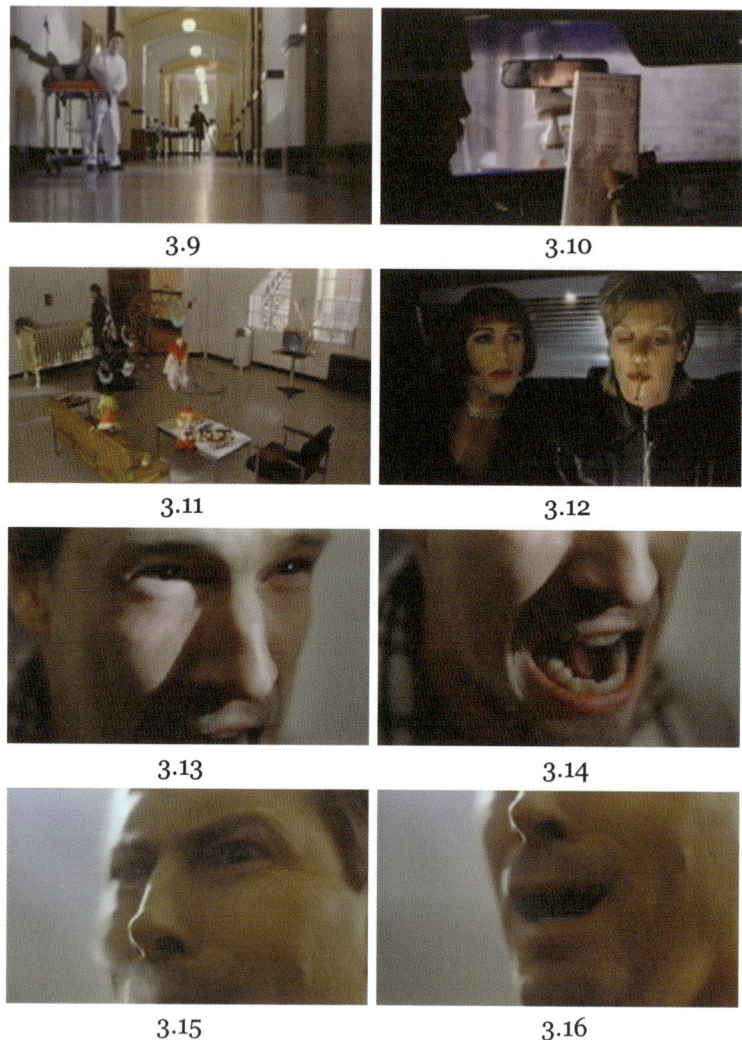

3.9   3.10

3.11   3.12

3.13   3.14

3.15   3.16

3.17

3.18

3.19

3.20

3.21

3.22

3.23

3.24

Talker (© Lloyd Martell)

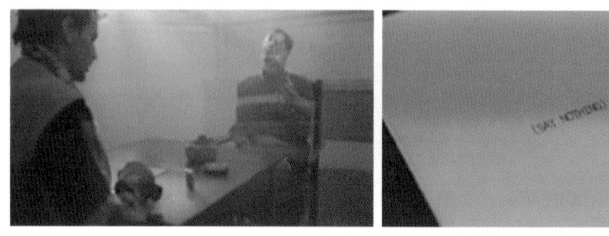

3.25   3.26

Tenacity (© Cheyenne/Arapaho Productions)

4.1

4.2

4.3

4.4

4.5

4.6

4.7

4.8

Tenacity (© Cheyenne/Arapaho Productions)

4.9

4.10

4.11

4.12

4.13

4.14

4.15

4.16

Tenacity (© Cheyenne/Arapaho Productions)

4.17   4.18

4.19

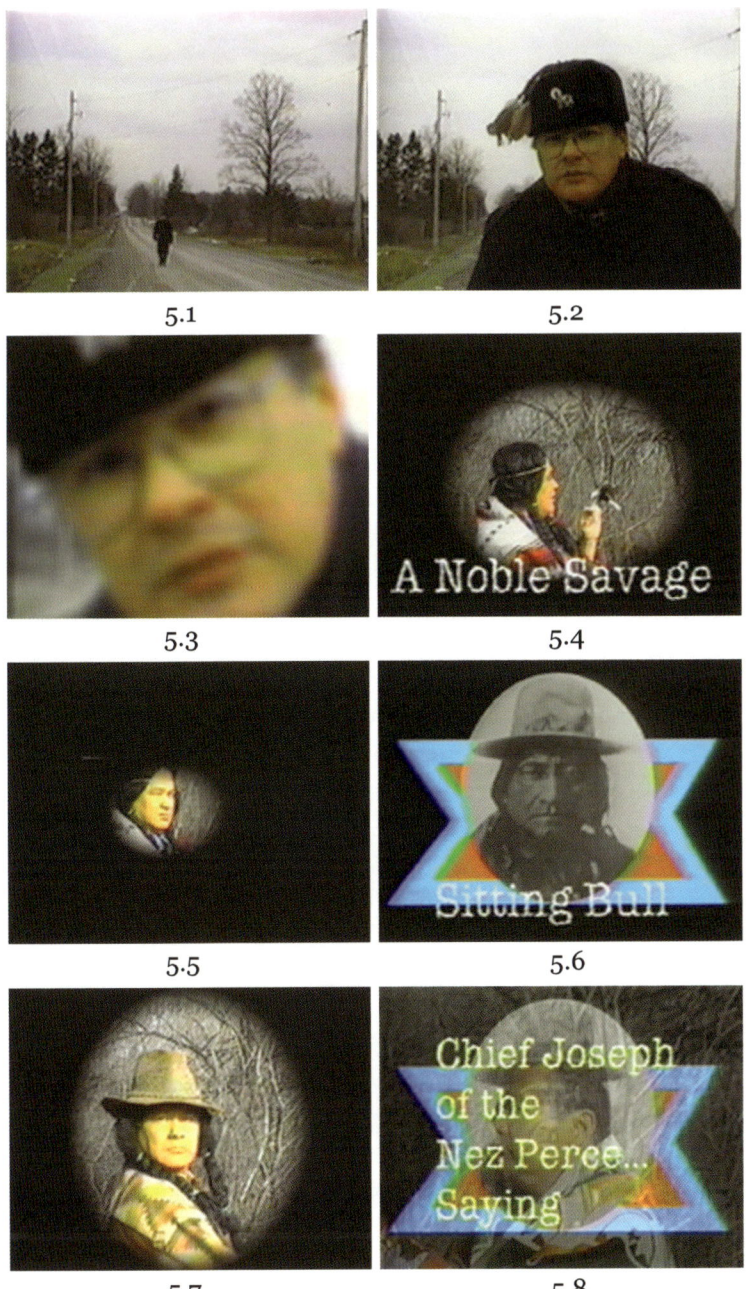

5.1   5.2

5.3   5.4

5.5   5.6

5.7   5.8

Overweight With Crooked Teeth (© Big Productions)

5.9

5.10

5.11

5.12

5.13

5.14

5.15

5.16

Overweight With Crooked Teeth (© Big Productions)

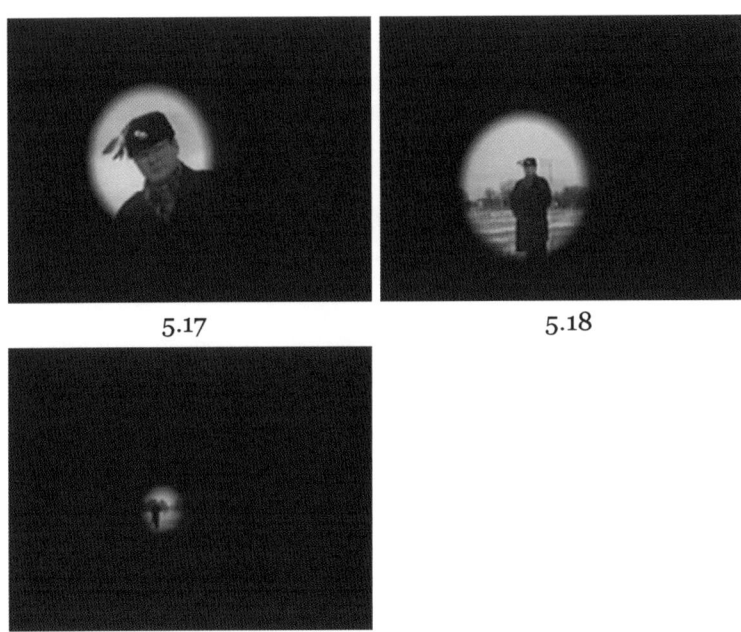

5.17   5.18

5.19

Honey Moccasin (© Turtle Night Productions)

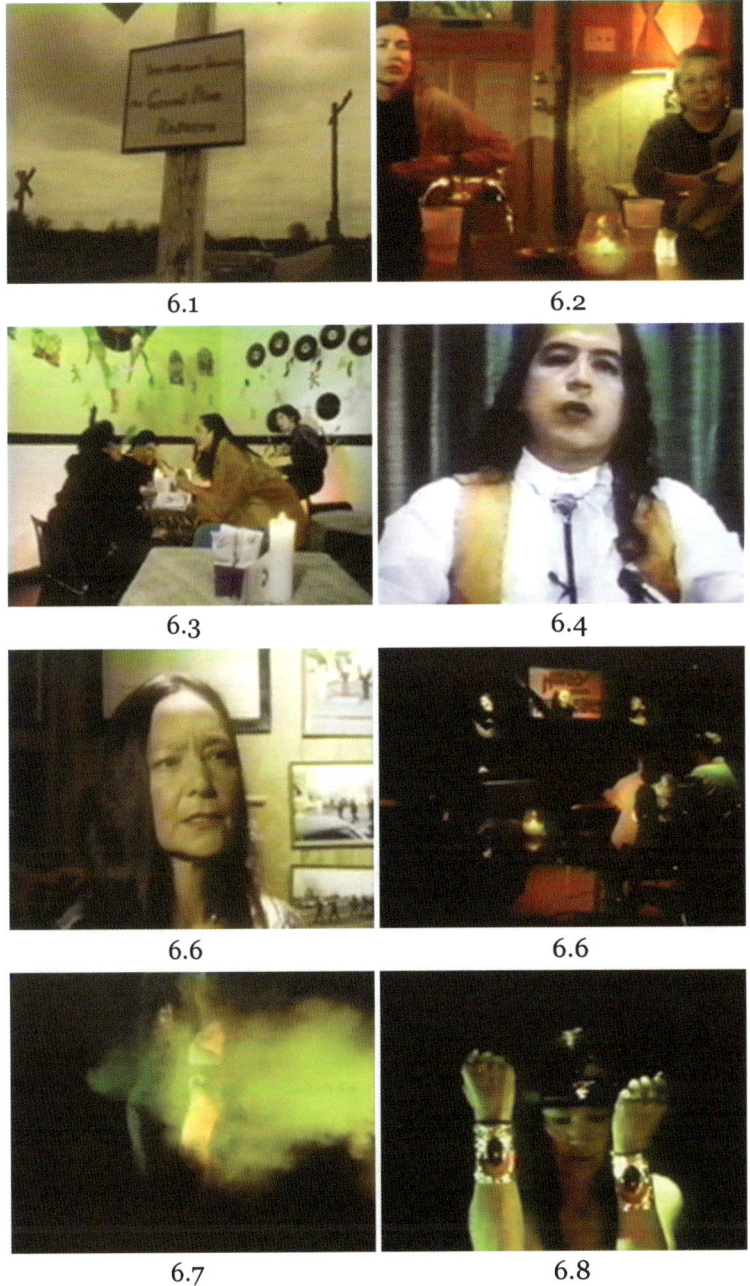

6.1

6.2

6.3

6.4

6.6

6.6

6.7

6.8

Honey Moccasin (© Turtle Night Productions)

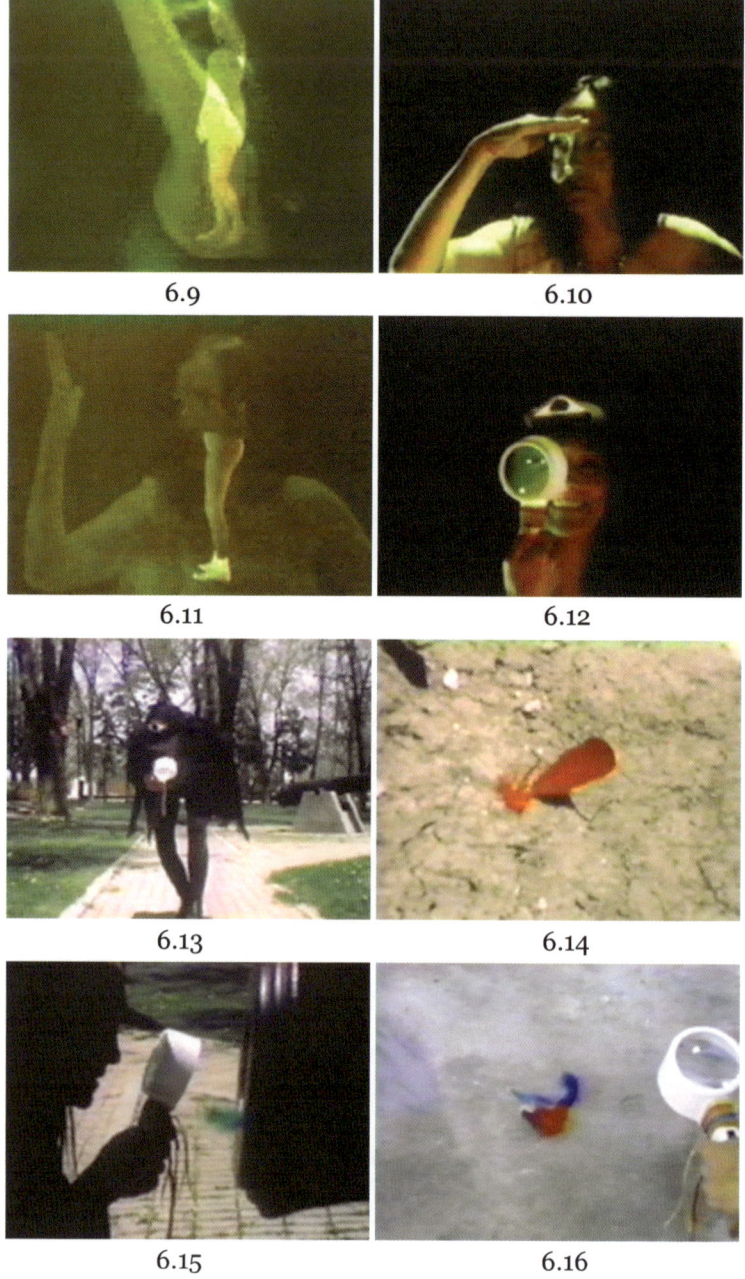

6.9   6.10

6.11   6.12

6.13   6.14

6.15   6.16

Honey Moccasin (© Turtle Night Productions)

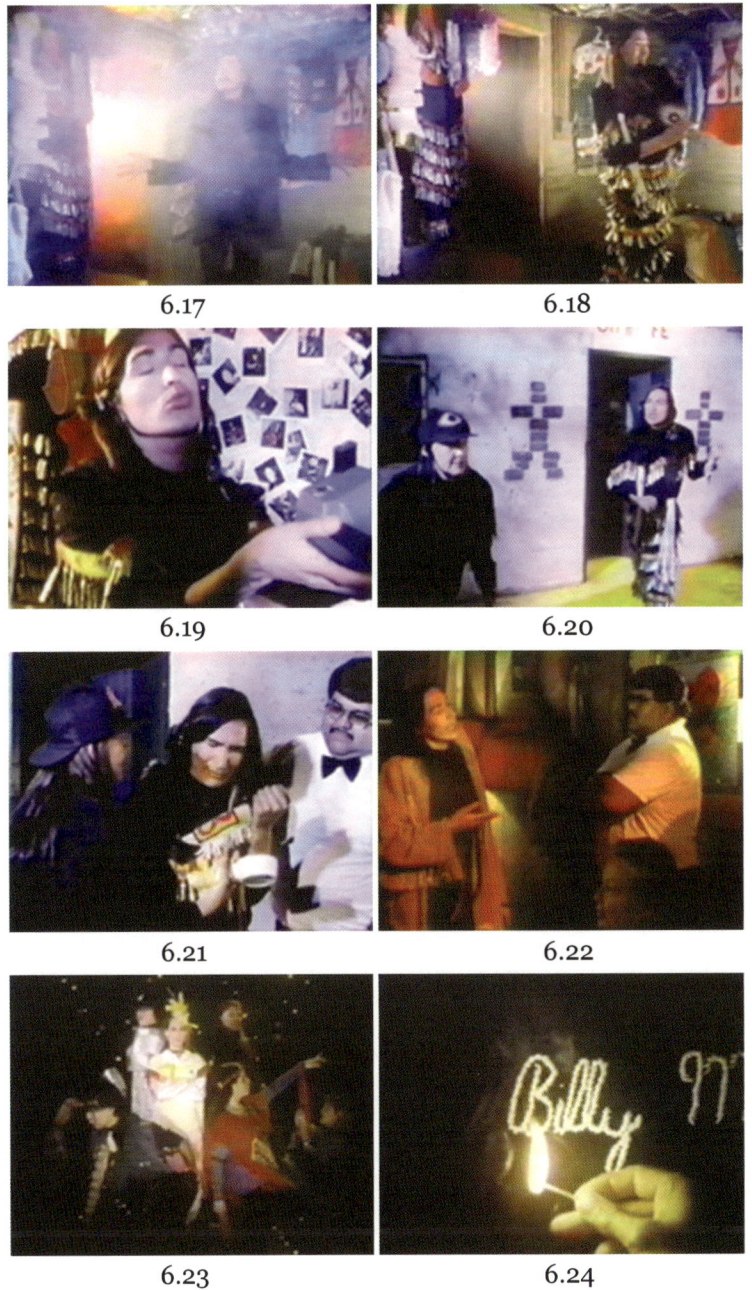

6.17

6.18

6.19

6.20

6.21

6.22

6.23

6.24

Honey Moccasin (© Turtle Night Productions)

6.25

6.26

6.27

6.28

6.29

6.30

6.31

6.32

Honey Moccasin (© Turtle Night Productions)

6.33   6.34

6.35   6.36

Smoke Signals (© Shadow Catcher Entertainment)

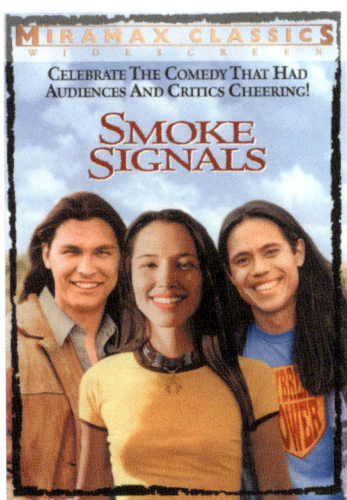

7.1

Big Bear (© Télé-Action Bear Inc. & Big Bear Film Inc.)

8.1

8.2

8.3

8.4

8.5

8.6

8.7

8.8

Big Bear (© Télé-Action Bear Inc. & Big Bear Film Inc.)

8.9

8.10

8.11

8.12

8.13

8.14

8.15

8.16

Big Bear (© Télé-Action Bear Inc. & Big Bear Film Inc.)

8.17

8.18

8.19

8.20

8.21

8.22

8.23

8.24

Big Bear (© Télé-Action Bear Inc. & Big Bear Film Inc.)

8.25

8.26

8.27

8.28

8.29

8.30

8.31

8.32

Big Bear (© Télé-Action Bear Inc. & Big Bear Film Inc.)

8.33

8.34

8.35

8.36

8.37

8.38

8.39

8.40

Big Bear (© Télé-Action Bear Inc. & Big Bear Film Inc.)

8.41

8.42

8.43

8.44

8.45

8.46

8.47

8.48

Big Bear (© Télé-Action Bear Inc. & Big Bear Film Inc.)

8.49

8.50

8.51

8.52

Atanarjuat: The Fast Runner (© Igloolik Isuma Productions)

9.1

9.2

9.3

9.4

9.5

9.6

9.7

9.8

Atanarjuat: The Fast Runner (© Igloolik Isuma Productions)

9.9   9.10

9.11   9.12

9.13   9.14

9.15   9.16

Atanarjuat: The Fast Runner (© Igloolik Isuma Productions)

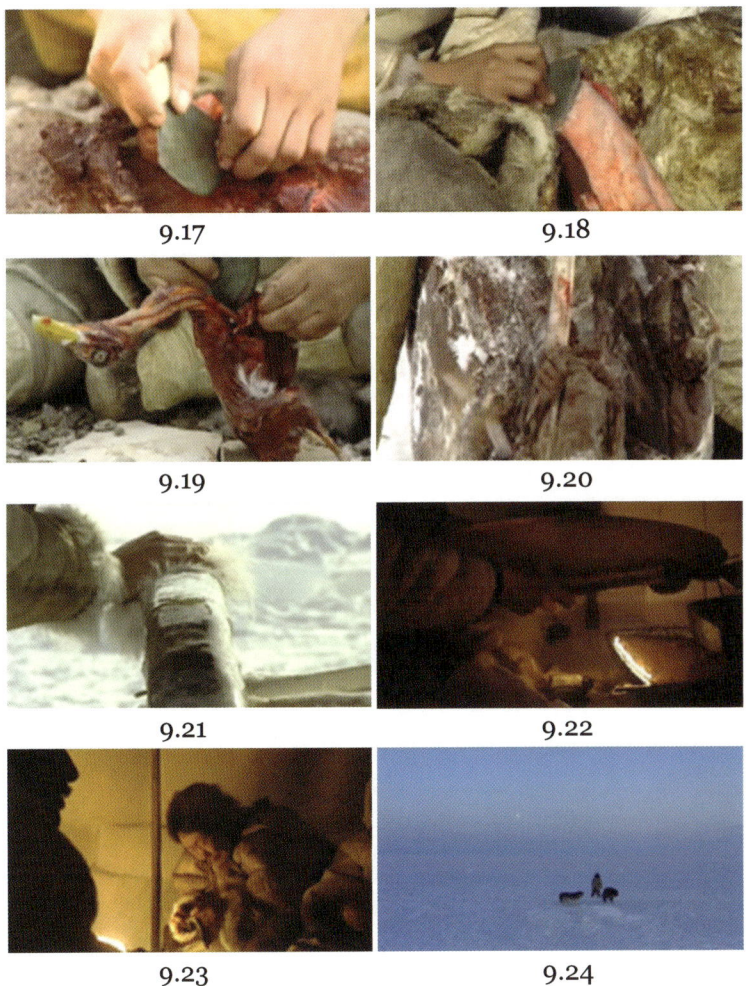

9.17

9.18

9.19

9.20

9.21

9.22

9.23

9.24

Atanarjuat: The Fast Runner (© Igloolik Isuma Productions)

9.25   9.26

9.27   9.28

9.29   9.30

9.31   9.32

Atanarjuat: The Fast Runner (© Igloolik Isuma Productions)

9·33   9·34

9·35   9·36

9·37   9.38

9·39   9.40

Atanarjuat: The Fast Runner (© Igloolik Isuma Productions)

9.41   9.42

9.43   9.44

9.45   9.46

9.47   9.48

5 Dramatic Films

THIS CHAPTER analyzes full-length fictional dramatizations by Indigenous filmmakers. *Honey Moccasin* falls outside the strict category of mainstream feature film, whereas *Smoke Signals*, *Big Bear* and *Atanarjuat: The Fast Runner* largely remain within the framework of mainstream conventions. The difference in the case of *Honey Moccasin* is partly due to the fact that the film was made on a small budget by a filmmaker with her own production company, ensuring independence from colonialist control by the mainstream film industry. However, this very independence has meant that the film misses out on the opportunities for distribution afforded by major networks, remaining limited to a small audience reached through film-festival screenings and minor distribution. *Atanarjuat: The Fast Runner*, similarly, was made by an independent Inuit production company but succeeded in achieving international acclaim. The other two films, the first major Indigenous film productions in the USA and Canada respectively, were either made in collaboration with large television companies (*Big Bear*) or were bought and financed by a Hollywood company (*Smoke Signals*). Such collaboration secures a large audience and major distribution in North America and Europe but also allows colonialist influences in the form of Western film conventions, among others, to enter the production process. In both cases, cooperation was sought by the filmmakers, who do not consider Indigenous filmmaking as an exclusive practice. Gil Cardinal and Doug Cuthand have made it clear in interviews (1998) that they retained control over the production process, and could thus limit direct colonialist influence.

Honey Moccasin

Shelley Niro's film *Honey Moccasin* is yet another example of the recent tradition of all-Indigenous filmmaking.[1] She wrote, directed, and produced it with her own film company, Turtle Night Productions. That means that, except for its realization via Western technology, it is an Indigenously autonomous product. Beyond its ethnocultural origins, the film defies easy categorization. The Métis filmmaker Marjorie Beaucage described it to me in private conversation as being "totally off the wall," and to me this seems to be the closest characterization possible upon first viewing. At times it is hilariously funny, ridiculing imposed and self-appropriated Indian stereo-types as well as widespread beliefs about reserve life. At other times, the film is sad and serious, reversing previously funny situations and pointing toward problems in Indigenous communities resulting from colonialism and marginalization. The film differs in aspects of its form and content from conventional narrative cinema. Asked to characterize her film, Niro has said:

> I think there's a lot of performance art in it, and it's based on entertaining. It takes on a lot of different layers and dimensions and does not necessarily stay within the narrative. [...] I'd like to think of the whole structure as being like a long poem, or what you call a tone poem. (interview, 1998)

Niro uses classical filmmaking techniques but does not abide by the rules of conventional filmmaking. *Honey Moccasin* employs a non-linear narra-tive, an uneven pace, and an indefinite narrative time and space. By setting the film in a contemporary Indigenous community, Niro confronts clichéd notions of Indigenous people that are centered on the traditional and historical, re-enacting oral storytelling with unconventional contemporary cinematic techniques, the rule-breaking of which yields alternatives to colo-nialist media discourse.

The sequence protocol in the Appendix gives a general idea of the plot as well as the temporal and spatial specifics of the sequences. The film runs about 49 minutes, a length that is quite unusual for a fiction-film. Not counting credits and titles, the ten sequences of the film (containing 51 shots of different length) run from 15 seconds up to 12 minutes, revealing

---

[1] The term 'all-Indigenous filmmaking' should not imply that there cannot be non-Indige-nous involvement in the crew or cast but that director, producer, scriptwriter, and/or a sub-stantial proportion of the crew is Indigenous.

the very uneven pace of the film. Some shots are linked by dissolves but most by a simple cut or fade. Except for the fades, all shots are connected either by sound bridges, the Native-tongue broadcast of one shot continuing in the background of the next, or by the characters indicating events in the next shot. The main characters are: Honey Moccasin (Tantoo Cardinal), owner of a bar called the "Smokin Moccasin"; her daughter Mabel (Florene Belmore), a filmmaker and performance artist; Zachary John (Billy Merasty), owner of the newly opened "Inukshuk Café"; his father Johnny John (Tom Hill); Bernelda Birch (Bernelda Wheeler) and Richard Rock (Paul Chaat–Smith), reporter and newscaster respectively at the Indigenous television station Native Tongue; and Beau Bradley (Kelly Henhawk), bouncer at the "Smokin Moccasin."

The Parody of Detective Stories as Digressive Narrative

The main narrative is a detective story, Honey's search for vanished pow-wow outfits. It is not a narrative in the classical sense because it is not clear and linear, nor is it driven by a consistent cause–effect chain.[2] Some sequences are not motivated by the previous sequence, and some narrative strands from one sequence are not taken up in the next or later in the film but are left 'unresolved.' It is a narrative that digresses and caricatures itself continually in its other form – the metanarrative, which describes and comments on the film *Honey Moccasin*. The metanarrative further reveals and emphasizes the techniques and tools of filmmaking, à la the Brechtian alienation effect, as well as providing an exemplary account of Indigenous filmmaking. Several subnarratives revolve around, cross over, and merge with the main narrative. These concern the rivalry between Honey and Zach, Zach's struggle with his gay identity, and Indigenous television, videomaking, and writing. The film presents a world full of vivid, and sometimes bizarre, characters.

Of the ten sequences, four are set in the "Smokin Moccasin," two in the "Inukshuk Café," one in a car, and one in the Native Tongue studio. The narrative space is therefore made up largely of interiors. The space of the reserve itself remains unclear. Only the flashbacks in sequences 1 and 3 are set outside, but they do not employ a long landscape shot in which a sense of the place where the film is set might have been conveyed. One long

---

[2] On the cause-and-effect chain, see David Bordwell & Kristin Thompson, *Film Art: An Introduction* (1979; New York: McGraw–Hill, 1997): 90–101.

landscape shot occurs in the Native Tongue clip featuring Hank singing (sequence 10). But apart from the fact that this shot appears only in the last sequence after the closing title, according to the narrative it belongs to a video clip, the location of which would not be valid in terms of the narrative space of the film. Thus, the narrative space remains unclear. Unlike fictitious reserves in movies and novels, this one is made to look unreal. The two flashbacks in sequence 1 show a sign, in a low angle and straight medium shot, reading "You are now leaving the Grand Pine Reserve" as a car drives by (Fig. 6.1). It is customary to find such signs upon entering and leaving reserves and reservations, but these are official signs, not handwritten and nailed on a St Andrew's Cross the way this one is. Very little of the environment is seen in either shot, so that the shots do not permit geographical localization. One device for creating a sense of an unreal narrative space is the 'distant planet' name of the neighboring town, Pluto. Imagine hearing: "I see we have some young people from Pluto here tonight" as Honey greets guests in her bar. Since Pluto is also the god of the underworld in Roman mythology, the place name 'Pluto' generates an unworldly narrative space in a twofold manner. Thus, Niro designs not only a fictitious narrative space but also an unreal one, and her cinematic devices indicate that the film has taken the viewers onto a reserve in a netherworld.

Just as the narrative space is kept obscure, so is the narrative time. The viewers can infer that the plot is set in May 1995. Honey tells them her age and birth year and the Native Tongue newscast refers to the end of WWII as fifty years ago. But apart from the point of time when the narrative takes place, there is no way of knowing how much time passes between the sequences and how long the detective narrative needs to develop and conclude, since no temporal clues are provided. Nor do the characters have fixed 'deadlines' in which they have to perform certain tasks or achieve specific goals, which would have provided a set time-frame. Instead, Niro employs temporal discontinuity at one point. Honey searches for the thief during the day, and right after this enters her bar at night with the same clothes on and the magnifying glass still in her hand. It seems as if Honey has jumped through time and space. The blurring of narrative time and space matches the unsteady narrative and the uneven pace, implying the use of alternative, unconventional filmmaking methods.

The "Smokin Moccasin" and the "Inukshuk Café," the sites of most of the action, serve as metonyms for two opposite spaces: the community space and the space of the outsider. Honey Moccasin is on good terms with everybody, her bar is a meeting-place for reserve residents, and she seems to be the center of the community. Zach, by contrast, coming from Pluto, is not fully integrated into the community. He opens a café with a karaoke machine and serves health food and non-alcoholic beverages exclusively. His readiness to adapt to modern developments and his practical comments on the problems of alcoholism, obesity, and diabetes that loom large in Indigenous communities do not meet with the approval of the community members. To have Zach coming from Pluto, associated with space or the underworld, also determines his otherness. As space and the underworld are the 'other' to the world, so is Zach the 'other' to the rest of the Grand Pine community. He also has to come to terms with his gay identity. His uneasiness shows in his encounters with Beau, who he thinks is continually threatening him. Zach is as much an 'outsider' as Honey is an 'insider'. This antagonism is further developed by Zach's lop-sided rivalry with Honey, a conflict introduced at the end of the first sequence when he tells a bar customer that he felt deprived of his inheritance by Honey, who bought the bar from his father. The reddish-yellowish light in Honey's bar give it an air of warmth and security, whereas the bright light in the café and the Inukshuk pattern[3] on the walls, as well as its plain interior, give off an air of coldness and discomfort (Figs. 6.2–6.3). In addition, the smoke in the bar adds a familiar atmosphere, as many Indigenous people are smokers. The smoke also invokes spirituality in Indigenous culture semantics, for ritual cleansing is usually done with the smoke of burning sweetgrass. The place names "Smokin Moccasin" and "Inukshuk Café" enhance this effect by referring to a smoky warmth and the cold Arctic. The space metaphor that defines Honey as insider and central and Zach as outsider and marginal reflects existing colonialist relations in North America, where Indigenous people are politically, socially, and economically marginalized and structurally relegated to the space of the 'other'. The mass media, especially, employ signifiers that associate Indigenous people with the notion of the 'other' and 'outsider', as is shown by the media coverage of the Oka and Caledonia crises, land-claim negotiations, discussions about taxation, and other such matters.

The opening sequence of the film introduces the viewer to the main narrative. The Native Tongue newscast announces that there have been mys-

---

[3] 'Inukshuk' is the Inuit term for a figure imitating a human being; it is made of several stones placed on top of each other. Such figures are usually erected as trail markings in the Arctic.

terious break-ins during recent weeks, and that powwow outfits have been stolen (Fig. 6.4). Then the film does a dog-leg (as I do now from the narrative line) to Honey introducing herself to the audience in the bar. She talks about her parents, her birth, her childhood, and her marriage with Hank. Her story is illustrated by two black-and-white flashbacks. After finishing her story she sings a song. At the beginning of this sequence, the viewer is cued to believe that Honey is the only person in this space and is introducing herself to her/him exclusively. Only towards the end, when the camera zooms out and pans through the room, is the viewer acquainted with the larger setting of the bar and the audience in the bar that was also listening to Honey's story (Figs. 6.5, 6.2, 6.6). The film has fooled the viewer into believing s/he was the only 'audience'. By revealing the whole setting only gradually with zooms and pans, the camera draws attention to itself. Through this sleight of hand, the film breaks up the seamless presentation of an illusionistic reality and discloses its metanarrative.

Only in the next sequence, when Richard Rock from Native Tongue demands the return of the powwow outfits in the name to the robbed, does the film return the viewer to the detective plot. A few sequences later they are reminded of the robberies again by the Native Tongue broadcast, when, at the end of his interview, Zach snatches the microphone from Bernelda and condemns the thief ferociously. Then Honey transforms herself into Wonder Woman, a figure resembling Pocahontas, and finally into an ironic copy of Sherlock Holmes, with Bernelda watching in awe (Figs. 6.7–6.12). In the next sequence, Honey re-enacts a 'search' for the outfits, sporting a ludicrous Sherlock Holmes outfit: black jacket and tights matched by a black hat with two peaks and a huge eye stitched on the front. She also carries an oversized magnifying glass with (stereo-)typical fringes and wears a (stereo-) typical fringe-jacket. This outfit (coupled with her stooped posture as she searches for clues through the magnifying glass) derides Sherlock Holmes movies rather than representing a serious detective search. Honey does not even have to look far for clues: a trail of bright-colored feathers leads her straight to the "Inukshuk Café" (Figs. 6.13–6.16). Thus, the main narrative is a burlesque; it is not a classical detective plot, which would be designed to maintain suspense until the very last frames. Instead, the way the 'search' is presented – as obvious, blatant, and easily trackable – deconstructs any suspense and parodies mysteries.

There is no suspense in *Honey Moccasin* whatsoever, because, before the search sequence, the viewer sees Zach steal a beaded knife and drop colored feathers, which links him with the crime. When he denounces the thief in the television interview, the viewer can read in his facial play that he knows more about the stolen powwow outfits than he admits. At these points the detective mystery turns into another kind of mystery: the narrative steers the attention of the viewer from the identity of the thief to the question of why he would steal the outfits. It then reveals this mystery by showing Zach descending into his basement, where he keeps the stolen powwow costumes. The descent stands for his withdrawal into a hide-out and his re-emergence into an imaginary (under)world. His uncanny surreal basement maintains the motif of the underworld associated with him through his home town Pluto. Upon entering the room, Zach breathes in the air of magic deeply, as if to initiate his transformation now into a jingle-dress dancer. In this costume he becomes the person he desires to be – a bewitching woman. Zach pathetically jingle-dances in a totally off-beat manner and takes his/her own Polaroids to nurture his/her illusion of being a beautiful woman. S/he has repeated the little ceremony of jingle-dancing and taking pictures of him/herself over and over again, as evidenced by the many photos on the wall where s/he pins the new ones (Figs. 6.17–6.19). The plot reaches a pseudo-dramatic 'climax' when Zach notices that s/he is being watched by Honey. S/he instantly changes back into Zach (though he still wears the jingle dress), for the magic of the moment is gone. In pursuit of the detective, he proceeds outside into a moonlit night, complete with the sound of howling coyotes. He attempts to kill Honey with a knife but is prevented from doing so by Beau, who wrestles with him until he collapses crying (Figs. 6.20–6.21). The closure of the 'detective plot' is represented by Zach's publicly returning the stolen outfits as part of the punishment imposed by the elders. Niro hereby offers an alternative punishment for crimes, reaching back to methods of precolonial Indigenous punishment dictated by the community.[4]

The pseudo-climax completes the main narrative as well as the first two subnarratives by providing resolutions for each one of them: the pseudo-mystery is solved and Zach is identified as the thief; Zach fails to get even with Honey; and Zach comes out and admits that he loves Beau. The dramatic point is not a climax in the classical sense, because Niro has not applied faster cutting and added rousing dramatic music, nor has she crea-

---

[4] Traditionally, offenders would most often be ridiculed publicly or ostracized. Recently, there has been a marked re-emergence of sentencing circles and alternative Indigenous punishment of offenders.

ted suspense leading towards the climax. Rather, the narrative works the opposite way, leading the viewer directly to the suspect by providing blatant hints throughout the film. Accordingly, the viewer is provided with unrestricted story information throughout the film.[5] The attempted murder cannot be taken seriously, either, for Zach raises a knife still covered by a sheath. This senseless action, coupled with the slow-motion movements of Honey and Zach in the 'killing' scene, work to undermine the detective plot as well. The moon and the howling coyotes also parody suspenseful scenes in murder mysteries. Honey's ridiculous detective outfit and the magnifying glass she needs to find clues make the parodic enactment of a classical detective story even more obvious. Niro creates an unreal surrealistic play within the film, the actors playing characters who, in turn, re-enact a play. Thus, the tragedy inevitably becomes comedy, the detective plot burlesque – metanarrative ridicules narrative.

The organization of the narrative in this film differs greatly from that in commercial mainstream films. The plot line often branches off to different events that do not seem to support the main narrative line. The main narrative line does not even sustain itself. It is modified in the course of the film by changing from the mystery around the vanished outfits into one about whether or not Zach can solve the problems centered on his gay identity, where it merges with one of its subnarratives. Whereas in classical filmmaking the characters often have clear-cut, long-range goals which create a conflict between them, none of the characters in *Honey Moccasin* has a clearly defined goal.[6] Zach's goal of 'getting even with Honey', which supplies the only conflict in the film, is only vaguely delineated. Other than this one conflict, characters' short-term goals, such as Honey trying to track down the thief and Johnny intending to host a fashion show, seem sporadically interspersed.

Classical filmmaking usually shortens inset artistic elements unless their full length is necessary for the plot. Niro however, includes two full-length songs (Honey, 2.43 min.; Hank, 1.15 min.), an art performance (Mabel's interpretation of "You Give Me Fever," 3.29 min.), and the screening of a short film (Mabel's film *Inukshuk*, 4.18 min.), making up more than one-fifth of the 49-minute film. These parts do not advance the narrative line,

---

[5] On restricted and unrestricted story information as a means of creating or denying suspense, see Bordwell & Thompson, *Film Art*, 102–108 and 388–93.

[6] French New Wave films likewise often lack goal-oriented protagonists (Bordwell & Thompson, *Film Art*, 466).

thus they become separate entities, generating their own meaning apart from the plot proper. This is another instance showing that the film does not necessarily employ a tightly organized and coherent narrative with goal-motivated characters. Rather, the stress on events outside the narrative, such as Honey's lengthy introduction, the screening of a home-video clip, the songs, and Mabel's performances, suggests that this film is not a narrative film in the conventional sense and that Niro's filmmaking relies on a more circular narrative weaving around the characters embedded in a community. *Honey Moccasin* is a medial form of community storytelling similar to the kind of storytelling Niro experiences in her own Indigenous environment. As the director herself says:

> What I find very often with Iroquois storytelling is that they start out, and it doesn't really have a conclusion. It might go from a beginning to a germ of the story but then the ending doesn't really end with a parable, or doesn't end with a moral or discovery of a universal truth. (interview, 1998)

Disrupting Western Clichés

Niro's modes of representation counter existing stereotypes and misrepresentations of Indigenous people in the mainstream media. She presents characters integrated into a larger community, where everybody seems to know everybody else and people call each other by their first names. Denying the film any historical references and setting it on a contemporary reserve in a netherworld, Niro attempts to free Indigenous presentation from its imprisonment in historical movies. Most films about 'Indians' are history dramas and come under either historical realism or historical romance. They "invariably situate Indians in the past, usually on the western frontier,"[7] with the result that Indigenous people exist mainly in a past-tense media discourse. Niro creates her own time-planes in an indefinite present, hence breaks with the 'tradition' of historical realism. The characters are not stereotyped victims but filmmakers, performers, television-makers, bar-owners and songwriters. No one-dimensional, rigid characters line up to illustrate some one-sided narrative, but a vivid, colorful community becomes the center of a narrative that explores various angles of contemporary Indigenous life. The only character who vaguely resembles the contemporary cliché Indian is Zach, who is a handsome, slender guy with long

---

[7] Daniel Francis, *The Imaginary Indian: The Image of the Indian in Canadian Culture* (Vancouver, British Columbia: Arsenal Pulp, 1992): 107.

hair and 'Indian-style' clothes. But since he is gay and the outsider, the film undercuts that cliché as well.

In the film, Niro plays with, and at the same time criticizes, notions that are part of a stereotypical North American mainstream construct of Indigenous people. Beau sports all the features of the 'stoic, non-talkative Indian', by generally standing in the doorway with folded arms and frozen stare (Fig. 6.22). At the end of the fashion show, three models assume this same 'Indian posture' and one model strikes the 'Indian' pose of gazing into the distance, one hand shading the eyes (Fig. 6.23). These interpretations cater to the familiar stereotypes but depart from the tradition of Indian presentation in mainstream photography and cinema. They are obviously being employed as a satirical undercutting of the same clichés. A subliminal critique resides in the fact that Zach opens the "Inukshuk Café" and applies an Arctic touch to its interior décor. By doing so, he exoticizes Arctic cultures in the same way as Western thought, writings, and films exoticize Indigenous cultures. Also, the notion of the bloodthirsty Indian, which still prevails in contemporary movies, is reduced to a ludicrous image when Zach, in his attempt to kill Honey, is not only unsuccessful but does not even remove the sheath from the knife.[8] Zach's character is a subversive presentation of the two opposing Indian clichés of the 'noble savage' and 'bloodthirsty Indian': a handsome Indigenous man who is gay and steals, and a killer who is unable to kill. The glaring absence of a wise old medicine wo/man or some sort of spiritual ceremony, which can be found in so many mainstream films that deal with Indigenous culture, either predominantly or marginally,[9] is a fact that speaks for itself about preconceived ideas of

---

[8] To illustrate the kind of thing Niro is up against, compare, for example, Ryszard Bugajski's *Clearcut* (Canada, 1991), in which Arthur (Graham Greene) is mysteriously guided by a medicine man (Floyd Red Crow Westerman), turns into a savage radical, and tortures his white hostage. The film very graphically illustrates this stereotype and reinforces the imagery of Indigenous North Americans as savages, predominant since first contact. The fierce Magua (Wes Studi) in *Last of the Mohicans* (USA, 1992) and the ruthless Pawnee (Wes Studi; this character does not even have a name but is called "Toughest Pawnee" in the closing titles) in *Dances With Wolves* (USA, 1990) also serve as examples. Because these are contemporary movies, supposedly conscious of how they are representing Indigenous cultures, they do more damage than older westerns, which portrayed Indians as 'savagely' attacking 'peaceful' European settlers but which, through their blatant presentation and historical setting, register more easily as misrepresentations.

[9] The films *Natural Born Killers* (USA, 1994), *Clearcut*, *Dances With Wolves*, and *Billy Jack* (USA, 1971) are good examples here. The couple in *Natural Born Killers*, on their lethal odyssey through the West, finally find their way into the house of an old Navajo (Russell Means), who gives them shelter and, in a feeble attempt to exorcize the demon in both,

Western filmmakers and Niro's response to such. It is usually the mystic
and spiritual aspect of Indigenous cultures that enthrals the mainstream
public – not contemporary issues. In a way, the ever-present medicine
wo/man in such movies serves to add exotic flavor, to attract viewers, and
to sell the product. Niro leaves out any spiritual aspect that invites the
romanticization of Indigenous cultures.

During her transformation, Honey briefly becomes a figure that resembles the romantic Western idea of an Indian princess. Because stereotypical
thinking usually associates a young Indigenous woman with Pocahontas, I
would argue that Niro has Honey slip into the role of the latter.[10] Jacquelyn

---

performs a ceremony because he 'mysteriously' knows what their problem is. The Navajo
does not speak English, though he is dressed in contemporary blue jeans and shirt. He has a
rattlesnake living in his hogan (a circumstance which Navajos would most likely refrain
from), which earns him the trust of the couple, for the snake is their self-declared power symbol. After they have killed him as well, there is a sea of rattlesnakes outside the hogan aveng-
ing the Indian's death; their own source of power has turned against them. The Navajo is the
first person the two do not mean to kill, which conveys that the Indigenous culture is romanticized as something special, separate from the hypocritical society the couple abhors. It is his
mystic and spiritual aura that secures the Indian's right to exist in the movie. Why these two,
who have not had any contact with Native American culture before, choose an Indian medicine man to be their healer is rather obvious: it expresses the unconscious search of Western
individuals for a spiritual and ecological dimension that is supposedly lacking in eurocentric
cultures. Through the story that the Navajo tells about a woman who nurses a sick snake and
later gets bitten by it, he foretells his own fate. The dying Navajo explains that he has been
expecting the demon for twenty years, which is similar to the Western myth of the Aztec
myth of the return of the white god Quetzalcoatl who 'materialized' in the shape of Cortez.
This myth of a myth served as colonial legitimization for genocide as rooted in Indigenous
mythology. In *Billy Jack*, the mixed-blood protagonist and returning soldier has to perform a
traditional rattlesnake ritual in order to acquire vision and to be fully initiated into Indian
culture. And, of course, a film like *Dances With Wolves*, which simultaneously sentimental-
izes a dying Indian culture and perpetuates stereotypes by polarizing the 'human' Sioux and
the 'savage' Pawnee, would not be right without a wise medicine man (Graham Greene).

[10]There is quite a body of critical work in literature and the media on the genesis of the
Pocahontas myth as well as on misrepresentations of the historical Pocahontas and her encounters with John Smith and John Rolfe. See, for example, Rebecca Blevins Faery, *Cartographies of Desire: Captivity, Race, and Sex in the Shaping of an American Nation* (Norman:
U of Oklahoma P, 1999); Beth Brant, "Grandmothers of a New World," in *Writing As Witness: Essay and Talk* (Toronto: Women's Press, 1994): 83–103; Rayna Green, "The Pocahontas Perplex: The Image of Indian Women in American Culture," *Massachusetts Review*
16.4 (Autumn 1975): 698–14; Rayna Green, "What is the Pocahontas Perplex?" *The Runner*
1.3 (Summer 1994): 9; Marianette Jaimes–Guerrero, "Savage Erotica Exotica: Media Imagery
of Native Women in North America," in *Native North America: Critical and Cultural Perspectives*, ed. Renée Hulan (Toronto: ECW, 1999): 187–210; Miles Morrisseau, "Disney's
Disgrace," *Aboriginal Voices* 2.3 (September–October 1995): 16–17; Jacquelyn Kilpatrick,
"Disney's 'Politically Correct' Pocahontas," *Cineaste* 21.4 (Fall 1995): 36; and Hartmut Lutz,

Kilpatrick writes pointedly about the 1995 Disney interpretation of the
"Pocahontas story":

> The visual is emotionally more compelling than the written word, to say
> nothing of being more accessible, and since few people will read about
> Pocahontas, this film will exist as "fact" in the minds of generations of
> American children. They will believe in the Romeo and Juliet in the wilds
> of North America that Disney has presented.[11]

Kilpatrick points out that visual media prove to be much more effective
than written media. As recent developments show, especially the younger
generations are 'schooled' to spend time with electronic media in the form
of computer and video games, internet, interactive media, television and
video, at the cost of reading. There are also many people who do not habi-
tually read books or are illiterate, so that their mode of information consumption is reduced to the visual as well. Thus, it is obvious that a stereotype that is perpetuated predominantly in the visual media can also be most
effectively disrupted in a visual medium – for example, film. It can break
down stereotypical ideas about Indigenous people in the minds of people
who otherwise consume cliché-saturated films. Such a film (*Honey Moccasin* being our present example) is trickster discourse, engaging in carnivalesque dialogue with romanticizing and cliché-laden films to ridicule and
subvert previous mainstream (mis)interpretations as well as mockingly
negotiating the traditional and modern Indigenous experience.

Just as Niro challenges Indian stereotypes, she also challenges stereotypical assumptions that homogenize homosexuals, crossdressers, and
transsexuals. Although Zach appears as a gay character at the start, one
cannot categorize him as such. Wanting to be a woman in order to be
attractive to men is not necessarily typical of gay men; it is, rather, common
among transsexuals. Also, the butterfly-like (dragonfly-like) posture Zach
assumes toward the end of Mabel's film can be read as a transsexual metaphor, for among transsexuals the butterfly symbolizes the metamorphosis
from one sex to the other,[12] and the dragonfly offers a metaphor for two-

---

"'Indiáns' and Native Americans in the Movies: A History of Stereotypes, Distortions, and
Displacements," *Visual Anthropology* 3 (1990): 31–48. However, there is also a trend among
Indigenous people to re-appropriate a eurocentric romanticization of their own culture.

[11] Jacquelyn Kilpatrick, "Disney's 'Politically Correct' Pocahontas," 36.

[12] I am indebted to Heike Gerds for this information.

spirit people.[13] In the character of Zach, Niro addresses the issue of gay, lesbian, and transgender individuals in Indigenous communities and the Western construct of the berdache.[14] Through Zach, she calls for more tolerance toward gay people in Indigenous communities but also links gayness and Indigeneity in Western thought. Berdaches or two-spirited people can be either women or men who, as one aspect of their being, assume the culturally defined role, life style, or personality traits of the opposite sex partially or completely.[15] Male berdaches have been documented in nearly 150 different Indigenous groups in North America.[16] Roscoe identifies three key features of berdache roles:

> *productive specialization* (crafts and domestic work for male berdaches and warfare, hunting and leadership roles in the case of female berdaches), *supernatural sanction* (in the form of an authorization and/or bestowal of powers from extrasocietal sources) and *gender variation* (in relation to normative cultural expectations for male and female genders).[17]

Cross-dressing as the most visible feature, however, does not prove to be the most reliable one for gauging berdache status. Studies imply that most berdaches are homosexual, to speak in Western terminology, but can also be bisexual and heterosexual.[18] Berdaches were integrated and revered

---

[13] Terry Tafoya, "M. Dragonfly: Two-Spirit and the Tafoya Principle of Uncertainty," in *Two-Spirit People: Native American Gender Identity, Sexuality, and Spirituality*, ed. Sue–Ellen Jacobs, Wesley Thomas & Sabine Lang (Urbana & Chicago: U of Illinois P, 1997): 193.

[14] Niro brought this fact to my attention in an email conversation.

[15] Sabine Lang, "Various Kinds of Two-Spirit People: Gender Variance and Homosexuality in Native American Communities," in *Two-Spirit People: Native American Gender Identity, Sexuality, and Spirituality*, ed. Sue–Ellen Jacobs, Wesley Thomas & Sabine Lang (Urbana & Chicago: U of Illinois P, 1997): 114.

[16] Will Roscoe, "How to Become a Berdache: Toward a Unified Analysis of Gender Diversity," in *Third Sex, Third Gender: Beyond Sexual Dimorphism in Culture and History*, ed. Gilbert Herdt (New York: Zone, 1994): 330.

[17] Roscoe, "How to Become a Berdache: Toward a Unified Analysis of Gender Diversity," 332; emphasis in original. The status of berdache can be also understood in terms of Indigenous concepts of gender and sex: "In traditional thought [...] masculine and feminine are considered cultural features rather than biological differences; gender is related to occupation and sexuality does not define [an] individual's position in the social structure"; Massimiliano Carocci, "The Berdache as Metahistorical Reference for the Urban Gay American Indian Community," in *Present is Past: Some Uses of Tradition in Native Societies*, ed. Marie Mauzé (Lanham MD: UP of America, 1997): 117.

[18] Sue–Ellen Jacobs, "Is the 'North American Berdache' Merely a Phantom in the Imagination of Western Social Scientists?" in *Two-Spirit People: Native American Gender Identity,*

members of their communities, who attributed to them spiritual and often supernatural powers. It is most important to note that the status of being berdache is not (only) a mode of gender variance; rather, it is defined by economic/occupational and religious/spiritual attributes.[19]

The term 'berdache' was originally a French term (from Arabic < Persian) for the younger male homosexual partner. It was introduced into accounts and studies of North America in the seventeenth century and was adopted into anthropological literature in the nineteenth century, which made it part of colonial discourse.[20] In Indigenous languages, no equivalent for 'berdache' existed in connection with sexual and gender identification.[21] Within the dominant discourse, the concept of berdache lost its original sense of signifying a different mode of social existence and underwent exotic reduction and ridicule. Berdaches were presented as creatures of failed biology (hermaphrodism), failed morals, and/or as not being able to meet expected norms.[22] In the process of colonialist appropriation of the concept, emphasis was shifted from the attributes of occupation, social role, and religious function to the attributes of sexuality and gender as defining features. This shift imposed a Western understanding of the concept of berdache and developed signifiers of difference and being other. Within Indigenous communities, the notion of biological and social otherness and 'immoral' behavior on the part of gay, lesbian, transgender, and berdache personalities gained a foothold with missionizing activities and the teaching of Victorian values and moral codes. Berdaches/two-spirit people lost their

---

Sexuality, and Spirituality, ed. Sue–Ellen Jacobs, Wesley Thomas & Sabine Lang (Urbana & Chicago: U of Illinois P, 1997): 29.

[19] Will Roscoe, "How to Become a Berdache," 332–36. About berdaches in various North American Indigenous societies, see several essays in *Two-Spirit People*, ed. Sue–Ellen Jacobs, Wesley Thomas & Sabine Lang. Similar modes of being exist in other Indigenous societies throughout the world – for example, in Tahiti/Hawai'i (*mahu*), Samoa (*fa'afafine*) and elsewhere in Polynesia, India (*hijra*), Zambia (*kwolu-aatmwol*), New Guinea, and the Balkans; Gilbert Herdt, "The Dilemmas of Desire: From 'Berdache' to Two Spirit," in *Two-Spirit People*, ed. Jacobs, Thomas & Lang, 276–83.

[20] Massimiliano Carocci holds that in Indigenous languages the term 'berdache' did not exist in relation to sexual and gender identification ("The Berdache as Metahistorical Reference for the Urban Gay American Indian Community," 117).

[21] Carocci, "The Berdache as Metahistorical Reference for the Urban Gay American Indian Community," 117.

[22] Gilbert Herdt, "The Dilemmas of Desire: From 'Berdache' to Two Spirit," 277, 280.

status of being respected and integrated and, instead, were often ostracized, even within their own communities.[23]

Anathematized by Indigenous gay/lesbian activists and at the same time appropriated into romantic discourse about transgender and gay/lesbian individuals in Indigenous and mainstream communities, the term 'berdache' gave way to the terms 'two-spirited' and 'two-spirit' people. Critics have come to understand divergent social, religious, and gender roles as 'third gender' and 'third and fourth gender'.[24] Ironically, within Indigenous gay and lesbian communities, the term 'berdache' as signifying the social, religious, and gender role of individuals has been generalized to the pan-Indian 'berdachism' in order to secure cultural identity and anchor individuals in both Indigenous and gay/lesbian communities. The concept of 'berdachism' has lost depth since the jettisoning of the social and religious aspect of the traditional mode of being berdache, and has thus become a mere category to signify gender variance.[25]

Referring to the liminal personalities of traditional berdaches, the term analogically denotes liminal personalities (gay/lesbian, transgender, modern/traditional Indigenous) in contemporary society. Zachary is such a liminal personality: he is in the liminal space between being gay and cross-dressing and between the modern and traditional. He is a male health-food café owner during the day and a female jingle-dress dancer at night. When he comes out, these oppositional aspects of his personality converge, and at the end Zach is included in the community. Thus, his figure becomes a signifier of the liminal space between insider and outsider, and his narrative function could be understood as a postcolonial cinematic strategy for overcoming oppositional binaries.

Cinematic Dialogue With Hollywood

Films very often contain quotations, references, motifs, and metaphors that are informed by an existing body of filmic and printed texts. Besides their professional training, filmmakers are intentionally or unintentionally influ-

---

[23] Cf. Sabine Lang, "Various Kinds of Two-Spirit People," 109. Such othering and exclusion of gay people within Indigenous communities is fictionalized by, for example, Jordan Wheeler in his novella "Exposure."

[24] Massimiliano Carocci, "The Berdache as Metahistorical Reference for the Urban Gay American Indian Community," 122, and Will Roscoe, "How to Become a Berdache," 338.

[25] Carocci, "The Berdache as Metahistorical Reference for the Urban Gay American Indian Community," 115.

enced in their ideas about film conventions and film codes by the mass of films they are familiar with. Every filmmaker draws on a corpus of film knowledge, comparable to the 'system of associated commonplaces' that, according to Max Black, defines the knowledge every human being accumulates in his or her social development.[26] Since such cross-references among texts are referred to as 'intertextuality', it makes sense to define similar cross-references among films as 'intermediality'.[27] In three intermedial references, the original material is ironized and/or imbued with additional meaning, so that these quotations become tools for Niro's playful treatment of mainstream film.

The sequence in Zach's basement (6) quotes from the film *Silence of the Lambs* (1991), in which the killer films himself dancing in front of a mirror in women's dresses and make-up. His darkened house, like Zach's basement, has a creepy ambience and functions as a retreat where he can transform himself into a woman. Also the fact that he, as a man who imagines himself to be a woman, creates his woman's outfit out of 'stolen' covers (he sews a dress out of the skin of women he has killed) is reminiscent of Zach (he wears stolen jingle dresses which are women's dress at powwows).[28] Zach's butterfly posture in Mabel's film is a further reference to *Silence of the Lambs*, where another insect – the moth – is the symbol of the metamorphosis from one stage to another that the killer aspires to. The film quotations are ambiguous: first, they might be paying homage to a well-crafted movie. But secondly, they might also be drawing on this movie to recontextualize critically the cliché of the scalping and cannibal-

---

[26] Max Black, *Models and Metaphors: Studies in Language and Philosophy* (Ithaca NY: Cornell UP, 1981): 40.

[27] Peter Drexler, too, defines the correlation between printed and filmic texts as well as among filmic texts as *Intermedialität* ('intermediality'), referring to writings by Brecht and Eidsvick; Drexler, "Erzählen in verschiedenen Medien – *Misery*: Stephen Kings Roman (1987) und Rob Reiners Film (1990)," in *Einführung in die Systematische Filmanalyse*, ed. Helmut Korte (Berlin: Erich Schmidt, 1999): 110–11. See also Joachim Paech, "Intermedialität" (1997), in *Texte zur Theorie des Films*, ed. Franz Joseph Albersmeier (Stuttgart: Reclam, 1998): 447–75. Kristin Thompson terms any form of reference to conventions of other works of art as "transtextual motivation." She explains this as a device that the film itself cannot sufficiently motivate and as one that is thus dependent on the viewer's ability to recognize it on the basis of prior aesthetic experience; Kristin Thompson, "A Neoformalist Approach to Film Analysis: One Approach, Many Methods," in Kristin Thompson, *Breaking the Glass Armor: Neoformalist Film Analysis* (Princeton NJ: Princeton UP, 1988): 18.

[28] See Sharon A. Desjarlais' documentary *Two Spirited* (2007), about a two-spirited jingle dress dancer.

istic Indian. Because the killer flays his victims, the police in *Silence of the Lambs* name him Buffalo Bill, confirming the discourse about the 'Wild West' in which the act of scalping served as one signifier of Indian 'savagery'.

The opening of *Honey Moccasin* is another reference to mainstream Hollywood cinema, when the camera shows the lighting of a match in close-up, with which the opening titles are illuminated (Fig. 6.24). David Lynch's *Wild at Heart* (1990) opens with the lighting of a match, which is repeated as a visual motif to identify scenes that describe the relationship between the protagonists. Rob Reiner's *Misery* (1990), Steven Spielberg's *Schindler's List* (1993), and Kenneth Branagh's *Henry V* (1989) also employ a shot of a match being lit.[29] Especially the latter film, in which the match is used to illuminate a dark film studio serving as the metafilmic space for Shakespeare's play, makes a similar use of the match: in *Honey Moccasin*, the match illuminates the diegetic titles, which are white beads stitched on black canvas that is part of the narrative space (probably a film studio as well). The technique of presenting some of the titles diegetically with concrete materials – black ground, white stitching, hand with burning match and flashlight – is uncommon in conventional filmmaking and serves as yet another device for metafilmic involvement.

Sequence 3 ends with Honey holding the magnifying glass in front of her eye to look at the sign "Inukshuk Café" at the door (Fig. 6.25). This image is a quotation from Orson Welles's *Mr. Arkadin* (1955), in which the professor (Mischa Auer), in a similar gesture, holds a magnifying glass, enlarging his eye. Monaco points out that there the irony resides in the fact that the magnifying glass is positioned for the viewer and not for the professor to look at something.[30] The viewer looks at the professor (his enlarged eye) and he looks at the viewer via the magnifying glass and the camera lens. In *Honey Moccasin*, the magnifying glass is positioned for both directions: the viewer looks at Honey's enlarged eye, and Honey looks at the door sign (implied by a cut) and at the viewer. The magnifying glass as second projecting lens within the film (second to the camera lens) visually supports the concept of the second camera gaze that critically looks at the imaginary Indian of Western film discourse and ironizes, undercuts, and/or destroys it through its manipulative and decolonizing potential. In

---

[29] Peter Drexler, "Erzählen in verschiedenen Medien," 144.

[30] James Monaco, *How to Read a Film: The Art, Technology, Language, History, and Theory of Film and Media* (1977; Oxford: Oxford UP, 1981): 163.

the realm of the symbolic, the magnifying glass enlarges and distorts the colonial on-screen Indian, which helps expose its flaws. But the on-screen Indian here (Honey) is an already decolonized image and, in this line of thought, the magnifying glass also enlarges and stresses decolonized film images and thus Indigenous film discourse. However, it does so while distorting the image – a metafilmic self-ironic look at Indigenous filmmaking. Both, the colonial and decolonized on-screen Indian (because the colonial inheres in the decolonized image) also look in the other direction at the viewer and self-confidentially return her/his observing gaze – they call for critical (self)reflection about colonial Indian and decolonized Indigenous images in film discourse. The irony is doubled, since above Honey's enlarged eye gawks the stitched eye from her cap.

Oral Tradition and Indigenous Television

The film *Honey Moccasin* draws heavily on the oral tradition. In Indigenous storytelling, there would usually be a storyteller surrounded by an audience watching him or her perform a story: i.e. acting out or illustrating the story with gestures and facial play. Niro projects modified oral storytelling situations into her film. In five sequences (four in Honey's bar, one in Zach's café), modified elements of the oral tradition can be detected. There are audiences in the film who watch various characters perform: Honey sings in her bar; Mabel performs a one-woman show and screens her film; Bernelda hosts a fashion show; and one character sings along with the karaoke machine in Zach's café. Before Honey performs, she introduces herself at length to her audience by talking about her life. This recalls storytelling with an Indigenous 'copyright system' based on trust, according to which the storyteller would introduce her/himself to the audience and then talk about where the story s/he is about to tell came from and who owns it. Since the flashbacks accompanying Honey's story cannot be seen by the bar audience but only by the film viewer, Niro splits the joined spectatorship and points to the postmodern structure of her film, which contains performances for audiences inside the film in addition to the audience outside the film. Here, the simple technique of the illustrated flashback caters to the metanarrative describing the making of the film. During Mabel's performance, the camera occasionally pans through the audience, thus pointing to the interaction between performer and spectator during this modified storytelling. As well as this, Niro reserves single shots for the slide projector in close-up from various angles, thereby foregrounding the technical equipment of the performance in a Brechtian way.

Much room in the film is given over to the Indigenous television station Native Tongue. Niro thus creates a space for Indigenous television to exist without guidelines and pressure from mainstream media. She gives Indigenous media an importance and recognition that it does not actually enjoy in contemporary society, and she allows it to grow with all the flaws and shortcomings that are part and parcel of new developments.[31] She also emphasizes the fact that watching television looms large in Indigenous communities, despite its being a major means for the dominant society to maintain control over Indigenous people:

> Watching television has probably been sort of a common denominator more than anything, because living on an Indian reserve you're isolated from other Indian people, you're isolated from people in general. But you still pretty well have this television there anyway, and in a way it sort of connects you. So, we all come to accept the fact that it is beckoning out information and instructions. (interview, 1998)

Niro juxtaposes the community-based Native Tongue programming, which includes the coverage of community news and world news, community events (e.g., the fashion show, the opening of Zach's café), and a home-video clip, with programming that the reserve residents were exposed to through mainstream television. She has Honey pondering the 'important' stuff she watched when she grew up: *Queen for the Day*, *I Love Lucy*, the Kraft Hour, and the Eichmann trials. Also, transforming herself into a Sherlock Holmes impersonator, Honey goes through different stages by very briefly becoming Wonder Woman and Pocahontas. These three figures, as much as the television programs, exemplify mainstream television, which on a large scale offers flat entertainment.[32] Underlining Niro's critique is the fact that Honey's parents die when their car gets run over by a train on their way to town to buy a new television antenna.[33] Both the railroad and television are metonymic elements in the process of the colonization of the North American continent. In the sense that infrastructural development

---

[31] APTN was launched in 1999, after the release of *Honey Moccasin*, so that APTN is not a model for Native Tongue.

[32] The qualitative value of the contextualized television programs varies, and it is not be the objective here to discuss the individual programs; it is just that this crosssection represents North American television discourse that Niro comments on.

[33] This fact was pointed to me out by Dirk Vanderbeke in a personal conversation.

enables the settling of a territory, the railroad facilitated the influx of ever more settlers into the West. Television is, in the majoritarian 'wrong hands', a means of manipulating and lulling people's minds and in recent history worked to alienate Indigenous people from their traditional culture (which is not exclusively negative) as well as to distract them from prevailing problems and from understanding existing power-structures. Mainstream television deludes marginalized people into thinking that they are part of the mainstream, thereby upholding colonialist relations.

The Native Tongue broadcast is a technical device adapted for Indigenous storytelling and oratory, for it is community-focussed programming, the community being the audience/receiver and the Native Tongue being the 'storyteller'/sender. Most often, Niro does not put a television frame around the Native Tongue broadcast sequences, nor does she show the projector and the projection screen when Mabel's film is screened. Thus, the broadcast and Mabel's film, in contrast to Mabel's performance, merge with the actual film. Likewise, the diegetic audiences merge with the non-diegetic audience of Niro's film. This effect is supported by Honey looking twice into the camera and smiling at the viewers of *Honey Moccasin*, thus involving them in the search for the thief (Figs. 6.26–6.27).[34] Not only does the actor's (and consequently the viewer's) eye-contact with the camera neglect 'unwritten' film conventions, but it also breaks up the narrative and enters the ridiculing metanarrative. Nevertheless, performance and enactment are, along with speech, the mechanisms by which oral tradition functions. Hence, the film *Honey Moccasin* uses modern electronic techniques to adapt Indigenous oral storytelling to a modern-day setting.

Niro not only criticizes mainstream television but also treats the presentation of the Native Tongue studio jokingly. She indicates pointedly its shortcomings in the tradition of Indigenous humor, which is often self-directed. When *Honey Moccasin* was made, Indigenous television, like Indigenous feature filmmaking, was still in its infancy and often had to struggle along on low budgets – a situation that has not changed all that much.[35]

---

[34] According to classical film convention, having the actors looking into the camera is a major flaw. For example, Godard in *À bout de souffle* [*Breathless*] (France, 1960) employs this violation as an aesthetic device and as a defiant deviation from the Hollywood norm.

[35] At the time of the making of *Honey Moccasin* in 1998, the first major Indigenous feature films (*Big Bear*, *Smoke Signals*) were still in the process of being made and Indigenous feature filmmaking was limited to smaller budget films which did not achieve national and international acclaim. Similarly, Indigenous television on a national scale did not yet exist.

Hence Native Tongue television appears somewhat unprofessional at times. Images are quite often shot out of frame: for example, the top of the news anchor, Richard Rock, is chopped off and, later, only half of Johnny John is visible, so that visual emphasis is put on his body with gesticulating hands, which looks quite funny (Figs. 6.6 and 6.28). The Native Tongue reporter Bernelda Birch does not have any specific questions while interviewing Zach, and instead issues global invitations: "So Zachary, tell us all about yourself" and "Zachary tell us all about the Inukshuk Café." Very unprofessionally, she sports grimaces of disgust and contempt when Zach's answers do not meet her expectations. The interview ends with a wonderful medium shot showing Zach smiling broadly into the camera beside Bernelda, who is wearing a long face (Fig. 6.29). In these instances, Niro mingles the subnarrative about the Native Tongue television station with the metanarrative about Indigenous media-making itself. Asked about these drafted flaws in an interview (1998), Niro has said: "I thought if it was a real Aboriginal station, the cameras wouldn't be set right and things would be off a little bit. It was intentional, but I think it's off a little bit too much in some of the parts." By creating a reality for Indigenous television in her film, Niro gives weight to the fact that one aspect of decolonizing the media is the development of Indigenous television on a national basis, an autonomously controlled media institution that centers on the Indigenous and presents an Indigenous perspective on contemporary issues.

Feathers, Inukshuk, and Other Cinematic Motifs

In addition to Indigenous television, various other binding motifs recur in the film. The motif of colored feathers, for example, appears in various places to support the detective plot. Feathers are the prime metonym of 'Indianness' in Western thought, the stereotypical epitome of North American Indigenous cultures. In order to break down this major stereotype, Niro has the feathers feed into the detective narrative being parodied, thus mocking the feather motif as well. Since the feathers are part of the stolen powwow outfits, the powwow itself becomes a motif that recurs with the feathers. Bernelda and Honey converse about last year's powwow, a home video of the powwow is broadcast, Zach returns the stolen outfits live on Native Tongue television, and, lastly, Johnny John discusses in a studio

---

Only in 1999 did the Aboriginal Peoples Television Network (A P T N) emerge from Television Northern Canada (T V N C) with a country-wide broadcast license.

interview the lack of understanding among the younger people for the work that goes into the preparation of traditional powwow costumes. The pow-wow motif reappears in modified guise during the fashion show, where, curiously enough, Johnny and the elders present powwow outfits that are made of materials such as wax, canvas, bottle caps, fruit loops, rubber tire tubes, and cardboard (Figs. 6.30–6.32). The outfits do not look traditional at all but eccentric and futuristic. Apparently, modern consumerism is even more a part of Indigenous life than traditionalism.[36] Puzzled film viewers see a fashion-show audience that seems to find nothing strange in these outfits and gives a big round of applause to the hosts. At this point, again, Niro detaches the film viewer from the diegetic audience and makes fun both of the expectations of the former concerning the fashion show and of the reactions of the latter. She pinpoints imaginary views of the Indian by making the viewer aware of clichéd expectations about Indigeneity. The extraterrestrial powwow costumes join with the town by the name of Pluto to help to create an unreal narrative space. The modified powwow motif indicates that a powwow does not have the spiritual or ritual connotation that is often applied to it. In fact, it has a social, competitive, and even eco-nomic character. Feathers and powwows, cliché-laden signifiers of 'Indian-ness' in the media, are turned by Niro into elements of a burlesque. The stolen powwow outfits and Zach's dressing up as jingle-dress dancer evoke "the traditions within mainstream society, too, when as at Halloween, cos-tume-hirers loan 'Indian dress' along with gorilla and Frankenstein suits."[37] Here, Niro denounces the commodification of Indigenous cultures and at the same time tells us that the 'Indian suit' is nothing more than a replace-able, imaginary, stereotypical signifier that lacks substance. Instead, she turns the untraditional powwow outfits into signifiers of modern Indigene-ity; they indicate cultural dynamism and creative adaptive negotiation of tradition. This redefinition of signifiers, like other elements in the film, tends to dismantle stereotypical ideologemes of the Indigenous traditional.

A third motif is reserved for Zach. The Inukshuk not only decorates the walls and the door of the "Inukshuk Café" but also recurs in Mabel's film. Zach, protagonist of the film, stands on a big rock, spreading out his arms in the posture of the Inuit figure. Here, he merges with the symbol that has

---

[36] See Heather Norris Nicholson, "Making Things Happen Through Parody and Visual Irony," *Screening Culture: Constructing Image and Identity*, ed. Heather Norris Nicholson (Lanham MD: Lexington, 2003): 165.

[37] Norris Nicholson, "Making Things Happen Through Parody and Visual Irony," 165.

characterized him throughout the film. This motif also blends the film with the film-within-the-film, thus blurring the boundaries between the two. In addition, the motif of the underworld is connected to Zach because of his home town Pluto and his mystic basement, as seen above. The motif of smoke, on the other hand, is connected to Honey because of the name of her bar and its cigarette smoke. This motif places Honey in the Grand Pine community, whereas the motifs of the underworld and the Arctic 'other' Zach from the community.

The lighting constitutes another motif in the film, since each setting is identified by a certain lighting color. The entrance to Honey's bar is lit by diegetic green light, the bar itself is bathed in diegetic reddish-yellowish light which creates a warm, cozy atmosphere (also supported by the low-key lighting), and Zach's café is flooded by bright yellow light which transmits a sense of impersonal coldness. The Native Tongue studio broadcast inconsistently appears in bluish light and greenish light, reinforcing the impression of a new and unprofessional Indigenous television station. The black-and-white flashbacks illustrating Honey's tale have the sepia tone of fading photographs, emphasizing the long time-span that lies between the events in the flashbacks and the events in the film. The sequence of Zach's attempted murder is lit by moonlight, conveying a sense of mystery. In the sequence where Zach descends into his basement to perform his transformation, Niro uses red background light and casts key light from a low source sideways onto his face without fill light in order to generate heavy shadows and to have Zach's face appear cruel and cold. His basement is bathed in blue light, picking up the foreboding of the red lighting to create an air of magic in the room. The lighting colors make the different settings look partly unnatural and surreal and support the mockery of detective movies. This technique draws attention to itself and to the fact that the events are staged. It disrupts the illusion of presented reality.

Like the deliberate use of color, the employment of sound connects the film's disparate sequences. Usually, the sound of one sequence carries over to the next as a sound bridge. There are two songs by Willi Dunn ("Half Empty Closet" and "Honey Moccasin in Blue") that start as diegetic songs and become non-diegetic, leading towards the next sequence and the closing titles respectively. Sound serves further to characterize the atmosphere in the individual sequences. For example, there is melancholy cello music accompanying the flashbacks showing Honey's birth and the death of her parents. The sound of Zach's voice and the powwow music in the basement echo off the walls, contributing to the magical atmosphere in the room. Juxtaposed with the powwow music is the sad cello tune at the end of this and in the 'climax' sequence. By using a sad and slow cello tune in the 'climax' sequence, Niro departs from classical filmmaking, which usually has a dramatic soundtrack heralding a climax or dramatic situation. Instead, she emphasizes the painfulness of a situation which is becoming a turning-point in Zach's life. Further, the sound in the bar sequences is in itself contrapuntal. On the one hand, there are typical diegetic bar noises: voices, music, and the soundtrack of the various performances seem to be real. On the other, the sound of applause is distorted and seems to be coming from far away – it is unreal for this place. This contrapuntal sound also comple-mentss Niro's interweaving of magic and reality and contributes to the dis-junctive nature of the film, which self-reflexively reveals its own construc-tedness.

The line between physical reality and magic is constantly blurred. Niro's blurring counters clear Western distinctions between the two concepts, classifying magical occurrences in Indigenous texts as either myth and legend or 'magical realism', a term that fails to denote the interplay of real-ity and magic in Indigenous thought.[38] Niro's film presents two 'magical' transformations, an apparition, futuristic powwow outfits, and an impos-sible 'detective search' in the narrative space of a netherworld. The magical transformations are not presented with Hollywood-like special effects but only with the respective character doing a spin in front of the camera (Honey and Zach), with added artificial smoke, and dissolves and a black frame respectively. Transformation is achieved through the viewer's believ-ing and producing a mental image and not through seeing and receiving a made-to-believe image as in traditional narrative cinema. In the sequence preceding the screening of her film, Mabel pays homage to the community and to the author of the poem that serves as the basis for her film – Daniel David Moses, a well-known Canadian poet and playwright. Niro not only includes a person from the empirical outside world in her film in a post-modern way, she also has him appear (D.D. Moses played by D.D. Moses) as an apparition surrounded by smoke in the bar where Mabel's film is about to be shown. But instead of being frozen with fright at this apparition, the audience looks in his direction, smiling and applauding. Here, Niro switches positions – the unreal space of the plot becomes a real place serv-

---

[38] See the discussion of magical realism in chapter 3 above, fn. 96.

ing as a backdrop against which a real person appears as an unreal vision. She thus further confuses the film viewer and reinforces the entanglement of magic with reality. Finally, she once again fools her viewers by enlisting the alienation effect to indicate the twofold audience.

Cinematic Postmodernism: Performance and Film Screening as Extrafilmic Elements

Niro's film draws on a postmodern tradition: transcending temporal and spatial levels, she creates an unstable, parodic narrative, visualizes the oscillation between magic and reality, underlines the continuous interplay between film and metafilm, creates a burlesque of mainstream and Indigenous television, and includes two items that could also be understood as non-diegetic: Mabel's performance and Mabel's film.

The performance is a structured piece of art in itself. Mabel's prop is an erected tipi, in which she sits with her head sticking out of an opening in the fabric. It seems as if she is looking out of one of those wooden boards with painted Indians where tourists can stick their heads through and have their pictures taken. Niro's replication here of such a culturally expropriative tourist device is a critical comment in itself. Only, here the opening is surrounded by painted flames, and various photographs are projected onto the tipi front (Figs. 6.33–6.34). Tipis are *the* Indian form of housing *per se* and the prop is an allusion to this pan-Indian cliché. Mabel is singing playback to Peggy Lee's love-song "You Give Me Fever," which in this context obtains a new meaning. While, right below her face, there appear such images as a nuclear explosion, a painting depicting the 'Columbian' erection of a cross after an early colonizer's landfall on the American continent, of nuns and Indigenous children in residential schools, of battles during the Indian wars, of Indigenous people poor and hungry, sick and dying, of treaty-making and demonstrations, she sings: "You give me fever / when you kiss me / fever when you hold me tight / fever in the morning / fever all through the night." Simultaneously with the words "When you put your arms around me / I get a fever that's so hard to bear / you give me fever," a photograph of three nuns holding three Indigenous babies wrapped in white cloth appears on the canvas, alluding to a missionizing embrace from which the Indigenous people could not escape. The photographs of nuns and residential schools are signifiers of christianization that are recontextualized to illustrate the creation of colonized minds through colonial discourse, via biblical and educational texts. But there are also two other photographs with Indigenous children dressed up as stereotypical Indians with fake war bonnets and smiling nuns behind them. These images insert a subversive playfulness into the performance and the film. They suggest, on the one hand, that Indigenous culture was not wholly erased by the residential school system and, on the other, that the concept of the Indian as inferior other was constructed in colonial institutions of knowledge and education (exemplified by the nuns as the colonial self and as signifiers of church-run residential and boarding schools, and the children with war bonnets as the exotic savage other). These images at the same time suggest that Indigenous people have absorbed this stereotypical hegemonic notion of the Indian other and see themselves as filtered through the lenses of colonial discourse. The cross in the painting can be considered as a sign of colonial power, as its erection on 'uninhabited' land (*terra nullius*) was a symbolic act of taking possession. The painting is one example of the visual side of colonial discourse that mapped the *terra incognita*, the unknown land thought to be uninhabited. Because the lyrics of the song, revolving around love, pain, sickness, and dependency, are interpreted via photographs containing signifiers of colonization and the resulting dependency of the Indigenous people, their literal meaning is broadened. According to this overwritten meaning, the lyrics tell of Christian 'love' and 'embrace', small-pox epidemics ('fever'), colonial military aggression, US-American nuclear imperialism, and colonial dependency. Thus they manifest Mabel's, and subsequently Niro's, indictment of the same. When Mabel sings: "Captain Smith and Pocahontas / had a very mad affair / when daddy tried to kill him she said: 'daddy, oh, don't you dare / he gives me fever / [...] / fever when he holds me tight / fever, I'm his missus / daddy won't you treat him right'," she clearly critiques the romantic Western idea of Powhatan's Indian court with kings and princesses and the exploited Western myth of the love affair between Pocahontas and John Smith. The word 'burn' in the repeated line "what a lovely way to burn" at the end of the song again refers to aggressive colonialist enterprises on the North American continent and thr resulting pain and suffering of its Indigenous inhabitants (both historical and contemporary), its linkage with 'lovely way' further supporting the ironic critique.

Niro recontextualizes Western photographs of Indigenous people in a twofold way: on the one hand, she pinpoints the staged character of Indian images and clichés developed in Western visual discourse by functionalizing the photographs in a staged performance; on the other hand, she creates subjectivities aside from the subjectivity of the presented fiction of *Honey Moccasin*. There is a second subjectivity (via Mabel's slide projector), and a third (via Niro's camera). The images of Indigenous people pass through three lenses – one colonialist (the camera of the Euro-American photographer) and two under Indigenous control (Mabel's slide projector and Niro's camera) – and thus their colonialist potential is undermined. This is Niro's decolonization of the Foucauldian lens of power.

One can read Mabel's one-woman show as both a separate piece of art and as belonging to a larger whole – the film *Honey Moccasin*. Supporting the first reading is the fact that this performance would make sense on its own. Supporting the latter reading is the fact that the performance takes up several motifs that also appear in the film: two facial photographs of powwow dancers repeat the powwow motif, the Captain Smith and Pocahontas line comes back to Honey's transformation, and finally the "Fever" song is also the theme song of *Honey Moccasin*, since it fills the soundtrack during the opening credits and returns once during the Native Tongue broadcast.

Mabel's film *Inukshuk*, a filmic interpretation of Daniel David Moses' poem "Inukshuk,"[39] is very different from its framing film *Honey Moccasin* and, at first sight, is reminiscent of German expressionism. It is black and white, has a slow pace, and uses mystic, melancholy, and partly abstract images, visualizing the metaphors of the poem. The choice of such a film fits in with Niro's strategy of polarizing the traditional and the postmodern as well as of setting contemporary spirituality against romanticized traditional spirituality. By heavily overexposing most shots and by adding the sound of howling wind and a slow, discordant cello tune, Niro creates sombre, abstract images and an alienated atmosphere that match the poem's content.

The ambience created in *Inukshuk* reiterates the Inukshuk motif in *Honey Moccasin*. It reappears in Mabel's film verbally in the form of the poem and visually in the form of a straight medium shot of an Inukshuk on a rock. This shot is cut together with a low-angle medium shot of Zach standing on a big rock with arms spread, so that both fuse symbolically (Figs. 6.35–6.36). Through its linkage with a helpful tool created by human beings, the figure of Zach similarly becomes positively connoted. His acting in Mabel's film leads to his being fully taken up into in the Grand

---

[39] Daniel David Moses, "Inukshuk," in *The White Line* (Saskatoon, Saskatchewan: Fifth House, 1990). For the text of the poem, see the Appendix.

Pine community. Mabel acknowledges Zach as a brother, and after the screening of the film both Mabel and Zach receive hearty applause and Zach is reconciled with his father.

Like the "Fever" performance, the *Inukshuk* film is a separate piece of art and at the same time it is an integral part of the film. On the one hand, it would have its own meaning beyond the framing film because it differs from it in regard to content, form, and the techniques employed. It has separate opening credits: "*Inukshuk* / a film by Mabel Moccasin / poetry by Daniel David Moses." On the other hand, it is shown within the setting of *Honey Moccasin*, the 'protagonist' of the film and the author of the poem are present during the screening, and the diegetic film takes up two of the framing film's motifs – the Inukshuk and coldness/alienation created by lighting and overexposure respectively. Furthermore, Zach merges with the Inukshuk, and his acting in *Inukshuk* connects with his enactment of his own role in *Honey Moccasin*. Thus, the Inukshuk and the cold ambience function both diegetically and non-diegetically to link the film to the metafilm.

Final Remarks

Honey Moccasin is ironic and funny about the mysterious issues happening on the imaginary Grand Pine reserve but is startlingly real and sad concerning the consequences of colonization that it exposes and that Indigenous people face in contemporary society. At the same time, the film does not lecture blatantly in order to keep the viewer's interest alive. As Niro says:

> I do want to make statements but I don't want it to be so serious that people get turned off by looking at it. [...] you want to say things and have them [the audience] enjoy at the same time. (interview, 1998)

She has Zach voice her concerns after Mabel's art performance:

> It's okay stuff, I guess. But a little on the weird side. It's just too heavy. It's supposed to be a night out for enjoyment and fun. Time to forget your problems, not to have somebody remind you over and over again of that depressing stuff. Drink, dance, be merry.

In this sense, *Honey Moccasin* is trickster discourse; it playfully and mockingly derides the bloodthirsty and stoic Indian, the romanticized vanishing Indian, the handsome exotic lover, and the Indian princess (as well as, in what Zach says above, both the 'carefree Indian' and the Indian drowning his sorrows in alcohol). Niro also ridicules and pokes fun at both Western and Indigenous media discourse, exposing their shortcomings. While juxtaposing Native Tongue television and Western media products in the narrative, in the metanarrative she juxtaposes her own film as part of Indigenous film discourse and Western media discourse and has them engage in Vizenor's dialogism. Niro adds humorous flavor to her complex film through little things: Honey recounts how, the night she was born, there was a heavy thunderstorm – but in the flashbacks the viewer does not notice any rain or storm at all; there is the sign "Honey Mock-A-Sin"[40] in the stage background of the bar; characters' names such as Richard Rock, Bernelda Birch, Honey Moccasin and Mabel Moccasin sound like an excerpt from an Indian museum index; Honey talks about her marriage to Hank, who is, according to her, an ugly guy; and, last but not least, Richard announces "the one and only Hank and his 'Band of No Goods'." When Hank enters the film played by the well-known songwriter Willi Dunn, the viewers have to ask themselves: What kind of songwriter calls his band 'Band of No Goods' and did Willi Dunn mind being called an ugly guy? The announcement and the song come after the words "The End"; the film carries on after its closing title in a postmodern way. It seems as if the film has escaped the grip of its master, the filmmaker. After the narrative ends, the metanarrative takes over and continuous in its own right. *Honey Moccasin* is neither a conventional short nor a feature film. Calling it experimental would depreciate its political and entertaining value. It is simply not classi-

---

[40] Literally, the sign supposedly means to ignore the concept of sin. On the other hand, this phrase might be a take-off on the Englishman Archie Belaney, who was one of the greatest impostors in Canadian history. He gave himself the name 'Wa-sha-quon-asin' – meaning 'Grey Owl'. The last three syllables in 'Honey mock a sin' and 'Wa-sha-quon-asin' are homophones; the first phrase might thus be alluding to Belaney. From 1931 until his death in 1938, Belaney managed to deceive the world's public and passed as Apache and / or Ojibway. During this time he was famous for his writings and lectures about the Canadian wilderness and for his mission to save the beavers. See esp. Daniel Francis, *The Imaginary Indian*, 131–41, Donald B. Smith, *Land of the Shadows: The Making of Grey Owl* (Saskatoon, Saskatchewan: Western Producer Prairie Books, 1990), and Armand Garnet Ruffo, *Grey Owl: the Mystery of Archie Belaney* (Regina, Saskatchewan: Coteau, 1996). Niro's reference to Belaney, however coincidental it is, appears ambiguous. On the one hand, it ridicules romantic tendencies among non-Indigenous people to appropriate an Indian identity and to achieve spiritual dimensions that Western cultures lack. On the other, it might be read positively, since Belaney as Grey Owl fought for the Indigenous cause as well. He spoke for the welfare of Canada's Indigenous people and lobbied for plans to set aside large parts of land for use by Indigenous people who still lived traditionally off the land (Smith, *Land of the Shadows: The Making of Grey Owl*, 208).

fiable as belonging to any known film genre. This fact indicates that Indigenous filmmaking can shape new film forms alongside classical ones, thereby questioning and breaking with established film conventions.

Niro creates her own ahistorical Indigenous reality apart from mainstream stereotyped representation. She works with filmic oppositions and
translates the colonial self/other dichotomy into filmic space and characters. With simple means she imparts the basic values of Indigenous cultures: honoring of elders and accomplished personalities from their own
ranks, honoring of achievements within a group, solving conflicts within a
group, and paying tribute to the originator of a story and to supporters of a
project. Like postmodern fiction, the film operates with several narratives
and artistic insertions and weaves different planes of reality into a complex
story. It is not a narrative film in the conventional sense, because the main
narrative is created, ridiculed, and destroyed continually. Magic and reality
are constantly interwoven and Indigenous traditions are reflected through
the modern world. Niro has commissioned an Indigenous songwriter (Willi
Dunn) and an Indigenous playwright (Daniel David Moses), the latter playing himself. Both roles, nevertheless, are ironically undermined. Moses appears magically out of the blue and Willi Dunn (alias Hank) is first labelled
ugly by Honey and is later deserted by his band members, who take off
with the band truck, leaving him singing alone in a field. The quotations
from the programs *Pocahontas, Wonder Woman,* and *Sherlock Holmes*
ironize mainstream television and cinema. By utilizing the strategy of
alienation created by Brecht, the film self-reflexively indicates its constructedness through artificial smoke in the bar, simple devices that imply
magic transformations, and the apparition of D.D. Moses. Similarly, the
conscious avoidance of 'proper' lighting and implementation of colored
narrative spaces and contrapuntal and often alienated sound create the surreal and mocking character of the film and disrupt seamless presentation.
Niro constantly merges the television program and the other performances
in the film with the film itself, only to separate them from each other in the
next instant with technical finesse, in this way also destroying any impression of illusionary reality. She plays with the medium of film and with
fiction being described and undermined by its metafiction. The actors are
not playing 'real' characters but their roles become unbelievable, as their
acting is a continual re-enactment of yet another role. This exaggerated enactment is also an aspect of the alienation effect, and becomes subversive
play.

The things mainstream viewers might find a nuisance, such as Honey's lengthy introduction and two full-length songs as well as the partly over-done acting, are filmic elements that go back to the oral tradition. *Honey Moccasin* is partly reminiscent of syncretic theatre, a dramatic performance practice in Africa, which is characterized by the incorporation of ritual and mythic elements and by the fusion of performance styles and forms – Indigenous (e.g., ceremonies, dances, funerals) and Western (e.g., drama, ballet, opera) ones.[41] The difference is that Niro subversively commissions Indigenous and Western performance forms, ironizing both. Her film code is hybrid; it is informed by established Western film conventions and by subversive play with these conventions. Discarding the classical film-making features of consistent narrative, cause–effect chain, goal-oriented characters, three-point lighting, and spatial and temporal continuity, the film shows how Indigenous filmmaking can use and re-invent mainstream filmmaking techniques. It creates an image of contemporary Indigenous life in the media, free from confining stereotypical notions and historical con-textualization, and provides a space in which to unfold Indigenous storytell-ing in the direction of playful mockery and critical contextualization of both the Indigenous and the Western experience.

Smoke Signals[42]

Smoke Signals (USA / Canada, 1998) is the first major motion picture in North America to be written, directed, and co-produced by and starring In-digenous people, and one that won national and international acclaim (Fig. 7.1). It is the director Chris Eyre's (Cheyenne / Arapaho) debut in Holly-wood. Sherman Alexie (Coeur d'Alene) wrote the script, basing it on his short-story collection *The Lone Ranger and Tonto Fistfight in Heaven*. The film was produced on a budget of four million US dollars[43] by Shadow Catcher Entertainment[44] and released by Miramax Films.[45] *Smoke Signals*

---

[41] Christopher Balme, "Inventive Syncretism: The Concept of the Syncretic in Intercultural Discourse," in *Fusion of Cultures?*, ed. Peter Stummer & Christopher Balme (Cross / Cultures 26, ASNEL Papers 2; Amsterdam & Atlanta GA: Rodopi, 1996): 15–16.

[42] Unfortunately, Miramax would not grant permission to print the 31 film stills that were selected to illustrate the arguments in this chapter.

[43] "Rauchzeichen aus Nordwest," *Der Spiegel* 19 (1998): 219.

[44] Other films by Shadow Catcher Entertainment are Michael Miner's *The Book of Stars* (USA, 2001) and Lisanne Shyler's *Getting to Know You* (USA, 1999).

stars such noted Canadian Indigenous professionals as Tantoo Cardinal (Arlene Joseph), Gary Farmer (Arnold Joseph), Irene Bedard (Suzy Song), Adam Beach (Victor Joseph), and Evan Adams (Thomas Builds-The-Fire).[46] The playwright Monique Mojica (Grandma Builds-The-Fire),[47] John Trudell (DJ Randy Peone), Michael Greyeyes (Junior Polatkin), Cody Lightning (young Victor), Simon Baker (young Thomas), Michelle St. John (Velma) and Elaine Miles (Lucy) complete the Indigenous cast.

The 89-minute film received favorable critiques and was considered a hit and trailblazer for other Indigenous productions. Canadian and German papers held that the makers were fine storytellers and compared their work to that of Quentin Tarantino and Jim Jarmusch. Victor's search for himself was compared to Kurtz's search in Conrad's *Heart of Darkness*. They noted that the makers shied away from simplistically charging mainstream society with committing crimes against Indigenous people during the course of five hundred years of colonization, that the film "is free of the oppressive weight of victim culture," and that it "offers an insight into native culture that most films made from the outside (Bruce McDonald's *Dance Me Outside* [1994], Kevin Costner's *Dances With Wolves* [1990], Disney's *Pocahontas* [1998]) could only dream of."[48] The film is not a counter-discourse which refurbishes or blatantly attacks old clichés but an answering discourse that presents Indigenous culture in its own right, offering a critique of colonization and misrepresentation of Indigenous cultures in a largely ironic way. It recontextualizes the Indian image of mainstream thought and responds with a freshly different representation.

---

[45] Miramax has also released other out-of-mainstream films such as *Trainspotting* (UK, 1996), *Artemisia* (France, Germany & Italy, 1997), *Next Stop Wonderland* (USA, 1998), and *Once Were Warriors* (New Zealand, 1994), the first feature film by a Maori director (Lee Tamahori) to recive widespread international acclaim (the first New Zealand feature film made chiefly by Maori was Barry Barclay's *Ngati*, 1987 – also the world's first feature film by an Indigenous culture living within a eurocentric majority culture).

[46] Although the screenwriter and director of *Smoke Signals* clearly make this film a US-American production, the casting of mainly Canadian actors permit the film to be regarded also as part-Canadian.

[47] Monique Mojica was born in New York City but resides in Toronto. She is a founding member of Native Earth Performing Arts and its former artistic director.

[48] In order of publication: Stephen Cole, "First All-Native Film Sends Good Signals," *Globe & Mail* (3 July 1998): A10; "Movie Cathartic for Native Actor," *Regina Leader Post* (4 July 1998): D7; Tobias Kniebe, "Reservate des Rückwärtsgangs," *Süddeutsche Zeitung* (8 December 1998): 15; Roger Ebert, "'Smoke Signals': American Indians Offer a Beacon to the Wire Culture," *Friday Magazine* (24 July 1998): 10; and Mike Boon, "Charismatic Cast Adds Fire to Smoke Signals," *Calgary Herald* (31 July 1998): C1.

Smoke Signals won the Dramatic Audience Award and the Filmmakers Trophy at the 1998 Sundance Film Festival and opened the international New Directors/New Films Festival at the New York Museum of Modern Art in March 1998. It was screened in program theatres in major cities in the USA and Canada. In Germany it was shown at the Munich Film Festival as well as in program theatres in larger cities. However, despite the wide acclaim and positive critiques it has received, it did not make it into the major movie houses, which perhaps deemed it not marketable enough. In Regina, for example, the capital of Saskatchewan with an Indigenous demographic of roughly 13.3 percent (8.3 percent in Regina, 9.1 percent in Saskatoon),[49] it opened only weeks after its US release but, aside from a first screening for invited guests, was shown only twice in a program theatre. When I made a telephone inquiry of a Calgary theatre, I was told that there were not enough copies made for Canadian screenings, which had resulted in a rather meagre release in Canada. The question of whether this can be explained by structural inequalities between Indigenous and mainstream cinema within the film industry in general or to a US-dominated film market must remain unanswered.

"Fire and Smoke": A Narrative of Loss

The sequence protocol in the Appendix provides a rough overview of the various sequences, indicating their content, temporal and spatial specifics, and transition devices.[50] A detailed shot analysis is not needed, because it would yield little further information relevant to analysis. For the discussion of style, a detailed analysis of selected sequences is also given in the Appendix. The script for *Smoke Signals* is a mixture of characters, plots, and settings from seven stories in Alexie's *The Lone Ranger and Tonto Fistfight in Heaven*.[51] The following analysis sets out neither to compare the film with the latter nor to discuss Alexie's screenplay adaptation.

---

[49] Cf. Canadian census of 2001 – "Aboriginal Peoples of Canada," at http://www12.statcan.ca /english/census01/Products/Analytic/companion/abor/canada.cfm#5.

[50] At some points, mainly through the flashbacks, the clear distinction between sequences according to their narrative time and space becomes blurred but is retained as a general guideline for the segmentation.

[51] The short story lending the film its basic narrative is "This Is What It Means to Say Phoenix, Arizona." The other six provide individual narrative elements that are woven into the first: "Every Little Hurricane," "Because My Father Always Said He Was the Only Indian Who Saw Jimi Hendrix Play 'The Star-Spangled Banner' at Woodstock," "The Only Traffic Signal on the Reservation Doesn't Flash Red Anymore," "The Trial of Thomas-Builds-the-

One reviewer has said that the narrative of the film is no more than any average film tale, but that its filmic translation makes it a special 'treat' with its "careful weave of recurring shots, isolated-but-comforting landscapes and full immersion in Indian culture and speech patterns."[52] *Smoke Signals* tells the story of Victor Joseph, a charismatic but sulky young man, who learns of the death of his father, Arnold. Arnold abandoned his family ten years earlier because he could not live with a lie that made his family gradually crumble. Victor could never forgive his father's desertion, which has made him the resentful and cynical man he is now. Victor sets out for Phoenix, Arizona, to claim his father's ashes. On his way he is accompanied by the goofy, irrepressible storyteller Thomas Builds-The-Fire. Both young men are connected by faith, for twenty-two years earlier Arnold had accidentally set the Builds-The-Fires' house on fire. Thomas's parents died in the fire, but Arnold saved baby Thomas from the flames by catching him in flight as he was thrown out of the first story of the house. The fire has ruined both families, physically killing the young parents and destroying Victor's family psychologically. After the incident, Arnold started to drink; withdrawing mentally from his wife Arlene and his son Victor, he finally left them. Thus, both Victor and Thomas are children born of flames and ashes, their lives scarred by the fire.

Thomas received a very sheltered upbringing by his grandma, which made him somewhat out of touch with the outer world. Although he grew up in an Indigenous community, what he knows about his people is his own interpretation of mainstream media products of Indians. On the reservation he is known as the unnerving village goof; and he has always been teased by Victor, who is the central figure in the group of young reservation males. In this respect, Victor is the 'ordinary' insider, and Thomas the 'weird' outsider. But of all people, it is the 'outsider' Thomas who offers to pay for Victor's trip to Phoenix on condition that Victor takes him along. Initially declining this offer contemptuously, Victor has no choice but to accept it, as he and his mother simply cannot otherwise afford the trip.

Not only are the two young men wholly different in character, but their perceptions of Arnold differ fundamentally. Victor has never forgiven his father for deserting him mentally and physically, for having become a

---

Fire," "Jesus Christ's Half-Brother Is Alive and Well on the Spokane Indian Reservation," and "The Approximate Size of My Favorite Tumor."

[52] Katherine Monk, "Real Native Culture Shines Through Smoke Signals," *Vancouver Sun* (17 July 1998): C 3.

choleric and a drunk, and for beating his mother. Thomas, however, wor-
ships Arnold as the hero who saved him from the flames and imagines him
as the ideal father he never had. Both are competitors in a posthumous
claim on Arnold as a father, which is the ground on which their opposition
is built. In search of a father, Thomas is the other to Victor's self. Alexie
has said in an interview that, in writing the script, he was very much affected by his relation to his own father:

> It's more about my relationship with my father than about my friend's rela-
> tionship with his father. My father is still alive, but he's had to struggle with
> alcoholism, as I have. It's also about the struggle within myself of being this
> storytelling geek like Thomas, as well as this big jock masculine guy like
> Victor, so it's a sort of schizophrenic multiple personality of myself that I
> develop within the movie.[53]

The two opposing personalities and minds continuously clash on the
road trip; still, they finally come to terms with each other. On the journey,
the naive and starry-eyed Thomas has to learn to get by in a non-Indigenous
world where he encounters open racism, bluff and boasting, exertion of
authoritarian power, but also understanding and recognition. Victor has to
learn to tolerate, forgive, help, and be considerate of others. He realizes that
not Arnold but he himself is to blame for his cynicism and anger. For both,
the trip to Phoenix becomes a journey to learning and healing. In picar-
esque fashion, the odd couple, an imaginative storyteller and a tough prag-
matist, travel through the country and have to pass various tests that teach
them both about themselves and about each other. These challenges bring
them closer to their goal, which they only learn about when they get home:
reconciliation with the ghosts of fire, fathers, and friendship.

In a trailer park near Phoenix, they meet the beautiful and enigmatic
Suzy Song, Arnold's neighbor, who seems to be the keeper of riddles and
ashes. It is through her that Victor learns of his father's love for him and his
mom, of his pride in Victor, and of his longing for home. And through
Suzy he learns how the fatal fire had started, hence about the reason for
Arnold's flight from his family. Suzy, too, saw Arnold as a father-figure,
and Arnold becomes the connecting factor between the three young people.
On their way back, an argument develops between Victor and Thomas that
prompts them to reveal their true feelings about Arnold and about each

---

[53] Dennis West & Joan M. West, "Sending Cinematic Smoke Signals: An Interview with
Sherman Alexie," *Cineaste* 23.4 (1998): 30.

other. At the climax of this argument (the climax of the narrative as well), they get into a car wreck, which abruptly ends their verbal fight. They argue with Burt, the driver responsible for the wreck, and help the two injured women, whereupon Victor embarks on a night-long run to get an ambulance. At the police station the next morning, they have to defend themselves against unjustified charges lodged by Burt. They are released; happy to have escaped custody, they resume their journey home and receive a warm welcome.

The Road Movie as Circular and Linear Narrative

Formally, the narrative is organized into 67 sequences lasting between 4 seconds and 4.16 minutes, which is not unusual in conventional film-making. Most of the sequences move in a time-span of between 30 seconds and 2.30 minutes, ensuring a quite steady film rhythm. The film follows the road-movie genre, which usually employs an uncomplicated plot that is catalyzed through its characters' journey. During the journey, Victor and Thomas discover certain social, political, and cultural realities,[54] and aside from their concrete goal, their purpose is self-discovery.[55] They experience racism and cultural differences, but, even more, they learn to come to terms with their past and with each other. As the basic rule for road movies dictates, the narrative space of the film changes constantly. It starts from the Coeur d'Alene reservation, moves through different localities, reaches the point of the characters' destination, the trailer park near Phoenix, and returns to the reservation. With regard to localities and the story-line, the narrative completes a circle, with Victor, Thomas, and Arnold leaving home and returning to it at the end. The journey presents the detour – the circle – that the characters have to travel for self-discovery and reconciliation. Through flashbacks, the filmmakers weave back and forth between several temporal levels, which supports the circular structure and transmits the circular sense of time and seamless transition between past, present, and future that Alexie wanted to emphasize.[56] In regard to filmic realization, the film is a linear narrative that relies on a classical cause–effect chain to further the action and that resolves all narrative threads in the end. Also typical

---

[54] Frank E. Beaver, *Dictionary of Film Terms* (New York: Twayne, 1994): 300.

[55] Susan Hayward, *Key Concepts in Cinema Studies* (London & New York: Routledge, 1996): 301.

[56] Dennis West & Joan M. West, "Sending Cinematic Smoke Signals: An Interview with Sherman Alexie," 31.

of the road movie genre, most of the film's action happens in the means of transportation and at the stops of the journey. Various characters that the protagonists meet (cowboys, Burt, Holly, Julie, Suzy, and a police officer) carry much of the plot as antagonists. The encounters with them as well as their being together on a journey create causalities important for Victor and Thomas's character development. As in other road movies, the journey episodes introduce wonderful landscapes, here in Idaho, Nevada, and Arizona, and they mirror a cross-section of non-Indigenous people in their encounters with Victor and Thomas. Matching the expanses of space, the narrative time is also expanded: the temporal plot development is realized through alternating sequences in 1998, 1988, and 1976 as well as through various flashbacks with no specification of time.

Jhon Warren Gilroy argues that the road-movie genre was chosen for its greater accessibility to both Western and Indigenous audiences and that a more experimental or postmodern film would have denied that large-scale accessibility. This accessibility is paramount for indicating stereotypes to both Western and Indigenous viewers.[57] According to Gilroy, the road-movie genre with its uncomplicated plot allows the viewer to focus on how the story is told and on its cultural otherness, achieved chiefly by replacing the genre's conventional Caucasian male heroes and story with Indigenous equivalents:

> In a very clever appropriation of the dominant discourse, the film creates a system of schemata that alerts the viewer to look beyond the surface level of the narrative for deeper philosophical meanings. [...] The use of non-traditional characters in stereotypically white male roles has the effect of holding a mirror up to the form itself; the viewer is made aware of the film as an act of representation through the incongruous nature of another subject occupying the space traditionally filled by white males.[58]

The dynamic in the film is generated through the inner conflicts between the characters, mainly Victor and Arnold, and Victor and Thomas. The central narrative tells the story of Victor and Thomas going to Phoenix to claim Arnold's ashes. One sub-narrative tells the story of Victor's family – how it disintegrates to the point that Arnold leaves, and of Victor's pain and hatred for his father. It embeds the main conflict in the film, that of father and son.

---

[57] Jhon Warren Gilroy, "Another Fine Example of the Oral Tradition? Identification and Subversion in Sherman Alexie's *Smoke Signals*," *Studies in American Indian Literatures* 13.1 (Spring 2001): 29–30.

[58] Gilroy, "Another Fine Example of the Oral Tradition?" 31.

A second sub-narrative deals with the animosity between Victor and Thomas, motivated by their unconscious competition for the right to claim Arnold as a father. Yet a third sub-narrative tells the story of the Coeur d'Alene community at the end of the twentieth century.[59] The first three narrative lines run parallel to, and interact with, each other, merging and reaching their climax when Victor and Thomas, on their way back, start fighting and are involved in the car wreck. After this point, the narratives find their resolution: Victor and Thomas are reconciled and a cautious friendship begins to develop between the two. Victor, apparently for the first time, sacrifices himself for another individual by starting out on a twenty-mile run to fetch help for the injured Julie. In the police station, again for the first time, Victor acknowledges Arnold as his father; he has forgiven him and is now reconciled with him. The reservation narrative is concentrated at the beginning and at the end of the film. In a few shots, it acquaints the viewer with the reservation and somewhat bizarre village characters, thus transporting the idea of a humorous and simultaneously sombre way of life that grows out of the need for plain survival. It lingers in the community at the beginning without providing essential information for the three other narratives. It exists in its own right, to create insights into reservation life.

Alexie's script tells a general story that can happen anywhere and at any time without ethnic specification; a story of a deserted son and lost father is possible in all cultures. Alexie says: "it's a very basic story, a road trip/buddy movie about a lost father, so I'm working with two very classical, mythic structures. You can find them in everything from *The Bible* to *The Iliad* and *The Odyssey*."[60] Such a universal story filled with Indigenous characters, happening on a contemporary reservation, however, is what cues the viewer into believing that this is an 'ordinary' Indigenous story, not exoticized by rituals, sweat lodges, feather and buckskin costumes, dances or the like – a conscious choice that counters the romanticized In-

---

[59] Also Spike Lee, for example, in his film *Do The Right Thing* (USA, 1989), embeds several narrative lines, one of which describes the African-American community in which the characters live. Whereas Lee limits his setting to the African-American part of Brooklyn, Eyre and Alexie extend the narrative space from the reservation to locations that the characters pass on their journey, conditioned by their story and the choice of the road-movie genre.

[60] Dennis West & Joan M. West, "Sending Cinematic Smoke Signals," 29.

dian images that fill Hollywood filmographies. Eyre and Alexie[61] further avoid including contemporary Indian clichés, such as modern-day vision quests, traditional singing somewhere in the countryside, and the generic AIM (American Indian Movement) political activism.[62] Simply setting the story in the present wards off the kind of historical contextualization that Indigenous cultures have been subjected to in Western film discourse. The contemporary setting can be understood as a statement critical of that practice, supplemented by individual satirical references to Indigenous–Western history. Cobb points out that Eyre and Alexie have succeeded in portraying "a fully realized [...] Native American experience without speaking for all Indians," in creating "a world that was at once recognizable as pan-Indian and tribally specific," and in creating "characters who were also recognizable as 'American', characters who were participants in mainstream America."[63]

The beginning of the film is crucial to its general message. Whereas one might expect to be introduced to the main characters in the opening sequence, here it acquaints the viewers with the Coeur d'Alene reservation. Similar to the beginning of Spike Lee's *Do The Right Thing*,[64] the film starts with a broadcast from the reservation radio station, presenting the setting, the weather forecast, a traffic report, and, most important, introductory information on the sequence to come (the house fire) as well as background information for the events portrayed in the film. As DJ Randy Peone talks, the camera travels from his old rusty trailer along deserted roads to Lester FallsApart transmitting his traffic report from a van "broken

---

[61] It is not customary in film analysis to include the script-writer as an agent of film production; however, *Smoke Signals* seems to be a collaboration between Alexie and Eyre in terms of content and cinematic translation so that both names are given as agents.

[62] Dennis West & Joan M. West, "Sending Cinematic Smoke Signals," 29.

[63] Amanda J. Cobb, "This Is What It Means to Say *Smoke Signals*: Native American Cultural Sovereignty," in *Hollywood's Indian: The Portrayal of the Native American in Film*, ed. Peter C. Rollins & John E. O'Connor (1998; Lexington: UP of Kentucky, rev. ed. 2003): 219.

[64] For example, the films *Thunderheart* (USA, 1992) and *Good Morning Vietnam* (USA, 1987) also begin with a radio broadcast. However, there are more similarities with the beginning of Spike Lee's *Do The Right Thing* (USA, 1989): a local radio broadcast accompanied by shots of the early-morning Brooklyn neighborhood. These similar beginnings support the analogy between the two films: their makers are the first in their cultures to enter mainstream cinema on a large scale. Lee was the first African-American director to receive the opportunity to make a film in Hollywood that is set in his own culture, *She's Gotta Have It* (USA, 1986).

down" at a desolate junction, before showing a reservation image. Peone's broadcast and FallsApart's traffic reports are contextualized along with images of the radio trailer, the traffic van, the reservation, and reservation residents, all of which embeds the narrative in an Indigenous socio-geographic and cultural context. The news is mostly limited to announcements of parties and usually there is no traffic at all, so that FallsApart instead describes the clouds that move above him and reports about an old woman who is speeding. Funny as this sequences is, it also shows how desolate and secluded the reservation is. It is so remote that the outside world barely notices it – something underscored by the amazement shown by the driver and passengers of the Greyhound bus when Victor and Thomas climb on board. Equipped with inside knowledge (Alexie is Coeur d'Alene), the filmmakers establish an ironic distance from the reservation in this sub-narrative and casts an ironic look at their own cultures, something that is maintained throughout the film. But this ironic distance also reveals affection for the rez, as Alexie comments: "We wanted to show, exactly, the beauty of this reservation."[65] As Niro does in *Honey Moccasin*, they resort to a rather mocking presentation of the Indigenous radio station. It begins with the rusty trailer that serves as the station's home, continues with Peone's funny talk, and ends with the figure of Lester FallsApart and his goofy traffic reports. The first sequence does not get the narrative going but presents the reservation sub-narrative. It could, in the broadest sense, be considered as establishing the setting for the main narrative. This introduction reveals a certain emphasis on the reservation setting and not necessarily on the main characters, who are introduced only in the sixth sequence.

Smoke Signals' story is narrated by Thomas, who also narrates various stories within the film. He is the narrator on two different levels: as a character in the story and as authorial/non-diegetic narrator of the film.[66] Thomas's voice-over narration at the beginning, intermittently, and at the end suggests that the viewers only know what he tells them and that the story is narrated from his viewpoint as a character. There may be more things about the various characters that could outline their traits but that

---

[65] Sherman Alexie, *Smoke Signals Screenplay* (Miramax Books; New York: Hyperion, 1998): 158.

[66] In the film classic *Citizen Kane* (USA, 1941) one character likewise has such a double function. There, the narrative is presented through the figure of the reporter Thompson, who explores the life of Kane. Although he is a figure in the movie, he occasionally falls into authorial narration.

Thomas (and the film) chooses not to tell. For example, Thomas accuses Victor of being mean to his mom and of deserting her mentally. The film, however, does not support this claim; it just shows how Victor and Arlene understand each other without words and how Victor treats his mom very gently. There are sequences (mainly the subjective memories of Suzy, Arnold, and Victor) that are beyond Thomas's knowledge as a character and thus belong to his knowledge as authorial narrator. The line between Thomas's authorial/non-diegetic and diegetic storytelling is constantly blurred and his figure becomes the interface between these two narrative modes and between narrative and metanarrative. As narrator of the film story, Thomas appears only as a voice; and as storyteller within the film he appears as a 'real' character. When he starts telling a story, he closes his eyes and concentrates hard, as if to immerse himself into the story before he tells it. He seems to be merging with the stories, as he is often part of them, and he always falls into his peculiar storytelling mode, in which his voice assumes a different rhythm, pitch, and timbre than it normally has. But he also ironizes his storytelling by overdoing it, play-acting, which is revealed when he at one point opens one eye to see how his audience is doing. Since Thomas's stories lack credibility and are equipped with a good deal of irony and yarning, his credibility as the teller of the film's story is analogously put in question. Aside from the fact that the film is fiction, a second level of fictitiousness is added by an unreliable narrator on the metanarrative level. The film contains two narrative levels: first, the narrative with its sub-narratives, which tell a story on various plot levels; and secondly, the metanarrative, which comments on the narrative and where the film describes its own constructedness. Through Thomas's double function, the metanarrative enters the viewer's perception and undermines the narrative by questioning its truthfulness.

Thomas is the vehicle of an essential element of Indigenous cultures that he translates into the film – that of oral storytelling. Like storytellers in Indigenous cultures, Thomas works as the keeper of oral knowledge, in this case of the community stories centered on Arnold and Arlene. In the nuclear family of Thomas and his grandma, Thomas is the visionary who unites past, present, and future in stories. He transports the circular character of time which, according to Alexie, connects with the seamless transition from past to present.[67] Grandma Builds-The-Fire has raised Thomas as

[67] Dennis West & Joan M. West, "Sending Cinematic Smoke Signals," 31.

a seer and storyteller who reflects his world through stories. This circumstance becomes clear when his grandma, upon his return, asks Thomas to
tell everything that has happened and everything that will happen. Thus,
Thomas is also the keeper of the events that happen during the journey, for
he will surely tell stories about the trip later on. He is also the timekeeper,
since he has for no real reason counted the days and hours he and Victor
were gone from the reservation (six days, twelve hours and thirty-two
minutes) – a trait that further serves to ironize his character.

The storytelling situations are adapted to particular circumstances.
Thomas tells stories wherever he is: on the road, in the bus, in the diner, in
the pickup. He does not need an assembly of spectators or some individual
to prompt his stories. Also, the stories about Arnold and Arlene are more or
less a product of Thomas's imagination, so he does not need to name the
originator of them, either. As in traditional oral accounts, the degree of
fictitiousness in Thomas's stories varies and the line between reality and
myth is constantly blurred. The stories are employed to pay respect to this
oral Indigenous tradition and to root this filmic story in it. But at the same
time they serve to examine this tradition ironically and are not to be taken
too seriously, since Thomas's storytelling mode gives many a reason for a
good laugh. When Thomas has traded a story for a ride, Velma and Lucy
are impressed by his story and admit that this "was a fine example of the
oral tradition." But that said, the women burst out laughing, thus making
fun of the situation and their reverence for this tradition. Whereas in the
oral tradition accounts are usually cultural knowledge packed into mythical
and community stories which are mainly believed to be true, Thomas's
accounts are his individual stories, which are not necessarily believed. This
is expressed in Victor's persistently negative reactions to them: "No, it's
not true, Thomas, you're so full of shit," and "Thomas, each time you tell
the story, it's different." Here, Victor voices his disgust and disbelief, and
above all, his contempt for his father. But the latter statement also points to
the fact that in oral storytelling the tellers stay in line with the basic structure, the 'scaffold', of a story but might change bits and pieces that belong
to the illustrative part each time they tell it.

Thomas, in fact, delivers some 'fine examples of the oral tradition' in a
modified way, and his figure subverts clichéd ideas of a romantic and
mythic oral tradition. Because his stories are a product of his own imagination, their truthfulness cannot be confirmed – neither in the sense of a Western concept of objective truth nor in the sense of an Indigenous concept of

subjective truth which preconditions belief. Thomas is an unreliable story-teller, for his stories are received differently: they are untrue and "shit" in Victor's eyes but are believed and liked by Velma and Lucy. Although Thomas's accounts are rooted in the oral tradition through their means of transmission – audio, sonic, and somatic effects – the tradition of storytelling is modernized by Thomas's alterations of the setting and his mode of telling. Thomas himself is not as accepted in the community as storytellers usually are; he is naive and starry-eyed, a sensitive romantic, someone inhabiting a fantasy world. He is too funny and weird to gain the respect that storytellers enjoy. In this figure, Eyre and Alexie are able to counter the Western construct of the mythological and spiritual Indian. Thomas imagines himself in a romanticized past with his second-hand media knowledge about Indigenous cultures, and it seems that he is not but likes to play the storyteller. His bizarre appearance and conduct, however, parody his notions of himself. On the journey, he is taught to adapt to contemporary forms of living in a westernized world while at the same time keeping his Indigenous heritage. The figure of Thomas escapes the preconceived mold of the Indian fully immersed in his or her traditional mythic past and develops into a mix of a traditional and modern person. Since Thomas's stories weave around different characters and their filmic illustrations depart from and return to the main narrative, these stories present cyclical narrative elements that support the circular character of the narrative.

The end of the movie does not present a typical happy ending, but it nevertheless offers hope. Victor has already apologized for treating Thomas meanly in the past by saying: "I'm sorry for the wreck. I mean for every wreck," referring to the fight in the pickup on the night of their accident. Accepting Thomas's claim to Arnold as a father, Victor pours some of Arnold's ashes into Thomas' piggy-bank, which he has ridiculed so often before. When Victor brings the ashes to Arlene he has reached his goal on the journey, and he has, in an abstract sense, also symbolically fulfilled his desire to reunite his family. The narrative lines are woven together at the end, the two main conflicts are settled; the narratives achieve closure. The last sequence is designed to relate the natural very tightly to the human. It features (partly in slow motion) some beautiful aerial tracking shots of the Spokane River as it grows larger until it reaches the Spokane Falls. Then the camera tilts up to reveal Victor standing on the bridge and pouring Arnold's ashes into the river, while screaming in pain. From a high angle it shows how Victor breaks down on the bridge. The whole sequence is com-

plemented by Thomas' non-diegetic recitation of the poem "Forgiving our
Fathers" by the poet–musician Dick Lourie.[68] It is a poem about how
forgiving can be a very painful experience which nevertheless helps in the
process of self-discovery. The monologue becomes the epilogue of the film
and an analogy to Victor's journey of coming to terms with his past and the
ghost of his father.

Disrupting Western Clichés

Humor has helped Indigenous people to bear the results of eurocentric colonization: the seizure of their traditional territories, marginalization, oppression, and personal and structural racism, among others. Alexie treats the
situation of Indigenous people in his works with such humor, and *Smoke
Signals'* script unmistakingly has Alexie's handwriting on it; it betrays his
acid irony, his irreverent sarcasm, and his anger. With *Smoke Signals*, Indigenous filmmaking arrives in Hollywood, which was and is the factory of
Indian stereotypes in movies *per se*, providing the visual and sonic side of
colonial discourse. Of course, the filmmakers cannot deconstruct this long
tradition of clichéd presentation, but they can use the same medium to
create self-controlled images as an answering discourse. Like the incongruence between the viewer's genre expectations and *Smoke Signals'* employment of the road-movie genre, the disjunction between preconceived ideas
about Indians and *Smoke Signals'* presentation of Indigenous people and
issues creates a space where subversion of such stereotypes and corrections
of biased historical and cultural knowledge can take place. By creating this
space of incongruence and dialogism mostly through humor, (self-)irony,
and satire, the filmmakers avoid having their film slip into plain lecturing
and moralizing about five hundred years of colonialism and colonial media
discourse. In Vizenor's sense, the filmmakers utilize strategies of trickster
discourse, engaging in subversive dialogue with Hollywood and Western
historical discourse and thereby revealing dissident views of Indigeneity
and colonial history and challenging stereotypical and monolithic narratives
thereof. "The political subtext succeeds because it is never *overtly* political," Amanda Cobb observes.[69] Thomas, for example, in a monologue describes in funny allegories the displacement of Indigenous cultures from

---

[68] For the text of the poem, see the Appendix.
[69] Amanda J. Cobb, "This Is What It Means to Say *Smoke Signals*," 213; emphasis in
original.

their territories by the settler culture, the (still continuing) nuclear testing close to reservations and sacred sites,[70] and US-American expansionist policies:

> We've been traveling a long time, enit? I mean, Columbus shows up and we start walking away from that beach, trying to get away, and then Custer moves into the neighborhood, driving down all the property values, and we have to walk some more, then old Harry Truman drops the bomb and we have to keep on walking somewhere, except it's all bright now so we can see exactly where we're going, and then you and I get a beach house on the moon, but old Neil Armstrong shows up and kicks us off into space.

Funny as these lines sound, some contemplation allows the filmmakers' acid cynicism to show through. Eyre and Alexie take this notion of movement of Indigenous people as a characteristic motif of their film and send Victor and Thomas 'on the road'. They are constantly moving, and Thomas's monologue is presented exactly when the two men are walking on an Arizona dirt road to find the trailer park. The image of the two men walking functions as a metonym of movements of several Indigenous cultures – not only forced by the colonizing culture (e.g., the Trail of Tears and the Flight of the Nez Perce) but also as an inherent element in the former way of life of some nations (e.g., the movement of the Dené/Navajo south and the seasonal movement of Plains cultures). Thomas's satirical talk about Indian movement at the same time points to the fatal stereotypical assumption that all Indigenous nations were nomads, on which basis the occupation of their territory found legitimization because they were not 'inhabiting the land' in the Western sense. If one subtracts Thomas's droning voice as well as the bizarre situation of the two walking through the desert, the rather amusing tirade becomes a serious indictment of the forced removal of Indigenous cultures from their traditional lands as well as of continual nuclear terror and the calculated

---

[70] Cf. the documentary *Trespassing* (2005) by Carlos DeMenezes, which explores the controversies around uranium mining, nuclear testing, and storage of nuclear waste close to reservations and Indigenous sacred sites, such as in Nevada's Yucca Mountains, in the Four-Corners area, and in California's Mojave Desert. The film, poetically and emotionally gripping, documents Indigenous and non-Indigenous protests against American nuclear policies and protesters' efforts to prevent further health risks of residents as well as further desecration of Indigenous lands, air, and water ("Tresspassing," at http://www.cinelasamericas.org /archivePROGRAMG/2006CLA9/festival9/filmPAGES/Trespassing.html). Cf., further, "The Making of *Trespassing*," at http://www.wsdp.org/trespassing.htm

risks of cancer cases, birth defects, and loss of lives and life-style of (non-
)Indigenous inhabitants of nuclear testing, mining, and storage areas.

Further, Eyre and Alexie recontextualize some of the most prevalent Indian stereotypes. Hartmut Lutz, in his study of Indian images in American
and West German children's thinking, singles out several as the most common clichés: Apaches and Sioux are the most familiar nations; Sitting Bull,
Crazy Horse, and Geronimo the most famous Indians; Pocahontas, Squan-
to, and Tonto the most popular mythical/fictional characters; living in tipis,
hunting buffalo, and fighting white invaders the main activities of Indians;
and 'firewater', 'scalp', 'squaw', 'wigwam', 'tomahawk', 'moccasin', and
'manitou' some of the best-known real or invented Indian terms.[71] One example of such a recontextualization is the conversation between Victor,
Junior Polatkin, and Boo in the indoor basketball court which ends in
Custer mockery song. Here, the film culls some aspects of colonialism
from its historical context and discusses them with basketball semantics.
When the young men debate who was the best basketball player ever, they
do not talk about contemporary first-rate African-American players such as
Michael Jordan, Earvine Johnson, Patrick Ewing, or Shaquille O'Neal, who
are exploited by the machinery of commercialized sport (and, of course, use
this commercialism for their own benefit). Instead, they come up with an
historical Indigenous figure, challenging the viewer's expectations and putting their culture at the center. The dialogue in the script reads as follows:

> *Junior Polatkin:* Hey Victor, who do you think is the best basketball player
> ever? *Victor:* That's easy. Geronimo. *Junior Polatkin:* Geronimo? He
> couldn't play basketball, man. He was Apache, man. Those suckers are
> about three feet tall. *Victor:* It's Geronimo, man. He was lean, mean, and
> bloody. Would have dunked on our flat Indian ass and then cut it off. *Junior
> Polatkin:* Yeah, some day it's a good day to die, some day it's a good day to
> play basketball.

This dialogue holds court with several aspects of clichéd views of Indian
people produced by the mainstream media. It endows Geronimo with all
the derogatory features that such colonial discourses attributed to the
Apaches as a reaction to the blows the US army received during Geroni-

---

[71] Hartmut Lutz, "'Indians' and Native Americans in the Movies," 31–32. This study draws
on Ralph Friar and Natasha Friar's work on the presentation of Indians in Hollywood movies
in *The Only Good Indian: The Hollywood Gospel Gospel* (New York: Drama Book Specialists, 1972).

mo's successful guerrilla warfare.[72] Especially in the media, the Apaches were fitted out with savage and belligerent characteristics that would mitigate the literal and moral losses of the US cavalry in the public realm as well as legitimate US military reactions to Geronimo's warfare. This description of Geronimo as presented by non-Indigenous filmmakers, members of the group that produces and controls colonialist images, would consolidate the very stereotypical notion. The sardonic description by Indigenous filmmakers, members of the group whose images are produced and controlled, however, subverts and saps the potency of the media cliché. The makers who present it are so sure that the stereotype is insubstantial that they feel safe repeating it by integrating it into their joking. In the same context, the players launch into their song about Custer:

> *[the young men are imitating a Powwow drum, Victor giving the rhythm by pounding the basketball]* Oh, I took the ball to the hoop and what did I see? Oh, I took the ball to the hoop and what did I see? General George Armstrong Custer was a-guarding me, a-guarding me!

The text here ventures into history, alluding to Custer's attack on the Sioux camped at the Little Big Horn in 1876 as well as paying homage to their victory in the ensuing battle, when Sioux and Cheyenne warriors defeated Custer and his troops. The filmmakers inscribe a modified Indigenous medium (song/dance) with ridicule of this American military 'hero', in this way poking fun at the "incessant Custer myth-making" that was the film industry's reaction to the traumatic losses at Little Big Horn, including twenty-two films between 1909 and 1971 alone.[73]

The narrative also brings up an issue that very often creates prejudices and slips into contemporary Indian cliché. The presentation of two heavy drinking parties (one in the Builds-The-Fires' home and one in the Josephs' home) contextualizes the alcohol problems that infiltrate Indigenous communities on a large scale. At this point the filmmakers might be accused of perpetuating the stereotype of the drunken Indian and catering to the 'blame the victim' idea that Indigenous people themselves are responsible for their disadvantaged situation in North America. In order to circumvent this trap without turning away from this issue, Eyre and Alexie portray its effect on families but, in contrast to the short stories in Alexie's *The Lone Ranger and Tonto Fistfight in Heaven*, cast all the younger characters as non-

---

[72] Lutz, "'Indians' and Native Americans in the Movies," 38.
[73] "'Indians' and Native Americans in the Movies," 38.

drinkers. This shift away from alcoholism is contextualized very subtly in the brief conversation between Victor and the police officer. When the latter informs Victor that he is accused of having caused the accident and of having been drunk, Victor replies that he never drinks, upon which the officer asks incredulously: "What kind of Indian are you exactly?" The question is employed ambiguously, because it not only asks what nation the two are from (Thomas sheepishly answers that they are Coeur d'Alene Indians) but it also implies that there is a common assumption that Indians drink and one who does not drink cannot be a 'real Indian'. Here, the film-makers play with the viewer's preconception about the contemporary drinking Indian. And they relate to the importance of tribal affiliation among Indigenous cultures, countering homogenizing practices in Western filmic discourse that created a pan-Indian mash,[74] where several distinct In-digenous cultures, distinct cultural and regional traits would be blended into one. Thomas's fear and Victor's aggressiveness during the interrogation and their great relief when they are released reveal their internalized as-sumptions of how Indigenous people and members of other minority groups are treated by government officials, especially the border patrol and the police.[75] Racial profiling, unjustified charges, inappropriate treatment, and other discriminatory practices are a common experience, a fact that the filmmakers subtly evoke. More ironically, the filmmakers return to this topic when Thomas tells the story of Arnold taking part in an anti-Vietnam War demonstration during which he supposedly beat up a National Guard private and got arrested. Thomas recounts:

> At first, they charged him with attempted murder. And then they plea-bargained that down to assault with a deadly weapon. And then they plea-bargained that down to being Indian in the twentieth century.

Arnold's 'crime of being Indian' in the twentieth century is exaggerated and designed to pinpoint discriminatory practices of government officials that are motivated by racist reactions to ethnic background. As Niro in *Overweight With Crooked Teeth* employs exaggeration and accumulation

---

[74] This term is derived from Hartmut Lutz's concept of 'pan-Indian Mash', the blending together of distinct Indigenous cultural and regional traits in Western discourses; Lutz, "'Indians' and Native Americans in the Movies: A History of Stereotypes, Distortions, and Repression," in Lutz, *Approaches: Essays in Native North American Studies and Literatures* (Augsburg: Wißner, 2002): 53.

[75] Jhon Warren Gilroy, "Another Fine Example of the Oral Tradition?," 27–28.

of stereotypes, Eyre and Alexie's strategy here is exaggeration of racist experience in order to critically reflect upon it.

Cinematic Dialogue With Hollywood

Intermedial references in *Smoke Signals* are another vehicle for conveying indirect criticism and making the film more entertaining through allusions to current pop culture. The most distinct criticism refers to the movie *Dances With Wolves*. Thomas has derived his image of Indians from watching this movie around a hundred times. Watching a Hollywood movie that is itself often rather absurd and doing so in order to gain knowledge about Indigenous cultures is pretty bizarre and shows Thomas's warped world-view. Victor ridicules Thomas's way of acquiring knowledge, and his mockery contains Eyre's and Alexie's critique of the movie. It is supposed to be a politically correct movie,[76] one that raises sensitivity toward Indian clichés and promotes a broader awareness of Indigenous issues in North America. Although the movie might have done this on the surface, it contains the same colonialist stereotypes packed neatly into benevolent images of Indians. There are, again, blood-thirsty, savage Pawnee set against peaceful, 'domesticated' Sioux. Emma LaRoque outlines the inherent dangers of such 'pan-Indian' movies and maintains that films like *Dances with Wolves* (1990), *Clearcut* (1991), and *The Last of the Mohicans* (1992),[77] which are regarded as fostering cross-cultural tolerance, use very seductive techniques to portray only fragments of Indigenous cultures.[78] According to her, these movies uphold the established dichotomy of the

---

[76] The term 'politically correct' comes with problematic connotations, as Ella Shohat and Robert Stam endeavour to clarify: "The phrase 'political correctness' (PC) evokes not only the neoconservative caricature of socialist, feminist, gay, lesbian, and multiculturalist politics but also a real tendency within the left – whence its effectiveness. Amplifying the preexisting association of the left with moralistic self-righteousness and puritanical antisensuality, the right wing has portrayed all politicized critique as the neurotic effluvium of whiny malcontents, the product of an uptight subculture of morbid guilt-tripping" (*Unthinking Eurocentrism*," 11).

[77] Amanda J. Cobb shows how such "Indian sympathy films" influenced North American public discourse and resulted in an upsurge of interest in Indigenous culture: "For example, during the wave of Indian sympathy films in the 1980s and early 1990s, Indian causes became popular with philanthropic foundations, and even with the U.S. leaders who construct important Indian policy and legislation [...] during the years *Dances With Wolves* won several Academy Awards, 'the Senate Select Committee on Indian Affairs had the highest number of senators wanting to serve on it'" ("This Is What It Means to Say *Smoke Signals*," 212).

[78] Thoughts of LaRoque presented in a paper at the Joint Annual Conference of the Western Literature Association and the Canadian Association for American Studies (Banff, 1998).

noble and the savage Indian (e.g., Sioux and Hurons, Sioux and Pawnee), present racist sexual images, and have contemporary Indigenous actors (such as Wes Studi and Graham Greene) perform savage acts so that Indian savagery is made very real and plastic. Instead of raising awareness about stereotypes, these films only perpetuate them, albeit in a very subtle way. They transport a false notion of fairness and political correctness toward Indigenous cultures. In this sense, the movie *Dances With Wolves* is highly dangerous, for it claims to present Indigenous people in a sensitive, correct way but maintains traditional stereotypes on a more subliminal level. Katherine Monk writes:

> Beyond the crystal-toting flakes, past the revisionism of dreamcatcher hippie chic and way, way deeper than even the most benevolent manifestations of white bourgeois guilt contained in the likes of *Dances With Wolves* lies a creature called genuine Indian culture. It's not easy to find. For the past century, we've beaten it into a pasty white pulp and poured it into readymade moulds of acceptable shapes and sizes – nothing too big and threatening, just something colourful enough to show us life in a different hue. The result has been a rather nauseating red-and-white collage of well-meaning stinkers such as designer sweat lodges, shrink-wrapped sweetgrass, Bruce McDonald's *Dance Me Outside* and Disney's *Pocahontas*. These things have successfully raised white awareness about the plight of the 20th century Indian, but they have once again translated the Indian experience into white terms.[79]

The media discourse described by Monk is the source of Thomas's romanticized picture of Indians, although a 'real' Indigenous culture is just outside his doorstep. But Victor's idea of Indian males also relies heavily on channelled media pictures. He has only partly shucked off the romanticized 'noble savage' (he insists on good looks and long unbound hair) and has kept the tough-warrior image, necessary, he thinks, for Indian males to make a stand against non-Indians. Thus, his perception of Indigeneity is warped as well. On their trip, Victor teaches Thomas how to dress and behave properly as a 'real Indian'. Victor's teachings, such as asserting that an Indian has to look stoical and mean like a warrior just returned from killing a buffalo, are informed by such clichéd colonial discourse. Victor, in the manner of Western thinking, reduces the variety of Indigenous cultures to the Plains Indian nations, who hunted buffalo. "From the mid-nineteenth century until today, the mounted Plains warrior has become the epitome of

---

[79] Katherine Monk, "Real Native Culture Shines Through Smoke Signals," C3.

the Indian par excellence," explains Lutz. "It is an exclusive stereotype that has influenced non-natives and natives alike, culminating in the gradual displacement of traditional headgear by the war bonnet as the Pan-Indian headdress in the 1950s."[80]

Thomas innocently replies that the Coeur d'Alene people never hunted buffalo but were fishermen, showing that he can nevertheless distinguish between his romantic idea of Indians and the cultural heritage of his people. But Victor stubbornly maintains that a fisherman would not look tough enough: "What? Do you want to look like you just returned from catching a fish? This ain't Dances With Salmon, you know? Thomas, you got to look like a warrior" – Victor admits, then, that his standard idea of a 'real Indian' also relies heavily on the dominant media discourse and the movie *Dances With Wolves*. Although Thomas takes Victor's teaching seriously and changes his clothes and his hair, he is not willing to put on Victor's 'stoical warrior' look, pretending to do so but again displaying a broad smile before he enters the bus. Just as Victor ridiculed Thomas for his romantic ideas about Indianness, Thomas now ridicules Victor for his insistence on similar clichéd ideas. Victor's notion of Indianness is put to the test in the encounter with two redneck cowboys in the bus who have taken their seats after a stop. Here, of course, his stoical conduct fails him, sarcastically and discouragingly summed up Thomas: "Guess your warrior look doesn't always work." Thus, the film plot itself corrects its characters' internalized autostereotyped notions of Indigenous cultures.

Thomas mentions the movie title *The Last of the Mohicans*, emphasizing its playful variation on the phrase "last of ... ": "When Indians go away, they don't come back – Last of Mohicans, Last of Winnebago, Last of ... ." The 1992 version of *The Last of the Mohicans* (and the first three movies as well) is based on Cooper's novel by the same title. It follows, like *Little Big Man* (1970), the narrative structure of the first genuinely American literary genre, the 'Indian captivity tale'.[81] The movie, like many others, presses one Indigenous nation (Huron) into the mold of a blood-thirsty savage people while polarizing them against a more docile Indian nation and Indigenous characters (Uncas, Chingachgook, Mohican). Apart from this, the notion of one Indian being the last of his or her culture suggests the extinction of a nation, which plainly does not apply here. Although U S and

---

[80] Hartmut Lutz, "'Indians' and Native Americans in the Movies," 36. He draws upon John Ewers, *Artists of the Old West* (1965; Garden City N Y : Doubleday, 1973).

[81] See also Lutz, "'Indians' and Native Americans in the Movies," 34.

Canadian colonialist policies for a long time aimed at the extinction of Indigenous cultures, only a few nations (e.g., Natchez and Beothuk) really
suffered this fate. Further, Hollywood presented Indigenous people via a
small range of stock characters, one of which was "the last of his dying
race."[82] Eyre and Alexie, through comical repetition, attack such stock
casting, along with the notion of Indigenous cultures having been on the
brink of extinction. Also, the phrase "last of Winnebago" is a critical allusion to the practice of mainstream culture of appropriating Indigenous
nations and terms to name objects – for example, the RV-trailer Winnebago, the army helicopter Apache, the Jeep Cherokee. Hand in hand with
this sort of terminology goes the naming of sports clubs such as the Cleve-
land Indians and Washington Redskins. Their mascots as well as the mas-
cot of the University of Illinois basketball team, Chief Illiniwek, and the
'tomahawk chop', an offensive arm gesture of Atlanta Braves fans,[83] are
pejorative replicas and signifiers of Indigenous cultures and uphold Indian
clichés in contemporary society. Such practices are not only unethical but
also wrongfully commercialize Indigenous cultures.
      Chief Dan George's famous line from the movie *Little Big Man*, "It's a
good day to die," is put to use as well. It reappears in modified guise in
Peone's morning broadcast: "It's a good day to be Indigenous," in Thomas's words "sometimes it's a good day to die, sometimes it's a good day
to have breakfast," and in Junior Polatkin's declaration: "yeah, sometimes
it's a good day to die, sometimes it's a good day to play basketball." The
quotational take-offs ridicule this silly romanticized Indian death drive.
Such often romantically tinged one-liners and statements by famous Indian
chiefs flood the mainstream market in little books and are almost invariably
found in many mainstream films featuring Indian topics. Thus, Indigenous
cultural knowledge and spirituality are commercialized and presented
selectively (only what is of interest to the West). Playful quotations such as
the ones in *Smoke Signals* ridicule the 'maxims of the wise' and strip them
of their lop-sided representation of Indians as having a unique claim on
natural wisdom and spirituality.[84]

---

[82] "'Indians' and Native Americans in the Movies," 39.

[83] Beverly Singer, *Wiping the War Paint Off the Lens: Native American Film and Video*
(Minneapolis: U of Minnesota P, 2001): 5, 10.

[84] Such collections of Indian proverbs and Indian speeches contextualize Indian wisdom
and Indian relation to Mother Earth, combined with beautiful natural images and romantic
photographs or paintings of Indigenous chiefs. These appear most often in the format of little

The genre of the American western is enlisted by Holly when she calls Thomas and Victor "the Lone Ranger and Tonto"; in her gratitude, she sees in them Indian saviours walking in the 'footsteps' of this male biracial couple. Thomas answers archly: "No, it's more like we are Tonto and Tonto." The story of the Lone Ranger and Tonto is a classic western fairy-tale, in which a masked ranger and his Indian friend ride out to serve justice.[85] The relation between the two men is characterized by their ethnic background, as such biracial partnerships often are elsewhere in literature and film (e.g., Defoe's Robinson Crusoe and Friday, Cooper's Natty Bumppo and Chingachgook, Thoreau's Henry and Wawatan): the Lone Ranger, a white man clad in white and wearing a white mask, guides his Indian friend Tonto, dressed of course in buckskin and fringes.[86] Their rela-

---

booklets, as Lee Schweninger pointed out in a paper presented at the Biennial Conference of the European Association for American Studies in Lisbon in 1998. Speeches by Indigenous leaders are very often put to use in environmentalist campaigns. "The Speech of Chief Seattle" is the most exploited example. For example, in a German edition of Indian proverbs, quotations from the speech are turned into four 'proverbs'; *Indianerweisheiten*, ed. Angelika Koller (Munich: arsedition, 1996): 11, 25, 44, and 47. Apart from being abridged and not correctly translated, they are taken out of the context of the whole speech, which is, rather, an apocalyptic vision of the Indigenous future and includes the omen that the spirits of his dead people will haunt the white men that live on the stolen land. I base my discussion on the version of Seattle's speech in *The Heath Anthology of American Literature*, vol. 1, ed. Paul Lauter (1990; Boston MA & New York: Houghton Mifflin, 1998): 1888–91. On the discrepancies in American versions and incorrect translations as well as their employment for environmentalist agendas in the European context, see Rudolf Kaiser, "Chief Seattle's Speech(es): American Origins and European Reception," in *Recovering the Word: Essays on Native American Literature*, ed. Brian Swann & Arnold Krupat (Berkeley: U of California P, 1987): 497–536.

[85] The Lone Ranger and Tonto story material was born as a radio series in 1932 and was made into a film series in 1939 and into a television series in 1949. In 1956, Stuart Heisler adapted it again for the screen under the title *The Lone Ranger*; Joe Hembus, *Das Western-lexikon* (Munich: Wilhelm Heine, 1997): 712.

[86] Leslie A. Fiedler explains that the forests of the New World were regarded as a natural Eden, lost when Christianity and woman intervened. According to him, the white men in such male biracial couples constitute the image of the runaway from civilization, while the Indian men are identified as the serpent in the natural Eden, as the name Chingachgook (Great Serpent) in Cooper illustrates; Fiedler, *The Return of the Vanishing American* (1968; New York: Stein & Day, 1976): 116–19. In the context of Cooper's Natty Bumppo and Chingachgook, Fiedler also illuminates the romantic aspect of such biracial male couples, who have turned their backs on civilization and enjoy their love of nature and the challenge of the American wilderness. He describes Natty as "a Protestant Noble Savage, worshipping in the Universalist Church of the Woods" and Chingachgook as presenting "whatever in the American psyche has been starved to death, whatever genteel Anglo-Saxondom has most ferociously repressed, whatever he himself had stifled to be worthy of his wife and daughters"; Fiedler, *Love and*

tion as leader and follower is even more defined through the name of the
Lone Ranger, given him by his friend Tonto: Kemo Sabe, meaning 'Leader
whom one trusts'.[87] Thus, the character Tonto submits to the role as docile
follower and ward of the colonial guard that non-Indigenous writers, script-
writers, and filmmakers have conceived for him. Lutz compares the figure
of Tonto with Chingachgook, "a 'Noble Savage' who is in the process of
becoming a domesticated, 'acculturated', 'good' Indian, serving European-
American expansionism and law-and-order ideology like the *Lone
Ranger*'s Tonto."[88] Thomas' reply that they are, rather, Tonto and Tonto
first of all denies any colonial guardianship; however, it also mocks his
own figure and that of Victor, since Tonto is the archetype of a good-
natured, docile Indian who is unable to think and decide for himself (after
all, *tonto* is Spanish for 'stupid'). On the one hand, *Smoke Signals* derides
the American western by quoting from it; on the other, it pokes postmodern
fun at its characters.

Smoke Signals, furthermore, cites the American western by mentioning
the two actors John Wayne and Charles Bronson. Thomas asserts that
Arnold looks like Charles Bronson (Paul Kersey) in *Death Wish V*, the title
chosen as a take-off on the Hollywood custom of producing several sequels
where one is often worse than its predecessor. Since Arnold does not look
like Charles Bronson at all and Thomas discloses his claim with such impossible seriousness, the statement turns into a joke. Eyre and Alexie can
use this comparison as a vehicle for pointing critically at the fact that in
western movies the main Indian part was seldom played by an Indigenous
actor but most often by an Italian, Asian, or American immigrant actor like
Charles Bronson.[89] John Wayne is parodied in a song in which Victor and
Thomas explore the riddle of his teeth, which, according to them, he never
shows in his movies (though he does). By making fun of two well-known
charismatic actors who are metonyms of the American western, Eyre and
Alexie attempt to reverse the Hollywood habit of humiliating, misrepresenting, and caricaturing Indigenous people and thereby asserting euro-

---

Death in the American Novel (1960; New York: Penguin, 1982): 192–95.

[87] Joe Hembus, *Das Westernlexikon*, 712.

[88] Hartmut Lutz, "'Indians' and Native Americans in the Movies," 34.

[89] Bronson played Indian and half-breed characters in several movies, such as *The Magnificent Seven* (USA, 1960), *Chato's Land* (USA, 1972), and *Valdez, il Mezzosangue* [*Chino*]
(France, Italy & Spain, 1973).

centric supremacy. The western could not but misrepresent the Indian, who would not fit into the Western myth of a lone individual

> heroically taming a frontier 'wilderness.' [...] The Hollywood western could at best present the Indian as the unknown 'Other', part of the forces threatening the onward march of civilization because for the native population there is no place within that dream.[90]

Still, many Indigenous people like to watch westerns just to see Indian images on the screen at all:

> You were so hungry for some sort of validation of your existence in the national consciousness that any images were acceptable, as long as they were brown. [...] So you watch cowboy movies because you at least see Indians. You still root for them and hope that this will be the movie where they finally win.[91]

In *Smoke Signals*, Alexie not only derides a genre that has a history of distorting Indigenous cultures, but also the fact that Indigenous people consume such representations. As Thomas, Victor, and Suzy watch a western on television, Thomas comments wittily: "You know, the only thing more pathetic than Indians on TV is Indians watching Indians on TV." The character Thomas criticizes his own act, becoming a commentator on the film's plot, feeding the metanarrative. In the same vein, he mocks the very film he is a character in, since *Smoke Signals* is certainly "Indians on television and the screen." Eyre and Alexie blend an American western scene (an Indian attack) into their film and with it the trail of Indian stereotypes that viewers associate with seeing such a scene. The images of the western have to pass through yet another camera, this time 'controlled' by Indigenous filmmakers. The western is embedded in the cultural Indigenous context of three Indigenous people having frybread for dinner, visually realized through a pan from the television set to the kitchen table. At the same time, the recontextualization of the western is embedded in the context of an autonomous Indigenous narrative and visual discourse where Thomas's statement criticizes the heterostereotyping of Indigenous cultures in westerns and the partial Indigenous autostereotyping found in the same discourse. The western thus becomes vulnerable to manipulations and sub-

---

[90] Hartmut Lutz, "'Indians' and Native Americans in the Movies," 39.
[91] Sherman Alexie, quoted in Rita Kempley, "No More Playing Dead for American Indian Filmmaker Sherman Alexie," *Washington Post* (3 July 1998): D1.

versive contextualization of the second camera, the second, anticolonial gaze which Eyre and Alexie relish engaging with. The way in which the western genre is quoted invites critical reflection, commenting as it does on this filmic tradition and undermining it. *Smoke Signals* becomes a piece of filmed criticism.

Last but not least, the characters Velma and Lucy are clearly a quotation of the road movie *Thelma & Louise* (1991), which broke with the road movie tradition of featuring male protagonists. Velma and Lucy are just driving on reservation roads; nevertheless, they are on the road like Thelma and Louise. "I wanted to put them in there as a homage to Thelma & Louise," says Alexie.[92] Their driving in reverse is an Indigenous metonym and metaphor simultaneously: first, because cars on the rez do not always work as they should, and secondly, because it alludes to a circular sense of time that Alexie attempts to accentuate: "'Sometimes to go forward you have to drive in reverse'."[93] To non-Indigenous viewers, not only the driving in reverse but even more so the dialogue and conduct of the two young women seem a bit overdone. Yet the two are a fresh illustration of rez characters and cater to the sub-narrative depicting reservation life in the twentieth century. Apparently, it is impossible nowadays to make a movie without directly or indirectly quoting from others, and Alexie comments on the numerous intermedial allusions and quotations as follows:

> Movies have never allowed us to be fully functioning members of the national consciousness and society. This movie shows that we are just as influenced by our own particular tribe of cultures as we are [by] pop cultures. That's how we live our lives. That's who we are.[94]

Roads, Movement, and Other Cinematic Motifs
Various motifs running through the film serve as a 'treat' for attentive viewers and tighten the film's texture. They can be grouped according to content and technique. The motifs associated with content appear on different narrative levels. At first, there is the motif of the road itself, realized through roughly twenty shots, partly aerial views of roads winding through

---

[92] Dennis West & Joan M. West, "Sending Cinematic Smoke Signals: An Interview with Sherman Alexie," 31.

[93] West & West, "Sending Cinematic Smoke Signals," 31.

[94] Alexie, quoted in Rita Kempley, "No More Playing Dead for American Indian Film-maker Sherman Alexie," D1.

the reservation and various landscapes. They provide the basic visual ingredient of the road movie. The high number of such shots reveals a certain emphasis on landscapes as set(ting), indicating the filmmakers' attempt to show the vastness and beauty they see in the land as well as the characters' integration into it. "You can let the landscape tell a lot of story," says Alexie.[95] Also, medium shots of the bus driver, close-ups of the gear shift lever and the bus tires, as well as rear-view-mirror shots of the driver and Victor, all serve as basic visual road-movie elements.

Closely linked to the road motif is that of the journey, with defining character for the movie. The dynamic of the journey, an essential feature of the road-movie genre, is here derived from Victor's goal of bringing back the ashes of his father. The journey motif is lent variety through the different vehicles the characters use (the Malibu, the Greyhound bus, Arnold's pickup, the police car). The walk through the desert and Victor's run are variations on the journey pattern, whereby the walk is employed rather parodically. Aside from supporting the journey motif, the different variations of running (young Victor running toward the house, sequence 12; running after leaving his father, 31; running down the road, 33, 34; and adult Victor running for help, 53) make this form of movement a motif relating to Indigenous tradition. In this tradition, young men ran in order to gain strength and endurance or to ensure good hunting and harvests, as in N. Scott Momaday's *House Made of Dawn*.[96] Whereas these runs were voluntary, Victor's run for help is forced by circumstances – he is being compelled to exhaust himself and, in a way, to move closer to traditional ways.

A fourth motif is developed through the clothes the characters wear. Arnold mainly wears a red T-shirt and blue jeans. Victor, in the 1988 as

---

[95] Dennis West & Joan M. West, "Sending Cinematic Smoke Signals," 29.

[96] Contemporary long runs attempt to revive traditions – for example, the annual 500-mile marathon to the Degannawidah-Quetzalcoatl University Davis (D-QU) in California, which aims to "unify American Indians spiritually through many exercises of the traditional Indian values of life, balanced with today's modern world"; Hartmut Lutz, *D-Q University: Native American Self-Determination in Higher Education* (Davis CA: Tecumseh Center Publications, 1980): 114. Political spin-offs of such runs were the 500-mile run from Davis, California to Los Angeles and the Longest Walk from Davis and San Francisco to Washington, D.C., both also initiated by D-QU. These were strong spiritual events which pursued political agendas, seeking to draw attention to political prisoners like Leonard Peltier and to demonstrate against bills in Congress which intended to terminate US American trust responsibilities toward Indigenous people (Lutz, *D-Q University*, 41–42). In this sense, Victor's run becomes the vehicle of a postmodern reference to Indigenous spiritual and political struggles.

well as in the 1998 sequences, most often wears a red T-shirt and blue jeans as well. Thus, father and son are linked through their clothes. The clothing motif recurs in the sequence in which Victor sifts through his father's belongings. He finds Arnold's blue jeans and red T-shirt lying on the bed where he has passed away. The color red also sets off the two characters from the others to echo visually the fact that the film's narrative revolves around the father–son conflict. Victor also wears checkered shirts which, conversely, connect him to his mother Arlene, who throughout the film appears in such shirts. The match on action cuts 27/28, 28/29, and 33/34 are supported by Victor's matching checkered shirts with almost the same color. Thomas as a juvenile and adult constantly wears a three-piece suit, rounded off by two tight braids, seemingly an absurd costume for a boy and young man in the twentieth century. It is reminiscent of the appearance of 'civilized' boys in colonialist residential and boarding schools. The 'Indian' in a three-piece suit and braids visually reiterates photographs of 'civilized Indians' in the late 1800s and early 1900s and comments critically on both the American and Canadian policy of 'civilizing Indians' and the of loss of tradition, cultural pride, language, parenting skills, self-assurance and self-respect that were the devastating consequences, still felt by contemporary generations.[97] Thomas's outfit, his awkwardness, and his 'talent' for storytelling, which he constantly puts to use, make him a weirdo who does not seem to fit into reservation life. After Victor has taught him how to dress and 'behave properly', Thomas changes his clothes to blue jeans and a blue T-shirt, with the words "Frybread Power" and wears his hair unbound, but later appears in his usual attire. Here, the sartorial motif might be understood as an indicator of a change in Thomas's personality as he learns to reconcile traditional and contemporary life.

Similarly, hair is a recurrent motif. Before the fatal house fire, Arnold has long black hair. Later in the film, he is seen with short grey hair, having turned into a prematurely ageing drunk. As non-diegetic narrator, Thomas

---

[97] Luther Standing Bear, in his book *Land of the Spotted Eagle*, includes a photograph of himself and his father in which his father is seen in a three-piece suit and braids and Standing Bear in a similar suit but with his hair cut. The hairdo here shows the break between the two generations and the degree of 'civilization'. Charles Alexander Eastman, in *From the Deep Woods to Civilization*, inserts photographs of himself with short hair and wearing a coat and a three-piece suit. Standing Bear rather disapprovingly describes his school years, drawing attention to their alienating consequences, while Eastman fully embraced 'white civilization', as his enthusiastic descriptions reveal. In the second text, the inclusion of the photographs may, rather, be motivated by pride in Eastman's achievements in Euro-American society.

explains that Arnold has cut his hair to mourn the dead of the fire. The viewer infers that he started to drink out of an inability to deal with his guilt. Later, when Victor enters Arnold's trailer in search of something that he can keep and that will reconnect him with his father, he finds a pocket knife with which he cuts his own hair, disclosing his grief for the loss of his father – physically and emotionally. The hair motif connects father and son by having Victor repeat Arnold's act of cutting his hair in grief. What mars Victor's act somewhat is the impossible wig he wears after this. The wig is one of the accessories belong to the production and is mocked by the narrator of the film: Thomas calls Victor's act ironically "butchering his hair" and a "ceremony." The comments work as yet another vehicle for merging narrative and metanarrative, where the narrator ironizes one of the characters. It is also a metafilmic comment on the rather poor prop and thus the making of the film.

Another motif is expressed in the character traits shared by Arnold and Victor: on the one hand, both are very gentle, able to express their love for their family. On the other, both tend to be choleric, with rapid mood-swings. This is shown most graphically when Arnold strikes Arlene in a fight and hits young Victor when he accidentally drops a beer. It reappears also in the young Victor's violent beating of Thomas, in the adult Victor's aggressive reactions to Thomas's stories, and in his standoffish behavior at the police station. Both men exercize verbal and physical violence upon others to release their suppressed anger and frustration. Throughout the film, father and son are linked by parallel presentation in regard to their clothes, their hair, their choleric nature, and their treatment of others.

Frybread is also a recurring pattern, being a traditional dish in many Indigenous cultures. Since frybread is the only thing eaten in the film, this pattern becomes a defining element in the film. The frybread is also a narrative element in one of Thomas's stories, in which Arlene miraculously turns fifty pieces of frybread into one hundred. In his story, Thomas compares frybread to the Jesus legend: "Arlene Joseph makes some Jesus frybread, frybread that can walk across water, frybread rising from the dead." This story, of course, leans heavily on the biblical account of Jesus feeding five thousand people on one loaf of bread only. Of course, it is a parodic allusion to its biblical model, for Arlene in no way acts miraculously – she just divides each piece into two halves. In the same way, the filmmakers' replace the biblical figure of Jesus with an Indigenous character and food item and thus secularize the biblical text. This sort of subversive mimicry of imperial texts is one strategy beloved of postcolonial writers, including Eyre and Alexie. Furthermore, the making of frybread is employed to parallel scenes in the houses of the Josephs and the Builds-The-Fires: after Thomas has offered to pay for Victor's trip, the film cuts back and forth between the two kitchens of the houses. Arlene makes frybread while Victor tells her of his plans and Thomas's offer; Thomas makes frybread while his grandma warns him against Victor. The film's polarized presentation of gender roles suggests that, like in non-Indigenous cultures, essentialist and 'naturalized' ideas about gender are being broken down. In the Joseph family, it is the woman who, very conventionally, makes the bread while the man grabs the first piece that is ready. By contrast, in the Builds-The-Fires family the man makes the bread, and both sit down very sophisticatedly to eat dinner. This scene indicates that Victor is still macho and needs to be fed, a passive person to be cared for, while Thomas takes an active part in caring for his grandma. Thomas is past that childish stage, and in this sense is the more mature of the two young men. When Thomas and his grandma eat dinner, the two intercut scenes merge with each other via the knock on the door that indicates Victor coming to their house to tell Thomas that he accepts his offer.

The "Frybread Power" T-shirt Thomas wears emphasizes this element of Indigenous food. In T-shirt form, however, this element is politicized as a take-off on the political movements Women's Power, Black Power, Bronze Power, and Red Power. This self-ironizing statement might be a postmodern interpretation of political changes and might suggest that these terms have become mere denotations of political movements whose content and methods have changed or, in case of the Red Power movement with its close association with AIM, are keenly questioned by some Indigenous people. Thus, the T-shirt is a sign that can be seen as conveying Alexie's critical attitude toward AIM, which he has also voiced in an interview with the *Süddeutsche Zeitung*.[98]

Thomas's stories are also a motif running through the film. The stories are essential for characterizing Thomas, providing background information on the two major conflicts, and livening up the film. Through their struc-

---

[98] Susan Vahabzadeh, "Weil oder obwohl Indianer? Warum Sherman Alexies Film 'Smoke Signals' erfolgreich ist," *Süddeutsche Zeitung* (8 December 1998): 16. Here, Alexie says that AIM has indeed drawn attention to Indigenous people but that he does not believe that Indigenous people needed AIM to become aware of themselves. The movement failed because of its violence, and he does not believe that any political objectives justify violence.

tural repetition, they become a neat vehicle to transport humor, for each time Thomas falls into his funny storytelling mode, the viewer can deduce what the content of the story will be and how Victor will react. The content of the stories does not vary much – it is always some sort of exaggerated presentation of Arnold and Arlene. Still, as funny as these stories may appear through Thomas's peculiar performance, they have a serious side as well: Thomas, who never had parents as Victor did, imagines an ideal family in these tales. Victor, however, has experienced family life and knows that it is never as idealistic as Thomas imagines it. These divergent ideas of parenthood as well as the competition for it are the moments that provide the inner conflict between Victor and Thomas.

The motif of fire and ashes is another characterizing element. Both fire and ashes become metaphors for destruction and death. A fire has destroyed Thomas's home and killed his parents. The same fire has destroyed Arnold's self-respect and has spiritually killed his family. The ashes of Arnold are a dynamizing force because they are the reason for Victor's and Thomas's trip. They become a symbol for Victor's and Thomas's search for a lost father and are also a unifying object by passing through the hands of Suzy, Thomas, Victor, the police officer, and Arlene. When Victor hands Arlene the urn, Arnold has emblematically arrived where he belongs, and where he was always longing to go – home. Arnold's ashes induce Victor to change his character, to forgive and reconcile. Shots of the fatal house fire are repeated in several flashbacks. This repetition enhances the fire as a key element in the plot. The burning house is visually paralleled by Arnold's burning trailer, their linking element being Arnold. Whereas the house fire is realized in several long and medium shots from straight angles, the trailer fire is first realized through a shot from within the burning trailer and then through an aerial shot, so that the escaping smoke is seen drifting through the air. This shot is the only reference to the title of the film, which awakens cliché-laden expectations that the film, however, does not meet. In this way, the film plays with possible viewer expectations and ironizes romanticized images of Indigenous cultures in the dominant media discourse.[99] The camera work of the first fire suggests Arnold's involvement in the fire and positions the viewers as possible participants or bystanders. The camera work of the second fire, especially the aerial shot,

---

[99] The title *Smoke Signals* also suggests the first major Indigenous signal on the horizon of colonial film discourse that the film was to become.

clearly leaves the viewers outside the plot in an observing position – a position that also Arnold's spirit assumes. Further, the sequence in which Suzy sets the trailer on fire, shot from within the trailer, is stressed by adding a slow-motion effect, giving the impression of its being a ceremonial act that serves to get rid of the ghost associated with the trailer: Arnold's flight from his family. The trailer-burning, finally, is designed to erase Arnold's presence in Phoenix and his absence from home.

Lastly, the basketball, too, becomes a defining motif, since basketball is the game par excellence in the film. At the beginning, Victor, Junior Polatkin, and Boo play in an indoor court, then Arnold seems to play by himself on a small court near the trailer park, and finally the flashback in this sequence shows the game in which Arnold and Victor play against two priests. Suzy alludes to this game when she throws Arnold's basketball to Victor and bets she can make a shot in order to make Victor go into Arnold's trailer and look for things that could link Victor's self to Arnold's. Victor takes the ball home and, in the police-station scene, where Victor is reconciled with the spirit of his father, both items, the ball and the urn, become objects of the interrogation and are thus linked. When Victor and Thomas reclaim the pickup at the impound yard, Victor shoots the ball away as if to get rid of his anger against Arnold. The ball follows Victor on his journey and accompanies his inner odyssey to find his father.

Apart from the visual motifs, there are sound motifs as well. For the soundtrack, Eyre and Alexie chose different songs that recur with certain situations. There are, for example, two alternating sad theme songs which appear when Arlene receives the news of Arnold's death (9), lead over the sequences in which Victor decides to go to Phoenix to claim his father's ashes (13–17), reappear when the men resume their journey at the impound yard and when Suzy sets Arnold's trailer on fire (57–58), and return when Victor arrives at home and presents Arlene with the ashes (61). These sound motifs are clearly connected with Arnold's death. Accelerated, more dramatic music is placed at pivotal moments, such as the sequences of Arnold leaving (31), of the young Victor beating the young Thomas, carrying over to the adult Victor remembering these scenes in the bus (33–34), of Suzy finding Arnold's corpse (45), of Victor's 'marathon' (53), and of the epilogue (63). The filmmakers also place songs so that their lyrics match the content of the respective sequence. For example, in sequences 24 through 26 "A Million Miles Away" (by Jim Boyd) comments on the geographical distance between the men and their homes. It illustrates the journey motif and interprets the party of the Josephs as the cause of Arnold's leaving. The lyrics also refer to the temporal distance between the adult and the young Victor as well as to the emotional distance between him and his father. Similarly, the song "Father and Farther" (by Jim Boyd) in sequences 58 through 60 interprets the geographical and emotional distance between Victor and Arnold, undercut through Arnold's death. Landscape visuals are complemented by guitar music, supporting the road-movie character. When the camera focusses on the gear shift while the bus is starting, drums dynamize the music and thus the action.

Furthermore, the filmmakers very carefully employ traditional Indigenous music. At times, they combine it with rock music, at other times it appears in its own right. A combination of the different music genres occurs right at the beginning to build up the necessary ambience, and at the end it closes the narrative accompanying Victor as he painfully empties the urn of ashes into the river. Traditional songs (by Ulali) are reserved for the visuals of the burning house (2), of Victor cutting his hair (49), and in the Custer and Wayne songs. In the Custer song, the three men imitate traditional drum songs to lyrics that embed the Custer figure in basketball semantics; in the Wayne song, Victor and Thomas start singing about John Wayne's teeth, continued non-diegetically by the Eaglebear Singers. Here, traditional singing and drums mixed with Western rhythms are interpreted with lyrics ridiculing a famous western star. Apart from conveying anticolonial parody, the combination of the traditional and the modern in both songs indicates changes in Indigenous cultures and caters more specifically to the dismantling of the frozen concept of tradition. Also, in Velma's and Lucy's brown Malibu, a non-diegetic song (but one prompted by its announcement by Randy Peone of the K R E Z radio station) becomes a diegetic song on the car radio. Through the device of mixing non-diegetic music and diegetic music, the film enters into the metafilm about its making because it alerts attention to the difference between the inside and outside space of the film.[100] On the other hand, the various songs in the film connect the se-

---

[100]Non-diegetic music in classical narrative film has played a considerable part in producing suture and rendering a seamless presentation of the filmic events. Its function as a device supporting continuity is complemented by its function in establishing a convincing atmosphere of time and place, underscoring the feelings or psychological states of characters, serving as neutral background filler to the action, accentuating the rising action of a scene, and rounding it off with a sense of finality. Because of its direct access to the viewers' psyche, film music is able to draw them into the events presented. Hollywood musical scores are composed according to specific guidelines that yield a subtle, elusive, and unobtrusive sound track

quences or even carry the narrative through several sequences, so that they become a means of creating coherence and supporting continuity. Alexie says that the songs are vehicles to carry complementary story information:

> I didn't want the music to be an afterthought, but an inherent and organic part of the film. Writing songs is another way of expressing ourselves. Just as I think screenplays are accessible poetry, I think songs are accessible poetry. [...] For me, writing songs is a way to reach a different kind of audience. Using those songs in the film, however, is also a way of telling the story, of adding more layers to the story, as you see things on screen.[101]

Magic Cuts and Sound Bridges as Stylistic Devices

One might expect from the filmic translation of the story a new, non-Hollywood, Indigenous filmmaking style. However, Eyre and Alexie largely adhere to a conventional filmmaking style to translate the universal story (father–son conflict) into a mainstream film genre (road movie). The narrative runs smoothly and steadily, is realized through a cause–effect chain, and narrative time and space are clearly identified. The number of main characters – Victor, Thomas, Arnold, Arlene, Suzy, and Grandma Builds-The-Fire – has been chosen in accordance with modern American screen-writing manuals, which suggest seven to eight main characters for a clearly

---

supporting the narrative, sealing continuity breaks, preventing viewers from noticing the technological construction of the film, and seldom drawing attention to itself; Jeff Smith, "Unheard Melodies? A Critique of Psychoanalytic Theories of Film Music," in *Post-Theory: Reconstructing Film Studies*, ed. David Bordwell & Noël Carroll (Madison: U of Wisconsin P, 1996): 232–35. Nevertheless, the inaudibility of musical scores that is claimed for classical filmmaking is contested by Smith, who argues that it is not a question of hearing or not hearing film music but the degree to which film music is perceived, or on what level. This perception functions through various different listening modes and depends on the competencies of listeners ("Unheard Melodies?" 236–37). At the moment when diegetic music is merged with non-diegetic music, this musical score adheres to its function of creating suture. But at the same time it breaks suture, since it reveals its two different sources – the inside and outside space of the filmic action – and thus identifies the technological basis of the film. In the case of the John Wayne song and the song from the car radio, the songs partly support the narrative in the sense of unobtrusive background music, but are also narrative elements to which characters draw attention. The John Wayne song carries some of the narrative's ridiculing criticism and the car-radio song is stressed by Velma: "Oh man I love that song."

[101] Dennis West & Joan M. West, "Sending Cinematic Smoke Signals," 31. Denise K. Cummings explains Alexie's concept of 'accessible poetry' and analyzes *Smoke' Signals*, *Dead Man* (USA, 1995) and *Ghost Dog: The Way of the Samurai* (USA, 1999) according to this concept; Cummings, "'Accessible Poetry'? Cultural Intersection and Exchange in Contemporary American Indian and American Independent Film," *Studies in American Indian Literatures* 13.1 (Spring 2001): 5–78.

comprehensible plot. The characters have well-defined goals and their actions and motivation are obvious. As in conventional filmmaking, contigu-
ous spatial and temporal structures as well as the film's style are subordinated to the narrative. In technical terms, Eyre and Alexie adhere to classical continuity and to the 180° system, carefully place the sound, use standard shot/reverse-shot cutting and a steady cutting rhythm, and the camera
work (distance, perspective, and movement) is fairly consistent with that of
mainstream feature films. What might strike the viewer as a different film
style is the deliberate usage of such salient techniques as technical motifs,
multiple flashbacks, aerial shots, and the transition devices of magic cuts
(match on action shots) and apparent sound bridges.

Of the transition devices applied, the six dissolves and five fades are
ordinary transitions alongside the simple cut.[102] Whereas dissolves are cus-
tomarily used for a brief time lapse and fades for a longer one,[103] Eyre and
Alexie apply them interchangeably and not according to this scheme. They
use two fades between a 1976 sequence, a flashback, and a 1998 sequence
(3/4/5). Two others are employed between three sequences occurring in
1998 (49/50/51). The dissolves come between sequences in 1976 (2/3), between a 1998 and a 1988 sequence (6/7), and between two 1998 sequences
(58/59). Thus, there is no special pattern at work in the time-related placement of fades and dissolves. However, both types are placed in clusters at
the beginning and at the end of the film, so there is a pattern in their formal
positioning. Eyre's and Alexie's transition devices for the time lapses
between 1976 and 1998 are mainly sound bridges and match on action cuts.
Of the nineteen temporal lapses, they four times connect shot A and B via a
simple cut (7/8, 25/26, 41/42, 47/48). Otherwise, they employ two fades
(3/4, 4/5), one dissolve (6/7), five sound bridges (26/27, 29/30, 40/41,
42/43, 46/47), two match cuts (25/26, 27/28), and five match on action
cuts (10/11, 12/13, 28/29, 33/34, 43/44). In the sequence of Victor's
nightly 'marathon' (53), a series of flashbacks is woven into the scene via
dissolves.

The two match cuts, six match on action cuts,[104] and nine apparent sound
bridges[105] are Eyre's and Alexie's distinctive techniques and form two

---

[102] Cf the sequence protocol in the Appendix.

[103] See Bordwell & Thompson, *Film Art*, 299.

[104] The seventh match on action cut 53/54 does not occur during a temporal lapse.

[105] To my mind, there are two different sorts of sound bridges. One type goes pretty well
unnoticed by the viewer. The sound of shot A may stay briefly with the visuals of shot B,

technical motifs that run through the film. The sound bridges of *Smoke Signals* are placed as follows: 7/8, 16/17, 26/27, 29/30, 40/41, 42/43, 44/45, 46/47, and 56/57. Besides functioning as transition devices, six of them carry pivotal plot material. The first sound bridge is the Custer mockery song (7/8) and is one of the subliminal references to historical and current colonization of Indigenous peoples contained in the film. The second sound bridge comprises the rules for Thomas's behavior that Victor sets up (16/17). It lends the scene a comical character and realizes a nice transition from the scene in Grandma Builds-The-Fire's house to Victor and Thomas on the road. The symbolic content of this sound bridge (Thomas's and Victor's opposition) takes up the opposition between the two young men that was achieved through intercutting between the Josephs' and the Builds-The-Fires' kitchens and is then confirmed by having the men walk on either side of the road. The third sound bridge, in which Thomas tells one of his stories about Arnold (26/27), and the fourth, which contains Victor's smashing of beer bottles (29/30), frame two match on action cuts, which again enclose the sequence in which Victor remembers his parents' drinking party, after which Arnold left the family. These two sound bridges and match on action cuts belong to the sub-narrative dealing with the father–son conflict and thus promote narrative development by carrying important story material.

Two other sound bridges contain Arnold's voice (42/43, 46/47) and are part of the same sub-narrative as well. In the first, Arnold – in Suzy's words – tells the story of the basketball match between Victor and Arnold and two priests. To Arnold, the match was the source of both his pride and his disappointment in Victor. The game was the point at which the woven threads of Victor and Arnold unravelled and split up. Arnold has lied, telling Suzy that Victor made the last shot which won them the game, whereas in reality Victor missed the shot. Arnold, apparently having told this story several times to Suzy or himself, kept trying to recapture that moment to undo the split between him and his son by believing his own version of the ending of the match. Arnold did not realize that he was looking at the wrong thing in

---

while the belonging sound is not yet dubbed in, or: the sound of shot B is dubbed in to the last visuals of shot A. Such sound bridges are usually employed to achieve smooth transitions between the sequences or to create certain expectations of the next scene (Bordwell & Thompson, *Film Art*, 338). There are also sound bridges created to be noticed by the viewer. Technically, they are no different from the first kind. However, here the sound contains key elements of the plot – in dialogue or noise – so that this form of non-simultaneous sound stresses these elements, and the sound bridge becomes apparent.

attempting to reconnect with Victor. By going back to that game again and again, he was reaching a dead end, constantly deceiving himself. One of the reasons why Arnold never went home while he was alive was that he was unable to get past that basketball game. On the metaphoric level, in this scene Eyre and Alexie translate the infiltration of Indigenous religions by Christianity into basketball semantics and iconography. Arnold says: "It was the Indians versus the Christians that day. And for at least one day the Indians won." This statement fortifies the thesis about Arnold's illusory thinking, because Indigenous people have not won against imposed Christianity, either. The unequal match (two adults versus a man and a boy) symbolizes the power relation between the colonizing forces and the colonized. The unequal match can also serve to show the unfair (in basketball semantics) and insidious (in literal terms) actions of the intruder – the infiltration of religion as well as gradual replacement of sacred items, religious symbols, and icons. The next sound bridge with Arnold's voice (46/47) holds the moment at which Arnold for the first time in his life reveals who set the Builds-The-Fires' house on fire that fatal night. To him, this revelation was the first step toward going home – which, however, he could never realize in his lifetime. Not only is it an essential element in the father–son sub-narrative but it also explains one of the film's initial secrets. Usually, filmmakers create such secrets or mysteries to generate suspense in movies. However, this is the only incident in which Eyre and Alexie rearrange the chronological order of narrative events for this purpose.

Looking at the placement of these sound bridges, one notices that six of them are grouped in little clusters. The first cluster (26/27, 29/30) frames Thomas's tale about the day when Arnold took him out for lunch, which triggers Victor's recollections of his father's leaving. The second (42/43, 44/45, 46/47) encloses Arnold's reminiscence of the basketball match against the priests and his revelation of his responsibility for Thomas's parents' death. Eyre and Alexie stress these story elements not only with the sound bridges but also by grouping them around two of the most pivotal narrative sections. Because the sound bridges narrate over temporal and spatial changes, they appear to the viewer as authorial insertions and support the authorial-narrative mode of the movie even though they do not feature Thomas's voice all the time. Instead, the authorial-narrative mode is interspersed with other persons' voices in these sound bridges (Victor, Junior Polatkin, Boo, Arnold, and the police officer).

The other conspicuous stylistic means are the match on action cuts. Alexie calls them "magic cuts" and says that they are employed "to make the flashbacks integral to the narrative of the film."[106] They also support the "sense of time in the movie, when the past, present, and future are all the same, that circular sense of time, which plays itself out in the seamless transitions from past to present."[107] Eyre and Alexie use two different types of matching cuts. The first type (match cut) occurs when graphic features of one shot (e.g., shapes, colors, compositions, movements) are repeated in the next to achieve smooth continuity or abrupt contrast.[108] Such match cuts include 25/26, in which the film cuts from a red blanket covering the sleeping Victor to a red shirt or blanket around a woman's shoulders at the Josephs' party, and 27/28, when both young and adult Victor wear checkered shirts. The other type is derived from matches on action which show the continuation of movement through two or more shots.[109] Eyre and Alexie extend this usage and show with these matches on action also movement across two or more different temporal levels and between filmic reality and characters' subjective thought. For example, in 43/44 a basketball links three different spatial and temporal levels, and in 53/54 Victor imagines himself being helped up by his father, but his taking the helping hand of a construction worker. Most of these "magic cuts" (in essence, matches on action) connect Victor's present with his past, by the adult Victor (in 1998) completing a movement by the young Victor (in 1988) and vice versa. The detailed analysis of the three match cuts 10/11, 12/13, and 33/34 in the Appendix gives some idea of how these are realized.

The filmmakers create the match cuts with simple means. For example, in match on action cut 12/13 they cut from the young Victor opening the door to the adult Victor closing the door. However, they use different camera positions (outside and inside the door) and camera distance, so that the cut does not appear unreal, but simply indicates the time-lapse. Camera movement and camera angle are the same between shots 3 and 4 in this match on action cut. In 10/11 and 33/34, the match is realized through a pan and a tilt and only a pan respectively, so that the term 'match on action cut'

[106] Alexie, quoted in Amanda J. Cobb, "This Is What It Means to Say *Smoke Signals*," 225.

[107] Dennis West & Joan M. West, "Sending Cinematic Smoke Signals," 31.

[108] On these match cuts, see Bordwell & Thompson, *Film Art*, 274–76. Bordwell & Thompson, *Film Art*, 289–90 and 273–74.

[109] See Bordwell & Thompson, *Film Art*, 289–90.

does not apply literally, for there is no cut at the point of the time-lapse.[110] Shot 4 in match on action cut 10/11 and shot 3 in match on action cut 33/34 are these transition shots which merge two different temporal levels. Both transition shots contain the images of the adult Thomas and the young Victor, as well as the young and the adult Victor, respectively. As a result, the characters on the different temporal levels appear in one shot, almost together on the screen, in order to make this transition more magical.[111] As Niro did, Eyre and Alexie engage the concept of magical transformation, but in a different way. Niro has Honey Moccasin do a 'magical' spin, and each time she comes to a halt she has changed into another being – realized through dissolves. She also has Zach become a jingle-dress dancer through a 'magical' spin, this time realized through a cut and black screen. Eyre and Alexie, as shown above, accomplish the transition via pans and tilts featuring the same character(s) on two different temporal levels in the same shot and almost together in one frame. Whereas Niro's transformations are clearly designed to insert 'magical occurrences' into a 'real' world, the transitions in *Smoke Signals* indicate a time-lapse involving the same characters.

In all three examples above, the sound supports the match on action cut, linking two temporal levels. In match cut 12/13, the sound of shot 3 is taken up in shot 4 (the squeaking of the door), while theme music begins to introduce the next sequence. In 10/11 and 33/34, camera position, distance, and perspective do not stay the same during the transition from one temporal level to the next, because of the pan and tilt; but the sound does. In match on action cut 10/11, the sound of the shot preceding the 'transition' shot (the door bell) continues into the latter, just as in 33/34 the dramatic music of the 'transition' shot starts in the shot before. In contrast to the sound carrying over the match on action cuts, verifiable conclusions regarding the lengths of the different shots cannot be drawn. Whereas in 10/11 the 'transition' shot measures about only one tenth of the following shot, in 33/34 the 'transition' shot has temporal priority and lasts about four times longer than the preceding and following shots. In 12/13, the two cuts that make up the match on action cut are of about the same length. Thus, there is no structural temporal pattern in these three match on action cuts.

---

[110] Nevertheless, the term 'match on action cut' will be employed, as terms such as 'match on action pan' and 'match on action tilt' would be really confusing.

[111] See Sherman Alexie, *Smoke Signals Screenplay* (Miramax Books; New York: Hyperion, 1998): 157.

Like the sound bridges, the match on action cuts are enlisted to carry important plot material and to realize visually pivotal transitions between Victor's childhood and the present. In the first match on action cut (10/11), Victor cashes a check at the trading post; and his encounter with Thomas takes his memories back to the Fourth of July 1988, on which he is picked up by Arnold, who takes him home in the truck. Arnold undeservedly slaps him in the face for spilling a beer and Victor runs crying into the house. His entering the house is realized through a second match on action cut (12/13). These two frame Victor's painful childhood recollections, which illuminate the father–son conflict and Victor's initial rejection of his father. The next three match on action cuts elucidate another one of Victor's painful child-hood memories: that of the day on which his father abandoned him and the party the previous night. The match cut featuring red blankets (25/26) leads from the sleeping Victor in the bus to his memories about the party at his parents' house. Upset by Thomas's idealized story about how Arnold had taken Thomas out for lunch – one of the things that fathers do and that Victor apparently missed – Victor walks into the bathroom of the diner and looks into the mirror. In a match on action shot, the film cuts to young Vic-tor looking in the mirror of his parents' bedroom to see his parents lying passed out on the bed after the party (27/28). Then, again in a match on action shot (28/29), the film cuts back to Victor looking in the bathroom mirror of the diner, bridging ten years. The sound bridge of the bottles being smashed carries over to the next shot, in which Arlene is shown waking up after the party and looking out the window to see her son throw-ing full beer bottles against his father's truck, unable to release his anger otherwise. To him, the alcohol and partying is killing his family, and so, in a feeble attempt, he tries to destroy the obvious source of his family's dis-integration. His parents have a fight, and Arnold prepares to leave the family with a choleric but determined disposition.

Another powerful scene follows, expressing Victor's immediate under-standing of the situation as well as his deep despair. He runs madly after his father's truck, Arnold stops to hug him briefly, then pushes him away. Arlene grabs the frantic boy to comfort him and the two gaze after the vanishing truck. In a similarly compelling scene that follows, Victor beats Thomas up violently. The violence in the Joseph family has transferred to the relation between the boys. This sequence is also a point at which the two sub-narratives of Arnold–Victor and Victor–Thomas merge. Extending

screen duration over plot duration,[112] Eyre and Alexie cut between Arlene
comforting young Thomas and Victor running down the road. Then the
camera shows young Victor running from another angle until it tilts up to
reveal the adult Victor sitting in the bus to Phoenix, watching his own self
desperately running along the roadside beside the bus (33/34). For a brief
moment, the young and the adult Victor appear in the same frame, which
would be a major flaw if there were not a reason for it. Eyre and Alexie
have blended the two different selves of one character in one frame to emphasize the fact that the reasons for Victor's spiritual and emotional problems lie in his childhood, especially in his father's leaving. They thus
demonstrate the causes of the father–son sub-narrative, which subliminally
drives the action of the film. The sequences discussed are powerful visual-
izations of the psychological effects of child, alcohol, and drug abuse in
dysfunctional families. These abuses are some of the major consequences
of the imposition on Indigenous nations of the reservation and welfare system by the US and Canadian governments.[113]

Match on action cut 43/44 is part of the father–son narrative as well. In
the flashback of sequence 43, Arnold is filmed on the desert basketball
court telling the story about the match against the priests, illustrated by
another inserted flashback showing the game. After Victor makes the last
shot in the second flashback, Arnold in the first one throws away the ball,
which rolls to Victor's feet in the framing sequence in which Suzy tells
Victor what she knows about Arnold. The ball very nicely links the three
different spatial and temporal frames of the main narrative in 1998 and
Arnold's and Suzy's embedded recollections. The last match on action cut
(53/54) closes Victor's nightly 'marathon' (sequence 53), in which images
of the burning house and of Arnold running for it, of Suzy talking, of
Arnold at the desert basketball court, of Victor running after his father's
truck, and of himself at the Spokane Falls bridge move before his mind's
eye. These images indicate his mixed-up thoughts and emotions as well as
his anger at Arnold and himself, which he digests during the run. Thus, the
film suggests that the run is an act of self-discovery. Victor wistfully imagines himself in the place of Thomas at the Falls, and in his vision reaches

---

[112] See Bordwell & Thompson, *Film Art*, 117.

[113] On the effects of alcohol and drug abuse in Indigenous communities and their contextualization in Indigenous poetry, see Stefanie von Berg, *"Uncomfortable Mirror": (De-)Kolo-
nisation in Gedichten zeitgenössischer indigener nordamerikanisher Autorinnen* (Aachen:
Shaker, 2001): 122–33.

out for Arnold's hand from below, but instead a road construction worker takes it and helps him up. This match on action cut metaphorically describes how Arnold has failed to give Victor paternal love and care. Instead, he picked up Thomas at the Falls and took him out for lunch, the story with which Thomas is constantly nagging Victor. The paternal hand that Victor missed so much is compensated for by the hand of a person unknown to him, indicating that Victor is on his way to coming to terms with his past through his own efforts.

The inserted shots in the 'marathon' sequence appear to be Victor's mental subjectivity, for they are rendered with the classical tools of slow motion, dissolves, and superimpositions,[114] and the echoing sound of traditional singing. However, some of these cannot be subjective shots of Victor's recollection, because he never saw the fire or Arnold at the desert basketball court, he did not see Suzy with another set of clothes, and he was not at the bridge with his father, either. None of these shots is born of Victor's mind, so they belong to the authorial narration of the film. Since a clear narrative would have rendered only Victor's mental subjectivity, this is yet another point at which narrative and metanarrative are intertwined. In the same way, in sequence 48 some previous shots are repeated, apparently for their expressive potential and importance to the story. These shots are the one in which the baby is thrown out of the window of the burning house in slow motion and the one of Arnold handing baby Thomas to Grandma Builds-The-Fire, their black silhouettes illuminated by the flames. Lastly, the visual match between Thomas and his grandma complements the technique of the matching cuts and adds a comical effect. Upon Thomas' return, both smile broadly at each other and the intercut faces reveal a matching physiognomy.

The use of flashbacks is a common filmmaking device; here it is employed to support the continual weaving of narrative time between 1976 and 1998. Disregard for temporal divisions is a characteristic feature of the oral tradition which Alexie tries to translate into film. He develops this stylistic use of flashbacks and several temporal levels to be able to take up the interplay of various time layers from his writing:

> In my books, I've always been fascinated with dreams and stories and flashing forward and flashing back and playing with conventions of time, so in adapting the screenplay, I always knew I would use those elements. [...] I

---

[114] See Bordwell & Thompson, *Film Art*, 107.

always knew that while the person was talking, we were going to see images from the story he or she was telling.[115]

Since all flashbacks illustrate something other characters (Arnold, Victor, Suzy) recount, these characters become the narrators of little stories, which in turn are part of Thomas's authorial narration. In this sense, the stories and flashbacks are interfaces between past and present and between the main narrative and its sub-narratives.

Eyre and Alexie realize most dialogue and indoor sequences in medium shots and with conventional shot/reverse-shot cutting.[116] At crucial moments, they have the camera move closer to its subject from a medium shot to a close-up.[117] The outdoor scenes (except those containing dialogues) are usually done in long shots, and the images of landscapes are mostly in extreme long shots combined with aerial shots. In sequences 4 (Arnold leaves in his pickup), 24 (Victor and Thomas travel to Phoenix in the Greyhound bus), 50 (Victor and Thomas go home in the pickup), 60 (Arnold's trailer burns), and 62 (Victor drives to his mother's house in the pickup), the aerial shots cater to the road-movie genre. They emphasize the vehicles of movement and mark stages in the development of the narrative.

There is no extraordinary use of pans, tilts, and zooms. Eyre and Alexie employ these camera movements whenever the narrative requires it, such as in landscape shots and shots in which the camera has to follow the characters' movements. Pans and tilts effectuate the technique of match on action cuts. In one instance, a zoom-in, in concert with a close-up (29), carries the visual implication of Victor remembering a childhood incident.

---

[115] Dennis West & Joan M. West, "Sending Cinematic Smoke Signals," 30.

[116] In sequences 6, 7, 8, 10, 12, 13, 15, 23, 27, 36, 40, 42, 44, 46, 48, 51, 56, 57, 58, and 61 they largely employ this pattern, sustaining the established axis of action and spatial continuity.

[117] Such moments are Victor's and Thomas's verbal fight as schoolboys (87), Arnold slapping Victor (12), the young men's encounter with the two rednecks (36), the climax sequence in the pickup (51), Victor catching the basketball in the police station and resolutely claiming the urn as being his father (57), and finally Victor and Thomas saying good-bye in the pickup (61). Eyre and Alexie, further, apply close-ups on faces at pivotal points, such as when Arlene receives the message of Arnold's death and she and Victor share a long understanding look (9), when Thomas tells a story (20), when Victor looks into the bathroom mirror (29 zoom-in), and when Arlene painfully watches her son smashing the beer bottles (30). Finally, when Victor lectures Thomas about how to behave as a 'real Indian' (34), The filmmakers switch between close-ups and medium shots of the two. Some essential visual elements, such as the basketball in Victor's hands (57), a piece of frybread (15), Arnold's wallet with the family photograph, and the knife with which Victor cuts his hair, are also shot in close-up.

The camera, and the viewers respectively, move closer to Victor's face as if to penetrate his thoughts. At the same time, the encroaching camera symbolizes the intruding childhood memories which Victor cannot escape, triggered by Thomas's heroic legends of Arnold. Similarly, but through a cut, the camera moves closer to Victor's face as he and Thomas quarrel in the climax sequence (51). Here, the movement toward his face supports the epitasis and the climactic dialogue.

Eyre and Alexie use deep-space photography to have several actions taking place on different planes in one shot. With this technique, they accentuate tensions between characters and other dynamizing situations. For example, the dialogue between Victor and Thomas in the trading post (10) is photographed in deep-space in concert with shot/reverse-shot cutting, Thomas moving about in the front and Victor and the cashier in the back plane. After Arnold has left (32), the directors arrange the mise-en-scène so that desolate-looking Arlene sits in an easy chair in the back of the room and Victor walks around in the front and then switches the front-porch light on and off in the rhythm of SOS in the Morse code. The filmmakers thereby compare mother and son visually and shows how both deal with their pain. Also in the sequence shot in the hospital (56), the complete mise-en-scène is photographed in deep focus: Julie in bed in the front, then Holly by the bed, the hospital room, Victor and Thomas at the door, and the hallway behind them. At the impound yard (57), Eyre and Alexie photograph Victor and Thomas getting out of the police car from inside Arnold's pickup, the windscreen wipers in the foreground, Thomas and Victor in the middle, and the police car in the background. At other points, the filmmakers conspicuously position different objects in the background and foreground. For example, in the first basketball sequence (6), they place Thomas's walking feet, and, later, a cassette recorder on a small table, in the foreground, shot from a low angle and framing the other young men playing in the back plane. By photographing Thomas's feet and the recorder out of proportion to the players (they are much smaller), the directors polarize Thomas and the other young men and visualize Thomas's position as an outsider. This is also underscored by Thomas's ridiculous appearance in a three-piece suit and his pointless action of bringing a small cassette player to the basketball court, where the drumming of the ball drowns out any sound from the appliance. Similarly, in sequence 7, the school building towers behind young Victor and Thomas, who are standing in the foreground, a burning garbage bin between them. The school building is very reminiscent of former boarding school buildings and thus can be understood as the bearer of a critical reference to the unwanted but inescapable christianizing and civilizing efforts of the colonizing Europeans in the form of the boarding school system and its devastating effects.

Upon first view, Eyre and Alexie design the climax sequence (51) in the way classical filmmaking demonstrates. In the course of the argument between Victor and Thomas, shot/reverse-shot cutting is used, the camera moves closer to Victor's face, dramatic and catalyzing music is employed, and it seems that accelerated cutting is applied. However, as the analysis table below shows, there is no continuous diminishing of the temporal length of shots and subsequently no constant accelerated cutting. the filmmakers clearly do not compose the climax sequence with all the dramatic devices of conventional filmmaking.

Analysis table for sequence 51

IMAGE	SHOT LENGTH	IMAGE	SHOT LENGTH
1. Thomas	5.41sec.	16. Victor	2.37sec.
2. Victor	6.56sec.	17. Thomas	1.78sec.
3. Thomas	3.31sec.	18. Victor	1.22sec.
4. Victor	10.44sec. (camera moves closer)	19. Thomas	2.94sec.
5. Thomas	3.25sec.	20. Victor	2.09sec.
6. Victor	3.97sec.	21. Thomas	3.87sec.
7. Thomas	3.60sec.	22. Victor	2.10sec.
8. Victor	3.06sec.	23. Thomas	3.09sec.
9. Thomas	5.50sec.	24. Victor	2.37sec.
10. Victor	4.15sec.	25. Thomas	5.43sec.
11. Thomas	5.41sec.	26. Victor	2.69sec.
12. Victor	2.65sec.	27. Thomas	5.31sec.
13. Thomas	4.97sec.	28. Victor	3.75sec.
14. Victor	2.91sec.	29. Road	1.60sec.
15. Thomas	3.28sec.	30. Victor	0.84sec.

Final Remarks

Since *Smoke Signals* is the first major feature film by Indigenous filmmakers in Hollywood, Eyre and Alexie bore a lot of responsibility to make it a success in order to break the barrier surrounding large-scale Indigenous film production. A flop would have confirmed critical opinion, such that major Indigenous filmmaking is rendered impossible by a lack of professionalism. Alexie says: "There needs to be that one film that proves that Indians can make a movie and it can be successful."[118] Also, being the first ones to reach international audiences with their film and get a foot in the door of Hollywood, their approach might serve as a model for followers. Eyre and Alexie deliberately commissioned Indigenous participants in the production team where it was possible and necessary. Writer and script-writer, director, co-producers, actors, most of the composers and musicians, and a considerable number of the film crew were Indigenous. The film was shot on Indigenous locations as far as the script allowed. However, the makers shied away from an 'exclusively Indigenous' policy and also en-gaged non-Indigenous producers, supporters, and crew. The film was bought by an acclaimed Hollywood company (Miramax) and was made possible through the Sundance Institute, both enabling the film to gain publicity and reach a large audience. Furthermore, the writer of the thematic poem about fathers, Dick Lourie, is not an Indigenous writer. The choice of his poem goes hand in hand with the filmmakers' approach of an Indigenous but non-exclusive production.

Summing up the filmmaking style of *Smoke Signals*, it has been seen that Eyre and Alexie avail themselves of classical film conventions. The filmmaking adheres to classical continuity, to the 180° system, and em-ploys standard shot/reverse-shot cutting, and customary camera work. Spatial and temporal continuity as well as conventionally placed sound support the classical creation of a filmic reality. The makers have applied a classical clear-cut narrative to the road-movie genre. The number of main characters remains within the limits of feature-film conventions and the characters have clearly defined aims, which they also achieve: Victor has the goal of going to Phoenix to claim the ashes of his late father, Thomas the goal of befriending Victor in order to be accepted by the other young men in the community. There are also several interpersonal conflicts which catalyze the plot and which are largely settled at the end. Three of the four narrative lines are resolved, so that the film achieves a sense of closure: Victor is reconciled with his father and Arnold's remains are brought home. Victor and Thomas have come to understand each other and their shared past so that they have created a basis for a possible friendship. The reserva-tion sub-narrative, of course, cannot be 'resolved', but has fragmentally

---

[118] Alexie, quoted in Jennifer Parham, "This is What it Means to Make Our Own Movies," *Aboriginal Voices* 4.5 (July–September 1997): 31.

described reservation life. Furthermore, the events in the film are connected by the cause-and-effect plot principle. Some of the usual transition devices (dissolves and fades) complement the simple cut. The stylistic devices such as matching cuts, apparent sound bridges, and flashbacks artfully weave between the sequences on the three temporal levels. Also the deep-space photography and the cinematic motifs support the narrative. These salient stylistic devices complement the conventional filmmaking style and characterize Eyre and Alexie's filmmaking. They are also found in mainstream narrative cinema, but gain a different dynamic, since they are part of an Indigenous film that responds to this established narrative cinema.

However, in some respects the filmmaking diverges from conventional rules. The lack of deadlines for characters to achieve their goals fails to create suspense, as does the editing. The makers allow their characters all the time they need to unfold the plot, which is running smoothly on Indian time. As in *Honey Moccasin*, one character (Velma in sequence 28) several times briefly looks into the camera, which is a blunt violation of conventional filmmaking rules and makes the viewer aware of the camera gaze. There is no love romance between a male and female protagonist, which in Hollywood cinema often serves as material for a second narrative. The filmmakers strenuously avoid having Victor and Suzy enter into a romance as Hollywood-trained viewers might expect. Rather, they apply a mystical erotic relationship to Arnold and Suzy which is not further developed. Victor does not fulfill what one usually expects of a tough Hollywood hero: he neither drinks nor smokes, he does not seduce women, he does not play cool in order to impress but because he cannot deal with the double loss of his father. The filmmakers avoid idealizing Indigenous cultures and moralizing about the effects of colonialism. Instead, they compose an anticolonial film discourse that either imitates, parodies, or subverts colonial media discourses and presents autonomous images. Film technology, a Western medium of cultural expression, with its most dominant form, the conventional Hollywood film style, is enlisted and complemented with individual stylistic means. The universal story (the search for a lost father) translated into a mainstream film genre (the road movie) is filled with Indigenous characters and a large dose of self-irony and satirical allusions to Euro-American colonization.

From the scenery to the soundtrack, *Smoke Signals* depicts contemporary and complex American Indian characters in a contemporary and complex

Indian world that exists both within and outside of the larger American culture.[119]

In this film, Hollywood filmmaking conventions and genre are turned into a vehicle for anticolonial self-expression. As a result, *Smoke Signals* in its mainstream form is a convincing feature of Indigenous media.

Big Bear

Big Bear, a three-hour mini-series[120] produced in 1998, is Canada's first major motion picture by an Indigenous director, Gil Cardinal, and Indigenous producer, Doug Cuthand. It is also the first major production to be largely shot on Indigenous land, the Pasqua First Nations reserve sixty kilometers northeast of Regina, Saskatchewan. The film is a collaborative project between a mainstream film company, Télé-Action Inc., and two Indigenous film companies, Kanata Productions Inc. (owned by Gil Cardinal and Dorothy Schreiber) and Blue Hill Productions (owned by Doug Cuthand), in association with the CBC. CBC aired the 8.5 million Canadian dollar budget film on prime time on 3 and 4 January 1999. The year before, it was screened at the San Francisco American Indian Film Festival, winning both the story award and the producer's award.[121] The mini-series is based on the 1973 novel *The Temptations of Big Bear* by Rudy Wiebe, which centers on the life and struggle of one of the most charismatic figures of the history in the Canadian Prairies. It traces the era of treaty-making on the prairies and chronicles Cree chief Big Bear's lengthy resistance to signing a treaty. He knew that the Cree would relinquish their rights to live and move freely on the prairies, that they would plunge into poverty and dependence, and that the treaty would destroy their traditional way of life. He and his band were finally starved into signing Treaty No. Six in winter 1882. Poundmaker, Sweetgrass, and other Cree chiefs had signed this treaty six years earlier.

In the mini-series, Cardinal, Cuthand, and Wiebe do three things. First, through the story of Big Bear's band they reflect Canadian prairie history during the late-nineteenth century from an Indigenous perspective. They

---

[119] Amanda J. Cobb, "This Is What It Means to Say *Smoke Signals*," 225.

[120] The production is marketed as a four-hour mini-series, but these four hours include commercial breaks; without them the film runs for about three hours.

[121] See Blue Hill Productions at http://www.Dougcuthand.com/project.html

also draw attention to Big Bear, one of the most important Cree leaders in Canadian history, and take him out of the shadow of his American counterparts such as Sitting Bull, Chief Joseph, and Geronimo. And, more importantly, they correct Canadian history writing, which has depicted Big Bear as either a foolish old man who could not control his warriors or as a troublemaker and bloodthirsty war leader.[122] They exemplarily present Big Bear's eloquent negotiations with the government for a better treaty and his struggles to keep all contact with government officials, police (the North West Mounted Police, N WM P), and settlers peaceful. As well as this, they show his efforts to unite all Cree into a powerful league and to establish one large Cree reserve instead of the scattered band reserves.

The film received nationwide attention even during production, with major and local papers reporting on its making. Generally, the production received good critiques. Some commented on the film's turning the tables on the conventional Hollywood treatment of Indigenous people, on the historical accuracy of costume design and sets, and on the filmmakers' attempt to revise Saskatchewan history from a Cree perspective. Others commented on the sometimes harsh weather conditions and the determination of the actors and crew to stay on schedule and on the fact that the film is an Indigenous production from top to bottom, and that being at the center of a movie production was a new and pleasant experience for the Indigenous actors.[123]

The Cree Approach
The filming of Big Bear's life itself has different underlying stories. The first is the long duration and hard work between Wiebe's published novel and the film release. Wiebe made several attempts with several film companies to turn the novel into a film on the basis of his various screenplay drafts. When Cardinal and Schreiber saw Wiebe's drafts they got involved in the screen adaptation. Endless meetings and collaborative rewritings of

---

[122] See Doug Cuthand (unpublished interview, 1998).

[123] In order of appearance: Richard Helm, "History Revisited: 'Big Bear' Turns a Few Tables on the T V Audience to Trace the Saga of a Native Hero," *Regina Leader Post T V* (2–8 January 1999): 46; Pat Shaver, "Made for T V Movie Spotlights Crees' Struggle," *Aboriginal Voices* (July–August, 1998): 53; Carmen Pauls, "Walking in His Moccasins: Filmmakers Re-Tell Big Bear's Story," *Prairie Dog* (July 1998): 14; Pamela Green, "Big Bear: Rain or Shine, the Show Must Go On," *SA G E* (July 1998), at http://www.ammsa.com/sage /JULY98.html#anchor222342; and Chris Dafoe, "The Resurrection of Big Bear," *Globe & Mail* (18 July 1998): C1.

the drafts followed, until in 1995/96 they were able to involve Télé-Action and the CBC in the project.[124] The collaboration with mainstream film and broadcast companies and the collaborative process of writing the script demonstrates that the filmmakers did not apply an 'exclusively Indigenous' approach. They were not concerned with the issue of whether Cree or non-Cree people had more or less influence but, rather, with the quality of that input.

Another story is the casting of the Cree actor Gordon Tootoosis as Big Bear. Although his appearance by no means qualified him to play the role of Big Bear (Tootoosis is a tall, broad-shouldered and charismatic man and Big Bear was rather short, thin and not very handsome), his personal connection with the story of Big Bear did. He grew up on the Poundmaker reserve with the tales about Big Bear, speaks Cree, and is actually able to sing the various Cree songs that his role requires; his great-grandfather was Poundmaker's brother and advisor, and his father was one of the founders of the Assembly of First Nations and also one of the people who supported Wiebe's research for the novel.[125] Cuthand, the producer, had a similar relation to the story of Big Bear, as he has made clear in an interview (1998). He grew up on the Little Pine reserve where Big Bear died, also influenced by the tales of this cultural hero. His great-grandfather and Big Bear were very close friends and they served in jail together for their involvement in the resistance to the Canadian government.

The approach to the film production is a related story. It was clear to Cardinal and Cuthand that they would shoot as much as possible on Indigenous land in the area where Big Bear lived, so that the filming would be a sort of homecoming for the hero and a step toward raising self-awareness among Indigenous people living on such reserves. The second thought behind that choice was more pragmatic. Communities such as the Pasqua reserve in Saskatchewan are usually affected by high unemployment rates and ensuing poverty. The filmmakers were trying to curb this situation, at least for a short time, by bringing money and jobs into the community. Land was rented from the Pasqua reserve and close to one hundred people from the reserve were employed as security guards, set decorators, painters, carpenters, community coordinator, and wardrobe assistant (interview with Cuthand, 1998). More than two thirds of the cast and almost all the extras

---

[124] See Gil Cardinal and Doug Cuthand (unpublished interviews, 1998); Chris Dafoe, "The Resurrection of Big Bear," C3.
[125] Chris Dafoe, "The Resurrection of Big Bear," C3.

came from reserves near Fort Qu'Appelle or from other areas in Saskatche-
wan.[126] The film stars two well-known Indigenous actors, Gordon Tootoo-
sis (Big Bear), and Tantoo Cardinal (Running Second). Others are Lorne
Cardinal (Little Bad Man), Kennetch Charlette (Lone Man), Patrick James
Bird (Kingbird), Michael Greyeyes (Wandering Spirit), Ben Cardinal
(Miserable Man), Michael Obey (Iron Body), Lorne Duquette (Round The
Sky), Simon Baker (Horsechild), Henry Beaudry (Sweetgrass), Tyronne
Tootoosis (Poundmaker), Harry Daniels (Gabriel Dumont), Gail Maurice
(Nowakich), Willene Tootoosis (Man's Woman), and Bernelda Wheeler
(Sayos).[127] For these Indigenous actors, the production also provided a
career boost and paved the way for more nationwide casting. A story
circulates that it was not easy to contract extras because candidates had to
have long hair, had to be slim, and could not have tattoos. Not only with the
choice of the location but also with the cast, the filmmakers stayed close to
this Cree historical narrative. Production money was benefiting Cree
people; within their means, the filmmakers financially supported the descendants of Big Bear's people (in a larger sense) and closed the circle.

The depiction of the spiritual aspect of Cree life was difficult to master.
Big Bear was a very spiritual man, and it was not an easy task to translate
this aspect into film without violating cultural taboos or capitalizing on
Cree spirituality. Tootoosis enacts songs and carefully mimes ceremonial
acts, as at the beginning when he ceremoniously opens his medicine bundle
and chants. Big Bear's visions are indicated through dissolves as transitions
from the 'real' world. The visions themselves are partly shot as realistic
scenes, sometimes technically modified by computer animation, sepia tone,
slow motion, blurring and multiple exposure, or distortion. The presentation of the Thirst Dance posed the most paramount problem. Cardinal and
Cuthand did not want to lose that pivotal scene (this Thirst Dance at the
Poundmaker reserve in 1884 attracted more than two thousand Cree), but
the filmmakers bowed to the Cree elders, who said that the dance could not
be shown. "I think by not showing it [the dance] we lose some of the essence of the man," says Tootoosis, "but to show those spiritual things

---

[126] *Regina Leader Post* (June 1998): A2.
[127] Tantoo Cardinal also played Honey Moccasin in *Honey Moccasin* and Arlene in *Smoke
Signals*. We also know Bernelda Wheeler as Bernelda Birch from *Honey Moccasin* and
Simon Baker as young Thomas from *Smoke Signals*.

would have been sacrilege."[128] It was a tough decision and the filmmakers decided to only allude to the dance. Cardinal explains:

> The solution we came up with was for them to start to prepare the Thirst Dance, and then to have the Governor Dewdney and the police come and stop them. Instead of being stopped, the people do a kind of dance anyway, right there, without being able to build the Thirst Lodge and without all of the components that go with a real Thirst Dance. Even though they couldn't do that they could still "dance" in the same spirit. (interview, 1998)

Thus, the film was shot with the utmost respect for cultural taboos and with attention to concerns about not commercializing Cree spirituality.

As an Indigenous film, *Big Bear* was produced with the same set structure as conventional narrative films. This is not due to the collaboration with a mainstream film company, but to the filmmaker's approach to filmmaking in general. Cuthand has said in interview (1998) that as professional filmmakers they took a professional approach, which includes the division into several separate units for photography, sound, set, and miscellaneous. Since this mini-series is not a studio production, most of the filming was realized on exterior locations. Here, the filmmakers worked with conventional lighting and sound-recording techniques for shooting outside. In post-production, sound was processed in a conventional sound studio (at CBC in Regina). One difference with this Indigenous production, Cuthand has mentioned (interview, 1998), is that a community coordinator (Neil Pasqua) was commissioned to work between the production and the band council of the Pasqua reserve.

Cree Historicity as Circular and Linear Narrative

The purpose of this section is not to analyze the content of the mini-series, since the script follows Wiebe's novel closely and much has already been written on this text.[129] This analysis instead explores how the filmmakers

---

[128] Chris Dafoe, "The Resurrection of Big Bear," C3.

[129] Cf. Brigitte Bossanne, "A Canadian Voice Within the Text: Rudy Wiebe's *The Temptations of Big Bear*," *Études Canadiennes / Canadian Studies: Revue Interdisciplinaire des Études Canadiennes en France* 7.10 (June 1981): 223–34; Allan Dueck, "Rudy Wiebe's Approach to Historical Fiction: A Study of *The Temptations of Big Bear* and *The Scorched-Wood People*," in *The Canadian Novel: Here and Now*, ed. John Moss (Toronto: NC Press, 1978): 182–200; Terry Goldie, "Comparative Views of an Aboriginal Past: Rudy Wiebe & Patrick White," *World Literature Written in English* 23.2 (Spring 1984) 429–39; Robert Lecker, "Trusting the Quintuplet Senses: Time and Form in *The Temptations of Big Bear*," *English Studies in Canada* 8.3 (September 1982): 333–48; Penny van Toorn, "Bakhtin and the Novel as Empire: Textual Poli-

translate into the medium of film the historical figure of Big Bear, some pivotal events of Canadian–Cree history, and Cree life in that era. The sequence protocol in the Appendix relates the content and structure of the film as well as temporal and spatial relations. It also gives an outline of Big Bear's family.

The narrative space of *Big Bear* is defined as the areas in Northern and Southern Saskatchewan where Big Bear lived. The narrative time is clearly specified as the time-span between 1875 and 1888. The authorial narrative chronologically reflects the events occurring in Big Bear's family and band within that time-frame. There are no unexplained time-lapses, no flash-backs, or movements between several temporal levels. Based on Wiebe's thorough research (he spent six years writing the novel), the film presents events as closely as possible to historical facts.[130] One must ask how Wiebe did his research: i.e. which sources he consulted. In the 1970s published Indigenous history writing was scarce, if not non-existent, so Wiebe's sources can only have been mainly mainstream Canadian ones. It is also speculative whether or not consultation with elders or drawing on the Cree oral tradition would have rendered considerably different results. However, the fact remains that the filmmakers as well as the leading actor were content with Wiebe's research and applied his version of the events. One difference between the novel and the film is that Wiebe shows both the Cree and the Canadian perspective, whereas the filmmakers concentrate on the Cree point of view. As seen above, both Cuthand and Tootoosis grew up in families and communities that have close relations with the historical figure of Big Bear; more importantly, they grew up with oral accounts of Big Bear.

---

tics in Robert Drewe's *The Savage Crows* and Rudy Wiebe's *The Temptations of Big Bear,*" *Journal of Commonwealth Literature* 27.1 (1992): 96–109; Penny van Toorn, *Rudy Wiebe and the Historicity of the Word* (Edmonton, Alberta: U of Alberta P, 1995); Carla Visser, "Historicity in Historical Fiction: *Burning Water* and *The Temptations of Big Bear,*" *Studies in Canadian Literature* 12.1 (1987): 90–111; and Susan Whaley, "Narrative Voices in *The Temptations of Big Bear,*" *Essays on Canadian Writing* 20 (Winter 1980–81): 134–48.

[130] See Doug Cuthand (unpublished interview, 1998). For example, on the negotiations and making of Treaty No. Six, see Alexander Morris, *The Treaties of Canada with the Indians of Manitoba and the North-West Territories Including the Negotiations on Which They Were Based* (1880; Saskatoon, Saskatchewan: Fifth House, 1991): 168–244. Wiebe and Rob Beal compiled eye-witness accounts and illustrative material (photographs and sketches) of the 1885 Northwest. On the Frog Lake incident and battle at Frenchmen Butte, see Rudy Wiebe & Rob Beal, *War in the West: Voices of the 1885 Rebellion* (Toronto: McClelland & Stewart, 1985). On the historical figure of Big Bear and his political negotiations and actions during the era of treaty-making and rebellion, see Hugh Dempsey, *Big Bear: The End of Freedom* (Vancouver, British Columbia & Toronto: Douglas & McIntyre, 1984): 277–91.

Therefore, their translation of Big Bear's life into film is also informed by this oral knowledge. In this respect, the filmmakers present the historical figure of Big Bear and Cree–Canadian history from various converging perspectives: a mainstream perspective, Wiebe's perspective, and a Cree perspective drawing on oral cultural and historical knowledge. In regard to the chronological presentation of the events in Big Bear's life in the speci-fied time span, the film is driven by a classical linear cause-and-effect nar-rative. However, considering the fact that the film presents Big Bear's movements and his life, the narrative can be understood as non-linear and circular, as Big Bear moves back and forth across the prairies and his body returns to the earth at the end, his life circle is thus completed. This is realized visually by Big Bear in his death vision laying himself to rest out on the prairies and then turning into a stone through a dissolve, then by the camera zooming out to reveal the prairie landscape (Fig. 8.1–8.2).

In *Big Bear*, Cardinal and Cuthand remain close to historical realism and to the tradition of historical films.[131] At the beginning, the title announces that the film will be giving an account of historical events: "This program is based on historical fact. It depicts events that occurred in Western Canada in the late 1800s that changed forever the way of life of the Cree people." The historical presentation is supported by inserted titles such as "Frog Lake Settlement April 2nd, 1885." The film ends with the camera zooming in on a photograph of Big Bear after the title: "Mistahi Muskwa; Big Bear; 1825–1888." At the end, then, the film drops into documentary mode by presenting an archival photograph, Cree name, and the epitaphic life-span of its historical protagonist. This connects the film character with the historical figure. Just as the events are depicted with historical accuracy, so are the costumes and locations that carry the narrative. The film production could not move around as Big Bear's band did, so the Pasqua reserve in the Qu'Appelle Valley served as the location for all sequences except those in winter, which were shot in Northern Quebec. Replicas of Fort Walsh and Fort Pitt as well as of reserve log shacks were constructed on the Pasqua reserve and old farm machinery brought there as well. The tipis were also re-created from historical models and their arrangement in the camp, as

---

[131] Here I work with Susan Hayward's definition of the 'historical film': the narrative focusses on a real event in the past or the life of a real person. The setting, costumes, and ob-jects must appear authentic, and the film's ideological function is to reflect national history through "great moments" or "great men or women"; Hayward, *Key Concepts in Cinema Stud-ies* (London & New York: Routledge, 1996): 172–73.

were their setting up and taking down. The clothes the Cree characters wear are a mixture of traditional Cree clothing and cottonware acquired through trading. The Cree clothing as well as the settlers' clothes and police and army uniforms are based on historical models. The Hudson's Bay Company (HBC) blanket (white with green, red, and yellow stripes), repeatedly contextualized in the film, had an almost symbolic meaning for Canadian–Indigenous relations in the nineteenth century. The film does not contain pan-Indian war bonnets nor any other item associated with clichéd and exoticized Indians. Instead, some of the Cree wear derby hats and other European headgear, partly embellished with feathers, and pelt hats that were acquired through trading and raiding. The close-to-history presentation, however, is flawed by the fact that all the clothes are too neat; they are never dirty, torn, ripped, or worn out. Except for the Frog Lake incident and the battle at Frenchmen's Butte, which left some traces on the clothes and faces, the characters are always neatly dressed. The wigs of Big Bear, Kingbird, and later Wandering Spirit mar the presentation as well, as they can be easily identified as artificial.

There is one digression from historical fact: the film says that Big Bear died on the Poundmaker reserve, whereas he actually died on the Little Pine reserve that borders on the former. Cuthand comments on this inaccuracy:

> In the story they say Big Bear died on Poundmaker's reserve. Poundmaker's and Little Pine border each other. The people from my reserve say he lived on my reserve and died on my reserve [Little Pine]. You see, chief Poundmaker was in the movie, so there is a connection that we're saying Big Bear died on Poundmaker's reserve. To say he died on Little Pine reserve, the people wouldn't know where it was, but in the context of this movie to say he died on Poundmaker's reserve is not really historically correct. But it completes the story, the cycle of the story. (interview, 1998)

Inverting the Hollywood Language Model

The filmmakers were very concerned about the language choice and struggled with the problems outlined in Chapter 2. The solution is a linguistic sleight of hand based on the fact that mainstream films usually assigned Standard English to the non-Indigenous characters and some substandard English to the Indians. Consequently, the Indigenous characters were defined as the inferior 'Others' through the language they spoke, which was either English interspersed with grammatical errors, English consisting of monosyllables, or English fitted out with a fictitious or exotic accent. Cardinal and Cuthand subvert that tradition by placing the Cree at the center of the narrative and the Canadians on the margin by having the Cree speak Standard English and the Canadians speak a non-existent, incomprehensible language. Many Cree people, including filmmakers, have censured Cardinal and Cuthand for not employing the Cree language and securing a culturally and linguistically appropriate context for the story. It would have been possible to film the characters speaking Cree, since Cuthand, Tootoosis, and some other actors, extras, and crew members recruited from Regina and nearby reserves are able to speak Cree. The filmmakers wanted to tell the story of the leader Big Bear from a Cree point of view, but dismissed the idea of having all Cree speak Cree and provide three hours of subtitles or voice-overs.

> In the way of the dramatic storytelling it would keep people removed, you'd always be listening to a narrator, or you'd have to always be watching the words on the screen. That sets up a distance, that sets up sort of an intellectual conscious dimension when what you want is you want people to become fully engaged in the story. (interview, 1998)

In order to engage the viewer with the Cree perspective without language barriers, they decided to have the Cree speak English. And since at that time the Cree could not understand the Canadians, the latter have to speak an unintelligible language. For this reason, Wiebe created a jabberwocky language with its own structure, out of Mennonite Low German, Dutch, and English words, and neologisms. In practice, this mishmash (pronounced as it is written) looks the way it does, in context, in the following excerpt from the treaty-making sequence (8):

> SWEETGRASS (Cont)
> When I take your hand and touch your heart, I say, let us all be one. May this earth never taste a White man's blood.
> *Morris smiles regally, and still holding Sweetgrass' right hand, looks about the circle slowly. All wait to hear him. Finally, Morris stares across at Big Bear: He seems a mound thrust up by the earth into the level light.*
> MORRIS
> Me humpret glee, grotle klings, du a wilmming depforth. O a scriple laguranteum Big Bear, du autom gratualayome ...
> *His voice carries on as Erasmus begins interpreting simultaneously in a high, carrying voice.*
> ERASMUS
> He says, "My heart is glad for you, great Chiefs, that you have behaved in the right way. And Big Bear has come, so I can tell him that the Treaty we have made is for him too, as if he were here – "

Sweetgrass coughs, Morris stops in mid-word and Erasmus stops as well;
undecided, the translator looks from one to the other. Sweetgrass' face
slowly loosens and goes blank; he drops his hands and shuffles to his place
at the center of the Chiefs; sits, makes himself comfortable and nods to Big
Bear. A waiting silence settles over the assembly. Finally Big Bear raises
his strong, scarred face. He ignores Morris and speaks, quietly intense but
not confrontational, across the half-circle of Chiefs to Sweetgrass.

BIG BEAR

I find it hard to speak. It is no small matter we have to consult about, and
already I see you dressed in these red coats, these shiny things.

He pauses, digs in the earth again with his fingers.

BIG BEAR (Cont)

I have come to speak for my people, far out on the plains hunting for food.

gestures to the Whites

Police Chief Crozier I know, Peter Erasmus I know, but who is this "Gov-
er-nor" standing there? I've never seen him before. Has anyone? Will we
ever see him again?

Through Erasmus, Morris has followed the dialogue; he announces loudly.

MORRIS

O e lagimororide Quanto, du me bregit dug remalation

fingers his blue coat

a simple. A Quanto ...

He continues as Erasmus picks up the translation.

ERASMUS

He says, "My blue coat shows I speak for your Great Grandmother, the
Queen. She tells you, 'I love my Red Children as well as my White.' She
knows it is hard for you to live in some parts of her lands, but she has long
arms, to help you, so you need never go hungry.

Morris stretches his arms out wide as Erasmus translates this, but Big Bear
still doesn't acknowledge him. He looks at Sweetgrass steadily.

BIG BEAR

She may have long arms, but are her *breasts* big enough to feed us all!?

A burst of immense laughter bounces from person to person until the hill-
side is rocketing with sound. Even the inner circle of Chiefs grin. Morris
looks to Erasmus, who does not dare translate. Angrily Morris demands:

MORRIS

Quat? Quat?[132]

---

[132] Rudy Wiebe & Gil Cardinal, *Big Bear* screenplay, script-ed. Jordan Wheeler (1998, unpublished): 25–27; ellipses and emphasis in original.

This passage reveals that the film pays much more attention to what the Cree say, even in negotiating situations such as this one. One would expect both parties and the translator to have the same share of speaking time. That the Canadians speak more than is written in the script and that Erasmus translates all they say is suggested by Morris's ellipses. Nevertheless, the greater share of Cree speaking-time in sequences in which both parties speak is partly due to the practical reason that it is hard to invent and speak this artificial language and that there is no need for dialogue in this language, since it does not transmit information. But it is even more due to the film's focus on the Cree perspective. The language differentiation makes it clear how hard communication (the negotiating and settling of conflict) between Indigenous people and the colonizers in North America was. It also shows a gradation of the Canadians' knowledge of Cree: whereas Crozier, another officer, and Governor Dewdney speak a broken Cree, the Métis translator Erasmus and Kitty, McLean's mixed-blood daughter, speak Cree fluently. Unfortunately, the clear association of Cree language skills is not kept up throughout the film. At times the viewer is confused about which Canadians are able to fluently speak Cree. For example, the Indian agent Quinn, HBC factor Simpson, HBC clerk Cameron, farm instructor Delaney, and Father Farfard at times speak broken Cree, whereas at other times they speak it more fluently.

The inversion of linguistic positions has several effects. It puts the audience in the vantage of the Cree, inducing them to associate and sympathize with the Cree because they are the only people they can understand.[133] Since there are no subtitles for the gibberish the Canadians speak, the viewer is made to feel the paranoia of not comprehending the language of intruders who turn out to be decision-makers through military and self-proclaimed political power. The European colonizers are defined as the 'other', the 'foreigners', and the 'outsiders' by virtue of the 'uncivil' and 'savage' language they speak, by the broken syntax when they use (Cree) English, and by their small share of speaking-time. Thus, the filmmakers

---

[133] Murray Smith distinguishes between two narrative processes: alignment as the way in which a film provides access to the actions, feelings, thoughts of characters; and allegiance as the way in which a film tries to guide the viewer's sympathies for or against characters. He states that in classical narrative cinema the viewer's sympathies are usually elicited for characters with whom the viewer is aligned; Smith, "The Logic and Legacy of Brechtianism," in *Post-Theory: Reconstructing Film Studies*, ed. David Bordwell & Noël Carroll (Madison: U of Wisconsin P, 1996): 141. In *Big Bear*, the filmmakers utilize this mainstream practice of merging alignment with allegiance in order to evoke empathy for the Cree.

reverse the traditional linguistic self/other positions of mainstream historical movies that contain imaginary Indians.

As is apparent from the excerpt, the filmmakers attempt to transmit the
humor that is inherent in the Cree language. It is partly based on analogies
and word-play and contains a substantial share of bodily and sexual
jokes.[134] On par with Big Bear's reference to the Queen's breasts is Miserable Man's question whether the government and the Queen are husband
and wife, accompanied by an explicit body gesture of moving his hips in an
earlier meeting between two reverends and the band (sequence 5). These
jokes display the Cree's unconventional contextualization of body functions and sexuality, even with regard to leaders. Little Bad Man and other
warriors once in a while use the word 'shit', illustrating the fact that Cree,
like any other language, contains swear words. It also makes the Cree more
sympathetic, as they are portrayed as human beings with a weak side. Paramount is the fact that the film presents the Cree as people with ordinary
conversational skills. In contact with Canadians, Big Bear, Little Bad Man,
and Wandering Spirit employ a few analogies and metaphors which the
Canadians do not understand. Apart from these, their dialogue exchanges
do not contain any of the baggage of romantic, poetic phrases and long
speeches that often weigh down the speech of Indigenous people in stereotypical Western media discourse. This latter discourse thrusts Indigenous
eloquence into a niche of cliché that falsifies and commercializes Indigenous wisdom and relation to nature.[135]

The jabberwocky language juxtaposed with Standard English creates an
unexpected value-gap between the colonizers and colonized. By assigning
the superior linguistic position to the Indigenous characters, Cardinal and
Cuthand use the colonial language in order to decolonize the prevalent Hollywood language model. But they fail to present the traditional language
that the people concerned spoke; simply using the Cree language would
have been enough to transmit Cree world-views.

---

[134] I came to know this Cree humor through Cree friends whom I met when I was doing research in Regina, Saskatchewan. See also Piapot (unpublished interview, 1996)

[135] The results were, among others, collections of Indian maxims that flooded Western
markets. See the discussion of such booklets in the section "Cinematic Dialogue With Hollywood," chapter 5 below.

Cinematic Historicity: Cree–Canadian History and Cree Culture
The signing of Treaty No. Six by the Cree chiefs and later by Big Bear
were pivotal events in Cree history; accordingly, special attention is given
to these scenes in the film. Sequence 7 opens with a close-up on several
sheets of white paper with Treaty No. Six written out, superimposed on a
group of Cree chiefs standing by the treaty tent, while Erasmus, in a loud,
clear voice, reads out the treaty (he translates during the whole sequence).
The treaty tent is surrounded by people of the five chiefs' bands, and a line
of warriors with arms raised and mounted on horses stand at a distance.
Then there is a cut to Governor Morris and Sweetgrass at a camp table in a
medium shot, with Sweetgrass in concentrated apprehension. Morris, dressed in a black army uniform, ceremoniously raises a quill, which Sweetgrass touches, and scratches an X beside the name "Sweetgrass" on the list
of Cree chiefs, shown in close-up. After showing Big Bear and three other
warriors riding toward the scene, the camera, in medium shot, cuts to Morris as he helps Sweetgrass into a red NWMP coat, which is too small for
him. When he buttons it, it seems as if Sweetgrass is putting himself into a
straitjacket.[136] Sweetgrass, again shown in a medium shot, receives from
Morris a treaty medal with the Queen's image, which is focussed on in a
close-up. Both 'confirm' the treaty with a handshake, Sweetgrass puts his
hand on Morris's chest and blesses the treaty and peace that is sealed, while
the other chiefs and their people watch in silence (Figs. 8.3–8.7). In a long
shot, Morris and Sweetgrass are shown side by side, the Cree chief now
almost completely trussed up in Canadian paraphernalia; his face seems
pinched and no longer confident.[137] Big Bear's arrival creates some unrest
among the chiefs and the rest of the Crees present. Morris and Crozier are
somewhat irritated and alarmed, but continue the ceremony anyway. The
treaty-signing of the other chiefs is omitted.

    After negotiations between Morris and Big Bear, the latter declines to
sign the treaty under the present conditions, whereupon Morris announces
that there will be no extra treaty for his band. Big Bear delivers a loud
speech, in which he explains why he will not sign. In several extreme long
shots, intercut with a close-up of Big Bear's stern and thoughtful face, the
camera shows a small NWMP brass band striking up "God Save the

---

[136] Rudy Wiebe & Gil Cardinal, *Big Bear* screenplay, script-ed. Jordan Wheeler (1998, unpublished): 22.
[137] Wiebe & Cardinal, *Big Bear* screenplay, 22.

Queen" (Figs. 8.8–8.9). The Canadians and the chiefs, save for Big Bear, rise – it is a somewhat comic and at the same time pitiful scene, reinforced visually by the long camera distance, which highlights the smallness of the Canadian camp in the wide open prairies that are still an Indigenous space. Here, the makers of *Big Bear* visualize a masquerade: the Cree chiefs are dressed in red NWMP coats and take part in the Canadian-anthem ceremony, rising from the ground and taking off their hats. They wear costumes in which they imitate Canadian military leaders. The Cree chiefs' subordination is visualized via ridiculous mimicry: by virtue of the red police coats and the medal, they are physically 'fettered' and symbolically confined to the laws of the Queen. The seriousness with which the Canadians conduct their ritual in the 'wilderness' inhabited by 'savages' is ludicrous. In the context of Great Britain, the rituals and uniforms make sense, but removed from their original environment and placed in a different 'wild and savage' space and another cultural context, their ritual and dress turn into a pathetic and comical performance, as suggested in the film, because it presents the events from the Cree perspective. Nevertheless, only a few years later the same ceremony and uniforms were to become major metonyms of colonial power, adapted to the space of the Canadian West.

Six years later, Big Bear signs Treaty No. Six because his people are gradually starving to death. His signing (sequence 22) is realized in a wholly different manner. The setting is a small room in Fort Walsh on a winter night and not a large meadow on a summer day as in the first treaty-signing sequence. An interpreter in the presence of a young officer as Governor Dewdney's representative carries out the act. Big Bear and Lone Man come alone in the darkness, as if they have to hide from something. From outside, the camera peeks into the room, where the two do not even take off their coats and hats. There is a cut inside to Big Bear looking at his reflection in the window while the interpreter, in a droning voice, reads out the treaty conditions:

> does hereby, transfer, relinquish and *surrender* to Her Majesty the Queen and for the use of the Government of Canada, that is does *extinguish forever* all his rights, titles, and privileges whatsoever to these lands, does *extinguish forever* all hold and use of said lands forever.[138]

Then the camera tracks from the window to the Treaty No. Six laid out on the table with a treaty medal lying on top of it. Via a cut, the camera closes

---

[138] Wiebe & Cardinal, *Big Bear* screenplay, 63; emphasis in original.

up on the medal and pans to the place with Big Bear's name. In a medium shot it shows Big Bear looking at the translator and the quill; a close-up focusses on the quill that Big Bear's hand touches and then on a hand scratching the X below Big Bear's name (Figs. 8.10–8.14). There is no ceremonial act to 'confirm' the treaty, and Lone Man and Big Bear immediately leave the office. The act of Big Bear's signing is not treated with appropriate ceremoniousness by both parties, possibly because of anger at Big Bear's resistance on the Canadian side and bitterness on Big Bear's side. Governor Dewdney's absence and the small side room in the fort instead of his office fail to give the act an appropriate setting. Big Bear is saved from the NWMP coat, the handshake, and the anthem. On the other hand, he is not 'honored' with this masquerade, either. Big Bear is no longer a proud and influential man. Instead, he is weak and desperate, knowing that his nation will become dependent and subservient.

In this sequence, the filmmakers do not show how the treaty medal is put on, and the two different treaty-making situations are translated cinematically with a different focus and pace and also with a different share of film-time. Whereas the first treaty-making scene is characterized by a calm venerableness and is portrayed in two sequences (actually, a single sequence divided by a commercial break) with many dialogues which together run for 10.23 minutes, the second sequence only runs for 1.29 minutes. Except for the reading-out of the treaty, nobody speaks a word, and an air of silent haste and resignation hovers over the scene. In both scenes, though, the filmmakers take care to focus visually on the X being scratched under the treaty and on the treaty medal, thereby transforming the X and the medal into cinematic signifiers of the Indigenous relinquishment of land rights and their subordination under British/Canadian law. Metaphorically, the X and medal 'confirmed' Indigenous dependence, welfare mentality, residential schooling, and the ensuing problems of health, substance abuse, and dysfunctional family.[139] Even more so, the translator reading out the treaty passage that specifies the surrender of land rights

---

[139] Other Indigenous artists have also metaphorically recontextualized Treaty-X. One example is a group of artists in the "In-X-Isle" exhibition at the Neutral Ground gallery in Regina in 2000, curated by Edward Poitras. Another example is the group of artists in the traveling exhibition "Reservation-X," organized by the Canadian Museum of Civilization. The latter was presented at the Hood Museum of Art at Dartmouth College in 2001. See Neutral Ground Gallery, Regina at http://www.neutralground.sk.ca/programming/2000/edward/index.shtml and the catalogue *Reservation X* (Hanover NH: Hood Museum of Art, Dartmouth College, 6 October – 16 December 2001.

forever sonically pinpoints the colonial injustice of such treaty, which is thus presented as legal land theft.

In the same vein, the filmmakers realize the killing of settlers in the Frog Lake settlement with careful attention. In sequence 44 they spend 18.07 minutes, a fairly large share of the film time, to depicting the Frog Lake incident where nine settlers were killed by Big Bear's warriors and where Big Bear attempted unsuccessfully to avert the disaster. Before sequence 44, Cardinal and Cuthand describe the events that led to this incident: the hunger of the people in Big Bear's band; the death of Man's Woman and Earth Girl; the refusal of the Indian agent Quinn and Governor Dewdney to provide the band with food; the arrest of He Speaks Our Tongue, where Poundmaker and Big Bear could hardly restrain the angered warriors; and the message that the Métis have engaged in armed resistance at Duck Lake. They illustrate how Big Bear gradually loses the respect of and control over the young warriors, since he always favors peaceful solutions to conflict. Cardinal and Cuthand succeed in conveying the tension among the men in the band, who are slowly splitting in two groups during the course of events. One group supports Big Bear, who still tries to avoid armed confrontation, and the other group supports Little Bad Man and Wandering Spirit, who are enraged by their treatment by government officials and who will no longer accept peaceful settlement. The filmmakers also illustrate the tension within Big Bear's family. The women reproach him for not signing the treaty and not accepting assignment to a reserve; the family and the other people from his band suffer constantly from hunger, and malnutrition is slowly killing the weakest among them.

Great care is taken to describe the treatment of captives in the camp.[140] During the Frog Lake incident, a few settlers, among them the widow of Delaney the farm instructor, are taken hostage by the warriors. So are the HBC factor McLean, his pregnant Cree wife, and their daughter Kitty after their surrender of Fort Pitt. When Miserable Man takes Theresa Delaney from her dead husband by force and brings her to the camp, Running Se-

---

[140] The location of Big Bear's camp near the north end of Frog Lake was verified through the discovery of the remains of the camp and a Woods Cree settlement in 1991. Prompted by an historical study of the area for a Husky Oil pipeline, the camp was located thanks to Fred Fidler, a Cree elder who learned about the camp from his grandfather. Along with the remains, several objects were found: a Northwest musket barrel, a forged-iron trade axehead, and several other artifacts, the use of which was dated around the time of the Frog Lake settlement and Big Bear's camp in that area; Diane Parrenteau, "Historic Study Uncovers Big Bear's Camp," *Windspeaker* 9.6 (7 June 1991): 3.

cond scolds him in front of everybody and immediately protects her. From
then on, Theresa Delaney and the McLeans are guests in Big Bear's lodge,
where they are provided with food. The captives are more or less integrated
into what is left of ordinary camp life. They are protected by Big Bear and
Lone Man when Wandering Spirit attempts to kill them. When Big Bear
tells the captives to flee, he even makes suggestions about where they could
go. Although they are released, Theresa Delaney and the McLeans stay
with them.[141] In this description of the Cree treatment of captives, the filmmakers undermine the tradition of captivity tales that created a demonized
cliché of Indians brutally taking captives and treating them with cruelty.
Captivity stories gradually acquired symbolic character as legends of colonial culture, the colonial experience being shown as the peril facing white
Christian women subjected to Indian cruelty in a 'savage' space. These
texts constructed Indigenous males as the brutal, uncivilized other, "with
the bodies and sexuality of white women captives as the contested border
zone."[142]

---

[141] For accounts by Theresa Delaney and Elizabeth McLean of their two-month's captivity
in Big Bear's band, see Rudy Wiebe & Bob Beal, *War in the West.* For accounts by Theresa
Gowanlock and Theresa Delaney of their two-month's captivity in Big Bear's band, see their
captivity narratives in *Two Months in the Camp of Big Bear: The Life and Adventures of
Theresa Gowanlock and Theresa Delaney* (Regina, Saskatchewan: Canadian Plains Research
Center, 1999). Cardinal and Cuthand's descriptions of the Frog Lake massacre and of the ensuing captivity of Frog Lake settlers differ in some points from Gowanlock and Delaney's
description of these events, mainly regarding John Delaney's relation to the Cree, the facts
about the lodge the captives stayed in and who protected them, and how they gained their
freedom. Delaney's account is more analytical and gives a more reasonable assessment of the
historical conditions behind the Frog Lake massacre. In her description of the Cree she is
more cautious than Gowanlock about attributing savage characteristics to the Indigenous
people, and she differentiates between those who were peaceful farmers and those who were
responsible for the killing and the taking of hostages. Nevertheless, both accounts, in the
tradition of captivity narratives, demonize their captors and assign to them the most
abominable and beast-like characteristics, describing their cultural traditions, here mostly
ways of cooking and living, division of labor, and dances, as uncivilized beyond hope. They
establish the fate of female captives as a double trial and tribulation: suffering from being
forcibly taken into another culture that they thought of as being inferior to their own, and
constantly fearing "inhuman treatment [...] even worse than a hundred deaths."
[142] Rebecca Blevins Faery, *Cartographies of Desire: Captivity, Race, and Sex in the Shaping of the American* (Norman: U of Oklahoma P, 1999): 40. On the genre of captivity tales,
see, for example, Barry Fruchter, "Den of Lions: Captivity and Ideology on the New American Frontier," *Journal of Nassau Community College* 7.5 (1999): 116–33, Hartmut Lutz, "*Indianer" und "Native Americans": Zur sozial- und literarhistorischen Vermittlung eines
Stereotyps* (Hildesheim, Zurich & New York: Georg Olms, 1985): 136–42, and Paul Neubauer, "Indian Captivity in American Children's Literature: A Pre-Civil War Set of Stereo-

Everyday Cree life, customs, and ceremonial acts (e.g., funerals, prayers, and songs) are not overtly displayed and commented on, as was typical of the ethnographic tradition. These cultural elements are depicted in the context of the historical events: i.e. they are subordinated to these events and provide a 'realistic cultural setting'. The film demonstrates the constant hunger suffered by the band, compounded by an upsurge in incoming settlers and the decrease of the buffalo. Both traditional methods of hunting buffalo – sneaking up on foot in wolf-skins, and driving and shooting them on horseback – are depicted, as well as the hunting of other game in winter. Funeral customs are not exoticized and presented with mourning, death songs, and wrapped bodies placed on funeral platforms. In one sequence (9), the tradition of oral storytelling during long winter nights is captured in Lone Man's telling of a story that Big Bear enacts with shadow-play (Fig. 8.15). This is not modified oral storytelling as in *Honey Moccasin* and *Smoke Signals*, but a demonstration strictly according to traditional models: a family is assembled around a fire in a lodge in winter, listening to a story that is enacted for entertainment.

The Father–Son Conflict
The conflict between Big Bear and his oldest son Little Bad Man is the most apparent interpersonal conflict that is grounded in the rising conflict among the men in the band. This conflict is centered on the issue of dealing with the settlers, government officials, and the NWMP. It is maintained and intensified throughout the film. It is not so much realized through dialogue as through glances between the two men and through depicted situations from which the viewer can infer what both men think and feel. At the beginning, Big Bear and Little Bad Man are still united in their disapproval of the treaty. In sequence 11, their views already split, when Little Bad Man suggests moving south because there are more buffalo. Big Bear rejects this plan for fear of too many Blackfoot and American soldiers in that area. Before Little Bad Man and Kingbird set out for a horse raid into the Blackfoot area (sequence 12), Big Bear warns them not to start a war, as he knows that Little Bad Man can act very impulsively (whether he means a war with the Blackfoot or with the US army remains unclear). As long as Little Bad Man is close to the band, Big Bear can still control him and curb

types," *The Lion and the Unicorn: A Critical Journal of Children's Literature* 25.1 (January 2001): 70–80.

his temper. At this point, Little Bad Man is already derisive of his father's goal to make peace with the Blackfoot: "I did not come south to Blackfoot country to sit on my ass and talk peace treaties, or to drink tea with the new white Governor 'Dewdney'." Understanding but trying to avoid conflict, Big Bear responds: "Ahh, old warriors have their work. Just like young warriors and beginners (*nods to Kingbird*) have theirs."[143] When his two sons return with a beautiful white mare and three other horses and Kingbird presents the mare to him (sequence 15), Big Bear is very proud of his sons and touched by their gift. He decides to follow Little Bad Man's suggestion of six months earlier and move south to where the buffalo are; he and Little Bad Man are again in union. During the buffalo hunt (sequence 16), Big Bear chooses one cow he wants to run down with bow and arrows. His sons and the other warriors, who are armed with rifles, leave the cow for him, for which Big Bear is very thankful after the hunt.

The harmony between father and son is again brought to a crisis when Big Bear announces after the hunt that he will not hunt buffalo anymore. In his vision, blood was streaming from the earth and Coyote was laughing at him, which he interprets as a bad omen. Little Bad Man is upset, arguing that up north Cree people are crowding around the forts and begging for food. As a proud warrior, such a situation is unthinkable for him. At the funeral of Earth Girl (sequence 20), he restrains himself, knowing that she died because the band had not signed a treaty and was therefore not entitled to receive food from the Indian agent. Although Lone Man, Big Bear's second son, is in favor of the treaty and a reserve and despite the fact that his daughter has just died, he does not dare to openly criticize his father. When Big Bear's resistance is finally broken because his people are starving, it is not his first son but his second son who accompanies him to sign the treaty (sequence 22). After Big Bear has decided to do a Thirst Dance on Poundmaker's reserve to ask for strength, wisdom, and guidance, Little Bad Man declares that he will support Big Bear out of obedience but will make his own vow. This announcement here demonstrates that Little Bad Man does not agree with Big Bear's plans to settle all conflict peacefully with the government and incoming settlers. On Poundmaker's reserve, Big Bear attempts to convince the other Cree that all Cree should establish a strong league in order to be respected by government officials and to

---

[143] Wiebe & Cardinal, *Big Bear* screenplay, script-ed. Jordan Wheeler (1998, unpublished): 40.

negotiate for one large reserve for all Cree bands (sequence 26). Meanwhile, Little Bad Man welcomes Gabriel Dumont, and both talk about how the NWMP and Canadian army can be defeated by the Cree and Métis together. Little Bad Man for the first time directly criticizes his father and undermines his plans. He agrees with Dumont, complaining that his father is a weak man who always talks peace with government officials. Here it becomes obvious that Little Bad Man has lost respect for his father and will from now on pursue his own goals.

At agent Craig's house (sequence 30), when armed conflict is imminent and the warriors and NWMP are pointing their weapons at each other, Poundmaker and Big Bear hold back the men, earning a contemptuous look from Little Bad Man (Fig. 8.16). At Man's Woman's funeral (sequence 37), Little Bad Man openly confronts Big Bear and makes a vow that he will not forget the death of his wife. Whereas some of Big Bear's family blame him for not signing the treaty, Little Bad Man ridicules his peaceful negotiations. Little Bad Man's solution is to drive back the settlers and thus secure their traditional food-source. He is not as wise as Big Bear and cannot foresee that this vision will never be realized. After the funeral, Little Bad Man leaves his family and moves into the Rattler lodge (the warrior lodge), where he later proclaims Wandering Spirit war chief (sequences 38, 39). When Lone Man brings the news that a war has started at Duck Lake and that Dumont wants them to join, Little Bad Man disregards Big Bear's chiefly status and, in Lone Man's words, agrees to join by smoking the tobacco offered (sequence 40). Big Bear is very concerned about this secret plan, and as he hears the war drum he knows that the warriors will engage in armed conflict. The power-struggle is now in the open and Little Bad Man strives for leadership within the band. Big Bear does not respond to the challenge, but instead employs the policy of passive resistance that he also pursues in his dealings with government. He and Lone Man try to undermine the warriors' plans, warning the Indian agent Quinn that the warriors are going to attack the Frog Lake settlement, but they are disregarded (sequence 42). They are also laughed at and called names when the warriors, in a dance, prepare for the attack the next day. Just as Little Bad Man shows Big Bear disrespect, Miserable Man ridicules him before the other men in the band. Of his adult sons, Little Bad Man and Kingbird side with the warriors, while Lone Man sides with Big Bear. In the face of the advancing catastrophe, such a split cannot be deeper within a family. Again, Big Bear is mocked the next morning, when he attempts to divert

the warriors from the forcible seizure of ammunition from the HBC store in
the settlement (sequence 44). He sends Lone Man to Fort Pitt to fetch food
supplies that he hopes might calm down the hot tempers, again crossing
Little Bad Man's plans. Nevertheless, he cannot prevent the killing of nine
settlers and the taking of hostages.

During negotiations outside Fort Pitt with McLean two weeks later
(46), both Big Bear and Little Bad Man are shown side by side, but their
goals are different. A pivotal moment in the father–son conflict is reached
when Big Bear passes the Council Pipe on to Little Bad Man. Despite his
age and lack of power, he verbally challenges Little Bad Man and Wandering Spirit (49), foretelling that soldiers and police will come and fight
them. He does not ceremoniously present the pipe to him with advice, as
is the custom, but does so grimly, with some contempt, and without blessings. Apparently he has no other choice – his son has challenged him, and
he is worried because he sees danger for the band with Little Bad Man as
chief. He undermines his son's power by telling the captives to leave after
the battle at Frenchmen Butte, when Little Bad Man is still determined to
fight the police and army (51). The whole band disperses after the battle
and, after most of the captives have left, only a fraction of the band and
his family are with Big Bear. With kind blessings, he passes his medicine
bundle on to Kingbird, leaving Lone Man out of the succession. Lone
Man reports that Little Bad Man now calls himself Little Bear and is leading fifteen families south. Big Bear understands, and ends their rivalry
with the words "It's a hard thing ... for a grown man to always be a son. But
now, Little Bad Man has decided what has to be done."[144] Perhaps the
chosen name reveals Little Bad Man's respect for his father and his token
submission. But for father and son, the family, and the band, this insight
comes too late, as they are split up and destroyed. In the course of the
film, Cardinal and Cuthand do not focus on this conflict, but subordinate
it to the historical events. Nevertheless, they give it appropriate attention
in order to convey the sense of rising tension and rivalry between the two
men, nourished by their diverging political ideas and by Little Bad Man's
striving for power and vengeance, which ends so disastrously. In their
complex depiction of the conflict between Big Bear and Little Bad Man,

---

[144] Wiebe & Cardinal, *Big Bear* screenplay, script-ed. Jordan Wheeler (1998, unpublished): 172; omission in original.

the filmmakers succeed in presenting Big Bear as a man of peace unable to prevent the killing at Frog Lake and the ensuing war.

Hunger, Rope, and Other Cinematic Motifs

Hunger is the most persistent motif dynamizing the narrative. Because ever more settlers entered the area, burned the grasslands, and slaughtered the buffalo, these animals, the Cree's subsistence food source, gradually vanished. The film shows this fateful process, whereby the Cree can no longer live in their traditional ways and have to adapt to new and adverse conditions. As displayed in the film, their food decreases steadily in terms of quantity and quality: from buffalo meat to deer that has been left by two wolves, to rabbits, dog- and horse-meat from killed camp animals, to the flour from the Indian agent and pork that Sits Green on the Earth acquires through prostitution. The people's self-respect, associated with the acquisition of food, also diminishes. The hunger depresses the people and resignation and irritability hover in the camp and Big Bear's lodge. It is hunger that makes Big Bear sign the treaty, and hunger and the unfair patronizing of the Indian agent that drives the warriors to start a war. The motif of death is associated with the hunger motif, with more people dying each winter of malnutrition (according to Big Bear, twenty-three in the winter of 1884/85 alone). The viewer witnesses two funerals (of Lone Man's daughter Earth Girl and of Little Bad Man's wife Man's Woman) through which death is brought starkly to their attention.

The rope metaphor is a recurrent verbal motif. During negotiations, Big Bear several times metaphorically defines the treaty as a "rope around his neck, choking his liberty."[145] One example crops up in the treaty-making sequence (8):

> BIG BEAR (Cont)
> I heard the Governor was to come, and I said that I shall see him; that I would tell him there is something I dread. To feel the rope around my neck, choking my liberty.
> *Sweetgrass understands and bows his head at this heavy thought. Other Cree in the crowd react much the same way. In his translation Erasmus literally gestures a person being hung. Morris, confused, then speaks quickly, impatiently.*

---

[145] On the historical accuracy of Big Bear's dictum, see Hugh Dempsey, *Big Bear: The End of Freedom*, 74, and Olive P. Dickason, *Canada's First Nations: A History of Founding Peoples from Earliest Times* (Don Mills, Ontario: Oxford U P Canada, 3rd ed. 2002): 277.

MORRIS

Lob! Il et drummin Grapple Sprilling, o et ...

ERASMUS

Rope! Why are you concerned with hanging? It is the punishment of murder, under the Queen's law.

*Big Bear, startled, looks at Morris, He tries to explain, speaking directly to
him.*

BIG BEAR

I speak of freedom, not of law.

MORRIS/ERASMUS

There can be only one law, the Great Grandmother's.

Morris still does not understand, so Big Bear starts again.

BIG BEAR

I find something very bitter in my mouth when our tongues should be sweet
today.

*Morris is again confused by Big Bear's symbolism, and responds with some
irritation.*

MORRIS/ERASMUS

We have handed out much sweet food to everyone who touches the pen,
and to their families.[146]

Big Bear believes the treaty will lead to the Cree's confinement to reserves,
subservience to government officials and Canadian laws, political and economic dependency, poverty, and patriarchal treatment by government representatives – all expressed through the metaphorical 'rope around his
neck'. This metaphor is introduced in sequence 5 when Big Bear names his
last-born son Horsechild, "like a colt running without a rope around its
neck to choke its liberty." It is taken up by Little Bad Man in sequence 23
when he responds to the commanding officer who attempts to forbid them
to visit Poundmaker. It is also used by Poundmaker in sequence 24, commenting on the reserve conditions: "My brother, the government rope is the
same for us all." As with other metaphors in Big Bear's speeches, government representatives misunderstand the meaning of 'the rope'. In this case,
perhaps due to Erasmus' gesture in the first treaty-making sequence, Morris
interprets it as Big Bear's concern with hanging as punishment. In the end,
this metaphoric motif becomes literal when Big Bear is tied in chains in the
Regina court room and Wandering Spirit and three other warriors are

---

[146] Wiebe & Cardinal, *Big Bear* screenplay, script-ed. Jordan Wheeler (1998, unpublished): 29–30; ellipsis in original.

hanged (Figs. 8.17–8.18). Other Indigenous leaders, including Louis Riel, were punished in the same way.[147] The defeat of the Cree is also visualized in the sequence where Big Bear's long hair, traditionally associated with strength and a strong spirit, is cut; the shot (Fig. 8.19), reinforced by the high angle, signifies Big Bear's and his people's disempowerment, humiliation, and bleak future under Canadian laws.

Instead of simply depicting events at the different locations and inserting titles informing the viewer where the narrative is moving, Cardinal and Cuthand include many brief sequences that show Big Bear's band taking down and putting up lodges and trekking to different places, in this way visualizing the nomadic life of the Plains Cree that would soon end. The trekking and walking become a binding motif. However, not all movements between the several locations could be visualized. Some movements are suggested by titles, and sequences 18, 23, 48, 56 show the trekking directly. As the trekking is not important for conveying narrative information, Western filmmaking would likely have omitted it, so that its repetition reveals the filmmakers' concern with this aspect of Plains Cree life. The trekking motif assumes the variant of running in the sequences where Little Bad Man and Kingbird run south to raid a Blackfoot camp (sequences 12, 14). The viewer cannot know how far it is into Blackfoot country, but via dissolves the men are shown running through changing daylight, suggesting that they run for a very long time. It is a run and raid for Kingbird to prove himself as a "worthy young man" and to be admitted among the warriors. For Little Bad Man, more pragmatically, the run is to acquire good horses, which Big Bear's band is in need of. Like Victor's run in *Smoke Signals*, this is a reference to the traditional runs of young men in order to test strength and endurance as well as to contemporary political runs and walks.

Visual motifs are the tipis at different locations. Whereas these are well-maintained tipis as long as Big Bear's band moves independently, on Poundmaker's reserve the film shows a run-down, patched-up tipi (Figs. 8.20–8.22) to visualize the people's decreasing pride and increased colonial dependency. Another visual motif is the HBC blanket as it has been widely put to use by the Cree, mostly to ward off the winter cold. Cinematic focus on these blankets, and likewise shots of treaty money being

---

[147] Blair Stonechild & Bill Waiser give an account of the punishments of Indigenous and Métis prisoners after the Battle of Batoche in 1885. They show that Indigenous prisoners were punished more severely than the Métis; Stonechild & Waiser, *Loyal till Death: Indians and the North-West Rebellion* (Calgary, Alberta: Fifth House, 1997).

handed out, similarly function as signifiers of colonial dependency and the
shift from the Cree's traditional hunter-gatherer economy to a capitalist
economy based on the exchange value of money and Western goods (Figs.
8.23–8.26). Whereas in the first image Big Bear wears a buffalo robe, he
later wears an HBC blanket, which contrast points up his state of economic
dependency. The various prairie skies are another visual motif, changing as
they do from bright to cloudy to dramatic skies heralding thunderstorms.
Similarly, various shots of the prairie landscape recur. As sky and prairie
are two parts of the same frame, the sky motif appears together with the
motif of the wide open plains (Figs. 8.27–8.29, Fig. 8.2).

The soundtrack of the production is one consistent composition by Clode
Hamelin. It is not a lavish musical score as with most Hollywood productions but nevertheless serves to support and underline the tension and character of the events presented and the emotional states of the characters. It is
mostly melancholy orchestral music with dramatic elements usually sig-
naled by drums. The cello, flute, and drums are the instruments that appear
most often in the foreground, and in the broadest sense can be regarded as
sound motifs.

Slowness and Movement as Stylistic Devices
The most salient features are the slow pace of the film, minimal employment of cross-cutting, the stress on the movement of the band, the long dissolves, and a large number of long shots and extreme long shots that take in
the panorama of the prairies. Although the film runs for roughly three
hours, it consists of sixty sequences only. By comparison, *Smoke Signals*
runs for about eighty-nine minutes and consists of sixty-three sequences.
Whereas the sequences in *Smoke Signals* have an average length of 1.3
minutes, in *Big Bear* they have an average length of 2.9 minutes.[148] Instead
of moving briskly through the narrative, the filmmakers concentrate longer
on one single scene. The Frog Lake sequence is the longest, as well as the
climax of the film. Favoring a slow pace, the filmmakers avoid accelerated
cutting as a device to create dramatic tension. The tension leading to the
climax is achieved by the content of the previous events only. Most obvious among these events is the dance of the warriors the night before when

---

[148] *Smoke Signals* is not to be considered as the standard film for the length of sequences.
Nevertheless, in this regard it can be taken as an example that is close to average mainstream
narrative films.

they declare that they will raid the settlement. Neither the dance sequence nor the Frog Lake sequence has shorter cuts than the other sequences. The climax sequence even begins with a 29-second pan as a long shot through the still sleeping settlement early in the morning. This image suggests peace instead of approaching disaster. It also ends almost as 'peacefully' with Horsechild walking for 1.20 minutes through the settlement, looking at dead bodies, and covering a bleeding wound on the dead Reverend Farfard. Only the slow, foreboding music supports the rising action. Tension is thus created largely through character play, causal events, presented action, and a careful musical score, and not with faster cutting or decreasing camera distance. Cuthand says that he learned to slow the pace while making a documentary with Cree elders, finding that he could not pace it as fast as he does others. He felt the need to give natural images and the elders more time within one individual shot in order to match the pace of their life and stories.[149] Cardinal and Cuthand apply a similar principle in *Big Bear*, endeavoring to show the long time Big Bear takes to consider the treaty, the calm sensibility with which he makes decisions, and the slow pace of Cree life, involving long winters, long walks, and so forth.

There is not much crosscutting between sequences, which are consistent entities cut together chronologically. Only twice does the film divide scenes to insert another sequence. Between the sequences of the young men's run south and Kingbird's raid in the Blackfoot camp, Cardinal and Cuthand insert the scene of the annual treaty payment and Big Bear's treaty negotiations at Fort Walsh (sequences 12–14). The Thirst Dance is 'interrupted' by the scene at the house of the Indian agent Craig, at this point to convey the fact that both events happen simultaneously (sequences 27–29). Within sequences, the filmmakers likewise largely refrain from crosscutting between situations. Shorter cuts are usually employed in concert with reverse-angle shooting during dialogue exchanges. Avoiding crosscutting and structuring the sequences chronologically support the slow pace of the film.

The transition devices fade and dissolve do not occur more often than in mainstream feature films, but the dissolves seem rather long, most of them between three and four seconds. Fades are almost exclusively deployed in transition to commercial breaks. The four exceptions are: after the treaty-making when other Cree follow Big Bear (8/9); after the Thirst Dance (29/30); after the warriors' dance, before the Frog Lake incident (43/44);

---

[149] See Doug Cuthand (unpublished interview, 1998).

and at the end. Except for the ending, there is no recognizable pattern in these three exceptions. The dissolves, however, are used in Big Bear's visions (16 and 60); between landscape shots (Sounding Lake, 38); before, after, and during trekking (18, 23/24, 47/48, 55/56); during the long run of Little Bad Man and Kingbird (12); after Earth Girl's funeral (20/21); after the incident with He Speaks Our Tongue when Poundmaker and Big Bear exchange a long look (30/31); and before Big Bear dies (59/60). The dissolves are thus associated with vision, land, movement, and death.

With many long shots, the filmmakers are able to show a certain unique quality of the prairies, the vastness of the wide open spaces. A horizontal line divides sky from earth and defines the image composition as in Masayesva's *Itam Hakim, Hopiit*, where the frame would show a small expanse of land and a large expanse of sky. In concert with these long shots, establishing shots of the camps, the Frog Lake settlement, and other locations are provided. In order to convey the quality of endless spaces, which Big Bear also had in mind when he spoke of his liberty being impaired by the 'rope around his neck', the filmmakers, especially the cinematographers, took great care in taking the shots. Cuthand explains:

> There is a quality, it's hard to tell you, but there is a quality about this production and the land.... Even if it was shot by White people, Georges Dufeaux and his daughter Sylvaine. Georges was the director of photography and Sylvaine was the camera operator. And Sylvaine told me that they had to be very careful to shoot it to show the size of the land, the hugeness of it. And it goes for miles, we got pictures out there that we couldn't get anywhere else, this wide, open prairie just goes for miles. And she had to shoot it with that in mind, 'cause she had to capture what the prairie was like a hundred years ago, it takes quite a bit of doing. (interview, 1998)

At some points, one expects to move closer to an object in order to 'really see' and scrutinize it when 'only' medium shots are provided. For example, when Little Bad Man and Kingbird return from the horse raid and Kingbird presents Big Bear with the white mare, one expects facial reaction shots to be in close-up. At other points, however, close-ups are indeed provided, usually to convey facial expression and subsequently to transmit the state of mind of the respective character. Most of the close-ups are of Big Bear's face, as he is the protagonist and the person who makes the most frequent and most momentous decisions. His pensive or mourning face in close-up thus becomes a visual motif as well (e.g., Figs. 8.30–8.33, Fig. 8.8). The shot in Fig. 8.8 is emphasized cinematically by an almost 180°

tracking shot around the crouching leader. Generally, close-ups, medium shots, and long shots are balanced and do not form salient patterns.

The four trekking sequences are chosen here for closer examination. A detailed shot analysis of these sequences is provided in the Appendix. In the first trekking sequence (18), the band moves north when Big Bear decides to cease hunting buffalo. In the second sequence (23), the band moves further north in order to choose a reserve after Big Bear has signed the treaty. In the third sequence (48), the band, now under Little Bad Man and Wandering Spirit's leadership, flees after the incidents at Frog Lake and Fort Pitt. And in the fourth sequence (56), the band and Big Bear's family are almost wiped out and Running Second leads the few survivors away. All of the trekking sequences focus on the exhaustion of the people, caused by hunger and too much movement without rest. They are realized by positioning the camera and having the people move toward or past it, mostly in medium shots and medium close-ups (e.g., Figs. 8.40–8.42). This technique underscores the people's movement and its effects, with the medium close-ups displaying tired faces. Often the riders do not sit up, but are shown with hanging heads. Everybody trots along dully; only in sequence 48 are the warriors alert because the band is in flight. There is no chatting among the people, except in sequence 18 when Sits Green and Kingbird flirt a little. The filmmakers are concerned to convey the harshness and deprivation of nomadic life, as the people usually walked on foot, always had to carry all their belongings, and could only own as much as they (and their horses) could carry.

Cinematic focus within the trekking sequences shifts with the events that change the life of the band. In the first (18), attention is paid to the movement across the prairie, while a single excursus (Sits Green and Kingbird's flirt) serves to lighten the sombre mood momentarily (Figs. 8.34–8.42). In the second (23), the presence of the four guarding NWMP and the tension between them and the Cree controls the scene (Fig. 8.43). In contrast to the first trekking sequence, which is dominated by natural colors, in this one the red NWMP coats visually 'disturb' the natural color composition. This contrast indicates that a momentous break, that of the signed treaty, has occurred before. The fact that in the third trekking sequence (48) Little Bad Man and Wandering Spirit lead the trek and Big Bear walks last makes it clear that a transfer of authority within the band has taken place. As the two are looking around alertly, it becomes obvious that they expect an attack by the NWMP (Figs. 8.44–8.46). Camera attention on their alertness and on the faces of the captives points to the dreadful incident at Frog Lake for which the two are responsible. Whereas in this sequence most of the shots are taken with a still camera and the camera distance does not shift, in the last shot featuring Big Bear walking behind, the camera distance shifts from medium shot to close-up and the shot is taken with a tracking camera (Fig. 8.47). Thus, camera work here centers on Big Bear and his facial expression. Finally, the last trekking sequence (56) focusses on the separation of the family, realized through reverse-angle shots between Big Bear and Running Second (taken with a still camera) and two sound bridges with Running Second's piercing wail (Figs. 8.48–8.49).

Shot length, camera movement, and camera distance also indicate changes in the situation of the band. In the first part of sequence 18, dissolves very nicely connect five shots of decreasing camera distance, from extreme long to medium. In the last three of these five, the dissolves are longer that the actual shot, so that one dissolve leads into the next and three images are on the screen simultaneously. The long dissolves underline the long distance that is covered between the two camps. Low camera angles put the prairie grass in the foreground, granting it special visual attention (Figs. 8.34–8.39). Other shots throughout the film have a similar compositional concentration on the prairie grass (e.g., Figs. 8.51–8.52). In order of their appearance, the four trekking sequences run for 1.28, 1.36, 1.09, and 1.08 minutes. Before the climax at the Frog Lake settlement, the trekking sequences 18 and 23 last longer than those after it (48 and 56). Although the last two sequences are shorter, they contain more shots, sixteen each, in contrast to thirteen and twelve in the first two. Subsequently, the length of the shots within the trekking sequences decreases as the length of the sequences itself decreases. The average shot-length of the first trekking sequence is 6.79 seconds, while the others are 7.94, 4.14, and 4.66 seconds. The first two contain dialogue, the last two do not. By controlling the pace of the trekking sequences, generating a slower pace in the first two and a faster one in the last two, the filmmakers indicate that there was still peace in sequences 18 and 23, while in 48 and 56 the Frog Lake incident had instilled war between the Cree and the NWMP. The Cree's pace of life has changed, too, also suggested by the decreased average shot length. In sequences 18, 23, and 48, the trekking people move toward the camera, and in sequence 56 they move away from it, as seen from Big Bear's POV (Fig. 8.50). Here, there are ten close-ups and medium close-ups of people's faces as opposed to three medium shots and three long shots. By contrast, there is only one close-up in sequence 18, none in sequence 23, and five close-ups in sequence 48. In the last trekking sequence there is no camera movement, whereas there are four, two, and three shots with camera movement in the first three. With these technical means, the filmmakers set the last trekking sequence off from the other three in order to convey the devastating sadness that hovers over the scene of the separating family. The close-ups of faces and, of course, Running Second's wail help to convey this sadness.

Final Remarks

Through the figure of Big Bear, Cardinal and Cuthand give a historical account of an important era in Cree–Canadian history from an inside perspective (this can, of course, not be a complete and universal account), and describe the Cree life concealed behind historical facts. They give insight into the drastic changes for the Cree caused by the colonization of the Canadian West. The film presents an historical narrative that counters Canadian historical portrayals of the figure of Big Bear, which previously depicted him as a belligerent and/or powerless chief. Producer Cuthand and leading actor Tootoosis were concerned with recontextualizing this narrative, having grown up with stories about the respected chief Big Bear, and they see him as a crucial part of the history of the Canadian prairies. For historical accuracy they rely on a body of Cree stories about Big Bear and on Wiebe's research for the novel *The Temptations of Big Bear*, thereby combining Cree oral tradition and Canadian creative history writing as sources for their historical film.

The film obeys classical film conventions, with the cinematic style subordinated to the narrative. This consistently linear narrative is driven by a cause-and-effect chain and embedded in clear narrative time and space, its characters are goal-oriented, and the narrative achieves closure at the end of the film. The two sub-narratives about the father–son conflict and about traditional Cree life and its transformation through colonialism complement the main narrative about Big Bear's life and related events of Cree–Canadian history. The film adheres to classical continuity and to the 180° system; camera work, musical score, sound, lighting, colors, editing, and mise-en-scène support the narrative and do not draw attention to the technical process of filming.

However, in contrast to conventional narrative films, the filmmakers do not create suspense and surprise as means of heightening tension. They deliberately avoid fast cutting and compose a slow pace through many long shots and longer takes, long sequences, long transitions between shots, and the contextualization of slow nomadic movement. Similarly, the chronological presentation, with avoidance of flashbacks and flashforwards, the absence of intimate camera positions when portraying sex or violence, the refusal to indulge in displays of Indian 'savagery' (even in battle scenes), the avoidance of any gloriously staging of warfare and 'heroic' individual characters – all this sets the film apart from its Hollywood models. There is no exoticizing and romanticizing of Cree spirituality, no medicine wo/man, no magical occurrence that would suggest possession of shamanic magical powers. Big Bear's spiritual power is carefully realized through his visions and his conducting of a Thirst Dance. The Cree elders' veto on cinematic depiction of the Thirst Dance was respected, and the dance was only intimated. The filmmakers refrain from focussing sub-narratives on romance between the Cree protagonists and present the relationships of the couples in a natural way. By contrast, prostitution in exchange for food is shown as a disgusting act. The filmmakers do not idealize Cree culture, do not ideologize historical events, and do not moralize about the effects of colonialism. This mini-series constitutes a film within the tradition of historical realism in North American cinema that for the first time contextualizes the colonized perspective. It thus subverts the colonialist gaze that has been informed by, and has itself informed, one-sided historical writing to create one-dimensional Indian characters. The filmmakers' gaze comes from outside in terms of the historicity of the events, but from inside in terms of cultural background.

Atanarjuat: The Fast Runner

The Inuit feature film *Atanarjuat: The Fast Runner* (Canada, 2001), is one of the most celebrated Canadian films of the past few years. It is the first Inuit dramatic film made in Inuktitut to receive nationwide and international attention. The film was screened at various film festivals and program theatres in the world and won six Genie Awards, including Best Picture, and the *Caméra d'Or* for Best First Feature at the Cannes Film Festival in 2001.[150] In Germany it premiered at the Documenta 11 in Kassel

---

[150] Paul Apak Angilirq, et al. *Atanarjuat: The Fast Runner* (Toronto: Coach House / Isuma, 2002): 7.

in September 2002. Critics throughout North America hailed this first Inuit epic, calling it a noteworthy and "must-see" picture. A.O. Scott of the *New York Times* calls it "a masterpiece" that is "by any standard, an extraordinary film, a work of narrative sweep and visual beauty that honors the history of the art form even as it extends its perspective." Margaret Atwood terms it a "knockout" and "a generational saga with many Homeric elements," and Katherine Monk writes in the *Vancouver Sun* that Kunuk's film "is nothing less than a complete revelation and reinvention of cinematic form." According to Rick Groen of the *Globe & Mail*, "it is a superb film" and "is both intriguingly exotic and uniquely Canadian," and Liam Lacey in the same newspaper labels it "a milestone, an unclassifiable mixture of drama – murder, adultery and supernatural forces – and a fascinating cultural document." Jim Hoberman of the *Village Voice* holds that "this three-hour movie is engrossing from first image to last, so devoid of stereotype and cosmic in its vision it could suggest the rebirth of cinema," and Desson Howe of the *Washington Post* admires its "unadulterated, free-flowing magic."[151]

Set in the area between Baffin Island and the Melville Peninsula, the film is a retelling of an ancient legend that is a central story in the Inuit oral tradition and one that the filmmakers heard as children. The story has didactic functions, admonishing the audience not to let envy, rivalry, and personal interests overtake the sense of responsibility and community that is of utmost importance for survival in the Arctic.[152] It is the legend of an unknown shaman putting a curse on a small nomadic Inuit community, infesting it with evil and upsetting the spiritual balance and solidarity. After the community leader Kumaglak[153] is killed by the evil shaman Tungajuaq,

---

[151] A.O. Scott, "Film Festival Review: A Far-Off Inuit World, in a Dozen Shades of White," *New York Times* (30 March 2002): 9, B3, Margaret Atwood, "Of Myths and Men: *Atanarjuat: The Fast Runner*," *Globe & Mail* (13 April 2002), repr. in Atwood, *Moving Targets* (Toronto: House of Anansi, 2004): 259–60, Rick Groen & Liam Lacey, *Globe & Mail* (19 July 2002), Jim Hoberman, "*Atanarjuat – The Fast Runner*," *Village Voice* (20 March 2002): 26, Desson Howe, "'Fast Runner' a Stunner," *Washington Post* (21 June 2002): WE44. Extracts from reviews in *Atanarjuat: The Fast Runner* – webpages at http://www.atanarjuat.com/media_centre/index.html and http://lot47.com/thefastrunner/reviews.html

[152] Zacharias Kunuk, "I First Heard the Story of Atanarjuat From My Mother," in Paul Apak Angilirq, et al. *Atanarjuat: The Fast Runner*, 13; Nancy Wachowich, "Interview with Paul Apak Angilirq," in Apak Angilirq, et al. *Atanarjuat: The Fast Runner*, 17; *Atanarjuat: The Fast Runner* – webpages at http://lot47.com/thefastrunner/about_Roots_of_project.html

[153] There is a difference in the spelling of names between the script and the subtitles in the film, owing to the fact that when Inuktitut is written in Roman letters very often the stan-

with the help of Kumaglak's son Sauri, Sauri himself becomes a manipulative leader, and lethal rivalry develops between two families.[154] Sauri
weakens Tulimaq through ridicule and mistreatment because Tulimaq and
his family are suffering from the curse that brings bad luck and bad hunting. Tulimaq's two sons Amaqjuaq and Atanarjuat and Sauri's daughter
Puja and son Oki grow up in this climate of rivalry and hatred. Amaqjuaq,
the Strong One, and Atanarjuat, the Fast Runner, soon change the power-
relations in the community by becoming the best hunters and ridiculing the
Sauri/Oki family. The main conflict now develops between the mean-
spirited, choleric, and devious Oki and the honest, calm, and observant
Atanarjuat, who has the right sense of justice. Community relations come to
a boiling point when the beautiful Atuat, Oki's wife-to-be, reveals her feelings for Atanarjuat, who then wins her in an Inuit boxing match. Oki is the
embittered loser on both a physical and an emotional level. Puja, Oki's
scheming sister, is also in love with Atanarjuat and, with Oki's encourage-
ment, manages to accompany Atanarjuat on his summer caribou hunt because his pregnant wife needs to stay at the summer camp. Puja seduces
Atanarjuat, who, apparently out of a sense of responsibility, takes her home
as his second wife. She turns out to be lazy, uncooperative, and fond of
taking long walks in the tundra, so that Uluriaq, Amaqjuaq's wife, accuses
her of fucking with spirits (*ijirait* – invisible human-like spirits).[155] When
Puja seduces her brother-in-law Amaqjuaq, the brothers' relationship is
seriously strained.[156] Puja walks to Oki's camp, complaining that Atanarjuat has tried to kill her, whereupon Oki resolves to avenge the 'shame' by
killing Atanarjuat, his hated rival. Returning to Atanarjuat's camp, Puja
manages to reconcile herself with Atuat and Uluriaq. Knowing that Oki

---

dardized spelling is simplified. The script (published in Apak Angilirq, et al. *Atanarjuat: The
Fast Runner*) uses the standard spelling, whereas the subtitles and the *Atanarjuat: The Fast
Runner* – webpages (www.atanarjuat.com; www.lot47.com/VideoDVD/thefastrunner.html)
use the simplified spelling. See Bernard Saladin d'Anglure, "An Ethnographic Commentary:
The Legend of Atanarjuat, Inuit and Shamanism," in Paul Apak Angilirq, et al. *Atanarjuat:
The Fast Runner*, 197.

[154] Cf. the genealogical trees of the Oki/Sauri and Atanarjuat/Tulimaq families preceding
the sequence analysis in the Appendix.

[155] D'Anglure, "An Ethnographic Commentary: The Legend of Atanarjuat, Inuit and
Shamanism," 211.

[156] According to Inuit custom, in-laws were strictly forbidden to talk to each other. Sexual
relations among in-laws was the paramount taboo and its violation could incur serious social
disorders and the wrath of the spirits, which would withhold game animals (d'Anglure, "An
Ethnographic Commentary: The Legend of Atanarjuat, Inuit and Shamanism," 221).

will take blood revenge, she arranges events so that the brothers are asleep in their tent after an exhausting hunt and the three women have gone to collect bird's eggs. The two brothers are attacked by Oki's gang while they are asleep. Amaqjuaq is speared to death but Atanarjuat escapes through the help of a good spirit. Naked and barefoot, he runs across the Arctic plain and ice for a long time, trying to escape from the three pursuers who want to murder him, and leaps across a wide crack in the pack ice. He succeeds in escaping and with the help of another good spirit finds his way to Qulitalik and his family, where he is hidden and nursed back to health. Years earlier, they had left the evil and embittered community. The shaman Qulitalik supports Atanarjuat's spiritual power and his endeavor to end this evil haunting curse. In the meantime, Oki has killed his father Sauri to become community leader and raped Atuat to claim her as his wife. Returning with Qulitalik, Atanarjuat defeats Oki and his friends in a final fight and restores peace and harmony in his community. He reunites with Atuat and Oki, Puja, Pakak, Pittiulaq and their families are sentenced to leave the community.

The Inuit Approach

The film *Atanarjuat* was made by the first independent Inuit-owned production company Igloolik Isuma Productions, founded in 1990 by the director and hunter Zacharias Kunuk, the late producer Paul Apak Angilirq, the elder and actor Paulossie Qulitalik, and the New York-born video artist Norman Cohn, the only non-Inuit member.[157] The film was co-produced and partly financed through the Aboriginal Filmmaking Program of the National Film Board of Canada[158] and co-financed through the Canadian Television Fund and Telefilm Canada. Directed by Kunuk, written by Apak Angilirq, and photographed by Cohn, the film was realized in an "Inuit-style of community-based media production."[159] Like the three-hour TV-

---

[157] Before *Atanarjuat: The Fast Runner*, Igloolik Isuma produced the three dramatic films *Qaggiq* (Canada, 1988), *Nunaqpa* (Canada, 1990), and *Saputi* (Canada, 1993) and the thirteen-part dramatic TV series *Nunavut: Our Land* (Canada, 1994–95). These dramatic productions won awards and special recognition in Canada and were also internationally acclaimed (*Atanarjuat: The Fast Runner* – webpage at http://www.atanarjuat.com/about_isuma /index .html).

[158] *Atanarjuat: The Fast Runner* – webpage at http://www.atanarjuat.com/production_diary /index.html

[159] The filmmakers of Igloolik Isuma Productions define this community-based media production as an approach to filmmaking that would "preserve and enhance Inuit culture, create

drama *Big Bear*, this film was shot on Indigenous land, here Nunavut, the first Indigenous-controlled territory in Canada. The all-Inuit cast consists entirely of Igloolik residents, being both experienced actors and first-time performers. The production also employed an almost exclusively Inuit crew, mixing expert filmmakers and film novices who trained hands-on on the set. A few southern professionals were involved in pre- and postproduction processes including music composition, foley effects, editing, and the training of Inuit film novices in make-up, sound recording, continuity, stunts, and special effects.[160] The 1.9-million-Canadian-dollar production employed sixty Igloolik Inuit as cast, crew, and support staff, and together with other production expenditures supported the local economy of the Igloolik community with 1.5 million Canadian dollar.[161] Just as the production money of *Big Bear* benefited the weak economy of a Cree reserve community, *Atanarjuat*'s production money supported the community of Igloolik that, like other Arctic communities, has an unemployment rate of sixty percent and suicide rates ten times higher than the national average.[162] The filmmakers open up this oral legend, an Inuit intellectual property, to a global market; but with their community approach to filmmaking, they also give something back: the film, national and international attention, jobs, money, and cultural pride. Financial means acquired for the film are returned to at least one Inuit community. The appropriation of this cultural knowledge for a market outside of the Inuit community is 'compensated' through finances that come from that outside community. The Inuit legend is processed by Inuit artists (the filmmaking team), and in this way it is turned into a modernized Inuit intellectual property. It may be accessed by

---

jobs in Igloolik and represent a distinctively Inuit point of view in the global communications marketplace" (*Atanarjuat: The Fast Runner* – webpage at http://lot47.com /thefastrunner/About _the_filmmakers.html).

[160] *Atanarjuat: The Fast Runner* – webpages at: http://lot47.com/thefastrunner/about_Inside _action.html; http://www.atanarjuat.com/production_diary/index.html

[161] *Atanarjuat: The Fast Runner* – webpage at http://www.atanarjuat.com/production_diary /index.html

[162] *Atanarjuat: The Fast Runner* – webpage at http://www.atanarjuat.com/production_diary /index.html. Statistics Canada of 2001 gives an employment rate for Igloolik of 40.0 percent and for Nunavut of 56.2 percent. Official unemployment rates in the same year are 28.4 percent for Igloolik and 27.8 percent for Nunavut ("Statistics Canada: Community Profile – Igloolik," at http://www12.statcan.ca/english/profil01 /Details/details1inc1.cfm?SEARCH=BEGINS&PSGC =62&SGC=6204012&A=&LANG=E&Province=62&PlaceName=igloolik&CSDNAME=Iglo olik&CMA=&SEARCH=BEGINS&DataType=1&TypeNameE=Hamlet&ID=13599).

the Western world, but even more so will be 'used' by the Inuit community and returned as 'their intellectual property'.

Adjusting the process of filmmaking to extreme arctic conditions meant to shoot on widescreen digital betacam and to transfer the material later to 35 mm film.[163] Kunuk clarifies this by saying that using film technology would have been impossible because it would have taken too much time to send the rushes south to get developed and back before the filmmakers could view their takes.[164] In an interview, he also explains that digital video is their choice because digital cameras, filming and projection equipment are much easier to handle and because they can avoid the high costs of film material.[165] Adjusting filmmaking to arctic conditions also meant having crew and cast living in conditions and dwellings similar to those of their ancestors while filming on location in the Igloolik area, in order to reduce the notoriously high production costs of arctic films.[166] Kunuk says that they hired hunters to provide food for crew and cast.[167]

The community approach also involves the remaking of traditional clothes, tools (*ulu* – curved women's knife; seal-oil lamps), hunting weapons (forked *kakivak* – fish spear; *unaaq* – spear; *sakku* – harpoon head), sleds (*qamutik* – sled made of caribou antlers, bone, and sinew), a kayak (*qajaq* – one-man canoe), caribou goggles (*iggak*), igloos (*qaggiq* – large ceremonial igloo), and seal-skin tents.[168] All of these items were re-created mostly by local artists and elders after traditional models, which either belong to cultural knowledge handed down orally from generation to generation or are based on the journals of William Edward Parry, leader of the British expedition to Igloolik in 1821–23, and on drawings made by Captain George Lyon, who took part in that expedition.[169] The kayak was

---

[163] Raúl Gavez, "In Conversation with Norman Cohn," *Montage* (Spring 2002): 12.

[164] Raúl Gavez, "Epic Inuit: In Conversation with Zacharias Kunuk," *Montage* (Spring 2002): 11.

[165] Zacharias Kunuk (2006, unpublished interview).

[166] *Atanarjuat: The Fast Runner* – webpage at http://www.atanarjuat.com/art_directions /sets/index.html.

[167] Zacharias Kunuk (2006, unpublished interview).

[168] *Atanarjuat: The Fast Runner* – webpages at:
http://www.atanarjuat.com/art_direction/props/caribou_goggles/index.html
http://www.atanarjuat.com/art_direction/props/hunting_tools/index.html
http://www.atanarjuat.com/art_direction/props/qamutik/index.html

[169] This expedition was part of Parry's second attempt of four to find the Northwest Passage, here via the Hudson Bay and Repulse Bay. Lyon's pen-and-ink sketches of Inuit proved to be of major importance to the filmmakers for the re-creation of the costumes, weapons,

rebuilt from drawings made of an almost two hundred year-old kayak in the British Museum, taken there by this expedition. The filmmakers relied on knowledge that has been made part of Western anthropological print and museum discourse. Thus, they restored Inuit cultural knowledge partly by detouring into colonial Western discourse. Because anthropologists and ethnographers can only read cultures that are different from their own within the mind-set of their own cultures, the knowledge that they transmit in their notebooks, film / video, and later print and museums is taken out of its cultural and philological context and is thus subject to misinformation and information gaps where the dimensions and material constitution of objects cease to be a relevant factor. For reconstruction, it is essential, as a corrective, to be familiar with the mind-set and traditional lore of the cultures studied. In the case of the kayak and other props, Inuit traditional knowledge was indispensable to knowing how these objects are made and how to acquire the materials. Thus, the re-appropriated anthropological knowledge about Inuit is only valid in combination with Inuit oral cultural knowledge. By reconstructing a pre-contact Inuit way of life and reviving the traditional making of costumes, tools, weapons, and means of transportation, the film production makes an active contribution toward preserving these traditions and supporting Inuit cultural knowledge.[170]

Cinematic Dialogue With Flaherty

As Indigenous filmmaking is in constant dialogue with colonial film discourse that has objectified and stereotypified colonized cultures and estab-

---

tools, and women's tattoos; Edward Struzik, *Northwest Passage: The Quest for an Arctic Route to the East* (Toronto: Key Porter, 1991): 69, 86; Bernard Saladin d'Anglure, "An Ethnographic Commentary: The Legend of Atanarjuat, Inuit and Shamanism," 205–207; *Atanarjuat: The Fast Runner* – webpages at:
    http://lot47.com/thefastrunner/about_Ancient_Crafts.html
    http://www.atanarjuat.com/art_direction/props/qajaq/index.html
    http://www.atanarjuat.com/cast_characters/index.html
[170] In an interview, Apak Angilirq explains that the research for the movie revealed many traditional activities that were no longer practiced. He points out that the remaking of traditional tools and clothes and revival of ancient cultural activities will help promote traditional Inuit culture in contemporary Arctic communities; Nancy Wachowich, "Interview with Paul Apak Angilirq," in Paul Apak Angilirq, et al. *Atanarjuat: The Fast Runner*, 21. Similarly, Wachowich recounts that actors were transforming into their characters, growing their hair long, learning rituals and rules of behavior, and practising Old Inuktitut. This transformation is not only a passive learning of cultural tradition and language through viewing a film, but an active revival and relearning of these; Wachowich, "Comments by Nancy Wachowich," in Paul Apak Angilirq, et al. *Atanarjuat: The Fast Runner*, 23.

lished them as the 'inferior other', an Arctic film must necessarily be in dialogue with Robert Flaherty's film *Nanook of the North* of 1922. As a pro-
spector, Flaherty undertook four expeditions (1910, 1911, 1913, 1915) to the
Arctic and sub-Arctic, all financed by Sir William Mackenzie, the Canadian railway magnate. During the latter two, Flaherty gathered impressions
and ideas and shot footage for a film about the North that was burned accidentally during editing in Toronto.[171] His fifth expedition, to Port Harrison (a Frères trading post) on the Eastern shore of the Hudson Bay in
1920, was subsidized by the French fur-trading company Revillon Frères, a
competitor of the Hudson's Bay Company that foresaw the advertising
potential of an Arctic film.[172] Here Flaherty set up camp, undertook filming
expeditions, and processed the filmed material that was to become the film
Nanook.

The film invokes the documentary format,[173] pretending to record Inuit
life by following Nanook and his family during their hunting trips and
everyday activities. At the beginning Flaherty announces that the people he
filmed were Itivimiut[174] from Hopewell Sound, Northern Ungara, and he
provides maps of their territory and hunting grounds, all of this data being

---

[171] Paul Rotha, "Nanook and the North," *Studies in Visual Communication* 6.2 (1980):
35–45.

[172] Sherrill E. Grace, "Exploration as Construction: Robert Flaherty and *Nanook of the
North*," *Essays on Canadian Writing* 59 (Fall 1996): 126. The opening titles of *Nanook* give
credit to Revillon Frères as the sponsor.

[173] John Grierson and Richard Griffith have discussed Flaherty's work as documentary,
and both referred to Flaherty as "the father of the documentary film," a 'fact' that entered film
history seemingly unquestioned. Correspondingly, Flaherty's 'realism' in *Nanook* was hailed
and *Nanook* 'became' a documentary film; Richard Griffith, *The World of Robert Flaherty*
(New York & Boston M A: Duell, Sloan & Pearce, Little, Brown, 1953): xiii; Erik Barnouw,
Documentary: A History of the Non-Fiction Film (Oxford: Oxford U P, 1993): 85, Sherrill
Grace, "Exploration as Construction," 127, 134, 137. Jay Ruby explains that Flaherty's contemporaries, except professional anthropologists, regarded Flaherty as an 'amateur' anthropologist and *Nanook* as anthropologically significant; likewise, Flaherty considered himself as
"being an anthropologist or his films as ethnographic"; Ruby, "A Reexamination of the Early
Career of Robert J. Flaherty," *Quarterly Review of Film Studies* 5.4 (Summer 1980): 447.
Brian Winston, on the other hand, distinguishes between critics who see Flaherty as the father
of documentary and prime 'poet' of the cinema and others who criticize his practice of reconstruction and his paternalistic attitude toward his filmed objects. He defines this attitude of
superiority and practice of dramatic re-enactment as "major factors in documentary's flawed
methodological and theoretical foundations"; Winston, "The White Man's Burden: The Example of Robert Flaherty," *Sight and Sound* 54.1 (1984): 58–59.

[174] Flaherty has some misspellings in his intertitles. He spells 'Itivimiuts' as 'Itivimuits'
and 'Cunayoo' as 'Cunayou'.

designed to support the supposed documentary character of his film. In reality, Flaherty instructed the participants to re-enact a traditional, pre-contact, primitive way of life without Western influence. As in Western ethnographic films, he presents everyday cultural activities such as hunting and eating, the making of a kayak and omiak (a bigger boat made of seal and walrus skin), the making of an igloo, glazing the runners of a sled with water, how moss is used as fuel for the hearthstone, while explaining what is done with intertitle cards. His approach entailed staging the events, adding dramatic effects, and erasing the identities of his characters. Nanook is introduced as The Bear, the chief of the Itivimiuts. The real name of Nanook was Allakariallak, and his 'wife' Nyla (played by Alice Nuvalinga) and 'son' Allegoo (played by Phillipoosie) were not Allakariallak's family in reality.[175] Instead, Nuvalinga and an Itivimiut woman who played the character of Cunayoo were Flaherty's common-law wives.[176] The actors were only allowed to wear traditional fur clothes and to use traditional tools and hunting weapons, as if to lend the film anthropological authenticity and to preserve a 'pure' culture that would soon vanish. Flaherty said:

> I am not going to make films about what the white man has made of primitive peoples … What I want to show is the former majesty and character of these people, while it is still possible – before the white man has destroyed not only their character, but the people as well. The urge that I had to make *Nanook* came from the way I felt about these people, my admiration for them; I wanted to tell others about them.[177]

Tobing Rony terms Flaherty's filmmaking "taxidermy" and "romantic preservationism." Drawing on Haraway, she explains taxidermy as a form of representation that presupposes the acknowledgement of death and that entails a desire for the whole and for protection against its loss. Because this ethnographic taxidermy is "'a politics of reproduction'," "in order to make a visual representation of indigenous peoples, one must believe that they are dying, as well as use artifice to make a picture which appears more

---

[175] Sherrill E. Grace, "Exploration as Construction: Robert Flaherty and *Nanook of the North*," 129, 135.
[176] Fatimah Tobing Rony, "Taxidermy and Romantic Ethnography: Robert Flaherty's *Nanook of the North*," in Fatimah Tobing Rony, *The Third Eye: Race, Cinema, and Ethnographic Spectacle* (Durham NC & London: Duke UP, 1996): 123.
[177] Robert J. Flaherty, from *The Flaherty Papers*, Box 59, quoted in Erik Barnouw, *Documentary: A History of the Non-Fiction Film*, 45; ellipsis in original.

true, more pure."[178] Flaherty managed to film a walrus hunt as it was done in pre-contact times without the use of guns,[179] and, likewise, Nanook arrives at the trading post with a large bundle of polar fox and polar bear furs in order to trade for knives (which we do not see him use), beads, and bright-colored candy – no other metal tools and guns. Almost every sign of Western contact that had already influenced Inuit cultural and economic activities was banned from his film,[180] although the Quebec Inuit in the 1920s were part of the fur-trading system and its cash economy, were using guns for hunting, wore Western clothes, and were certainly acquainted with Western diseases.[181] This essentializing attempt to preserve 'authentic' pre-contact Indigenous cultures on celluloid only reflects the maker's constructed, clichéd, and ethnocentric image of 'the Inuit'.

Flaherty was infatuated with the universal theme of man fighting against natural forces, of people living and surviving in harsh environments. In *Nanook*, he is very careful to describe the Arctic landscape dramatically in intertitles as "mysterious Barren Lands – desolate, boulder-strewn, wind-swept – illimitable spaces which top the world" and the Arctic winter as "long nights – the wail of the wind – short, bitter days – snow smoking fields of sea and plain – the brass ball of sun a mockery in the sky – the mercury near bottom." To him, the North has a "melancholic spirit," expressed by the "shrill piping of the wind, the rasp and hiss of driving snow, the mournful wolf howls of Nanook's master dog." He complements these intertitles with dull dark images of Arctic plains, drifting ice floes, and the family fighting their way through a blizzard, all of which helps establish this melancholy space. However, Flaherty also has scenes that were filmed in bright Arctic sunlight and that compromise somewhat his illusion of a gloomy atmosphere. He tells the viewer that only one 'race', the "most

---

[178] Tobing Rony, "Taxidermy and Romantic Ethnography," 102, 244.

[179] This scene was, according to Flaherty, suggested by the Inuk Wetalltok; Robert J. Flaherty in collaboration with Frances Flaherty, *My Eskimo Friends* (Garden City NY: Doubleday, 1924): 126–27, quoted in Jay Ruby, "A Reexamination of the Early Career of Robert J. Flaherty," 449–50.

[180] Although Flaherty's objective was to stage a 'pure' pre-contact Inuit way of life, as shown by his refusal to allow the Inuit own Western clothes, tools, and firearms, he was not careful enough to keep fully to this objective. Thus, the walrus hunters use something like field glasses to spot out the walrus, Allegoo has a little toboggan that definitely needs nails to keep its wooden parts together, and in the winter sequence Flaherty shows dwellings that are set up close to a church building.

[181] Tobing Rony, "Taxidermy and Romantic Ethnography," 109.

cheerful people in all the world – the fearless, lovable, happy-go-lucky Eskimo," can survive in this space characterized by a "sterility of the soil and the rigor of the climate." Flaherty more than once stresses that the people live constantly under the threat of death, as when he says that "the desert interior, if deer hunting fails, is the country of death – for there is no food," "Nanook's band already on the thin edge of starvation," and "almost perishing from the ice blasts and unable to reach their own house." He presents the Arctic as a desolate, uninviting, very cold space, subject to the whims of northern winds, where people might feel insignificant and powerless in the face of the brutal forces of nature.

So how does Flaherty reconcile the "most cheerful people in all the world" with this rough unrelenting natural environment? He introduces Nanook, the great hunter, who withstands all hardships and masters hunting in challenging Arctic conditions. While Flaherty correctly underscores the harsh Inuit reality with the daily struggle for food and, consequently, survival, he seems to overdo it here and there in order to have his hero Nanook appear even more heroic – almost like a superhero. When Nanook comes to the trading post, Flaherty almost brags about Nanook's having killed seven polar bears that year, "which in hand to hand encounters he killed with nothing more formidable than his harpoon." When an ice field seals the coast, Flaherty depicts how the great Nanook is able to manoeuver his kayak through the ice floes, to traverse them, to find a good fishing spot, and finally to make a good catch with a fish spear and without live bait. The intertitle reads "Though Nanook's band, already on the thin edge of starvation, is unable to move, Nanook, great hunter that he is, saves the day," revealing that these intertitles are often strategically placed in order to enhance dramatic tension. In the same vein, the first intertitle during the walrus-hunt scene reads: "with the discovery of a group asleep on shore the suspense begins," literally betraying Flaherty's aim to give the filmed hunt a suspenseful feel. Similarly, he describes the walrus as a ferocious animal that is "well called the 'tiger of the North'" and appropriate game for the great Nanook and his mates. That the 'actors' at one point were in considerable danger of being drawn into the sea as they were not used to the traditional hunting method anymore is an unpleasant aspect that is too easily glossed over. The hunters asked Flaherty to intervene with a rifle, which he refused to do for the sake of his picture.[182] On a closer look,

---

[182] Erik Barnouw, *Documentary: A History of the Non-Fiction Film*, 36–37.

however, one can assume that the two men who turn their heads several times in the direction of the camera were asking for help. Allakariallak died of hunger two years after *Nanook* was made. This fact exposes the gap between Flaherty's idealistic Nanook and the real Allakariallak, who lost the battle for survival.

The theme of man fighting for survival in hostile environments was to become the central theme of two other films by Flaherty, *Moana: A Romance of the Golden Age* (1926) and *Man of Aran* (1934). The latter is a dramatic story set on the Aran islands off the coast of Ireland, portraying a fictitious nuclear family that tries to make a living in the barren environment by fishing in the rough sea and farming land that has no fertile soil. The custom of shark hunting, abandoned ninety years before, was re-enacted for the film, delivering some exciting and thrilling pictures.[183] *Moana* is shot on the Samoan islands, where Flaherty sought out communities who had not yet been exposed to Western contact; he draw a blank, however – the missionaries were always one step ahead of him. Because this environment was not so hostile as in *Nanook* and *Man of Aran* (except for a group of wild boars), the story of man fighting against unrelenting natural forces would not have worked as nicely. Thus, *Moana* is focussed on a love story and the tattooing initiation ceremony of Ta'avale alias Moana, a custom that was almost extinct by the time of Flaherty's filming.[184] The very subtitle *A Romance of the Golden Age* is a romantic revitalization of the 'Golden Age' trope, now inscribed by Flaherty in colonial film discourse.[185]

Flaherty's three films are clearly reflections of colonialist policies: exploration of foreign, exotic worlds, mapping these 'other' worlds in film discourse and objectifying them in films that combine an anthropological thirst for knowledge and narrative with preconceived eurocentric notions of these worlds. The cultural and natural background of these films varies, but the taxidermic preservation with patterns are the same: a fictitious family with invented names is followed during the course of everyday activities, most of which are staged. Abandoned customs are reintroduced and signs of Western influence banned wherever possible. Consequently, all three films are nostalgic re-enactments of an exoticized, 'pure' past of the three

---

[183] "Flaherty's *Man of Aran*," at http://www.iol.ie/~galfilm/filmwest/19aran.htm
[184] Barnouw, *Documentary: A History of the Non-Fiction Film*, 47–48; Frances Flaherty, "Flaherty: Samoa," *Filmkritik* 5.245 (1977): 255–60.
[185] For the discourse of the Golden Age, see above, chapter 3, fn 96.

different cultures. The paradox is that Flaherty was aware of the devastating influences of Western contact and that he, as explorer and filmmaker,
was part of the colonizing process. Like the anthropologists, he resolved "to
capture on film the nature of rapidly vanishing cultures," a practice that became known as 'salvage ethnography'.[186] On the one hand, Flaherty expressed reverence for and sensitivity toward the cultures he studied, as
demonstrated by his (nevertheless paternalistic) practice of filming in a way
that enlisted the collaboration of the people being filmed[187] and by the fact
that he had spent considerable time living with these cultures (sixteen
months at Port Harrison – now Inukjual – and more than a year in Safune,
Samoa).[188] By including the Inuit in the production process of *Nanook*,
"from acting, to the repair of cameras, to the printing and developing of the
film, to the suggestion of film scenes,"[189] and by showing film rushes to the
crew to see their reaction, Flaherty established the myth of 'ethnographic
participant observation' that purportedly showed the ethnographer's and
also the filmed subjects' view of themselves.[190] On the other hand, he
fostered the idea that the people being studied should revere him, even consider him as the 'Big White Chief' or Angarooka, 'the white master', in the
case of the Inuit.[191] This idea was conditioned by his attitude of being a
member of a superior culture and having the right to film 'vanishing' inferior cultures. Brian Winston terms this attitude the "divine right of filmmakers,"[192] which aligns anthropological filmmaking with the colonial concept of Manifest Destiny. Flaherty's sense of superiority also comes to the
fore in the way in which he presents the Itivimiuts. Throughout the film

---

[186] Erik Barnouw, *Documentary: A History of the Non-Fiction Film*, 45.

[187] In his own words, he saw them as "partners" and was aware of the fact that his project
depended upon them: "My work had been built up along with them; I couldn't have done
anything without them"; Robert J. Flaherty, "Robert Flaherty Talking," in *Cinema 1950*, ed.
Roger Manvell (Harmondsworth: Pelican, 1950): 13–14, 18–19, quoted in in Jay Ruby, "A
Reexamination of the Early Career of Robert J. Flaherty," 449, 437.

[188] Paul Rotha, "Nanook and the North," *Studies in Visual Communication* 6.2 (1980): 45;
Frances Flaherty, "Flaherty: Samoa," 260.

[189] Flaherty acknowledges the support of the Itivimiut in the opening titles, which might
have supported the belief in the myth of 'ethnographic participant observation'. He also made
sure in his contract with Revillon Frères that the (participating) Inuit would receive a $3,000
credit at Port Harrison as remuneration; Jay Ruby, "A Reexamination of the Early Career of
Robert J. Flaherty," 449.

[190] Fatimah Tobing Rony, "Taxidermy and Romantic Ethnography," 118.

[191] Tobing Rony, "Taxidermy and Romantic Ethnography," 120.

[192] Brian Winston, "The White Man's Burden: The Example of Robert Flaherty," 59.

there is the sense of the benevolent fatherly filmmaker who is proud to be able to present his happy yet tough children, something underscored by Flaherty's calling them the "cheerful [...] fearless, lovable, happy-go-lucky Eskimo."

As in Flaherty's *Nanook*, Kunuk's *Atanarjuat* also exhibits ethnographic traits, since he presents pre-contact Inuit culture, remade traditional props, and traditional women's facial tattoos. He takes time to show everyday cultural activities in the camp, such as eating raw meat, skinning animals, preparing the runners of a sled, and building ceremonial igloos. Further, he contextualizes traditional competitions and entertainment games such as women's throat singing, Inuit boxing,[193] a singing contest, and a contest in which the corner of the opponent's mouth is pulled until one gives up. Kunuk does not, however, present traditional weddings, initiation rituals, burial ceremonies or the like, which are generally essential elements of Western ethnographic films (not *Nanook*, though), and which would have been legitimized by the film's plot as one generation grows up, Atanarjuat and Amaqjuaq marry, and Kumaglak, Amaqjuaq, and Sauri die. Thus we can conclude that Kunuk is not interested in giving a complete ethnographic picture of his Inuit culture. In contrast to Flaherty's film, which gives the impression of a documentary but is largely staged, Kunuk embeds these 'ethnographic facts' in a dramatic story that is set in pre-contact times, thereby necessarily involving the staging of a pre-contact life-style. In accordance with the character and dramatic potential of the legend, he emphasizes the tensions between the characters, but he does not, as Flaherty does, enhance dramatic tension during hunts. Kunuk shows aspects of traditional Inuit life from an inside perspective, without commentary, and unobtrusively. These aspects support a narrative, instead of being the sole purpose of a film that looks at an 'other', 'exotic' culture from the outside perspective. Thus, he weaves traditional cultural knowledge into the mythic narrative to acquaint non-Inuit viewers *en passant* with fundamental cultural aspects.

In a documentary by Claude Massot that revisits Inukjuak (Port Harrison), the location of Flaherty's film, the manager of the local TV-station,

---

[193] Traditionally, conflicts and personal animosities were settled through a singing contest (not throat-singing), where each side would present a song that ridiculed the other side and where the audience would decide the winner. If this contest could not settle the conflict, physical competitions such as Inuit boxing would have to straighten out the fronts. During an Inuit boxing match, both opponents take turns punching the other on the temple while the other has to hold still; whoever knocks the other out has won (d'Anglure, "An Ethnographic Commentary," 223).

Moses Nowkawalk, presents some clips of *Nanook of the North* and comments on serious flaws and misrepresentations on Flaherty's part. He explains that the characters in *Nanook* wear polar-bear pants, although they were not typical of the region where he filmed and that for lighting reasons the tops of the igloo props were cut off and that the characters were filmed in these igloo props practically outside in the cold.[194] A closer look at these 'inside' scenes also reveals that the sunlight illuminates the igloo set.

Furthermore, the character of Nanook is ridiculed, as he has to pretend at the trading post that he had never seen a gramophone before; Flaherty shows him wondering at it and actually biting into the record. This trading-post scene is a staged example of the first contact game 'I give you an object and you will certainly misuse it, making a fool out of yourself but making me laugh' – and this is the whole intention. Flaherty here is playing on the animal instinct of checking out whether or not objects encountered are food by sniffing or tasting, thereby attributing a non-human trait to the Inuit. In this way, he characterizes them as savage-like, naive, and instinctual and excludes them from the category of human beings equipped with the capacity for abstract thought. Tobing Rony states that the gramophone incident "reassures the viewer of the contrast between the Primitive and the Modern" and that "this conceit, of course, obscures the Inuit's own appropriation of the new technology, their participation in the production of the film."[195] The intertitle tells us that "in deference to Nanook, the great hunter, the trader entertains and attempts to explain the principle of a gramophone – how the white man 'cans' his voice." The caption is pure hegemonic irony, because we are aware that Allakariallak knew gramophones, and because the phrase 'in deference' ridicules the Itivimiuts with Flaherty pretending that the trader 'humbles himself' to an 'ignorant' Itivimiut, switching positions in the racial hierarchy constructed in Western discourse. Similarly, the phrase "'cans' his voice" betrays Flaherty's conviction that the childlike Itivimiut could not understand the concept of sound storage and need an oversimplified explanation within 'their own' framework of thought. Flaherty addresses the Western viewer in the same way, as though to give an idea of how the Inuit 'need to be addressed'. Another intertitle in the trading-post sequence equates an Itivimiut child with a dog, announcing that "Nyla [...] displays her young husky, too"

---

[194] Claude Massot, dir., *Nanook Revisited* (USA, 1994).
[195] Fatimah Tobing Rony, "Taxidermy and Romantic Ethnography," 112–13.

after she is seen with her newborn in her hood. Also at the trading post, the character of Allegoo takes a spoonful of castor oil because he has supposedly eaten too many sea biscuits; he smiles broadly and pretends that he actually likes it. In the record and castor-oil incidents, Flaherty represents the Itivimiuts as ignorant children, who need lessons from their well-meaning parents, thus catering further to the father-and-child relation of filmmaker and filmed in *Nanook*. Furthermore, Flaherty staged a seal hunt by having two ice holes connected by a rope beneath the ice; Nanook, pretending, after having harpooned 'the seal', pulls at one end of the rope while others off-screen pull at the other end to imitate a seal first resisting and finally being hauled out of the water. The seal-hunt scene functions to parody this Inuit hunting activity by rendering it as slapstick comedy – 2.40 minutes of tug-of-war before they are able to haul 'the seal' out of the water. In both the trading-post and the seal-hunt scenes, the Western filmmaker ridicules individuals of the 'other' culture to present them as deficient, animalistic, childlike, and unable to engage in cultural activities, clearly constructing his own culture as superior and the one studied as inferior.

Flaherty said in a BBC interview in 1945:

> [Films] are very well suited to portraying the lives of primitive people whose lives are simply lived and who feel strongly, but whose activities are external and dramatic rather than internal and complicated. I don't think you could make a good film of the love affairs of an Eskimo [...] because they never show much feeling in their faces, but you can make a very good film of Eskimos spearing a walrus.[196]

Nevertheless, at the beginning of his film Flaherty includes a ten-second close-up of Allakariallak's face and an eight-seconds medium close-up of Alice Nuvalinga's face – for what reason must remain unclear, as, according to him, the Inuit show hardly any emotion in their faces. His opinion of Inuit as film subjects seems to be diametrically opposed to Kunuk's view, not least thanks to Kunuk's inside perspective and Flaherty's outside perspective. Flaherty felt that Inuit are only good at showing their external activities; Kunuk felt the opposite, and made a film about spiritual conflicts

---

[196] Robert J. Flaherty, Recorded BBC Talks, London 14 June, 25 July, 5 September 1949, quoted in Jay Ruby, "A Reexamination of the Early Career of Robert J. Flaherty," 448, and Tobing Rony, "Taxidermy and Romantic Ethnography: Robert Flaherty's *Nanook of the North*," 104.

and human relations set in a melodramatic plot about love, hate, murder, and revenge. In doing so, he very often works with close-ups on faces in order to suggest thoughts and feelings. Unlike Flaherty, Kunuk also manages to convey the humoristic side of Inuit social life. There are many bodily jokes and sexual references in conversations and songs, as when Oki and Atanarjuat, before their boxing match, ridicule each other in their songs, which attempt to mock the other's sex life. Kunuk also includes sex scenes and a quite humorous scene in which men are seen, from behind, urinating. Here *Atanarjuat*, like *Big Bear*, resonates with the straightforward treatment of sexuality and bodily functions that is characteristic of most Indigenous cultures. Hence, Kunuk normalizes Flaherty's immaculate Inuit superhero and the notion of the noble savage without bodily needs.

In his references to Flaherty's film *Nanook*, Kunuk uses the strategy of subversive quotation. In one scene, he quotes directly from Nanook's arrival at a shoreline, when Atanarjuat returns from a hunting/fishing trip (sequence 16) and paddles ashore (Figs. 9.1–9.2). Whereas, in Flaherty's film, this scene prompts laughter and again borders on mockery of the Itivimiuts as Nanook's whole family (wife, baby, second wife) and a puppy one after the other emerge from the one-man canoe (the son Allegoo was perched on the bow), Kunuk neutralizes the scene by creating a rather idyllic and romantic picture of the hunter/fisherman returning home to his family. Kunuk, too, uses polar-bear pants, but instead of having everybody wear them and creating a pan-Inuit mash,[197] he has only the evil shaman wear such pants in order to distinguish him as a shaman and to stress that he is a stranger from other parts.[198] Similarly, Kunuk merely hints at a seal hunt by showing his characters waiting patiently at various breathing holes (sequence 33), again neutralizing Flaherty's parody through calm images (Fig. 9.3). In stark contrast to Flaherty's *Nanook*, which centers on hunting activities, in *Atanarjuat* we often see men bringing home the catch on sleds, but we do not see an animal being killed. This is not a case of cinematic political correctness in the sense of 'No animals were harmed during or in connection with the production of this film', because the animals killed in the film are the game that was shot by commissioned hunters to provide food for crew and cast. As Kunuk says in an interview, the acts of hunting as such were not crucial elements of the legends, supporting the thesis that

---

[197] For this term, see this chapter, fn 74 above.

[198] *Atanarjuat: The Fast Runner* – webpage at http://www.atanarjuat.com/art_direction /costumes/index.html

the presentation of ethnographic details was not the objective of the film. What, however, are indeed crucial narrative elements are the many close-ups of various kinds of raw meat and fish being prepared and eaten, as well as other everyday activities. In the same interview, Kunuk explains that they wanted to show how the Inuit lived.[199] By emphasizing some cultural elements and ignoring others, Kunuk denies the objectifying, ethnographic colonial gaze any opportunity by creating an autonomous gaze at his own culture, choosing not to give a complete picture.

Last but not least, the endings of the films differ greatly. Flaherty has the family seeking refuge from a blizzard in an abandoned igloo and go to sleep as they were "[a]lmost perishing from the icy blasts and unable to reach their own snowhouse." The last images show the sleeping family, the raging storm, and the sled dogs in the cold with the "mournful wolf howls of Nanook's master dog" that "typify the melancholy spirit of the North." He thus caters to the trope of the 'vanishing Indian' and announces the end of traditional Inuit life that he, with his film, tried to preserve and reproduce as taxidermy. Kunuk ends his film with the family having assembled in a sod house and driving the evil spirits away. The ending suggests that Ata-narjuat's son Kumaglak will be the future leader in the spirit of old Kuma-glak as young Kumaglak enters the sod house at the moment in which Panikpak calls for the old Kumaglak.[200] While Flaherty metaphorically indicates death, Kunuk indicates continuation of life.

Translating Oral Tradition into Film[201]

When Indigenous filmmakers translate oral knowledge into the medium of film and video, they have to be aware of certain changes that they subject the material to. Oral tradition is kept alive through the continuous 'live' re-telling of the same legends, each telling responding to immediate condi-tions, atmosphere, audience, and teller by introducing minor adjustments and changes. Oral tradition, unlike Western modes of knowledge transfor-

---

[199] Zacharias Kunuk (2006, unpublished interview).

[200] According to Inuit belief, dead parents could be reincarnated by naming babies after them. In *Atanarjuat*, Panikpak names Atuat after her own dead mother and Atuat's son Kumaglak after her dead husband; Bernard Saladin d'Anglure, "An Ethnographic Commen-tary: The legend of Atanarjuat, Inuit and Shamanism," in Paul Apak Angilirq et al., *Atanar-juat: The Fast Runner* (Toronto: Coach House/Isuma, 2002): 213.

[201] This first paragraph is a summary of the concerns and issues that filmmakers face when translating an oral legend into film that were discussed in the section on "Filming Oral Tradi-tion" in chapter 3.

mation – print, film – is a medium of the moment. As soon as words are
spoken, they are gone, and with them, the information they contain; this can
only be retrieved later in the same mode through a renewed telling. Only
when oral information is transformed into the Western media of video/film
and print can it be retrieved again and again without the authority of the
sender/storyteller. The filming of such a legend removes this oral knowledge from its original narrative context. The immediate and primary quality
of the mythtelling is lost and replaced, through the mediation of the filmmaker, by a secondary mythtelling. The words and performance of one
storyteller now become an authorially narrated story constructed, acted out,
and realized by a group of people. The means of transmitting information,
the audiovisual impulse, is put at a further remove by electronic recording.
Furthermore, the filming freezes one version of the legend and breaks with
the continuum of change and adaptation of the story as transmitted in oral
tradition. Screening the film for a non-Inuit audience also removes this oral
knowledge from the cultural context necessary to maintain its full compre-
hension and function. For filmmakers, there is also the issue of the lan-
guage(s) in which the oral knowledge is to be rendered; employing English
subjects oral knowledge to colonialist influence and risks a loss of the
cultural context of the spoken words. Employing the traditional language
secures the cultural context of the spoken words but limits the film audience. The filmmaking team of *Atanarjuat* has solved this problem by
having all the characters speak Inuktitut and providing English subtitles. Of
course, the subtitles distract the viewers' attention from the visuals, but
they seem to be the best pragmatic option for getting around the language
problem. There are increasingly fewer among the younger Inuit generation
who are capable of speaking their traditional language; by choosing to film
in Inuktitut, the filmmakers foster pride in, and the survival of, this language.[202]

---

[202] In spite of the development of a formal Canadian education system in the 1950s, which
at the beginning exclusively employed English and discouraged the use of Inuktitut (this
policy was gradually abandoned in the present-day Nunavut area in the 1970s), the use of
Inuktitut remained rather strong among adults. In 1984, more than ninety percent of Inuit in
the eastern Arctic were reporting Inuktitut as their home language; Jean–Philippe Chartrand,
"Survival and Adaptation of the Inuit Ethnic Identity: The Importance of Inuktitut," in *Native
People, Native Lands: Canadian Indians, Inuit and Metis*, ed. Bruce Alden Cox (Ottawa:
Carleton U P, 1992): 242–47. Roughly thirty years later, in 2001, about seventy percent of
Nunavut's population speak Inuktitut as their first language. English is the working language
of Nunavut's government, and is used as intercultural lingua franca and increasingly among
Inuit as well. In places like Iqaluit, where home bilingualism is widespread, Inuit children,

Kunuk and his team have taken great pains to render this legend with as much fidelity as possible to its model in Inuit oral tradition. The team recorded eight Igloolik elders telling their versions of the legend and combined these into one final version. Elders were also consulted for cultural and linguistic accuracy during the various stages of the scriptwriting process.[203] At no point does the film allow the viewer to draw any conclusion about the time period in which the story takes place, reinforcing the fact that this is a timeless myth. The story is narrated by Panikpak, wife of the community leader and the shaman Kumaglak, who is killed in a spiritual contest at the beginning. That she is the narrator is not as obvious as in *Smoke Signals*, where Thomas's voice-over narration at the beginning, intermittently, and at the end clearly identifies him as the narrator. Panikpak only has one small part of voice-over narration, partly as a sound bridge between sequences 3 and 4 and at the beginning of sequence 4, when Qulitalik and Nirinuniq prepare to leave the community to settle elsewhere (3) and when Kumaglak and Tungajuaq have their spiritual contest and Tungajuaq casts his evil spell on the community (4). She recounts: "We never knew what he was or why it happened. Evil came to us like Death. It just happened and we had to live with it." But at this moment, her narrative role is asserted.[204] Throughout the film, this role is supported by cinematic means, her face being framed repeatedly in close-up, the camera trying to explore her thoughts and conveying her view of the events occurring. Often, sequences end with such a shot, focussing on her even though she has no part in the immediate action. At the end of the film, she is the one who bans Puja, Oki, his friends and their families from the community.

---

adolescents, and young adults to a larger extent use English, not least because school instruction in Inuktitut ends after grade four; Julie Tomiak, "Talking Power: Language Policies and Practices in Nunavut," paper presented at the CINSA National Conference (Peterborough, Ontario: Trent University, 2005): 3–7. More drastically, Alexina Kublu & Mick Mallon warn that today very few Inuit children in Western Nunavut speak, or even understand, Inuktitut, and that the survival of Inuktitut depends on the younger generations. They make it clear that parents have to show strong commitment to maintain Inuktitut as the home language and that instilling pride in the language and a determination to use it, especially with younger generations, is essential for the survival of Inuktitut; Kublu & Mallon, "Our Language, Our Selves," at http://www.nunavut.com/nunavut99/english/our.html#3

[203] Nancy Wachowich, "Interview with Paul Apak Angilirq," in Paul Apak Angilirq, et al. *Atanarjuat: The Fast Runner*, 19; Norman Cohn, "The Art of Community-Based Filmmaking," in Paul Apak Angilirq, et al. *Atanarjuat: The Fast Runner*, 25.

[204] See the discussion of three roles of storytellers in the section on "Filming Oral Tradition" in chapter 3 above.

During her speech, she is first photographed from a low angle, then from a slight low angle, and finally from a straight angle in close-up, these shots being intercut with shots of the community members. At this point, the story and cinematography lend more importance to her character than to others. Thus, of the characters who do not belong to the inner circle around whom the main conflict revolves (Atanarjuat, Oki, Atuat), Panikpak is the one who is most highlighted. Because her role in the legend does not qualify her to be given any greater emphasis cinematically than, for example, Qulitalik, Sauri, or Tulimaq, we must conclude that in addition to Panikpak's brief voice-over this filmic emphasis designates her as the storyteller and confirms her narrative role.

The narrative of *Atanarjuat* develops as in classical drama. There is the exposition (sequences 1–5), where the cause of the evil spell and the rivalry is introduced. The conflict is developed with rising dramatic action in sequences 6 through 24, and with the catastrophe and climax in the murder sequence (25) and Atanarjuat's escape sequence (27). The rest of the narrative develops with falling dramatic action in sequences 28 through 41 and the resolution of the conflict in sequences 42 and 43. These last two also form minor climaxes, with Atanarjuat fighting Oki's gang and Qulitalik and Panikpak successfully driving away the evil spirit. The latter part of sequence 43 functions as an epilogue in which the mean-spirited characters Oki, Puja, Pakak, Pittiulaq and their families are sentenced to leave the community.

The film *Atanarjuat* takes the non-Inuit viewer into a cultural and contextual limbo which it is difficult to relate to. Nor will such a viewer be familiar with the legend. For the non-Inuit viewer, this mythic space is constructed in a threefold way. First, the viewer is aware that this is an Inuit legend translated into film, where a DVD-player, VCR, or computer is the storyteller. The film is viewed from within cultural contexts that differ from the one being represented, and it is understood that the myth is taking place in a non-Western, almost non-rational space in which it assumes greater credibility. Secondly, the film contextualizes shamanic activities and displays items that have shamanic power (e.g., the polar-bear and walrus-necklaces of the two shamans). Here, Western viewers are confronted with activities and objects that in their cultures are usually exoticized and most often defined as belonging to the sphere of myth. Thirdly, much of the story's action is motivated by prophecies and shamanic powers which are again understood as supernatural. Atanarjuat's escape from Oki's gang

across the Arctic snow and ice, running naked and barefoot for an incre-
dibly long distance,[205] is also made possible by good spirits and superhuman strength, unreal in a Western context.

Prophecies have the function of foretelling what is going to happen,
which usually becomes 'true' within the realm of myth. In *Atanarjuat*,
Qulitalik prophesies twice, after the visit of the evil shaman and Kumaglak's death, that "Tulimaq is the one they'll go after now," meaning that
Tulimaq and his family will be the ones who will suffer from the influence
of bad spirits. Upon leaving the community and saying good-bye to his sister after the fatal night, Qulitalik and Panikpak prophesy that there will be
times when Qulitalik's spiritual help is necessary and that he will be able to
help:

QULITALIK
Sister, if you ever need me....

PANIKPAK
Yes, I know you'll come when I call for help in my heart. Take my husband's rabbit's foot. You'll need it some day.

This prophecy comes true: Panikpak calls her brother for help when Atuat,
out of the need to provide for Panikpak and Kumaglak, resolves tearfully to
offer herself to Oki (sequence 35) and when Qulitalik changes Oki's personality with a rabbit spirit. Also fulfilled are Panikpak's and Tulimaq's
prophecies that one day Tulimaq's sons will end Tulimaq's constant ridicule and will help the community (sequence 8).

Doubtlessly, the presentation of Inuit shamanism[206] posed a major challenge for the filmmakers. According to the legend, an evil shaman lays a
curse on a small community, and the film likewise starts with the evil
shaman visiting and entering into a spiritual contest with Kumaglak, the
community's shaman. In such a contest, the hands and feet of both shamans
would be tied, they would fall into a *sakaniq* (shaman's trance), and their
spirits would have to fight. As such a spiritual contest is hard to present in a
film, the viewers see only the two shamans being tied, sitting face to face,

---

[205] The filmmakers provide a map of the localities of the myth. According to the map,
Atanarjuat fled approximately thirty kilometers from Qikirtaarjuk to Siuraq across the pack
ice. Accordingly, d'Anglure holds that Atanarjuat ran about twenty miles to Qulitalik's camp
on the island of Siuraq ("An Ethnographic Commentary," 201; *Atanarjuat: The Fast Runner*
– webpage at http://atanarjuat.com/legend/esp_legend/legend_land.html).
[206] On Inuit shamanism, see d'Anglure, "An Ethnographic Commentary," 209–15.

falling into a trance, and imitating the sounds of their helping animal spirits (polar bear and walrus) until Kumaglak falls down motionless because his spirit has not returned to his body (Fig. 9.4). Here, the filmmakers clearly avoid a kitschy and special-effects presentation of spirits; the viewer has to rely on facial close-ups that show the people's reactions in order to know that spirits are in the room. For a Western viewer it is almost impossible to understand why and how Kumaglak is killed, because visual access to the two shamans is partly blocked and viewers cannot quite see what is going on and because there is no 'clear' explanation of this event. Also, killing somebody in Western cultures usually involves using chemicals or physical force and the notion of being able to kill with spiritual force is wellnigh incomprehensible to a rationalistic Western mind. At this point, the filmmakers are clearly dividing the audience into those who do and those who do not grasp the events of this sequence.

Later, Kumaglak's spirit helps Atanarjuat win the Inuit boxing match (sequence 15) and distracts the murderers' attention so that Atanarjuat can escape after his brother is killed (sequence 25). Qulitalik's spirit appears to help Atanarjuat find his way to his camp during this escape (sequence 27). These and other spirits are usually photographed as 'real' people, sometimes rendered with the help of dissolves, superimposition, strange sounds, and alienated voices that seem to come from far away (Figs. 9.5–9.6). But the viewer mostly has to deduce from the context when a spirit appears. In the case of the evil shaman's spirit, help is afforded by the accompanying idiosyncratic giggle. The evoking of the spirits of remote or dead relatives is effected either by the caller looking aside and calling or calling through seal-oil lamps, neither of which is realized with special effects but with shots of the lamps and of the faces of the caller and the spirit being called, supported by the alienated sound of the voices. Atanarjuat's superhuman jump across the crack in the pack ice and Qulitalik's rounding a stone cairn to change Oki's personality with a rabbit spirit are rendered in slow motion, also an indication that supernatural events are occurring. At the end, the evil spirit in the sod house simply vanishes by means of a dissolve. The upshot of all this is that the appearance of spirits as human beings, the limited use of the post-production effects of alienating sounds, dissolves, superimposition, and slow motion, and the avoidance of special-effects magical occurrences present these shamanic and spiritual activities as 'ordinary' and rooted in Inuit philosophy and as anchored in the everyday life of the people in this timeless myth. The shamanic and spiritual activities are nothing special and absolutely believable within the realm of the filmic world. Thus, the film re-introduces the traditional shamanic heritage into contemporary Inuit cultural knowledge and counters the colonialist erasure of this heritage.

Arctic Colors, Movement, and Other Cinematic Motifs

The film contains different motifs that connect the sequences and help to create a cinematic whole. The most obvious is the visual motif of the various different color nuances in Arctic ice and snow. The film opens with a striking extreme long shot (49 sec.) of a bluish snowy landscape in the Arctic twilight, where the sky and the ground merge at the horizon and a pale sun hovers above the scene. We see a male Inuit figure walking with a few sled dogs, accompanied by the eerie sound of the blowing wind and the howling dogs. This scene works very nicely to set the stage for mythic events occurring in a timeless suspended world. Also throughout the film, the camera highlights the sometimes whitish, bluish, greyish, and golden refractions of snow and ice in the unique Arctic light. In sequences set on sunny days, the snow assumes a blindingly bright white, set off from the blue sky and the bluish shadows of little snow mounds and snow drifts. During the two sequences in the *qaggiq* (13 and 15), the sun renders the igloo walls translucent with the bright Arctic light entering the interior space. Sequence 13 contains a wonderful low-angle shot that shows a man from below inserting the last snow blocks to finish off the dome-shaped roof of the *qaggiq*. Again, the sun makes the snow blocks look like glass (Fig. 9.7). In other interior scenes, the bluish Arctic twilight sometimes shines through the igloo walls (e.g., sequence 8). During daylight sequences without sun, the snow becomes an indefinite shapeless white. In contre-jour shots during summer sequences (e.g., 20 and 22) the snow assumes a white-to-golden quality set off against brownish stripes of exposed earth. During summer sequences realized with natural backlight, the quality of the snow varies between a shapeless white and a white-bluish color that draw the contours of the surface. After Tulimaq's return from his hunt toward the end of the day (sequence 6), sky and snow become a milky light-blue. Arctic whiteness in its numerous shades is balanced against subdued brownish and greyish colors of earth and washed-out rocks in summer camps, seagrass, and the also often dark interior of igloos and sod houses. Thus, the filmmakers very carefully depict the various qualities of Arctic colors and Arctic light and highlight the beauty of their interplay.

Although the Artic generally might suggest that people are in a state of frozen mobility, the film counters such an impression. It contextualizes the frequent hunting trips and implies, through the various locations, the current movements of people between winter, summer, and hunting camps according to the availability and migratory patterns of Arctic animals. Thus, movement becomes another unifying motif in *Atanarjuat*. Although the film does not feature people's movements between the camps as in *Big Bear*, it strongly emphasizes the hunting activities. In six sequences (6, 12, 16, 17, 24, 34), men either return from or leave for a hunt (Figs. 9.8–9.14). These scenes are sometimes realized by filming the hunters from various angles and at different camera distances, intercut with shots of the people at the camp awaiting them.[207] Sequence 16 opens with a contre-jour shot of Atanarjuat paddling toward the shore and singing an old song, his silhouette set off against the dark cliffs and the white and golden glittering water (Atanarjuat's return takes 1.48 min.; Fig. 9.1). The other movements leaving for or returning from hunts are not depicted as idyllic and romantic but, rather, reveal the harshness of Arctic life. When Atanarjuat and Puja move to the summer caribou-hunting ground (sequence 18), they are shown walking along a shoreline and having to carry the tent, provisions, and hunting gear on their backs. When Tulimaq returns from a hunt (sequence 6; 2.30 min.), his empty sled stands in stark contrast to the rich bag that the other hunters unload. Also, disappointment and sadness on the faces of Pittaluk and Tulimaq because he did not bring home any game are polarized against the happiness about the good hunt on the faces of the other people. Later in the film, the situation is revised. When Oki and Atanarjuat return from a hunt (sequence 12; Oki's return screen-time 27 sec.; Atanarjuat's 32 sec.), Oki can hardly conceal his frustration about his bad luck and his slow dogs, whereas Atanarjuat and his parents are very happy about Atanarjuat's rich catch and Tulimaq announces that he will host a feast for everyone.

In such sequences, the film underlines the fact that hunting is the prime subsistence activity, that continual good hunts are necessary for survival, and that bad luck in hunting can result in starvation if there is no community to share their meat resources. The ridicule that Tulimaq experiences and the fact that he keeps getting the leftovers of the hunted seals also indicate that a bad or unlucky hunter becomes wholly dependent on the mercy of the others and furthermore risks subjecting himself and his family to

---

[207] See the detailed shot analysis of sequence 6 in the Appendix.

public mockery. The film also stresses movement when Qulitalik and Niri-nuniq leave the community (sequence 3), when Atanarjuat flees across the Arctic plain and ice (sequence 27; 4.23 min.), when he returns home to Igloolik (39; 2.29 min.), and when Oki's gang arrives at Qulitalik's camp (28; 37 sec.). Usually, the movement sequences feature the characters either from the side or from the front, but in sequence 3 they are seen from behind because they are not arriving at some place or are returning to the community but leaving it for good. In sequence 39, Atanarjuat is shown in slow motion from behind, motivated by the fact that although he is returning home nobody is awaiting him. As part of the movement motif, the framing of people arriving and leaving with dog teams becomes a major visual element as well. The cinematographic stress on movement and the screen-time of people's movements of up to four and a half minutes suggests that the filmmakers were concerned to emphasize people's movement, particularly in the centrally important activity of hunting.

Connected with the motif of movement and hunting are recurring shots of raw meat. Seven sequences contain close-up shots of raw meat either being cut up, prepared for consumption, being consumed, or the animal skin being cleaned (sequences 7, 11, 20, 23, 29, 38, 42). Six of these even begin with this close-up shot (Figs. 9.15–9.20). Similarly, five other sequences begin with the preparation or making of something, most often shown in close-up: Qulitalik glazes the runners of his sled with water (sequence 3; Fig. 9.21), three men and Atanarjuat respectively make a *qaggiq* (sequences 13, 40; Fig. 9.7), Atanarjuat and Amaqjuaq prepare their drum for the feast, while Uluriaq sews a shoe (sequence 14; Fig. 9.22), and Niri-nuniq also sews (sequence 32; Fig. 9.23). Close-up and medium shots of meat being prepared and eaten and things being made or prepared, placed at the beginning of sequences, form a stylistic motif that recurs eleven times altogether. Clearly, the filmmakers wish to stress the most important food source for Arctic people and also the fact that it needed to be eaten raw. These shots have two different effects: they anchor this eating habit in Arctic life without exoticizing it but presenting it as customary and necessary; and they work toward weakening the widespread disgust among non-Inuit viewers at this habit. The stereotyped colonialist discourse branding the Inuit as "animal-like, savage, and cannibalistic" due to their diet of raw meat is undermined.[208]

---

[208] Fatimah Tobing Rony, "Taxidermy and Romantic Ethnography," 105.

Other recurring visual motifs conditioned by the setting are the igloos, seal-skin tents, and sod houses in various locations, women's facial tattoos and hair styles, and the perhaps unexpected variety of the clothing. Garments are made of such different materials as polar-bear skin, seal skin, caribou skin, and eider-duck feathers, with often beautiful designs. Their greyish, brownish, and whitish colors complement the established space of whiteness. The many long shots and extreme long shots of Arctic landscapes, often with people and dwellings, also make up a visual motif (Figs. 9.24–9.27, Fig. 9.3, Fig. 9.47). The soundtrack of the film contains, besides the spoken Inuktitut, a mix of traditional songs and a musical score that features a Jew's harp, flute, and percussion. Traditional songs and these instruments constitute a coherent and typifying sound motif.

The Film Atanarjuat *as Electronic Mythtelling*
The film can be understood as electronic mythtelling, with the filmmakers taking a story from the oral tradition and retelling it with electronic means, here digital video/film technology. Translating this legend into video/film is a modified continuation of the storytelling tradition, likewise preserving this oral knowledge for future generations. In interviews, both filmmakers, Apak Angilirq and Kunuk, expressed their view that filming traditional oral knowledge is a way of collecting these old stories and retaining them for the future; this film, says Kunuk, is "one way of bringing back lost traditions." [209] One of the reasons why the filmmakers chose to translate a legend into film and chose drama was that there is no footage that cinematically depicts the stories and legends that elders tell when they are recorded on camera. Kunuk holds further that video technology is a perfect tool to render oral history. [210]

The most apparent difference from the average Western narrative film is the very slow pace, reminiscent of long, slow processes of storytelling. It takes a long time for the narrative to unfold, the camera often remains still to convey cultural details, and the film contains long stretches with nobody speaking, allowing the viewer to take in the gorgeous landscape images. In fact, the slow pace is very pleasant and relaxing for viewers who are used to fast-cut movies with an overwhelming mass of information that needs to

---

[209] Nancy Wachowich, "Interview with Paul Apak Angilirq," 19–21; Raúl Gavez, "Epic Inuit: In Conversation with Zacharias Kunuk."

[210] Zacharias Kunuk (2006, unpublished interview).

be processed quickly. Eric Beltmann says: "the deceptive 'slowness' of *Atanarjuat* is, for me, its greatest thrill," and Katherine Monk suggests rightly that "Kunuk slows his narrative pace to match the landscape and the aboriginal oral tradition."[211] The 161 minutes of the film embrace only 43 sequences, with the average sequence taking 3.7 minutes. Thus, the individual sequences are longer than those of today's average narrative films. In comparison, the sequences of *Big Bear*, also a very slow film, have an average length of 2.9 minutes and those of *Smoke Signals*, a film comparable to contemporary narrative films as far as pace is concerned, have an average length of 1.3 minutes. The filmmakers avoid fast cuts, and most shots are realized as longer takes. More than half of the transitions between sequences in *Atanarjuat* are realized through dissolves, outnumbering the simple cut and contributing to the slow character of the film. The filmmakers let the camera linger on the mise-en-scène for a while at the beginning and at the end of sequences to give the viewer time to grasp the setting and situation and to digest the events presented. One could speculate that the screen-time of 161 minutes is close to the time it would actually take to tell this legend. Thus, the length and slow pace help to position the film in the sphere of oral tradition.

The cinematography is largely conditioned by the Arctic setting. In many long shots and extreme long shots, the filmmakers reveal the vastness and beauty of the Arctic landscape that is photographed at different times, weather and lighting conditions, presenting a whole spectrum of sky and snow colors. The frame compositions of most outside sequences are similar, determined by the flatness of the terrain. They usually have a horizontal line dividing the screen, showing land / ice / snow and sky in varying proportions.[212] Besides the many long shots, there is an unusually high number of close-ups of objects and faces, feet, and other body parts. Sometimes characters move so close to the camera that the viewer flinches, as in the sequence of the Inuit boxing match. This effect is only partly due to the fact that the team filmed in constricted interiors; it is, rather, a style feature.

Often in concert with the short camera distance, the filmmakers work extensively with POV shots, most of which are reserved for Atanarjuat – for example, when he and Oki box and Atanarjuat is almost knocked out (se-

---

[211] Eric Beltmann, "*Atanarjuat: The Fast Runner*," *Flipside Movie Emporium* (15 August 2002), at http://www.flipsidemovies .com/atanarjuat.html, and Katherine Monk at *Atanarjuat: The Fast Runner* – webpage at http://www .atanarjuat.com/media_centre/index.html

[212] Cf. shots 10 and 11 in the detailed shot analysis of sequence 6, in the Appendix.

quence 15; Figs. 9.28–9.29), after he and Puja have just made love
(sequence 19), when he is angry with Puja for having sex with his brother
and he tries to attack her (sequence 24), when he collapses after his flight,
and when he recovers consciousness to find the three heads of Qulitalik,
Nirinuniq, and Kigutikaajuk looking down at him (both in sequence 28;
Fig. 9.30). During his final fight with Oki in sequence 42, there are POVs
of him and Oki, showing the respective opponent. We also have Atuat's
POV when she is raped by Oki (sequence 30; Fig. 9.31) and Qulitalik's
when Oki attacks him, throws him to the ground, and threatens to kill him
(sequence 28; Figs. 9.32–9.33). The POV shots are enlisted to underscore
dramatic action when the characters fight and when they are more emotionally involved than in other scenes. They lend the actions more immediacy;
the viewer is practically transported into the bodies of the characters, seeing
an opponent as close as the characters do, and might feel like acting along
with the character. At such moments, the viewer can see the events differently from the usual outside perspective, and can see what other characters
cannot. Even more, the POV shots align the viewer more intimately with
the vantage-point of the characters whose POV is being registered and for
whom more empathy can thus develop. As we mostly have Atanarjuat's
POV, this device, too, helps designate him as the main character. By
switching between inside and outside views, the filmmakers on the meta-
level make the viewer conscious of the divergent Inuit and non-Inuit perspectives as well as of the divergent contexts of production and reception.
The switching can thus be understood as warning Western filmmakers not
to tell Indigenous stories from their outside perspectives and as calling
upon more Indigenous filmmakers to tell these stories themselves on
film/video.

   Throughout the film, the filmmakers largely employ a hand-held camera.
When filming running or walking movements, the camera is tied to a sled
or Cohn is positioned on a sled with the camera. During competitions,
fights, running movements, and dramatic unrest, the images often become
shaky, which further helps to convey a sense of action and agitation. In dialogue sequences, the camera often pans back and forth between the dialogue partners instead of intercutting between them. The techniques of the
hand-held camera and mobile framing also create a sense of closeness that
helps bridge the cultural and spatial difference between filming and viewing contexts.

Close-ups of feet walking and running and long walking and running sequences align the film with early Navajo films[213] and Victor Masayesva's
Itam Hakim, Hopiit. Examples here are the sequences of Tulimaq returning
from a hunt (sequence 6; 3.51 min.) and of Atanarjuat escaping across the
Arctic plain and ice (sequence 27; 4.23 min.). In both sequences, movement is given relatively much screen time and is thus underscored, as suggested earlier. Closer analysis of these two sequences[214] reveals that in the
first shot of sequence 6 alone the camera is trained on Tulimaq's walking
feet for 43 seconds (Fig. 9.34). In sequence 27, the camera shows Atanarjuat's running and, later, bloody feet for 26 seconds altogether over several
shots, not least to underline the pain he must feel when, with each step, the
harsh snow cuts his flesh anew. In sequence 28, his bloody feet, hands, and
knees are featured even more prominently (Figs. 9.35–9.39). In accord
with these shots, close-ups of his increasingly exhausted and desperate face
throughout the escape sequence show that he is running for life, that the
success of this run means plain survival (Figs. 9.40–9.41). In the same
vein, the screen-time of this run (4.23 min.), beside its dramatic potential,
helps establish this sequence as the climax sequence.

The close-ups on Tulimaq's and Atanarjuat's feet are taken from low
camera angles, as are some shots featuring Tulimaq's face or body and two
shots of his sled dogs in close-up, for 19 seconds altogether (Figs. 9.42–
9.45).[215] Other low-angle shots follow in Atanarjuat's escape sequence
(27); the camera is positioned on the ground in two shots (10, 11), showing
Oki and his friends one after the other running through a water hole from
the water level, then Atanarjuat and his pursuers as tiny little figures moving within the vast Arctic landscape (Figs. 9.46–9.47). These latter low-
angle shots, together with a still camera, allow frame compositions with
two thirds of ground (snow and water) and one third of sky that beautifully
render a doubled sky as it is reflected in the water. By positioning the cam-

---

[213] Mike Anderson, *Old Antelope Lake* (15 min.); Susan Benally, *A Navajo Weaver* (20
min.); Johnny Nelson, *The Navajo Silversmith* (20 min.); Maxine Tsosie & Mary Jane Tsosie,
The Spirit of the Navajo (20 min.). All of these films are part of the "Navajos Film Them-
selves" project carried out by Sol Worth and John Adair in 1966; see Worth & Adair,
Through Navajo Eyes. See also the discussion of Masayesva's *Itam Hakim, Hopiit* and the
Navajo films in chapter 3.

[214] The detailed shot analyses of these two sequences are provided in the Appendix, below.

[215] In the movie *Never Cry Wolf* (USA, 1983), for example, the camera also focusses on
the sled dogs of a musher – however, not as intensely, as the shots are shorter and not
executed in close-up.

era on the ground, the filmmakers can focus neatly on the water and can even take in the part of the ground that is immediately before the camera and which would have been cut off if filmed from a straight angle. In the second of the three shots rendering Atanarjuat's superhuman jump across the crack in the pack ice (shot 18), the camera points vertically upward to show his leaping body in slow motion from below (Fig. 9.48). Low-angle shots also feature prominently in other sequences. As mentioned earlier, in sequence 13 the camera is pointed upward, in several shots featuring a man from below completing the roof of the *qaggiq*, against the background of the translucent *qaggiq* roof (Fig. 9.7). After the men's fight in sequence 10, Amaqjuaq, Oki, and several bystanders are photographed from a low angle, roughly from the spot where they have just fought.

The camera movement in sequence 6 differentiates between shots that feature forward movement towards the camp and shots in the camp where there is no forward movement respectively (e.g., when Tulimaq fights with one dog). The former are photographed with a mobile camera (tracks, pans, tilts), the latter with a still camera. Thus, the waiting Pittaluk is contrasted with the returning Tulimaq. Both are joined in shot 20 as Pittaluk and their sons is shown from behind waiting for Tulimaq, who approaches the camera with his dog team. In sequence 27, there seems to be no pattern for the camera movement. Still, there is a tendency to feature the movement of Atanarjuat and his pursuers with mobile frames, as 15 shots out of the 25 are photographed with a mobile camera. The cutting rhythm of both sequences is rather unsteady, with the first shot in sequence 6 lasting 66 seconds and the others taking between 2 and 16 seconds. Sequence 27, too, begins with an unsteady rhythm, one shot lasting 73 seconds and the others between 2 and 24 seconds. However, towards Atanarjuat's jump the cutting speed accelerates between shots 11 and 17, and after the jump the shots become continuously longer again. This accelerated cutting serves to highlight the climax shot within this sequence. In Tulimaq's return sequence, the filmmakers employ metonymic takes, the camera showing the feet of Tulimaq in close-up, then tilting up quickly to show his legs, hips, upper body, and finally the head, with feet and head being stressed, as they are much longer on the screen (Figs. 9.42–9.44). This fragmentary introduction of Tulimaq is reminiscent of character introduction in Martell's *Talker* and Masayesva's *Itam Hakim, Hopiit*. At these moments, the film resists presenting the whole body, as if to frustrate any outside gaze that might wish to 'study' the whole at a (necessarily greater) distance.

The lighting in *Atanarjuat* is more reminiscent of Dogma films than of conventional narrative films. Since the bright Arctic light is of sufficient quality for filming day scenes, there is no artificial light used and most exteriors are rendered in high-key lighting. Quite a few contre-jour shots, which are considered flaws in classical filmmaking or would be employed only for a special reason, enhance this sense of natural lighting. In sequences taking place inside igloos at night or sod houses, the filmmakers used seal-oil lamps as diegetic light-sources and a 200-watt flicker master hooked to a dimmer to match the light from the lamps.[216] These sequences are usually rendered in low-key lighting. It is difficult to assess whether or not artificial light is used here, but it is obvious that the filmmakers have deviated from the classical three-point lighting system, which is partly due to the arctic conditions but which is also a stylistic choice.

Because of the hand-held camera and extreme mobile framing, very often the framing is not exact and the camera fails to keep track of the moving characters – for example, the head of Tulimaq in sequence 6 often moves in and out of the frame. Sometimes characters move into a still frame from off-screen, as Atuat does in sequence 16. Also the fact that the filmmakers employed many non-professional actors to a large degree shows at various points. All these 'flaws' in a Western understanding of filmmaking are not necessarily so; rather, they indicate conscious creative insouciance toward established artifices of conventional filmmaking – and perhaps even some of the kind of deliberately imposed rigor and 'natural' restrictions typical of the Dogma school. In *Atanarjuat*, the people behind and in front of the camera as well as people working on the set form a horizontally organized team, as opposed to vertically organized film teams as in most Western filmmaking.[217] The people being filmed cease to be objects studied and become creative subjects. In this way, the film team subverts the ethnographic subject/object relation to undermine the self/other dichotomy inherent in Western films about Indigenous cultures.

---

[216] Zacharias Kunuk (2006, unpublished interview).

[217] *Atanarjuat: The Fast Runner* – webpage at http://lot47.com/thefastrunner/about_Inside_action.html

Final Remarks

Atanarjuat: The Fast Runner is a hybrid film in the sense of integrating components of Inuit and Western/non-Inuit cultural origin. The Inuit film-makers[218] avail themselves of Western film technology and apply it according to Arctic conditions and their own modes and concepts of film in order to translate the traditional legend into this medium. This film presents the universal themes of love and hate, passion and revenge, sex and rape, envy and rivalry, pride and resentment as elements of a legend rooted in Inuit cultural lore. These themes are not unique to Inuit culture but are also part of other world mythologies and literatures. The props are careful reconstructions on the basis of Inuit cultural knowledge and the Western anthropological and ethnographic research accessible in museums and print. Traditional storytelling is adapted to Western modes of storytelling (here video/filmmaking), and Inuit filmmakers become modern electronic storytellers, whereas in their traditional cultures they would not have necessarily been such. The film itself is a bilingual product, both Inuktitut and English being spoken during the making of the film and both languages being present in the final product.[219] In terms of location and character movement, the film has a circular structure, as the people move among several localities (not shown but only implied) and Atanarjuat is driven from his home and returns to it. Also the weaving among several temporal levels emphasizes, as in *Smoke Signals*, a circular sense of time and a seamless transition from past to present and back, which in turn supports the mythic character of the narrative.

In its basic aspects, the film cleaves close to Western film conventions; it has a clear-cut narrative and a classical cause-and-effect structure with interpersonal conflicts dynamizing the plot. It has temporal and spatial continuity, continuity editing, and a conventional placement of sound with a composed musical score that also integrates traditional music. These basic aspects of classical filmmaking are complemented and realized via such individualistic techniques as the slow pace, long dissolves, many long shots

---

[218] Although Cohn is the only non-Inuit member of Igloolik Isuma Productions, here he is seen as belonging to the group of Inuit filmmakers.

[219] The spoken language in the film is Inuktitut and an English translation is provided in subtitles. The script was written parallel in Inuktitut and English, the Inuktitut script being the basis for the filming, the instructions, and dialogue for the actors and the English script for the proposals submitted to the Canadian funding institutions; Norman Cohn, "The Art of Community-Based Filmmaking," 25.

and close-ups, cinematic emphasis on movement, many low-angle and POV shots, a hand-held camera and extensive mobile framing, no classical lighting, and slow-motion effects. These salient stylistic techniques are not unique to Indigenous filmmaking and might also be found in Western narrative films, but their distinctive combination creates a unique Inuit film style conditioned by the Arctic. The mythic story embedded in an Inuit cultural context and realized with these individual stylistic techniques and an Inuit community-based approach to filmmaking results in a hybrid film code existing at the interface between Inuit cultural activities and oral knowledge, Arctic conditions, Western filmmaking conventions, and colonial influences. The autonomous presentation of Inuit culture from an inside perspective helps to de-exoticize the filmed material and its cultural context. In consequence, the film belongs to a decolonized film discourse that consciously merges Indigenous and Western cultures.

℘ ᐊ

Conclusion

T HE PRECEDING ANALYSIS of Indigenous films has indicated in some depth several of the strategies adopted by subaltern film-makers as outlined by Shohat and Stam.[1] The 'aesthetic of hunger' is noticeable in *The Road Allowance People* and *Honey Moccasin*. In the first of these two films, this strategy is conditioned by the very limited budget rather than constituting the conscious employment of this aesthetic style. Video technology, community actors, and a basic audio track consisting of dialogue and a musical score originating in the Métis community (for which probably no copyright payments had to be made) distinguish the film qualitatively from Western narrative films and reveal a focus on community storytelling where such qualitative aspects are less important. In the second example, the low budget produced similar results: no three-point lighting and a basic audio track (the songs in the film were all written and performed by Indigenous artists; if any payments were made, they were, in all probability, pretty low). The difference is that some of the Indigenous actors were professionals and film technology was used. The expensive film stock meant that repeat takes were not the norm; Shelley Niro has commented in an interview (1998) that the first shot taken often had to be used regardless of minor flaws. At some points, however, this imperfection is stretched into a consciously deployed strategy. Diegetic titles, character transformations achieved with simple means, the film con-tinuing after the announced 'end', partly overdone acting, and the presenta-tion of a non-professional Indigenous television station in *Honey Moccasin* – all are deliberate stylistic elements that mirror the 'aesthetic of hunger'.

Oral tradition is integrated as narrative formula in *The Road Allowance People* and *Itam Hakim, Hopiit*, dramatized in the former and recorded and

---

[1] See the section "Strategies of Postcolonial Filmmaking" in chapter 2.

partly staged in the latter. Modernized versions of the oral tradition appear
in *Honey Moccasin*, where there are five modified oral storytelling situations and performances. Here and in *The Road Allowance People*, oral
tradition also operates as a structuring formula, resulting in a non-linear,
digressive narrative in *Honey Moccasin* and in a digressive and circular
narrative in *The Road Allowance People*. *Talker* goes back to the oral tradition by dramatizing a trickster myth; similarly, *Atanarjuat: The Fast Runner* dramatizes an Inuit legend for cinema. In *Honey Moccasin*, characteristic elements of the oral tradition, such as lengthy introductions of the
storyteller/performer, songs, and overdone acting, find their way into the
narrative in an adapted form. In *Big Bear*, one scene of oral storytelling as
narrative element is also included. Here and in *Atanarjuat: The Fast
Runner*, a slow rhythm (a style-feature of the oral tradition) was created
through long takes and a slow editing pace in order to reflect a traditional
understanding of time and the slower pace of life in traditional Indigenous
communities.

A deliberate community approach was taken for the making of *The Road
Allowance People*, *Big Bear*, *Atanarjuat: The Fast Runner*, and *Itam
Hakim, Hopiit*. In the first film, members of a Métis community were involved as actors and set decorators, and this community served as the location for the film. *Big Bear* was filmed on the Pasqua reserve near Regina,
Saskatchewan, on Indigenous land. The film project supported the community financially, since the land of the location was rented from the band
council and close to a hundred people from the community were hired to
work on the production. Similarly, *Atanarjuat: The Fast Runner* was filmed
in Nunavut, an autonomous Indigenous territory, involved actors, artists,
elders, and crew members from the Igloolik area, and its production supported Igloolik's local economy. Masayesva, for *Itam Hakim, Hopiit*, involved community members on a much smaller basis: the storyteller Ross
Macaya and the children who formed his audience are filmed in his house,
complemented by shots from the Hopi land surrounding this community.

Four films (*Itam Hakim, Hopiit*, *Talker*, *Overweight With Crooked
Teeth*, and *Honey Moccasin*) deploy a Brechtian alienation effect in order
to disrupt the illusion of reality that characterizes established narrative cinema. This effect draws attention to the medium of film itself, indicating that
'filmic reality' is constructed and can at most only be reflected reality. It
undermines the Hollywood practice of seamless presentation. This effect is
achieved through jump cuts, extreme camera angles, the blurring of images,

mobile frames,[2] fragmentary filming, iris shots and masks over images, characters looking directly into the camera and/or winking at the viewer,[3] the interplay of magic and reality, character transformations achieved with simple means, overdone acting, re-enactment of roles to transform the narrative into subversive play, quotations from mainstream films, and, finally, the convergence of filmic space with outside space by merging an audience in the film with the audience of the film. The alienation effect enables the filmmakers to focus on the process of filming, comment on the making of the film, and create a self-reflexive metafilm about Indigenous filmmaking.

The strategy of carnivalesque subversion is not so common as the other strategies. None of the films discussed thematizes carnival, as it is not a cultural characteristic of Indigenous North America. *Big Bear*, in the treaty-making sequence, visualizes a masquerade with which the British/Canadian military are subversively parodied. In *Overweight With Crooked Teeth*, the only actor is dressed up in carnivalesque fashion to grotesquely reflect various Indian clichés. A carnivalesque film aesthetic, as Shohat and Stam understand it, is employed only in *Overweight With Crooked Teeth* and *Honey Moccasin*, where Niro consciously disregards some of the classical filmmaking conventions.

The three dramatic films *Smoke Signals*, *Big Bear*, and *Atanarjuat: The Fast Runner* are the most conspicuous in their selective employment of classical filmmaking conventions. In the first two films, a clear-cut narrative is applied to a film genre of the dominant media discourse (road movie, historical movie), and inscribed with an Indigenous story. The main narratives unfold according to the cause-and-effect principle and are complemented with several sub-narratives. In *Smoke Signals*, one sub-narrative addresses contemporary reservation life and in *Big Bear* one sub-narrative addresses traditional life transformed into dependent reserve life. However, in contrast to classical narrative cinema, both films avoid mainstream devices for generating suspense and surprise. *Atanarjuat: The Fast Runner* also has a clear-cut causally motivated narrative, and, like *Smoke Signals*, has a circular structure in terms of character movement and continual weaving among several temporal levels. In all three films, the filmmakers have

---

[2] *Atanarjuat: The Fast Runner* also employs extreme mobile framing and extensive low angles, but still largely upholds seamless presentation.

[3] In *Smoke Signals*, a character looks into the camera several times, which can be understood as a break in filmic illusion. However, in the rest of the film such alienating effects are absent; hence this film is not listed with the other four.

combined a classical filmmaking style with individual stylistic techniques. In *Smoke Signals*, the most salient individual techniques are matching cuts and apparent sound bridges, and in *Big Bear* and *Atanarjuat: The Fast Runner* they are a slow pace achieved through long sequences, longer takes, dissolves, many long shots, and the avoidance of fast cutting. *Atanarjuat: The Fast Runner*, further, employs extensive mobile framing and hand-held camera, low-angle shots and POV shots, and slow-motion effects. As in the Navajo films and *Itam Hakim, Hopiit*, walking and other degrees of movement are contextualized and emphasized: in *Smoke Signals*, movement as an element intrinsic to the road-movie genre; in *Big Bear*, walking and nomadic movement in the literal sense; and in *Atanarjuat: The Fast Runner* nomadic movement and movement associated with hunting, flight, and pursuit as well as cinematographic stress on walking and running feet.

The films respond to colonialist media discourse in different ways: whereas *Big Bear* presents an historical narrative from an Indigenous point of view and disrupts the stereotyped (mis)representations of Indigenous culture and history typical of the same Western narrative, *Smoke Signals* avoids historical contextualization, presenting instead a contemporary narrative interlaced with subversive and humorous references to the imaginary and ideological Indian of Western film discourse. Although *Atanarjuat: The Fast Runner* presents an Inuit legend, it nevertheless engages in oppositional dialogue with Robert Flaherty's semi-ethnographic *Nanook of the North*, as well as correcting the flat and clichéd portrayals of Inuit people and culture that issue from Hollywood. All three films refrain from heroizing their protagonists and do not present them as tough and infallible. In light of the dominant media's history of presenting one-dimensional Indian characters, they apply the "critique-of-stereotypes" approach, as Shohat and Stam call it, and create three-dimensional characters within a realist dramatic aesthetic.[4] The production of all these films entailed the hiring of largely Indigenous crews, but did not exclude mainstream involvement and financing (the Sundance Institute, Miramax, CBC, Télé-Action, and the NFB). Thanks to their deliberate employment of conventional filmmaking rules and a striving for seamless presentation, the three films, as conventional narratives, largely uphold the illusion of filmic reality.

---

[4] Ella Shohat & Robert Stam, *Unthinking Eurocentrism: Multiculturalism and the Media* (1994; London & New York: Routledge, 1997): 210.

The short films *Talker* and *Tenacity* also adhere to classical film conventions, which they blend with individual stylistic techniques. In *Tenacity*, these include the deployment of POV shots and high and low camera angles as well as the blurring of images. Cinematography and mise-en-scène are designed to create filmic oppositions. In *Talker* these are extreme lighting, extreme camera angles, extreme facial close-ups, mobile frames, rear-view mirror shots, and a 360° shot. Both filmmakers obscure narrative time and space in order to create a vague background with symbolic mise-en-scène elements in the service of abstract metaphoric narratives.

The two films that translate the medium of oral tradition into that of film differ in their approach. *The Road Allowance People* dramatizes oral storytelling (fictional film) and *Itam Hakim, Hopiit* records the Hopi elder Ross Macaya conveying oral knowledge to a group of children (documentary). Both films, however, blur genre conventions: whereas the former at three points complements the dramatic mode with a documentary mode, the latter stages parts of the storytelling situation. In the two films, the narratives are subordinated to their purpose of relaying oral tradition: i.e. the storytelling provides the only narrative material and dynamic. In both examples, oral narrative patterns are mediated, indirectly through scripted and directed enactment in *The Road Allowance People*, and directly through recording in *Itam Hakim, Hopiit*. Structural features of the oral tradition also find their way into the making of the films. Campbell organizes the narrative in a circular structure by staging a main sequence of storytelling from which sub-sequences illustrating the content of the stories depart and return. Masayesva merely hints at a circular structure, by positioning the same shot at the beginning and the end of the film. But he visualizes natural cycles (dry earth, rain clouds, rain, wet plants) and the Hopi agricultural cycle (corn being planted, the watering of plants, corn being harvested, ground, and processed into bread). This visualized cyclical continuum is made up of several sub-narratives complementing the main narrative of Macaya's talk. The repetitions, pauses, and songs characteristic of oral rhetoric are directly reproduced.

These two films largely adhere to conventional filmmaking and its basic rules. However, Campbell abstains from creating suspense, surprise, and a climax as principles of dramatized films. Masayesva avoids the conventional 'cuts-only-talking-head' documentary format, narrative voice commentary, and a line-up of facts and/or arguments typical of documentary film. Instead, he employs a very slow editing pace (except in the harvest-

festival sequence) with many long takes and dissolves, a rather high average shot length; he also edits long talking sequences with largely organic
images and images that reflect the content what is said. His mobile frames,
blurring of images, fast-motion effects, high and low camera angles, and
stress on close-ups and long shots counter the ethnographic film method of
objectifying and scrutinizing. In concert, his fragmenting style, which is
also employed in *Talker*, avoids any evocation of the ethnographic gaze.
Only the sequences that depict daily chores are realized in medium shots,
because Masayesva is concerned, like the Navajo filmmakers, with showing how these things are done. Color posterization and visual and sonic
breaks, together with the stylistic elements already indicated, promote the
creation of an individual documentary style. For both films, language use is
of paramount importance. In Masayesva's film, the cultural knowledge is
conveyed in Hopi with summarizing subtitles, and in Campbell's film it is
mediated in a Métis vernacular of English. In this way, both films succeed
in subjecting oral knowledge to colonialist influence to a lesser degree than
they would have by using Standard English. At the same time, they reach
both Indigenous and non-Indigenous viewers because they deploy forms of
the lingua franca, an English vernacular and German/English subtitles.

    Niro's approach to filming is different from that of the other filmmakers,
since she consciously disregards classical film conventions. Because she
made the films independently with her own production company and a low
budget, she was able to experiment with narrative forms and film techniques and create films that contrast with mainstream products. *Overweight
With Crooked Teeth* consists of vignettes that are related to each other only
through the fact that they spoof established Indian stereotypes, blatantly
and ostentatiously. Through a minimalistic approach, she creates the impression of an amateur home video. She adds iris shots, color posterization,
and a contrapuntal voice-over in order to abstract the images and lay stress
on the camera gaze and the medium of film. *Honey Moccasin* also breaks
with established narrative film conventions by introducing a non-linear
main narrative that is repeatedly created and destroyed and that contains a
pseudo-dramatic climax. The narrative itself is a burlesque 'whodunit' that
cannot be taken seriously. The issues that Niro deals with in sub-narratives,
however, are serious. They include the status of gay people in Indigenous
communities, problems of alcohol, diabetes, and obesity, as well as Indian
clichés prevalent in mainstream media. As in *Talker* and *Tenacity*, an unspecified space and time serve as a stage for an abstract plot. The narrative

intertwines magic and reality by including magical character transformations as necessary plot elements. The two films *The Road Allowance People* and *Honey Moccasin* create a new dramatic film form, first through their unconventional length of forty-five to fifty minutes, and secondly through their unconventional digressive narratives without dramatic climaxes, suspense and surprise.

The films discussed engage in dialogue with the dominant film discourse in various ways. Among these are the inclusion or exclusion of dominant media involvement and the enlisting or avoiding of classical film conventions, and the blending of classical conventions and individual styles. The degree of hybridization of film discourse varies but is always present. This dialogic engagement, further, shows in the contextualization of established stereotypes and in the probing of their validity, as Bhabha has suggested. Through subversive quotations, mimicry, allusions, jokes, and other references, the filmmakers respond first and foremost to the stereotypical and imaginary Indians established in colonial film discourse, redirect its construction of subject positions, of both colonial and colonized, thereby fashioning an answering filmic discourse. The dramatized films analyzed (except *Big Bear* and *Atanarjuat: The Fast Runner*) introduce a diversity of contemporary Indigenous characters who are not the stereotyped and objectified victims or attackers, frozen in the past, that originate in dominant media discourse. *Overweight With Crooked Teeth* stands out for its implementation of Bhabha's idea of employing the effectivity of colonial stereotypes, the 'dynamic of clichés', for their deconstruction by presenting them (they are recognized) and ridiculing them an instant later (the effectivity of the cliché is redirected). *Honey Moccasin* engages with the power of stereotypes structurally: i.e. elements of clichéd colonial discourse furnish a springboard for a subversive narrative of parody. Visually, Niro employs the dynamic of clichés for ironic effect: e.g., in the fashion show, the search for the thief, and the transformation sequences. By quoting from mainstream films, she comments playfully on dominant media discourse. She thematizes not only cultural stereotyping but also gender stereotyping with the figure of Zach, which makes her film stand out even more from the others. *Smoke Signals* verbally subverts the power of stereotypes by deploying humor and satire, with references to and quotations from colonial media discourse. Bhabha's effectivity of stereotypes ties in closely with Vizenor's trickster discourse. *Overweight With Crooked Teeth*, *Honey Moccasin*, and *Smoke Signals* are trickster discourse because they mockingly and playfully pinpoint aspects of the imaginary and ideological Indian that viewers (both colonizing and colonized subjects) have internalized via the colonial lens of Western media discourse. These films engage Western and Indigenous media discourse in a dialogue, in the sense of Vizenor's dialogism, to expose the ironies and disparities between these discourses on the subject of the Western on-screen Indian and colonial history. The films are thus able to break down such stereotypical and hegemonic assumptions and subvert and renegotiate the on-screen Indigenous experience.

At this point, it is necessary to point out that all the individual techniques used by Indigenous filmmakers and manifest in the analyses could also be used by mainstream filmmakers to add certain individual touches, to experiment with style and form, and to create formal diversity beyond the realms of content. These techniques do not in themselves define an Indigenous film aesthetic. There is an Indigenous film discourse made up of the numerous Indigenous films, but there cannot be a universal Indigenous film aesthetic or a 'characteristic Indigenous' filmmaking style. As I hope to have shown in this book, filmmakers apply various approaches: either they make independent and consequently low-budget films,[5] or they collaborate with mainstream filmmakers and/or companies because they need financial backing and do not regard an 'exclusively Indigenous' approach to be a creative *sine qua non*.[6] Such collaborations result in mixed alliances of filmmakers – script-writers or producers (usually not both, and not the director) can be a member of the dominant group, and a large number of crew members can be non-Indigenous as well. As long as the subaltern filmmakers remain in control of the product, they often welcome mainstream cinematic experience and financial power. In regard to filmmaking conventions, the approaches likewise vary. They navigate between adherence to filmmaking rules established in dominant film discourse and their

---

[5] To my knowledge, *Naturally Native* (USA, 1998) is the only Indigenous feature film so far that has been financed solely by Indigenous money, here casino profits from the Mashantucket Pequots. At the present time, it is hard to imagine a situation in which Indigenous feature films secure funding from Indigenous sources on a scale similar to the budget dimensions of mainstream feature films.

[6] For example Gil Cardinal, Doug Cuthand, and Rodger Ross say in interviews that they had positive experiences from cooperations with non-Indigenous filmmakers/companies and would continue such cooperation. Neil Pasqua and Lloyd Martell, despite negative experiences, were willing to enter into such cooperations again. Martell later worked in association with a Regina company and described this relation as having been very good (Gil Cardinal, Doug Cuthand, Rodger Ross, Neil Pasqua, and Lloyd Martell, unpublished interviews, 1996 and 1998).

negation. Indigenous filmmaking must be understood as a hybrid practice between these two modes, in which various ways of combining and merging divergent cultural experiences, film conventions, and film technologies are explored and negotiated. As Western film technology is inscribed with individual Indigenous styles, so is the dominant film discourse inscribed with Indigenous film discourse. To talk about hybridization of discourses would be too farfetched; however, influence will ultimately cease to be one-directional and both discourses will come to influence each other.

Indigenous filmmaking largely began in the documentary genre, partly because this genre requires much lower budgets and smaller crews and because there was great interest in documentaries on Indigenous issues as the descendants of ethnographic films. Increased awareness of Indigenous issues, including that of the appropriation of Indigenous cultures and spirituality, prompted Indigenous filmmakers to make such films. The policy of various agencies and film companies of funding documentaries almost exclusively was another factor encouraging concentration on this genre. Nevertheless, funded and promoted documentary films (e.g., those made at the NFB in Canada) could at least secure nationwide distribution. Broadcasts on education channels and work commissioned by band and tribal councils and the government also furthered the production of Indigenous documentaries. Via short films, Indigenous filmmakers began exploring the genre of dramatic films. As funding and support for dramatic Indigenous films was scarce, filmmakers were initially confined to shorts. Most of these were created independently, thus, apart from screenings at film festivals, could seldom hope for broad distribution.[7] In the past few years, Indigenous filmmakers have been able to acquire funding for higher-budget films from various sources, gaining support from mainstream film companies, broadcasters, and distributors, and/or making films in collaboration with them. The rapid development of Indigenous feature filmmaking (e.g., *Tushka, Naturally Native, Smoke Signals, Big Bear, Honey Moccasin, Backroads, Atanarjuat: The Fast Runner, Kusah Hakwaan, The Business of Fancydancing, Skins, Skinwalkers, A Thief of Time, Johnny Tootall, Indian Summer: The Oka Crisis, The Journals of Knud Rasmussen, Four Sheets to the Wind,* and *Tkaronto*) shows that the creation of decolonized films now

---

[7] These are general statements about tendencies in the Indigenous film industry and do not claim final authority and comprehensive character. Of course, there are exceptions to these tendencies.

also involves the feature-film format. This format is the most influential and marketable, as it is the most widely distributed. In consequence, the deconstruction of stereotypical presentations of Indigenous cultures is at its most effective in this film format.

The work that has been and is being done within the field of Indigenous film indicates that filmmakers are keenly aware of the colonial gaze/lens that has created forms of media discourse that have objectified, fetishized, misrepresented, and generated stereotypical images of Indigenous cultures. They cannot change colonialistic hegemonic discourse practices, but they can create an Indigenous discourse that dismantles and defies these practices. They cannot undo constructed clichés, but they can offer autonomous images that subvert these colonialist presentations. In the films discussed, underlying oppositional binaries of self/other and center/margin are either undermined and blurred, reversed by centering the Indigenous perspective, or emphasized in order to point up colonialist relations. Similarly, the subject/object relation, established through colonial discourse practices, is undermined and/or reversed as well. To this (considerable) extent, an answering Indigenous film discourse is creatively returning the gaze of power. Indigenous filmmakers are turning Western filmmaking techniques into an instrument for the dissemination of anticolonialist media; instead of the inflexible distorting lens of colonialist power, the world and Indigenous people now have a powerful, multifocal lens of cultural truth – a decolonized lens of power.

ॳ ॳ

Works Cited

Achebe, Chinua. "The African Writer and the English Language" (1975), in *Colonial Discourse and Post-Colonial Theory*, ed. Williams & Chrisman, 428–34.

Acoose, Janice. *Iskwewak. Kah' Ki Yaw Ni Wahkomakanak: Neither Indian Princesses nor Easy Squaws* (Toronto: Women's Press, 1995).

Adair, John, & Sol Worth. "The Navajo as Filmmaker," *American Anthropologist* 69.1 (1967): 76–78.

Adams, Howard. *Prison of Grass: Canada from a Native Point of View* (Saskatoon, Saskatchewan: Fifth House, 1989).

Agness, Jack, ed. *Behind Closed Doors: Stories from the Kamloops Indian Residential School* (Kamloops, British Columbia: Secwepemc Cultural Education Society, 2000).

Ahenakew, Edward. *Voices of the Plains Cree*, ed. Ruth M. Buck (1973; Regina, Saskatchewan: Canadian Plains Research Center, U of Regina, 1995).

Albersmeier, Franz Joseph. *Texte zur Theorie des Films* (Stuttgart: Reclam, 1998).

Alexie, Sherman. *The Lone Ranger and Tonto Fistfight in Heaven* (New York: HarperPerennial, 1994).

——. *Smoke Signals* Screenplay. Miramax Books (New York: Hyperion, 1998).

Apak Angilirq, Paul et al. *Atanarjuat: The Fast Runner* (Toronto: Coach House/ Isuma, 2002).

Appiah, Kwame Anthony. "Is the Post- in Postmodernism the Post- in Postcolonial?" *Critical Inquiry* 17.2 (Winter 1991): 336–57.

Asch, Timothy. "Ethnographic Film Production," *Film Comment* 7.1 (1971): 40–42.

——. "The ethics of ethnographic film-making," in *Film as Ethnography*, ed. Peter Ian Crawford & David Turton (Manchester & New York: Manchester UP, 1992): 196–204.

Asch, Timothy, John Marshall & Peter Spier. "Ethnographic Film: Structure and Function," *Annual Review of Anthropology* 2 (1973): 179–87.

Ashcroft, Bill, Gareth Griffiths & Helen Tiffin, ed. *The Empire Writes Back: Theory and Practice in Post-Colonial Literatures* (London & New York: Routledge, 1989).

——. *Key Concepts in Post-Colonial Studies* (London & New York: Routledge, 1998).

Ashcroft, W.D. (= Bill Ashcroft). "Is That The Congo? Language as Metonomy in the Post-Colonial Text," *World Literature Written in English* 29.2 (1990): 3–10.

Atwood, Margaret. "Of Myths and Men: *Atanarjuat: The Fast Runner*," *Globe & Mail* (13 April 2002), repr. in Atwood, *Moving Targets* (Toronto: House of Anansi, 2004): 259–62.

Bahn–Coblans, Sonja. "Reading with a Eurocentric Eye the 'Seeing with a Native Eye': Victor Masayesva's *Itam Hakim, Hopiit*," *Studies in American Indian Literatures* 8.4 (Winter 1996): 47–60.

Bailey, Cameron. "A Cinema of Duty: The Films of Jennifer Hodge de Silva," *Cine-Action* 23 (Winter 1990–91): 4–12.

Balme, Christopher. "Inventive Syncretism: The Concept of the Syncretic in Intercultural Discourse," in *Fusion of Cultures?* ed. Peter Stummer & Christopher Balme (Cross/Cultures 26, ASNEL Papers 2; Amsterdam & Atlanta GA: Rodopi, 1996): 9–18.

Bannerji, Himani, ed. *Returning the Gaze: Essays on Racism, Feminism and Politics* (Toronto: Sister Vision, 1993).

——. "Returning the Gaze: An Introduction," in *Returning the Gaze*, ed. Bannerji, ix–xxiv.

Barnouw, Erik. *Documentary: A History of the Non-Fiction Film* (Oxford: Oxford UP, 1993).

Barsam, Richard M. *Nonfiction Film: A Critical History* (Bloomington & Indianapolis: Indiana UP, 1992).

Barthes, Roland. "The Death of the Author," in Barthes, *Image – Music – Text*, ed. Steven Heath (New York: Hill & Wang, 1977): 142–48.

Bataille, Gretchen, & Charles L.P. Silet. "The Entertaining Anachronism: Indians in American Film," in *The Kaleidoscopic Lens: How Hollywood Views Ethnic Groups*, ed. Randall M. Miller (n.p.: Jerome S. Ozer, 1980): 36–53.

Bath, C. Richard, & Dilmus D. James. "Dependency Analysis of Latin America: Some Criticism, Some Suggestions," *Latin American Research Review* 11.3 (1976): 3–54.

Beaver, Frank E. *Dictionary of Film Terms* (New York: Twayne, 1994).

Beaucage, Marjorie. "Aboriginal Voices: Entitlement Through Storytelling," in *Mirror Machine: Video and Identity*, ed. Janine Marchessault (Toronto: YYZ, 1995): 214–26.

——. "Self-Government in Art to Create Anew.../ Être autonome... être autochtone... se re-créer," in *Video re/View*, ed. Peggy Gale & Lisa Steele (Toronto: Art Metropole & Vtape, 1996): 72–83.

——. Interview, cond. Kerstin Knopf (1998, unpublished).

Benjamin, Walter. *Das Kunstwerk im Zeitalter seiner beliebigen Reproduzierbarkeit* (*Zeitschrift für Sozialforschung* 5.1, 1936; Frankfurt am Main: Suhrkamp, 1963). Tr. by Harry Zohn as "The Work of Art in the Age of Mechanical Reproduction," in Benjamin, *Illuminations*, ed. & intro. Hannah Arendt (tr. 1968; New York: Schocken, 2007): 217–51.

Berkhofer, Robert F. *The White Man's Indian* (New York: Vintage, 1978).

Bhabha, Homi K. *The Location of Culture* (London & New York: Routledge, 1994).

——. "The Other Question: Difference, Discrimination and the Discourse of Colonialism," in *Out There: Marginalization and Contemporary Cultures*, ed. Russel Ferguson et al. (New York: New Museum of Contemporary Art & Cambridge MA: MIT Press, 1990): 71–87.

——. "Signs Taken for Wonders: Questions of Ambivalence and Authority under a Tree outside Delhi, May 1817," *Critical Inquiry* 12.1 (Autumn 1985) 144–65, repr. in Bhabha. *The Location of Culture*, 102–22.

——. "The Third Space: Interview with Homi Bhabha," in *Identity: Community, Culture, Difference*, ed. Jonathan Rutherford (London: Lawrence & Wishart, 1990): 207–21.

Black, Max. *Models and Metaphors: Studies in Language and Philosophy* (Ithaca NY: Cornell UP, 1981).

Blevins Faery, Rebecca. *Cartographies of Desire: Captivity, Race, and Sex in the Shaping of an American Nation* (Norman: U of Oklahoma P, 1999).

Boon, Mike. "Charismatic Cast Adds Fire to Smoke Signals," *Calgary Herald* (31 July 1998): C1.

Bordwell, David. "Classical Hollywood Cinema: Narrational Principles and Procedures," in *Narrative, Apparatus, Ideology: A Film Theory Reader*, ed. Philip Rosen (New York: Columbia UP, 1986): 17–34.

——. "Contemporary Film Studies and the Vicissitudes of Grand Theory," in *Post-Theory: Reconstructing Film Studies*, ed. David Bordwell & Noël Carroll (Madison: U of Wisconsin P, 1996): 3–36.

——, & Noël Carroll. "Introduction" (1996), to *Post-Theory: Reconstructing Film Studies*, ed. Bordwell & Carroll, xiii–xvii.

——, & Noël Carroll, ed. *Post-Theory: Reconstructing Film Studies* (Madison: U of Wisconsin P, 1996).

——, & Kristin Thompson. *Film Art: An Introduction* (1979; New York: McGraw–Hill, 4th ed. 1997).

Borofsky, Robert. "Valuing the Pacific: An Interview with James Clifford," in *Remembrance of Pacific Pasts: An Invitation to Remake History*, ed. Robert Borofsky (Honolulu: U of Hawai'i P, 2000): 92–99.

Bossanne, Brigitte. "A Canadian Voice Within the Text: Rudy Wiebe's *The Temptations of Big Bear*," *Études Canadiennes / Canadian Studies: Revue Interdisciplinaire des Études Canadiennes en France* 7.10 (June 1981): 223–34.

Bourgeault, Ron. "Women in Egalitarian Society," *New Breed Journal* (Métis Society of Saskatchewan; January–April 1983): 3–8.

——. "Race, Class and Gender: Colonial Domination of Indian Women," in *Race, Class, Gender: Bonds and Barriers*, ed. Jesse Vorst et al. (Society for Socialist Studies: A Canadian Annual 5, 1989): 87–115.

Bowannie, Mary K. "Tenacious Focus," *Aboriginal Voices* 1.4 (Fall 1994): 10–11.

Brant, Beth. "Grandmothers of a New World," *Writing As Witness: Essay and Talk* (Toronto: Women's Press, 1994): 83–103.

Breinig, Helmbrecht, & Klaus Lösch. "Introduction: Difference and Transdifference," in *Multiculturalism in Contemporary Societies: Perspectives on Difference and Transdifference*, ed. Helmbrecht Breinig, Jürgen Gebhardt & Klaus Lösch (Erlangen: Univ.-Bund Erlangen–Nürnberg, 2002): 11–36.

Brotherston, Gordon. *Book of the Fourth World: Reading Native Americans Through Their Literature* (Cambridge: Cambridge UP, 1992).

Bruchac, Joseph. *The Faithful Hunter: Abenaki Stories* (New York: Greenfield Review Press, 1985).

——. *The Wind Eagle and other Abenaki Stories* (New York: Bowman, 1985).

Bumsted, J.M., ed. *Interpreting Canada's Past*, vol. 1 (Toronto: Oxford UP, 1993).

Burke, Seán. *The Death and Return of the Author: Criticism and Subjectivity in Barthes, Foucault and Derrida* (1992; Edinburgh: Edinburgh UP, 1999).

Burton, Julianne. "Marginal Cinemas and Mainstream Critical Theory," *Screen* 26.3–4 (1985): 2–21.

Campbell, Maria. *Stories of the Road Allowance People* (Penticton, British Columbia: Theytus, 1995).

Cardinal, Gil. Interview, cond. Kerstin Knopf (1998, unpublished).

Cardozo, Christopher, ed. *Native Nations: First Americans as Seen by E.S. Curtis* (Boston MA: Bulfinch, 1993).

Carlson, Marta. Interview, cond. Kerstin Knopf (1999, unpublished).

Carocci, Massimiliano. "The Berdache as Metahistorical Reference for the Urban Gay American Indian Community," in *Present is Past: Some Uses of Tradition in Native Societies*, ed. Marie Mauzé (Lanham MD: UP of America, 1997): 113–29.

Carroll, John B., ed. *Language, Thought, and Reality: Selected Writings of Benjamin Lee Whorf* (Cambridge MA: MIT Press, 1962).

Carpentier, Alejo. "On the Marvelous Real in America" (1949), tr. Tanya Huntington & Lois Parkinson Zamora, in *Magical Realism: Theory, History, Community*, ed. Lois Parkinson Zamora & Wendy B. Faris (Durham NC & London: Duke UP, 1995): 75–108.

Cashmore, Ellis, ed. *Dictionary of Race and Ethnic Relations* (1984, London & New York: Routledge, 4th ed. 1996).

Césaire, Aimé. "From *Discourse on Colonialism*" (1972), in *Colonial Discourse and Post-Colonial Theory*, ed. Williams & Chrisman, 172–80.

Chardon, Francis A. *Chardon's Journal at Fort Clark, 1834–1839*, ed. & intro. Annie Heloise Abel, intro. William R. Swagerty (Lincoln: U of Nebraska P, 1997).

Chartrand, Jean–Philippe. "Survival and Adaptation of the Inuit Ethnic Identity: The Importance of Inuktitut," in *Native People, Native Lands: Canadian Indians, Inuit and Metis*, ed. Bruce Alden Cox (Ottawa: Carleton UP, 1992): 241–55.

Chiampi, Irlemar. *El realismo maravilloso* (Caracas: Monte Ávila, 1983).

Churchill, Ward. *Fantasies of the Master Race: Literature, Cinema and the Colonization of American Indians* (San Francisco: City Lights, 1998).

——. "Fantasies of the Master Race: The Cinematic Colonization of American Indians" (1998), in Churchill, *Fantasies of the Master Race*, 167–224.

——, & Winona LaDuke. "Native North America: The Political Economy of Radioactive Colonialism," in *The State of Native America: Genocide, Colonization, and Resistance*, ed. M. Annette Jaimes (Boston MA: South End, 1992): 241–66.

Cipolla, John. "Mass Media as Language: The Sapir–Whorf Hypothesis and Electronic Media," in *Universalism versus Relativism in Language and Thought: Proceedings of a Colloquium on the Sapir–Whorf Hypothesis*, ed. Rik Pinxten (The Hague: Mouton, 1976): 303–10.

Clifford, James. "Introduction: Partial Truths," in *Writing Culture: The Poetics and Politics of Ethnography*, ed. James Clifford & George E. Marcus (Berkeley: U of California P, 1986): 1–26.

——. *The Predicament of Culture: Twentieth-Century Ethnography, Literature, Art* (Cambridge MA: Harvard UP, 1988).

Clutesi, George. *Son of Raven, Son of Deer: Fables of the Tse-Shaht People* (Sidney, British Columbia: Gray's Publishing, 1967).

Cobb, Amanda J. "This Is What It Means to Say *Smoke Signals*: Native American Cultural Sovereignty," in *Hollywood's Indian: The Portrayal of the Native American in Film*, ed. Peter C. Rollins & John E. O'Connor (Lexington: UP of Kentucky, 2003): 206–28.

Cohn, Norman. "The Art of Community-Based Filmmaking" (2002), in Apak Angilirq et al., *Atanarjuat: The Fast Runner*, 24–27.

Cole, Stephen. "First All-Native Film Sends Good Signals," *Globe & Mail* (3 July 1998): A10.

Collier's Encyclopedia, vol.19 (New York: Macmillan Education, 1990).

Conrad, Margaret, Alvin Finkel & Cornelius Jaenen. *History of the Canadian Peoples*, vol. 1: *Beginnings to 1867* (Toronto: Copp Clark Pitman, 1993).

Corbin, Amy Lynn. "Native American Narrative and Experimental Film: Aesthetics of Activism and Resistance" (BA Hons. thesis, College of William & Mary, 1997).

Cruikshank, Julie. "Oral Tradition and Oral History: Reviewing Some Issues," *Canadian Historical Review* 75.3 (1994): 403–18.

Cuddon, J.A. *A Dictionary of Literary Terms and Literary Theory* (1976, Oxford: Basil Blackwell, 3rd ed. 1991).

Cummings, Denise K. "'Accessible Poetry'? Cultural Intersection and Exchange in Contemporary American Indian and American Independent Film," *Studies in American Indian Literatures* 13.1 (Spring 2001): 57–78.

Currie, Gregory. "Film, Reality, and Illusion," in *Post-Theory: Reconstructing Film Studies*, ed. Bordwell & Carroll, 325–44.

Curtis, Edward S. *The North American Indian: Photographic Images* (1907–30; Cologne: Taschen, 1997).

Cuthand, Doug. Interview, cond. Kerstin Knopf (1998, unpublished).

d'Anglure, Bernard Saladin. "An Ethnographic Commentary: The Legend of Atanarjuat, Inuit and Shamanism" (2002), in Apak Angilirq et al., *Atanarjuat: The Fast Runner*, 196–228.

Darwin, Charles. *The Origin of Species, By Means of Natural Selection* (1859; London: John Murray, 1921).

——. *The Descent of Man, and Selection in Relation to Sex* (London: John Murray, 1871).

Dafoe, Chris. "The Resurrection of Big Bear," *Globe & Mail* (18 July 1998): C1, C3.

Deloria, Vine, Jr. "Trouble in High Places: Erosion of American Indian Rights to Religious Freedom in the United States," in *The State of Native America*, ed. M. Annette Jaimes (Boston MA: South End, 1992): 267–90.

——, *God is Red: A Native View of Religion* (Golden CO: Fulcrum, 1994).

——, *Red Earth, White Lies* (Golden CO: Fulcrum, 1997).

——, & Clifford M. Lytle. *American Indians, American Justice* (Austin: U of Texas P, 1983).

Dempsey, Hugh. *Big Bear: The End of Freedom* (Vancouver, British Columbia, & Toronto: Douglas & McIntyre, 1984).

Dickason, Olive Patricia. *Canada's First Nations: A History of Founding Peoples from Earliest Times* (Don Mills, Ontario: Oxford UP Canada, 3rd ed. 2002).

Dirlik, Arif. "The Past as Legacy and Project: Postcolonial Criticism in the Perspective of Indigenous Historicism," *American Indian Culture and Research Journal* 20.2 (1996): 1–31.

Drexler, Peter. "Erzählen in verschiedenen Medien – *Misery*: Stephen Kings Roman (1987) und Rob Reiners Film (1990)," in *Einführung in die Systematische Filmanalyse*, ed. Helmut Korte (Berlin: Erich Schmidt, 1999): 107–46.

Dueck, Allan. "Rudy Wiebe's Approach to Historical Fiction: A Study of *The Temptations of Big Bear* and *The Scorched-Wood People*," in *The Canadian Novel: Here and Now*, ed. John Moss (Toronto: NC Press, 1978): 182–200.

Eastman, Charles Alexander. *From the Deep Woods to Civilization* (1916; Lincoln & London: U of Nebraska P, 1977).

Ebert, Roger. "'Smoke Signals': American Indians Offer a Beacon to the Wire Culture," *Friday Magazine* (24 July 1998): 10.

Eccles, William J. "The French Fur Trade in the Eighteenth Century," in *Interpreting Canada's Past*, vol. 1: *Pre-Confederation*, ed. J.M. Bumsted (Toronto: Oxford UP, 1993): 207–30.

Eco, Umberto. *A Theory of Semiotics* (Bloomington & London: Indiana UP, 1976).

Eisenstein, Sergei. *The Film Sense*, tr. Jay Leda (New York: Harcourt, Brace, 1947).

Emberley, Julia. *Thresholds of Difference: Feminist Critique, Native Women's Writings, Postcolonial Theory* (Toronto: U of Toronto P, 1993).

Encarta. *World English Dictionary* (London: Bloomsbury, 1999).

Ewers, John. *Artists of the Old West* (1965; Garden City NY: Doubleday, 1973).

Fanon, Frantz. *The Wretched of the Earth*, tr. Constance Farrington, intro. Jean-Paul Sartre (*Les damnés de la terre*, 1961; New York: Grove, 1963).

——. *Black Skin, White Masks*, tr. Charles L. Markman (*Peau noire, masques blancs*, 1952; tr. New York: Grove, 1967).

——. "On National Culture" (excerpt from *The Wretched of the Earth*, 1961), in *Colonial Discourse and Post-Colonial Theory*, ed. Williams & Chrisman, 36–52.

Faris, James C. "Photographing the Navajo: Scanning Abuse," *American Indian Culture and Research Journal* 20.3 (1996): 65–81.

Fiedler, Leslie A. *Love and Death in the American Novel* (1960; New York: Penguin, 1982).

——. *The Return of the Vanishing American* (1968; New York: Stein & Day, 1976).

Fisher, Robin. "Indian Control of the Maritime Fur Trade and the Northwest Coast," in *Readings in Canadian History*, vol. 1: *Pre-Confederation*, ed. R. Douglas Francis & Donald B. Smith (Toronto: Holt, Rinehart & Winston of Canada, 1990): 79–92.

Flaherty, Frances. "Flaherty: *Samoa*," *Filmkritik* 5.245 (1977): 255–67.

Fludernik, Monika. "Introduction" to *Hybridity and Postcolonialism: Twentieth-Century Indian Literature*, ed. Monika Fludernik (Tübingen: Stauffenburg, 1998): 9–18.

——. "The Constitution of Hybridity: Postcolonial Interventions," in *Hybridity and Postcolonialism*, ed. Fludernik, 19–53.

Forbes, John. "Postcolonial Biscuit," *Meanjin* 56.1 (1997): 196–97.

Foucault, Michel. *Madness and Civilization: A History of Insanity in the Age of Reason* (*Folie et déraison: Histoire de la folie à l'âge classique*, 1961; New York: Pantheon, 1965).

——. *The Birth of the Clinic: An Archaeology of Medical Perception* (1963; *Naissance de la clinique: Une archéologie du regard medical*, 1963; New York: Pantheon, 1973).

——. "Orders of Discourse," tr. Rupert Swyer ("L'ordre du discours") *Social Science Information* 10.2 (1971): 7–30.

——. *Discipline and Punish: The Birth of the Prison* (*Surveiller et punir: La naissance de la prison*, 1975; New York: Vintage, 1979).

——. *The Order of Things: An Archaeology of the Human Sciences* (*Les Mots et les choses: Une archéologie des sciences humaines*, 1966; London & New York: Routledge, 2007).

Francis, Daniel. *The Imaginary Indian: The Image of the Indian in Canadian Culture* (Vancouver, British Columbia: Arsenal Pulp, 1992).

Francis, R. Douglas, & Donald B. Smith, ed. *Readings in Canadian History*, vol. 1: *Pre-Confederation* (Toronto: Holt, Rinehart & Winston of Canada, 1990).

Franco, Jean. "Beyond Ethnocentrism: Gender, Power and the Third-World Intelligentsia" (1988), in *Colonial Discourse and Post-Colonial Theory*, ed. Williams & Chrisman, 359–69.

Frase–Blunt, Martha. "New Regard for Hispanic Authors," *ASN* 34 (September 1994): 40–43.

French, Philip. "The Indian in the Western Movie," *Art in America* 60 (July–August 1972): 32–39.

Friar, Ralph, & Natasha Friar. *The Only Good Indian: The Hollywood Gospel* (New York: Drama Book Specialists, 1972).

Frideres, James S. *Native Peoples in Canada: Contemporary Conflicts* (Scarborough, Ontario: Prentice Hall Canada, 1993).

Fruchter, Barry. "Den of Lions: Captivity and Ideology on the New American Frontier," *Journal of Nassau Community College* 7.5 (1999): 116–33.

Gabriel, Teshome H. "Towards a Critical Theory of Third World Films" (1989), in *Colonial Discourse and Post-Colonial Theory*, ed. Williams & Chrisman, 340–58.

Galarce, Carmen J. *La novela chilena de exílio, 1973–1987: El caso de Isabel Allende* (Santiago de Chile: Departamento de Estudios Humanísticos, 1993).

Gavez, Raúl. "Epic Inuit: In Conversation with Zacharias Kunuk," *Montage* (Spring 2002): 10–14.

——. "In Conversation with Norman Cohn," *Montage* (Spring 2002): 12–13.

Gilbert, Helen, & Joanne Tompkins. *Post-Colonial Drama: Theory, Practice, Politics* (London & New York: Routledge, 1996).

Gilroy, Jhon Warren. "Another Fine Example of the Oral Tradition? Identification and Subversion in Sherman Alexie's *Smoke Signals*," *Studies in American Indian Literatures* 13.1 (Spring 2001): 23–42.

Ginsberg, Faye. "Indigenous Media: Faustian Contract or Global Village?" *Cultural Anthropology* 6.1 (1991): 92–112.

Gipper, Helmut. "Is There a Linguistic Relativity Principle?" in *Universalism versus Relativism in Language and Thought: Proceedings of a Colloquium on the Sapir–Whorf Hypothesis*, ed. Rik Pinxten (The Hague: Mouton, 1976): 217–28.

Gish, Robert Franklin. *Beyond Bounds: Crosscultural Essays on Anglo, American Indian, and Chicano Literature* (Albuquerque: U of New Mexico P, 1996).

Goldie, Terry. "Comparative Views of an Aboriginal Past: Rudy Wiebe & Patrick White," *World Literature Written in English* 23.2 (Spring 1984): 429–39.

Gowanlock, Theresa, & Theresa Delaney. *Two Months in the Camp of Big Bear: The Life and Adventures of Theresa Gowanlock and Theresa Delaney* (Regina, Saskatchewan: Canadian Plains Research Center, 1999).

Grace, Sherrill E. "Exploration as Construction: Robert Flaherty and *Nanook of the North*," *Essays on Canadian Writing* 59 (Fall 1996): 123–46.

Green, Rayna. "The Pocahontas Perplex: The Image of Indian Women in American Culture," *Massachusetts Review* 16.4 (Autumn 1975): 698–714.

——. "What is the Pocahontas Perplex?" *The Runner* 1.3 (Summer 1994): 9.

Greyson, John, & Lisa Steele. "The Inukshuk Project/Inuit TV: The Satellite Solution," in *Video re/View: The (Best) Source for Critical Writings on Canadian Artists' Video*, ed. Peggy Gale & Lisa Steele (Toronto: Art Metropole & Vtape, 1996): 57–63.

Griffiths, Gareth. "The Myth of Authenticity: Representation, Discourse and Social Practice," in *De-Scribing Empire: Post-Colonialism and Textuality*, ed. Chris Tiffin & Alan Lawson (London & New York: Routledge, 1994): 70–85.

Gross, Elizabeth. "Criticism, Feminism and the Institution: An Interview with Gayatri Chakravorty Spivak," *Thesis Eleven* 10–11 (1984–85): 175–87.

Grossberg, Lawrence. "On Postmodernism and Articulation: An Interview with Stuart Hall," *Journal of Commonwealth Inquiry* 10 (1986): 45–60.

Hakluyt, Richard. *Divers Voyages Touching the Discoverie of America* (1582; Ann Arbor MI: facs., 1966.

——. *The Principall Navigations, Voiages and Discoveries of the English Nation*, 2 vols. (1589; London & Cambridge: facs., 1965).

Hall, Stuart. "Cultural Identity and Cinematic Representation," *Framework: A Film Journal* 36 (1989): 68–81.

——. "When Was 'The Post-Colonial'? Thinking at the Limit," in *The Post-Colonial Question: Common Skies, Divided Horizons*, ed. Iain Chambers & Lidia Curti (London & New York: Routledge, 1996): 242–60.

——, & Paul du Gay, ed. *Questions of Cultural Identity* (London: Sage, 1996).

Hayward, Susan. *Key Concepts in Cinema Studies* (London & New York: Routledge, 1996).

Helm, Richard. "History Revisited: 'Big Bear' Turns a Few Tables on the TV Audience to Trace the Saga of a Native Hero," *Regina Leader-Post TV* (2 January–8 January 1999).

Hembus, Joe. *Das Westernlexikon* (Munich: Wilhelm Heine, 1997).

Henley, Paul. "Fly in the Soup," *London Review of Books* (21 June 2001): 35–37.

Herdt, Gilbert, ed. *Third Sex, Third Gender: Beyond Sexual Dimorphism in Culture and History* (New York: Zone, 1994).

——. "The Dilemmas of Desire: From 'Berdache' to Two Spirit" (1997), in *Two-Spirit People*, ed. Jacobs, Thomas & Lang, 276–83.

Hoberman, Jim. "*Atanarjuat – The Fast Runner*," *Village Voice* (20 March 2002): 26.

Hochbruck, Wolfgang. *"I have Spoken": Die Darstellung und ideologische Funktion indianischer Mündlichkeit in der nordamerikanischen Literatur* (Tübingen: Gunter Narr, 1991).

Hohenberger, Eva. *Die Wirklichkeit des Films: Dokumentarfilm, Ethnografischer Film* (Hildesheim, Zurich & New York: Georg Olms, 1988).

Honneth, Axel. *Kritik der Macht: Reflexionsstufen einer kritischen Gesellschaftstheorie* (Frankfurt am Main: Suhrkamp, 1994).

Hood Museum of Art. *Reservation X* (exh. cat., 6 October–16 December 2001; Hanover NH: Hood Museum of Art, Dartmouth College, 2001).

Howe, Desson. "'Fast Runner' a Stunner," *Washington Post* (21 June 2002): WE44.

Hulan, Renée, ed. *Native North America. Critical and Cultural Perspectives* (Toronto: ECW, 1999).

Hulme, Peter. *Colonial Encounters: Europe and the Native Caribbean, 1492–1797* (London: Methuen, 1986).

——. "Including America," *ARIEL: A Review of International English Literature* 26.1 (January 1995): 117–23.

Huntsman, Jeffrey F. "Traditional Native American Literature: The Translation Dilemma" (1983), in *Smoothing the Ground*, ed. Swann, 87–97.

Hymes, Dell, ed. *Reinventing Anthropology* (New York: Pantheon, 1972).

Ikegami, Yoshihiko. "From the Sapir–Whorf Hypothesis to Cultural Semiotics – Some Considerations on the 'Language–Culture Problem'," in *Scientific and Humanistic Dimensions of Language*, ed. Kurt Jankowsky (Amsterdam & Philadelphia PA: John Benjamins, 1985): 215–22.

Jacobs, Sue–Ellen. "Is the 'North American Berdache' Merely a Phantom in the Imagination of Western Social Scientists?" (1997), in *Two-Spirit People*, ed. Jacobs, Thomas & Lang, 21–43.

——, Wesley Thomas & Sabine Lang, ed. *Two-Spirit People: Native American Gender Identity, Sexuality, and Spirituality* (Urbana & Chicago: U of Illinois P, 1997)

Jaimes, M. Annette, ed. *The State of Native America: Genocide, Colonization, and Resistance* (Boston MA: South End, 1992).

Jaimes–Guerrero, Marianette. "Savage Erotica Exotica: Media Imagery of Native Women in North America," in *Native North America: Critical and Cultural Perspectives*, ed. Renée Hulan (Toronto: ECW, 1999): 187–210.

Jay, Martin. "In the Empire of the Gaze: Foucault and the Denigration of Vision in Twentieth-Century French Thought," in *Michel Foucault: Critical Assessments*, ed. Barry Smart (New York & London: Routledge, 1994), vol. 1: 201–23.

Johnston, Basil. *Indian School Days* (Toronto: Key Porter Books, 1988).

——. *The Manitous: The Spiritual World of the Ojibway* (Toronto: Key Porter Books, 1995).

——. *Tales of the Anishinaubaek* (Toronto: Royal Ontario Musum, 1993).

Kaiser, Rudolf. "Chief Seattle's Speech(es): American Origins and European Reception," in *Recovering the Word: Essays on Native American Literature*, ed. Brian Swann & Arnold Krupat (Berkeley: U of California P, 1987): 497–536.

Kawaja, Jennifer. "Process Video, Self Reference and Social Change," in *Mirror Machine: Video and Identity*, ed. Janine Marchessault (Toronto: YYZ, 1995): 203–13.

Kehoe, Alice B. *North American Indians: A Comprehensive Account* (Englewood Cliffs NJ: Prentice Hall, 1992).

Kempley, Rita. "No More Playing Dead for American Indian Filmmaker Sherman Alexie," *Washington Post* (3 July 1998): D1.

Kilpatrick, Jacquelyn. "Disney's 'Politically Correct' Pocahontas," *Cineaste* 21.4 (Fall 1995): 36.

——. *Celluloid Indians: Native Americans and Film* (Lincoln: U of Nebraska P, 1999).

King, Thomas. *Green Grass, Running Water* (New York: Bantam, 1994).

——. "Godzilla vs. Post-Colonial," *World Literature Written in English* 30.2 (1990): 10–16.

Kniebe, Tobias. "Reservate des Rückwärtsgangs," *Süddeutsche Zeitung* (8 December 1998): 15.

Knopf, Kerstin. "Aboriginal Women and Film in Canada" (MA thesis, University of Greifswald, 1996).

——. "Geschichte filmen: Die Perspektive kanadischer indigener Filmemacher(innen)," *Zeitschrift für Kanada-Studien* 19.1/35 (1999): 175–85.

Kögler, Hans Herbert. *Michel Foucault* (Sammlung Metzler 281: Realien zur Philosophie; Stuttgart & Weimar: J.B. Metzler, 1994).

Kohl, Karl–Heinz. "Abwehr und Verlangen: Der Eurozentrismus in der Ethnologie," *Berliner Hefte* 12 (1979): 28–42.

Koller, Angelika, ed. *Indianerweisheiten* (Munich: arsedition, 1996).

Kroeber, Karl. "Oral Narrative in an Age of Mechanical Reproduction," *Studies in American Indian Literature* 11.2 (Spring 1987): 61–91.

Krupat, Arnold. "Nationalism, Indigenism, Cosmopolitanism: Critical Perspectives on Native American Literatures," *Centennial Review* 42.3 (Fall 1998): 617–26.

——. "Postcoloniality and Native American Literature," *Yale Journal of Criticism* 7.1 (1994): 163–80.

Kuehnast, Kathleen. "Visual Imperialism and the Export of Prejudice: An Exploration of Ethnographic Film," in *Film as Ethnography*, ed. Peter Ian Crawford & David Turton (Manchester & New York: Manchester UP, 1992): 183–95.

Kunuk, Zacharias. "I First Heard the Story of Atanarjuat From my Mother" (2002), in Apak Angilirq et al. *Atanarjuat: The Fast Runner*, 12–15.

Lang, Sabine. "Various Kinds of Two-Spirit People: Gender Variance and Homosexuality in Native American Communities" (1997), in *Two-Spirit People*, ed. Jacobs, Thomas & Lang, 100–18.

Lauter, Paul, gen. ed. *The Heath Anthology of American Literature*, vol. I (1990; Boston MA & New York: Houghton Mifflin, 1998).

Lecker, Robert. "Trusting the Quintuplet Senses: Time and Form in *The Temptations of Big Bear*," *English Studies in Canada* 8.3 (September 1982): 333–48.

Leuthold, Steven. "An Indigenous Aesthetic? Two Noted Videographers: George Burdeau and Victor Masayesva," *Wicazo Sa Review* 10.1 (Spring 1994): 40–51.

——. *Indigenous Aesthetics: Native Art, Media and Identity* (Austin: U of Texas P, 1998).

——. *'Telling Our Own Story': The Aesthetic Expression of Collective Identity in Native American Documentary* (Ann Arbor MI: UMI, 1992).

Levy, Jerrold E. "Hopi Shamans: A Reappraisal," in *North American Indian Anthropology: Essays on Society and Culture*, ed. Raymond J. DeMallie & Alfonso Ortiz (Norman & London: U of Oklahoma P, 1994): 307–27.

Littlejohn, Catherine Isabel. "The Indian Oral Tradition: A Model for Teachers" (MA thesis, University of Saskatchewan, College of Education, 1975).

Lutz, Hartmut. *Approaches: Essays in Native North American Studies and Literatures* (Beiträge zur Kanadistik 11; Augsburg: Wissner, 2002).

——. "Canadian Native Literature and the Sixties: A Historical and Bibliographical Survey," *Canadian Literature* 152–53 (Spring–Summer 1997): 167–91; repr. in Lutz, *Approaches*, 154–71.

——. "The Circle as Philosophical and Structural Concept in Native American Fiction Today," in *Native American Literatures*, ed. Laura Cotelli (Pisa: Servicio Editoriale Universitario, 1989): 85–100; repr. in Lutz, *Approaches*, 195–208.

——. "Confronting Cultural Imperialism: First Nations People are Combating Continued Cultural Theft," in *Multiculturalism in North America and Europe: Social Practices – Literary Visions*, ed. Hans Braun & Wolfgang Klooss (Trier: WVT, 1995): 132–51; repr. in Lutz, *Approaches*, 83–97.

——. *Contemporary Challenges: Conversations with Canadian Native Authors* (Saskatoon, Saskatchewan: Fifth House, 1991).

——. "Cultural Appropriation as a Process of Displacing Peoples and History," *Canadian Journal of Native Studies* 10.2 (1990): 167–82; repr. as "Cultural Appropriation as a Repression of Peoples and Histories," in Lutz, *Approaches*, 75–82.

——. *D–Q University: Native American Self-Determination in Higher Education* (Davis CA: Tecumseh Center Publications, 1980).

——. *"Indianer" und "Native Americans": Zur sozial- und literarhistorischen Vermittlung eines Stereotyps* (Hildesheim, Zurich & New York: Georg Olms, 1985).

——. "'Indians' and Native Americans in the Movies: A History of Stereotypes, Distortions, and Displacements," *Visual Anthropology* 3 (1990): 31–48; repr. in Lutz, *Approaches*, 48–61.

——. "Native Literatures in Canada Today: An Introduction," *Zeitschrift der Gesellschaft für Kanada-Studien* 10.1/17 (1990): 27–47.

———. "First Nations Literature in Canada and the Voice of Survival," *London Journal of Canadian Studies* 11 (Special Issue on Aboriginal Peoples, 1995): 60–76.

———, et al. *Achte Deines Bruders Traum: Gespräche mit nordamerikanischen Indianern 1978–1985* (1987; Osnabrück: Druck- und Verlagskooperative, 1997).

MacDougall, David. "Ethnographic Film: Failure and Promise," *Annual Review of Anthropology* 7 (1978): 405–25.

Mackenthun, Gesa. *Metaphors of Dispossession: American Beginnings and the Translation of Empire, 1492–1637* (Norman & London: U of Oklahoma P, 1997).

Malik, Sarita. "Beyond 'The Cinema of Duty'? The Pleasures of Hybridity: Black British Film of the 1980s and 1990s," in *Dissolving Views: Key Writings on British Cinema*, ed. Andrew Higson (London & New York: Cassell, 1996): 202–15.

Manuel, George, & Michael Posluns. *The Fourth World: An Indian Reality* (Don Mills, Ontario: Collier–Macmillan Canada, 1974).

Maracle, Lee. *Sojourner's Truth and Other Stories* (Vancouver, British Columbia: Press Gang, 1990).

Marchessault, Janine, ed. *Mirror Machine: Video and Identity* (Toronto: YYZ, 1995).

Martell, Lloyd. Interview, cond. Kerstin Knopf (1996, unpublished).

———. Interview, cond. Kerstin Knopf (1998, unpublished).

Masayesva, Victor, Jr. "The Emerging Native American Aesthetics in Film and Video," *Film and Video Monthly Independent* (December 1994): 20–21, 27.

———. *Hopi Photography, Hopi Images* (Tucson: Sun Tracks/U of Arizona P, 1984).

———. *Husk of Time: The Photography of Victor Masayesva* (Tucson: U of Arizona P, 2006).

———. Interview, cond. Kerstin Knopf (2001, unpublished).

Mayne, Judith. *Kino and the Woman Question* (Columbus: Ohio State UP, 1989).

McClintock, Anne. "The Angel of Progress: Pitfalls of the Term 'Post-Colonialism'" (1992), in *Colonial Discourse and Post-Colonial Theory*, ed. Williams & Chrisman, 291–304.

McLuhan, Marshall. *Understanding Media: The Extensions of Man* (New York & Scarborough, Ontario: Mentor, 1964).

Michaels, Eric. "Constraints on Knowledge in an Economy of Oral Information," *Current Anthropology* 26.4 (1985): 505–10.

Miller, J.R. "Reserves, Residential Schools, and the Threat of Assimilation," in Miller, *Skyscrapers Hide the Heavens: A History of Indian–White Relations in Canada* (1989; Toronto: U of Toronto P, 2000): 125–47.

Mishra, Vijay, & Bob Hodge. "What is Post (-) Colonialism?" (1991), in *Colonial Discourse and Post-Colonial Theory*, ed. Williams & Chrisman, 276–90.

Momaday, Scott N. *House Made of Dawn* (1966; Tucson: U of Arizona P, 1968).

——. "The Man Made of Words," in *The Remembered Earth: An Anthology of Contemporary Native American Literature*, ed. Geary Hobson (Albuquerque NM: Red Earth, 1979): 162–73.

Monaco, James. *How to Read a Film: The Art, Technology, Language, History, and Theory of Film and Media* (1977; Oxford: Oxford UP, 1981).

Monk, Katherine. "First Takes: Our Home and Native Land," in Monk, *Weird Sex and Snowshoes*, 45–62.

——. "Real Native Culture Shines Through Smoke Signals," Vancouver Sun (17 July 1998): C 3.

——. *Weird Sex and Snowshoes and Other Canadian Film Phenomena* (Vancouver CA: Raincoast, 2001).

Morris, Alexander. *The Treaties of Canada with the Indians of Manitoba and the North-West Territories Including the Negotiations on Which They Were Based* (1880; Saskatoon, Saskatchewan: Fifth House, 1991).

Morris, Glenn T. "International Law and Politics: Toward a Right to Self-Determination for Indigenous Peoples," in *The State of Native America*, ed. M. Annette Jaimes (Boston MA: South End Press, 1992): 55–86.

Morris, Rosalind C. *New Worlds from Fragments: Film, Ethnography, and the Representation of Northwest Coast Culture* (Boulder CO: Westview, 1994).

Morrisseau, Miles. "Disney's Disgrace," *Aboriginal Voices* 2.3 (September–October 1995): 16–17.

——. "Review: *Dance Me Outside*," *Aboriginal Voices* 2.2 (May–July 1995): 56.

Moses, Daniel David. "Inukshuk," in *The White Line* (Saskatoon, Saskatchewan: Fifth House, 1990): np.

"Movie Cathartic for Native Actor," *Regina Leader-Post* (4 July 1998): D7.

Nelson, Emmanuel. "Fourth World Fictions: A Comparative Commentary on James Welch's *Winter in the Blood* and Mudrooroo Narogin's *Wild Cat Falling*," in *Critical Perspectives on Native American Fiction*, ed. Richard F. Fleck (Washington DC: Three Continents, 1993): 57–63.

Nelson, Robert M. *Place and Vision: The Function of Landscape in Native American Fiction*, vol. 1 (New York: Peter Lang, 1993).

Neubauer, Paul. "Indian Captivity in American Children's Literature: A Pre-Civil War Set of Stereotypes," *The Lion and the Unicorn: A Critical Journal of Children's Literature* 25.1 (January 2001): 70–80.

Ngũgĩ wa Thiong'o. *Decolonising the Mind: The Politics of Language in African Literature* (Portsmouth NH: Heinemann, 1981).

——. "The Language of African Literature" (1981), in *Colonial Discourse and Post-Colonial Theory*, ed. Williams & Chrisman, 435–55.

Niro, Shelley. Interview, cond. Kerstin Knopf (1998, unpublished).

Noriega, Jorge. "American Indian Education in the United States: Indoctrination for Subordination to Colonialism," in *The State of Native America: Genocide, Colonization, and Resistance*, ed. M. Annette Jaimes (Boston MA: South End, 1992): 371–402.

Norris Nicholson, Heather. "Introduction" (2003) to *Screening Culture*, ed. Norris Nicholson, 1–10.

——. "Making Things Happen Through Parody and Visual Irony" (2003), in *Screening Culture*, ed. Norris Nicholson, 157–68.

——, ed. *Screening Culture: Constructing Image and Identity* (Lanham MD: Lexington, 2003).

Obomsawin, Alanis. Interview, cond. Kerstin Knopf (1996, unpublished).

O'Connor, John E. *The Hollywood Indian: Stereotypes of Native Americans in Films* (Trenton NJ: New Jersey State Museum, 1980).

Ong, Walter J. *Orality and Literacy: The Technologizing of the Word* (New York: Routledge, 1982).

Ortiz, Alfonso. "The Dynamics of Pueblo Cultural Survival," in *North American Indian Anthropology. Essays on Society and Culture*, ed. Raymond J. DeMallie & Alfonso Ortiz (Norman & London: U of Oklahoma P, 1994): 296–306.

——, & Richard Erdoes. *American Indian Myths and Legends* (New York: Pantheon, 1984).

Owens, Louis. *Mixedblood Messages: Literature, Film, Family, Place* (Norman: U of Oklahoma P, 1998).

Parham, Jennifer. "This is What it Means to Make Our Own Movies," *Aboriginal Voices* 4.5 (July–September 1997): 30–31.

Parrenteau, Diane. "Historic Study Uncovers Big Bear's Camp," *Windspeaker* 9.6 (7 June 1991): 3.

Pasqua, Neil. Interview, cond. Kerstin Knopf (1998, unpublished).

Pasquaretta, Paul. *Gambling and Survival in Native North America* (Tucaon: U of Arizona P, 2003).

Pauls, Carmen. "Walking in His Moccasins: Filmmakers Re-Tell Big Bear's Story," *Prairie Dog* (July 1998): 14–15.

Peabody, Berkley. *The Winged Word: A Study in the Technique of Ancient Greek Oral Composition as Seen Principally through Hesiod's "Works and Days"* (Albany: State U of New York P, 1975).

Peipp, Matthias, & Bernhard Springer. *Edle Wilde, Rote Teufel: Indianer im Film* (Munich: Wilhelm Heyne, 1997).

Perkins, V.F. *Film as Film: Understanding and Judging Movies* (1964; Harmondsworth & Baltimore MD: Penguin, 1972).

Piapot, Debra. Interview, cond. Kerstin Knopf (1996, unpublished).

Poitras, Evelyn. Interview, cond. Kerstin Knopf (1998, unpublished).

"Rauchzeichen aus Nordwest," *Der Spiegel* 19 (1998): 214–15.

Ray, Arthur J. "Fur Trade History as an Aspect of Native History," in *Readings in Canadian History*, vol. 1: *Pre-Confederation*, ed. R. Douglas Francis & Donald B. Smith (Toronto: Holt, Rinehart & Winston of Canada, 1990): 49–63.

Ray, Sangeeta, & Henry Schwarz. "Postcolonial Discourse: The Raw and the Cooked," *ARIEL: A Review of International English Literature* 26.1 (January 1995): 147–66.

Red Earth, Michael. "Traditional Influences on a Contemporary Gay-Identified Sisseton Dakota" (1997), in *Two-Spirit People*, ed. Jacobs, Thomas & Lang, 210–16.

Reichard, Gladys A. *Navaho Religion: A Study of Symbolism* (Tucson: U of Arizona P, 1983).

Renov, Michael, ed. *Theorizing Documentary* (New York & London: Routledge, 1993).

Ressner, Jeffrey. "They've Gotta Have It: What Spike Lee's Film Did For African Americans, *Smoke Signals* Aims to Do For Native Americans," *TIME* (29 June 1998): 2.

Roberts Powers, Willow. "Images Across Boundaries: History, Use, and Ethics of Photographs of American Indians," *American Indian Culture and Research Journal* 20.3 (1996): 129–36.

Robins, Robert H. "The Current Relevance of the Sapir–Whorf Hypothesis," in *Universalism versus Relativism in Language and Thought: Proceedings of a Colloquium on the Sapir–Whorf Hypothesis*, ed. Rik Pinxten (The Hague: Mouton, 1976): 99–107.

Robinson, Harry. *Write It On Your Heart: The Epic World of an Okanagan Storyteller*, ed. Wendy Wickwire (Vancouver, British Columbia: Talonbooks/Theytus, 1989).

Rodenberg, Hans–Peter. *Der imaginierte Indianer: Zur Dynamik von Kulturkonflikt und Vergesellschaftung des Fremden* (Frankfurt am Main: Suhrkamp, 1994).

Roemer, Kenneth M. "Native American Oral Narratives: Context and Continuity" (1983), in *Smoothing the Ground*, ed. Swann, 39–54.

Rollins, Peter C., & John E. O'Connor, ed. *Hollywood's Indian: The Portrayal of the Native American in Film* (Lexington: UP of Kentucky, 2003).

Rosaldo, Renato. "Doing Oral History," *Social Analysis* 4 (September 1980): 89–99.

Roscoe, Will. "How to Become a Berdache: Toward a Unified Analysis of Gender Diversity," in *Third Sex, Third Gender: Beyond Sexual Dimorphism in Culture and History*, ed. Gilbert Herdt (New York: Zone, 1994): 329–72.

Rosen, Philip, ed. *Narrative, Apparatus, Ideology: A Film Theory Reader* (New York: Columbia UP, 1986).

Ross, Rodger. Interview, cond. Kerstin Knopf (1996, unpublished).

——. Interview, cond. Kerstin Knopf (1998, unpublished).

Roth, Lorna. "Television Broadcasting North of 60," *Images of Canadianness: Visions on Canada's Politics, Culture, Economics*, ed. Leen d'Haenens (Ottawa: U of Ottawa P, 1998): 148–66.

——. *Something New in the Air: The Story of First Peoples Television Broadcasting in Canada* (Montreal & Kingston, Ontario: McGill–Queen's UP, 2005).

——. "The Aboriginal Peoples Television Network (APTN) – Going National," in Roth, *Something New in the Air*, 201–18.

Rotha, Paul. "Nanook and the North," *Studies in Visual Communication* 6.2 (1980): 34–60.

Ruby, Jay. "A Reexamination of the Early Career of Robert J. Flaherty," *Quarterly Review of Film Studies* 5.4 (Summer 1980): 431–57.

Ruffo, Armand Garnet. *Grey Owl: the Mystery of Archie Belaney* (Regina, Saskatchewan: Coteau, 1996).

Rushdie, Salman. *Imaginary Homelands: Essays and Criticism, 1981–1991* (New York: Granta, 1992).

Said, Edward W. "Foucault and the Imagination of Power," in *Foucault: A Critical Reader*, ed. David Couzens Hoy (Oxford & New York: Basil Blackwell, 1986): 149–55.

——. *Orientalism* (London: Routledge, 1978).

Sands, Kathleen M., & Allison Sekaquaptewa Lewis. "Seeing with a Native Eye: A Hopi Film on Hopi," *American Indian Quarterly* 14.4 (1990): 387–96.

Scholte, Bob. "Toward a Reflexive and Critical Anthropology," in *Reinventing Anthropology*, ed. Dell Hymes (New York: Pantheon, 1972): 430–57.

Schulte, Bernd. "Kulturelle Hybridität: Kulturanthropologische Anmerkungen zu einem 'Normalzustand'," in *Hybridkultur: Medien, Netze, Künste*, ed. Irmela Schneider & Christian W. Thomsen (Cologne: Wienand, 1997): 245–63.

Schweickle, Günther, & Irmgard Schweickle. *Metzler Literatur Lexikon* (Stuttgart: J.B. Metzler, 1990).

Scott, A.O. "Film Festival Review: A Far-Off Inuit World, in a Dozen Shades of White," *New York Times* (30 March 2002): 9, B3.

Shaver, Pat. "Made for TV Movie Spotlights Crees' Struggle," *Aboriginal Voices* (July–August, 1998): 52–53.

Shohat, Ella, & Robert Stam. *Unthinking Eurocentrism: Multiculturalism and the Media* (1994; London & New York: Routledge, 1997).

Silberman, Robert. "Victor Masayesva and the Question of a Native American Aesthetic," paper presented at College Art Association Conference, Chicago, 1992; unpublished.

Silbermann, Alphons, Michael Schaaf & Gerhard Adam. "Theoreme der Filmanalyse," in *Filmanalyse: Grundlagen – Methoden – Didaktik* (Munich: Oldenbourg, 1980):48–57.

Silko, Leslie Marmon. "Videomakers and Basketmakers," *Aperture* 119 (Summer 1990): 72–73.

Singer, Beverly R. *Wiping the War Paint Off the Lens: Native American Film and Video* (Minneapolis: U of Minnesota P, 2001).

Sioui, Georges E. *For an Amerindian Autohistory*, tr. Sheila Fischman (*Pour une autohistoire amérindienne*, 1991; Montreal & Kingston, Ontario: McGill–Queen's UP, 1992).

Slemon, Stephen. "Modernism's Last Post," *ARIEL: A Review of International English Literature* 20.4 (1989): 3–17.

Smith, Donald B. *Land of the Shadows: The Making of Grey Owl* (Saskatoon, Saskatchewan: Western Producer Prairie Books, 1990).

Smith, Jeff. "Unheard Melodies? A Critique of Psychoanalytic Theories of Film Music," in *Post-Theory: Reconstructing Film Studies*, ed. Bordwell & Carroll, 230–47.

Smith, Murray. "The Logic and Legacy of Brechtianism," in *Post-Theory: Reconstructing Film Studies*, ed. Bordwell & Carroll, 130–48.

Sollors, Werner. *Beyond Ethnicity: Consent and Descent in American Culture* (New York & Oxford: Oxford U P, 1986).

——. "Foreword: Theories of Ethnicity" (1996), in *Theories of Ethnicity*, ed. Sollors, x–xliv.

——. "Introduction: The Invention of Ethnicity" (1989), in *The Invention of Ethnicity*, ed. Sollors, ix–xx.

——, ed. *The Invention of Ethnicity* (New York & Oxford: Oxford U P, 1989).

——, ed. *Theories of Ethnicity: A Classical Reader* (Houndmills & London: Macmillan, 1996).

Spivak, Gayatri Chakravorty. "Acting Bits/Identity Talk," *Critical Inquiry* 18 (Summer 1992): 770–803.

——. "Can the Subaltern Speak?" (1988), in *Colonial Discourse and Post-Colonial Theory*, ed. Williams & Chrisman, 66–111.

Standing Bear, Luther. *Land of the Spotted Eagle* (1933; Lincoln & London: U of Nebraska P, 1978).

Stearn, E. Wagner, & Allen E. Stearn. *The Effects of Small Pox on the Destiny of the Amerindian* (Boston M A: Bruce Humphries, 1945).

Stiffarm, Lenore A., & Phil Lane, Jr. "The Demography of Native North America: A Question of American Indian Survival," in *The State of Native America*, ed. M. Annette Jaimes (Boston M A: South End, 1992): 23–53.

Stonechild, Blair & Bill Waiser. *Loyal Till Death: Indians and the North-West Rebellion* (Calgary, Alberta: Fifth House, 1997).

Strain, Ellen. "Exotic Bodies, Distant Landscapes: Touristic Viewing and Popularized Anthropology in the Nineteenth Century," *Wide Angle* 18.2 (April 1996): 70–100.

Struzik, Edward. *Northwest Passage: The Quest for an Arctic Route to the East* (Toronto: Key Porter, 1991).

Suleri, Sara. "Women Skin Deep: Feminism and the Postcolonial Condition," *Critical Inquiry* 18 (Summer 1992): 756–69.

Sutherland, Linda. "Citizen Minus: Aboriginal Women and Indian Self-Government, Race, Nation, Class and Gender" (M A thesis, University of Regina, 1995).

——. Interview, cond. Kerstin Knopf. (1996, unpublished).

Swann, Brian. *Coming to Light: Contemporary Translations of the Native Literature of North America* (New York: Vintage, 1994).

——, ed. *Smoothing the Ground: Essays on Native American Oral Literature* (Berkeley: U of California P, 1983).

Tafoya, Terry. "M. Dragonfly: Two-Spirit and the Tafoya Principle of Uncertainty" (1997), in *Two-Spirit People*, ed. Jacobs, Thomas & Lang, 192–200.

Tedlock, Dennis. "On the Translation of Style in Oral Narrative" (1983), in *Smoothing the Ground*, ed. Swann, 57–77.

Thompson, Kristin. "A Neoformalist Approach to Film Analysis: One Approach, Many Methods," in Kristin Thompson, *Breaking the Glass Armor: Neoformalist Film Analysis* (Princeton NJ: Princeton UP, 1988): 3–46.

Tiffin, Chris, & Alan Lawson, ed. *De-Scribing Empire: Post-Colonialism and Textuality* (London & New York: Routledge, 1994).

Tobing Rony, Fatimah. "Victor Masayesva, Jr., and the Politics of Imagining Indians," *Film Quarterly* 48.2 (1994–95): 20–33.

——. *The Third Eye: Race, Cinema, and Ethnographic Spectacle* (Durham NC & London: Duke UP, 1996).

——. "Taxidermy and Romantic Ethnography. Robert Flaherty's *Nanook of the North*" (1996), in Tobing Rony, *The Third Eye*, 99–126.

Todd, Loretta. "Three Moments After Savage Graces," *Harbour* 9 (1993): 57–62.

——. Interview, cond. Kerstin Knopf (1998, unpublished).

Tomiak, Julie. "Talking Power: Language Policies and Practices in Nunavut," paper presented at the CINSA National Conference (Trent University, Peterborough, Ontario, 2005).

Vahabzadeh, Susan. "Weil oder obwohl Indianer? Warum Sherman Alexies Film 'Smoke Signals' erfolgreich ist," *Süddeutsche Zeitung* (8 December 1998): 16.

van Kirk, Silvia. *Many Tender Ties: Women in Fur-Trade Society, 1670–1870* (Winnipeg, Manitoba: Watson & Dwyer, 1980).

——. "'Women in Between': Indian Women in Fur Trade Society in Western Canada," in *Out of the Background: Readings on Canadian Native History*, ed. Robin Fisher & Ken S. Coates (1988; Toronto: Copp Clark, 1996): 102–17.

van Toorn, Penny. "Bakhtin and the Novel as Empire: Textual Politics in Robert Drewe's *The Savage Crows* and Rudy Wiebe's *The Temptations of Big Bear*," *Journal of Commonwealth Literature* 27.1 (1992): 96–109.

——. *Rudy Wiebe and the Historicity of the Word* (Edmonton: U of Alberta P, 1995).

Visser, Carla. "Historicity in Historical Fiction: *Burning Water* and *The Temptations of Big Bear*," *Studies in Canadian Literature* 12.1 (1987): 90–111.

Vizenor, Gerald. *Manifest Manners: Narratives on Postindian Survivance* (1994; Lincoln & London: U of Nebraska P, 1999).

——. *Manifest Manners: Postindian Warriors of Survivance* (Hanover NH & London: Wesleyan UP & UP of New England, 1994).

——. "A Postmodern Introduction," in *Narrative Chance: Postmoden Discourse on Native American Indian Literatures*, ed. Gerald Vizenor (Norman & London: U of Oklahoma P, 1993): 3–16.

——. "Trickster Discourse," *American Indian Quarterly* 14.3 (Summer 1990): 277–87.

——. "Trickster Discourse: Comic Holotropes and Language Games," in *Narrative Chance: Postmodern Discourse on Native American Indian Literatures*, ed. Gerald Vizenor (Norman & London, U of Oklahoma P, 1993): 187–211.

von Berg, Stefanie. "*Uncomfortable Mirror": (De-)Kolonisation in Gedichten zeitgenössischer indigener nordamerikanisher Autorinnen* (Aachen: Shaker, 2001).

VOX of Dartmouth (5 November 2001): 8.

Wachowich, Nancy. "Interview with Paul Apak Angilirq" (2002), in Apak Angilirq et al. *Atanarjuat: The Fast Runner*, 16–21.

——. "Comments by Nancy Wachowich" (2002), in Apak Angilirq et al. *Atanarjuat: The Fast Runner*, 22–23.

Wallace, Jo–Ann. "De-Scribing *The Water-Babies*: 'The Child' in Post-Colonial Theory" (1994), in *De-Scribing Empire*, ed. Tiffin & Lawson, 171–84.

Walters, Anna Lee. *Talking Indian: Reflections on Survival and Writing* (Ithaca NY: Firebrand, 1992).

Weatherford, Elizabeth. "Currents: Film and Video in Native America" (1988), in *Native Americans on Film and Video*, ed. Weatherford & Seubert, 7–8.

——. "The Public Eye, Native Media-Making: A Growing Potential," *Native Americas: Akwe:kon's Journal of Indigenous Issues* (Spring 1996): 56–59.

——. "To End and Begin Again: The Work of Victor Masayesva," *Art Journal* (Winter 1995): 48–52.

——, ed. *Native Americans on Film and Video* (New York: Museum of the American Indian, 1981).

——, & Emelia Seubert, ed. *Native Americans on Film and Video*, vol. 2 (New York: Museum of the American Indian, 1988).

Welsh, Christine. "Voices of the Grandmothers: Reclaiming a Métis Heritage," *Canadian Literature* 131 (Winter 1991): 15–24.

West, Dennis, & Joan M. West. "Sending Cinematic Smoke Signals: An Interview with Sherman Alexie," *Cineaste* 23.4 (1998): 28–31, 37.

Whaley, Susan. "Narrative Voices in *The Temptations of Big Bear*," *Essays on Canadian Writing* 20 (Winter 1980–81): 134–48.

Wheeler, Jordan. "Exposure," in Wheeler, *Brothers in Arms* (Winnipeg, Manitoba: Pemmican, 1989): 157–223.

Whorf, Benjamin Lee. *Language, Thought, and Reality*, ed. John B. Carroll (London: Chapman & Hall, New York: John Wiley & Sons & Cambridge MA: Technology Press of MIT, 1956).

Wickwire, Wendy C. "To See Ourselves as the Other's Other: Nlaka's pamux Contact Narratives," *Canadian Historical Review* 75 (1994): 1–20.

Wiebe, Rudy. *The Temptations of Big Bear* (Toronto: McClelland & Stewart, 1973).

——, & Bob Beal. *War in the West: Voices of the 1885 Rebellion* (Toronto: McClelland & Stewart, 1985).

——, & Gil Cardinal. *Big Bear*: screenplay, script ed. Jordan Wheeler (1998, unpublished).

Wiget, Andrew. *Native American Literature* (Boston MA: Twayne, 1985).

——. "Native American Oral Literatures: A Critical Orientation" (1994), in *Dictionary of Native American Literature*, ed. Wiget, 3–18.

——. "Telling the Tale: A Performance Analysis of a Hopi Coyote Story," in *Recovering the Word: Essays on Native American Literature*, ed. Brian Swann & Arnold Krupat (Berkeley, Los Angeles & London: U of California P, 1987): 297–336.

——, ed. *Dictionary of Native American Literature* (New York & London: Garland, 1994).

Willhelm, Sidney. "Red Man, Black Man, and White America: The Constitutional Approach to Genocide," *Catalyst* 4 (Spring 1969): 1–62.

Williams, Patrick, & Laura Chrisman, ed. *Colonial Discourse and Post-Colonial Theory* (1993; New York: Columbia UP, 1994).

——. "Colonial Discourse and Post-Colonial Theory: An Introduction" (1993), in *Colonial Discourse and Post-Colonial Theory*, ed. Williams & Chrisman, 1–20.

Winston, Brian. "The White Man's Burden: The Example of Robert Flaherty," *Sight and Sound* 54.1 (1984): 58–60.

Witherspoon, Gary. "Cultural Motifs in Navajo Weaving," in *North American Indian Anthropology: Essays on Society and Culture*, ed. Raymond J. DeMallie & Alfonso Ortiz (Norman & London: U of Oklahoma P, 1994): 355–76.

Wolfe, Alexander. *Earth Elder Stories: The Pinayzitt Path* (Saskatoon, Saskatchewan: Fifth House, 1988).

Worth, Sol, & John Adair. "Navajo Filmmakers," *American Anthropologist* 72 (1970): 9–34.

——, & John Adair. *Through Navajo Eyes: An Exploration in Film Communication and Anthropology* (1972; Albuquerque: U of New Mexico P, 1997).

Yoshimoto, Mitsuhiro. "The Difficulty of Being Radical: The Discipline of Film Studies and the Postcolonial World Order," *boundary 2* 18.3 (Fall 1991): 242–57.

Young, Robert J.C. *Colonial Desire: Hybridity in Theory, Culture and Race* (London & New York: Routledge, 1995).

Filmography[1]

Indigenous Productions

Alexie, Sherman, dir./writ.[2] *The Business of Fancydancing* (USA 2002; 103 min.).

Anderson, Mike. *Old Antelope Lake* ("Navajos Film Themselves" project, Sol Worth & John Adair, USA 1966; 15 min.).

Barclay, Barry, dir. *Ngati*, writ. Tama Poata, Pacific Films (New Zealand 1987; 92 min.).

Beaucage, Marjorie, dir./prod./writ. *Speaking to their Mother* (Canada 1992; 25 min.).

Belcourt, Shane, dir./writ. *Tkaronto* (Canada 2007; 105 min.).

Benally, Susan. *A Navajo Weaver* ("Navajos Film Themselves" project, Sol Worth & John Adair, USA 1966; 20 min.).

Campbell, Maria, dir./prod./writ. *The Road Allowance People* (Halfbreed, Inc. (Canada 1988; 48 min.).

——, dir. *Journey to Healing*, prod. Maria Campbell & Linda Jane (Gabriel Productions & Indigenous Peoples Program, Extension Division U of Saskatchewan (Canada 1992; 45 min.).

Cardinal, Gil, dir. *Big Bear*, prod. Doug Cuthand, writ. Rudy Wiebe & Gil Cardinal (Télé-Action Bear Inc. & Big Bear Films (Canada 1998; 180 min.).

Cheechoo, Shirley, dir./writ. *Bearwalker* (Canada & USA 1999; re-released as *Backroads*, 2000; 80 min.).

Clah, Al. *Intrepid Shadows* ("Navajos Film Themselves" project, Sol Worth & John Adair, USA 1966; 15 min.).

Cohn, Norman: see under Zacharias Kunuk.

DeMenezes, Carlos, dir. *Trespassing*, prod. Susana Lagudis (USA 2005; 116 min.).

Desjarlais, Sharon A., dir./writ. *Two-Spirited* (Canada 2007; 6.47 min.).

Eyre, Chris, dir. *Tenacity*, prod. Paul S. Mezey (NYU TSOA GFTV & Cheyenne Arapaho Productions, USA 1994; 9 min.).

——, dir. *Smoke Signals*, writ. Sherman Alexie (Shadow Catcher Entertainment, USA & Canada 1998; 88 min.).

——, dir, *Skins*, writ. Jennifer D. Lyne & Adrian C. Louis (USA 2002; 84 min.).

——, dir. *Skinwalkers*, writ. James Redford & Tony Hillerman (USA 2002; 94 min.).

---

[1] Sometimes the listed running time of films does not correspond to the actual running time – as in the case of Flaherty's *Nanook of the North* and Kunuk's *Atanarjuat: The Fast Runner*. The difference results from the fact that for my analysis I only took into account the running time without credits. The running time of most films in this filmography is taken from the Internet Movie Database at http://www.imdb.com.

[2] The writers of the screenplays and writers of texts on which the film is based, where applicable, are listed as writers.

——, dir. *Edge of America*, writ. Willy Holtzman (U S A 2003; 105 min.).

——, dir. *A Thief of Time*, writ. Alice Arlene & Tony Hillerman (U S A 2004; 94 min.).

——, dir. *A Thousand Roads*, writ. Scott Garen & Joy Harjo (U S A 2005; 40 min.; signature film for the Smithsonian's National Museum of the American Indian in Washington D C).

Harjo, Sterlin, dir./writ. *Four Sheets to the Wind* (U S A 2007; 81 min.).

Kahn, Alta. Untitled film ("Navajos Film Themselves" project, Sol Worth & John Adair, U S A 1966; 10 min.).

Kunuk, Zacharias, dir./writ. *Qaggiq* (Igloolik Isuma Productions, Canada 1989; 58min.).

——, dir./writ. *Nunaqpa* (Igloolik Isuma Productions, Canada 1991; 58 min.).

——, dir./writ. *Saputi* (Igloolik Isuma Productions, Canada 1993; 30 min.).

——, dir./writ. *Nunavut: Our Land* (Igloolik Isuma Productions, Canada 1994–95)

——, dir. *Atanarjuat: The Fast Runner*, writ. Paul Apak Angilirq & Norman Cohn (Igloolik Isuma Productions, Canada 2001; 172 min.).

——, & Norman Cohn, dirs. *The Journals of Knud Rasmussen*, prod. Norman Cohn, Zacharias Kunuk, Elise Lund Larsen, Vibeke Vogel & Stephane Rituit (Igloolik Isuma Productions & Bartok Film, Canada & Denmark 2006; 112 min.).

Lucas, Phil, & Robert Hagopian, dir./prod./writ. *Images of Indians* (K C T S /9, U S A 1980; five-part series: *The Great Movie Massacre, Heathen Injuns and the Hollywood Gospel, How Hollywood Wins the West, The Movie Reel Indians, Warpaint and Wigs*).

Martell, Lloyd, prod. *Talker*, dir./writ. Rob King (Media House Productions, Canada 1996; 9 min.).

Masayesva, Victor, dir./prod./writ. *Hopiit* (I S Productions, U S A 1981; 15 min.).

——, dir./prod./writ. *Itam Hakim, Hopiit* (I S Productions, U S A 1984; 58 min.).

——, dir./prod./writ. *Ritual Clowns* (I S Productions, U S A 1988; 15 min.).

——, dir./prod./writ. *Pot Starr* (I S Productions, U S A n.d.; 6 min.).

——, dir./prod./writ. *Imagining Indians* (I S Productions, U S A 1992; 86 min.).

Morris, Sean, dir. *Kusah Hakwaan*, writ. Sean Morris & Bryan Davidson (U S A 2001; 75 min.).

Nelson, Johnny. *The Navajo Silversmith* ("Navajos Film Themselves" project, Sol Worth & John Adair, U S A 1966; 20 min.).

Niro, Shelley, dir/writ. *Overweight With Crooked Teeth*, prod. Shelley Niro & Dan Big Bee, Jr. (Big Productions, Canada 1997): 5 min.).

——, dir./writ. *Honey Moccasin*, prod. Lynn Hutchison & Shelley Niro (Turtle Night Productions, Canada 1998): 49 min.).

Niro, Shelley & Anna Gronau, dir./writ./prod. *It Starts With a Whisper* (Baye of Quinte Productions, Canada 1993): 28 min.).

Obomsawin, Alanis, dir./writ. *Christmas at Moose Factory* (National Film Board – N F B , Canada 1971; 13 min.).

——, dir./prod./writ. *Mother of Many Children* [*Sounds From Our People*] (NFB, Canada 1977; 58 min.).

——, dir./co-prod./writ. *Incident at Restigouche* (NFB, Canada 1984; 46 min.).

——, dir./co-prod./writ. *No Address* (NFB, Canada 1988; 56 min.).

——, dir./co-prod./writ. *Kanehsatake: 270 Years of Resistance* (NFB, Canada 1993; 119 min.).

Osawa, Sandra, dir./co-prod./writ. *The Native American Series* (NBC-TV, USA 1974).

Red Horse, Valerie, & Jennifer Wynne Farmer, dir. *Naturally Native*, writ. Valerie Red Horse (USA 1998; 107 min.).

Sanjines, Jorge, dir. *Yawar Mallku* [*Blood of the Condor*], writ. Jorge Sanjines & Óscar Soria (Bolivia 1969; 85 min.).

——, dir. *Ukamau*, writ. Jorge Sanjines & Óscar Soria (Bolivia 1966; 85 min.).

Skorodin, Ian, dir. *Tushka* (USA 1996).

Solito, Auraeus (Kanakan Balintagos), dir. *The Blossoming of Maximo Oliveros* writ. Michiko Yamamoto (Philippines 2005; 100 min.).

——, dir. *Tuli*, writ. Jimmy Flores (Philippines 2006; 113 min.).

Todd, Loretta, dir./writ. *Through the Lens: Changing Voices*, prod. Gretchen Jordan Basto & Fumik Kiyooka (Canadian Broadcasting Corporation, Canada 1998; 60 min.).

Tsosie, Maxine, & Mary Jane Tsosie. *The Spirit of the Navajo* ("Navajos Film Themselves" project, Sol Worth & John Adair, USA 1966; 20 min.).

African American Productions

Lee, Spike, dir./prod. *She's Gotta Have It* (USA 1986; 84 min.).

——, dir./prod. *Do the Right Thing* (USA 1989; 120 min.).

Maori Productions

Tamahori, Lee, dir. *Once Were Warriors*, writ. Riwia Brown (New Zealand 1994; 99 min.).

Non-Indigenous Productions

Anderson, Brad, dir. *Next Stop Wonderland*, writ. Brad Anderson & Lyn Vaus (USA 1998; 104 min.).

Apted, Michael, dir. *Thunderheart*, writ. John Fusco (USA 1992; 119 min.).

Ballard, Carroll, dir. *Never Cry Wolf*, writ. Ralph Furmaniak & Farley Mowat (USA 1983; 91 min.).

Bergman, Ingmar, dir./writ. *Persona* (Sweden 1966; 85 min.).

——, dir./writ. *Viskningar och Rop* [*Cries and Whispers*] (Sweden 1972; 91 min.).

Boyle, Danny, dir. *Trainspotting*, writ. John Hodge (UK 1996; 94 min.).

Branagh, Kenneth, dir./writ. *Henry V* (UK 1989; 137 min.).

Bugajski, Ryszard, dir. *Clearcut*, writs. Rob Forsyth & M.T. Kelly (Canada 1991; 100 min.).

Coletti, Duilio & John Sturges, dir. *Valdez, il Mezzosangue* [*Chino*], writ. Massimo De Rita (France, Italy & Spain 1973; 97 min.).

Costner, Kevin, dir. *Dances With Wolves*, writ. Michael Blake (USA 1990; 182 min.).

Demme, Jonathan, dir. *Silence of the Lambs*, writ. Ted Tally (USA 1991; 118 min.).

Egleson, Jan, dir. *Coyote Waits*, writs. Lloyd Gold & Tony Hillerman (USA 2003; 107 min.).

Elder, Sarah & Leonard Kamerling. *The Alaska Native Heritage Series* (USA 1972).

Ellerly, Tom & Bradley Raymont, dir. *Pocahontas II: Journey to a New World*, writ. Allen Estrin & Cindy Marcus, Walt Disney (USA 1998; 72 min.).

Flaherty, Robert, dir./writ. *Nanook of the North* (USA 1922; 79 min.).

——, dir./writ. *Moana: A Romance of the Golden Age* (USA 1926; 77 min.).

——, dir./writ. *Man of Aran* (USA 1934; 76 min.).

Forman, Milos, dir. *One Flew Over the Cuckoo's Nest*, writ. Bo Goldman & Lawrence Hauben (USA 1975): 133 min.).

Gabriel, Mike & Eric Goldberg, dir. *Pocahontas*, writ. Carl Binder & Joe Grant, Walt Disney (USA 1995; 81 min.).

Godard, Jean–Luc, dir./writ. *À bout de souffle* [*Breathless*] (France 1960; 87 min.).

Heisler, Stuart, dir. *The Lone Ranger*, writ. Herb Meadow (USA 1956; 86 min.).

Jarmusch, Jim, dir./writ. *Dead Man* (USA 1995; 121 min.).

——, dir./writ. *Ghost Dog: The Way of the Samurai* (USA 1999; 116 min.).

Johnson, Lamont, dir. *Fear on Trial*, writ. David W. Rintels (USA 1975; 100 min.).

Laughlin, Tom (alias T.C. Frank), dir. *Billy Jack*, writs. Tom Laughlin (alias T.C. Frank) & Delores Taylor (USA 1971; 115 min.).

Leone, Sergio, dir. *C'era una Volta il West* [*Once Upon a Time in the West*], writ. Dario Argento, Bernardo Bertolucci, Sergio Donati & Sergio Leone (Italy & USA 1968; 165 min.).

——, & Tonino Valeri, dir. *Il Mio Nome è Nessuno* [*My Name is Nobody*] (Italy, France & West Germany 1973; 117 min.).

Levinson, Barry, dir. *Good Morning Vietnam*, writ. Mitch Markowitz (USA 1987; 119 min.).

Lynch, David, dir./writ. *Wild at Heart* (USA 1990; 124 min.).

Mann, Michael, dir. *The Last of the Mohicans*, writ. John L. Balderston (USA 1992; 122 min.).

Marston, William M. *Wonder Woman* television series (USA 1976–79).

Massot, Claude, dir. *Nanook Revisited*, writ. Claude Massot & Sebastien Regnier (USA 1994; 60 min.).

McDonald, Bruce, dir. *Dance Me Outside*, writ. John Frizzell & W.P. Kinsella (Canada 1994; 84 min.).

Merlet, Agnès, dir. *Artemisia*, writ. Patrick Amos & Agnès Merlet (France, Germany & Italy 1997; 98 min.).

Miner, Michael, dir. *The Book of Stars*, writ. Tasca Shadix (USA 2001; 111 min.).

Morris, Errol, dir. *The Dark Wind*, writs. Neal Jimenez & Tony Hillerman (USA 1991; 104 min.).

Page, Anthony, dir. *The Missiles of October*, writ. Stanley R. Greenberg & Robert F. Kennedy (USA 1974; 150 min.).

Penn, Arthur, dir. *Little Big Man*, writ. Calder Willingham (USA 1970; 147 min.).

Pontecorvo, Gillo, dir. *La Battaglia di Algeri* [*The Battle of Algiers*], writ. Gillo Pontecorvo & Franco Solinas (Algeria & Italy 1966; 117 min.).

Reiner, Rob, dir. *Misery*, writ. William Goldman (USA 1990; 107 min.).

Scott, Ridley, dir. *Thelma and Louise*, writ. Callie Khouri (USA 1991; 129 min.).

Sholder, Jack, dir. *Renegades*, writ. David Rich (USA 1989; 106 min.).

Shyler, Lisanne, dir. *Getting to Know You*, writs. Joyce Carol Oates & Lisanne Shyler (USA 1999; 96 min.).

Silverstein, Elliot, dir. *A Man Called Horse*, writs. Jack DeWitt & Dorothy M. Johnson (USA 1970; 114 min.).

Spielberg, Steven, dir. *Schindler's List*, writ. Steven Zaillian (USA 1993; 197 min.).

Stone, Oliver, dir. *JFK*, writ. Jim Marrs & Jim Garrison (USA & France 1991; 206 min.).

——, *Natural Born Killers*, writ. David Veloz & Quentin Tarantino (USA 1994; 122 min.).

Sturges, John, dir. *The Magnificent Seven*, writ. William Roberts & Walter Newman (USA 1960; 128 min.).

Welles, Orson, dir. *Citizen Kane*, writ. Orson Welles & Herman J. Mankiewicz (USA 1941; 119 min.).

——, dir./writ. *Mr. Arkadin* (France, Spain & Switzerland 1955; 105 min.).

Winner, Michael, dir. *Chato's Land*, writ. Gerald Wilson (USA 1972; 110 min.).

Witney, William & John English, dir. *The Lone Ranger*, writ. Franklin Adreon & Ronald Davidson, fifteen episodes (USA 1938; 264 min.).

Internet Sources

American Indian Film Festival in San Francisco:
   http://www.aifisf.com

Annual Taos Talking Picture Festival:
   http://www.ttpix.org/native_copy.html

Aboriginal Peoples of Canada: A Demographic Profile, 2001 Census: analysis series:
   http://www12.statcan.ca/english/census01/products/analytic/companion/abor/pdf
   /96F0030XIE2001007.pdf

Aboriginal Peoples Television Network:

http://www.aptn.ca/corporate/corporate_home_html
Atanarjuat: The Fast Runner – webpages:
  http://www.atanarjuat.com/about_isuma/index.html
  http://www.atanarjuat.com/art_direction/costumes/index.html
  http://www.atanarjuat.com/art_direction/props/caribou_goggles/index.html
  http://www.atanarjuat.com/art_direction/props/hunting_tools/index.html
  http://www.atanarjuat.com/art_direction/props/qamutik/index.html
  http://www.atanarjuat.com/art_direction/props/qajaq/index.html
  http://www.atanarjuat.com/art_direction/sets/index.html
  http://www.atanarjuat.com/cast_characters/index.html
  http://www.atanarjuat.com/legend/esp_legend/legend_land.html
  http://www.atanarjuat.com/media_centre/index.html
  http://www.atanarjuat.com/production_diary/index.html
  http://lot47.com/thefastrunner/about_Ancient_Crafts.html
  http://lot47.com/thefastrunner/about_Inside_action.html
  http://lot47.com/thefastrunner/about_Roots_of_project.html
  http://lot47.com/thefastrunner/About_the_filmmakers.html
  http://lot47.com/thefastrunner/reviews.html

Beltmann, Eric. *"Atanarjuat: The Fast Runner*: A Lot 47 Film":
  http://www.flipsidemovies.com/atanarjuat.html

Blue Hill Productions:
  http://www.Dougcuthand.com/project.html
  http://www.dougcuthand.com/index.html

Canadian census of 2001 – Aboriginal Peoples of Canada:
  http://www12.statcan.ca/english/censuso1/Products/Analytic/companion/abor/canada.cfm#5

Churchill, Ward. "Smoke Signals: A History of Native Americans in Cinema," *LiP Magazine* (1998):
  http://www.lipmagazine.org/articles/revichurchill_35_p.htm

David, Jennifer. *Aboriginal Language Broadcasting in Canada: An overview and recommendations to the Task Force on Aboriginal Languages and Cultures*, Debwe Communications Inc., 26 November 2004, 1–45:
  http://www.aptn.ca

Documentary Educational Resources:
  http://www.der.org/films/itam-hakim-hopiit.html

"Explore North: Milestones in Television Broadcasting in Northern Canada":
  http://www.explorenorth.com/library/weekly/more/bl-milestones.htm.

"Flaherty's Man of Aran":
  http://www.iol.ie/~galfilm/filmwest/19aran.htm

Green, Pamela. "Big Bear: Rain or Shine, the Show Must Go On," *SAGE* (July 1998):
  http://www.ammsa.com/sage/JULY98.html#anchor222342.

History of the Inuit Broadcasting Corporation:
   http://www.inuitbroadcasting.ca/history_e.htm
The Hopi Tribe – Office of Mining and Mineral Resources:
   http://www.hopi.nsn.us/mining.asp.
The Internet Movie Data Base:
   http://www.us.imdb.com
IS Productions:
   http://www.infomagic.net/~isprods/index.html
Kublu, Alexina, & Mick Mallon. "Nunavut: Our Language, Our Selves":
   http://www.nunavut.com/nunavut99/english/our.html#3
Neutral Ground Gallery, Regina:
   http://www.neutralground.sk.ca/ programming/2000/edward/index.shtml
NMAI Film Festival:
   http://www.nmai.si.edu/fv/festival/index.html
NSI Drama Prize Teams:
   http://www.nsi-canada.ca/dramaprize/participants.html
Roth, Lorna. "First Peoples' Television Broadcasting in Canada":
   http://www.museum.tv/archives/etv/F/htmlF/firstpeople/firstpeople.htm
SAGE:
   http://www.ammsa.com/sage/JULY98.html#anchor222342.
Statistics Canada – "Indigenous Language Use":
   http://www.statcan.ca/Daily/English/980113/d980113.htm#ART1
Statistics Canada: Community Profile – Igloolik:
   http://www12.statcan.ca/english/profil01/Details/details1inc1.cfm?SEARCH=BE
   GINS&PSGC=62&SGC=6204012&A=&LANG=E&Province=62&PlaceNam
   e=igloolik&CSDNAME=Igloolik&CMA=&SEARCH=BEGINS&DataType=1
   &TypeNameE=Hamlet&ID=13599
Sundance Channel:
   http://www.sundancechannel.com
Talking Dog Studios:
   http://www.talkingdogstudios.com/awards/
Taos Talking Picture Festival – Native Cinema Showcase (2002):
   http://www.ttpix.org/native_copy.html
V-tape – Online Catalogue:
   http://www.vtape.org/catalogue.htm
Whiteduck Resources Inc. and Consilium *Northern Native Broadcast Access Program (NNBAP) & Northern Distribution Program (NDP) Evaluation. Final Report*:
   http://www.aptn.ca.

֍ ֎

Appendix

Glossary[1]

180° SYSTEM
The continuity approach to editing dictates that the camera should stay on one side of the action to ensure consistent left–right spatial relations between objects from shot to shot. The 180° line is the same as the AXIS OF ACTION.

ACCELERATED MONTAGE
The use of editing to add to the effect of increased speed of action in a motion picture. By decreasing the length of the individual shots in an action or chase sequence, it is possible to quicken the pace of the film and to impose an external pace on the rhythm of the film.[2]

AMERICAN SHOT
A shot in which the human figure is framed from the knees up.

AXIS OF ACTION
In the CONTINUITY EDITING system, the imaginary line that passes from side to side through the main actors, defining the spatial relations of all the elements of the scene as being to the right or left. The camera is not supposed to cross the axis at a cut and thus reverse those spatial relations. Cf. 180° SYSTEM.

BACKLIGHTING
Illumination cast onto the figures in the scene from the side opposite the camera, usually creating a thin outline of highlighting on those figures.

---

[1] If not otherwise specified, the definitions are taken from the glossary of David Bordwell & Kristin Thompson, *Film Art: An Introduction* (1979; New York: McGraw–Hill, 1997): 477–82.
[2] Frank E. Beaver, *Dictionary of Film Terms: The Aesthetic Companion to Film Analysis* (New York: Twayne, 1994): 235.

BILATERAL SYMMETRY
The extreme type of balancing the left and right halves of a frame.

CAMERA DISTANCE / DISTANCE OF FRAMING
The apparent distance of the frame from the mise-en-scène elements. [...]
See also CLOSE-UP, EXTREME CLOSE-UP, EXTREME LONG SHOT,
MEDIUM CLOSE-UP, MEDIUM SHOT, PLAN AMÉRICAIN.

CANTED FRAMING
A view in which the frame is not level; either the right of left side is
lower than the other, causing objects in the scene to appear slanted out of
an upright position.

CAUSE–EFFECT CHAIN
A narrative formed through a chain of events in cause-and-effect relationship occurring in time and space.

CLOSE-UP
A framing in which the scale of the object shown is relatively large; most
commonly a person's head seen from the neck up, or an object of a comparable size that fills most of the screen.

CLOSURE
The degree to which the ending of a narrative film reveals the effects of
all causal events and resolves (or 'closes off') all lines of action.

COMPOSITIONAL BALANCE
Compositional balance refers to the extent to which the areas of screen
space have equally distributed masses and points of interest.

CONTINUITY EDITING
A system of cutting to maintain continuous and clear narrative action.
Continuity editing relies upon matching screen direction, position, and
temporal relations from shot to shot.

CROSSCUTTING/ INTERCUTTING
Editing that alternates shots of two or more lines of action occurring in
different planes, usually simultaneously.

CUTAWAY
A shot of another event elsewhere that will not last as long as the elided
action.

DEEP-FOCUS PHOTOGRAPHY
A use of the camera lens and lighting that keeps both the close and the
distant planes being photographed in sharp focus.

DEEP-SPACE PHOTOGRAPHY
An arrangement of MISE-EN-SCÈNE elements so that there is a considerable distance between the plane closest to the camera and the one farthest away. Any or all of these planes may be in focus.

DIEGETIC SOUND
Any voice, musical passage, or sound effect presented as originating from a source within the film's world.

DISSOLVE
A transition between two shots during which the first image gradually disappears while the second image gradually appears; for a moment both images blend in SUPERIMPOSITION.

DOCUDRAMA
A term for the narrative blending of documentary and fictional elements to create a film drama based on historical, news-inspired actuality.[3]

DOLLY
A camera support with wheels, used in making TRACKING SHOTS.

DYNAMIC CUT – Cf. JUMP CUT.

ELLIPSIS
In a narrative film, the shortening of plot duration achieved by omitting intervals of story duration.

ELLIPTICAL EDITING
Shot transitions that omit parts of an event, causing an ellipsis in plot and story duration.

ESTABLISHING SHOT
A shot, usually involving a distant framing, that shows the spatial relations among the important figures, objects, and setting in a scene.

EXTREME CLOSE-UP
A framing in which the scale of an object shown is very large; most commonly a small object or a part of the body.

EXTREME LONG SHOT
A framing in which the scale of an object shown is very small; a building, landscape, or crowd of people would fill the screen.

EYELINE MATCH
A cut obeying the AXIS OF ACTION principle, in which the first shot shows a person looking off in one direction and the second shows a

---

[3] Beaver, *Dictionary of Film Terms*, 116.

nearby space containing what he or she sees. If the person looks left, the following shot should imply that that the looker is offscreen right.

FADE
1. Fade-in: a dark screen that gradually brightens as a shot appears. 2. Fade-out: a shot gradually darkens as the screen goes black. Occasionally fade-outs brighten to pure white or to a color.

FAITHFUL SOUND
Sound that belongs to a certain image, i.e. the sound of a barking dog and the image of a barking dog. The image of a meowing cat with the sound of a barking dog would be a LACK OF FIDELITY.

FILL LIGHT
Illumination from a source less bright than the KEY LIGHT, used to soften deep shadows in a scene.

FISH-EYE LENS
The fish-eye lens, an extremely wide-angle lens, photographs an angle of view approaching 180°, with corresponding distortion of both linear and depth perception.[4]

FOCAL LENGTH
The distance from the center of the lens to the point at which the light rays meet in sharp focus. The focal length determines the perspective relations of the space represented on the flat screen.

FRAME
A single image on the strip of film. When a series of frames is projected onto a screen in quick succession, an illusion of movement is created by the spectator.

GRAPHIC MATCH
Two successive shots joined so as to create a strong similarity of compositional elements (e.g., color, shape).

HEAD-ON SHOT
A shot on the AXIS OF ACTION, the action moving toward the camera.

HIGH-KEY LIGHTING
Illumination that creates comparatively little contrast between light and dark areas of the shot. Shadows are fairly transparent and brightened by FILL LIGHT.

INTERCUTTING — Cf. CROSSCUTTING

---

[4] James Monaco, *How to Read a Film: The Art, Technology, Language, History, and Theory of Film and Media* (1977; Oxford: Oxford UP, 1981): 60.

IRIS
A round, moving MASK that can close down to end a scene (iris-out) or emphasize a detail, or it can open to begin a scene (iris-in) or to reveal more space around a detail.

JUMP CUT
An ELLIPTICAL CUT that appears to be an interruption of a single shot. Either the figures seem to change instantly against a constant background, or the background changes instantly while the figures remain constant.

KEY LIGHT
In the THREE-POINT LIGHTING system, the brightest illumination coming into the scene.

LACK OF FIDELITY — Cf. FAITHFUL SOUND.

LONG SHOT
A framing in which the scale of the object shown is small; a standing human figure would appear nearly the height of the screen.

LONG TAKE
A shot that continues for an unusually lengthy time before the transition to the next shot.

LOW-KEY LIGHTING
Illumination that creates strong contrast between light and dark areas of the shot with deep shadows and little FILL LIGHT.

MASK
An opaque screen placed in the camera or printer that blocks part of the frame off and changes the shape of the photographed image, leaving part of the frame a solid color. As seen on the screen, most masks are black, although they can be white or colored.

MATCH CUT/GRAPHIC MATCH
Shots linked by graphic similarities. Shapes, colors, overall composition, or movement in shot A may be picked up in the composition of shot B.

MATCH ON ACTION
A continuity cut which splices two different views of the same action together at the same moment in the movement, making it seem to continue uninterrupted.

MEDIUM CLOSE-UP
A framing in which the scale of the object shown is fairly large; a human figure seen from the chest up would fill most of the screen.

MEDIUM LONG SHOT
A shot of non-human objects in the same frame size as an American shot.

MEDIUM SHOT
A framing in which the scale of the object shown is of moderate size; a human figure seen from the waist up would fill most of the screen.

MISE-EN-SCÈNE
All of the elements placed in front of the camera to be photographed: the settings and props, lighting, costumes, make-up, and figure behavior.

MOBILE FRAME
The effect on the screen of the moving camera, a zoom lens, or certain special effects; the framing shifts in relation to the scene being photographed.

MOTIF
An element in a film that is repeated in a significant way.

NON-DIEGETIC SOUND
Sound, such as mood music or a narrator's commentary, represented as coming from a source outside the space of the narrative.

OVEREXPOSURE
The act of exposing each frame of film to more light or for a longer period of time than would be required to produce a 'normal' exposure of the same subject. There is little or no visible detail in the highlights – the bright areas of the picture – and images appear bleached, more or less washed out.[5]

PAN
A camera movement with the camera body turning to the right or left. On the screen, it produces a mobile framing which scans the space horizontally.

---

[5] Beaver, *Dictionary of Film Terms*, 140.

POSTERIZATION
The technique involves restricting the vibration of light waves on the film strip so that they have different amplitudes on different planes and, therefore, show distorted outlines and distorted colors.[6]

POV SHOT (POINT-OF-VIEW SHOT)
A shot taken with the camera placed approximately where the character's eyes would be, showing what the character would see; usually cut in before or after the character looking.

RACKING FOCUS
Shifting the area of sharp focus from one plane to another during a shot; the effect on the screen is called "rack focus."

REACTION SHOT
A shot within a scene that shows a character's reaction to a dramatic situation. The reaction shot is usually achieved through a close-up or medium shot of the character.[7]

REVERSE-ANGLE SHOT — Cf. SHOT/REVERSE SHOT

ROUGH CUT
An early version of an edited film in which shots and sequences are placed in general order. Precise cutting points have yet to be made.[8]

SCENE
A segment in a narrative film that takes place in one time and space or that uses crosscutting to show two or more simultaneous actions.

SEAMLESSNESS
Used to refer to the Hollywood film style where – in the name of realism – the editing does not draw attention to itself. The spectator is presented with a narrative that is edited in such a way that it appears to have no breaks, no disconcerting unexplained transitions in time and space.[9]

SEQUENCE
Term commonly used for a moderately large segment of a film, involving one complete stretch of action. In a narrative film, often equivalent to a SCENE. In this thesis, a sequence is generally assigned as a piece of

---

[6] Sonja Bahn–Coblans, "Reading with a Eurocentric Eye the 'Seeing with a Native Eye': Victor Masayesva's *Itam Hakim, Hopiit*," *Studies in American Indian Literatures* 8.4 (Winter 1996): 55.

[7] Beaver, *Dictionary of Film Terms*, 291.

[8] Beaver, *Dictionary of Film Terms*, 300.

[9] Susan Hayward, *Key Concepts in Cinema Studies* (London & New York: Routledge, 1996): 307.

action happening at the same time and locale. Whenever there is a change
in time or location, a new sequence starts.

SHOT
1. In shooting, one uninterrupted run of the camera to expose a series of
frames. Also called a take. 2. In the finished film, one uninterrupted
image with a single static or MOBILE FRAMING.

SHOT/REVERSE SHOT
Two or more shots edited together that alternate characters, typically in a
conversation situation. In CONTINUITY EDITING, characters in one
framing usually look left, in the other framing, right.

SOUND BRIDGE
1. At the beginning of one scene, the sound from the previous scene
carries over briefly before the sound from the new scene begins. 2. At the
end of one scene, the sound from the next is heard, leading into that
scene.

STYLE
The repeated and salient uses of film techniques characteristic of a single
film or a group of films (for example, a filmmaker's work or a national
movement).

SUPERIMPOSITION
The exposure of more than one image on the same film strip.

TAIL-ON SHOT
A shot on the AXIS OF ACTION, the action moving away from the
camera.

THREE-POINT LIGHTING
A common arrangement using three directions of light on a scene: from
behind the subjects (BACKLIGHTING), from one bright source (KEY
LIGHT), and from a less bright source balancing the key light (FILL
LIGHT).

TILT
A camera movement with the camera body swiveling upward or down-
ward on a stationary support. It produces a mobile framing that scans the
space vertically.

TRACKING SHOT
A mobile frame [camera movement] that travels through space forward,
backward, or laterally.

ॐ ॐ

Sequence Protocols and Detailed Shot Analyses

Abbreviations employed in the following tables:

C/Dist	Camera Distance	C/Angle	Camera Angle
C/Move	Camera Movement	Shot/L	Shot Length
sc. = scene			

Itam Hakim, Hopiit: Detailed Shot Analysis

No.	Content of Shot	C/Dist	C/Angle	C/Move	Sound	Shot/L
0	frozen frame: two silhou-ettes working in a cornfield against backdrop of morn-ing sky; credits	medium shot	straight	still	no sound	
1	earth, feet, and lower legs walking; buckets	close-up	straight	left track	Macaya's voice	9 sec.
2	same (jump from close to a little farther)	close-up	straight	left track	Macaya's voice	3 sec.
3	same, buckets are put down	close-up	straight	left track, still	Macaya's voice, faithful sound	10 sec.
4	horiz. line, upper frame: mesa sand, feet, lower legs, lower part of bucket; lower frame: water, reflecting lower legs; hand drawing water in bucket twice; buckets lifted, feet start walking; buckets whole, legs up to knees; earth, man from rear up to back; Maca-ya exits frame to upper left; mesa earth; Macaya enters frame in upper left; body to neck; whole body, low scrub, rocks; (Macaya walks away from camera)	medium close-up, medium shot, long shot	oblique left, straight, oblique left	still, tilt up, left pan, tilt up, right pan	Macaya's voice, howling wind, faithful sound	1.05 min.
5	horizontal line in lower part of frame (1/4 mesa-grass, earth, rocks, 3/4 sky); Ma-caya walks from the middle to the right, puts buckets down, pours water on very dry reddish earth	long shot	straight	still, right pan	Macaya's voice, howling wind	36 sec.

6	horizontal line: 3/4 mesa earth, water holes in fgd, 1/4 sky and other mesas in bkgd	long shot	changes with pan	still, right pan	Macaya's voice, howling wind	20 sec.
7	horizontal line: 3/4 mesa; yellow reddish earth and plants, 1/4 sky and other mesas in bkgd; tiny figure near middle of frame; figure in upper left middle	extreme long shot, long shot	straight	still, zoom in	Macaya's voice, howling wind	24 sec.
8	inside a house: cast-iron stove, two poles; back of Macaya enters frame and fills almost whole frame	medium close-up	straight	still, tilt down, right pan	Macaya's voice, faithful sound	34 sec.
9	fragment of loom, hands and forearms weave; fore-head of Macaya enters frame from right briefly	medium close-up	right side	still	Macaya's voice, faithful sound	15 sec.
10	fragment of loom; upper part of Macaya's body, he weaves	medium close-up	oblique right, high angle	still	Macaya's voice, faithful sound	16 sec.
11	hand and tin; fragment of right hip from behind; whole body from behind, stove	close-up, medium shot	changes with pan	zoom out, right pan	Macaya's voice	15 sec.
12	face of Macaya fills right part of frame; looks into camera briefly, then longer	close-up	straight	still	no sound, then howling wind, children's voices	9 sec.
13	horizontal line: 1/4 sky, 3/4 grassy mesa with wooden shack; children emerge from shack and play; 1/3 sky, 2/3 mesa	medium shot, long shot	straight	still, zoom out	howling wind, children's voices	21 sec.
14	splintered wood, axe, hands, knee, leg, breast, head (Macaya chops wood)	close-up	straight	tilt up	howling wind, faithful sound	20 sec.
15	four children run towards camera; pile of wood that children pick up	medium shot, long shot	straight	zoom out	howling wind, children's voices	18 sec.
16	children in front of house from behind; they enter carrying wood; child exits	medium shot	oblique left	still, zoom in, tilt up	howling wind	21 sec.

17	faces of two children; faces of all four children	close-up	changes with pan	still, right pan	Macaya talks to children, children talk	15 sec.
18	hands of Macaya; drums rhythm of song with fist into palm of other hand	close-up	high angle	still	Macaya chanting	23 sec.
19	heads and upper bodies of two children; table with pots and pans in right fgd	medium shot	oblique right	still, zoom out	Macaya and children laughing	13 sec.
20	head and upper body of Macaya sitting in front of stove; talks	medium shot	oblique left	still	Macaya starts telling story of emergence	8 sec.
21	face of boy; faces of other three boys; face of first boy – looks briefly into camera	close-up	changes with pan	zoom in, right pan, left pan	Macaya's voice	36 sec.
22	interior of room; children on bunk	long shot, medium shot	changes with pan	left pan, zoom in	Macaya's voice	12 sec.
23	red, blue, yellow corn; hand runs through corn	extreme close-up	straight	still	Macaya's voice, faithful sound	20 sec.
24	basket with blue corn emptied into tin bowl; falling corn against bkgd of mesa earth is somewhat blurry – like rain; blue corn in tin bowl fills frame	close-up	straight	zoom out, tilt down	Macaya's voice, faithful sound	23 sec.
25	full moon in upper right frame; clouds	long shot	straight	still	howling wind, Macaya's voice, cry of animal	59 sec.
26	full moon in lower mid-frame; clouds gradually cover moon and dissolve; darkness and lighting	long shot	straight	still, zoom out	Macaya's voice, howling wind, thunder	2.06 min.
27	rain, muddy earth	close-up	straight	still	Macaya's voice, rain	8 sec.
28	eagle with spread wings on roof of house; it is raining	long shot, close-up	straight	still, zoom in	Macaya's voice, rain	25 sec.
29	eagle flapping its wings on roof of house; it is raining	long shot	straight	still	Macaya's voice, rain	17 sec.
30	eagle on roof	medium shot	straight	still, zoom out	Macaya's voice, rain	23 sec.

31	eagle on roof	close-up, extreme close-up	high angle	zoom in	Macaya's voice, eagle's cry	11 sec.
32	eagle against backdrop of the sky	close-up	straight	zoom out	Macaya's voice	25 sec.
33	pieces of raw meat, legs of eagle, bows head down to eat meat	extreme close-up	straight	still	Macaya's voice, eagle's cry	18 sec.
34	mesa wall of sand; rain washes down great chunks of earth	long shot	straight	still, zoom out	Macaya's voice, faithful sound	16 sec.
35	sea water, waves (fill whole frame)	long shot	straight	zoom out	Macaya's voice, surf	18 sec.
36	horiz. line: 2/3 beach sand, 1/3 water; waves rolling upon a beach	medium shot	straight	still	Macaya's voice, surf, drums and singing	25 sec.
37	face of boy lit from one side; same boy on chair, interior of room	close-up, medium shot	oblique right	zoom out	Macaya's voice, surf, drums and singing	20 sec.
38	face of one boy; single faces of all four boys	extreme close-up	changes with pan	still, right pan, zoom out	Macaya's voice, surf	26 sec.
39	one boy chewing gum, one asleep	medium shot	oblique left	still	Macaya's voice	12 sec.
40	face of boy chewing gum; he makes gum bubbles	close-up	low angle	still	Macaya's voice, children laughing and talking	10 sec.
41	lower part of kerosene lamp; lower part of glass lamp shade being put on	close-up	straight	still, tilt up	Macaya's voice, children laughing and talking	13 sec.
42	boy's face, nose and mouth; boy plays with lamp, lights matches and throws them into lamp	extreme close-up; medium shot	straight	still, zoom out, still	Macaya's voice, children laughing and talking	35 sec.
43	glowing flame in lower part of lamp; blurred	extreme close-up	straight	still	Macaya's voice, children laughing and talking	10 sec.
44	almost darkness; two boys play with lamp; one boy drops glass lamp shade	medium shot	straight	still, zoom in	Macaya's voice, children laugh, talk, sound of shattering glass	22 sec.

45	base of nose and right eye of Macaya; full moon right in the curve of the base of the nose	extreme close-up; close-up	oblique right	still, zoom out, still, zoom out	Macaya's voice	29 sec.
46	sunset, clouds, lake, forest, sun rays reflected in water	long shot medium shot	straight	zoom in	Macaya's voice, surf	32 sec.
47	ruin at center of frame; bushes on sides of path	long shot	straight	track fwd, hand-held	Macaya's voice	12 sec.
48	Anasazi ruins from rim of Canyon de Chelly – wall and rims on both sides; horiz. line: 1/5 sky, 4/5 canyon	long shot extreme long shot	high angle, straight	zoom out	Macaya's voice	14 sec.
49	hands knock corn off blue corncob; horiz. line: 1/4 sky, 3/4 mesa earth, bushes; woman sits and works	close-up; medium shot	straight	still, zoom out	Macaya's voice, faithful sound	30 sec.
50	hands shake basket with blue corn	close-up	straight	still, tilt up	Macaya's voice, faithful sound	16 sec.
51	blue corn; rim of basket; corn poured out; falling corn against bkgd of sky; looks like rain (not same shot as 24)	close-up	straight	still, tilt down	Macaya's voice	17 sec.
52	field, yellow-red earth and green mesa valley; horiz. line: 1/3 field, 2/3 mesa valley in bkgd; boy digging holes; woman planting corn; several people working in the field	long shot	changes with pan	still, right pan, still	Macaya's voice, bird whistle, howling wind	39 sec.
53	two boys working in the field; their heads and upper parts of the body; they move out of frame; people in bkgd working	close-up, long shot	high angle	still, zoom out	Macaya's voice, howling wind	18 sec.
54	dry reddish earth; planting stick, shoe; somebody digs holes	extreme close-up, close-up	high angle	still, zoom out	Macaya's voice, howling wind	14 sec.
55	earth, white plastic bucket, hand counts seeds into other hand; boy moves into frame; kneels, plants corn	close-up	high angle	still, zoom in	howling wind	22 sec.

56	yellow earth, bushes; image becomes blurred	long shot	straight	zoom in	Macaya's voice, wind howls	25 sec.
57	wet earth, feet, lower legs, and knees of several people walking to left	medium shot	high angle	right pan	Macaya's voice, drums and singing	5 sec.
58	reflection of legs walking in the water	medium shot	changes with pan	right pan	Macaya's voice, drums and singing	5 sec.
59	leaves; trees in small pine forest	close-up, medium shot	straight	right track, zoom out	Macaya's voice, drums and singing	17 sec.
60	single conifer trees in fgd; mountains with trees in bkgd	medium shot	straight	right track	Macaya's voice, drums and singing	10 sec.
61	image is milky; birch trunks, later blurry; twigs in fgd birch trunks in bkgd	long shot close-up	straight	zoom in, rack focus	Macaya's voice, drums and singing	20 sec.
62	image is milky; birch forest in snow	medium shot	straight	right track	Macaya's voice, drums and singing	1.34 min.
63	deer grazing on snowy grass	long shot	changes with pan	right pan	Macaya's voice, drums and singing	12 sec.
64	snow; herd of sheep; one figure and three dogs moving towards camera	long shot	changes with pan	still, right pan	Macaya's voice, drums and singing	14 sec.
65	horiz. line: 1/4 snow, 3/4 white sky, gray sheep; white-in-white composition; sheep walking away from camera; image blurs	long shot	oblique right	still	Macaya's voice, drums and singing	29 sec.
66	deer (stags)	medium shot	changes with pan	left pan	Macaya's voice, drums and singing	23 sec.
67	dark sky, clouds, mountain tops at bottom of frame	long shot	straight	still	Macaya's voice, drums and singing	20 sec.
68	horiz. line: below: grassy meadow; above: dark green mountains	long shot	straight	still, zoom out	Macaya's voice, drums and singing	11 sec.
69	pine forest, 1/3 sky	long shot	high angle	zoom out	Macaya's voice, drums and singing	13 sec.

70	high alpine mountain tops; mesa rim enters frame	long shot	changes with pan	right pan, zoom out	Macaya's voice, drums, singing	25 sec.
71	horiz. line: 1/2 earth, 1/2 sky; sunset; one mountain range	long shot	straight	still, zoom in	Macaya's voice, drums, singing	11 sec.
72	horiz. line: 1/3 trees, 1/3 sky; evening sky with clouds; lake, trees, sky	long shot	changes with pan	right pan, zoom out	Macaya's voice, geese crying	14 sec.
73	horiz. line: 1/2 water, 1/2 sky; evening; geese flying low across lake	long shot	changes with pan	right pan	Macaya's voice, geese crying	21 sec.
74	1/2 earth, 1/2 sky; mountain far out; mountain with Old Oraibi on top	long shot	straight	zoom in	Macaya's voice, howling wind	18 sec.
75	horiz. line: 4/5 earth, 1/5 ground; four grass stalks in fgd focus; earth in bkgd	close-up, long shot	straight	rack focus	Macaya's voice, howling wind	18 sec.
76	Macaya's face in half-shade	close-up	oblique left	still	Macaya's voice, crickets	14 sec.
77	horiz. line: 3/4 earth, 1/4 sky; moon rises, upper right frame	long shot	straight	still	Macaya's voice, crickets	42 sec.
78	grassy earth, Alosaka mountain, sky, clouds	long shot	straight	track in, hand-held	Macaya's voice, wind	25 sec.
79	rattlesnake moving down dry tree trunk; its whole body moves past camera	close-up	oblique right	tilt down, still	Macaya's voice, howling wind, rattling snake	14 sec.
80	Anasazi ruin	long shot	low angle	right pan	Macaya's voice, howling wind, birds singing	10 sec.
81	Anasazi ruin from canyon rim	extreme long shot	high angle	tilt up	Macaya's voice, howling wind, birds singing	7 sec.
82	canyon walls, sky	long shot	low angle	left pan	Macaya's voice, howling wind, birds singing	13 sec.
83	canyon walls, sky (not the same shot)	long shot	low angle	left pan	Macaya's voice, howling wind, birds singing	10 sec.
84	corn plants	close-up, medium shot	changes with pan	right pan	voices of Macaya, playing children	16 sec.

85	corn field; children running around	long shot	changes with pan	right pan	Macaya's voice, voices of playing children	6 sec.
86	children playing in corn field	medium shot	changes with pan	left pan, tracking children	voices of Macaya, playing children	14 sec.
87	deer in front of birch trees	long shot	straight	zoom in, following deer	Macaya's voice, crickets	49 sec.
88	rain clouds, grassy mesa, dry mesa earth; houses in bkgd	long shot	low angle	right pan, zoom in	Macaya's voice, crickets	32 sec.
89	old photo with round white mask; Hopi wrapped in blankets from behind	close-up	straight	still	Macaya's voice, howling wind	3 sec.
90	old photo with round white mask; dance in a village	close-up, extreme close-up	straight	zoom in, still	Macaya's voice, howling wind	17 sec.
91	photo of religious dancers	extreme close-up	straight	still	Macaya's voice, howling wind	11 sec.
92	photo of two Koshare clowns walking to the right	extreme close-up	straight	still	Macaya's voice, howling wind	7 sec.
93	same photo, closer	extreme close-up	straight	tilt up	Macaya's voice, howling wind	10 sec.
94	photo of person in ceremonial clothes holding basket of feathers & other ritual items	extreme close-up	straight	still	Macaya's voice, howling wind	10 sec.
95	same photo; basket and content in detail	extreme close-up	straight	still	Macaya's voice, howling wind	4 sec.
96	same photo; head of man in detail	extreme close-up	straight	zoom out	Macaya's voice, howling wind	10 sec.
97	photo of Hopi kneeling; white round mask around photo	extreme close-up, close-up	straight	zoom out	Macaya's voice, howling wind	10 sec.
98	drum, blurry, focussed, then blurry	extreme close-up	straight	rack focus	Macaya sings chant of Ahl brotherhood	8 sec.
99	photo of two pairs of naked feet dancing	extreme close-up	straight	still	Macaya chanting	3 sec.
100	photo of priests performing dance; torsoes in detail, drum	extreme close-up	changes with pan	left pan	Macaya chanting	17 sec.

101	same photo	close-up	straight	still, zoom in, right pan, still	Macaya chanting	34 sec.
102	Macaya's face	close-up	oblique right	still	Macaya chanting	12 sec.
103	one stag	long shot	changes with pan	right pan	Macaya chanting	21 sec.
104	buffalo, blurry, then focussed	medium shot	straight	slow focus	Macaya chanting	16 sec.
105	photo of priests performing a dance	extreme close-up	straight	zoom out	Macaya chanting	14 sec.
106	spider spinning web around grasshopper	close-up	straight	still	silence; birdcall; baroque Spanish. military music	30 sec.
107	posterization: greyish grass, purple sky; mesa grass in fgd; helmets; Spanish riders moving to left in bkgd	close-up, long shot	low angle	left pan	Span. military music	23 sec.
108	posterization: greyish grass, purple sky; riders traverse landscape towards right	long shot	low angle	right pan	Span. military music	15 sec.
109	posterization: greyish grass, purple sky; lower half of frame fgd: grass and earth; riders move to left	long shot	low angle	track backward, left pan	Span. military music, horseshoes and harness rattle	30 sec.
110	posterization: greyish grass, purple sky; horiz. line: 1/2 earth, grass, 1/2 sky, riders	long shot	low angle	right pan	Span. military music, horseshoes and harness rattle	18 sec.
111	posterization: bright green grass, purple sky; horiz. line: 3/4 earth, 1/4 sky; riders approach camera	long shot medium shot	straight	camera follows riders	Span. military music, horseshoes and harness rattle	26 sec.
112	posterization: grayish grass, purple sky; yellow armour; rider fills out frame; moves to left	medium shot	straight	left track	rattling of horseshoes and harness	16 sec.
113	posterization: purple; wolf in a trap	close-up	straight	zoom out	Macaya's voice, rattling of horseshoes, harness	10 sec.

114	soft posterization: only part of the sky is purple; lop-sided horizon; two riders move to left	long shot	high angle	left track, camera held lop-sided	Macaya's voice, rattling of horses	16 sec.
115	dark sky, strip of yellow light in lower frame; lighting	long shot	straight	still	Macaya's voice	12 sec.
116	two riders moving towards camera	medium shot	straight	still, track backward	Macaya's voice	15 sec.
117	Macaya's head and upper body against bkgd of mesa sand; hands with cane pound the earth	medium shot	left side	still	Macaya's voice	28 sec.
118	horiz. line: 1/3 water, 2/3 sky; 1/2 earth, water, 1/2 rain clouds	long shot	straight	zoom out	Macaya's voice	15 sec.
119	Macaya's hands pounding with cane	close-up	left side	still	Macaya's voice	4 sec.
120	small ruin oblique right, shack in back; Macaya's head enters frame	medium shot, long shot,	left side	zoom out	Macaya's voice	15 sec.
121	slow motion: legs of run-ning white horse; foot of a rider; body and head of horse	close-up	straight	track back-ward, tilt up	Macaya's voice, rattling of horses	20 sec.
123	back and tail of white horse	close-up	straight	left track	Macaya's voice, rattling of horses	4 sec.
124	mesa landscape, two riders move to left	long shot	changes with the pan	left pan	Macaya's voice, rattling of horses	19 sec.
125	sky; three flying birds	long shot	straight	still	Macaya's voice, Span. military music	6 sec.
126	fast motion, posterization: black silhouettes against red bkgd; Span. riders beat-ing or killing Hopi people	medium shot	straight	still	Macaya's voice, Span. military music	13 sec.
127	dark sky, rainclouds, strip of orange-yellow light in lower frame; lighting	long shot	straight	still	Macaya's voice, Span. military music	9 sec.

128	race track around lake; runners on the track; runners coming up the hill	long shot	high angle	still	Macaya's voice, Span. military music, runners are cheered	13 sec.
129	horiz. line: 1/3 earth, 2/3 sky; sun sets on horizon in left frame	long shot	straight	still	Macaya's voice, runners are cheered	8 sec.
130	bushes; four runners with corn plants coming uphill	medium shot	high angle	still	Macaya's voice, runners are cheered	6 sec.
131	boy runner with corn plant running uphill from behind	medium shot	straight	tilt up	Macaya's voice, runners are cheered	9 sec.
132	rattlesnake moving down dry tree trunk (not same shot as 79)	close-up	straight	tilt down	Macaya's voice, runners are cheered	11 sec.
133	cornfield with clothesline; runner at back moves to right, filmed between pieces of laundry; later alone	long shot	changes with pan	zoom in, right pan	Macaya's voice cheers runners	48 sec.
134	corn plants moving in rain storm	close-up, medium shot	straight	zoom out	Macaya's voice, sound of rain	26 sec.
135	two riders against bkgd of mesa landscape moving to left	extreme long shot, long shot, extreme long shot	changes with pan	still, left pan, zoom in, zoom out	Macaya's voice, Vivaldi's *Concerto for Baroque Trumpet*	1.24 min.
136	Macaya's face	close-up	left side	still	Macaya's voice, concerto	17 sec.
137	dry mesa earth, village in bkgd	long shot	low angle	zoom out	Macaya's voice	6 sec.
138	sky with clouds, single bird; landscape in lower frame	long shot	changes with the pan	tilt down, left pan, zoom out	traditional dance songs and music	27 sec.
139	full moon in lower middle frame	long shot	straight	still	dance songs and music	9 sec.
140	sun setting on horizon in middle of frame; small strip of light; 4/5 dark	long shot	changes with pan	still, right pan	dance songs and music	22 sec.
141	burning fire; pot with sth. boiling	close-up	high angle, straight	tilt up	dance songs and music	14 sec.

142	boy cuts throat of a sheep; somebody holds a bowl for the blood	medium shot	high angle	still	dance songs and music	19 sec.
143	three people skin the sheep	medium shot, close-up	high angle	zoom in	dance songs and music	10 sec.
144	inside a house, a woman puts pieces of sth. into pot	medium shot	oblique right	still	dance songs and music, women talking	17 sec.
145	two hands knock corn off cobs	close-up	straight	still, zoom in	dance songs and music, faithful sound	10 sec.
146	open box with grindstone; blue corn poured into box; woman starts grinding corn	medium shot	high angle, oblique left	still	dance songs and music	20 sec.
147	box with ground corn; hands brush cornmeal from grinding stone and interior	close-up	high angle, oblique left	still	dance songs and music	15 sec.
148	yellow plastic bowl with cornmeal; two hands make dough	close-up	oblique right	still	dance songs and music	7 sec.
149	head of woman who makes dough	close-up	oblique right	still	dance songs and music	4 sec.
150	sth. is poured into blue corn dough; dough kneaded; two girls make the dough	close-up, medium shot	straight	zoom out	dance songs and music	25 sec.
151	contre-jour shot: girl takes bread from earth oven to right against bkgd of mesa	long shot	changes with pan	left pan	dance songs and music	12 sec.
152	bread, blurry, then focussed	close-up	straight	still	dance songs and music	6 sec.
153	body fragments of dancers in village arena; heads, then torsoes, then feet of dancers; drums in bkgd	close-up	changes with pan	still, left pan, tilt down, tilt up, zoom out, zoom in	dance songs and music	2.40 min.
154	sky, cloud shapes; corn leaves in lower right corner; corn plants in lower half	long shot, medium shot	straight	still, tilt down	dance songs and music	22 sec.

155	sky with rain clouds, lightning, and rainbow; 1/5 earth	long shot	changes with pan	left pan	dance songs and music	28 sec.
156	flower stalk with blossoms	close-up	straight	still	dance songs and music	9 sec.
157	two white flowers	close-up	straight	still	dance songs and music	6 sec.
158	butterfly on flowers	close-up	straight	still	dance songs and music	6 sec.
159	corn leaves moving in the wind	close-up	high angle	still	dance songs and music	20 sec.
160	shot from the back of white pickup – drives through cornfield; corn plants on loading space	long shot, close-up	straight	track forward, tilt down	dance songs and music	13 sec.
161	wheels drive through earth of cornfield, pulling a plow	close-up	low angle	still	dance songs and music	5 sec.
162	body fragments of dancers in village arena; audience in the back	close-up, long shot	straight	zoom out	dance songs and music	18 sec.
163	water; face of girl splashed with water	close-up	straight	hand-held	dance songs and music	8 sec.
164	body fragments of dancers in slow motion	close-up	straight	hand-held	dance songs and music	7 sec.
165	boy katchina dancer, face and upper body	medium shot	changes with pan	right pan	dance songs and music	3 sec.
166	pile of blue corncobs; pile of yellow corncobs	medium shot	low angle	right pan	dance songs and music	16 sec.
167	children corn dancers in village arena; spectators in bkgd; one little boy dancer	close-up, long shot		zoom out, dancers tracked, zoom in	dance songs and music	1.16 min.
168	little boy dancer	medium shot	changes with pan	right pan	dance songs and music	2 sec.
169	adult dancers in village arena; heads, feet, torsoes, whole bodies of dancers; fast motion begins	close-up, medium shot, long shot	changes with pans	pans, tilts	dance songs and music, sped-up noise & drum beat	45 sec.
170	heads and upper bodies of dancers	close-up, medium shot	low angle, straight	pan, tilts, zoom out	fast-motion noise, sped-up drum beat	9 sec.

171	heads and upper bodies of dancers	close-up, medium shot	changes with pans	zoom out, pans	fast-motion noise, sped-up drum beat	11 sec.
172	torsoes and whole bodies of dancers	close-up, medium shot	straight	zoom out	fast-motion noise, sped-up drum beat	2 sec.
173	heads of dancers	close-up	changes with pan	left pan	fast-motion noise, sped-up drum beat	4 sec.
174	whole bodies of dancers	medium shot	changes with pan	right pan	fast-motion noise, sped-up drum beat	3 sec.
175	torsoes and whole bodies of dancers	medium shot	changes with pan	right pan	fast-motion noise, sped-up drum beat	4 sec.
176	head of one dancer	close-up	low angle	still	fast-motion noise, sped-up drum beat	2 sec.
177	head of one dancer (not the same shot)	close-up	low angle	still	fast-motion noise	2 sec.
178	heads, upper bodies, whole bodies, torsoes of dancers	close-up, medium shot, long shot	straight	zoom out	fast-motion noise, sped-up drum beat	4 sec.
179	torso of dancer	medium shot	straight	zoom out	fast-motion noise, sped-up drum beat	3 sec.
180	head of dancer	close-up	straight	still	fast motion noise, sped-up drum beat	1 sec.
181	silhouettes of two people against morning sky; they sort corncobs, credits	medium shot	straight	still	Macaya's voice, voices of the two people	

ಐ ঽ

Talker: Detailed Shot Analysis

No.	Content of the Shot	C/Dist	C/Angle	C/Move	Shot/L	Pattern
1	opening credits			still		
2 1st sc.	cabbie's eyes, calm	extreme close-up	straight	still	8.37 sec.	a
3	dashboard between the seats, cab driver ID	close-up	changes with pan	left pan ⇓10	5.10 sec.	b
	cabbie's head from behind	close-up	oblique right			b2
4	hooker and pimp in rear-view mirror, street through windshield	not clear – several planes	oblique left	still	2.69 sec.	c
5	hooker and pimp on back seat talking, pimp puts cigarette in her mouth	medium close-up	oblique right	still	7.60 sec.	d
6	title: *Talker*			still	6.28 sec.	
7	still the same shot (5), pimp lights cigarette	medium close-up	oblique right	still	7.50 sec.	d
8	cabbie's eyes, nervous and alert	extreme close-up	straight	still	1.22 sec.	a
9	through windshield framed by steering wheel and upper dash-board: street and woman on left sidewalk	long shot	changes with pan	left pan, camera moves forward through cab ⇓	0.90 sec.	e
10	cabbie's eyes, startled	extreme close-up	straight	still	0.75 sec.	a
11	left side of hood with woman's hands and purse, she was almost run over by cab	medium close-up	oblique right	still	0.44 sec.	e
12	woman blurred on left side	medium close-up	oblique right	still	0.72 sec.	e
13	hooker and pimp on back seat turning their heads	medium close-up	straight	still	1.12 sec.	d

---

[10] The arrow indicates that this camera movement continues through the whole shot.

14	image of gesticulating woman in left wing mirror, framed by street and left car window	not clear – several planes	oblique right	still	2.34 sec.	e
15	hooker and pimp on back seat turning their heads back	medium close-up	straight	still	3.66 sec.	d
16	cabbie's eyes, exhausted	extreme close-up	straight	still	2.28 sec.	a
17	dashboard between the seats, cab driver ID, cab driver's right hand switching off radio	close-up	straight	still	1.90 sec.	b
18	pimp and hooker on back seat, pimp talking to cabbie	medium close-up	oblique left	still	8.25 sec.	d
19	hooker and pimp in rear-view mirror, street through windshield	not clear – several planes	oblique left	still	2.03 sec.	c
20	hooker and pimp on back seat, pimp leaning forward and yelling at cabbie, back of cabbie's head	medium close-up	changes with pan	right pan	4.18 sec.	d
21	hooker on back seat, pimp leaning back again, hooker leaving car, then pimp leaving car, empty back seat briefly	medium close-up	straight	still	13.63 sec.	d
22	car door, hooker walking away and turning around, talking to pimp, pimp turning back at car and spitting on the windshield, both walking away, people on the street through windshield, wiper blades smearing the spit, back of cabbie's head blurred on the left of frame	medium shot	changes with pan	left pan	19.38 sec.	f
23 2nd sc.	snow, roofs of houses, store: Western Furs Ltd., a backyard with garbage bins, the cab	long shot	extreme high angle, oblique right	tilt down	13.13 sec.	a
24	front of the car from left side, passage between two houses with garbage bins and garbage lying around, three tramps rummage in bins	medium shot	straight	still	5.22 sec.	b

25	inside of cab from back seat, a pair of white miniature shoes dangling from rear-view mirror, cabbie's head in the left of frame, his forehead and eyes alternately in rear-view mirror, cabbie following a buzzing fly with his eyes and chasing it	medium close-up	straight	still	22.28 sec.	c
26	fly on dash board, killed by slap with newspaper	close-up	straight	still	1.97 sec.	d
27	same shot as 25, cabbie picking up newspaper, seeing an ad where the dead fly sticks, reading ad (by mental hospital seeking professional talk therapists), calls number of hospital	medium close-up	changes with pan	right pan ⇓	51.75 sec.	c
	tramps at the right front of car, one tramp entering car and telling cabbie where to go	medium close-up		still		c2
28	cab from above, other two tramps entering car from right, cabbie leaving car on left side, left door being pushed open, cabbie jamming it closed, hitting the door window	medium shot	extreme high angle, oblique right	still	18.65 sec.	a
29 3rd sc.	hospital front, cabbie from behind entering the door	long shot	straight	tilt up	17.41 sec.	a
30	cabbie's feet walking toward reception desk	medium close-up	high angle, waist-high	tilt up ⇓	26.28 sec.	a2
	his hands waist-high clutching newspaper, camera stays there briefly	medium close-up	changes with pan	left pan ⇓		a3
	reception desk with two telephones, cup with a bunch of sharpened pencils, sharpener in the shape of a doll's head being turned around by two hands	medium close-up	oblique left	tilt up ⇓		b
	head of receptionist with headphones and mike talking	medium close-up	oblique left	still		b2

31	cabbie's hands with newspaper waist-high	medium close-up	straight	still	1.72 sec.	a3
32	head of receptionist talking to cabbie	medium close-up	oblique left	still	5.90 sec.	b2
33	cabbie's left eye and surrounding facial parts	extreme close-up	oblique right	still	3.00 sec.	a4
34	head of receptionist talking to cabbie	medium close-up	changes with track	track around her to right	8.57 sec.	b2
35	hallway, male nurse wheeling a stretcher, receptionist at desk, cabbie walking down hallway, person in white coat moving around in the back	long shot	low angle, straight	still	8.03 sec.	c
36	observation room, mobile with clowns in fgd, a chained TV, a garbage bin, a children's cot, armchairs, a couch, and a table with magazines in the room, cabbie moving around in the room	long shot	high angle, oblique right	still	33.56 sec.	d
37	magazine: *The Year in Pictures 1972*	close-up	high angle, oblique right	tilt up ⇓	23.22 sec.	f
	his hands picking up the magazine	close-up	changes with pan	right pan ⇓		a3
	his leather jacket, TV, his hands moving the chain	close-up	changes with track	track around cabbie ⇓		a5
	cabbie's right arm in sudden movement, doctor and his assistant standing behind him	medium close-up	straight	still		a5
38	heads of doctor and assistant	close-up	straight	still	2.28 sec.	g
39	cabbie's startled face	close-up	straight	still	2.37 sec.	a4

40	sterile white stairway, doctor, assistant, and cabbie descending the stairs, doctor starting to take off surgical clothes	medium shot	low angle, oblique right	camera tracks the figures as they descend	20.22 sec.	h
	the three walking past the camera to the right	medium close-up	low angle	still		h2
41	stairway from behind, the three descending and doctor continuing to take off his surgical clothes	medium shot	low angle, oblique left	camera tracks the figures as they descend	21.47 sec.	h
	the three approaching camera, staying there briefly	medium close-up	low angle	still		h2
42	the three descending, doctor has almost finished taking off his surgical clothes	medium shot	low angle, oblique right	camera tracks the figures as they descend	20.72 sec.	h
	an empty picture frame on the wall, doctor and assistant off to left behind cabbie who is turning to the right in fgd, assistant motioning him to the left, cabbie is completing a full turn and off to left, assistant off to right	medium shot	low angle	still		h2
43	cellar corridor with pipes on the ceiling, another assistant in the left of frame	long shot	low angle	slight right pan, tilt down ⇊	15.94 sec.	i
	doctor and cabbie entering the picture in right of frame through another corridor	long shot	changes with the pan	camera pulls forward, right pan ⇊		i2
	doctor, assistant, and cabbie standing in corridor, doctor handing cabbie some papers and asking him to sign	medium shot	straight	still		i3
44	cabbie's hands signing the paper	close-up	oblique left	still	2.06 sec.	a3
45	doctor, assistant, and cabbie standing in corridor, doctor gives last instructions	medium shot	straight	still	9.47 sec.	i3

46	cabbie looking confused	medium close-up	oblique left	still	1.28 sec.	a4
47	the three standing in corridor, doctor off to left, cabbie, still confused, moving in direction the assistant motions	medium shot	straight	camera tracks cabbie ⇓	22.91 sec.	i3
	cabbie walking around left corner into another cellar corridor, turning around to reassure himself	medium shot		still		b5
48 4th sc.	cabbie entering room and looking around	medium shot	oblique right	camera pulls back ⇓	14.65 sec.	a
	cabbie standing and back of patient's head unfocussed on right			still		a2
49	patient strapped to chair, middle part of cabbie's body from behind unfocussed to the left, between them diagonally a table with cigarettes, an ashtray, and an envelope with the cabbie's instructions	medium shot	oblique right	still	50.97 sec.	b
	cabbie moving forward, taking a cigarette, and lighting it for patient, starting to walk around patient, who keeps craning his neck toward him, cabbie taking off his jacket and sitting down	medium shot ⇒ medium close-up ⇒ medium shot	changes with track	camera tracks movements of cabbie, then moves around table counter-clock-wise, focussing patient		b2
	both sitting opposite to each other at the table, cabbie from behind in lower right of frame, patient in upper left	medium shot	oblique right	camera pulls away from patient		b
50	cabbie looking at patient, lighting a cigarette but is interrupted by buzzer, stops smoking	medium shot	oblique left	still	8.91 sec.	c

51	patient at table talking and smoking	medium shot	oblique right	still	4.72 sec.	d
52	cabbie at table looking irritated and confused at patient	medium shot	oblique left	still	2.25 sec.	c
53	patient at table talking and smoking	medium shot	oblique right	still	7.31 sec.	d
54	cabbie at table looking around irritated and confused	medium shot	oblique left	still	6.18 sec.	c
55	patient at table talking and smoking	medium shot	oblique right	still	14.15 sec.	d
56	cabbie at table looking irritated and confused at patient	medium shot	oblique left	still	3.66 sec.	c
57	patient at table talking and smoking	medium shot	oblique right	still	17.90 sec.	d
58	cabbie at table looking irritated and confused at patient	medium shot	oblique left	still	4.03 sec.	c
59	patient at table, talking and smoking	medium shot	oblique right	still	5.97 sec.	d
60	cabbie's hands opening the envelope	close-up	oblique left	tilt up ⇓	9.69 sec.	c2
	cabbie's face, astounded and horrified	close-up	oblique left	still		c
61	patient's face; he is talking and smoking	medium close-up	oblique right	still	6.19 sec.	d
62	cabbie's face; he is grinning	medium close-up	oblique left	still	9.25 sec.	c
63	patient's face, he is talking and smoking	medium close-up	oblique right	still	4.62 sec.	d
64	cabbie's face, he is sneering	medium close-up	oblique left	still	3.43 sec.	c
65	patient's face, he is talking and smoking, starting to get frightened	close-up	oblique right, slight low angle	still	5.53 sec.	d

66	cabbie's face, he is gazing into space	close-up	oblique left, slight high angle	still	2.41 sec.	c
67	patient's face frightened, he is talking and smoking	close-up	oblique right, slight low angle	still	6.41 sec.	d
68	cabbie's face showing fright and anger	close-up	oblique left, slight high angle	still	1.90 sec.	c
69	patient's face, he is talking and smoking, becoming more and more frightened and nervous	close-up	oblique right, slight low angle	still	3.19 sec.	d
70	cabbie's face showing fright and anger	close-up	oblique left, slight high angle	still	1.97 sec.	c
71	white paper, instructions: (SAY NOTHING)	close-up	oblique left, slight high angle	still	2.00 sec.	e
72	patient's face, he is yelling and smoking, being frightened and nervous	close-up	oblique right, slight low angle	still	2.19 sec.	d
73	cabbie's face showing fright and anger, his nose and mouth starting to tremble	close-up	oblique left, slight high angle	still	2.62 sec.	c
74	patient's face, he is yelling and smoking, frightened and nervous	close-up	oblique right, slight low angle	still	2.47 sec.	d

75	cabbie's eyes and nose, eyes narrowed to slit s	extreme close-up	oblique left, slight high angle	still	2.44 sec.	c
76	patient's eyes and nose, eyes wide open	extreme close-up	oblique right, slight low angle	still	3.25 sec.	d
77	cabbie's eyes and nose	extreme close-up	oblique left, slight high angle	tilt down ⇓	2.66 sec.	c
	cabbie's mouth opened to scream	extreme close-up	oblique left, slight high angle			c
78	patient's eyes and nose	extreme close-up	oblique right, slight low angle	tilt down ⇓	3.04 sec.	d
	patient's mouth opened to scream	extreme close-up	oblique right, slight low angle	still		d
79	red ashtray made of clay in the shape of a face with open mouth	close-up	oblique right, slight high angle	still	2.28 sec.	e
80	closing credits					

✆ ৯

Honey Moccasin: Sequence Protocol

0:00 – opening CREDITS
in white beadwork on black ground, illuminated by a hand with burning matches and later a flashlight

1.) 1:46 – "Smokin Moccasin," night
Native Tongue television covers a mysterious disappearance of powwow outfits; Honey Moccasin introduces herself to the audience; flashbacks illustrate her story; she performs a song, Bernelda and Mabel are background singers; Zach has his first encounter with Beau

2.) 13:46 – "Smokin Moccasin," day
Honey watches the Native Tongue broadcast and is later joined by Bernelda; Native Tongue programming includes the screening of a home video about the previous year's powwow, Bernelda on location in Zach's café interviewing him, and Bernelda interviewing Johnny John, Zach's father, in the Native Tongue studio about the meaning of traditional powwow outfits; Honey transforms herself into an ironic made-up of Sherlock Holmes

3.) 20:46 – somewhere outside, day
Honey as detective follows a track of colored feathers which take her to a WWII veteran memorial and eventually to the "Inukshuk Café"

4.) 23:43 – "Smokin Moccasin," night
elders host a fashion show moderated by Bernelda; Mabel gives an art performance

5.) 31:07 – "Inukshuk Café," night, shortly after previous sequence
one of the three guests in the bar tries out Zach's new Karaoke machine while the other two laugh heartily, Beau returns Zach's wallet – it is the second of the "feared" encounters with Beau

6.) 32:50 – "Inukshuk café," after closing
Zach turns out the lights and descends into his basement where he keeps the stolen powwow outfits; he transforms into a jingle dress dancer; Honey peeks in from outside; Zach attempts to kill Honey and is prevented by Beau

7.) 38:14 – inside a car, night
Zach and his father sit silently in the back seat, Zach cries, Johnny shakes his head in displeasure

8.) 38:29 – Native Tongue studio, time unspecified

stolen powwow outfits are on display, Zach returns outfits live on Native Tongue broadcast

39:20 – TITLE "one year later"
in white beadwork on black ground illuminated by diegetic source

9.) 39:24 – "Smokin Moccasin," night
Mabel gives words of thanks to community; her film is screened

45:41 – TITLE "the end"
in white beadwork on black ground illuminated by a diegetic source

10.) 45:45 – Native Tongue broadcast
a clip of Hank and his "Band of No-Goods" playing a song for Honey; clip: location unspecified, Hank outside in the back of a tour truck, he steps out while singing, his two helpers close the back door and leave with the truck

Smoke Signals: Sequence Protocol

1.) 00:00 – July 4th, 1976, INTRODUCTION[11]
Randy Peone in K–REZ radio station, which is an old rusty trailer; reservation road; Lester FallsApart on traffic van parked at a desolate crossroads transmits the traffic report; opening CREDITS are superimposed

dissolve
00:40 – TITLE *Smoke Signals*

dissolve
2.) 00:40 – July 4th, 1976, The Fire, night
burning house; people run around disorientedly; hands in the first floor throw out a baby – Thomas Builds-The-Fire (slow motion); Arnold runs and dives to catch it which is heavily reminiscent of a football-catch; he hands the baby to Grandma Builds-The-Fire, their silhouettes against the flames of the burning house

dissolve
3.) 02:48 – 1976, The Morning After
people walk through the ashes; Arnold (long hair) stands between Grandma Builds-The-Fire holding baby Thomas and Arlene Joseph holding baby

---

[11] When the time of the day is not indicated, the events happen during daylight. Also, when the year is not given, the events in the sequence happen in 1998, the year of the film's narrative present. The sequences are usually divided by a cut if not specified otherwise.

Victor; Grandma Builds-The-Fire thanks Arnold for saving Thomas from the flames

fade

4.) 04:00 – n.d., Arnold's Grief – flashback
Arnold Joseph (short hair) in pickup; aerial shot of his yellow pickup driving down a road

fade

5.) 04:15 – The Reservation
K–REZ radio station; Velma and Lucy in their brown Malibu drive in reverse; Lester FallsApart on the roof of the traffic van; K–REZ radio station

6.) 05:14 – Basketball
Victor, Junior Polatkin, and Boo play basketball, Victor in a red T-shirt and cut-off blue jeans; Thomas with traditional braids, thick glasses and dressed in a three-piece suit watches them; Victor claims to have been fouled by another player; ball bounces off the court and comes to a stop at Thomas's feet; Thomas throws it back awkwardly to Victor, who makes fun of Thomas's clumsiness and his outfit

dissolve

7.) 06:13 – 1988, Schoolboys
young Thomas and Victor stand at a burning garbage bin in the school yard; Thomas lectures Victor about how things burn in different colors and nags him about his father, who has left his family – Victor is hurt; Victor counters by asking Thomas in what colors his parents burned up in the house fire of 1976 – Thomas is now hurt as well

sound bridge: mockery song

8.) 07:17 – Basketball
the three young men start a mockery song about Custer, providing the rhythm by dribbling the ball; then they joke around about who the best basketball player is (Geronimo)

9.) 08:08 – Bad News
the phone rings in Arlene's house; she picks up the receiver and her face reflects shock as Suzy Song gives her the news of Arnold's death; Victor enters in time to see his mother's shocked face; they exchange a long look; dissolve to Arnold's trailer near Phoenix; dissolve back

10.) 08:45 – Trading Post
Victor cashes a forty-US-dollar check for his mom; Thomas enters and offers his condolences; he also offers to help Victor out with some money

to go down to Phoenix to claim his father's ashes, provided he takes Thomas along; Victor laughs and declines this offer and leaves the store

match on action cut
11.) 10:11 – 1988, Trading Post
young Victor (red T-shirt, blue jeans, and hair unbound) walks out of the trading post; Thomas (traditional braids, glasses, three-piece suit) comes running around the corner, holding a burning sparkler firework, and wishes Victor a happy Fourth of July; Victor is picked up from behind by his father; Arnold sends Thomas home and takes Victor to his pickup, doing a magic trick with a coin

12.) 10:52 – 1988, In the Pickup
Victor is holding a beer as they drive along; Arnold is engaged in a monologue about spiriting away white people, white cities, white Catholics, reservations, Indians etc.; Victor is a little scared and confused; Arnold stops in front of their house; he motions Victor to hand the beer back but it slips from his hands; Arnold's mood changes instantly from being over-excited to angry: he slaps young Victor in the face, upon which Victor runs toward the house

match on action cut
13.) 12:50 – In the Josephs' House, evening
Victor enters the house and walks into the kitchen, where Arlene is making frybread; she is sorry that she has not enough money for Victor to go to Phoenix; Victor takes her hands in his

14.) 13:31 – In Grandma Builds-The-Fire's House, evening
Thomas is making frybread and talking to his grandma; she warns him about Victor's meanness; they sit down to eat

15.) 13:52 – In the Josephs' House, evening
Arlene puts pieces of hot frybread in basket; Victor grabs one piece and starts eating while he is telling his mother about Thomas' offer; Arlene talks about how she listens to the advice of people on how to make the frybread taste better and asks Victor to promise he will come back

16.) 15:11 – In Grandma Builds-The-Fire's House, evening
Thomas and his grandma eating dinner; there is a knock at the door and they grin at each other knowingly

sound bridge: the rules that Thomas has to follow on their trip to Phoenix
17.) 15:46 – Reservation Road

Thomas (three-piece suit, braids, glasses) and Victor (red T-shirt, blue jeans, hair unbound) try to hitchhike out of the reservation to the bus stop; they walk on opposite sides of the road

18.) 15:54 – K–REZ Radio Station
Randy Peone's morning show; images of the reservation

19.) 16:16 – K–REZ Traffic Van
Lester FallsApart on top of the van gives his traffic report by cell phone

20.) 16:48 – Velma and Lucy
Velma and Lucy drive their brown Malibu strangely in reverse; they pick up Victor and Thomas, on condition that Thomas trade a story for the ride; Thomas starts telling a story about Arnold as a hippie demonstrating against the Vietnam war; Velma and Lucy are amazed by the story; Victor becomes angry; the story is considered appropriate for the trade, and the two take Victor and Thomas to the bus stop; Velma and Lucy say good bye, with some jokes along the way

21.) 20:40 – Bus stop
the bus pulls in; Thomas is about to enter the bus; Victor hesitates and asks Thomas whether or not he is sure about paying for their trip; they enter the bus

22.) 21:21 – Bus Interior
the passengers are, among others, a black soldier, a white man, a female punk, a male biker, and a young woman; all the passengers follow Thomas and Victor with their eyes as they walk down the aisle and take a seat next to the young woman, who turns out to be a gymnast

23.) 22:22 – Bus Interior, later
Cathy is ostentatiously stretching her legs; Thomas stares at her and Victor is seemingly embarrassed about this; Thomas starts talking to her; Cathy brags about having been on the 1980 Olympic team; Thomas is very impressed; Victor shuts her up by telling her she is just bragging; Cathy, hurt, moves to another seat; Victor lectures Thomas about his naivety and tells him not to trust anybody

24.) 25:19 – Idaho Landscape
the bus rolls through wheat fields at sunset

25.) 25:33 – Bus Interior, night
Victor and Thomas sleep in their seats

match cut
26.) 25:42 – 1988, the Josephs' House, night

there is a party; Arlene and Arnold are pretty drunk and dance together; young Victor upsets his father by answering with "nobody" the question who his favorite Indian would be; Arlene tries to calm Victor down; Arnold drifts away, upset and amused at the same time

sound bridge: Thomas' story about Arnold
27.) 27:30 – In a Diner, night
Thomas starts telling the story about how Arnold found Thomas at Spokane Falls and took him to Denny's; Victor replies that he has heard the story a thousand times; Thomas tells it nevertheless; flashback: young Thomas is sitting at the Falls and staring at the water when Arnold appears from behind and starts talking to him; Thomas continues his story; Victor (checkered shirt) looks at him, pretty pissed off; he gets up and walks to the bathroom

match cut
28.) 29:45 – 1988, the Josephs' Bedroom
young Victor (checkered shirt) looks in the bedroom mirror and turns around to see the bed where both his parents are sleeping after the party with their clothes still on; he looks again at the reflection in the mirror

match on action cut
29.) 29:56 – In the Diner Bathroom
Victor looks at his reflection in the mirror

sound bridge: bottles being smashed
30.) 30:23 – 1988, the Josephs' House, inside
Arlene wakes up from the noise of smashing bottles; she goes to the window to see young Victor throwing full beer bottles against his father's pickup; Arlene yells at Arnold (red T-shirt, blue jeans) that they have to stop partying and drinking; they argue in front of Victor; Arnold wants to buy booze; Arlene tries to stop him; he slaps her and she falls to the floor

31.) 31:22 – 1988, the Josephs' House, outside
Arnold comes storming out of the house; determined and silent, he climbs into the truck and drives off; young Victor runs after him and climbs into the back of the pickup; Arnold stops, hugs Victor for a moment, pushes him away, and takes off; Arlene grabs the crying Victor to comfort him and herself

32.) 32:24 – 1988, the Josephs' House, later the same day
Arlene sits in an easy chair; young Victor walks around; he switches the lamp outside on and off in the rhythm of the Morse code for SOS; they

share the moment of sadness; young Thomas appears and calls Victor outside

33.) 33:12 – 1988, the Josephs' House, outside
Thomas relentlessly questions Victor about Arnold's leaving; Victor suddenly leaps at Thomas, pushes him to the ground, and starts beating him violently; Arlene comes running out and pulls Victor off Thomas; she holds the kicking and screaming Victor briefly until he breaks free and runs away; Arlene comforts the bruised and bleeding Thomas and hushes his nagging questions; Victor (checkered shirt) runs down the road

match on action cut
34.) 34:03 – Bus Interior
Victor (checkered shirt) looks out of the bus window and sees himself as young Victor running beside the bus; Thomas starts asking questions and talking about Arnold again; Victor ignores him at first, then reacts sourly by asking why he always babbles on without sense; he accuses him of behaving and talking like an Indian frozen in the past and mocks him for having constructed his idea of "Indianness" from the movie *Dances with Wolves*; Victor lectures Thomas about how to act like a "real" Indian

35.) 36:24 – Convenience Store
the whole bus waits for Thomas, Victor and the driver standing outside; then Thomas emerges (slow motion): he wears a blue T-shirt with the letters "Fry Bread Power," blue jeans, his hair unbound, no glasses, and he looks very stoic; just before he reaches the bus, he cannot hold it any longer, and flashes the broad smile that Victor has just criticized

36.) 37:03 – Bus Interior
Thomas and Victor walk to their seats, which are occupied by two cowboys; they try to reclaim them but get stonewalled by the cowboys' racist behavior; they take two other seats; Thomas teases that the stoic Indian stare does not always work and complains about the cowboys always winning; both start a song mocking John Wayne's teeth; the passengers turn around and look at them; shots of the passing landscape

37.) 39:35 – Phoenix
the bus rolls into the station; Thomas and Victor get off

38.) 40:25 – The Walk
Thomas and Victor walk down a deserted road, Thomas again talking on and on about Arnold and moving Indians in his storytelling mode; Victor becomes frustrated; Thomas offers Victor a drink from his army canteen twice, and twice Victor angrily throws it away

39.) 42:31 – Suzy's Trailer
through the window Suzy can see the two walking towards her trailer; they introduce each other, and both men are overwhelmed by her beauty; Victor asks for his dad; Suzy disappears and returns with a silver urn; Victor looks puzzled; Suzy offers the urn to Victor, who steps back and averts his gaze from it; Thomas finally takes it; Victor, rather impolitely, makes to leave; Suzy, a little puzzled at this, invites them to stay for a while

40.) 44:39 – Suzy's trailer, night
Thomas sits on the couch with a basket of frybread, and Victor and Suzy at the kitchen table; they watch a western; Thomas talks about the good frybread Arlene makes; Victor is obviously uncomfortable, finally he grabs a piece of frybread and eats it; Thomas starts telling the story about how Arlene magically turned 50 pieces of frybread into 100; flashback illustrating the story; Suzy likes the story and Victor is angry again; then Thomas asks Suzy to tell how she met Arnold

sound bridge: sound of a car which is being started
41.) 48:55 – n.d., A Road – flashback
Suzy and Arnold in his pickup: he wants to give her a ride; they talk, and Arnold tries to start the car but it will not start; both walk down the road, Suzy with a bag of groceries; they talk about the bad things they did in their lives; Arnold says that he broke three hearts

42.) 51:20 – Suzy's Trailer, night
Thomas has fallen asleep on the couch with the silver urn in his arms; Suzy continues to talk about Arnold; Victor asks if Arnold had ever talked about him; Suzy replies that Arnold always talked about how he and Victor played basketball against two priests

sound bridge: Arnold's voice
43.) 51:48 – n.d., Arnold and Basketball – flashback
basketball court out in the desert close to the trailer park; Arnold tells himself the story about the game; second flashback: Victor and Arnold on an indoor basketball court playing against the two priests; the score is very tight, next basket wins; Victor makes a shot; Arnold on the outdoor basketball court throws the ball away

match on action cut
44.) 53:55 – Suzy's Trailer, outside, night
Victor catches the ball as it rolls toward his feet; they talk and Suzy admits that she loved Arnold like a father, which upsets Victor very much; Suzy tells how she and Arnold went to a big Powwow; Arnold's dog Kafka returns

sound bridge: Kafka's barking and Suzy's voice calling him
45.) 56:15 – Arnold's Death – flashback
Suzy walks over to Arnold's trailer and finds him lying dead on his bed

46.) 57:03 – Suzy's Trailer, outside, night
Suzy tries to persuade Victor to go into the trailer to look at Arnold's belongings; Suzy tells Victor how the fire started that killed Thomas's parents – she knows the story from Arnold, who has not talked about it to anybody else

sound bridge: Arnold's voice
47.) 58:41 – 1976, The Party, July 4th, night
Arnold is drunk and stumbles out of the house with a burning firework; he stands close to the window and a fireball shoots right into the house; soon the interior of the house catches fire and the house goes up in flames; Arnold does not notice the fire

48.) 59:14 – Suzy's Trailer, outside, night
at first Victor does not believe the story, then he is shocked by the fact that it was his dad who started the fire; flashback: the baby being tossed out of the first-story window; silhouettes of Arnold and Grandma Builds-The-Fire against the flames as he hands her the baby; Arnold turns around and runs for the burning house; Suzy persuades Victor to go into his father's trailer by telling him that Arnold always loved Victor and that he meant to go back home

49.) 1.00:26 – Arnold's Trailer, night
Victor enters and is appalled by the smell of his dead father; he searches through the trailer; a red T-shirt and blue jeans lie on the edge of the bed; in Arnold's wallet Victor finds a photograph of Arlene, Arnold, and himself as a child, the back of the photograph reads: HOME; in Arnold's blue jeans he finds a pocketknife; slowly he starts to cut his hair with it

fade
50.) 1.02:36 – Arizona and Nevada Landscape, day-night
Thomas and Victor drive home; landscapes move by

fade
51.) 1.03:10 – Yellow Pickup, night
Thomas and Victor inside; Thomas starts a romantic story about Arnold again; Victor is fed up and loses his temper; he tells Thomas that his father left him and his mom, that he was a drunk, and that he beat him and Arlene; they get into an argument; Thomas accuses Victor of doing nothing and making his mom cry; Victor says that Thomas took his dad away and that

he really loved Thomas and not Victor; he is very much enraged and shouts that he wished Arnold had not saved Thomas in the fire so he would not have left his family; as they argue, the car goes faster and faster; too late, Victor sees a car turned sideways in the middle of the road; Victor slams on the brakes and turns the wheel to avoid the car

52.) 1.05:10 – The Car Wreck, night
Victor and Thomas and the white couple in the other car are not injured; Burt, the driver, accuses Victor of having caused the wreck and orders his wife Penny to stay in the car; Thomas runs toward another very damaged car off the road and finds two young white women, one of whom seems to be seriously injured; an argument breaks out between Victor and Burt; Thomas tries to talk to the injured girl to keep her awake; Victor says, and then screams, that he wants to go for help; Burt dismisses his intention by announcing that the closest town must be 20 miles away; Thomas and Victor share a long, understanding look

53.) 1.06:43 – The Run, night
Victor starts to run along the desert highway; while running, he becomes considerably weaker until he just stumbles forward and finally breaks down exhausted at dawn; the run-sequence is intercut (through dissolves) with shots of the burning house, of Suzy, of Arnold standing on the desert basketball court, of young Victor running down the road, of Arnold running for the burning house, and of young Victor at the Fall's bridge, looking up at his father, who reaches out for him

match on action cut
54.) 1.08:22 – The Rescue, dawn
Victor reaches for the hand of a male construction worker

55.) 1.08:26 – In the Hospital, morning
Thomas clumsily pushes Victor down the hallway in a wheelchair, Victor has his feet bandaged; Holly and Julie are in a hospital room, Julie is in bed sleeping, wrapped in bandages, Holly sits beside her; she tells Victor and Thomas that Burt asserted that the wreck was Victor's fault because he was chasing and trying to kill them; Victor and Thomas decide to leave town instantly; they find themselves confronted by a police officer

sound bridge: voice of police officer': "you boys got yourself into some serious trouble"
56.) 1.10:06 – At the Police Station
the police officer tells them that Burt has charged Victor with having caused the accident; the police officer is calm, Victor is on aggressive defense; the officer questions them about the incident and then quotes from

Penny's testimony that her husband is "a complete asshole"; he dismisses Burt's allegations and asks what is in the silver urn; Victor replies that the urn is his father – for the first time acknowledging him

57.) 1.12:21 – In the Impound Yard, dusk
Victor and Thomas get out of a police car and turn to their battered pickup; Victor wants to hold his father's ashes for the first time; he also apologizes for the car wreck, for their fight, and indirectly also for the years of his teasing and not acknowledging Thomas

58.) 1.13:30 – Suzy at Arnold's Trailer
she walks to the door and lights up a cloth bundle to set the trailer on fire; intercut are shots of Victor and Thomas trying to start the pickup; when Suzy lights the bundle, the pickup starts as well

dissolve

59.) 1.14:39 – The Ride Home
aerial shots of the car as it crosses the Idaho landscape; aerial shot of Arnold's trailer burning; shots of reservation and pickup rolling into reservation

60.) 1.15:40 – Grandma Builds-The-Fire's House, outside, morning
the pickup pulls in; Victor thanks Thomas for his support; neither of them knows how to say good bye; Thomas and Victor are uncomfortable; Victor opens the silver urn and pours a third of the ashes into Thomas' now-empty glass jar; Thomas is touched by this gesture; he says that he will travel to the Spokane Falls and throw the ashes into the river so that Arnold will "rise like a salmon"; Victor laughs quietly and says that he had the same thing in mind but to him it would be more like "cleaning out the attic"; Thomas gets out of the car and walks toward the house while Victor starts the car; he suddenly remembers something, turns around, and runs toward the car; Victor stops and Thomas asks one last question: why did Arnold really leave?; Victor very calmly replies that Arnold did not mean to, and both agree in silence; Thomas walks to the house; Victor leaves

61.) 1.19:03 – the Josephs' House, outside
aerial shot of the pickup as it rolls along the reservation road; the pickup pulls into the Josephs' yard; Arlene comes out of the house welcoming Victor, she is glad to have him back; Victor hands her the urn with Arnold's ashes and she holds it up in grief

62.) 1.19:58 – Grandma Builds-The-Fire's House
Thomas enters the house; his grandma's face lights up and she takes him in her arms; she has exactly the same broad smile as Thomas and asks him to tell her everything that happened and that will happen

dissolve
63.) 1.20:35 – EPILOGUE
aerial shots of Spokane river as it grows larger; Victor at Spokane Falls
emptying the silver urn with his father's ashes into the river (slow motion);
Thomas' voice over recites a poem about how to forgive our fathers

fade
1.22:36 – CREDITS

Smoke Signals: Detailed Shot Analysis

Match on Action Cut 10/11

No.	Content of Shot	C/Dist	C/Angle	C/Move	Sound	Shot/L
1	inside trading post: Victor and Thomas in conversation, Thomas from behind, Victor frontal; Victor turns to go	medium shot	oblique right	pan right	Victor: "You're funny!"	4.39 sec.
2	inside the trading post, reverse shot: Thomas looks at Victor; Victor moves out of frame	medium shot	oblique left	still	Victor's footsteps	2.03 sec.
3	inside trading post: Victor walks out door; Thomas's head moves into lower left angle of frame	medium shot	oblique right	still	Victor's footsteps, jingling doorbell	1.81 sec.
4	outside trading post: Thomas frontal on doorstep, watches Victor leaving; he becomes blurred; later, young Victor at front turns to adult Thomas (adult Thomas and young Victor in same shot)	medium shot	straight	left pan, tilt down	Victor's footsteps, jingling doorbell	3.57 sec.

| 5 | outside trading post: young Victor still turned around; turns back, he looks puzzled at the image of adult Thomas; Arnold's pickup in bkgd; young Victor walks toward camera; young Thomas comes into shot from left out of the trading post with a burning sparkler, gives it to young Victor; Arnold appears from behind; while he is moving towards the boys he is photographed symmetrically right between the two boys | medium shot | left | still, slow left pan, tilt up and tracking forward with young Victor | door snaps shut; young Thomas: "Victor, look at this, ain't it cool... Here"; young Victor: "Nah, you keep it"; Arnold: "Hey Thomas, you better get home, your grandma is looking for you"; Arnold talks to Victor as they walk to truck; guitar music | 40.53 sec. |

Match on Action Cut 12/13

No.	Content of Shot	C/Dist	C/Angle	C/Move	Sound	Shot/L
1	outside the Josephs' house, in the pickup: Arnold has just slapped young Victor for spilling a beer; young Victor leaves the truck; Arnold grabs another beer from the cooler	medium shot	from left	still	young Victor's groaning; Arnold: "Quit your crying, I didn't hit you that hard. Go in the house, tell your mom I'll be right in"; truck door opening and closing; ice cooler opened and shut	18.90 sec
2	Arnold's POV: young Victor runs towards house	long shot		right pan		2.97 sec.
3	hall inside house, through door window, day: Arnold's pickup in bkgd, young Victor comes up steps, opens door	long shot ⇓ close-up	straight	still	Victor's footsteps; squeaking of the door being opened	3.56 sec.

4	kitchen inside house, night: door opens, adult Victor comes in, closes door, walks toward Arlene	medium shot	straight	still	squeaking of door being shut; beginning of sad theme song about Arnold and Arlene	4.94 sec.

Match on Action Cut 33/34

No.	Content of Shot	C/Dist	C/Angle	C/Move	Sound	Shot/L
1	outside the Josephs' house: Arlene kneels and holds young Thomas, who has just been beaten up by young Victor; she wipes his bleeding nose	medium shot	high angle	still	young Thomas: "Why'd Arnold leave?" Arlene: "Hush now Thomas, just hush"; dramatic music with drums	6.34 sec.
2	Arlene's POV: young Victor from behind, running down rez road	long shot	straight	still	dramatic music	3.87 sec.
3	inside the bus: young Victor runs beside the bus; adult Victor in the window seat looks out of window at his younger self, turns his face around; he looks confused and thoughtful	medium shot ⇓ close-up	high angle ⇓ oblique left	right pan, zoom out	dramatic music; adult Thomas: "Hey Victor, what do you remember about your dad?"	13.72sec.
4	in the bus: Thomas sits beside Victor; he starts a story about Arnold	close-up	straight	still	Thomas: "I remember one time we had this frybread eating contest..."	3.22sec.

℘ ℘

Big Bear: Sequence Protocol

Big Bear's family:

WIVES	SONS	DAUGHTERS
+ Sayos:	Little Bad Man	+ Man's Woman
	Lone Man	+ Nowakich
+ Running Second:	Kingbird	+ Sits Green on the Earth
	Horsechild	

TITLE: This program is based on historical fact. It depicts events that occurred in Western Canada in the late 1800's that changed forever the way of life of the Cree people.

part I
1.) 00:00 – Big Bear's Lodge, inside[12]
Big Bear ceremonially opens a power bundle with several layers; in the innermost layer there is a bear claw with a necklace; he starts chanting and with his muddy fingers paints four streaks on his face; then he puts the necklace with claw around his neck

TITLE *Big Bear* and opening credits superimposed on the following images

Southern Saskatchewan, 1875
2.) 00:44 – Prairies
Big Bear, Lone Man, Round the Sky, Little Bad Man, and a small group of armed warriors ride towards a hill where surveyors are driving red-flagged stakes into the ground; Little Bad Man gallops along the line of stakes and knocks them out; Big Bear's party meets North West Mounted Police (NWMP) Superintendent Lief Crozier and Métis translator Peter Erasmus; the Cree, outnumbering the surveyors and NWMP, succeed in turning them back

sound bridge: drum
3.) 03:04 – Big Bear's Summer Camp, South Saskatchewan River
a group of young warriors in a circle are 'dancing' by standing in place; Big Bear watches the dancers; he is told by Lone Man that the NWMP are

---

[12] When the time of day is not indicated, the events happen during daylight. The sequences are divided by a cut if not specified otherwise.

going to build a fort in the Cypress Hills; Kingbird asks him to ride with the warriors to hunt

4.) 05:21 – Prairies
Miserable Man and Little Bad Man in wolf-skins are trying to hunt buffalo by sneaking up on them; the buffalo are scared away by a buggy that comes over the hill; furious, they stop the buggy; Reverend John McDougall and Reverend George McDougall tell them that they intend to visit Big Bear and bring him an important treaty message; the two let them pass

fade; commercial break (cb)
5.) 07:05 – Big Bear's Lodge
inside: Running Second is kneeling surrounded by several women, she is giving birth
outside: Big Bear and the two Reverends are sitting on the ground facing each other, surrounded by warriors; the Reverends present a sealed document and tell Big Bear that the government representatives will come the next year in order to make a treaty; Big Bear demands to see and speak to the government;
inside: the baby son is passed around the family to receive their blessings; Big Bear names it Horsechild

6.) 11:50 – Big Bear's Lodge, night
camera pans through the lodge: Lone Man and Nowakich are asleep, Little Bad Man and Man's Woman are kissing and cuddling, Kingbird is wide awake, Big Bear is in a fitful sleep between Sayos and Running Second; he is dreaming of a herd of buffalo galloping across the prairie, then tumbling into a crater in the earth
later at dawn: Big Bear sits cross-legged and looks thoughtfully at the river; Sayos comes, puts a blanket around him, and sits down beside him; Big Bear talks about his dream; he is very disturbed

7.) 14:02 – Treaty-Making, Fort Pitt, Sept. 13th, 1876
close-up on several sheets of white paper with Treaty No. Six written out, superimposed on the group of Cree chiefs standing by the treaty tent; Governor Morris and Sweetgrass at a camp table; Morris raises a quill, which Sweetgrass touches, and makes an X beside the name Sweetgrass on the list of Cree chiefs; Morris helps Sweetgrass into a red NWMP coat and Sweetgrass receives a medal with the Queen's image, while Big Bear and his warriors arrive; Morris and Sweetgrass 'confirm' the treaty with a handshake while the other five chiefs and their people watch in silence;

Big Bear's arrival causes some unrest; during the whole sequence Erasmus translates;
some time later: a thunderstorm brews; the other chiefs have signed the treaty and now wear the red coats; Big Bear watches the last chief, Poundmaker, receiving the Queen's medal

fade; cb
8.) 16:26 – Treaty-Making, Fort Pitt, same day later
Big Bear and the other Cree chiefs sit down and discuss the treaty; Morris speaks to those assembled about the treaty and the Queen's promises; Big Bear gets up and speaks to everybody; he declines the grandmother Queen's offer in the treaty to feed them, and says that Mother Earth feeds him and his people and that he will not live with a rope around his neck; Morris does not understand this metaphor or the next one; Morris tells Big Bear that the Queen will not negotiate a treaty for a single chief only; a small NWMP brass band starts playing "God Save the Queen," the Canadians and the chiefs except Big Bear rise – it is a ridiculous and pitiful scene; in the distance Big Bear's warriors are lined up on horseback and with raised guns; Wandering Spirit, one of Poundmaker's warriors, rides up to Big Bear and declares that he wants to join him because Poundmaker has signed the treaty and there is no need for a warrior on a reserve; he is accepted; Big Bear leaves and a group of Cree from the other bands follow him

fade
Winter Camp, Near Frog Lake, 1877
9.) 24:25 – Big Bear's Lodge, evening
the family together; Lone Man tells a story while Big Bear enacts it with shadow-play

10.) 25:28 – Prairies
Big Bear and Kingbird are out hunting; they encounter two wolves which are feasting on a deer; Big Bear outstares the wolf; the two return to the camp with two deer legs

11.) 26:40 – Big Bear's Lodge
the family eats deer meat; Sayos tells Big Bear of Sweetgrass's death – his son-in-law's gun, a treaty gift, went off and killed him; Running Second complains that there is not enough food and that more and more people from Sweetgrass's camp are joining them because they do not want the treaty; Little Bad Man suggests going south where the buffalo went; Big Bear replies that there are too many Blackfoot and Sioux

South Saskatchewan River, Summer, 1877

12.) 28:35 – Prairies, The Raid
Little Bad Man and Kingbird are about to go on a horse raid for Kingbird
to prove himself; Big Bear admonishes him not to take too big a risk;
several shots in changing daylight connected by dissolves suggest that the
two men go south for a long time; at dawn, Little Bad Man prepares
Kingbird for the raid and applies paint to his face

13.) 31:09 – Fort Walsh
close-up on money being counted; many Cree people are in line to
receive the annual five-dollar payment; close by, traders display all kinds
of items: clothes, blankets, sacks of flour etc.; in a tent, Big Bear sitting
cross-legged on the ground and talks with Governor Edgar Dewdney,
who sits in a chair; Erasmus stands beside Dewdney and translates; Big
Bear questions Dewdney about a two-million-dollar payment that the
Hudson's Bay Company (HBC) received from the government for trading
rights; he asks who gave the HBC and the king the right to transfer
trading rights and sell the land and asks whether or not the Cree would
receive even more money for all the land they "sell" in the treaties;
Dewdney becomes annoyed, and repeats that the Queen will not negotiate
a treaty for Big Bear alone

14.) 34:40 – A Blackfoot Camp, early morning
Kingbird sneaks into the camp, where he finds a beautiful white mare; he
signals two circles with his arms and body, then cuts the rein that a
Blackfoot is holding, and with a war whoop leaves the camp

fade; cb
15.) 36:47 – Big Bear's Summer Camp
Little Bad Man and Kingbird return with three horses and the white mare;
they are welcomed with loud approval; Kingbird offers his father the
white mare as a gift; Big Bear proudly rides through the camp in circles
and loudly thanks Kingbird; he announces that they will go south where
the buffalo are

Montana, Summer, 1881
16.) 39:05 – Prairies, A Buffalo Hunt
Big Bear and Kingbird spy a small group of thin buffalo; Big Bear regrets
that they must kill the whole group; Kingbird suggests breeding buffalo
the way settlers do; Big Bear disapproves of this; he turns toward the sky
and prays for a good hunt;
a short time later: a group of Cree are hunting the buffalo, the warriors
with guns, Big Bear with bow and arrow; Big Bear kills a large cow and
sits down in front of it; in prayer he thanks the buffalo spirit and asks for

forgiveness; in his vision, a coyote close by seems to laugh at him and blood comes streaming out of the earth; he sits there for a very long time, realized through dissolves

17.) 44:02 – Big Bear's Lodge
the family eats, except for Big Bear; there is not enough meat left for the next day; they talk: hunger has already killed many of them, including Sayos, the settlers have burned the prairies and killed the buffalo, there is not enough game to hunt as in earlier days, the people are starving, even in summer; Big Bear tells them of his vision, he announces that he has killed his last buffalo and that they would have to go back north; everybody is surprised and upset, and Little Bad Man argues that up north the people crowd around the forts and beg for food

18.) 46:21 – The Trail North
Big Bear's band slowly treks north, the people hungry and tired; close to the camp, Nowakich desperately tries to lure a dog with a piece of meat, she succeeds, and kills it with a wooden stick

fade; cb
Fort Walsh, Late Summer, 1882
19.) 48:26 – Governor Dewdney's Office
in his Victorian-style living room-cum-office, Dewdney sits in a comfortable chair by a fireplace; Big Bear is obviously uncomfortable sitting on a chair; nobody speaks as they wait for Erasmus, who comes rushing through the door; Big Bear asks for food supplies because his people are starving; Dewdney refuses and makes it clear that they will not get any food unless Big Bear signs the treaty

sound bridge: death song
20.) 50:35 – Funeral Platform near Fort Walsh; Winter
the camera shows a dead tree and tilts down to reveal a platform with wrapped dead bodies; Big Bear sings a Cree death song; Nowakich and Lone Man stand mournfully before the platform, where a small wrapped body, their daughter Earth Girl, is placed by the warriors; all wear their hair unbound in mourning

dissolve
21.) 53:12 – Big Bear's Lodge
the family mourns for Earth Girl, who has died of hunger; Nowakich falls into a wailing song; she accuses Big Bear and Lone Man of not signing the treaty, which would have ensured food supplies

22.) 54:55 – Big Bear Signs the Treaty; Fort Walsh, small office, 1882, night

Big Bear looks at his reflection in the window while an interpreter, in a droning voice, reads out the treaty conditions: "... does hereby, transfer, relinquish, surrender to Her Majesty the Queen and for the use of the Government of Canada, that it does extinguish forever all his rights, titles and privileges whatsoever to these lands..."; close-up on the sheet of paper, on the quill that Big Bear's hand touches, and on a hand that puts the X below Big Bear's name; Lone Man and Big Bear, now weak and desperate, immediately leave the office; there is no ceremonial act to 'confirm' the treaty

fade; cb

23.) 56:24 – Prairies

Big Bear's band wearily treks up north to Frog Lake, where they are to choose a reserve; they are guarded by four NWMP men, and a small herd of cows follows; Big Bear announces that close by is Poundmaker's reserve and that they will visit; the NWMP men forbid this, but Big Bear goes anyway

dissolve

24.) 58:00 – Poundmaker Reserve

the reserve consists of a few scattered log shacks and patched lodges; there are all kinds of abandoned treaty gifts: rusting farm machinery, the remains of carts etc.; entering the reserve, they see Indian agent John Craig ordering around He Speaks Our Tongue, who is building a fence around a nice white farm house; Poundmaker welcomes Big Bear and tells him that the Indian agent controls everything on the reserve; their life has changed considerably: they are trying to become farmers and the government has become very strict; he tells Big Bear that the people on the reserve need someone to tell them who they are; Big Bear imitates a buffalo hunt and people gather to watch

sound bridge: Big Bear speaking

25.) 1.03:10 – Poundmaker's Lodge, night

Big Bear's family is visiting; they discuss how the coming of the settlers and the treaty has changed their lives; Big Bear makes a vow to do a Thirst Dance in order to pray for strength and wisdom and to seek guidance; he wants to prevent the Cree from becoming helpless beggars

26.) 1.05:00 – Poundmaker Reserve

Little Bad Man welcomes Gabriel Dumont and two other Métis in the camp; Dumont brings Riel's regards; a group of men sits in a circle and listens to Big Bear, who speaks about their situation as dependent on the government; he wishes to unite the Cree, and wants a large reserve for all Cree people together in order for them to become stronger, the next spring he wants the chiefs to go to Ottawa and speak to the highest government official; Little Bad Man and Dumont sit a little bit off and talk about how the NWMP can be attacked; Little Bad Man welcomes Dumont's plans and regrets that his father only talks peace with the government officials

27.) 1.07:10 – Thirst Dance
Big Bear leads a large group of people into the prairie to cut the center tree for the dance; everybody is in high spirits; Big Bear offers a prayer to the Great Spirit; Dewdney and Tom Quinn, the new agent, arrive in a buggy accompanied by three NWMP men, Crozier, their leader, speaks Cree; they tell Big Bear to leave the reserve and move north, otherwise they will cut his rations; they also prohibit the Thirst Dance; Big Bear stares at them defiantly; he then raises a power bundle to the four directions and starts singing in resistance, the others join in

sound bridge: singing of Thirst Dance
28.) 1.11:19 – meanwhile at Agent Craig's House
He Speaks Our Tongue shows Craig a small flour sack to indicate that his payment was not enough, he does not have enough food for his family; Craig violently pushes him off his porch so that he falls backwards; He Speaks Our Tongue throws an axe handle at Craig, it hits him on the leg, he stumbles and falls; He Speaks Our Tongue furiously smashes the axe handle down beside Craig's head and runs away

fade; cb
29.) 1.11:45 – Thirst Dance
Big Bear and his group continue to sing and dance; Craig arrives and tells Crozier what has happened; Crozier tries to stop the dance but is prevented from doing so by Little Bad Man and other warriors; he tells Little Bad Man that they will have to finish the dance soon, then leave the reserve, and that they also have to deliver up He Speaks Our Tongue the next day because he broke the law, otherwise they will come and get him

fade
30.) 1.13:20 – Poundmaker Reserve, Agent Craig's house barricaded with flour sacks, June 1884
a large group of warriors armed with long sticks and guns, some of them painted, move toward the house where the NWMP men have lined up; the NWMP men and warriors move towards each other; Little Bad Man,

Wandering Spirit, and two other warriors encircle He Speaks Our Tongue; Little Bad Man issues a war whoop; they meet Crozier, backed by his men; He Speaks Our Tongue explains what had happened; Crozier still wants to take him and put him on trial; Poundmaker tries to mediate; the tension rises, the warriors' guns are now pointing at the NWMP men and vice versa; Crozier pulls He Speaks Our Tongue out of the group; Poundmaker and Big Bear try to hold back the warriors; Crozier manages to take He Speaks Our Tongue with him; when everybody retreats, Little Bad Man looks angrily at Big Bear; he and Poundmaker share a long look

dissolve
31.) 1.17:12 – Winter Camp at Frog Lake, Big Bear's Lodge
the people are hungry, there is no food; Man's Woman lies sick, wrapped in blankets with her baby beside her; Little Bad Man and Kingbird return with a small deer; all of the hunters together failed to get much

32.) 1.18:41 – Agent Quinn's house at Fort Pitt
Nowakich and Horsechild, followed by Quinn, come out of the storeroom with a sack of flour; they request more and better food because Man's Woman and her baby are dying; Quinn denies their request and reproaches Big Bear for not choosing a reserve and sending women to ask for food; as they leave, the farm instructor John Delaney touches Nowakich lecherously; she pushes his hand away; Delaney and Quinn laugh

33.) 1.19:38 – Winter Prairies
Big Bear and Kingbird return wearily from a hunt, they only have one rabbit

34.) 1.20:04 – Big Bear's Lodge, night
the pregnant Sits Green on the Earth, now Kingbird's wife, rises and leaves the lodge; Running Second looks at her thoughtfully;
outside by the lake: Delaney runs his hands lasciviously over her face and rips off her clothes; he takes her violently from behind; Sits Green returns sobbing and presents a bundle with pork meat to Running Second; Running Second hugs her understandingly; Kingbird is wide awake

fade; cb
35.) 1.22:31 – Big Bear's Lodge, day
outside: Lone Man shoots a horse;
inside: Nowakich makes a broth with horse meat; she tells Big Bear reproachfully that the bands who chose reserves have enough food and clothing for the winter; Running Second joins in these arguments; Man's Woman is still very sick; Big Bear declares that he will visit the new HBC boss at Fort Pitt the next morning

36.) 1.24:21 – HBC Factor William McLean's House at Fort Pitt
Big Bear sits down across from McLean on a chair and accepts tea that
his Cree wife brings; their daughter Kitty, who speaks Cree fluently,
translates; Big Bear asks for food, as his people are starving, twenty-two
have already died that winter; McLean decides to have three cows slaughtered for Big Bear

37.) 1.27:04 – Funeral Platform, Frog Lake, Winter
as Big Bear returns, he hears loud wailing, and finally sees the small
group of his family walking toward the platform, led by Little Bad Man,
who leads a horse and travois with a wrapped dead body; when Big Bear
comes near, Little Bad Man looks at him hard and angrily; he opens the
bundle and cuts off Man's Woman's braids; clenching them in his fist, he
tells Big Bear sternly that he will not forget; Big Bear mourns; all wear
their hair unbound in mourning

fade: part II
38.) 1.28:55 – Big Bear's Lodge, night
Little Bad Man gathers his belongings, he hugs his daughter Summer and
leaves her in the care of Lone Man and Nowakich, he moves to the
Rattler lodge, the warrior lodge; upon his departure, Big Bear tells them
that they will choose a reserve at Sounding Lake; dissolve to some
beautiful panning long shots of the area around Sounding Lake

sound bridge: war drum
39.) 1.31:12 – Rattler Lodge, night
the lodge is packed with warriors; the drum beat accelerates and the
tension rises; Little Bad Man places the war pipe before Wandering Spirit
and declares him war chief; Wandering Spirit raises the pipe and makes a
vow

sound bridge: war drum
40.) 1.32:24 – Big Bear's Lodge
Lone Man comes in, very upset, and tells Big Bear that a messenger from
the Métis came and told them that the NWMP had intended to arrest Riel
and that when Dumont tried to hold them up at Duck Lake, the NWMP
started shooting, Dumont asks Big Bear to help him fight the NWMP;
Little Bad Man has already agreed, Big Bear refuses but is very
concerned because the war drum is heard from the Rattler lodge

fade; cb
41.) 1.34:17 – Frog Lake Settlement, Alberta, Spring 1885
Iron Body and Round the Sky watch settlers coming out of the church;
among them are Quinn, Delaney, the HBC clerk Cameron, and two Reve-

rends; Quinn sends the two NWMP men off to Fort Pitt; now there are no police left in the settlement

42.) 1.34:48 – Quinn's Front Room
Big Bear and Lone Man are trying to warn Quinn that a war has started at Duck Lake and that their warriors are ready to join the Métis; they advise him to bring all the settlers to Fort Pitt; Quinn does not understand Big Bear's analogy, cynically rejects their advice, and tells them they will stay

43.) 1.36:31 – Rattler Lodge
outside: a fire, war drums, and a war song; Wandering Spirit dances, more and more armed warriors, including Kingbird, join in; Lone Man and a few others leave amid mocking laughter

fade
44.) 1.38:16 – Frog Lake Settlement, early morning, April 2nd, 1885
the rattlers arrive and stride straight to the HBC building;
intercut the camp: Big Bear and Running Second discuss what to do;
HBC building: the rattlers enter and request that Cameron give them all the ammunition and gunpowder in the store; Big Bear, in trading regalia, enters and tries to prevent the forcible seizure of ammunition;
Quinn's front room: Wandering Spirit speaks in obscure war metaphors; Quinn, pretending not to understand, orders Delaney to give them all breakfast; Big Bear sends Lone Man to Fort Pitt to fetch Simpson
Delaney's kitchen: Delaney, flanked by two warriors, tries to eat breakfast and keep his composure; Little Bad Man and Miserable Man eat, too, and mock Delaney; his wife, who is very frightened, serves tea;
church: the settlers are gathered for Easter mass; Wandering Spirit and his men enter and disturb the mass, he clubs down one Reverend and takes everybody hostage; he wants to take them to the camp; Big Bear cannot do anything;

fade; cb
Big Bear tries to dissuade Kingbird from taking part; the men take the hostages to Quinn's porch; Wandering Spirit requests that Quinn gives out all the food he is storing and come along as a hostage; Quinn refuses, and is shot by Wandering Spirit; this triggers the other warriors to shoot down other settlers at random, who scatter in panic; Big Bear feebly runs around and tries to stop the killing; Horsechild walks around and finds dead bodies, among them Delaney and one Reverend; nine settlers are killed; Simpson arrives with supplies and is stopped by two warriors who order him to come to the camp as well

45.) 1.56:23 – Wandering Spirit's Camp (Wandering Spirit now leads the people as war chief)
the warriors return with Delaney's widow as hostage; Running Second angrily protects her; Simpson tells Big Bear that he will be held responsible for the killings;
at Rattler lodge: Wandering Spirit and Little Bad Man discuss what to do; they will go to Fort Pitt to get more food

fade; cb

46.) 1.57:33 – Fort Pitt, two weeks later
outside: the warriors are lined up at some distance; McLean and Kitty sit across from Big Bear and Little Bad Man; they negotiate; if the Cree let the NWMP men go without shooting, McLean will surrender himself and the whole fort to Wandering Spirit

47.) 1.58:55 – Fort Pitt, night
the warriors sack the fort, while McLean and his family load a buggy with a few belongings; the warriors have dragged a pedal organ outside and Miserable Man randomly hits the keys; the young men dance around the organ to terrible music; Big Bear turns away in disgust; Little Bad Man finds that all the guns have been destroyed; Iron Body sets the HBC store in the fort on fire

dissolve

48.) 2.03:07 – North Saskatchewan River
the Cree party and their hostages trek along the river; they are led by Wandering Spirit and Little Bad Man; Teresa Delaney is with Running Second; Big Bear is trudging behind

49.) 2.04:16 – Wandering Spirit's Camp
all are seated outside, listening to Little Bad Man, who wants to go to Batoche and join the Métis; Wandering Spirit wants to fulfill his vow and kill all whites; he aims at McLean but is thwarted by Little Bad Man; Big Bear pleads for the lives of the settlers and warns the two warriors that the NWMP will soon be arriving; he sternly presents the Council Pipe to Little Bad Man – a sign that he will no longer speak for his people; apparently Big Bear has no good advice and blessings for his son

fade; cb

50.) 2.09:54 – Frenchmen Butte, Saskatchewan May 28th, 1885
Iron Body, on lookout, espies advancing NWMP and Canadian soldiers; the people hurriedly dismantle the camp and hide in the bush; the warriors form a line behind a rifle pit made of tree branches; police and soldiers advance; in the ensuing battle, cannonballs hit the bush where the people are hiding; they leave their belongings and scatter about, frigh-

tened; the last cannonball kills the warrior beside Wandering Spirit; police and soldiers retreat; a few warriors and policemen are killed

51.) 2.17:17 – After the Battle
people move hastily away from the battle site, they have only a very few belongings; Wandering Spirit comes to his senses and tells Little Bad Man that they would have to protect the people from the destructive cannon; Little Bad Man is still determined to fight;

fade; cb
Big Bear tells the hostages to leave, they are to go either to Fort Pitt or to the agency at Cold Lake; some hostages and Cree leave; Teresa Delaney and the McLeans stay
at night: a few people remaining from Big Bear's band are sleeping by campfires, they have lost their lodges; Wandering Spirit sits at a fire beside Mrs McLean, his hair with white streaks now; he asks whether or not a white god would forgive him for what he has done.

52.) 2.23:34 – Big Bear and Kitty, Turtle Lake
Kitty follows Big Bear to the lake, she obviously admires him; he says that they have come to know the Cree and reminds her that it will not be like that again

53.) 2.25:22 – Big Bear and Horsechild, Turtle Lake Shore
Horsechild tells Big Bear of his vision; Big Bear explains it to him and tells him of a man's vision quest; because the man wanted to live forever he was turned into a rock, which is the first and last of all being

fade; cb
54.) 2.28:36 – Kingbird and Sits Green on the Earth, A Brush Shelter
Sits Green is highly pregnant; for the first time they talk about her prostituting herself for food; Kingbird can hardly keep his composure

55.) 2.31:14 – A Brush Shelter, Turtle Lake
Big Bear's family sits at a small fire; Lone Man brings news: there are many soldiers at Fort Pitt, they have arrested some warriors, most of the scattered Cree went to Fort Pitt, Little Bad Man leads fifteen families south to Montana; Big Bear presents his medicine bundle to Kingbird and says that he will teach him the songs; he says that he will stay there on the land where his ancestors lived
at night: Running Second asks him to come with them; he declines to do so

dissolve
56.) 2.34.53 – Turtle Lake

Running Second leads the rest of the family away; some way down, she turns and issues a piercing, wailing cry; Big Bear and Horsechild remain at the beach

57.) 2.36:01 – Fort Pitt
outside: policemen are rebuilding the fort; Big Bear comes to the gate and gives himself up; Horsechild is still with him;
fade; cb
inside: Big Bear sits on a chair with an expressionless face; his hair is being cut

58.) 2.37:16 – Regina, court room, Sept., 1885
Big Bear dressed in prison garb, hands and feet chained; he is accused of starting a war against the Queen; Erasmus translates;
intercut: Big Bear in his cell lying on a cot; he shivers, coughs, and prays
court room: Big Bear is given the opportunity to speak; he talks about the land, and that the settlers took it from them; he asks for forgiveness for his people, who are scattered in the bush; the judge answers sharply that the land always belonged to the Queen and that she was generous enough to let them choose their own strips of land; Big Bear says that he lived well before the settlers arrived and that he hunted buffalo at the place where the court building now is, he shared that buffalo meat with the first settlers; the sentence is three years in prison

59.) 2.44:27 – Stony Mountain Prison
Big Bear is led along a long prison tract;
in his mind: he sees how Miserable Man, Iron Body, Round the Sky, and Wandering Spirit are hanged; Wandering Spirit has stark white hair; the young men sing their death song while a priest recites his prayer;
prison: a priest with a big cross sprinkles water over Big Bear's shorn head, he makes the sign of the cross on his forehead; Big Bear does not resist the baptism – he is an old and broken man now
dissolve

60.) 2.46:20 – Poundmaker Reserve, Winter 1888
in a log house, the weak and ailing Big Bear lies down to rest; his legs stiff from the years in prison, he can no longer sit cross-legged; Horsechild cares for him; Big Bear dies;
his Death Vision: he rides the white mare over the prairies in different seasons to a river; he releases the steed and raises his arms in prayer to the four directions; he lies down, the camera tracks back, and his figure seems to turn into a big rock
fade

2.51:41 – TITLE: Mistahi Muskwa; Big Bear; 1825–1885
camera zooms into close-up of an archival photograph of the historical Big Bear

fade

2.52:25 – CREDITS

Big Bear: Detailed Shot Analysis

Sequence 18 (1.29 min.)

No.	Content of Shot	C/Dist	C/Angle	C/Move	Sound	Shot/L
1	1/3 sky, 2/3 prairie grass; grass in fgd; line of heads moving towards camera *dissolve*[13]	extreme long shot	low angle	still	sad string orchestra and a cello in fgd	8.03 sec.
2	1/3 sky, 2/3 prairie grass; grass in fgd; line of heads and upper bodies move towards camera *dissolve*	long shot	low angle	still	⇓	5.11 sec.
3	1/2 sky, 1/2 prairie grass; people from knees upwards, horses, and travois *dissolve*	long shot, closer	slight low angle	still	⇓	3.65 sec.
4	2/3 sky, 1/3 prairie grass; Running Second with her horse and travois leads trek *dissolve*	medium long shot	straight	still	⇓	2.44 sec.
5	3/4 sky, 1/2 prairie grass; Running Second with her horse and travois leads trek	medium shot	straight	still	⇓	7.90 sec.
6	sky; horseman moving slowly off right, more trekkers walk in from right and off to left	medium shot	low angle, oblique right	right pan, tilt down, still	⇓	9.50 sec.
7	Nowakich, Earth Girl walk from right to left	medium shot	oblique right	track left	⇓	3.12 sec.
8	Earth Girl's face as she is lifted up by Nowakich, who looks exhausted	close-up	oblique right	track left, left pan	⇓	4.81 sec.

---

[13] When a transition device is not specified, the shots are connected by a cut.

9	prairie grass in fgd; women walk from right to left	medium shot	low angle, oblique right	still	⇓	3.31 sec.
10	Kingbird, Little Bad Man, Sits Green, warrior on horseback with head hung low move from right to left	medium shot	oblique right	still	⇓	10.11 sec.
11	Kingbird falls back in order to flirt with Sits Green	medium shot	oblique right	track left	SG: "Tired... you wanna trade?" K: "You couldn't carry this. It's too heavy." SG: "I wouldn't carry it like you."	22.18 sec.
12	Big Bear and Running Second in from right and off to left	medium shot	oblique right	still	sad string orchestra and cello in fgd	4.31 sec.
13	group moving toward camera	extreme long shot	oblique right	still	⇓	3.75 sec.

Sequence 23 (1.36 min.)

No.	Content of Shot	C/Dist	C/Angle	C/Move	Sound	Shot/L
1	the band treks sullenly; Big Bear leads trek, flanked by two NWMPs, all framed symmetrically moving toward the camera	long shot	straight	still	same sad string orchestra and cello in fgd as in sequence 18	7.85 sec.
2	Kingbird, Sits Green, other Cree trek slowly; a cart with treaty payments with them; policemen among them; Little Bad Man, Iron Body, Round The Sky, and Miserable Man are the last; all in low spirits	medium shot	straight	still, right pan, tilt down	⇓	22.62 sec.
3	Big Bear leads his mare; he stops to consider, prepares to mount the mare	medium shot	straight	still	⇓	9.64 sec.

4	commanding officer stops, turns around	medium shot	oblique right	still	⇓	2.40 sec.
5	Big Bear mounts mare; turns around, motions his warriors to come forward	medium shot	straight	still	⇓	4.09 sec.
6	commanding officer motions other police men to come forward	medium shot	oblique right	still	music grows more dramatic	2.19 sec.
7	Little Bad Man and Wandering Spirit come forward; Big Bear speaks to police	medium shot	straight	still	Big Bear: "The reserve of my young friend Poundmaker is nearby. We'll have a visit."	14.74 sec.
8	commanding officer replies	medium shot	oblique right	still	commanding officer in broken Cree: "No... orders... you go...choose reserve... Frog Lake."	4.50 sec.
9	Little Bad Man speaks; Little Bad Man and Big Bear fill the screen	medium shot	straight	still	LBM: "We don't have the rope around our neck yet."	3.10 sec.
10	commanding officer replies	medium shot	oblique right	still	commanding officer: "Food there... reserve... you go"	2.37 sec.
11	Big Bear turns his horse, leads warriors and band off to left; N W M P do not intervene	medium shot ⇓ long shot	oblique right	right pan	drum and flute music	15.85 sec.
12	the band's trek from behind as they move in another direction; two policemen among them	long shot	straight	still	⇓	5.97 sec.

Sequence 48 (1.09 min.)

No.	Content of Shot	C/Dist	C/Angle	C/Move	Sound	Shot/L
1	band treks wearily toward camera; each carries bundle; warriors mounted; all sullen, silent	medium shot	straight	still	clattering of horses, squeaking of carts	4.10 sec.

2	face of woman leading horse off to right; horse's head, horse's back with leg and rifle butt; face of another man	close-up	oblique left	still	⇓	5.91 sec.
3	warrior watchfully turning around	medium shot	straight	still	⇓	1.54 sec.
4	mounted warrior off to right; Simpson and others pull the HBC cart with supplies	medium shot	slight low angle	still, tilt down	⇓	6.43 sec.
5	Little Bad Man and Wandering Spirit lead trek, both in derby hats	long shot	straight	still	⇓	6.25 sec.
6	Little Bad Man looking around alertly	medium shot	straight	still	⇓	2.09 sec.
7	Wandering Spirit looking around alertly	medium shot	straight	still	⇓	2.88 sec.
8	Kitty looking at Wandering Spirit from among the crowd	medium shot	straight	still	⇓	1.85 sec.
9	McLean in the crowd; the faces of the people before him out of focus		straight	still	⇓	2.44 sec.
10	McLean's wife, exhausted, eyes closed	close-up	oblique left	still	⇓	1.78 sec.
11	face of a man	close-up	oblique left	still	⇓	2.43 sec.
12	faces of women as they move to right of frame	close-up	oblique left	still	⇓	3.21 sec.
13	women walking toward camera; warriors behind	medium long shot	straight	still	⇓	3.28 sec.
14	a man leads a horse with travois	medium shot	oblique left	still, left pan	⇓	6.87 sec.
15	Running Second leads horse with travois; Teresa Delaney beside her; Big Bear behind	medium long shot	oblique left	still	⇓	5.58 sec.
16	Big Bear leads his mare; close-up on his face as he walks behind	medium shot ⇓ close-up	oblique left	track backward	⇓	9.56 sec.

Sequence 56 (1.08 min.)

No.	Content of Shot	C/Dist	C/Angle	C/Move	Sound	Shot/L
1	the rest of family treks along the shore of Turtle Lake; all are devastated by the battle, flight, and separation of the family; Running Second leads the small group	medium shot	straight	still	sad cello music	7.00 sec.
2	face of Sits Green with baby on her back	close-up	straight	still	⇓	3.34 sec.
3	face of Kingbird	close-up	straight	still	⇓	3.25 sec.
4	faces of Nowakich and Lone Man behind her	close-up	straight	still	⇓	3.44 sec.
5	face of Lone Man	close-up	straight	still	⇓	2.38 sec.
6	Big Bear and Horsechild at lakeshore, gazing after them	long shot	straight	still	⇓	2.75 sec.
7	small group from behind	long shot	oblique right	still	⇓	3.38 sec.
8	Running Second turns around and looks painfully at Big Bear	medium close-up	oblique right	still	⇓	2.31 sec.
9	little trek with Running Second looking painfully at Big Bear	medium shot	oblique right	still	⇓	5.81 sec.
10	Big Bear sadly looks at Running Second	medium close-up	straight	still	⇓	2.38 sec.
11	Running Second issues a piercing wail *sound bridge: wail*	medium close-up	oblique right	still	⇓	3.03 sec.
12	Big Bear looks sadly at Running Second *sound bridge: wail*	medium close-up	straight	still	⇓	5.08 sec.
13	in despair, Running Second turns around and moves on	medium close-up	oblique right	still	sad orchestra music sets in with drums	8.69 sec.
14	the little group from behind	medium shot	oblique right	still,	⇓	2.88 sec.

| 15 | the little group from behind | long shot | oblique right | still | ⇓ | 7.58 sec. |
| 16 | Big Bear sadly gazes after Running Second and his departing family | medium lose-up | straight | still | ⇓ | 4.37 sec. |

Atanarjuat: The Fast Runner: Sequence Protocol

Atanarjuat/Tulimaq family[14]

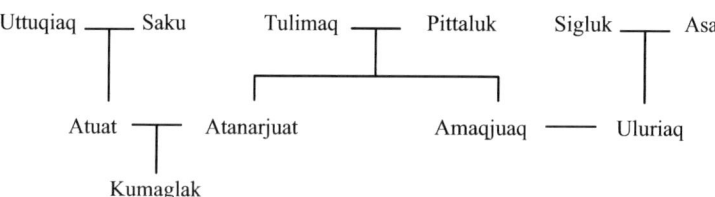

Tungajuaq (*evil Shaman*)

Uttuqiaq —— Saku   Tulimaq —— Pittaluk   Sigluk —— Asa

Atuat —— Atanarjuat   Amaqjuaq —— Uluriaq

Kumaglak

Oki/Sauri family

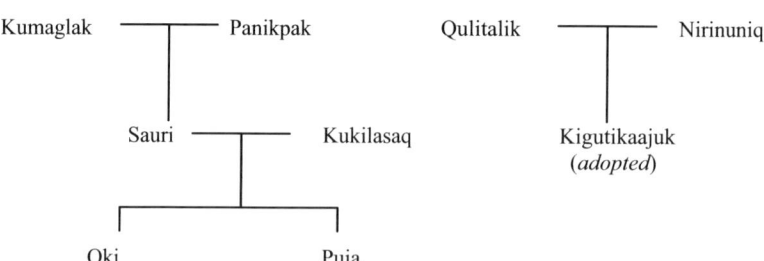

Atuat

Kumaglak —— Panikpak   Qulitalik —— Nirinuniq

Sauri —— Kukilasaq   Kigutikaajuk (*adopted*)

Oki   Puja

---

[14] The family trees are taken from http://www.atanarjuat.com/cast_characters/genealogy /photo2.html.

1.) 00:00 – Canadian Arctic, unspecified location, time unspecified[15]
bluish snowy landscape in Arctic twilight, sky and ground merge at the
horizon, a pale sun hovers above the scene, a male Inuit walks in the distance with a few sled dogs

OPENING TITLES: Igloolik Isuma Productions presents / A National Film
Board of Canada co-production

sound bridge: people in igloo talking
2.) 01:03 – The Evil Shaman, interior of sod house, night
an extended family spends the evening, the igloo is lit with seal oil lamps;
the people are visited by a stranger from up north, Tungajuaq (who turns
out to be an evil shaman), who is Kumaglak's 'opposite', as Kumaglak is
the community's shaman; each shows the other his coat, both of which
have special designs; a spiritual confrontation is about to follow; Tulimaq
has to take out the children, Oki, Amaqjuaq, and Atanarjuat

02:27 – TITLE on black ground: *The Fast Runner*

3.) 02:40 – Leaving, bright day
close-up on Qulitalik glazing the runners of his sled with water, he and his
wife Nirinuniq are about to leave the camp; Panikpak brings water for the
journey, she gives Qulitalik her husband Kumaglak's rabbit's foot as a
talisman; Qulitalik reminds her that he will help her as soon as she calls for
him and prophesies that the spirits will be after Tulimaq now; Qulitalik and
Nirinuniq leave with their dog team and move into the vast Arctic spaces

*soundbridge: Panikpak starts telling about the evil shaman visiting their
community*
4.) 04:47 – The Evil Shaman, interior of sod house, night; sequence 2
continued
Kumaglak and Tungajuaq are prepared for the spiritual contest, their hands
and feet are tied, they lie side by side, heads facing feet; Kumaglak dies
during the contest; Tungajuaq presents Sauri, Kumaglak's son, with the
walrus necklace; it is not clear why the disappointed Tulimaq feels left out
of the succession, he accuses Sauri of having helped the shaman to kill
Kumaglak

5.) 06:48 – Leaving, bright day
Panikpak watches her brother and sister-in-law leave

dissolve

---

[15] The time and location in the Canadian Arctic remains unspecified throughout the film.
The sequences are usually divided by a cut if not indicated otherwise.

6.) 07:03 – The Hunt, bright sunny day

Tulimaq and other men return from hunt, in close-up and extreme close-up shots of Tulimaq's feet walking, his face, the empty sled, and faces of sled dogs; cut to Pittaluk with their two sons in igloo; other men pass Tulimaq and tease him; Pittaluk, now in bluish Arctic twilight, waits at the camp; the other men return, unpack their catch; much later, Tulimaq returns with nothing, he tells her that he is sick of his bad luck, the others tease him and tell him to get some meat for his family

7.) 12:14 – The Humiliation, interior of Sauri's igloo, night

close-up on meat being eaten, Sauri's family has dinner; upon entering, Tulimaq sees the different frozen seal in the entrance tunnel; Oki tells him that his share is the rear end as usual; the men tease him: maybe his wife is a better hunter and he should stay home and do the cooking and sewing; Panikpak disapproves of this humiliation

8.) 13:44 – The Prophecy, interior of Tulimaq's igloo, night

family in igloo; Tulimaq is sharpening a new knife; Panikpak enters with some walrus heart; Pittaluk feeds Amaqjuaq first, then has Amaqjuaq feed Atanarjuat; Tulimaq prophesies that when his sons are grown up his family will never have to face humiliation again

fade to black, fade in; sound bridge: howling wind

9.) 15:57 – The Attack and Retribution, exterior, years later, day

grown-up Amaqjuaq, the Strong One, and Atanarjuat, the Fast One, lift heavy stones; Oki and his two friends Pakak and Pittiulaq approach; they have lost their dog team and take that of the two brothers; Atanarjuat runs them out and stops the team while Amaqjuaq throws the three men off the sled; the two leave laughing at Oki's gang

dissolve

10.) 18:07 – The Marriage Conflict, exterior of the camp, day

a few adults and children are playing 'wolf on the skin', with Atanarjuat as the wolf; Atuat runs away, Atanarjuat follows, they lie down behind a snow floe, they are obviously in love; Oki confronts Amaqjuaq with the assertion that his brother is standing in the way of his marrying Atuat, his promised wife-to-be, they have a fight; Atanarjuat and Atuat return; Oki confronts Atanarjuat; Puja avoids a fight by pulling Atanarjuat away, she also seems to be in love with Atanarjuat; Atuat looks on sadly

dissolve

11.) 22:02 – Women's Resistance against the Marriage Match, exterior of the camp, day close-up on raw meat being pounded by Panikpak; Panikpak compares Atuat to her own mother Atuat, she has named Atuat after her; she tells Atuat not to marry Oki, because he is a mean man, since the evil shaman has killed Kumaglak; Atuat needs to know how she can get out of the marriage match

dissolve

12.) 24:07 – The Marriage Conflict, exterior of the camp, day
Oki's gang returns from hunt; Sauri's family and other community members await them; Oki angrily beats and kicks one of the sled dogs, he also barks at the onlookers; tension rises; Amaqjuaq teases Oki about his slow dogs; Atanarjuat returns with a rich catch; Tulimaq and Pittaluk are happy and Tulimaq announces that he will give a feast the next day; Oki furiously approaches Atanarjuat and threatens him: in order to get Atuat he will have to defeat him first

13.) 29:56 – Building of the Qaggiq, interior, day
a few men of the camp are finishing the building of the qaggiq by putting in the last snow blocks; Puja brings Atanarjuat something to drink; when he drinks, Oki pushes him so that he falls; angered, Atanarjuat almost enters into a fight with Oki but is held back by his brother; the onlookers are amused

14.) 32:16 – Oki's Threat, interior of Amaqjuaq's igloo, night
close-up of drum being heated, Amaqjuaq and Atanarjuat prepare their drum for the feast; Amaqjuaq tells Atanarjuat that Oki has threatened to kill him, he says that he is not afraid; instead, Atanarjuat is afraid of being killed by Oki, as Oki is a lot stronger than Atanarjuat

dissolve

15.) 34:15 – The Feast, interior of qaggiq, day
the feast starts; Sauri asks his wife to sing his father's song; intercut shots of two contests: Atuat and Puja throat singing and Amaqjuaq and Pittiulaq pulling the corner of their opponent's mouth; Oki starts a song ridiculing Atanarjuat, in accordance with the custom that two opponents have to ridicule each other before they fight physically to see whether the conflict can be solved without a fight; then Atanarjuat starts his song ridiculing Oki; both songs have strong sexual contents, community members join the singers; Atanarjuat and Oki have their 'Inuit boxing' contest (they take turns punching the other upon the temple while the one being struck has to hold still; whoever knocks the other out has won); it seems to be agreed that whoever wins will be married to Atuat; while Atanarjuat and Oki deal out their blows, there are brief intercuts of the evil shaman giggling and

Panikpak calling her husband for help – the bad spirit is among them again!; because of Panikpak's help, Atanarjuat is able to land his final blow and knock Oki out; Sauri immediately protests against the outcome, but Atanarjuat and Atuat are very happy and Panikpak decides for this match; Oki and his family can only angrily witness the new development

dissolve

16.) 43:37 – The Summer Camp, sea shore, day
contre-jour shot of Atanarjuat on the water returning from a hunting/fishing trip in his kayak; on the shore, the pregnant Atuat awaits him; in the camp, Atanarjuat skins the seal; Tulimaq says that he needs Amaqjuaq for the walrus hunt that year and that Atanarjuat will have to go caribou hunting on his own; Pittaluk explains that in her time men used to have two wives; the camp members start joking about Atanarjuat getting a second wife on his way to the summer hunt; Atuat looks very concerned

dissolve

17.) 48:21 – The Offer, exterior of Sauri's camp, day
Atanarjuat approaches Sauri's camp with his hunting gear; Puja and Oki, and later the others, welcome him; Oki and his friend introduce their new wives, whom Atanarjuat acknowledges; when they sit down to eat, Sauri invites Puja to accompany Atanarjuat on his hunt, as the pregnant Atuat needs to stay in the camp; happy at this, Puja consents and it is agreed upon; Panikpak is concerned about this development

dissolve

18.) 52:58 – The First Day Together, day⇒night
Atanarjuat and Puja with their hunting gear walk along a shore line, pausing to rest; later, Atanarjuat sets up camp and Puja collects weeds for the fire; she makes advances to him; they tease each other and later sing a love song

dissolve

19.) 58:28 – The Seduction, summer tent, night
outside the tent they have a fire going, but Puja keeps saying that she is cold until Atanarjuat tries to warm her with his hands; later, their silhouettes making love are seen through the walls of the sealskin tent; inside close-ups and medium close-ups of their love-making

dissolve

20.) 1:02:01 – Atanarjuat's Two Wives, exterior of Atanarjuat's and Amaqjuaq's summer camp, day
camp on frozen sea shore; Atuat calls her little son Kumaglak; Puja, now the second wife, leaves the tent for a walk; later, the two families eat,

except for Puja; close-up on meat being cut up; Atanarjuat asks what is wrong with the family, since everybody seems so silent; Atuat tells him that Puja is lazy and bossy and that she and Uluriaq have to do all the work; Uluriaq accuses Puja of having intercourse with the spirits (ijirait – invisible human-like spirits) on her long walks

21.) 1:05:40 – The Seduction, interior of summer tent, morning
the two families are sleeping side by side, from left to right: Kumaglak, Atuat, Atanarjuat, Puja, Amaqjuaq, Uluriaq; Puja wakes up, moves closer to Amaqjuaq, he wakes up, too, and they have sex; Uluriaq, waking up, starts screaming and beating Amaqjuaq; Atanarjuat means to hit Puja but is prevented by Amaqjuaq; Puja and Amaqjuaq have violated a serious taboo – as in-laws they are not even supposed to talk to each other, let alone have sex

dissolve

22.) 1:08:00 – Puja's Scheming, interior of Sauri's summer tent, day
Puja walks to her father's camp, complaining; she says that Atanarjuat has tried to kill her although she did not do anything; Oki resolves to kill Atanarjuat; his father ridicules him, which makes him even more determined

dissolve

23.) 1:10:31 – Puja's Apology, exterior of Atanarjuat's and Amaqjuaq's summer camp, day
close-up of animal skin being cleaned, Atuat and Uluriaq clean skins and talk about the incident; both are afraid that the incident has broken up the family, as the two brothers are no longer talking to each other; Puja returns whining and apologizes, asking to be taken into the family again and promising to be more helpful; Uluriaq forgives her; Puja asks Atuat to be allowed to clean the skin for her, she is pretty slow in comparison to Uluriaq

24.) 1:16:56 – Puja's Scheming, exterior of Atanarjuat's and Amaqjuaq's summer camp, day
Atanarjuat and Amaqjuaq return from a hunt; upon seeing Puja, Atanarjuat becomes very angry; Atuat protects her and tells him that the women have forgiven her, and she asks him to be generous; Uluriaq forgives Amaqjuaq; Puja suggest that she dry the men's clothes while the men go to sleep, that the two other women go egg-hunting, and that she join them later; the two first wives leave and the two brothers undress and go to sleep, they make up with each other; Puja puts out their clothes to dry; seeing Oki's gang approaching, she continues with her tasks, putting the boots outside the tent to mark the spot where the men are sleeping, and leaves

25.) 1:23:10 – The Assault, exterior of Atanarjuat's and Amaqjuaq's summer camp, day
Oki, Pakak, and Pittiulaq approach; Oki motions Pakak to take the tent down, whereupon the three start thrusting their spears into the collapsed tent several times; Oki seems to have killed someone; the sound of the evil shaman laughing is heard and the spirit of Kumaglak distracts the attackers; Atanarjuat uses the momentary distraction to jump out of the collapsed tent stark naked and flee; the three set off after him in hot pursuit

dissolve

26.) 1:27:22 – The Murder without Killer, exterior of Atanarjuat's and Amaqjuaq's summer camp, day
the women return to the camp to find the murdered Amaqjuaq; Uluriaq wails; Atuat weeps, too, and calls out for Atanarjuat, assuming that the latter has killed his brother out of revenge

cut to black

27.) 1:30:19 – The Flight, Arctic landscape, day
Atanarjuat tries to escape, running naked and barefoot across the Arctic snow and ice; his flight is filmed from various angles and with various camera distances: close-ups of his running feet and his face, long shots and extreme long shots showing him and his pursuers with their spears. A dissolve indicates that time has passed. Atanarjuat falls into a shallow pool; the spirit of Qulitalik shows him the way; a wide crack in the pack ice opens up: without thinking, Atanarjuat jumps and miraculously makes it across the crack; Oki falls into the crack and has to stop his pursuit, furious, he swears he will kill Atanarjuat and calls to his friends to get the dog teams; in an extreme long shot, Atanarjuat is seen running away; in the end, he reaches the island of Siuraq, where Qulitalik and his family live, he has covered a distance of roughly thirty kilometres

dissolve

28.) 1:34:43 – The Deception, exterior of Qulitalik's camp, day
Qulitalik is collecting bird's eggs; he senses Atanarjuat approaching, and tells his wife to cook all the eggs although there are too many for the small family (Qulitalik, Nirinuniq, and their adopted daughter Kigutikaajuk); close to Qulitalik's camp, Atanarjuat collapses, his feet, knees, and hands bloody; he wakes up in the camp, the three having rescued him; Oki's gang approaches from the other direction; Qulitalik hides Atanarjuat under the seaweed; Oki and his men search the camp for traces of Atanarjuat; the tension heightens, since Oki does not believe Qulitalik when he says there is nobody else there; Oki takes a piss right on the seaweed above Atanarjuat's concealed face; Qulitalik asks about Oki's family to distract him

and almost gets killed by Oki; then he invites them to eat eggs; the three pursuers leave and Atanarjuat emerges from his hiding-place

dissolve

29.) 1:46:48 – Life without Support, exterior of Sauri's camp, day
close-up on burning fire and seabird being cut into edible pieces; Atuat, Kumaglak, and Panikpak now live together; Puja brings the rear end of a seal from Sauri; Oki asks his father why he cannot have Atuat now that her husband is dead; Sauri is against this, saying that they do not take women by force and nobody can be sure that Atanarjuat is dead, he says that Oki would be incapable of killing Atanarjuat, which angers Oki

dissolve

30.) 1:50:20 – Atanarjuat's Recovery and Atuat's Misery, exterior of Qulitalik's camp and the vicinity of Sauri's camp, day
Atanarjuat slowly recovers; he is picked up by Kigutikaajuk in a sea of purple Arctic heather; she walks the limping Atanarjuat back to the camp; a dissolve indicates the change of location; seemingly at the same time, Atuat and Panikpak walk across a meadow with purple Arctic heather; Panikpak leaves with Kumaglak; Atuat, now alone, picks some heather and sits by a creek; there she is attacked by Oki's gang and raped by Oki; afterwards, she sits alone; Panikpak later tries to console her

dissolve

31.) 1:56:17 – Atanarjuat Longs for Home, bluish Arctic twilight
Atanarjuat arrives with dog team at a shore line, he probes to see whether the ice is thick enough for him to cross the sound to return home to Igloolik

32.) 1:59:38 – Atanarjuat Decides to Return Home, interior of Qulitalik's igloo, night
close-up on Nirinuniq sewing; Qulitalik asks how the ice is, Atanarjuat tells him that he has decided to return home to Igloolik to face Oki

33.) 2:00:52 – The Murder, Arctic landscape, day
close-up on Sauri waiting patiently at a breathing-hole for a seal to appear; a long shot reveals several men at various breathing-holes; Oki comes up to his father and complains that his breathing-hole is no good, he takes Sauri's knife and kills him, saying that Sauri will no longer be in his way to get Atuat; when the others arrive he pretends that Sauri tripped, got caught in a rope, and fell on his knife; they return to camp with the dead Sauri on a sled

dissolve

34.) 2:02:52 – Oki Becomes Leader, exterior of Sauri's camp, twilight

the men bring home the dead body of Sauri; all start wailing; Panikpak is doubtful about Oki's story; Sauri's walrus necklace is passed on to Oki, who will now be camp leader

35.) 2:05:24 – Atuat's Decision, interior of Atuat's tent, day
with Sauri gone to protect and feed Atuat, Panikpak, and Kumaglak, Atuat, in tears, resolves to go to Oki and offer herself; Panikpak calls her brother for help through a seal-oil lamp; Qulitalik hears her call and resolves to accompany Atanarjuat to Igloolik

dissolve

36.) 2:07:55 – The Rabbit Spell, exterior of Qulitalik's camp, day
in slow motion Qulitalik rounds a stone cairn in hopping motion with rabbit's feet in his hands, he throws them away, in order for the rabbit's spirit to find Oki's camp, he intends to change Oki's personality with the rabbit's spirit

dissolve

37.) 2:08:56 – The Rabbit Spell, exterior of Oki's camp, day
Oki catches a strange white rabbit, and teases Atuat for being dressed very poorly and not having enough food; Atuat responds that he can choke on the rabbit; Panikpak sees that this is a strange rabbit

38.) 2:09:52 – The Rabbit Spell, interior of Oki's sod house, night
the rabbit is prepared; Oki eats the rabbit himself and does not share, he all of a sudden falls asleep, his body shakes in sleep, he awakes and says he feels great now; his friends look on, wondering

39.) 2:12:09 – Atanarjuat's Return, exterior of Oki's camp, day
in slow motion, Atanarjuat and his dog team are seen from behind running toward Igloolik; intercut are shots of Atuat and other camp members awaiting the strange dog team; Puja recognizes Atanarjuat and Atuat runs to meet him, they have a happy reunion; Atanarjuat rips apart her shabby coat and presents her with a beautifully adorned coat; Puja also runs to meet Atanarjuat, but his conduct toward her is hostile: he cuts up her new coat and sends her to her family just like that; Pakak and Pittiulaq wonder about Oki, who wants to welcome Atanarjuat as a friend, they cannot understand his change of character

dissolve

40.) 2:19:29 – Building of Qaggiq, interior, day
Atanarjuat prepares a qaggiq for his feast, he makes the ground slippery by spilling water over it that immediately freezes, he has made crampons for himself that he hides underneath the snow outside close to the entrance

41.) 2:21:22 – The Invitation, interior of Oki's sod house, day
Pakak and Pittiulaq worry that Atanarjuat will seek revenge; Oki is not
worried at all; Atuat enters and invites everybody to a feast on condition
that Oki and his two friends come alone first; she says that Atanarjuat
wants to put behind all bad feelings between them; Oki agrees; the other
two hesitate

42.) 2:23:34 – Reconciliation, exterior and interior of Atanarjuat's Qaggiq,
day
close-up on caribou leg and large pieces being chopped off by Atanarjuat;
Oki and his friends arrive at qaggiq and are welcomed by Atanarjuat;
inside, they feast on meat and have small talk; Atanarjuat goes outside to
put on the crampons, then comes back inside and fights all three men,
almost getting killed; finally he has the opportunity to kill Oki but instead
hits the ground beside Oki's head; Atanarjuat shouts that the killing must
now stop; Oki and his friends meekly walk outside, where they are awaited
by the others; Qulitalik announces that at night they all will meet to drive
away the evil spirit that has haunted their community for so long; he takes
the walrus necklace from Oki

43.) 2:29:25 – Reconciliation and Requital, interior of sod house, day
Qulitalik attempts to drive away the evil spirit that is haunting the camp, but
is unsuccessful: the spirit even enters and scares everybody; they have a
spiritual contest, and later, Qulitalik, helped by Panikpak, drives out the
spirit; Panikpak gets up and announces that she has forgiven her
grandchildren Oki and Puja for their mean behavior in lying and killing;
nevertheless, she orders the two of them, Pakak and Pittiulaq, to leave the
camp together with their families and never return, which is a harsh sentence
in the Arctic; through a seal-oil lamp, Kumaglak calls his sister and asks her
to sing his song; she calls Kumaglak, but instead little Kumaglak enters;
together, the rest of the community sing old Kumaglak's song

fade to black
　　2:37:31 - CREDITS

Atanarjuat: The Fast Runner: Detailed Shot Analysis

from Sequence 6 (3.51 min.)

No.	Content of Shot	C/Dist	C/Angle	C/Move[16]	Sound	Shot/L
1	Tulimaq's feet walking beside sled in snow, then his body, his head against blue sky, again his feet, head, back; moves from right to left	medium close-up alternating with close-up	low angle, oblique left	track left + alternating tilt-up, tilt down, left & right pan	Jew's harp and percussion music	66 sec.
2	head and front part of sled dog, two sled dogs in left fgd and Tulimaq with sled in right bkgd	medium close-up ⇒ medium long shot	low angle, oblique left	track left + right pan	⇓	12 sec.
3	Tulimaq's head against blue sky *dissolve*[17]	medium close-up	low, oblique left	track left	⇓	3 sec.
4	seal-oil lamp	medium close-up	straight	still	same music + baby Atanarjuat's voice	2 sec.
5	Pittaluk with baby Atanarjuat in hood and little Amaqjuaq in left fgd in their igloo	medium shot	straight, oblique right	still	same music + Pittaluk singing	4 sec.
6	face of Amaqjuaq *dissolve*	close-up	straight, oblique right	still	⇓	3 sec.
7	head and upper body of Tulimaq against blue sky; he moves from right to left	medium close-up	low, oblique left	track left	Jew's harp and percussion music	3 sec.
8	muzzle of sled dog	close-up ⇒ extreme close-up	low angle, oblique left	track left	⇓	7 sec.
9	Tulimaq in right fgd is passed by another hunter in bkgd; they move to left	medium long shot, long shot	straight, oblique left	track left + slight pan right and left	⇓	16 sec.

---

[16] All mobile frames in this sequence are photographed with a hand-held camera.

[17] When a transition device is not specified, the shots are connected by a cut.

10	the other hunter's face	close-up	straight, oblique left	track left + left pan	same music + hunter: "Tulimaq! Their balls are too big!" + his laughter[18]	5 sec.
11	Tulimaq in fgd fights with limping dog, two other hunters pass in bkgd *dissolve*	medium shot, long shot	straight, oblique left	still	Jew's harp, percussion music + hunters' laughter	9 sec.
12	Pittaluk, Atanarjuat, Amaqjuaq await Tulimaq; bkgd of snow in bluish Arctic twilight	medium shot	straight	still	Jew's harp, percussion music	9 sec.
13	two dog teams and several people move towards camp in bluish Arctic twilight	long shot	straight	left pan	same music + distant talk and laughter of people	7 sec.
14	several dead frozen seal, one being lifted	close-up	low angle	still	same music + talk and laughter of people	2 sec.
15	in fgd people pick up dead seal and carry them off right; dog team in middle ground; Pittaluk with Atanarjuat and Amaqjuaq in bkgd	medium close-up, long shot	straight	still	⇓	10 sec.
16	Pittaluk with Atanarjuat and Amaqjuaq; someone carries dead seal in fgd, left to right	long shot (closer than 15)	straight	still	same music + someone: "Where is Tulimaq?"	9 sec.
17	face and upper body of hunter	medium close-up	straight	shaky camera, tilt down, tilt up	same music + hunter: "With those starving dogs maybe he'll get home tomorrow!" + his laughter	12 sec.

---

[18] When someone is speaking, the English translation for the 'sound' column is taken from the subtitles, whereas the soundtrack has Inuktitut words.

18	same frame as in 15; in fgd people carry dead seal off right; dog team in middle ground; Pittaluk, Atanarjuat and Amaqjuaq in bkgd *dissolve*	medium close-up, long shot	straight	still	Jew's harp and percussion music	10 sec.
19	moon against blue twilight sky *dissolve*	long shot	low angle	still	⇓	7 sec.
20	Pittaluk, Atanarjuat, Amaqjuaq from behind in right fgd; Tulimaq returns with dog team; a few dogs run toward them	close-up, extreme long shot	straight	still	dogs bark and howl	9 sec.
21	Tulimaq returns with dog team	long shot	straight	zoom-out	dogs bark and howl, Tuli-maq's voice soothing them, snow crunch-ing	9 sec.
22	Pittaluk's disappointed face	close-up	straight	still		4 sec.

Sequence 27 (4:23 min.)

No.	Content of Shot	C/Dist	C/Angle	C/Move	Sound	Shot/L
1	Atanarjuat's bare feet running across snow, from right to left	close-up	low angle, oblique left	left track[19]	flute and percussion music, breathing, crunching snow	22 sec.
2	Atanarjuat's face while running, he turns to look at his pursuers	close-up	straight, oblique left	shaky camera, left track	⇓	16 sec.
3	Oki's face while running	close-up	straight, oblique left	shaky camera, left track	⇓	9 sec.
4	Atanarjuat's bare feet running through water	close-up	low angle, oblique left	left track	⇓	2 sec.

---

[19] All mobile frames in this sequence are photographed with a hand-held camera.

5	Atanarjuat's face while running: twice turns to look back; Oki, Pakak, and Pitti-ulaq in bkgd pursue him *dissolve*	close-up, long shot	straight angle, oblique left	shaky camera, left track	⇓	19 sec.
6	naked Atanarjuat runs toward camera; 3 pursuers in bkgd; he falls into water hole, stops to drink, looks behind at pursuers; runs off to left; Oki runs toward camera, stops at same spot, turns to look back	extreme long shot ⇒ medium close-up	straight	almost still, slight tilt down & right pan, tilt-up, tilt down, right pan	⇓	73 sec.
7	naked Atanarjuat from behind, runs from left to right	long shot	straight angle, oblique left	shaky camera, left track	⇓	7 sec.
8	three pursuers in middle ground from behind; Atanarjuat in bkgd runs away from camera	extreme long shot	straight	still	same music + voice: "He's trapped by the crack! He can't get away."	7 sec.
9	faces and upper bodies of Oki and Pakak; they move off to left	medium shot	straight	left pan	flute and percussion music, breathing	3 sec.
10	1/3 sky, 2/3 ground, snow and water whole, sky and sun reflected; Oki, Pakak, and Pittiulaq from behind, one after the other run through water *dissolve*	medium shot, long shot	very low angle	still	flute and percussion music, breathing, water splashing	24 sec.
11	1/3 sky, 2/3 water with snow rim, Atanarjuat and his three pursuers on horizon as tiny figures moving to left *long dissolve*	extreme long shot	very low angle	still	flute music, Qulitalik: "This way."	8 sec.
12	Qulitalik beckons	long shot	low angle ⇒ straight angle	tilt up	women singing, Qulitalik: "This way."	8 sec.

13	Atanarjuat runs across snow and water	long shot	straight angle, oblique left	shaky camera, left track	women singing, human breathing Qulitalik: "This way."	6 sec.
14	Qulitalik beckons	long shot	straight angle	still	women singing, human breathing, Qulitalik: "This way."	2 sec.
15	Atanarjuat's bloody feet running through water	close-up	low angle, oblique left	left track	⇓	2 sec.
16	Atanarjuat's face while running	close-up	straight, oblique left	shaky camera, left track	⇓	3 sec.
17	1/3 sky, 2/3 water with snow rim, Atanarjuat runs toward camera, sees huge crack in the ice, accelerates and jumps off, his body reflected in the water	long shot ⇒ medium shot	straight	still, slow motion at end of shot	female voices rise dramatically, human breathing	3 sec.
18	Atanarjuat from below jumping, against backdrop of blue sky	medium shot	very low angle, camera > sky	tilt down, slow motion	echo of singing	2 sec.
19	Atanarjuat lands on other side of crack, stumbles, steadies himself, looks back at his pursuers	long shot	straight	still	Qulitalik: "Just keep running and you'll find it!"	9 sec.
20	Oki's face and upper body, he sees crack and is startled, starts sliding	medium shot	straight	tilt down	human breathing, water splashing	3 sec.
21	1/3 sky, 2/3 water, Oki slides into water and struggles	medium close-up	low angle	still	⇓	3 sec.
22	Oki struggles in the water	medium close-up	slight high angle	still	water splashing, Oki's angry voice	5 sec.
23	same frame as in shot 19, Atanarjuat turns and runs off	long shot	straight	still	water splashing	3 sec.

| 24 | Oki is pulled out of water, his face as he speaks | medium shot | high angle ⇒straight | right pan, tilt up | human breathing, Oki: "I won't sleep until you are dead." | 18 sec. |
| 25 | same frame as in shot 19, Atanarjuat runs off into distance *dissolve* | extreme long shot | straight | still | human breathing, Oki: "Get the dogs." | 16 sec. |

Poems

Overweight With Crooked Teeth[20]

What were you expecting anyway
A noble savage
Sitting Bull
Chief Joseph of the Nez Perce
Saying…
The earth and I are one
Like we're not supposed to think
Just react
Like we're peripatetic pagans
Scrolling through a steaming forest after a June rain
Not supposed to fart
Or screw
Or be what we're supposed to be…
People with weaknesses
Victims of a lotta bad breaks
Like the repeating carbine rifle
Charles Darwin
Same thing
Small pox
Influenza
Halley's comet
What were you expecting anyway

— MICHAEL DOXTATER

---

[20] The poem is taken from the film *Overweight With Crooked Teeth* by Shirley Niro.

Inukshuk[21]

You were built from the stones,
they say, positioned
alone against the sky
here so they might take
you for something human

checking the migrations.
That's how you manage this,
standing upright despite
the blue wind that snow is,
this close to Polaris.

Still, the wind worries
you some. It's your niches
which ought to be empty.
Nothing but lichen grows
there usually. Now

they're home to dreams. Most come
from the south, a few from
further north – but what flows
out of their mouths comes from
no direction you know.

They keep singing about
the Great Blue Whale the world
is; how it swims through space
having nightmares about
hunters who only hunt
their brothers – each after
the other's snow-white face.

---

[21] Daniel David Moses, "Inukshuk," in *The White Line* (Saskatoon, Saskatchewan: Fifth House, 1990).

How beautiful frozen
flesh is! Like ivory,
like carved bone, like the light

of Polaris in hand.
So it goes on and on,
the hunting refrain. Dead
silence would be better,
the Pole Star overhead.

The wind agrees, at least
wants to stop up each niche.
How long can you stand it
– that song, the cold, the stones
that no longer hold you

up now that they hold you
down? Soon the migrations
recommence. How steady
are you? Dreams, so they say,
also sing on the wing.

— DANIEL DAVID MOSES

Forgiving Our Fathers[22]

How do we forgive our fathers? Maybe in a dream

Do we forgive our fathers for leaving us too often or
forever when we were little? Maybe for scaring us with
unexpected rage or making us nervous because there never
seemed to be any rage there at all?

Do we forgive our fathers for marrying or not marrying
our mothers? For divorcing or not divorcing our mothers?
And shall we forgive them for their excesses of warmth or
coldness?

Shall we forgive them for pushing or leaning? For shutting
doors? For speaking through walls, or never
speaking, or never being silent?

Do we forgive our Fathers in our age or in theirs? Or in
their deaths? Saying it to them or not saying it? If we
forgive our fathers, what is left?

— DICK LOURIE

---

[22] This lyric is taken from the screenplay for *Smoke Signals* – Sherman Alexie, *Smoke Signals* Screenplay (Miramax Books; New York: Hyperion, 1998): 147–49 – but was shortened and changed according to the actual words spoken in Thomas' epilogue.

Index